THE WORKSHEET

1. *The open-file icon.* Displays the File Open dialog box.
2. *The save-file icon.* Saves or updates the current file to disk.
3. *The print-range icon.* Sends the currently defined print range to the printer.
4. *The preview icon.* Displays a preview of the currently defined print range.
5. *The undo icon.* Performs the Edit Undo command.
6. *The cut-to-clipboard icon.* Deletes the current selection and copies it to the clipboard.
7. *The copy-to-clipboard icon.* Copies the current selection to the clipboard.
8. *The paste-from-clipboard icon.* Pastes the contents of the clipboard to the current location.
9. *The range-copy icon.* Copies the current selection to a location you select.
10. *The range-move icon.* Moves the current selection to a location you select.
11. *The summation icon.* Enters @SUM functions in an empty last row and/or column.
12. *The bold icon.* Applies the boldface style to the entries in the current selection.
13. *The italics icon.* Applies the italics style to the entries in the current selection.
14. *The underline icon.* Underlines the entries in the current selection.
15. *The align-left icon.* Left-aligns labels within their cells in the current selection.
16. *The center icon.* Centers labels within their cells in the current selection.
17. *The align-right icon.* Right-aligns labels within their cells in the current selection.
18. *The outline icon.* Applies the Outline and Drop shadow options (from the Style Border command).
19. *The currency-format icon.* Applies the currency format to values in the current selection.
20. *The comma-format icon.* Applies the comma format to values in the current selection.
21. *The percent-format icon.* Applies the percent format to values in the current selection.
22. *The apply-formats icon.* Duplicates the current formats in a location you select.
23. *The create-graph icon.* Opens a graph window and draws a graph of the selection.
24. *The perspective-view icon.* Displays three worksheets in the current window.
25. *The next-worksheet icon.* Moves the cell pointer to the next worksheet.
26. *The previous-worksheet icon.* Moves the cell pointer to the previous worksheet.

Computer users are not all alike.
Neither are SYBEX books.

We know our customers have a variety of needs. They've told us so. And because we've listened, we've developed several distinct types of books to meet the needs of each of our customers. What are you looking for in computer help?

If you're looking for the basics, try the **ABC's** series. You'll find short, unintimidating tutorials and helpful illustrations. For a more visual approach, select **Teach Yourself,** featuring screen-by-screen illustrations of how to use your latest software purchase.

Mastering and **Understanding** titles offer you a step-by-step introduction, plus an in-depth examination of intermediate-level features, to use as you progress.

Our **Up & Running** series is designed for computer-literate consumers who want a no-nonsense overview of new programs. Just 20 basic lessons, and you're on your way.

We also publish two types of reference books. Our **Instant References** provide quick access to each of a program's commands and functions. SYBEX **Encyclopedias** and **Desktop References** provide a *comprehensive reference* and explanation of all of the commands, features and functions of the subject software.

Sometimes a subject requires a special treatment that our standard series don't provide. So you'll find we have titles like **Advanced Techniques, Handbooks, Tips & Tricks,** and others that are specifically tailored to satisfy a unique need.

We carefully select our authors for their in-depth understanding of the software they're writing about, as well as their ability to write clearly and communicate effectively. Each manuscript is thoroughly reviewed by our technical staff to ensure its complete accuracy. Our production department makes sure it's easy to use. All of this adds up to the highest quality books available, consistently appearing on best-seller charts worldwide.

You'll find SYBEX publishes a variety of books on every popular software package. Looking for computer help? Help Yourself to SYBEX.

For a complete catalog of our publications:

SYBEX Inc.
2021 Challenger Drive, Alameda, CA 94501
Tel: (510) 523-8233/(800) 227-2346 Telex: 336311
Fax: (510) 523-2373

SYBEX is committed to using natural resources wisely to preserve and improve our environment. As a leader in the computer book publishing industry, we are aware that over 40% of America's solid waste is paper. This is why we have been printing the text of books like this one on recycled paper since 1982.

This year our use of recycled paper will result in the saving of more than 15,300 trees. We will lower air pollution effluents by 54,000 pounds, save 6,300,000 gallons of water, and reduce landfill by 2,700 cubic yards.

In choosing a SYBEX book you are not only making a choice for the best in skills and information, you are also choosing to enhance the quality of life for all of us.

UNDERSTANDING 1-2-3 FOR WINDOWS

UNDERSTANDING
1-2-3® FOR WINDOWS™

Douglas Hergert

SYBEX®

San Francisco • Paris • Düsseldorf • Soest

ACQUISITIONS EDITOR: *David Clark*
DEVELOPMENTAL EDITOR: *Christian T.S. Crumlish*
EDITOR: *Savitha Varadan*
TECHNICAL EDITOR: *Sheila Dienes*
WORD PROCESSORS: *Ann Dunn, Susan Trybull*
BOOK DESIGNER: *Amparo del Rio*
PRODUCTION ARTIST: *Lisa Jaffe*
SCREEN GRAPHICS: *Cuong Le*
DESKTOP PUBLISHING SPECIALISTS: *Deborah Maizels, Dina F. Quan*
PROOFREADER/PRODUCTION ASSISTANT: *Catherine Mahoney*
INDEXER: *Sandi Schroeder*
COVER DESIGNER: *Ingalls + Associates*
COVER PHOTOGRAPHER: *Michael Lamotte*

SYBEX is a registered trademark of SYBEX, Inc.

TRADEMARKS: SYBEX has attempted throughout this book to distinguish proprietary trademarks from descriptive terms by following the capitalization style used by the manufacturer.

SYBEX is not affiliated with any manufacturer.

Every effort has been made to supply complete and accurate information. However, SYBEX assumes no responsibility for its use, nor for any infringement of the intellectual property rights of third parties which would result from such use.

Copyright ©1992 SYBEX Inc., 2021 Challenger Drive, Alameda, CA 94501. World rights reserved. No part of this publication may be stored in a retrieval system, transmitted, or reproduced in any way, including but not limited to photocopy, photograph, magnetic or other record, without the prior agreement and written permission of the publisher.

Library of Congress Card Number: 91-66572
ISBN: 0-89588-845-9

Manufactured in the United States of America
10 9 8 7 6 5 4 3 2 1

ACKNOWLEDGMENTS

At the outset, David Clark and Dianne King were instrumental in getting me started on this book. Christian Crumlish helped devise an overall plan for the contents, and was always ready with levelheaded advice.

Savitha Varadan edited the manuscript with great skill and patience, and deftly guided the book through the various stages of publication. Sheila Dienes provided an exceptionally thorough and useful technical review, and made many important suggestions. Barbara Gordon and Rudolph Langer stepped in at key moments and helped to make pivotal decisions about the book. Kim Twist of Lotus Development Corporation furnished beta software and timely information. Claudette Moore of Moore Literary Agency offered counsel, encouragement, and guidance. In addition, the following people had important roles in the process of producing this book: Ann Dunn, Lisa Jaffe, Cuong Le, Catherine Mahoney, Deborah Maizels, Dina Quan, and Susan Trybull. My sincere thanks to all.

CONTENTS AT A GLANCE

Introduction xvii

PART ONE

LOTUS 1-2-3 IN THE WINDOWS ENVIRONMENT
Chapter 1   Working with Lotus 1-2-3 for Windows 5
Chapter 2   Lotus 1-2-3 and the Windows Interface 51

PART TWO

ESSENTIAL 1-2-3 FOR WINDOWS
Chapter 3   Worksheet Essentials 105
Chapter 4   Worksheet Formatting and Printing 161
Chapter 5   Worksheet Formulas and Functions 237
Chapter 6   Graphs 307
Chapter 7   Database Essentials 353
Chapter 8   Database Calculations and Operations . . . 395
Chapter 9   Introduction to Macros 429

PART THREE

ADVANCED 1-2-3 FOR WINDOWS
Chapter 10   Advanced Worksheet Tools 465
Chapter 11   Links between Files 513
Chapter 12   Macro Programming 539

APPENDICES

Appendix A   Installing Lotus 1-2-3 for Windows 573
Appendix B   The @ Functions 579

Index 593

INTRODUCTION xvii

PART ONE
LOTUS 1-2-3 IN THE WINDOWS ENVIRONMENT

Chapter 1
WORKING WITH LOTUS 1-2-3 FOR WINDOWS 5

Exploring the Lotus 1-2-3 Interface 6
    The Dimensions of a Worksheet 7
    The Menu Bar 11
    The Icon Palette 17
    The 1-2-3 Classic Window 20
    Data Entry and the Mode Indicator 22

Planning a Worksheet 24

Developing a 1-2-3 Worksheet 26
    Entering Labels and Data 27
    Writing Formulas 29
    Preparing the Worksheet for Presentation . . . 32
    Making Changes in the Data 34

Creating Graphs from a Worksheet 36
    Designing a Graph 37

Performing Database Operations 40
    Defining a Database 41
    Performing Sort and Search Operations in the Database . . 42

Summary 45

Chapter 2
LOTUS 1-2-3 AND THE WINDOWS INTERFACE 51

Exploring the 1-2-3 Application Window 52
    The 1-2-3 Window Title Bar 54
    The Menu Bar 59
    The Format Line 77
    The Edit Line 79
    The Icon Palette 81
    The Status Line 84

TABLE OF CONTENTS

Performing Operations on Worksheet Windows	86
Dividing a Worksheet Window into Panes	88
Opening More Than One Worksheet Window	91
Getting Help in Lotus 1-2-3 for Windows	93
Exploring the Help Menu	94
Finding Context-Sensitive Help	96
The Help Window	97
Summary	98

PART TWO
ESSENTIAL 1-2-3 FOR WINDOWS

Chapter 3
WORKSHEET ESSENTIALS — 105

Developing a Worksheet	108
Entering Labels	108
Entering Numbers	114
Selecting Ranges	115
Finding Totals	119
Creating Range Names	121
Copying a Range of Values	124
Saving the Worksheet	128
Using the Save As Command	129
Using the Save Command	132
Changing the Worksheet	132
Moving Ranges of Data	133
Inserting Rows and Columns	136
Working with Formulas in the Worksheet	139
Entering Formulas	141
Copying Formulas	144
Controlling the Order of Operations	153
Examining "What-If" Scenarios	154
Summary	156

Chapter 4

WORSHEET FORMATTING AND PRINTING **161**

Resuming Work on an Existing Worksheet 162
    Setting a Default Directory 163
    Using the Go To Command 164

Making Adjustments in the Worksheet 166
    Changing Column Widths 166
    Selecting Label Alignments 173
    Holding Worksheet Titles on the Screen 178
    Removing Grid Lines 180

Formatting Values on the Worksheet 184
    Selecting Global and Range Formats 188
    Entering Date Values into a Worksheet 192
    Entering Time Values into a Worksheet 199
    Protecting the Worksheet 205

Using Commands in the Style Menu 208
    Fonts, Type Styles, Shadings, and Borders 209
    Defining Style Names 215
    Applying Colors to the Worksheet 218

Printing the Worksheet 220
    Using the Page Setup Command 222
    Printing the Conference Worksheet 227

Summary 231

Chapter 5

WORKSHEET FORMULAS AND FUNCTIONS **237**

Writing Formulas 240
    Understanding Categories of Formulas 242
    Finding Errors in Formulas 251

Using Functions 253
    Entering a Function into a Cell 254
    Understanding Categories of Functions 257

Summary 302

Chapter 6

GRAPHS **307**

Creating a Graph from Worksheet Data 309
    Understanding Data Ranges for Graphs 311

    Choosing Commands from the Graph Menu 312
    Using the Graph Window's Menu Bar and Icon Palette . . 317
    Creating a Graph in the Rowwise Format 322
    Performing "What-If" Experiments with a Graph 325
Adding Features to the Graph 326
    Adding Titles and a Legend 326
    Adding Objects to the Graph 330
    Making Other Changes in the Graph 334
Adding the Graph to the Worksheet 336
Working with Other Graph Types 337
    Creating Line Graphs and Area Graphs 339
    Creating Pie Charts 340
    Creating XY Graphs and Mixed Graphs 343
    Creating HLCO Graphs 347
Summary 348

Chapter 7
DATABASE ESSENTIALS 353

Defining a Database 354
    Entering the Database 358
Sorting the Database 364
    Using the Data Sort Command 365
Performing Query Operations 373
    Preparing the Input, Criteria, and Output Ranges 375
    Using the Data Query Commands 377
    Writing Formulas as Criteria 388
Summary 390

Chapter 8
DATABASE CALCULATIONS AND OPERATIONS 395

Performing Calculations on Database Records 396
    Using the Database Functions 396
    Creating Computed Columns 402
    Creating Aggregate Columns 406
Joining Multiple Databases 408
    Preparing the Ranges for a Two-Table Query 409

Performing the Two-Table Query Operation 411
　Working with External Databases 413
　　　Using the Data Connect to External Command 415
　　　Using Database Functions with an External Database . . . 417
　　　Performing Queries on an External Database 418
　　　Performing Other External Database Operations 420
　Summary 424

Chapter 9
INTRODUCTION TO MACROS 429

　Creating Keystroke Macros 430
　　　Using Macro Key Names 431
　　　Entering Macros into a Worksheet 433
　　　Using the Tools Macro Run Command 436
　　　Using Macros as Subroutines 438
　Writing Macros as Menu Shortcuts 440
　　　Using {Alt} to Select Options from Dialog Boxes 443
　　　Using the Transcript Window to Develop Macros 445
　　　Attaching a Macro to an Icon 449
　Writing Macro Programs 453
　　　The Memo Macro 454
　Summary 459

PART THREE
ADVANCED 1-2-3 FOR WINDOWS

Chapter 10
ADVANCED WORKSHEET TOOLS 465

　Using the Data Matrix Commands 467
　　　Understanding Matrix Arithmetic 469
　　　Solving the Simultaneous Equations 470
　　　Using the Range Transpose Command 473
　　　Using the Range Annotate Command 474
　Using the Data Parse Command 476

Using the Data Distribution Command 482
Using the Data Regression Command 484
Using the Data What-if Table Commands 487
    Creating a One-Way What-If Table 491
    Creating Two-Way and Three-Way What-If Tables 495
Using the Tools Backsolver Command 499
Using the Solver 502
Summary 508

Chapter 11
LINKS BETWEEN FILES **513**

Creating Links between Worksheets 516
    Building a Totals Worksheet from the
    Four Source Worksheets 518
    Revising a Source Worksheet 521
    Revising a Source File When the
    Destination File is Closed 522
    Using the File Combine From Command 525
Creating Links between Documents in Different Applications . 527
    Transferring Data from a Worksheet to Another Document 528
    Transferring Data from Another Document
    to a 1-2-3 Worksheet 532
Summary 535

Chapter 12
MACRO PROGRAMMING **539**

Writing Programs That Interact with the User 542
    Using the {MenuCall} Command 548
    Using the {Let} Command 551
Working with Loops, Decisions, and Branches of Control . . 552
    Using the {For} Command 556
    Using the {If} and {Branch} Commands 558
    Debugging a Macro 561
Creating a Database Macro 563
    Using Text File Commands in a Macro 568
Summary 570

APPENDICES

Appendix A
INSTALLING LOTUS 1-2-3 FOR WINDOWS **573**

Appendix B
THE @ FUNCTIONS **579**

INDEX **593**

INTRODUCTION

otus 1-2-3 for Windows Release 1.0 is the latest release of the world's most popular spreadsheet program for IBM PCs and compatible personal computers. More than just a new version of the program, 1-2-3 for Windows is a splendid adaptation of existing application software to the graphical user interface of Microsoft Windows 3.0. Enhanced with a complete set of Windows-style menus and dialog boxes, a powerful collection of new visual tools known as SmartIcons, and a comprehensive online help system, 1-2-3 meets the highest potential for a major Windows application program.

This book, *Understanding 1-2-3 for Windows,* guides you through the stages of mastering this powerful new program. In twelve tutorial-style chapters, you'll learn all the essential details of the 1-2-3 software, while you work through complete business examples on your own computer. In these hands-on exercises, you'll learn to:

- ◆ Produce clear, accurate, and flexible worksheet documents.
- ◆ Generate presentation-quality graphs and charts from worksheet data.
- ◆ Build accessible databases and perform varieties of query operations on your data.
- ◆ Create custom macro tools, adapting 1-2-3 to your own work patterns.

Each chapter in this book begins with a learning feature called a Fast Track, designed both as a preview of the material to come and a quick reference guide to essential 1-2-3 procedures. Within the chapters, you'll find hundreds of screen illustrations, showing you exactly what happens in 1-2-3 when you perform the steps of specific worksheet, graph, and database operations.

This book is divided into three parts. Part 1, "Lotus 1-2-3 in the Windows Environment," gives you an overview of the product and an introduction to its new appearance in the Windows interface. Part 1 contains two chapters. Chapter 1, "Working with Lotus 1-2-3 for Windows," presents an introductory application designed to illustrate the spreadsheet, graph, and database components of 1-2-3. This application serves as a preview of the features you'll be studying individually in later chapters. In the hands-on portion of Chapter 1, you'll begin working with worksheet windows, the icon palette, and other features of the 1-2-3 window.

Chapter 2, "Lotus 1-2-3 and the Windows Interface," explores the elements of 1-2-3 in the Windows environment. In particular, you'll learn to work with menus, dialog boxes, and the visual tools that are common to all Windows applications. You'll practice the mouse and keyboard techniques for selecting and using these tools. Finally, you'll learn to take advantage of the comprehensive Windows-style Help system that is an integral part of 1-2-3 for Windows.

Part 2, "Essential 1-2-3 for Windows," contains seven tutorial-style chapters that introduce the basics of 1-2-3—the spreadsheet, the graphics capabilities, the database, and macros. Chapter 3, "Worksheet Essentials," takes you through the initial steps of building a worksheet for a business application. You'll learn how to enter labels and numeric data into the worksheet; to calculate totals; to perform important range operations, such as assigning range names and moving data; and to write formulas and copy them from one location to another in the worksheet. Along the way, you'll master the essential distinctions between absolute, relative, and mixed references in formulas; and you'll learn how to plan a worksheet as an effective "what-if" tool. You'll also learn to save your worksheet to disk. Throughout this chapter, you'll concentrate on using 1-2-3's impressive new icon palette tools, which streamline dozens of the most essential operations on a worksheet.

Chapter 4, "Worksheet Formatting and Printing," continues your introduction to basic spreadsheet operations. You'll learn to apply formats and type styles to numbers and labels on your worksheet, and to make adjustments in the appearance of the worksheet itself to accommodate your data. You'll also begin working with date and time values, and you'll begin learning the tools and techniques of date and time arithmetic. Finally, you'll work through the steps of printing your worksheet, and you'll concentrate on producing effective presentations of your data on paper.

Chapter 5, "Worksheet Formulas and Functions," guides you further into the large library of calculation tools that 1-2-3 provides for your use in worksheets. First, you'll expand your understanding of numeric, chronological, logical, and text formulas. Then you'll begin studying 1-2-3's collections of built-in @ functions for uses in specific applications—including statistical, financial, mathematical, chronological, logical, string, and lookup functions. Chapter 5 includes dozens of worksheet exercises for you to examine and work with as you master the use of these important spreadsheet tools.

Chapter 6, "Graphs," introduces the second component of the 1-2-3 package. In this chapter, you'll learn to create varieties of graphs from numeric data—including bar graphs, line graphs, area graphs, pie charts, and other pictorial formats for presenting information. You'll also explore the important tools of 1-2-3's graph window. In particular, you'll discover a completely new set of tools in the graph window's icon palette, and a new set of menu commands dealing specifically with graphs. You'll find out how to incorporate text elements and other objects into a graph window to make your graphs clear and attractive: You'll add titles, legends, and labels, and you'll draw objects such as arrows and boxes. Along the way, you'll learn to use a graph as a tool for exploring "what-if" scenarios. Finally, you'll work through the steps for adding a graph to a worksheet, and you'll learn to combine data and graphics in a final printed document.

Chapter 7, "Database Essentials," takes up the third major component in 1-2-3, the database management tools. This chapter introduces you to essential database concepts, and guides you through a series of hands-on exercises in which you create and work with a database. In particular, you'll learn to define fields, enter records, and create calculated fields. Then you'll begin mastering the database tools in the 1-2-3 Data menu, including the Data Sort command and the assortment of tools in the Data Query dialog box. You'll find out how to plan criteria and output ranges for effective database queries, and you'll practice performing the Find, Extract, Delete, and Modify operations on a sample database.

Chapter 8, "Database Calculations and Operations," teaches you more about 1-2-3's database capabilities. You'll begin by learning to use the special library of statistical functions designed for database queries, including @DCOUNT, @DSUM, @DAVG, and @DSTD. You'll also learn the steps for extracting other kinds of calculations from numeric fields in a database, and creating special output ranges known as computed and aggregate columns. Perhaps most important of all, you'll learn how to perform queries on multiple database tables and to create output ranges that combine data from two or more databases. Finally, you'll explore 1-2-3's special DataLens drivers that allow you to establish connections between external databases—such as dBASE IV and Paradox—and a 1-2-3 worksheet. Specifically, you'll learn to extract data from an external database and use the data to create an equivalent 1-2-3 database.

Chapter 9, "Introduction to Macros," shows you how to create your own library of 1-2-3 macro tools to streamline your work in worksheets, graphs, and databases. The macros you'll create in this chapter are shortcuts for specific operations that you may find yourself performing frequently during your work in 1-2-3. By creating a macro, you can reduce the steps for almost any 1-2-3 procedure to a couple of simple keystrokes. For example, you'll learn to create macros to enter a company name and address instantly into a range of worksheet cells, to apply formats and type styles to values and labels on your worksheet, and to choose other options from the 1-2-3 menu commands. Finally, in the ultimate step for customizing your copy of 1-2-3, you'll learn to create your own icons to represent macros in the icon palette. After completing this step, you can perform a macro simply by clicking a custom icon with the mouse. This chapter also contains a brief introduction to macro programming, a topic that is taken up again in Chapter 12.

Part 3, "Advanced 1-2-3 for Windows," introduces some of the most powerful tools in the 1-2-3 software package, including advanced worksheet tools, links between worksheets and other applications, and macro programming. This final part of the book includes three chapters. Chapter 10, "Advanced Worksheet Tools," conducts you through a series of exercises that will help you master the sophisticated 1-2-3 tools available in the Data and Tools menus. These include Data Matrix, for solving simultaneous equations; Data Parse for converting text files into usable worksheet data tables; Data Distribution for examining the frequency of values on a worksheet; Data Regression for exploring the correlation between numeric data sets; the Data What-if Table commands for performing multiple what-if calculations in a single operation; the Tools Backsolver command for finding an input value that produces a desired bottom-line calculation; and finally, the elaborate Solver facility for examining scenarios that match specific constraints in worksheet problems that you define. The details of these valuable worksheet tools are all illustrated in step-by-step exercises that you'll complete in this chapter.

Chapter 11, "Links between Files," shows you how to work with multifile applications in 1-2-3 and Windows. Lotus 1-2-3 allows you to open more than one worksheet file at a time, and to write special formulas to create links between worksheets. With a link formula, one worksheet can read data from another, whether the source worksheet is open or not. In an example presented in this chapter, you'll learn to take advantage of worksheet links to create a business summary from data contained in four different regional office worksheets. In addition, 1-2-3 supports a special Windows feature known as Dynamic Data Exchange (DDE), which allows you to transfer data between documents that you create in different Windows applications. For example, you can use DDE to copy a worksheet table to a word-processed document; then, as long as 1-2-3 and your word-processing program are both open in the Windows environment, any changes that take place in the worksheet data will automatically appear in your word-processed document. Chapter 11 helps you explore DDE links between different Windows applications.

Chapter 12, "Macro Programming," is an introduction to 1-2-3's complete macro language. You'll learn to use a variety of macro commands for programming operations such as loops, decisions, subroutines, and branches of control. You'll also learn to write interactive macro programs that elicit input from the user via input windows and custom menus. The sample programs presented in this chapter include a macro that creates daily appointment worksheets, and a macro that produces a file of mailing labels from an address database. In this chapter's final example, you'll learn to write a macro that creates data files on disk.

The book ends with two appendices and an index. Appendix A guides you through the steps of installing 1-2-3 on your computer. This appendix shows you how to select your own preferences for default options in the installation process—in particular, to activate 1-2-3's special Edit Undo feature. Appendix B lists and describes all of the 1-2-3 @ functions, providing you with a quick reference tool for reviewing the arguments and return values from each of the over one hundred tools in 1-2-3's function library.

A note about Release 1.0a: Not long after introducing Release 1.0, Lotus Development Corporation made several improvements in the performance of 1-2-3 for Windows and presented these revisions as Release 1.0a. If you switch from Release 1.0 to 1.0a, you'll notice a few differences in the product. For example:

◆ The Transcript window in Release 1.0a records keystroke macros in greater detail than in Release 1.0. (See Chapter 9, Figures 9.16 and 9.17.)

◆ The Install program for Release 1.0a activates the Edit Undo command by default. (See Appendix A.)

◆ The default setting for the Zoom option in the Window Display Options command is now 87% rather than 100%. (See Chapter 4, Figure 4.23.) You may want to increase this setting to 100% in Release 1.0a if you open a worksheet that you originally developed in Release 1.0.

Lotus Development Corporation has made the Release 1.0a update available free of charge to registered users of Lotus 1-2-3 for Windows.

PART ONE

FAST TRACK

To expand the size of a worksheet window, ... 8
click the maximize button (located at the upper-right corner of the window); or press Alt-Hyphen from the keyboard to open the control menu, and then type **X** to choose the Maximize command.

To move the cell pointer in the worksheet, ... 9
press an arrow key at the keyboard, or click the target cell with the mouse.

To scroll within the active area of a worksheet, ... 10
drag the scroll box to the right or left in the horizontal scroll bar or up or down in the vertical scroll bar.

To activate the 1-2-3 menu bar and pull down a menu, ... 11
press the Alt key plus the letter that represents the menu, or click the menu name with the mouse.

To view three worksheets in one window, ... 12
click the perspective icon in the icon palette; or pull down the Window menu, choose the Split command, and activate the Perspective option.

To insert worksheets into a worksheet window, ... 14
pull down the Worksheet menu and choose the Insert command. In the resulting dialog box, choose the Sheet option, and then enter the number of worksheets into the Quantity box.

**To move the cell pointer into a worksheet in a
window that contains multiple worksheets,** 15

perform one of the following three actions: Press Ctrl-PgUp or Ctrl-PgDn from the keyboard; click the next-worksheet or previous-worksheet icon in the icon palette; or click the target worksheet with the mouse if you are working in the perspective view.

**To read a brief description of any icon in the icon
palette,** 17

position the mouse pointer over the target icon, and hold down the right mouse button. The description appears in the title bar at the top of the 1-2-3 window.

To view the 1-2-3 Classic window, ... 20

press the slash key from the keyboard.

**To determine whether 1-2-3 is accepting a cell
entry as a label or as a value,** 22

look at the mode indicator (located at the upper-right corner of the screen, just below the menu bar) after you begin the entry. You will see either *LABEL* or *VALUE*.

To exit from 1-2-3, ... 24

pull down the File menu and choose the Exit command.

CHAPTER 1

Working with Lotus 1-2-3 for Windows

otus 1-2-3 for Windows contains the following three interrelated software components, known by the familiar terms *spreadsheet, graphics,* and *database:*

- ◆ The spreadsheet provides a rich variety of efficient tools designed to help you organize and work with tables of numbers.
- ◆ The graphics component allows you to create and print visual representations of numeric data, such as bar graphs and pie charts.
- ◆ The database gives you simple but effective techniques for storing and managing records of information.

These remarkable software tools have been available in the previous versions of Lotus 1-2-3—most recently, in Releases 2.2, 2.3, and 3.1. What is new and important about the latest version of 1-2-3 is its integration within the *graphical user interface* of Microsoft Windows 3.0. Running within the Windows environment, 1-2-3 has many significant advantages. Here are a few of the most important:

- ◆ The new style and appearance of 1-2-3 matches the general interface of other Windows applications. Windows programs have certain visual and functional elements in common—such as pull-down menus, dialog boxes, special-purpose keyboard functions, mouse control, and elaborate help systems. Lotus 1-2-3 for Windows includes all of these features, making the program easy to learn alongside other Windows applications that you might already be using.

◆ You can run Lotus 1-2-3 at the same time that you run other Windows application programs—such as a word processor, a desktop publishing program, or even a programming language compiler—and you can easily switch back and forth between one program and another.

◆ You can exchange data between Lotus 1-2-3 and other applications in a variety of important new ways. For example, you can use the Windows *clipboard* to copy data or graphs from Lotus 1-2-3 to other Windows programs.

This chapter introduces the three major components of 1-2-3 for Windows—spreadsheet, graphics, and database. You'll begin examining the features of these three components and learning how they interact with one another. Of course, you'll be studying each component in much greater detail throughout this book; this first chapter is an opportunity to gain a general understanding of the product's usefulness and to gather ideas for applying 1-2-3 to your own work.

You'll also begin exploring the elements of Lotus 1-2-3 in the Windows environment. A variety of hands-on exercises presented throughout the chapter will help you start using the keyboard and the mouse to explore the dimensions, features, and appearance of Lotus 1-2-3 for Windows.

EXPLORING THE LOTUS 1-2-3 INTERFACE

The Lotus spreadsheet provides on-screen *worksheets*—large grids of individual data cells—for organizing and analyzing tables of information. The terms worksheet and spreadsheet are sometimes used synonymously; in this book, however, *spreadsheet* refers to one of the three major software components of Lotus 1-2-3, and *worksheet* refers to an individual grid displayed on the screen for entering and working with tables of data.

Figure 1.1 shows the worksheet that appears on the screen when you first start Lotus 1-2-3 for Windows. (If you haven't yet followed the instructions presented in Appendix A for installing and starting Lotus 1-2-3 on your own computer, do so now. What you see on your screen will match the general appearance of Figure 1.1, although there may be some differences, depending on the characteristics of your display hardware.)

A worksheet is displayed inside a *window*. The worksheet window itself has all the characteristics and features that you may already be familiar with in the Windows environment, including a control menu, maximize and minimize buttons, scroll bars, and a title bar. If you don't know these Windows terms yet, you'll begin learning about them shortly, and you'll study them in greater detail in Chapter 2.

In an upcoming series of hands-on exercises, you'll explore the characteristics of a worksheet window. First of all, notice that the worksheet window's initial name is *Untitled*. This name, which appears on the *title bar* at the top of the window, is the default name for the first worksheet window that Lotus 1-2-3 displays on the screen at the beginning of a new session with the spreadsheet. When you begin developing a table of data inside a worksheet window, you'll ultimately want to save the worksheet as a file on disk. When you do so, you'll supply a file name that has meaning in the context of the work you are doing. But until you do so, the default title remains displayed on the title bar.

THE DIMENSIONS OF A WORKSHEET

The interior of the worksheet window is divided into rows and columns. Each row is identified by a number; you can initially see fewer than 20 rows, numbered 1, 2, 3, and so on. Each column is identified by a letter of the alphabet—A, B, C, and so on. A *cell* is the intersection of a row and a column, and is a

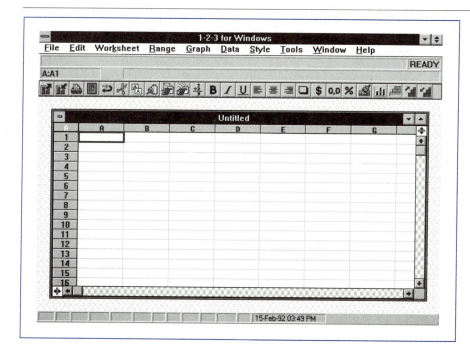

FIGURE 1.1:
A Lotus 1-2-3 worksheet

location in which you can enter a single data value. Each cell in the worksheet has an *address,* made up of the corresponding column letter and row number. For example, the cell at the intersection of column D and row 9 is identified by the address D9.

The *current cell*—that is, the cell in which 1-2-3 is ready to receive a data entry—contains a visual highlight known as the *cell pointer*. The cell pointer is a double-line border around the current cell. As you can see in Figure 1.1, cell A1 starts out as the current cell when you first begin your work in Lotus 1-2-3 or when you open a new worksheet window.

At the left and right ends of the worksheet window's title bar you can see some special icons. The rectangular icon located at the left side of the title bar is called the *control menu box;* and the pair of arrowhead icons at the right side are called the *minimize* and *maximize buttons*. (The *1-2-3 window*—that is, the application window in which the 1-2-3 environment is displayed—also has these three icons on its own title bar. When you get ready to use these window tools, make sure you distinguish correctly between the 1-2-3 window and the current worksheet window.) In addition, the right border of the worksheet window displays a *vertical scroll bar* and the lower border of the window displays a *horizontal scroll bar*.

In the following exercise, you'll use the maximize and minimize buttons, the control menu, and the scroll bars to explore the dimensions of the worksheet:

1. Click the maximize button, the up-arrow icon located at the upper-right corner of the worksheet window. (The *click* action means moving the mouse pointer to a particular target on the screen, and clicking the left mouse button once.) Alternatively, if you don't have a mouse, press Alt-Hyphen at the keyboard to pull down the control menu, and type **X** to select the Maximize command. The worksheet window expands to take up the available space within the 1-2-3 window (see Figure 1.2). Note that the worksheet window has temporarily lost its title bar. Instead, the title of the worksheet is included in the 1-2-3 title bar, in the following form:

   1-2-3 for Windows -[Untitled]

   In addition, the control box and the size button for the worksheet window are now displayed at the left and right sides of the 1-2-3 *menu bar,* just beneath the 1-2-3 window's title bar. (The *restore button* now appears as a two-headed arrow icon located at the right side of the menu bar. Clicking the restore button returns the worksheet window to its original size.)

2. Click the control menu box, the icon now located at the left side of the menu bar (or press Alt-Hyphen at the keyboard.) The control menu drops down over the worksheet window, as you can see in Figure 1.2. Click the Restore command with the mouse, or type **R** from the keyboard. The worksheet window shrinks back to its original size.

   3. Use either the maximize button or the Maximize command in the control menu to expand the worksheet window again.

   4. Press → once on your keyboard. The cell pointer moves one position to the right, to cell B1. Repeat this action six times, moving the cell pointer to H1. Column H is at the right side of the current worksheet window.

   5. Now move the cell pointer one more column to the right and watch what happens to the worksheet. Column A disappears from the left side of the window, making room for column I to be displayed on the right side of the worksheet. As this action begins to demonstrate, the worksheet contains many more columns and rows than can be displayed in the window at one time.

   6. Press ↓ key at the keyboard. Notice that the cell pointer moves down one position, to cell I2. Repeat this action until the cell pointer reaches I20,

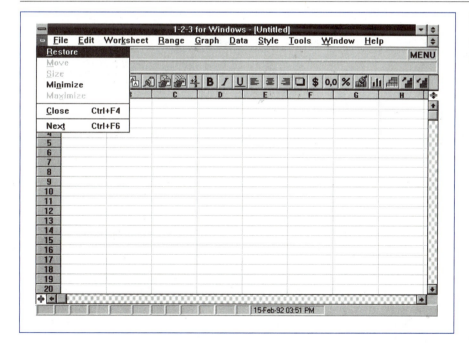

FIGURE 1.2:

The control menu of the worksheet window

then move the pointer down by one more cell. Notice that row 1 disappears from the worksheet window, making room for row 21.

7. Drag the *scroll box* part of the way across the horizontal scroll bar. The scroll box is a small, square button that indicates your current position in the *active* portion of your worksheet; for example, when the scroll box is located halfway across the scroll bar, you are at the approximate center of your current work. In this case, the *drag* action means moving the mouse pointer to the scroll box, holding down the left mouse button, and moving the pointer to the right; the scroll box moves along with the mouse pointer.

8. Press the End key and then press →. On this empty worksheet, the cell pointer moves to a column identified as IV, the last column in the worksheet. Note that the first 26 columns of the worksheet are identified by the letters A through Z; the next 26 by AA though AZ; the next 26 by BA through BZ; and so on, to the columns IA through IV. This lettering scheme gives the worksheet a total of 256 columns.

9. Press End and then ↓ at the keyboard. The final row on the worksheet is numbered 8192. The cell at the bottom-right corner of the worksheet therefore has the address IV8192, as shown in Figure 1.3.

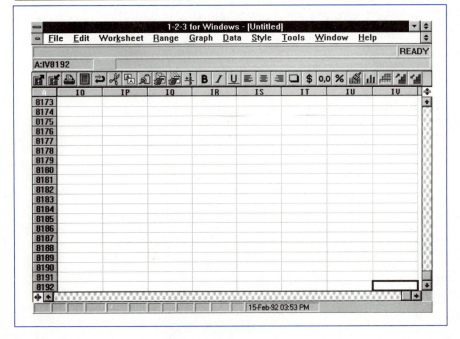

FIGURE 1.3:

The lower-right corner of the worksheet

10. Press the Home key on the keyboard. This action moves the cell pointer back to its beginning position, cell A1.

In summary, a Lotus 1-2-3 worksheet is a huge grid of rows and columns, with over two million individual cell addresses (256 columns times 8192 rows). The worksheet window displays only a small section of the worksheet at a time, but you can scroll the worksheet to view any group of cells that you want to work with.

One of the advanced features that Lotus 1-2-3 for Windows inherits from Release 3.1 is the capacity for *multiple worksheets* within a single worksheet window. This means that a worksheet window—and ultimately a worksheet file that you store on disk—can contain two or more worksheets. Furthermore, you can establish specific relationships among multiple worksheets by writing formulas that refer to data values in more than one worksheet. This useful arrangement is sometimes known as *three-dimensional worksheets*. In the next exercises, you'll begin exploring this feature; along the way, you'll have your first opportunity to try working with commands in the Lotus 1-2-3 menu.

THE MENU BAR

As in most Windows applications, the *menu bar* is the horizontal arrangement of commands displayed at the top of the screen, just below the 1-2-3 title bar:

File   Edit   Worksheet   Range   Graph   Data   Style   Tools   Window   Help

Each of these commands represents a *pull-down menu* containing a vertical list of subcommands. For example, Figure 1.4 shows the File menu. Mastering this system of menus and the dozens of commands they contain is a large part of the process of learning Lotus 1-2-3 for Windows.

There are several mouse and keyboard techniques available for choosing commands from the 1-2-3 menu system:

◆ From the keyboard, you press the Alt key—or the F10 function key—to activate the menu bar. Then you can press → or ← to highlight one of the main menu commands and ↵ to pull down the menu. (As you highlight a command on the main menu or within a pull-down menu, you'll notice that a brief description of the command is temporarily displayed at the top of the Lotus 1-2-3 window.) A keyboard shortcut for selecting a menu command is simply to press the Alt key followed by the single underscored letter that represents a particular command. For example, pressing Alt-F pulls down the File menu.

- With the mouse, you pull down a menu by simply clicking the corresponding command in the menu bar. For example, to pull down the File menu, you position the mouse pointer over File in the menu bar and click the left mouse button.

To back out of the menu system and return to your work in the current worksheet window, press the Escape key twice. Alternatively, you can click the worksheet window with the mouse to return to your data. As you switch between menus and worksheets, you'll notice changes in the *mode indicator,* the box near the upper-right corner of the 1-2-3 window, just below the menu bar. When the worksheet is active, this box displays the word *READY* (see Figure 1.3), but when a menu is active, the box displays *MENU* (see Figure 1.4). READY and MENU are two of several different *modes* that 1-2-3 switches between during your work in the program. You'll see other changes in the mode indicator later in this chapter.

Using Menu Commands to View Multiple Worksheets

In the following exercise, you'll use menu commands to explore 1-2-3's multiple worksheet feature.

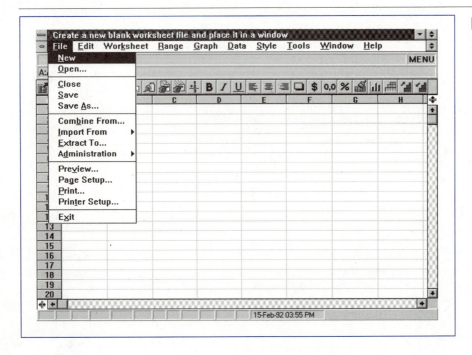

FIGURE 1.4:
The File menu

1. Pull down the Window menu by pressing Alt-W from the keyboard, or by clicking Window with the mouse.

2. On the pull-down menu, choose the Split command. (Type **S** at the keyboard, or click the command with the mouse.) This command gives you options for changing the appearance of the current worksheet window. The options are displayed on the *dialog box* that appears on the screen, shown in Figure 1.5. You'll find that many 1-2-3 commands produce dialog boxes. (Chapter 2 surveys the variety of graphic tools that Windows applications, including 1-2-3, display inside dialog boxes to represent particular options.)

3. Select the Perspective option button inside the Type box. This option allows you to view multiple worksheets inside the current window. To activate the option, you can type **P** from the keyboard or click the option with the mouse. When you make the selection, the round button at the left of the option is filled with a black bullet. To confirm the new option, press ↵, or click the rectangular OK button with the mouse. When you do so, the dialog box disappears from the screen, and the worksheet window is divided into sections for three worksheets (see Figure 1.6).

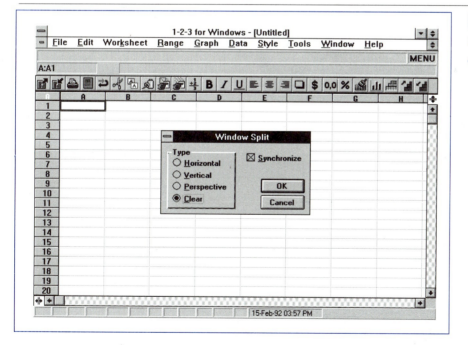

FIGURE 1.5:

The Window Split dialog box

4. Notice that the two upper worksheet sections are empty. To fill them with grids, your next step is to insert two new worksheets into the window. The Worksheet Insert command provides options for accomplishing this task. Use the mouse or the keyboard to pull down the Worksheet menu and select the Insert command. The resulting dialog box is shown in Figure 1.7.

5. Choose the Sheet option by typing **S** at the keyboard or by clicking Sheet with the mouse. (The Worksheet Insert command also has options for inserting columns or rows at a particular location in a worksheet, but in this case you want to insert entire new worksheets instead.)

6. Activate the Quantity box. (Type **Q** or click the mouse inside the rectangular box located beneath the word Quantity.) This is a *text box* into which you enter the number of worksheets that you want to insert. As you can see, the *default value* displayed inside the box is *1*. Enter a value of **2** into the box, instructing 1-2-3 to insert two new worksheets into the window. Press ↵ or click the OK button to confirm your entry. As a result, the two additional sections in the window are filled with new worksheet grids (see Figure 1.8).

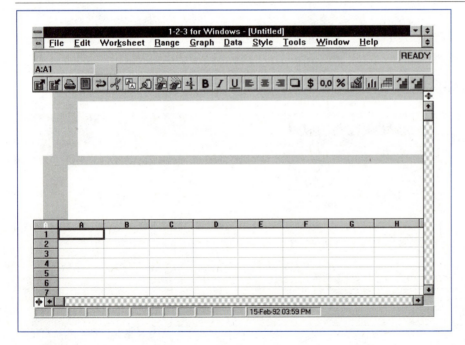

FIGURE 1.6:

The perspective view of the worksheet window

7. Press Ctrl-PgUp to move the cell pointer to the top worksheet, then press Ctrl-PgDn twice to move the cell pointer to each of the other two worksheets in turn. One worksheet in a window is current at a time. Notice that the worksheets are identified by the letters A, B, and C; as you move the cell pointer to each window, you'll see the *current cell address* displayed as *A:A1, B:A1,* or *C:A1* in the *address box,* located two lines below the menu bar. After you have experimented with the three worksheets, move the cell pointer to worksheet A.

8. Pull down the Window menu and select the Split command again. In the resulting dialog box, select the Clear option and press ↵. This action restores the original single-worksheet display in the window. However, the two worksheets that you inserted are still there. You can confirm this by pressing Ctrl-PgUp from the keyboard.

Take a moment to review what you've learned in these initial hands-on exercises. A worksheet window has the capacity for storing multiple worksheets—actually as many as 256. Every new worksheet window starts out with only one worksheet. You use the Worksheet Insert command to add new worksheets to a window. By activating the Perspective option in the Window Split dialog box, you can view three worksheets at once in a single window. Regardless of how many worksheets are actually displayed, you can use the

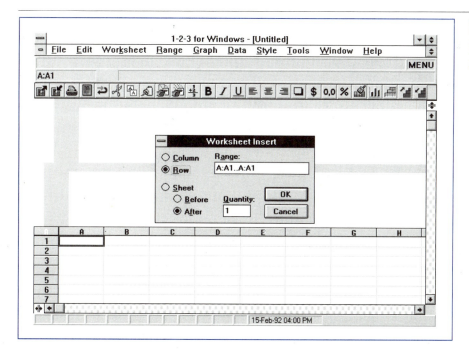

FIGURE 1.7:

The Worksheet Insert dialog box

Ctrl-PgUp and Ctrl-PgDn keyboard commands to view the previous or next worksheet in a window.

Like the columns in a worksheet, multiple worksheets in a window are identified by letters of the alphabet, from A, B, and C for the first three worksheets, up to IV for the 256th. A *complete cell address* therefore consists of three elements:

- The worksheet letter, followed by a colon
- The column letter
- The row number

For example, the following address refers to the cell at the intersection of column E and row 29, on the third worksheet in a window:

C:E29

Up to now, you have used menu commands—and their corresponding dialog boxes—to make changes in the appearance and content of a worksheet window. To make your work as easy and efficient as possible, Lotus 1-2-3 for Windows offers alternative tools for accomplishing particular tasks.

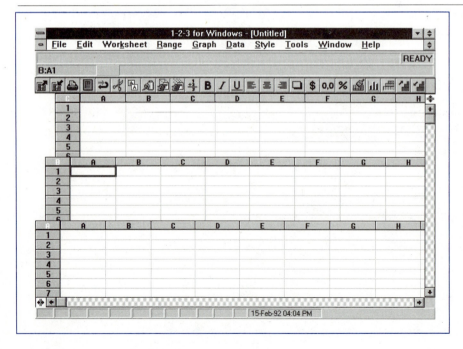

FIGURE 1.8:
Three worksheets in a window

Depending on your own preferences and work patterns, these alternatives can be quicker and simpler than the standard menu commands. You'll examine some of these tools in the upcoming sections of this chapter.

THE ICON PALETTE

One of the most engaging new features in 1-2-3 is the *icon palette*—the row of icons initially displayed above the worksheet area in the top portion of the 1-2-3 window. These tools—called *SmartIcons* in the Lotus documentation—give you one-step shortcuts for accomplishing some of the most commonly used menu commands. The icon palette has tools that perform a variety of tasks, including file storage, printing, copying, graphing, formatting, and so on. You'll learn the purpose of each icon as you study the corresponding menu commands in subsequent chapters. To perform the action that an icon represents, you simply click the icon with the mouse. (There is no keyboard access to the icon palette.)

In most cases, the drawings depicted in the icons themselves give you a good hint about the purpose of each icon. For example, the third icon from the right side of the palette seems to represent three overlapping worksheets. As you might guess, this icon switches the current window into the perspective view. In other words, the icon is a shortcut for selecting an option in the Window Split command. Try clicking this icon now with the mouse. As a result of the click, the three worksheets of the current window are once again displayed on the screen, as in Figure 1.8. Worksheet A is the current worksheet.

Conveniently, 1-2-3 for Windows offers you a simple technique for exploring the meaning and use of each of the tools in the icon palette. To find out what a particular icon does, follow these steps:

1. Position the mouse pointer over the icon you want to learn about.

2. Press and hold down the *right* mouse button. As long as you hold down the button, 1-2-3 displays a brief description of the selected icon on the title bar at the top of the 1-2-3 window.

When you try these steps on the perspective icon, you'll see the words *Perspective view* appear in the 1-2-3 title bar, as shown in Figure 1.9.

Take a few moments now to explore the other icons displayed in the icon palette. Press the right mouse button over each tool in turn, and note the description that 1-2-3 displays at the top of the window. Here is a list of the descriptions you'll read for the 26 icons initially displayed in the icon palette, from left to right:

Open an existing file

Save the current file

Print a range

Preview the print range

Undo last command or action

Cut to the clipboard

Copy to the clipboard

Paste from the clipboard

Select the range to copy to

Select the range to move to

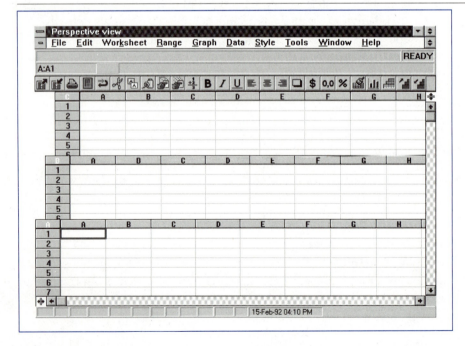

FIGURE 1.9:

The description of an icon in the icon palette

Sum the nearest adjacent range

Bold

Italics

Underline

Align left

Center

Align right

Outline and drop shadow

Currency format

Comma format

Percent format

Select range to apply current formats to

Create a new graph

Perspective view

Go to the next worksheet

Go to the previous worksheet

As you'll learn in Chapter 2, 1-2-3 for Windows allows you to *customize* the icon palette. The Tools Icon Palette command offers a large library of predefined *standard icons*. From this library, you can select the group of icons that seems most useful to you in your own work. You can also remove icons that you don't expect to use.

As an additional exercise with the icon palette, try performing the following steps:

1. Click the second-to-last icon on the right side of the icon palette. Clicking this icon ("Go to the next worksheet") moves the cell pointer to worksheet B. Click it again to move the cell pointer to worksheet C. (You'll recall that the Ctrl-PgUp sequence performs this same action from the keyboard.)

2. Click the last icon ("Go to the previous worksheet") twice. Worksheet A is current once again. (Ctrl-PgDn is the keyboard equivalent for this icon.)

3. Click the "Perspective view" icon (third from the right). You'll discover that this icon is a *toggle*—that is, clicking it once puts the current worksheet window in the perspective view, and clicking it again switches the window back into the single-worksheet view. Only worksheet A is now visible in the window.

4. Click the "Go to the next worksheet" and "Go to the previous worksheet" icons twice each in turn. As you'll see, these icons work both in the perspective view and in the single-worksheet view. (As you complete this exercise, make sure worksheet A is current.)

You'll learn much more about the tools in the icon palette as you continue working with 1-2-3 for Windows.

Another special feature included in this new version of Lotus 1-2-3 is the 1-2-3 Classic window, which you'll begin exploring in the next secion of this chapter.

THE 1-2-3 CLASSIC WINDOW

The 1-2-3 Classic window is a special alternate menu system for users who are upgrading from 1-2-3 Release 3.1, or from an earlier release of the program. This menu appears on the screen when you press the slash key—the key that has traditionally accessed menus in all previous versions of Lotus 1-2-3. (Alternatively, you can press Shift-<.) Press the slash key now, and you will see the 1-2-3 Classic window at the top of the screen, as in Figure 1.10. If you have worked extensively in a previous version of 1-2-3, the commands in this menu may seem comfortably familiar. This alternate menu system is accessible only from the keyboard, not with the mouse.

As an exercise with the Classic menu system, try switching between the perspective mode and the single-worksheet view in the current window:

1. With the 1-2-3 Classic menu currently displayed on the screen, type **W** to choose the Worksheet command.

2. Type **W** to choose the Window command.

3. Type **P** to choose the Perspective command. The result is the same as selecting the Perspective option in the Window Split dialog box: The current window displays three worksheets. Also notice that the 1-2-3 Classic menu disappears after you complete the action of selecting a command.

4. Now press the following four keys in sequence: **/WWC**. (This is the traditional notation for representing command selections

from the 1-2-3 Classic menus. In this case, the notation represents the /Worksheet Window Clear command from the 1-2-3 Classic menu.) The current window once again displays a single worksheet.

Here are a few words of advice about the 1-2-3 Classic window: Use it if you need to while you are first adjusting to the new 1-2-3 for Windows interface. But try to wean yourself from it as quickly as possible. Learn to use the standard menu bar and the practical new icon palette to accomplish tasks in this new environment. In the long run, you'll become a much more efficient Windows user if you adjust yourself to the standard ways of accomplishing tasks in Windows.

By the way, another part of the 1-2-3 Classic menu appears on the screen when you press the Shift-: keyboard combination. This second Classic menu contains commands related to formatting and preparing a worksheet for printing and publication. By contrast, the standard 1-2-3 for Windows menu contains all of the program's commands in a single convenient system of pull-down menus—another strong argument in favor of using the Windows-style menu rather than the Classic menus.

As a final introductory exercise, you'll next try entering data values into some of the cells of the worksheet you've been examining.

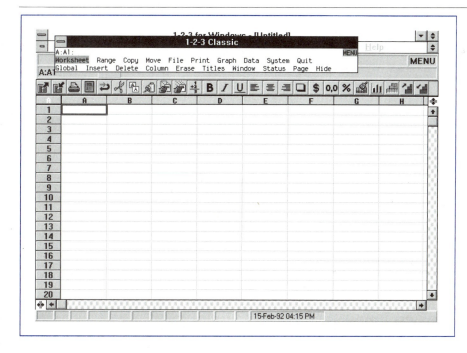

FIGURE 1.10:

The 1-2-3 Classic window

Data Entry and the Mode Indicator

Lotus 1-2-3 recognizes two general types of data for entry into the cells of a worksheet: *labels* and *values*. A label is a nonnumeric entry beginning with a letter of the alphabet or with one of several special symbols that 1-2-3 recognizes as the beginning of a label. A value is a number or the numeric result of a formula. (Actually, Lotus also recognizes date and time entries, and translates them into numeric values; you'll learn about such values in Chapter 4.)

Several interesting changes take place in the 1-2-3 program window when you begin entering a data item into a cell. You'll explore these changes in the following brief exercise, as you enter the word Profit as a label into cell A1 and the value 9876 into cell A2:

1. Press the Home key, if necessary, to select cell A1.

2. From the keyboard, hold down the Shift key and type the letter **P**. Examine the mode indicator; it now displays the word *LABEL*, indicating that 1-2-3 is accepting your entry as a nonnumeric data item (see Figure 1.11). The uppercase P that you have typed appears on the line just below the mode indicator, in an area called the *contents box*. The contents box displays data or formulas that you are in the process of entering from the keyboard. (You'll learn in Chapter 2 that the contents box is also a place where you can edit a data item or formula that is already stored in a cell.) Just to the left of the contents box are two small boxes, one containing an X and the other a check mark. These are called the *cancel button* and the *confirm button*, respectively.

3. Complete the label by typing the remaining letters of the word Profit. If you make a typing mistake, you can press the Backspace key to erase the last character you typed.

4. Confirm the entry either by clicking the confirm button with the mouse, or by pressing ↵ from the keyboard. Once again, notice the changes that occur on your worksheet and in the 1-2-3 window. The cancel button and the confirm button disappear, and the data item you entered into the contents box is copied into the current cell, A1. The label is left-justified inside the cell, following the default *alignment* for labels in 1-2-3. (In Chapter 4, you'll learn about other ways of aligning labels within cells.) The mode indicator now displays the word *READY*.

5. Press ↓ once to select cell A2.

6. Type the four digits **9876** from the keyboard. This time the mode indicator displays the word *VALUE*, indicating that 1-2-3 is accepting your data entry as a numeric value (see Figure 1.12). As before, the entry appears inside the contents box, and the cancel and confirm buttons are displayed just to the left of this box.

7. Press ↓ once on the keyboard. This action accomplishes two steps at once: It completes the data entry and moves the cell pointer down to cell A3. Notice that the value *9876* is displayed right-justified inside cell A2. Numeric values are always right-justified in Lotus 1-2-3.

8. In cell A3, begin the following label entry: **ABC**. (Do not press ↵.) Now cancel the entry by clicking the cancel button with the mouse, or by pressing the Escape key from the keyboard.

In summary, you can always check the mode indicator during data entry to make sure that 1-2-3 is accepting your data the way you are expecting it to—that is, as a label or a value. You can complete an entry by pressing ↵, by pressing a direction key (such as ↑ or ↓), or by clicking the confirm button with the mouse. Cancel an entry by clicking the cancel button or by pressing the Escape key.

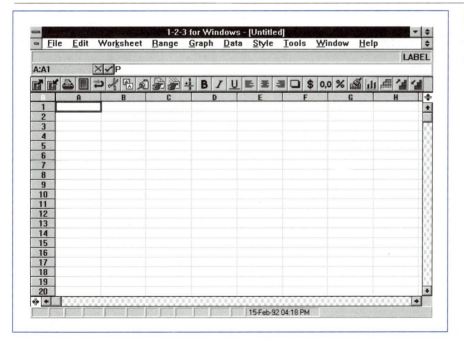

FIGURE 1.11:

Entering a label into a cell

This is the end of the hands-on portion of this chapter. If you wish to exit from 1-2-3 before you continue reading, here are the steps:

1. Pull down the File menu and select the Exit command.

2. In the File Exit dialog box, click the No button to indicate that you wish to exit without saving your current work.

After these steps, you remain in Windows, but the 1-2-3 application window is no longer open.

In the remainder of this chapter, you'll examine a set of sample applications that have been organized and solved within 1-2-3. In the context of these examples, you'll begin exploring the use of the three major 1-2-3 components—spreadsheet, graphics, and database.

PLANNING A WORKSHEET

As you have begun to learn, you can enter labels, numbers, and chronological values (dates and times) as the data values on a worksheet. You can also enter *formulas* that instruct Lotus to perform specific arithmetic operations with

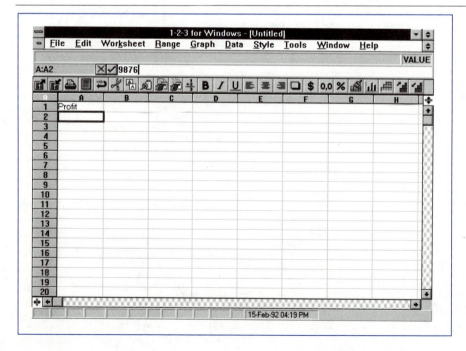

FIGURE 1.12:
Entering a value into a cell

your data. Given a table of raw data, a worksheet simplifies all kinds of calculations from finding bottom-line numeric totals to performing complex statistical and financial formulas. Perhaps the single most important feature of the Lotus spreadsheet is this:

> Worksheets automatically recalculate totals and other formulas whenever you make changes in the raw data.

This quintessential characteristic is what distinguishes an "electronic spreadsheet" from paper, pencil, and eraser. You can make changes in data values whenever you want, without having to face the task of redoing the rest of your work. If you plan and write your formulas appropriately, Lotus recalculates any numeric value that depends upon the raw data you have changed.

Spreadsheet users sometimes refer to this essential characteristic as 1-2-3's "what-if" capability. You can use this feature to find out what happens to a specific set of calculations when you make changes in the data that affect the calculations. "What-if" questions come up in an infinite variety of common business applications; for example,

- What is the new break-even point in the projected sales of a product if costs increase by a specific amount per unit?
- What happens to your projected tax rate this year if you purchase a major depreciable asset, such as a new computer for your business?
- What is the new monthly payment on a particular business loan if you can double the term of the loan and decrease the interest rate by one percent?

In calculations that are done by hand, finding the answers to questions like these can take a lot of time and effort—especially when there are many intermediate calculations that lead up to a final value. But in Lotus 1-2-3 you simply change the appropriate data parameters in your worksheet, and the rest of the work is done for you. As you gain experience with worksheets, you'll quickly learn to organize your work to take full advantage of the "what-if" feature in the context of business calculations.

The examples you'll be examining in the upcoming sections of this chapter describe an application that is less typical than the business calculations listed above—but nonetheless apt for illustrating the power of 1-2-3. The imaginary situation for these examples is as follows: A company has invited a nutritionist named Barbara Johnson to conduct a series of lunchtime seminars to which all employees are invited. The planned focus of the seminars is good nutrition for health-conscious working people. In particular, employees have expressed an interest in a somewhat confusing diet-related subject that has been frequently covered in recent media reports: the fat content in typical fast-food lunch menus, and the impact of this factor on health. There has been much talk about the so-called 30-percent fat diet, and many of the employees would like some clarification.

In anticipation of these seminars, Johnson is using Lotus 1-2-3 for Windows to prepare a series of handouts on which to base her discussion. These handouts are taking the form of worksheets, graphs, and databases. She begins her preparations by designing some worksheets that analyze the caloric and fat content of what she expects are typical lunches for the employees in her audience.

As you examine the nutritionist's work, keep in mind your own goals for this first chapter: To gain a general understanding of the elements of Lotus 1-2-3, and to begin imagining your own uses for the program. For the moment, focus on broad capabilities and features rather than on the specific techniques involved in creating these examples.

DEVELOPING A 1-2-3 WORKSHEET

Ultimately, most worksheets that you create are likely to become tools for presenting information to other people. Whether you are simply sharing data with the person who sits at the desk next to yours, or communicating ideas to a conference room full of managers, you will want your data to be not only accurate, but also clearly organized, attractively presented, and easy to understand. Lotus 1-2-3 for Windows includes a great number of tools designed to help you meet these requirements.

Accordingly, the process of creating a successful worksheet typically includes several tasks:

1. Place a descriptive title near the top of your worksheet.

2. Enter column headings and row labels that describe the categories of numeric data that you'll be including in your worksheet table.

3. Enter the numeric data values themselves.

4. Write formulas that perform specific calculations on the numeric data values. When appropriate, copy these formulas to additional cells on your worksheet to perform the same calculations on other columns or rows of data.

5. Improve the appearance of your data—both labels and numbers— by applying specific display formats and styles to particular cells.

For example, you might want to display certain numbers in a currency format or a percentage format. Titles, labels, and numbers can also be displayed in special type styles for clarity and emphasis. For example, you can display data in boldface, italic, and underlined styles.

You'll see this progression of tasks illustrated in Barbara Johnson's worksheet examples. Her initial goal is to explain the meaning of the 30-percent fat diet and, in the context of this diet, to analyze typical lunches that employees are likely to buy in fast-food restaurants or to bring to work in brown bags.

ENTERING LABELS AND DATA

As the starting point for her research, Johnson stops off at the fast-food restaurant across the street from the company's building. She knows that a lot of the employees come here for quick and inexpensive lunches. Johnson asks for nutritional information about several items on the restaurant's menu. The manager of the restaurant gives her a copy of a printed nutritional report that is always available, but provided only on request. A quick glance at the report confirms that it contains the data Johnson will need for her presentation—in particular, the calories and fat content of each item on the restaurant's menu.

Back at her office, Johnson formulates what she guesses is a typical lunch for someone who goes to the restaurant: a hamburger, an order of French fries, some cookies, and a diet soda. She starts up Lotus 1-2-3 for Windows, and begins designing a worksheet on which she can present nutritional information about this particular meal. She begins by entering a title for the worksheet in cells A3 and B3:

Lunch #1   Fast-Food Restaurant

Because she is planning to create additional worksheets for other menus, she identifies this one as "Lunch #1."

Her purpose in this worksheet is to analyze the fat content of a meal and to compare this content with the recommended fat intake for a healthy adult. Secondarily, she wants to demonstrate the importance of translating available nutritional information into meaningful data. The two major nutritional facts that she will be presenting in her seminar are as follows:

◆ Nutritionists recommend that the daily fat intake for a healthy adult should be 30 percent or less of the total daily caloric consumption.

♦ One gram of fat—regardless of its source—is equivalent to nine calories.

On the nutritional panels provided on food packages, the fat content per serving is usually stated in grams, rather than as a percentage of total calories. For this reason, the health-conscious consumer needs to do some arithmetic to figure out whether a given food item is a reasonable part of a 30-percent fat diet. Johnson will eventually express this arithmetic in formulas that she enters onto her worksheet.

She continues her work by entering labels in rows 5 and 6 for four columns of information:

	Total	Fat	% Fat
Item	Calories	in grams	Calories

The first column is for the name of the food item. The second and third columns will display data copied from the nutritional information Johnson received at the restaurant: The total calories of a given food item, and the total fat contained in the item, expressed in grams. The final column is for a value that will be calculated from the available nutritional data: the percent of total calories represented by the fat content in the food item.

Next, Johnson enters four rows of data for the four items she has included on her sample menu. She also plans a Total line at the bottom of the table, to provide the total of each column; but she leaves the numeric columns blank in this row as well.

Figure 1.13 shows Johnson's work up to this point. You'll immediately notice two interesting features of her worksheet: She has increased the display width of column A, to accommodate the names of the food items; and she has eliminated the display of *grid lines*—the vertical and horizontal lines that initially separate columns and rows in a worksheet. These characteristics illustrate two of the ways in which Lotus 1-2-3 gives the user control over the appearance of a worksheet; you'll learn how to accomplish these changes in Chapter 4.

In short, the nutritionist has completed the first few steps of designing her worksheet. She has created a title; she has entered descriptive column headings and row labels to identify the numeric data in the table; and she has copied the basic numeric data into the table. Her next step is to begin writing formulas to perform calculations. She'll enter formulas at two different locations on the worksheet: the Total line at the bottom of the table, and the % Fat Calories column at the right side of the table.

WRITING FORMULAS

The purpose of a formula in a worksheet is to calculate a value, usually using existing numbers on the worksheet as the parts of the operation. When you enter a successful formula into a cell, 1-2-3 displays the *result* of the formula in the cell. The contents box at the top of the 1-2-3 window displays the formula itself whenever you select the cell that contains a formula.

Lotus 1-2-3 recognizes specific formats for formulas and enforces precise rules regarding the correctness of those formats. Here are some of the most common elements you'll use in writing formulas:

◆ Literal numeric values, such as 9 or 365.

◆ Cell addresses, such as D5 or B4. In a formula, an address *represents* the value that is currently stored in the corresponding cell. (If you have ever worked with a programming language such as Basic or Pascal, you'll recognize that a cell address is roughly equivalent to a *variable* name in a computer program.)

◆ Arithmetic operators, such as + (addition), – (subtraction), * (multiplication), and / (division).

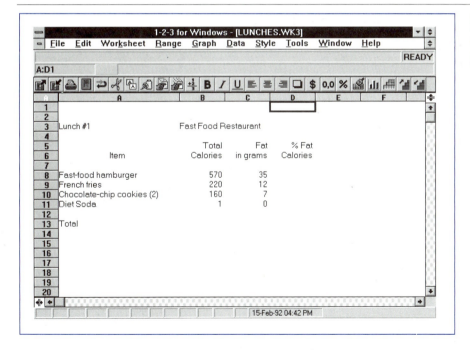

FIGURE 1.13:
The first stage of the lunch worksheet

◆ Functions from 1-2-3's large function library. A function is a built-in tool designed to perform a specific calculation. All of the 1-2-3 functions have names that begin with the @ character. For example, the @SUM function—one of the simplest and most commonly used of all the 1-2-3 functions—finds the sum of a group of numbers. (Chapter 5 presents a survey and summary of the 1-2-3 worksheet functions.)

You'll find examples of all of these elements in the formulas Barbara Johnson enters into her Lunch #1 worksheet. Her first task is to find the total calories and the total grams of fat contained in the meal. To accomplish this, she begins by entering the following formula into cell B13:

@SUM(B8..B11)

As you might have guessed, B8..B11 inside parentheses tells the @SUM function to find the total of all the values stored in the cells B8, B9, B10, and B11. An expression like B8..B11 represents a *range* of cells; you'll find many contexts in which ranges are important during your work with 1-2-3.

The result of the @SUM function is displayed in cell B13 as *951*. Similarly, Johnson enters an @SUM expression in cell C13 to find the total grams of fat in the meal. (Actually, she has the option of entering a new version of the formula directly from the keyboard, or *copying* the formula from cell B13 to cell C13. You'll learn the significance of copying formulas in Chapter 3.) The resulting value in cell C13 is 54.

Next, Johnson has to devise a formula that will calculate the fat calories in each food item as a percentage of the total calories. Given that there are nine calories in each gram of fat, here is the formula for finding the ratio of fat calories to total calories:

(Fat Grams × 9) ÷ Total Calories

Johnson's task is to translate this into a formula that 1-2-3 can accept and perform. She moves to cell D8 and enters the following:

+C8*9/B8

Cell C8 contains the number of grams of fat in a hamburger. Multiplying this value by 9 gives the calories of fat, and dividing the product by the total calories (stored in cell B8) gives the ratio. (Keep in mind that * represents multiplication in a 1-2-3 formula.) When Johnson first enters this formula into cell D8, this calculated value appears in the cell: 0.552632.

This is the decimal format of the ratio; but Johnson wants to display the ratio as a percentage. While D8 is still the current cell, she clicks the % icon in the icon palette at the top of the 1-2-3 window. This icon changes the display format of the value in D8 to a percentage, which now appears as *55.26%*.

Although Johnson appreciates the convenience of the percent icon, she decides that this predefined format is not exactly what she wants; she would prefer to display the percent as a rounded integer—that is, with no digits after the decimal point. To achieve this display format, she selects options from the Format command in the Range menu. As a result of her selections, the percentage is displayed simply as *55%*. (You'll work with the Range Format command in Chapter 4.)

Johnson has written a successful formula. The fat calories account for 55 percent of the total calories in the hamburger. Now she copies this formula down column D—first to find the percent of fat calories for the other food items on the menu, and then to find the total percent of fat calories for the entire meal. Figure 1.14 shows the result of her work. Notice that fat calories for the meal amount to 51 percent of the total calories—far above the recommended 30 percent. As Johnson notes with satisfaction, this worksheet will easily prove a point about the nutritional value of fast-food lunches!

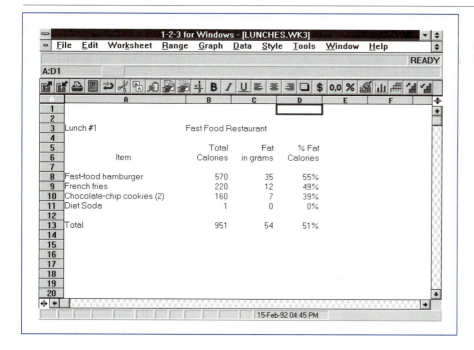

FIGURE 1.14:

Adding formulas to the worksheet

PREPARING THE WORKSHEET FOR PRESENTATION

Up to now, Barbara Johnson has concentrated on entering data and writing formulas, without worrying much about the appearance of her worksheet. With two exceptions, she has left data items in their default formats, alignments, and display styles. One exception is the percent format that she applied to the fourth column in her data table. The second exception is in the alignments of the four column headings; can you see that these labels are not displayed in their default alignments? (Recall that 1-2-3 initially left-justifies a label entry in a cell.)

Now the nutritionist is ready to give some thought to the appearance of her worksheet. Lotus 1-2-3 for Windows offers her a rich variety of options in this regard. For example, she can choose from among a great variety of formats for numeric values, including currency, decimal, and percentage. Values and labels can both be displayed in *styles*—such as bold, italics, and underlined—that provide emphasis in a worksheet. Furthermore, 1-2-3 offers a selection of type fonts and font sizes for displaying and printing the information in a worksheet. You'll learn about all these options—and the final step of printing a completed worksheet—in Chapter 4.

Johnson decides to use combinations of bold, italic, and underlined styles—along with increased type size for selected data items—to prepare her worksheet for presentation. You can see the result of her work in Figure 1.15.

Some of these options are available at the click of the mouse, thanks to style icons available in the icon palette. For example, here are the steps Johnson takes to change the column of food items to bold italic type style:

1. Select the target range of cells—in this case, from A8 down to A11—by positioning the mouse pointer at A8 and dragging the mouse down to A11. In response, 1-2-3 highlights the entire range.

2. Click the bold icon in the icon palette. The bold style is applied to all the labels in the selected range.

3. Click the italic icon in the icon palette. The italic style is applied to the labels.

Notice the actions performed in these steps: first selecting a range of cells and then choosing specific options for this range. As you continue working with 1-2-3, you'll find that this is one typical way of accomplishing many kinds of tasks in a worksheet. Conveniently, Lotus 1-2-3 for Windows often lets you choose between the following two approaches:

◆ Select a range first, then choose a command that applies to the range.

◆ Choose a command, then use the command's dialog box to specify the range over which the command will act.

Your choice between these two approaches is a matter of personal preference and convenience. The end result is always the same.

The nutritionist has now completed her first version of the lunch worksheet. She takes care to save her work to disk by pulling down the File menu and selecting the Save As command. She supplies the name Lunches for her worksheet, and 1-2-3 accordingly saves the file as LUNCHES.WK3. (.WK3 is the default extension name for worksheets saved from this version of 1-2-3.)

She is now ready to begin formulating other lunch menus to include in her presentation on fat intake in a healthy diet. Clearly there is nothing particularly healthy about this first menu. She decides to prepare two additional lunch menus, the first a combination of items purchased from the fast-food restaurant and food prepared at home; and the second consisting completely of "brown bag" items carried from home.

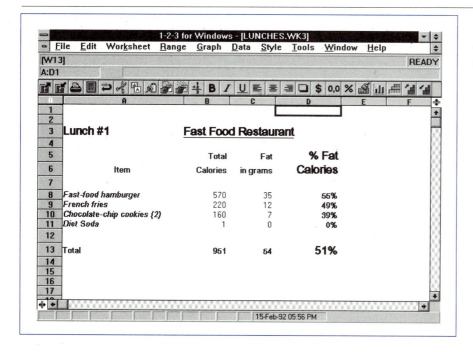

FIGURE 1.15:
Applying formats and type styles to the worksheet

This is where 1-2-3's "what-if" facility becomes central to her work. As you'll see, the nutritionist can create the two new lunch worksheets simply by changing a few data items in the original. Whenever she enters new numeric data values to describe a particular food item, 1-2-3 automatically recalculates the applicable formulas.

Making Changes in the Data

For lunch #2, Johnson decides to make two changes in the menu. She substitutes a turkey sandwich for the fast-food hamburger and a carton of milk for the diet soda. She begins by entering the names of the two new food items in cells A8 and A11:

A8	**Turkey sandwich (with mayo)**
A11	**Low-fat milk (1/2 pint)**

To change the contents of a cell in a worksheet, you can simply select the cell and enter a new label or value. When you confirm the new entry, the previous data item disappears, and the new item takes its place. Any display style that you have previously applied to the cell is retained. In this case, the two new food items are still displayed in bold italic type.

Next, Johnson determines the approximate caloric and fat contents of these two new menu items. She enters the calories into column B (cell B8 for the turkey sandwich and B11 for the milk); and the fat content, in grams, into column C (cell C8 for the sandwich and C11 for the milk). Each time she enters a new numeric data value, three additional changes take place instantly on her worksheet:

◆ A new column total appears in the Total line at the bottom of the worksheet (row 13).

◆ A new fat percentage appears in the final column of the worksheet (column D).

◆ The new total fat percentage for the meal appears in cell D13.

In effect, these are the "what-if" factors for her worksheet: What happens to the total calories, the total fat content, and the fat percentages if she changes an item in the menu? Thanks to 1-2-3's ability to recalculate formulas, the answers appear immediately when the nutritionist makes changes in the worksheet data. Figure 1.16 shows the second lunch menu, with the revised nutritional information. (Notice that the title of the worksheet has also been changed.) In terms of fat calories, this meal is an improvement over the first menu, but it still does not meet the goal of the 30-percent fat diet.

For her third menu, the nutritionist wants to illustrate the importance of simple but careful dietary decisions. After revising the title again, she makes two more changes in the menu, first removing the mayonnaise from the turkey sandwich and second substituting an apple for the French fries. She enters the new calories and fat data into columns B and C for these revised food items. Once again, 1-2-3 recalculates her formulas as she changes nutritional data. The final result (shown in Figure 1.17) is a dramatically reduced fat percentage, well below the 30-percent goal.

For convenience, Barbara Johnson decides to save all three of the lunch worksheets in a single file. She uses the Window Insert command to add two worksheets to the current window, and copies the current version of the lunch menu to each of the two new worksheets. She reformulates the first two menus in worksheets A and B, and retains the final menu in worksheet C. When she saves her work to disk, LUNCHES.WK3 contains three worksheets, one for each of the lunch menus that she will present in her seminar. Figure 1.18 shows how these worksheets appear in the pespective mode.

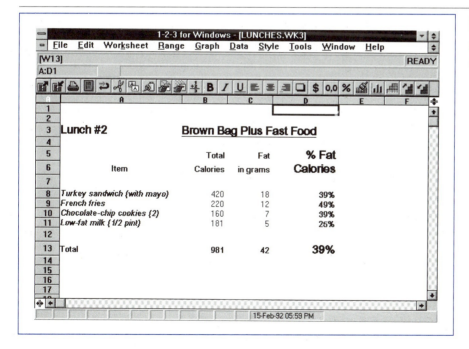

FIGURE 1.16:

Revised data and recalculated formulas

CREATING GRAPHS FROM A WORKSHEET

The graphics component of 1-2-3 gives you efficient tools for creating graphs and charts from your worksheet data. Lotus 1-2-3 for Windows supports an impressive variety of two- and three-dimensional graph types, including line graphs, bar graphs, and pie charts. The initial steps for creating a graph are simple:

1. Select the worksheet range containing the numbers and labels you want to represent in your graph.

2. Issue a command to create a new graph from the current range selection.

Again, notice the familiar pattern of these steps: First select a worksheet range, then give a command. The graph appears in a new window on the screen. In addition, 1-2-3 displays a new set of graph-related commands on the menu bar, and a new collection of icons in the icon palette.

Once you create an initial graph from a table of data, you can change the graph type and customize your presentation by adding titles, labels, a

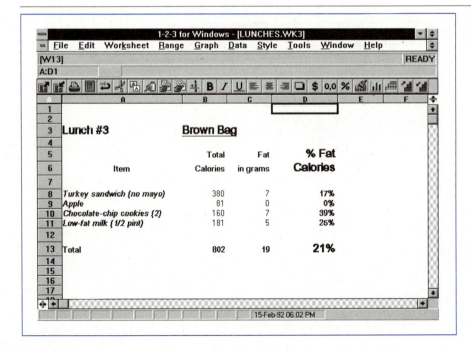

FIGURE 1.17:
The final lunch menu

legend, and other graph objects such as arrows and frames. The graph menu and icon palette include options for all these features.

Like the formulas in a worksheet, graphs are dependent upon the original raw data. If you make changes in your data, 1-2-3 automatically rebuilds the graphs you have created. This is perhaps the ultimate in "what-if" experiments: You can change a data value on your worksheet and immediately see the effect on the corresponding graph.

A graph is always associated with the worksheet from which it was originally created in Lotus 1-2-3. When you save a worksheet file to disk, any graphs you have created are saved with the worksheet. Furthermore, 1-2-3 allows you to copy a graph directly onto a worksheet so that you can view—and print—the worksheet table along with its graph.

DESIGNING A GRAPH

Barbara Johnson now turns her attention to a related topic that she wants to cover in her seminar. She realizes that many people have trouble interpreting the nutritional information that appears on the labels of food purchased in supermarkets. In regards to fat content, the problem is simple: Labels normally disclose the number of *grams* of fat per serving, whereas the important factor

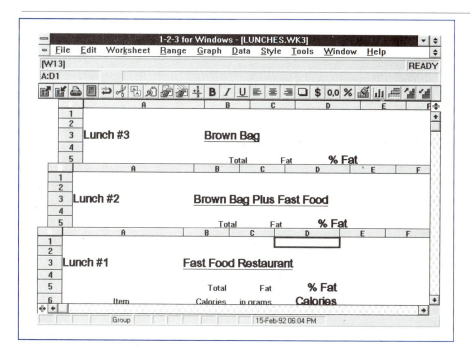

FIGURE 1.18:
The three lunch worksheets in a single window

is the *percent* of fat calories in the serving. For example, Johnson has found the following information on a package of bologna:

Serving size:	1 slice (30 grams)
Calories per serving:	90
Fat per serving:	8 grams

In this example, the fat content (8 grams) is less than a third of the total weight of a serving (30 grams). But the significant factor is not the weight of the fat, but rather the fat calories in proportion to the total calories. The 8 grams of fat are equivalent to 72 calories, or more than three-quarters of the total caloric content of a serving.

To underscore the importance of this distinction, Johnson decides to create some simple graphics that she can hand out to the participants in her seminar. The graphs should illustrate clearly the discrepancy between the *weight* content and the *caloric* content of fat in a particular food item.

For this second topic, the nutritionist will take advantage of the second major component of Lotus 1-2-3—graphics. She begins by creating a small worksheet table containing the information about a slice of bologna. As shown in Figure 1.19, the worksheet contains two rows of numeric data, recording the weight and caloric content of the food serving. There are three columns of numbers. The first two columns display the fat content and the total serving data. The final column is a calculation of the percentage of fat: While the fat is only 27 percent of the weight of a serving, it is a full 80 percent of the caloric content.

After completing this worksheet, the nutritionist follows a quick and easy sequence of steps to create her graphs. (You'll learn about these steps in detail in Chapter 6, which introduces the graphics component of 1-2-3.) She decides to create one bar graph to represent the relationship between the total weight of a serving and the fat weight in the serving; and a second graph to represent the relationship between total calories and fat calories.

For each graph in turn, she first selects the range of worksheet data that she wants to include in the graph: A5..C5 for the weight and A6..C6 for the calories. These ranges include labels (in column A) that will identify the elements of the graph, along with two columns of numeric data (columns B and C). Next, she clicks the graph icon in the icon palette. In response, 1-2-3 opens a new graph window and displays an initial line graph depicting the data she has selected on the worksheet.

But Johnson has decided that the best way to illustrate this particular set of data is with three-dimensional bar graphs. She selects this graph type in a dialog box that 1-2-3 presents when she pulls down the Chart menu and chooses the Type command. (The Chart menu is one of the new entries that 1-2-3 presents on the menu bar when the active window is a graph.) Finally, she uses other commands from the graph menu bar to add titles and *legends* to the graphs. A legend identifies the meaning of elements within the graph; in this case, the legend indicates the colors of the bars that represent fat weight and calories, and total weight and calories.

The entire job of creating the graphs takes only a few minutes. The result of Johnson's work appears in Figure 1.20. Each graph contains a cluster of two bars. The first graph shows the relationship between the fat weight and the total weight of a serving, and the second graph shows the relationship between fat calories and total calories. The contrast between these two relationships is dramatic, and the nutritionist is satisfied that this handout will adequately illustrate her point to her seminar participants.

For the final topic in her seminar on lunchtime nutrition for business people, Barbara Johnson wants to apply the 30-percent fat diet specifically to a group of people with differing nutritional needs. For this purpose, she has created a *database* of imaginary, but representive, clients who have varying caloric and fat requirements for a given day. She wants to compare these individual requirements with the nutritional content of one of the lunch menus

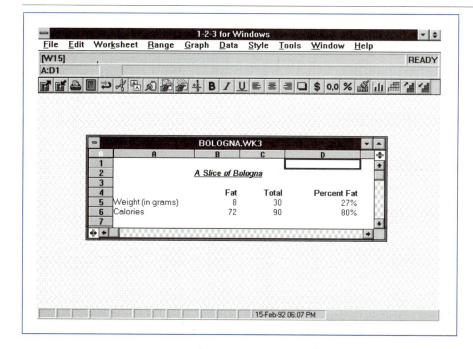

FIGURE 1.19:
The bologna worksheet

she devised earlier. Her goal is to demonstrate the suitability—or inadequacy—of this menu for meeting specific nutritional needs.

PERFORMING DATABASE OPERATIONS

A Lotus *database* is a collection of *records* stored in the rows and columns of a worksheet—for example, a client address directory, a group of employee records, or a list of inventory items. Each row displays one record of information, and a group of consecutive rows make up the database. The worksheet columns contain the *fields* of the database—that is, the categories of information supplied for each record. The *field names* are column headings that describe each category of information. For example, an inventory database might include the following fields:

Item   Quantity   ReorderDate   ReorderAmount   Price

In general, each record in the database contains a data entry for each field. Some field items are labels or numbers that you enter directly from the keyboard. Others may be *calculated fields*—that is, numeric or chronological items that are calculated from the data in other fields.

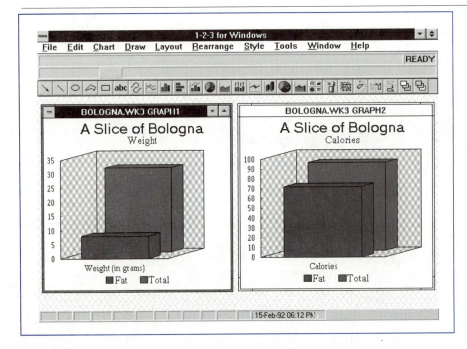

FIGURE 1.20:

The bologna graphs

The length of a database is equal to the number of records currently stored in the table. For example, an inventory database might have a length of a few dozen, or a few thousand, records. Over time, the length of a database might change, as you insert or append new records, or as you perform operations that delete records.

After developing a database in a worksheet, you can perform a variety of operations on the records in the database. A *query* is a database operation that isolates records that match specific *selection criteria*. Commands in the 1-2-3 Data menu are designed to simplify the query process, regardless of the length of your database. After writing expressions that represent your selection criteria, you can choose commands that perform the following queries:

- ◆ The Find operation simply highlights records that match your selection criteria.

- ◆ The Delete operation removes selected records from the database.

- ◆ The Extract operation copies matching records from the database to another table location that you specify.

- ◆ The Modify operation also extracts matching records, but keeps track of the locations of the extracted records. You can make changes in the extracted data table and then instruct 1-2-3 to return the modified records to their original places in the database.

Lotus 1-2-3 offers other important database operations. For example, you can rearrange, or *sort,* the database records in alphabetical, numeric, or chronological order. You can also apply statistical functions to selected records. Significantly, 1-2-3 offers a complete set of built-in functions that apply specifically to databases.

You'll begin learning about database operations in detail in Chapters 7 and 8. For the purposes of this introduction, you'll examine a short (and imaginary) database that the nutritionist Barbara Johnson might develop to describe the nutritional requirements of a specific group of her clients.

Defining a Database

The first step in designing a database is to determine the number and types of data fields the table will contain, and to choose a name for each field. Field names play several important roles in query operations and criteria formulas. Because of this, you must carefully follow the rules that 1-2-3 establishes for the form of a field name. Essentially, a field name is a one-word label (no spaces) consisting of letters and digits.

The nutritionist wants to include seven fields in her database of imaginary clients. On the first row of her database table, she enters the field names *Name, Age, Sex, Weight, TotalCalories, FatCalories,* and *FatGrams.* The first four fields will contain personal information about each client. The final three fields will represent selected nutritional guidelines:

◆ TotalCalories is the recommended daily caloric intake needed to maintain the current weight level. The nutritionist will enter this value directly from the keyboard for each client.

◆ FatCalories is the recommended maximum daily fat consumption for a patient. To calculate the value of this field for each patient, Johnson will write a formula based on the principles of the 30-percent fat diet.

◆ FatGrams is the recommended maximum daily fat consumption in grams. This will also be a calculated field, found by dividing FatCalories by 9. (You'll recall that a gram of fat is equal to nine calories.)

After creating the field names, Johnson begins entering the individual records of the database. Each client record takes up one row of the table. She begins by entering the fields that are not calculated, including Name, Age, Sex, Weight, and TotalCalories. When these fields are filled in for each record, she writes and copies formulas for the two calculated fields, FatCalories and FatGrams.

Her completed database appears in Figure 1.21. Notice that she has entered the records in alphabetical order by clients' names. To work more effectively with the information, she may sometimes want to view the database in a different order. Lotus 1-2-3 has an efficient Sort command that she can use to rearrange the records quickly. She will also want to perform other database operations to create a meaningful handout for the participants of her seminar. The 1-2-3 Data menu has a variety of commands that she will use to accomplish specific tasks with her database.

PERFORMING SORT AND SEARCH OPERATIONS IN THE DATABASE

Sorting a database requires just a few simple steps in Lotus 1-2-3:

1. Select the range containing all the database records, but *not* the database fields.

2. Choose the Sort command in the Data menu.

3. In the command's dialog box, specify a *key* field for the sort—that is, the field by which the records will be reordered. In addition, specify whether you want to sort the database in ascending or descending order.

The nutritionist begins her work by performing these three steps to rearrange the clients from youngest to oldest—in other words, to sort the database in ascending order by the Age field. Figure 1.22 shows the result of the sort operation.

Johnson realizes that there might be other useful ways of ordering the records. For example, she might want to sort the records by the Weight field, but divide the database into male and female patients. In effect, this sort requires *two* key fields: The Sex field is the *primary* key and the Weight field is the *secondary* key. Figure 1.23 shows the database after this two-key sort has been completed.

Finally, the nutritionist would like to produce a second database table that is a subset of the first. For this second table, she wants to extract client records that meet a particular selection criterion. To formulate this criterion, she will borrow data from her Lunches worksheet to answer the following question: Which clients can use the menu from Lunch #3 as a satisfactory way of staying within their maximum fat guidelines?

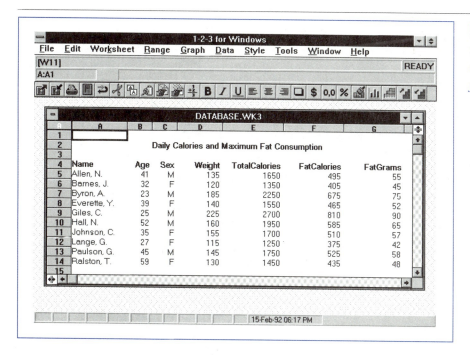

FIGURE 1.21:

The database of nutritional guidelines for individual clients

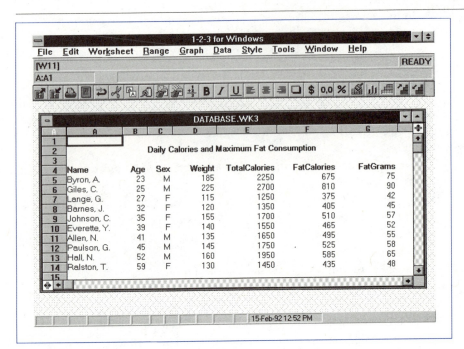

FIGURE 1.23:
Sorting the database by one key field

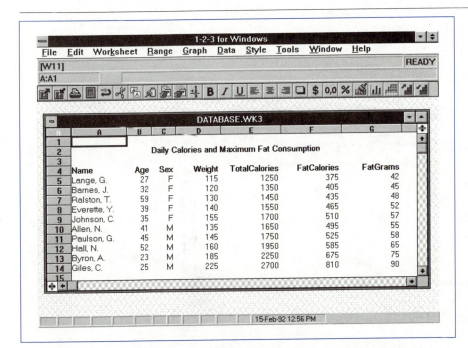

FIGURE 1.22:
Sorting the database by two key fields

The nutritionist starts with the assumption that fat consumed during lunch should be no more than one-third of the total consumption for the day. She writes a criterion formula that reflects this assumption, and then uses 1-2-3's Data Query Extract command to create the second database table. Figure 1.24 shows the resulting table.

As you can see, only half of the patients in the sample database meet this particular selection criterion. Barbara Johnson will use this database extract table to illustrate a final point to her seminar participants: Each client must look at total caloric and fat intake in relation to individual nutritional requirements and personal weight goals.

SUMMARY

The three components of Lotus 1-2-3 for Windows—spreadsheet, graphics, and database—have distinct individual features, and yet are designed to work smoothly together in a carefully integrated environment. In many business applications, you may find yourself using all three of the components together to create interrelated tables and documents.

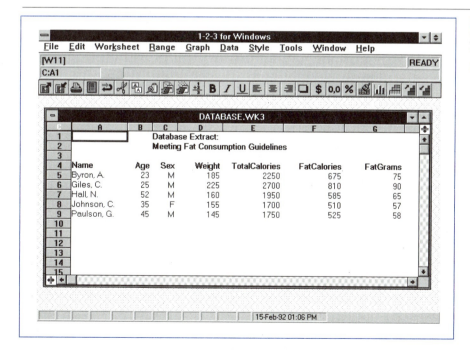

FIGURE 1.24:
Extracting records from the database

Perhaps the single most important characteristic of a 1-2-3 worksheet is its ability to recalculate formulas based on changes in raw data. This so-called "what-if" capability is a feature you will be seeing in many different forms and contexts throughout this book. In all of your work with 1-2-3 worksheets, graphs, and even databases, you will want to find ways to take full advantage of formula recalculation.

In Part 2 of this book, you'll begin examining the three components in detail. But first, Chapter 2 will help you orient yourself to the operations of 1-2-3 in the environment of the Windows graphic interface.

FAST TRACK

To switch to another application while you are working in 1-2-3, ... 58

pull down the control menu and select the Switch to command (or press Ctrl-Escape). In the resulting Task List dialog box, select the application you want to switch to and click the Switch To button. Alternatively, press Alt-Escape to step through the open application windows.

To select or activate a particular tool in a dialog box, ... 65

press Tab or Shift-Tab until the target tool has the focus, or press Alt plus the tool's underlined *access key*.

To enter a range into a text box (inside a dialog box), ... 67

select the range text box and type a period if you want to begin by anchoring the range (if the range is not already anchored). Then use →, ←, ↑, or ↓ to begin defining the target range. In response, 1-2-3 temporarily closes the dialog box and activates the current worksheet. As you continue pressing arrow keys, 1-2-3 highlights the range you are defining. When the target range is highlighted, press ↵ to return to the dialog box; 1-2-3 copies the range notation into the text box.

To edit the entry in a cell, ... 79

select the cell and press the F2 function key. Editing takes place in the contents box.

To change the position of the icon palette, ... 82

choose the SmartIcons command in the Tools menu and select one of the option buttons in the Palette position frame.

To split a worksheet into two panes, ... 90
  drag the vertical splitter icon across the horizontal scroll bar, or the horizontal splitter icon down the vertical scroll bar. Stop dragging at the point where you want the window to be divided. (Alternatively, select a cell in the row or column where you want the split to occur, and click Horizontal or Vertical in the Window Split dialog box.)

To switch between panes in a split worksheet, ... 90
  press the F6 function key or use the mouse to select a cell in either pane.

To open a new worksheet window, ... 92
  pull down the File menu and choose the New command.

To view worksheet windows in a tiled arrangement, ... 93
  pull down the Window menu and select the Tile command.

To view worksheet windows in a cascading arrangement, ... 93
  pull down the Window menu and select the Cascade command.

To get context-sensitive help about almost any command or activity, ... 96
  press the F1 function key.

To search for a particular help topic by name, ... 98
  click the Search button in the help window, and use the resulting Search dialog box to find the topic.

CHAPTER 2

Lotus 1-2-3 and the Windows Interface

The Windows interface promotes a visual and logical consistency among all applications that run within its environment. This is not to say that there is any lack of variety in the programs developed for Windows; but you can often perform equivalent tasks in similar ways, regardless of the application. From your point of view as a user, the uniformity has a distinct advantage: Because different Windows programs have many elements in common, you can apply much of what you know about one program to all the other applications you need to learn. In short, each new Windows application should be easier to master than the previous one.

In this chapter, you'll review some of the features and properties that Windows applications share, and you'll see how these characteristics are implemented and used in Lotus 1-2-3. In particular, you'll examine these features:

- The main properties of the 1-2-3 application window
- The visual and functional elements of menus, dialog boxes, and icons
- The properties of individual worksheet windows—and the mouse and keyboard techniques for performing specific operations on windows
- The elements of a Windows-style help system

If you are a veteran Windows user, you'll move quickly through this chapter, focusing only on details that are new or unfamiliar to you. On the other hand, if Lotus 1-2-3 is your first Windows application, you'll want to read this chapter from beginning to end, and work carefully through each exercise presented.

EXPLORING THE 1-2-3 APPLICATION WINDOW

As you've seen, two windows appear on the screen when you first start Lotus 1-2-3 for Windows:

- The outer 1-2-3 application window
- A worksheet window initially named Untitled, located inside the application window.

In Chapter 1, you began identifying and working with the elements of both the 1-2-3 window and the worksheet window. Now you'll examine these two windows in greater detail.

Figure 2.1 shows the elements of the 1-2-3 application window. Notice that there are five distinct lines (containing information, icons, and other tools) *above* the worksheet window. These lines are known as:

- The 1-2-3 window title bar
- The menu bar
- The format line
- The edit line
- The icon palette

The first four lines, known collectively as the *control panel,* all remain fixed in place at the top of the window throughout your work in 1-2-3. The fifth line, containing the icon palette, is in a slightly different category; as you'll learn later in this chapter, you can move the icon palette to different places in the 1-2-3 window.

There is a sixth line of information located *below* the worksheet area. This is called the *status line.* In the upcoming sections of this chapter, you'll begin examining each of these six lines and the many features they represent. For now, concentrate on simply recognizing the variety of visual tools found in 1-2-3. In later chapters, you'll focus on the significance of these tools in the context of 1-2-3 worksheets, graphs, and databases.

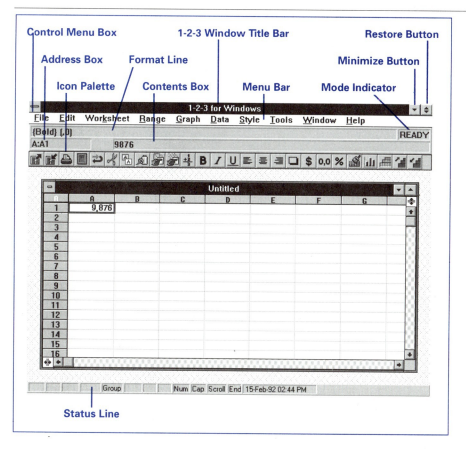

FIGURE 2.1:
The 1-2-3 application window

THE 1-2-3 WINDOW TITLE BAR

The title bar identifies the 1-2-3 application window. Initially, the title bar displays the application name:

1-2-3 for Windows

When you save a worksheet to disk and maximize the worksheet window, the 1-2-3 title bar also displays the name of the worksheet file, for example:

1-2-3 for Windows - [LUNCHES.WK3]

In several contexts, the format of the title bar changes in order to supply you with other kinds of information. For example, when you choose a menu or command in the 1-2-3 menu system, the title bar gives you a description of the highlighted menu or command. To review this feature, try the following brief exercise:

1. Press the Alt key to activate the menu bar, then press → several times. Each time you highlight a new command in the menu bar, the description in the title bar changes accordingly. For example, when you highlight the Style menu, the title bar displays the following general description of the tools supplied in this menu:

   Control the appearance of data on screen and in print

2. Now highlight the Tools menu and press ↵ to pull down the menu. Press ↓ several times and notice the description that the title bar displays for each individual command in the pull-down menu. For example, here is the description of the SmartIcons command:

   Reposition, hide, or customize SmartIcons on the icon palette

3. Press the Escape key twice to close the menu and deactivate the menu bar. The application name is redisplayed in the title bar.

You'll recall that the title bar also changes when you click an icon in the icon palette with the right mouse button. Again, the bar shows you a description of the tool you have selected.

Minimize, Maximize, and Restore Buttons—Sizing and Moving the Window

At the right side of the 1-2-3 title bar are the minimize button, an arrowhead icon pointing down; and the restore button, a double arrowhead icon. These buttons allow you to size the 1-2-3 application window, or to reduce the application to an icon while you work with other Windows applications.

Experiment with these buttons in the following exercise:

1. Click the restore button. The 1-2-3 window shrinks down to smaller dimensions within the Windows environment, and the restore button itself is replaced by a maximize button—an arrowhead icon pointing up.

2. Position the mouse pointer over the right border of the 1-2-3 window. The mouse pointer becomes a double arrowhead icon, pointing left and right. Drag the border to the left, toward the center of the screen. Release the mouse button, and you'll see that you have reduced the 1-2-3 window to about half its horizontal width. Notice how 1-2-3 rearranges the menu bar so that you can still see all of the commands.

3. Position the mouse pointer over the bottom border of the window, and drag the border up to the center of the screen. Now you have reduced the vertical length of the window by half.

4. Use the window's title bar to move the window to a new location on the Windows screen: Position the mouse pointer over the 1-2-3 window's title bar, and drag the window toward the center of the screen. When you complete this operation, 1-2-3 appears as shown in Figure 2.2. Reducing the size of the application window gives you the opportunity to view more than one application at a time in the Windows environment.

5. Click the maximize button. The 1-2-3 window returns to its full-screen dimensions.

6. Click the minimize button. The 1-2-3 window disappears altogether, and is represented instead by the 1-2-3 icon near the bottom of the Windows screen.

7. Double-click the 1-2-3 icon. (Position the mouse pointer over the icon and click the left mouse button twice in quick succession.) The 1-2-3 window reappears in its original dimensions.

Using the 1-2-3 window's control menu, you can perform these same window operations with the keyboard rather than the mouse, as you'll learn in the next section.

The 1-2-3 Window Control Menu

At the left side of the 1-2-3 title bar is the application's control menu box. You can pull down the application's control menu by either of two actions:

- Click the control menu box with the mouse
- Press Alt-Spacebar from the keyboard.

The control menu contains the following list of commands:

Restore

Move

Size

Minimize

Maximize

FIGURE 2.2:
Moving and sizing the 1-2-3 window

Close   Alt-F4

Switch to... Ctrl-Esc

Some of the control-menu commands are dimmed in certain contexts; that is, the commands appear in light gray text. A dimmed entry in any pull-down menu means that the command is not currently available for use.

The Restore, Minimize, and Maximize commands are equivalent to the buttons that appear on the right side of the title bar. The Move and Size commands are tools you use to move and size the application window. Try working with these commands in the following exercise:

1. Press Alt-Spacebar to pull down the 1-2-3 control menu, and then type **R** to choose the Restore command. The 1-2-3 window returns to the location and size you gave it in the previous exercise (shown in Figure 2.2).

2. Pull down the control menu and type **M** to choose the Move command. A four-headed pointer appears over the window, indicating that you can now move the window in any of four directions. Press ↑ on your keyboard; a shadow border moves up beyond the current position of the 1-2-3 window. Keep pressing ↑ until the top of the shadow border window is near the top of the screen. Then press ← until the left side of the shadow border is near the left side of the screen. Press ↵ to complete the move operation.

3. Pull down the 1-2-3 control menu and type **S** to choose the Size command. Press → and ↓ repeatedly to expand the right and bottom borders of the 1-2-3 window, until the border extends almost to the full dimensions of the screen. As you perform the size operation, a shadow border extends from the 1-2-3 window itself, and the pointer becomes a two-headed arrow. Press ↵ to complete the size operation.

4. Pull down the 1-2-3 control menu and type **X** to choose the Maximize command. The window returns to its original full-screen dimensions.

The 1-2-3 control menu also contains a Close command. This command closes the 1-2-3 window, effectively ending the application. Close is equivalent to the Exit command in the File menu. In fact, you can use any of the following mouse or keyboard techniques to exit from 1-2-3 for Windows:

◆ Pull down the File menu and choose the Exit command.

◆ Pull down the 1-2-3 control menu and choose the Close command.

- Press Alt-F4 from the keyboard. (This is the keyboard shortcut for the Close command.)

- Double-click the 1-2-3 control menu box.

All of these actions have the same effect, ending your current session with the 1-2-3 program. Before ending, however, 1-2-3 checks your current worksheets to see if you have made any changes that have not yet been saved to disk. If so, a dialog box appears on the screen, giving you the option of saving or abandoning your work (see Figure 2.3). Alternatively, you can cancel the exit by clicking the Cancel button.

Finally, the Switch to command is a tool for activating another application in the Windows environment. When you choose this command, the Task List dialog box appears on the screen, as shown in Figure 2.4. This box lists all the programs that you are currently running in your Windows environment. To switch to another application, highlight the program's name in the list, and click the Switch to button. (Alternatively, press Alt-Escape to step through the open application windows.)

As you saw in Chapter 1, worksheet windows have their own control menus, with command lists that are similar to the commands in the 1-2-3 control menu. You'll learn more about worksheet windows later in this chapter.

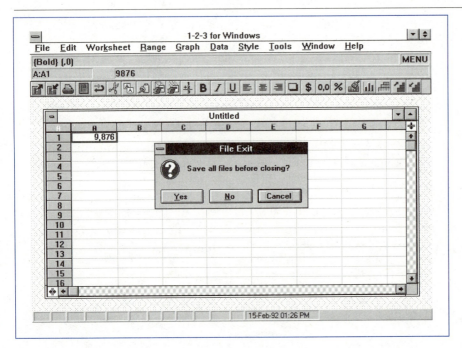

FIGURE 2.3:
Exiting from 1-2-3

The Menu Bar

The menu bar is located immediately below the 1-2-3 title bar. As you'll recall, you can activate the menu bar by pressing either the Alt key or the F10 function key. Alternatively, you can view a particular pull-down menu by clicking a command in the menu bar with the mouse.

The worksheet menu bar contains ten entries, each representing a pull-down menu. Here is a selective overview of these menus:

◆ The File menu contains the commands you use to save worksheets to disk and to retrieve previously saved worksheets. This menu also contains commands for printing worksheets and graphs, and for previewing printed pages before you actually start the printing process. In addition, several commands in the File menu relate to the administration of a network.

◆ The Edit menu has an extremely useful Undo command that reverses the effect of your last action in 1-2-3. In addition, you use commands in the Edit menu to perform cut-and-paste and copy-and-paste operations (via the Windows clipboard); to establish dynamic links for data exchange between 1-2-3 worksheets and documents created in other

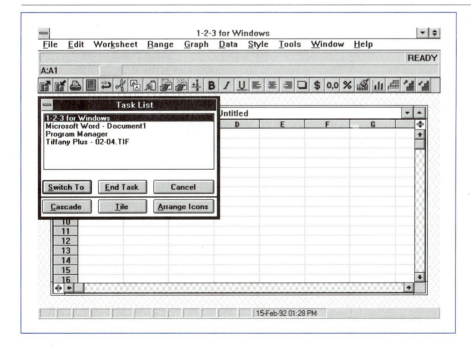

FIGURE 2.4:
The Task List dialog box

applications; to find specific data values in a worksheet, or to perform search-and-replace operations; and to copy formulas across ranges of cells in a worksheet.

- The Worksheet menu gives you ways to establish default global settings such as column widths, data alignments, and display formats for all the cells of a given worksheet. In addition, you can use commands in this menu to insert, delete, and hide specified rows or columns in a worksheet.

- The Range menu contains commands that you use to apply selected formats to specific ranges of data in a worksheet. Another important command in the range menu allows you to create names for ranges in a worksheet. You'll begin learning about the importance of range names in Chapter 3.

- The Graph menu has the commands you use to create new graphs from worksheet data, to view graphs that you have previously created, and to incorporate graphs into a worksheet.

- The Data menu contains the commands for database operations, including sorts and queries. In addition, this menu has a number of advanced and sophisticated calculation tools.

- The Style menu supplies options for changing the appearance of data on the screen and on the printed page, including fonts, alignments, colors, border styles, and shadings.

- The Tools menu offers a miscellaneous variety of 1-2-3 tools, including several related to advanced worksheet operations, and others that allow you to select general settings for 1-2-3 operations.

- The Windows menu has commands that you use to control the size, shape, and appearance of multiple worksheet and graph windows, as you'll see later in this chapter.

- The Help menu provides a variety of entry points into the 1-2-3 help system. (You'll also learn more about this menu later in this chapter.)

Before reading on, take a few minutes to browse through the worksheet menu system, and examine the brief descriptions that 1-2-3 displays (in the title bar) for individual commands in the pull-down menus.

Interestingly enough, this is not the only set of commands that you will see in the menu bar during your work in 1-2-3. The menu selections change in two situations. First, 1-2-3 has a different menu for working with graphs. You can examine this menu by simply clicking the graph icon in the icon palette. Even though your worksheet currently contains no data to graph, 1-2-3 opens a graph window, and displays the graph commands in the menu bar, as shown in Figure 2.5. Also notice that a new set of icons appears in the icon palette when a graph window is active. (When you are finished examining the Graph menu and icons, close this graph window by pulling down the File menu and choosing the Close command. The Untitled worksheet again becomes the active window.)

Yet another set of commands appears in the menu bar when you are working in a special tool called the Transcript window. This window records keystrokes and mouse actions in a way that allows you to play them back in the form of *macros*. A macro is a program you create to record a sequence of 1-2-3 commands. You'll learn about macros and the Transcript window in Chapter 9.

Using 1-2-3 Menu Commands

To represent specific menu options that are available for worksheet, graph, and database operations, 1-2-3 displays a variety of Windows-style tools on the screen. As you have seen, the menu system initially appears as a horizontal arrangement of commands in the menu bar; each of these commands in turn represents a vertical pull-down menu. Some commands in the pull-down

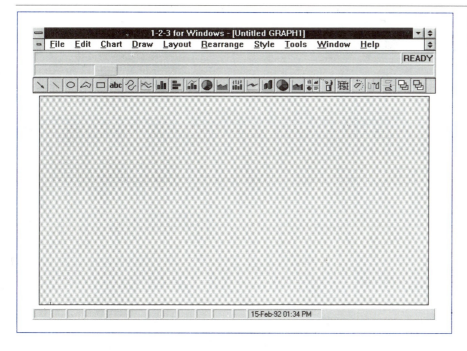

FIGURE 2.5:
The Graph menu and the graph icon palette

menus result in additional lists of commands called *cascade menus*. An arrowhead icon, displayed at the right of a command, indicates the presence of an associated cascade menu. Follow these steps to see an example of a cascade menu:

1. Pull down the Range menu. Notice the small right-pointing arrowhead icon displayed next to the Name command, as in Figure 2.6.

2. Select the Name command. The resulting cascade menu contains a list of four commands, as you can see in Figure 2.7.

When a cascade menu appears on the screen, you can select a command from it in the same ways you choose commands from a pull-down menu: Click a command with the mouse, press the underlined letter at the keyboard, or highlight a command and press ↵.

Dialog Boxes

Dialog boxes prompt you for the detailed information necessary to carry out particular operations in 1-2-3. A command that produces a dialog box on the screen is followed by an ellipsis in the corresponding menu list. For example,

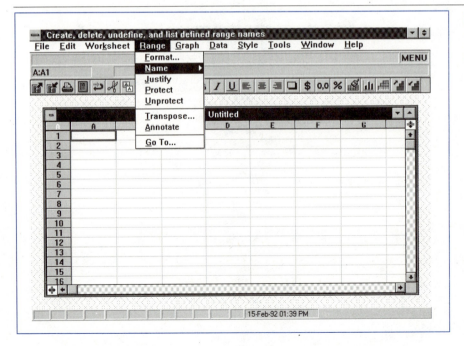

FIGURE 2.6:

The Name command in the Range menu

looking back at Figure 2.6 you can see the three commands in the Range menu that supply dialog boxes: Format, Transpose, and Goto. When you choose any one of these commands, 1-2-3 displays the associated dialog box on the screen.

Figure 2.8 shows the dialog box for the Range Format command. Follow these steps for displaying this dialog box on your own screen:

1. Press Alt-R from the keyboard to pull down the Range menu.

2. Type **F** to choose the Format command.

Notice that a dialog box is a window with its own title bar. The name of a dialog box is the same as the sequence of menu commands that you choose to display the box. Accordingly, the Range Format dialog box appears when you pull down the Range menu and select Format.

Dialog boxes displayed in 1-2-3 have certain features in common:

◆ A dialog box initially appears at the center of the screen, but can always be moved aside to a new position so that you can view other parts of your work. To move a dialog box, you can drag the box by its title bar.

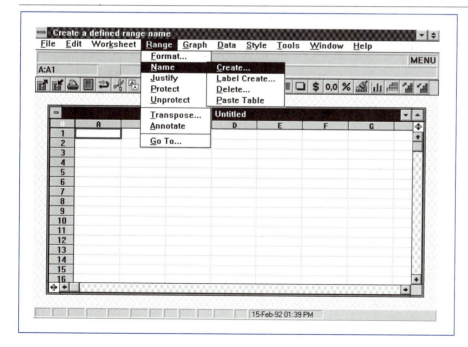

FIGURE 2.7:

A cascade menu

◆ A dialog box has its own control menu, represented by the control menu box at the upper-left corner of the window. The dialog box control menu has only two commands: Move and Close. (Dialog boxes cannot be resized, minimized, or maximized.)

◆ The graphic and textual elements displayed inside dialog boxes are standard Windows tools that operate in familiar and intuitive ways. These tools include *labels, command buttons, text boxes, check boxes, list boxes, frames, option buttons, drop-down boxes, file list boxes, directory list boxes,* and *drive list boxes*. A given dialog box may have any assortment or combination of these elements, depending upon the options that are relevant to the command at hand. As you can see in Figure 2.8, the Range Format dialog box contains examples of the following tools: labels, command buttons, text boxes, a check box, and a list box.

In the sections ahead, you'll look briefly at the variety of Windows tools that appear in 1-2-3 dialog boxes, and you'll gain a general sense of their function and use. But before examining these tools individually, consider a few characteristics that they have in common in the context of a particular dialog box.

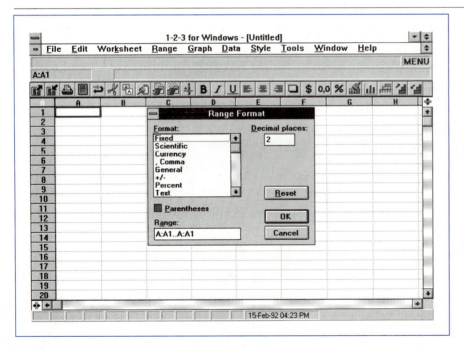

FIGURE 2.8:
The Range Format dialog box

First of all, you'll see that one tool inside a dialog box *has the focus* at a given time—that is, one tool is active for use. Dialog boxes display a combination of *highlights* and *dotted boxes* to indicate the current focus. For example, when a text box has the focus, the contents of the box may appear highlighted against a dark background. When a command button has the focus, the button's caption is enclosed in a light dotted box and the button's border is darkened. You will quickly get used to recognizing these particular graphic effects inside dialog boxes.

There are a number of ways to activate a new tool in a dialog box. From the keyboard, you can press the Tab key to move the focus from one tool to the next, or Shift-Tab to move backward through the elements of the dialog box. In some cases, you can activate a tool by clicking it with the mouse. However, a mouse click can mean different things to different tools in a dialog box, as you'll learn in the sections ahead. Pressing the Tab key is a neutral way of changing the focus without completing any particular action.

Another way to activate a particular tool in a dialog box—or, in some cases, to select the option that the tool represents—is to press an Alt-Key combination at the keyboard. Most tools in a dialog box have an associated *label* or *caption,* and this text usually has an underlined character that represents the *access key*. To activate the tool, you can hold down the Alt key and press the access key. For example, in the Range Format dialog box (shown in Figure 2.8), you can press Alt-D to activate the Decimal places text box, so you can enter a new value into the box. In contrast, pressing Alt-R is the equivalent of *clicking* the Reset button.

As you read the following descriptions of 1-2-3's dialog box tools, concentrate on the general use of each tool. For now, don't worry about the specifics of particular dialog boxes that appear as examples. You'll have the opportunity to study 1-2-3's menu commands and dialog boxes in upcoming chapters.

Command Buttons A command button is one of the simplest and most common tools you'll find in 1-2-3 dialog boxes. Command buttons represent actions you can carry out at the click of a mouse. For example, the Range Format dialog box shown in Figure 2.8 has three command buttons, labeled Reset, OK, and Cancel. When you click one of these buttons with the mouse, a graphic push-button effect occurs on the screen, and 1-2-3 immediately carries out the action that the button represents. In this particular dialog box, the Reset button resets the selected cell or cells to the current global format. The

OK button confirms whatever format specifications you have made in the dialog box, and the Cancel button closes the dialog box without changing any formats.

If you prefer to use the keyboard to select a command button, there are several techniques for doing so. First, as you already know, you can press Alt plus the corresponding access key. For example, pressing Alt-R is equivalent to clicking the Reset button. Alternatively, you can press the Tab key (or Shift-Tab) until the target button has the focus, then press ↵. In a dialog box that has OK and Cancel buttons, these two tools have a special status: Pressing ↵ selects the OK button, even when some other element of the dialog box (except for another command button) has the focus; and pressing the Escape key selects the Cancel button.

Sometimes a command button results in the display of a new dialog box on the screen. For example, consider the File Print dialog box, shown in Figure 2.9. At the right side of this box you can see four command buttons, labeled Page setup, Preview, OK, and Cancel. The ellipsis after Page setup indicates that a click of this button produces a new dialog box on the screen. Notice that the keyboard access to this command button is Alt-G.

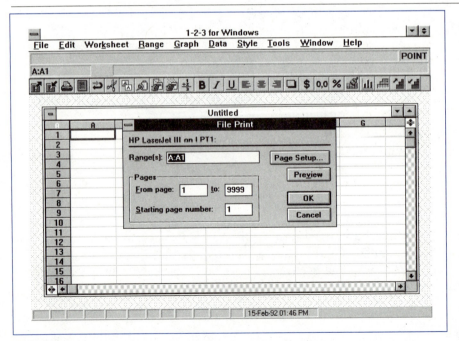

FIGURE 2.9:

Command buttons in the File Print dialog box

As an exercise with command buttons, try the following steps:

1. Pull down the File menu and select the Print command. The File Print dialog box appears on the screen.

2. Click the Page Setup button with the mouse, or press Alt-G from the keyboard. (If you use the mouse, notice the graphic push-button effect that takes place on the screen.) A new dialog box named File Page Setup appears on the screen, superimposed over the Page Setup dialog box.

3. For now, click the Cancel button on this new dialog box. The box disappears and you once again see the File Print box. Click Cancel or press the Escape key and this box also disappears from the screen.

Text Boxes A text box is a bordered rectangle into which you enter an item of information from the keyboard. The information might be a number, a text item, or a range, depending upon the requirements of a particular dialog box. For example, the Range Format dialog box in Figure 2.8 contains two text boxes, labeled Decimal places and Range. In the first of these you can enter the number of decimal places for a numeric display format you have selected; in the second, you enter the range of cells to which the new format will apply. In general, a text box has a *default* value at the time a dialog box is first displayed on the screen; this is the value that will apply if you make no changes in the text box.

To enter a value into a text box, you first activate the box by double-clicking it with the mouse or by pressing the Tab key repeatedly until the box has the focus. Then you can enter the expected type of information directly from the keyboard. Some dialog boxes also contain text boxes in which 1-2-3 displays information about options you have chosen. This kind of tool is sometimes known as an *information box*. Like other text boxes, an information box generally has a label that tells you what kind of information you can expect to find in the box. But an information box never receives the focus, because you cannot enter data directly into the box.

A range box is a special kind of text box. If you select a range of cells in the current worksheet *before* selecting a menu command that applies to a range, the range box displays your selected range as its default value. Alternatively, if you want to enter a new range into a text box when a dialog box is already displayed on the screen, 1-2-3 provides special pointing techniques for doing so. As an introduction to these techniques, try the following exercise in the File Print dialog box:

1. Press the Home key, if necessary, to select cell A1 in the current worksheet.

2. Pull down the File menu and choose the Print command. The dialog box appears on the screen. The Range(s) text box initially has the focus, and the current cell name, A:A1, is highlighted inside the box (as in Figure 2.9). In the File Print command, the Range box is where you specify the portion of your worksheet that you want to print.

3. Type a period (.) to *anchor* the range. (Anchoring simply means that you intend to use the current cell—in this case A1—as the corner in a range of cells.) When you do so, you may be surprised to find that the File Print dialog box disappears temporarily from the screen. The range notation *A:A1..A:A1* appears in the contents box of the edit line.

4. Press → on your keyboard five times, then press ↓ five times. As you do so, the range of cells from A1 to F6 is framed on the active worksheet, and the range notation *A:A1..A:F6* appears in the contents box, as shown in Figure 2.10. Also, a new mode name appears in the mode indicator: *POINT*. The POINT mode means that you are currently in the process of selecting a range.

5. Press ↵ to return to the dialog box. Notice that the Range(s) text box now displays the notation for the range that you have selected in the worksheet. If you were actually ready to print your worksheet, this is the range that 1-2-3 would send to your printer.

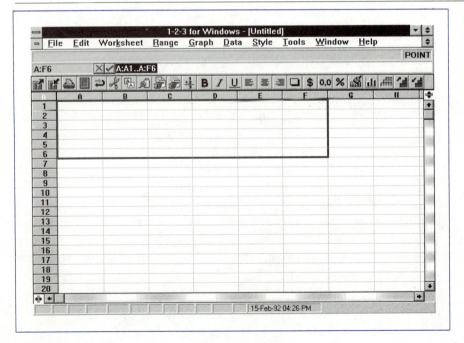

FIGURE 2.10:

Selecting a range of cells

6. For now, click the Cancel button or press the Escape key from the keyboard to cancel this operation.

1-2-3 also allows you to use the mouse to point to a range, or even to type a range notation directly from the keyboard into any text box that requires a range entry. You'll learn much more about ranges and the techniques for selecting them in Chapter 3.

List Boxes A list box is a bordered rectangle containing a vertical list from which you can select one item. If the list is too long to be displayed at once in its entirety, a vertical scroll bar appears at the right side of the list box.

For example, the Range Format dialog box in Figure 2.8 contains a list box labeled Format. This box contains the list of predefined formats that 1-2-3 supplies for you to choose from. You can select a format from this list to change the appearance of a range of values on your worksheet.

Here are the general steps for using a list box:

1. Activate the list box. (Click the box with the mouse, or press the Tab key until the list box has the focus.)

2. Scroll up or down the list until the item you want to select is visible in the box. To scroll through the box, click the scroll bar's up- or down-arrow icon with the mouse, or drag the scroll box up or down the length of the bar.

3. Click the target list item with the mouse. The selected item is highlighted in the list. (Alternatively, press ↑ or ↓ repeatedly from the keyboard to scroll through the list and select the previous or next item in the list.)

Most list boxes—like the Format box in the Range Format dialog box—contain lists of predefined options supplied by 1-2-3. But some contain names or other items that you have defined yourself. For example, the Range Name Create dialog box has a list of all the names you have defined to identify areas of the current worksheet. An example of such a list appears in Figure 2.11. (You'll examine the use of range names in Chapter 3.)

Check Boxes Check boxes represent options that you can turn on or off. A check box consists of a small square box with a caption displayed at its right. A check box has three states: *on, off,* or *undetermined*. When the option is on, the check box contains an X; when the option is off, the text box is empty. When 1-2-3 cannot determine the current status of a particular option, the corresponding check box is filled with a dark gray background. For example, the Range Format dialog box contains one text box, labeled Parentheses. You turn this option on if you want 1-2-3 to display numeric values within parentheses in your worksheet.

When a check box has the focus, the caption next to the box is enclosed in a dotted box. At this point, you can press the Spacebar on the keyboard to step through the three states. Alternatively, you can click a check box repeatedly with the mouse to step through the three states, or you can press the Alt key plus the underlined access key.

Some dialog boxes display lists of check boxes that are grouped together. For example, the Style Font dialog box contains check boxes labeled Bold, Italics, and Underlined (see Figure 2.12). Each of the check boxes in such a group operates independently of the others—that is, you can choose any combination of on, off, or undertermined states for the options represented in the group. Changing the status of one check box has no effect on the other check boxes.

Try this exercise with the check boxes of the Style Font dialog box:

1. Pull down the Style menu and choose the Font command.

2. Press the Tab key once to move the focus to the Bold check box. Notice that a dotted box encloses the Bold caption.

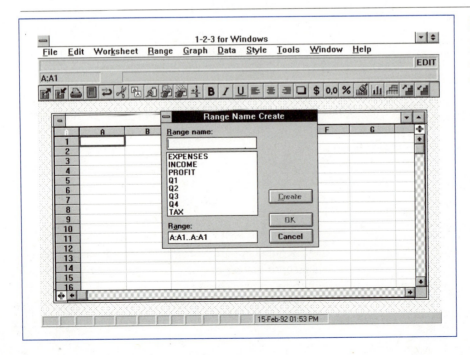

FIGURE 2.11:

The list box in the Range Name Create dialog box

3. Press the Spacebar on the keyboard several times and watch the Bold check box rotate through its three defined settings.

4. Press the Tab key again to move the focus to the Italics check box.

5. Again press the Spacebar several times, this time changing the setting of the Italics check box. Note that you can set Italics without affecting the current setting of the other two check boxes.

6. Click the Cancel button or press the Escape key to close the dialog box.

Option Buttons In contrast to check boxes, a group of option buttons represents mutually exclusive options available in a dialog box. In any list of option buttons, only one option can be on at once; all the others are off. An option button appears as a circle with a caption displayed at its right. When the option is *on,* the circle is filled with a bold black dot; when the option is *off,* the circle is empty. These are the only two settings available for an option button.

When a list of option buttons has the focus, you can select a new option in the group simply by pressing ↑ or ↓. Alternatively, you can click an option button with the mouse, or you can press the corresponding access key. Keep in mind the essential characteristic of option buttons: Only one

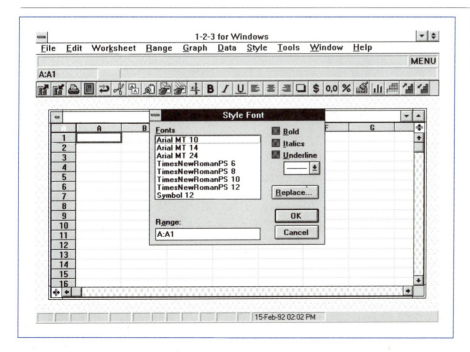

FIGURE 2.12:

Check boxes in the Style Font dialog box

option in a group can be on at a time. When a new option button becomes the selected option, the previous selection loses its bold dot.

The Tools SmartIcons dialog box, shown in Figure 2.13, contains a set of option buttons. This dialog box, which you'll be returning to later in this chapter, allows you to control the location, appearance, and contents of the icon palette. In particular, you can change the palette's position in the 1-2-3 window by choosing one of the five option buttons displayed at the left side of the dialog box. As you can see, the default option is Top, meaning that the icon palette appears as a horizontal line of tools displayed near the top of the 1-2-3 window.

Try the following exercise with this dialog box:

1. Pull down the Tools menu and choose the SmartIcons command. The dialog box appears on the screen, and the initial focus is on the group of option buttons.

2. Press ↑ at the keyboard. This action simultaneously turns on the Right option button and turns off the Top button.

3. Type **T** at the keyboard. The Top button is turned on once again.

4. Click the Cancel button or press Escape to close the dialog box.

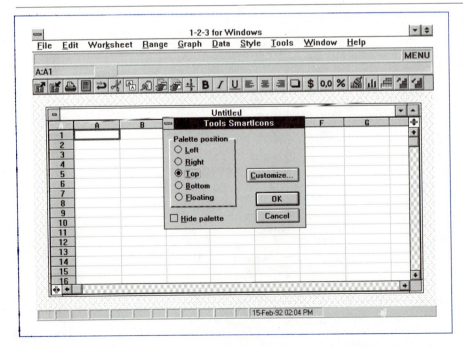

FIGURE 2.13:
Option buttons in the Tools Icon Palette dialog box

Frames When a dialog box contains more than one group of option buttons, each separate group is generally enclosed in a *frame*. A frame is a rectangular box that has a caption embedded in its top border line. For example, pull down the Worksheet menu and choose the Global Settings command. The resulting dialog box, presented in Figure 2.14, contains two groups of option buttons, each enclosed within a frame. In this case, each *group* of option buttons is independent from the other; that is, you can select and activate one option in each of the two groups.

Drop-down Boxes A text box with an attached pull-down list is known as a *drop-down box*. Whenever you see a ↓ button displayed at the right side of a text box, you know that the box has a pull-down list. There are two ways for you to enter a text value into a drop-down box:

◆ You can often enter information directly into the text box from the keyboard, although the legal entries are restricted to relevant values.

◆ You can pull down the attached list, and select an entry from the list. Your selection is automatically copied to the text box.

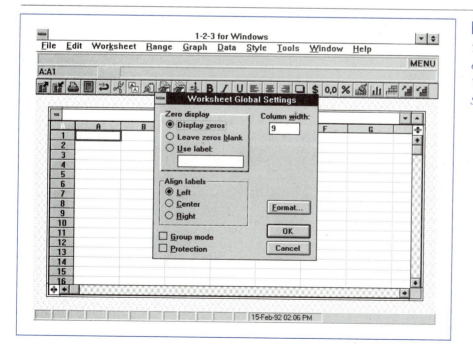

FIGURE 2.14:

Two framed groups of option buttons in the Worksheet Global Settings dialog box

To pull down the attached list, you simply click the down-arrow button with the mouse. Alternatively, you can press Alt-↓ from the keyboard when the drop-down box has the focus.

One example of a drop-down box appears in the File Open dialog box (see Figure 2.15). The Drives box is the text box in which you enter the name of the drive (A, B, C, and so on) containing the file you want to open. You'll have a chance to experiment with this box in the next section.

File List, Directory List, and Drive List Boxes Several 1-2-3 commands require you to identify a file name that becomes the object of a particular disk operation. For example, in the File Open command you specify the name of an existing worksheet file that you want to open into the 1-2-3 window. One way to specify a file is to type the complete path and file name directly into the File name text box from the keyboard. However, this entry can be long and tedious if the file you want to open is located somewhere other than the current directory and disk. For example, you might find yourself typing a complete path and file name such as:

D:\BUDGETS\WORK91\BUDG91.WK3

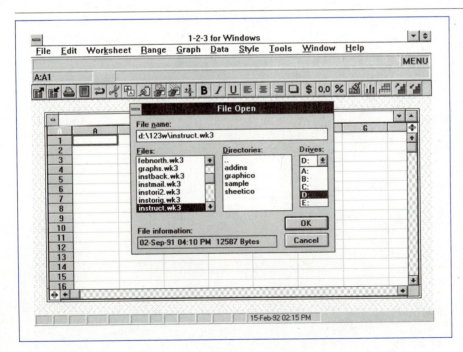

FIGURE 2.15:

The File Open dialog box

To simplify the task of identifying and selecting a target file on disk, Windows supplies three dialog box tools known as *file list, directory list,* and *drive list* boxes. Examples of these three boxes appear in the File Open dialog box (Figure 2.15). These three tools are always logically linked together in a given dialog box, so that they operate in a coordinated manner; when you change the drive selection in the drive list box, the directories list box subsequently displays a list of directories from the new drive. Likewise, when you change the selection in the directory list box, the file list box automatically displays the worksheet files from the selected directory on disk.

Opening and saving files are basic operations in almost all major Windows applications. If you have worked with other Windows applications, you probably already know how to select a file name in a File Open dialog box. But if 1-2-3 is your first Windows application—or if you just want to review the procedure—try the exercise of opening one of the sample files that the 1-2-3 installation program has copied onto your hard disk. In the following steps, the assumption is that you have installed 1-2-3 in the default installation directory, named \123W. (The sample 1-2-3 files are stored in a subdirectory named SAMPLE.) If this is not the case, substitute the correct directory name in the appropriate steps of the exercise:

1. Pull down the File menu and select the Open command. The File Open dialog box appears on the screen, as shown in Figure 2.15.

2. Activate the Drives box by clicking the box with the mouse or pressing Alt-V from the keyboard. Click the down-arrow icon at the left side of the Drives box (or press Alt-↓ from the keyboard). A list of all the drives available on your system appears. Select the C drive, or the name of the hard drive on which you have installed Lotus 1-2-3. As a result, the File name box displays the current path on the selected drive.

3. Activate the Directories box by clicking inside the box with the mouse, or by pressing Alt-D from the keyboard. At the top of the box is a pair of periods (see Figure 2.16); this entry represents the parent directory of the current directory list. As an experiment, double-click these two periods with the mouse, or highlight the entry and press ↵. Then double-click again on the two periods at the top of the resulting directory list. This action moves you *up* the directory path—in this case, to the root directory. In the resulting directory list, you will find the 123W entry. To reopen the directory that contains the 1-2-3 program, double-click the 123W entry, or highlight the entry and press ↵.

4. Now find the SAMPLE subdirectory in the directory list box. Double-click the entry, or highlight the entry and press ↵. As a result, the Files box displays a list of all the 1-2-3 worksheet files that are stored in the \123W\SAMPLE\ path. These are the sample worksheet files supplied with the 1-2-3 package.

5. Activate the files box by pressing Alt-F from the keyboard. Press ↓ until the file named LESSON1.WK3 is highlighted. Notice two important changes that take place in the File Open dialog box when you make this selection (see Figure 2.16). First, the File name text box now contains the full path name of the selected file: \123W\SAMPLE\LESSON1.WK3. This entry in the text box means that the Open command is now prepared to open this file. Second, the File information text box displays specific information about the file you have selected—the date and time of the last revision and the size in bytes of the file.

6. Click the OK button or press ↵ to complete the Open operation. As a result, 1-2-3 opens the LESSON1 worksheet, and displays it as the active window. Examine the worksheet if you wish, then double-click its control menu box to close the worksheet window again.

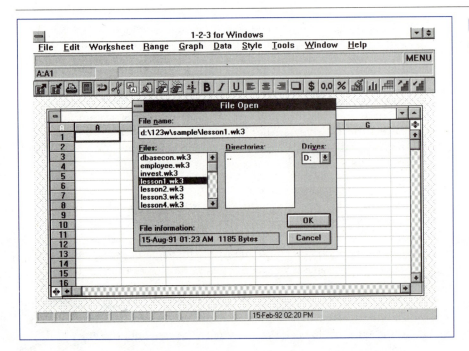

FIGURE 2.16:

Opening a worksheet file

You'll learn more about the Save and Open operations in Chapters 3 and 4. For now, simply keep in mind that windows applications typically display file list, directory list, and drive list boxes whenever you are expected to select a file name for a disk operation.

After this extended detour into menus, dialog boxes, and their characteristic tools, return your attention now to the 1-2-3 application window. You have examined the first two lines at the top of the window—the title bar and the menu bar. the next line down the control panel is called the *format line*.

THE FORMAT LINE

The format line identifies the formats and styles you have assigned to the current cell or range of cells in the active worksheet. This line can include information about any or all of the following properties:

- The font name and point size
- The type styles (such as bold or italics)
- The numeric format (such as percentage or dollar-and-cent formats)
- The shading and drop shadow settings
- The color
- The row height and column width
- The cell protection scheme

You'll learn about these characteristics in Chapter 4. If the current cell has the default settings for all of these properties, the format line displays no information.

Look back at Figure 2.1 for a simple example of a format line entry. Cell A1 is the current selection on the worksheet. The following notation is displayed in the format line:

{BOLD} (,0)

This means that the numeric value stored in A1 is displayed in bold type and in a comma format. You can confirm this information by examining the number displayed in the cell. The cells's value, 9876, is displayed as:

9,876

Follow these steps to duplicate this display on your own worksheet:

1. Press Home, if necessary, to select cell A1.
2. Enter the value **9876** into the cell.
3. Click the bold icon (**B**) in the icon palette, then click the comma-format icon (0,0).

In summary, the display in an individual worksheet cell is controlled both by the data entry itself, and by the variety of styles and formats you assign to the cell. The purpose of the format line is to identify the current style and format settings.

At the right side of the format line is the mode indicator.

The Mode Indicator

As you learned in Chapter 1, the mode indicator displays a single word that tells you what 1-2-3 is currently doing, or gives you information about your own activity. About a dozen different modes exist in 1-2-3 for windows. You have already seen some of the most common modes:

- The READY mode means that 1-2-3 is ready for your next action—for example, a data entry or a menu selection.
- The VALUE and LABEL modes tell you how 1-2-3 is accepting your current data entry—that is, as a number or a text entry.
- You are in MENU mode while in the process of choosing a menu command or selecting options from a 1-2-3 dialog box.
- The POINT mode indicates that you are currently selecting a range of cells.

You'll see other modes in later chapters. As you gain experience in 1-2-3, you'll easily come to recognize the most common modes. Learn to check the mode indicator first whenever you are confused about what is happening at any juncture in your work. Sometimes you'll find that you are in a different mode than you expected to be. In many cases, pressing the Escape key takes you back to the READY mode, or you may have to press Ctrl-Break.

THE EDIT LINE

The edit line—the fourth line in the control panel—is divided into two sections:

- The *address box* is the smaller section at the left side of the edit line. This box displays the complete address of the current cell in the active worksheet. As you've learned, a complete address includes the name of the active worksheet (A, B, C, and so on), followed by a colon and then the column letter and the row number.

- The *contents box* is the large section located at the right of the address box. This box displays the value, label, or formula that is stored in the current cell. The contents box is not affected by formatting; in other words, this box shows you what is actually *stored* in the cell rather than what is *displayed* in the cell. For example, you'll notice in Figure 2.1 that the contents box displays the number *9876* rather than the formatted value *9,876*.

The contents box also displays new entries as you are typing them into a cell. As you saw in Chapter 1, 1-2-3 displays two special buttons just to the left of the contents box as soon as you begin a new entry into a cell. These buttons are known as the *cancel button* and the *confirm button*. The cancel button contains a bold X; clicking this button (or pressing the Escape key) cancels the current data entry, without changing the contents of the current cell. The confirm button contains a check mark. Clicking this button (or pressing ↵) completes the current entry and copies the result to the current cell.

Finally, 1-2-3 also allows you to use the contents box to *edit* the contents of the current cell. Rather than completely retyping a value or label that is currently stored in a cell, you can switch into the EDIT mode with a single keystroke: To edit the current contents of a cell, select the cell and press the F2 function key. When you press F2, several things happen on the screen:

- The mode indicator displays the word *EDIT*.

- The entry stored in the current cell is copied to the contents box.

- The cancel and confirm buttons appear just to the left of the contents box on the edit line.

◆ A flashing vertical bar cursor appears in the contents box, indicating that 1-2-3 is ready for you to edit the value, label, or formula stored in the cell.

Here is a brief exercise that demonstrates the use of the F2 function key to switch to the EDIT mode:

1. Press the Home key to select cell A1, in which you entered the value 9876 in the previous exercise. (Enter this value now if you have not already done so.)

2. Press the F2 function key. The value of the cell appears in the contents line, followed by the flashing cursor (see Figure 2.17). Also notice the word *EDIT* displayed in the mode indicator.

3. Type a **0** (zero) at the keyboard. This entry appears as a fifth digit at the end of the number in the contents box.

4. Complete the edit by clicking the confirm button with the mouse, or by pressing ↵ from the keyboard. 1-2-3 returns to the READY mode.

When you complete these steps, the new entry *98,760* appears in cell A1. Notice that formats you previously applied to the cell—bold type and the

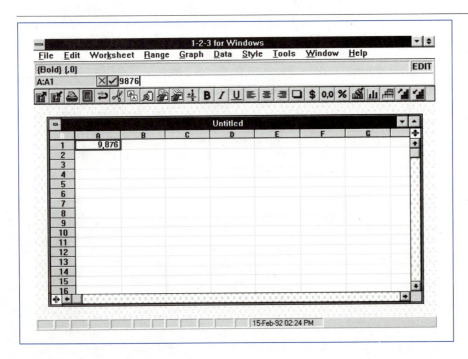

FIGURE 2.17:

Editing the entry in a cell

comma format—are still in effect. Editing the contents of a cell does not change the current formats applied to the cell.

In short, you use the contents box whenever you are entering or editing a value, label, or formula in a cell. The keys that you use while this box is active are standard Windows editing keys:

◆ The ← and → keys move the flashing cursor to the left or right by one character position at a time.

◆ The Home key moves the cursor to the beginning of the entry displayed in the contents line.

◆ The End key moves the cursor to the end of the entry displayed in the contents line.

◆ The Backspace key deletes the character located just to the left of the cursor.

◆ The Del key deletes the character located to the right of the cursor.

THE ICON PALETTE

The fifth line in the 1-2-3 application window contains the useful collection of icons (or "SmartIcons") that you've already begun experimenting with in this chapter and Chapter 1. Each of the tools in this palette is a one-click shortcut for a particular menu command, or for a common keyboard action.

You can customize this line in three different ways:

◆ Move the icon palette to a different position on the screen, or convert it into a free-floating window that you can then move to any location.

◆ Select a new set of icons to represent the commands that you perform the most often in your own work.

◆ Create new icons altogether, and write your own macros to carry out specific actions when you click your icons.

You carry out all three of these tasks within the SmartIcons command in the Tools menu. You'll learn about the first two customizations here in this chapter. The process of creating new icons—and programming them with macros—will be covered in Chapter 9.

Looking back at Figure 2.13, you can see the Tools SmartIcons dialog box. You can change the location of the palette inside the 1-2-3 window by making a new selection among the group of option buttons in the Palette position frame. As you see, the default position is Top. Here are the steps to move the palette to the bottom of the screen:

1. Pull down the Tools menu and choose SmartIcons.
2. On the resulting dialog box, click the Bottom option button, or type **B** from the keyboard.
3. Click the OK button, or press ↵.

Figure 2.18 shows what happens to the 1-2-3 window when you complete this action. The horizontal icon palette is now arranged across the bottom of the window, just above the status line.

If you want even more control over the position and the shape of the icon palette, choose the Floating option in the Tools Icon Palette dialog box. The palette becomes a free-floating window that you can resize with the mouse, and move to any location within the 1-2-3 window. Figure 2.19 shows one possible arrangement of the icon palette window along with a worksheet window.

Clicking the Customize button on the Tools SmartIcons dialog box produces another dialog box on the screen. Figure 2.20 shows the Tools SmartIcons Customize dialog box. This box contains the tools and resources

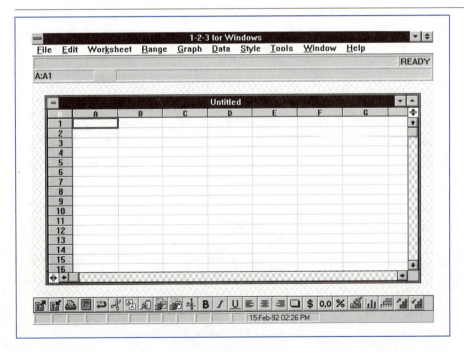

FIGURE 2.18:

Changing the position of the icon palette

you need to add new predefined icons to the palette, to remove existing icons, and to program your own custom icons.

The Standard icons box is a scrollable list containing dozens of predefined icons that you can add to your icon palette. Here are the steps for adding each new icon:

1. Scroll horizontally through the Standard icons box until you find the icon that you want to add.

2. Select the target icon by clicking it with the mouse. When you do so, a brief description of the selected icon appears in the Description text box, at the bottom of the Tools Icon Palette Customize dialog box.

3. Click the Add button to add the icon to your current palette.

The Current palette box displays the selection of icons that are currently in your icon palette. To remove one of these icons, follow these steps:

1. Scroll horizontally through the Current palette box until you find the icon that you want to remove.

2. Click the target icon with the mouse. When you do so, the Description text box displays a brief description of the selected icon.

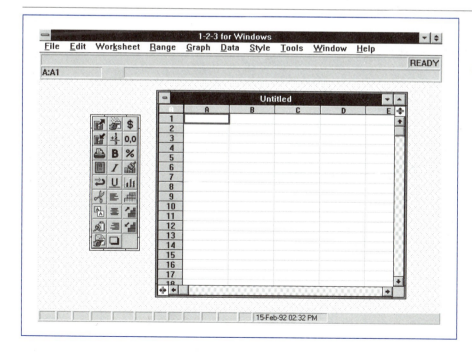

FIGURE 2.19:

The free-floating icon palette window

3. Click the Remove button to remove the icon from the palette.

You can always return a particular icon back to the palette if you change your mind after removing it. The complete set of available icons remains in the Standard icons box, even when you remove an icon from the Current palette box.

While the Tools SmartIcons Customize box is on the screen, you can perform as many Add and Remove operations as you wish. To confirm your work, click the OK button, then click OK on the Tools SmartIcons box.

THE STATUS LINE

The status line always remains in its fixed position at the bottom of the 1-2-3 window. Its purpose is to display information about current software and hardware settings that may affect your work. The line is divided into several panels, each of which is devoted to a particular setting or status. The information on the status line includes:

1. The current date and time, read from the system calendar and clock settings.

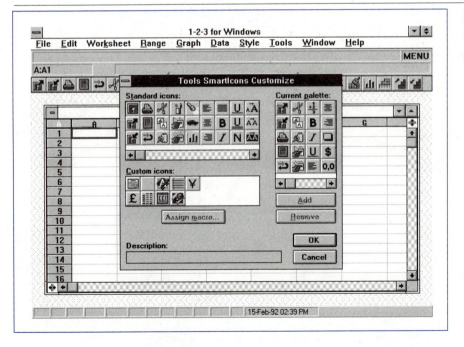

FIGURE 2.20:

The Tools SmartIcons Customize dialog box

2. The status of special toggle keys on your keyboard, including NumLock, CapsLock, ScrollLock, and End. (Looking back at Figure 2.1, you can see that all four of these keys have been toggled on.)

3. Other settings and conditions that may change during the course of your work in 1-2-3.

Along with the mode indicator, the status line can often give you essential information to help you through moments of confusion. For this reason, you should check the status line regularly to see if some condition has changed that requires a response from you.

You have now examined the six lines of tools and information that characterize the appearance and functionality of the 1-2-3 window. Take a moment to review what you've learned:

- Depending upon the context of your current activity, the title bar displays the application name, the current worksheet name, or a brief description of a menu command or icon.

- The menu bar is your primary entry point into a vast system of pull-down menus and Windows-style dialog boxes that represent the 1-2-3 command set.

- The format line gives you information about current format settings in a worksheet. At the right side of the format line, the mode indicator displays a one-word description of 1-2-3's current condition or activity.

- The edit line contains an address box that gives the current cell address, and a contents box that displays the value, label, or formula entry in the current cell.

- The icon palette is a useful and versatile selection of tools that you can use to streamline your work with worksheets, databases, and graphs.

- The status bar displays the date, the current status of keyboard toggles, and other conditions that may be relevant to your work in 1-2-3.

Aside from these six lines, most of the 1-2-3 window is normally taken up by at least one worksheet window. In the sections ahead, you'll focus on the features of this window.

PERFORMING OPERATIONS ON WORKSHEET WINDOWS

The mouse and keyboard actions that you use to change the size and position of a worksheet window are just about the same as for the 1-2-3 window. As you first learned in Chapter 1, a worksheet window has its own title bar, its own minimize, maximize, and restore buttons, and its own control menu—all of which operate in familiar ways:

- ◆ You can pull down a worksheet window's control menu (as shown in Figure 2.21) by pressing Alt-Hyphen at the keyboard, or by clicking the control menu box with the mouse. (Recall that the Alt-Spacebar keyboard sequence pulls down the control menu of the 1-2-3 window.)

- ◆ To maximize the size of a worksheet window, select the Maximize command in the control menu, or click the maximize button. Keep in mind that a worksheet window loses its title bar when you maximize the window. Instead, the window's control menu box and Restore button appear on either end of the menu bar, and the window's name appears in brackets on the title bar of the 1-2-3 window. The Move and Size operations are not available for a maximized worksheet window; to perform these operations, you must first click the Restore button to return the window to its original size.

- ◆ The mouse is the best tool for moving a window and changing its size. To move a worksheet window, drag it by its title bar. To increase or decrease the size of one dimension, position the mouse pointer along a vertical or horizontal border, and drag the border to the new size. (The mouse pointer becomes a double arrowhead icon, pointing vertically or horizontally.) To change both dimensions at once, position the mouse pointer at any one of the window's four corners and drag the corner to the new size. (The mouse pointer becomes a double arrowhead icon, this time pointing diagonally.) Alternatively, you can perform these operations by choosing the Move or Size command from the worksheet window's control menu; then use the keyboard's ↑, ↓, →, and ← keys to move or size the worksheet.

- ◆ Minimize a worksheet window (or a graph window) by clicking the minimize button or by choosing the Minimize command in the control menu. When you do so, the window is represented by an icon inside the 1-2-3 window. For example, Figure 2.22 shows two minimized windows—a worksheet and a graph. Whenever several worksheet files are open at once, you may want to minimize the windows that you are not currently working with. To restore the size of a minimized window, double-click the window's icon.

◆ Just as with the 1-2-3 window, there are several ways to close a worksheet window: Pull down the window's control menu and choose the Close command, or press Ctrl-F4 from the keyboard; double-click the window's control menu box; or activate the window and then choose the Close command from the File menu. If you have made unsaved changes in the window, 1-2-3 displays a dialog box asking you for instructions. You can save the changes before closing the window, abandon the changes, or cancel the Close operation. When you close the last open worksheet window, 1-2-3 automatically opens a new window named Untitled.

In the following sections, you'll learn about two additional operations related to worksheet windows: splitting windows into panes, and opening multiple worksheet windows concurrently.

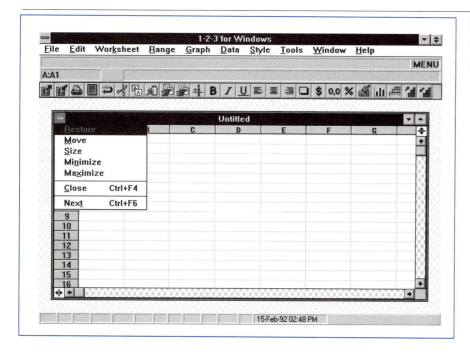

FIGURE 2.21:

Using the control menu of a worksheet window

DIVIDING A WORKSHEET WINDOW INTO PANES

Sometimes you may want to examine two distant sections of a worksheet at once. For example, imagine a worksheet on which you have entered a group of labels in column A and a corresponding group of calculated totals in some other column far to the right of A. Many columns of intermediate data values could separate the column of totals from the labels in column A, but at some point you might want to view the labels and the totals side by side.

One simple way to accomplish this effect is to divide the worksheet vertically into two separate *panes*. Panes are individual views of a single worksheet. Splitting a worksheet into panes allows you to look at two noncontiguous worksheet ranges at one time. For example, consider the Lunches worksheet that you examined in Chapter 1. You'll recall that the worksheet contains four columns of data: the labels in column A, numeric data entries in columns B and C, and calculated fat percentages in column D (as in Figure 2.23). Imagine that you want to view columns A and D side by side. To do so, you split the worksheet into panes. Then you display column A in the first pane and column D in the second pane. The result might look like Figure 2.24.

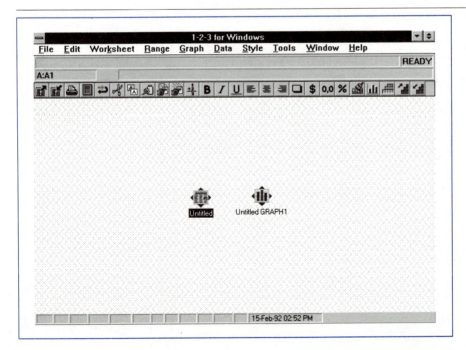

FIGURE 2.22:
Minimizing worksheet and graph windows

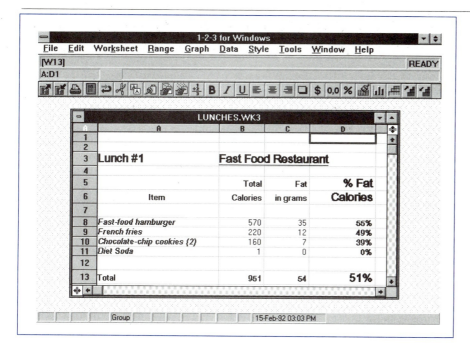

FIGURE 2.23:
The Lunches worksheet, before the pane division

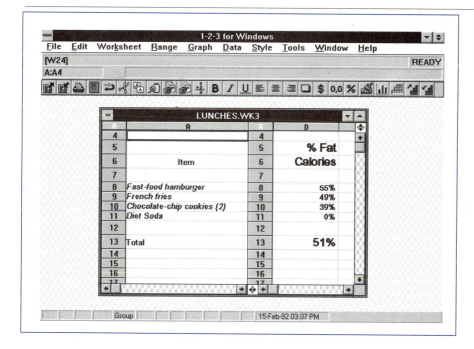

FIGURE 2.24:
The Lunches worksheet split vertically into panes

As you might expect, there are two techniques available for splitting a worksheet into panes, one using the mouse, and the other using a menu command. The mouse technique is simpler and more direct. It involves dragging one of the two icons known as *splitters*. The vertical splitter, located immediately to the left of the horizontal scroll bar, is depicted as a pair of left- and right-pointing arrowheads attached to two short vertical lines. Conversely, the horizontal splitter, located just above the vertical scroll bar, appears as up- and down-pointing arrowheads attached to horizontal lines. When you point to either of these two icons, the mouse pointer becomes a solid black version of the splitter icon. Here is how you use the splitters:

◆ To produce a vertical split like the one shown in Figure 2.24, you drag the vertical splitter across the horizontal scroll bar until you reach the point where you want to split the panes.

◆ Conversely, to create a horizontal split you drag the horizontal splitter down the vertical scroll line.

Try both of these actions now on an empty worksheet. You'll notice that 1-2-3 allows only one split at a time—either a vertical split or a horizontal split, but not both.

Only one pane in a split worksheet is current at once. To switch between panes, you can click inside either pane with the mouse, or you can press the F6 function key.

The other way to divide a worksheet window into panes is to choose the Split command in the Window menu. This command produces the dialog box shown in Figure 2.25. Here are the steps for creating a split:

1. On the active worksheet, select a cell in the column or row where you want to create the split. (A selected column will become the first column in the right-hand pane. A selected row will become the first row in the lower pane.)

2. Pull down the Window menu and select the Split command.

3. On the Window Split dialog box, choose either the Horizontal or the Vertical option, and then click the OK button or press ↵ to confirm your selection.

Notice one additional option in the Window Split dialog box: The Synchronize check box determines whether or not scrolling occurs simultaneously in the two panes of the window. This option is checked by default: In a vertically split worksheet, vertical scrolling is synchronized; that is, both panes always display the same range of rows. In a horizontally split worksheet, horizontal scrolling is synchronized—both panes always display the same range of columns. However, if you uncheck the Synchronize option, scrolling in the two panes is completely independent.

OPENING MORE THAN ONE WORKSHEET WINDOW

In Lotus 1-2-3 for Windows, you can open and work with multiple worksheet files at once. This feature is quite distinct from the *multiple-worksheet window* feature that you learned about in Chapter 1. Here is a summary of these two capabilities:

◆ A single worksheet window may contain as many as 256 worksheets. To insert one or more new worksheets into a window, you use the Worksheet Insert command, as you saw in Chapter 1. When you save such a worksheet window to disk, all the worksheets in the window are saved in a single file, under one file name. In the perspective view, you can view three worksheets at a time inside the same worksheet window.

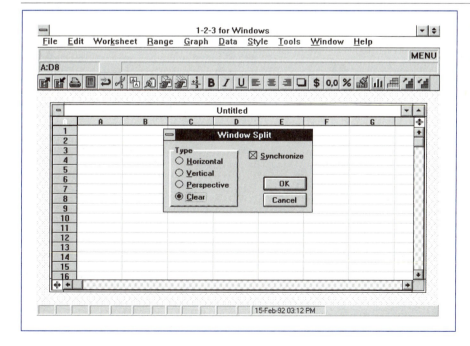

FIGURE 2.25:
The Window Split dialog box

◆ Two or more worksheet files can be open concurrently inside the 1-2-3 environment. Each open file occupies its own window. (The File New command opens a new worksheet window, and the File Open command opens an existing worksheet file from disk; in either case, you view the newly opened window alongside any other windows that are already open.) There are several ways to view and manage multiple open windows: You can minimize windows to icons (as in Figure 2.22); or, you can view multiple windows in *tiled* or *cascading* arrangements.

As a first experiment with multiple worksheet files, perform the steps of the following exercise:

1. Pull down the File menu and choose the New command. A new worksheet window, with the default name FILE0001.WK3 opens over the existing worksheet named Untitled.

2. Choose the New command two more times, creating files with default names of FILE0002.WK3 and FILE0003.WK3.

3. Pull down the Window menu. Notice the list of file names in the bottom section of the menu list, as in Figure 2.26. These are the windows that are currently open. Select any one of these file names to

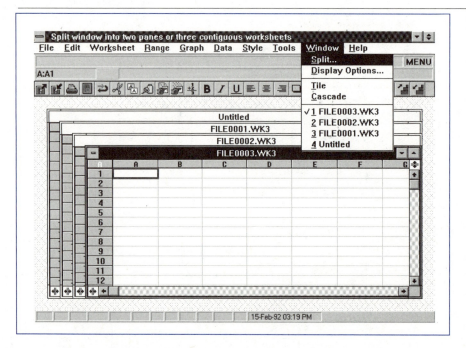

FIGURE 2.26:

The Window menu with a list of open worksheet windows

activate the corresponding worksheet window. (Alternatively, you can press Ctrl-PgUp or Ctrl-PgDn from the keyboard in the READY mode to activate the previous or the next worksheet window in sequence.)

4. Pull down the Window menu again and choose the Tile command. This command arranges the open worksheet files as windows of equal size, each viewed in its entirety (see Figure 2.27).

5. Pull down the Window menu yet again, and choose the Cascade command. This command arranges the open worksheet files as overlapping windows displayed one in front of another (see Figure 2.28).

One of the reasons you might want to open multiple files concurrently is to view worksheets that are *linked* together by formulas. You'll study this technique in Chapter 10.

GETTING HELP IN LOTUS 1-2-3 FOR WINDOWS

A complete and systematic help system is a vital element in any major Windows application; you should expect to find clear and relevant on-screen help

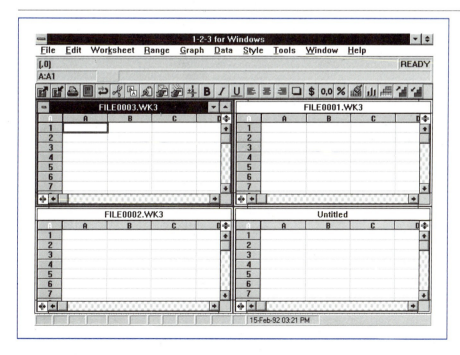

FIGURE 2.27:
A tiled view of four worksheet windows

at the click of a mouse button or the stroke of a key. Lotus 1-2-3 for Windows meets the highest standards for this expectation. While you are working in 1-2-3, you can bring up detailed information about virtually any topic, command, function, procedure, tool, or technique.

If 1-2-3 is your first Windows application, you should take the time to explore the help system early in your work with the program. One way to begin is simply to examine the Help menu (shown in Figure 2.29), which provides several entry points into the help system. Most of the commands in the Help menu open a special window named 1-2-3 for Windows Help. This window in turn displays individual help topics and lists of cross-referenced help categories. As you'll see shortly, the help window has its own unique menu bar and command buttons.

EXPLORING THE HELP MENU

Here is a brief summary of the eight commands in the Help menu:

◆ The Index command provides an alphabetized list of all major help categories (see Figure 2.30). You can click any underlined category in the list to jump directly to the corresponding help topic.

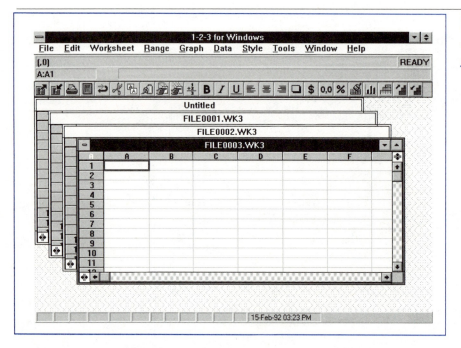

FIGURE 2.28:
A cascading view of four worksheet windows

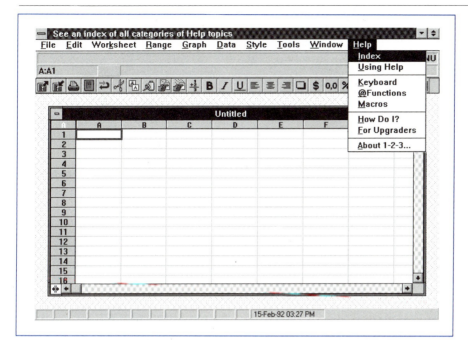

FIGURE 2.29:
The Help menu

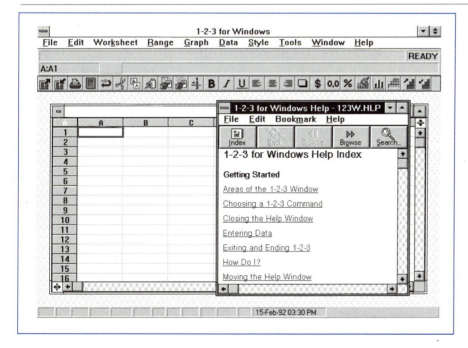

FIGURE 2.30:
The Help Index

◆ The Using Help command gives you a general introduction to the elements of the help system, a topic worth studying carefully. It also provides cross references to specific help features.

◆ The Keyboard, @ Functions, and Macros commands display special-purpose lists and indexes of help categories. The Keyboard index provides a general orientation to the use of the keyboard in 1-2-3. The @Functions and Macros indexes are more specialized and advanced; you can postpone exploring them until you arrive at these topics in later chapters of this book.

◆ The How Do I? command gives you access to useful lists of general 1-2-3 procedures, organized alphabetically. Under each procedure is a cross-referenced list of relevant help topics. The How Do I? command is a good place to start whenever you need to review the steps of a particular task involving worksheets, graphs, or databases.

◆ The For Upgraders command is an orientation for users of previous 1-2-3 releases. In particular, this help topic explains the 1-2-3 Classic menus, and provides cross-references to commands in these menus.

◆ About 1-2-3 is the only command in the Help menu that does *not* open the help window. Instead, it displays a small dialog box that gives you information about the current release of 1-2-3 for Windows.

FINDING CONTEXT-SENSITIVE HELP

Context-sensitive help is probably the single most useful feature of a Windows-style help system. You can get instant help relevant to your current activity by pressing the F1 function key at almost any point during your work in 1-2-3.

For example, imagine that you are selecting options in a dialog box, but you can't recall exactly how to use some aspect of the command in question. To get help you press F1. The resulting help window contains specific information about the dialog box you are viewing on the screen.

Here is a brief exercise that demonstrates the context-sensitive help feature:

1. Pull down the Tools menu and choose the SmartIcons command. The Tools SmartIcons dialog box appears.

2. Press the F1 function key. The help topic for the Tools SmartIcons command immediately appears, as shown in Figure 2.31. You can now scroll through this topic and read all you need to know about the command.

3. When you are ready to return to your work, click the minimize button on the title bar of the help window. The window disappears, and you can continue selecting options in the Tools SmartIcons dialog box. (For now, press Escape to cancel the command and to end this exercise.)

Try pressing F1 for context-sensitive help whenever you are not sure what to do next in a 1-2-3 procedure.

THE HELP WINDOW

As you saw in the previous exercise, the help window has its own title bar, control menu box, and minimize and maximize buttons. These features have the same functions as they do in other windows. For example, you may sometimes find it convenient to expand the size of the help window so that you can read more information at once. To do so, click the maximize button.

The help window also has its own menu bar, with four commands representing pull-down menus:

File   Edit   Bookmark   Help

The File menu contains commands for printing the current help topic, for opening the help system files for other Windows applications, and for exiting

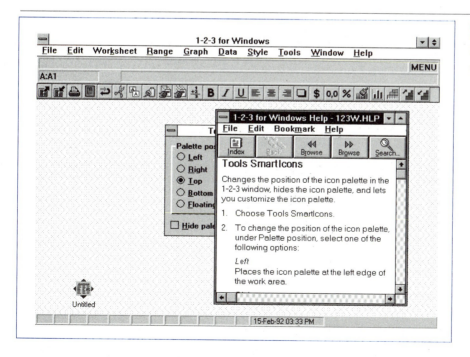

FIGURE 2.31:

Getting context-sensitive help

from Help. Commands in the Edit menu allow you to copy the current help topic to the Windows clipboard, and to insert your own annotations into a particular help topic. The Bookmark menu has a command for marking particular passages in the help system so you can find them quickly. The Help menu gives you access to the Using Windows Help window, a general description of the Windows help facility.

Finally, the help window has five special command buttons, each with its own icon and caption. Look back at Figure 2.31 to examine these buttons, located immediately below the help menu bar. Clicking the Index button takes you to the general Help Index. The Back button returns you to the help topic that you viewed just before the current topic. The two Browse buttons allow you to browse forward or backward through all the topics within a general help category.

The Search button represents a special tool for locating information in the help system. When you click this button, the Search dialog box appears on the screen. This feature gives you a quick way to search by name for any topic that you want to read about. For example, imagine that you want to review the features of the control panel. Here are the steps for using the Search dialog box:

1. In the Search For text box, enter the words **Control panel**. As you do so, the index list beneath the text box automatically scrolls to the alphabetic position of this topic.

2. Click the Search button, or simply press ↵. The Topics Found list at the bottom of the dialog box displays all the help topics related to the control panel, as in Figure 2.32.

3. Select one of these topics and click the Go To button. The Search dialog box is closed, and the selected topic appears in the help window. To see other related topics, you can click either of the Browse buttons.

4. When you have finished reading the help topic, click the minimize button on the help window's title bar to return to your work in 1-2-3.

SUMMARY

The Lotus 1-2-3 application window presents many tools and properties that are common to all Windows applications. If you have worked with almost any other major program in Windows, many of these elements will seem comfortably familiar and easy to use.

The application window itself contains six essential lines of tools and information that you will focus on throughout your work in 1-2-3. These are the title bar, the menu bar, the edit line, the format line, the icon palette, and the status line. In addition, most windows you encounter in 1-2-3—including the application window, worksheet windows, and even dialog boxes—have control menus and other common tools designed for managing the windows themselves.

Lotus 1-2-3 gives you two versatile ways to work with multiple worksheets. On the one hand, a single window—representing one worksheet file on disk—can itself contain as many as 256 worksheets. In addition, you can open and work with mulitple worksheet files concurrently in the 1-2-3 environment. Another useful feature allows you to divide a given worksheet window into panes, to view two noncontiguous portions of a worksheet at the same time.

One of the most important resources of the 1-2-3 application is its comprehensive help system. The Help menu and the help window itself both give you many ways to search for the help topic that you need at any given point in your work. You should learn to take advantage of the 1-2-3 for Windows Help window to guide you in your efforts with worksheets, graphs, and databases.

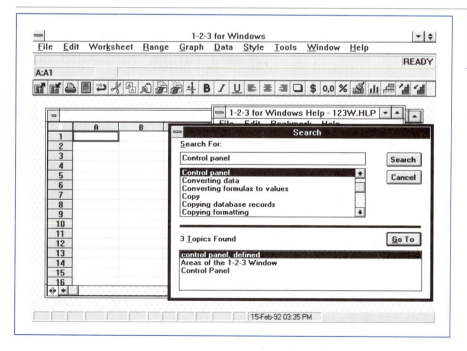

FIGURE 2.32:

The Search dialog box for the help system

PART TWO

FAST TRACK

CHAPTER 3

To preselect a range with the mouse, ... 117

point to one corner of the target range and drag the mouse pointer to the opposite corner. To highlight your selection, 1-2-3 displays a double-line border around the range.

To preselect a range with the keyboard, ... 118

press the F4 function key to switch to the POINT mode, then use arrow keys to define the range. (Use Ctrl-PgUp or Ctrl-PgDn to define a three-dimensional range over adjacent worksheets in a window.) Press ↵ to complete the range selection and return to the READY mode.

To compute the total of a range of numbers, ... 119

preselect the range plus a blank cell at the end of the range, then click the summation icon in the icon palette. Alternatively, enter a @SUM function directly into the worksheet.

To assign a name to a range of cells, ... 121

preselect the range and choose the Range Name Create command.

To copy a range of data from one position to another in the worksheet, ... 124

preselect the range and click the range-copy icon; then click the upper-left corner cell of the range to which you want to copy the data. (Alternatively, use the Edit Quick Copy command.)

To assign a password to a worksheet file, ... **131**
    select the Password protect option in the File Save As dialog box and then enter the password (twice) into the new dialog box that appears.

To update an existing file after you have made changes in the active worksheet, ... **132**
    click the save-file icon or choose the Save command from the File menu.

To move a range of data from one place to another in a worksheet, ... **133**
    preselect the source range, click the range-move icon, and then click the upper-left corner of the destination range.

To insert a blank row or column at a specific position on the worksheet, ... **136**
    select a cell at the target position and choose the Insert command from the Worksheet menu. Select either the Column or Row option and click OK.

To change the reference type of an address in a formula entry, ... **146**
    press the F4 function key in the POINT, EDIT, or VALUE mode. Each time you press F4, the address changes to the next reference type—from relative to absolute to mixed.

CHAPTER 3

Worksheet Essentials

ne of the most remarkable qualities of the Lotus 1-2-3 spreadsheet is its flexibility. Rather than dictating how you should arrange your work, 1-2-3 offers you a multitude of tools and options for presenting data and performing calculations. As soon as you begin entering information into the empty grid that first appears inside the worksheet window, the results quickly begin to reflect your own work requirements, formatting preferences, and organizational style.

In this chapter, you'll master the basic procedures for entering and calculating information in the 1-2-3 worksheet window. You'll work through the initial tasks of developing a complete worksheet example:

- ◆ Entering labels and values
- ◆ Selecting ranges on a worksheet
- ◆ Calculating totals
- ◆ Assigning names to ranges on a worksheet
- ◆ Copying ranges of data

- Saving your worksheet to disk
- Inserting, deleting, and moving blocks of data
- Developing formulas and copying them to new ranges
- Selecting appropriate reference types for addresses in formulas
- Using parentheses to establish the order of operations in formulas
- Exploring "what-if" scenarios

In Chapter 4, you'll continue developing your worksheet skills as you turn your attention to the steps of formatting and printing.

Throughout this chapter and the next, you'll work on one worksheet example, producing a document for an imaginary firm named Computing Conferences, Inc. As its main activity, this company organizes and conducts one-day training conferences that focus on the specific computing needs of various types of businesses. The worksheet you'll be developing is designed to compute the projected revenues, expenses, and profits for a one-day conference.

Figure 3.1 shows a sample of the final worksheet—a document that you'll create yourself by the time you finish Chapter 4. The worksheet is divided into sections. The top section gives general information about a planned one-day conference that the company will conduct in the future: the name of the conference, location, date, and per-person attendance price, and two estimates of the number of people who are likely to attend—a low attendance estimate (labeled *Minimum* on the worksheet) and a high estimate (labeled *Maximum*). The next two sections down the worksheet display the projected revenues and expenses for the conference, based on the attendance estimates. The two columns on the right side of the worksheet show financial figures based on the low and high attendance estimates, respectively. Finally, the bottom line of the worksheet gives the anticipated profit, again with projections based on the two different attendance estimates.

This document contains the data for a specific one-day conference planned for a date in the future—a St. Louis conference designed to introduce computer skills to the owners and managers of video rental stores. However, the worksheet itself is carefully designed as a general-purpose template for any one-day event that Computing Conferences, Inc. is in the process of planning.

The worksheet areas displayed in light gray shading are, in effect, the input ranges for data about a given conference. All the unshaded numeric values are calculated from the input data. A person using this worksheet simply enters information into the shaded ranges; for each new numeric data entry, 1-2-3 recalculates the formulas contained in the worksheet, based on the data entries for the new conference.

This general-purpose template represents an important approach to developing worksheets in Lotus 1-2-3. You can ultimately simplify and streamline your work if you think of each new worksheet you develop as a template for similar tasks that you might need to accomplish in the future. Of course, not all worksheets lend themselves to this kind of planning. But each time you start a new worksheet, you should ask yourself whether you are likely to perform a similar job on a daily, weekly, monthly, quarterly, or even yearly basis. If so, you should take care to organize your work so that you can reuse the worksheet to solve future computational tasks.

Prepare now for the hands-on exercises that you'll be working on in this chapter. Start up 1-2-3 for Windows if you have not already done so, and click the maximize button on the default worksheet named Untitled. In the sections ahead, you'll enter labels, values, and formulas onto the worksheet.

FIGURE 3.1:

The conference worksheet

Computing Conferences, Inc.
Profit Projection for a One-Day Conference

Conference: *Computing for Video Stores*
Place: *St. Louis*
Date: *15-Oct-92*

Expected attendance:

	Minimum	Maximum
	80	150

Price: *$195.00*

	Per Person	Min. Total	Max. Total
Projected Revenues			
Attendance		$15,600.00	$29,250.00
Video Sales	$35.00	$1,400.00	$2,625.00
Total Revenues		$17,000.00	$31,875.00
Projected Expenses -- Fixed			
Conference room		$1,500.00	$2,000.00
Video production		$1,000.00	$1,000.00
Promotion		$3,500.00	$3,500.00
Travel		$800.00	$800.00
Total Fixed Expenses		$6,800.00	$7,300.00
Projected Expenses -- Variable by Attendance			
Conference materials	$8.25	$660.00	$1,237.50
Coffee and pastries	$3.25	$260.00	$487.50
Box lunch	$4.75	$380.00	$712.50
Total Variable Expenses		$1,300.00	$2,437.50
Projected Profit		$8,900.00	$22,137.50

DEVELOPING A WORKSHEET

As you begin creating a worksheet, you may sometimes find yourself entering data in a temporary position or order. Because 1-2-3 gives you simple ways to move blocks of data from one point to another in the worksheet and to insert rows or columns if you need to, you can create the sections of your worksheet in any order that is convenient.

Accordingly, you'll begin your work in the following exercise by entering data for the fixed expenses associated with the training conference. When you are later ready to develop other parts of the worksheet, including the projected revenues, you will make room by moving the fixed expense section down to its correct position.

ENTERING LABELS

You'll recall that a label is a nonnumeric data entry in a cell. Labels appear on a worksheet as titles, column headings, and row descriptions. When you begin entering a label, 1-2-3 switches into the LABEL mode. By default, 1-2-3 left-justifies a label entry in a cell, but you can change this alignment in a number of ways, as you'll learn in Chapter 4.

Lotus 1-2-3 has an interesting way of handling *long* labels. When a label entry contains more characters than will fit in a given cell, 1-2-3 extends the label display into adjacent cells to the right if those cells are empty. Otherwise, if the cells to the right already contain data themselves, the display of a long label is cut off at the end of its own cell. You'll explore this feature now as you enter the two title lines at the top of the conference worksheet:

1. Select cell B1 by pressing → (assuming A1 is initially selected), or by clicking the cell with the mouse.

2. Type **Computing Conferences, Inc.** into this cell as the company name. As you type, your entry appears in the contents box, and the mode indicator displays the word *LABEL*.

3. Press ↵ to complete your entry, and 1-2-3 copies the entry into cell B1. But because the entry is too long to be displayed completely in B1, the display extends across row 1 into cells C1 and D1, as in Figure 3.2.

4. Press ↓ to select cell B2, and type the worksheet title **Profit Projection for a One-Day Conference**.

5. Press ↵ to complete this entry. Again, the display of this long label extends across the row, into cells C2, D2, and E2.

Now notice how the contents box displays the entry in cell B2 (see Figure 3.2):

'Profit Projection for a One-Day Conference

Even though this label is *displayed* across cells ranging from B2 to E2, its actual storage location is cell B2 alone. By the way, the single quotation mark at the beginning of the label in the contents box is 1-2-3's notation for a left-aligned label. You'll learn about other alignment symbols in Chapter 4.

What happens to a long label if you enter data in a cell located to the immediate right of the label? To answer this question, try the following exercise:

1. Press → to select cell C2. Notice that the contents box displays no entry for this cell: C2 is in fact empty, even though the display of the long label from cell B2 extends into C2.

2. Type **abc** as a temporary label into cell C2.

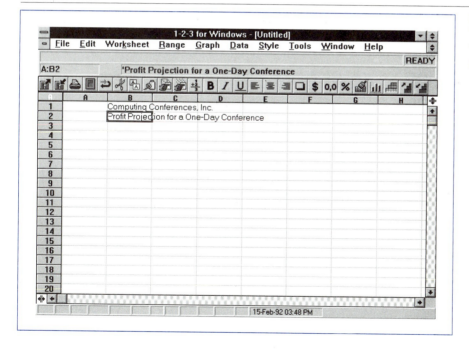

FIGURE 3.2:

Entering long labels into worksheet cells

3. Press ↵ to complete the entry. Notice what happens to the long label display from cell B2: It is now cut off at the end of its own cell, and C2 now displays its own label.

4. Press ← to select cell B2 again. The contents box displays the entire long label that you originally entered into B2, even though the cell itself can now display only the first several letters of this entry (see Figure 3.3).

In summary, the display of a long label extends into the cells to the right as long as those cells are empty. But the long label display is cut off, or *truncated*, if a cell to the right contains an entry of its own.

As a result of this experiment, you now have an unwanted label entry in cell C2. Deleting this entry is a simple step.

Deleting an Entry

To delete a label or value in 1-2-3, select the cell that contains the entry and press the Delete key on your keyboard. Alternatively, pull down the Edit menu and choose the Clear command. (The Delete key is the shortcut for the Clear command.) The program clears the entry itself, along with any styles or formats that you may have previously assigned to the cell.

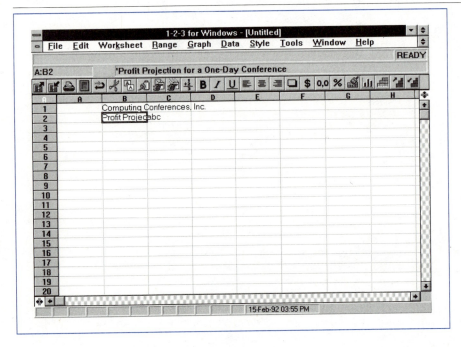

FIGURE 3.3:
Interrupting the display of a long label

Follow these steps to delete the temporary entry from cell C2:

1. Press → to select C2.
2. Press the Delete key to delete the cell's entry.

When you do so, the long label in cell B2 regains its full display across row 2. There is now no entry in cell C2 to interrupt this display.

Now pull down the Edit menu (shown in Figure 3.4) and you'll see other commands that delete the contents of a cell or range of cells. The Cut command deletes an entry and copies it to the Windows clipboard; this is the first step in a *cut-and-paste* procedure. In contrast, the Clear Special command produces a dialog box on the screen (shown in Figure 3.5) that allows you to specify exactly what you want to delete from a cell or range of cells: contents, formats, styles, or a graph. The Clear Special and Clear commands delete entries without copying them to the clipboard.

Because the Delete key is so readily available for deleting the contents of a cell or range of cells, you might sometimes perform deletions unintentionally. If this happens—or if you make any other mistakes during your work in 1-2-3—you can use the Undo command to restore your worksheet to its state before the last action. (The Edit Undo command is available if you

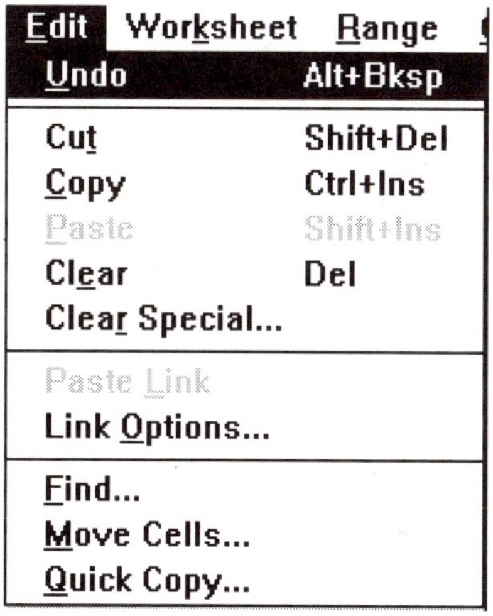

FIGURE 3.4:
The Edit menu

selected your own default preferences during installation, as described in Appendix A. Otherwise, you can activate the command by choosing Tools User Setup and clicking the Enable Edit Undo option.)

Using the Undo Command

To undo the effect of your last action at the keyboard or with the mouse, you can pull down the Edit menu and select Undo (see Figure 3.4). Alternatively, use the keyboard shortcut for this command, Alt-Backspace. Or simplest of all, you can click the undo icon in the icon palette. This icon depicts a pair of horizontal arrows pointing in opposite directions; see Figure 3.6.

Try this exercise with the Undo command:

1. Press ← to select cell B2. This is the cell that currently contains the second line of the worksheet title.

2. Press the Delete key. The entry in the cell disappears. Imagine that you had performed this action by mistake. You would now want a quick way to correct your error.

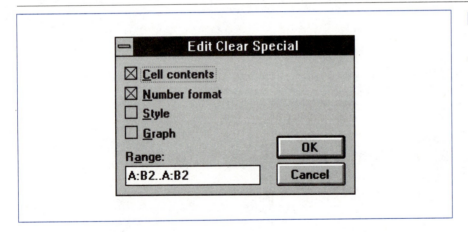

FIGURE 3.5:
The Edit Clear Special dialog box

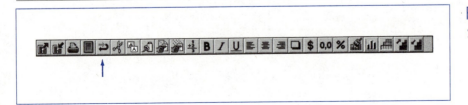

FIGURE 3.6:
The undo icon

3. Pull down the Edit menu and choose the Undo command, or click the undo icon. The label entry in cell B2 reappears.

There is one thing to remember about Undo: To use the command successfully, you must correct a mistake before you perform another action. Undo operates only on an action you perform just previous to choosing the command.

Next, you will continue entering labels into the conference worksheet to produce the contents shown in Figure 3.7. As you do so, keep in mind that you can press an arrow key (→, ←, ↑, or ↓) instead of ↵ to complete an entry. An arrow key performs two actions at once: It completes your entry into the current cell and selects a new cell for the next entry. This can considerably streamline the process of entering a column or row of data into a worksheet.

1. Enter the label **Conference:** into cell A4 and **Place:** into A5.

2. At the right of these entries, you will enter the name and place of the current conference. In cell B4 type **Computing for Video Stores**, and in B5 type **St. Louis**.

3. Enter the subtitle **Projected Expenses -- Fixed** into cell A7.

4. Finally, enter these labels, representing the fixed expense categories, into the range of cells from B8 to B12:

   Conference room
   Video production
   Promotion

	A	B	C	D	E	F	G	H
1		Computing Conferences, Inc.						
2		Profit Projection for a One-Day Conference						
3								
4	Conference:	Computing for Video Stores						
5	Place:	St. Louis						
6								
7	Projected Expenses -- Fixed							
8		Conference room						
9		Video production						
10		Promotion						
11		Travel						
12		Total Fixed Expenses						
13								
14								
15								
16								
17								
18								
19								
20								

FIGURE 3.7:
Columns of labels in the conference worksheet

Travel
Total Fixed Expenses

These categories represent the expenses that remain unchanged regardless of the number of people who attend the conference. Among these expenses are the rental price for the conference room, the cost of producing a video of the conference, the pre-conference promotion costs, and the amount spent on travel to the conference site. Later, you'll enter a group of *variable expenses* that depend directly on attendance.

The next step is to begin entering numeric values for the fixed expenses.

ENTERING NUMBERS

As you'll recall, a *value* is an entry that 1-2-3 accepts as a number. A value can become part of an arithmetic formula in your worksheet.

Normally, any entry that begins with a digit switches 1-2-3 into the VALUE mode. But digits sometimes also appear as characters in a label—for example, in an address:

456 Flower Street

When a label begins with a digit, you have to notify 1-2-3 to accept the entry as a label rather than a value. One way to do this is to begin the label with a single quote character:

'456 Flower Street

As soon as you enter the single quote, 1-2-3 switches into the LABEL mode and you can successfully complete the label entry.

A problem occurs when you begin an entry in the VALUE mode, and then type one or more characters that 1-2-3 cannot accept as part of a value. For example, imagine that you are entering the number 4321 into a worksheet cell. When you arrive at the last digit in this number, your finger slips and you inadvertently type **423q** instead. Because this entry ends in a nondigital character, 1-2-3 cannot accept the entry as a numeric value. When you press ↵, 1-2-3 beeps and automatically switches into the EDIT mode so that you can correct your entry before continuing. You'll have an opportunity to experience this feature firsthand in the following exercise, as you enter the column of fixed-expense figures into the conference worksheet:

1. Select cell D8, the top cell of the column range where you will enter the expense figures.

2. Type **1500** into D8. Notice that the word *VALUE* appears in the mode indicator as soon as you type the first digit of this number. To complete the entry and select the next cell down, press ↓.

3. Type **1000a** into cell D9. In this case, you have *intentionally* introduced an unacceptable character into the entry, but this kind of input error is very common. Press ↵ to attempt to complete the entry. You'll hear the beep, and then you'll see 1-2-3 switch into the EDIT mode. Your entry remains in the contents box, where you can examine it and figure out what has gone wrong. Press the Backspace key to delete the character *a*, then press ↵ again. This time 1-2-3 accepts your entry as a value, and copies the value to the current cell, D9.

4. Press ↓ to select cell D10. When you enter a dollar value into a cell, you might be tempted to begin the entry with a dollar sign. To see what 1-2-3's response is, try entering **$3500** into D10; press ↓ to complete the entry. You'll discover that 1-2-3 ignores the dollar sign, and omits it from the entry. The value displayed in the cell is simply *3500*. As you'll learn in Chapter 4, you must assign a numeric format to a cell in order to produce a dollar-and-cent display.

5. Enter the final expense value, **800**, into cell D11.

Now that you have entered an entire column of numbers, you need to compute the total for the column and display the total in cell D12. Calculating the total of a column or row of numbers is a common spreadsheet operation—so common that 1-2-3's icon palette includes a tool that makes the process almost automatic. But before you use this icon you must select the range of values that you want to total. In the next section, you'll expand your understanding of worksheet ranges, and you'll learn the techniques available for selecting a range. Then you'll return to the conference worksheet to find the total of the expense column.

SELECTING RANGES

As you know by now, a range is a rectangular area of worksheet cells that you select for a particular operation. Many of 1-2-3's menu commands and functions work with ranges. A range consists of any of the following arrangements of cells in a worksheet window:

◆ A single cell

◆ A group of contiguous cells contained within one row or one column

◆ A two-dimensional rectangle of cells within multiple rows and columns in a worksheet

◆ A three-dimensional group of cells, consisting of identically addressed ranges from adjacent worksheets in a worksheet window

The familiar notation for a range in 1-2-3 consists of two cell's addresses separated by two dots. For a range on a single worksheet, this notation can appear with or without the worksheet name. For instance, a range of cells on worksheet A might be identified either as A:B2..A:F6, or simply as B2..F6 if there is no possibility of confusing this range with the same ranges on other worksheets.

Here are some examples of ranges, as illustrated in Figures 3.8 through 3.12:

◆ B4..B4 is a range consisting of a single cell on a worksheet, at address B4 (see Figure 3.8).

◆ C5..C10 is a column range, or a range of cells all contained within a single worksheet column, C in this case (see Figure 3.9). C5 is the top of the range and C10 is the bottom.

◆ A6..E6 is a row range—a range of cells contained within row 6 (see Figure 3.10). A6 is the first cell at the left side of the range and E6 is the last cell at the right.

◆ B2..F6 is a two-dimensional range (see Figure 3.11). B2 is the upper-left corner of the range, and F6 is the lower-right corner.

◆ A:B2..C:F6 is a three-dimensional range, consisting of cells from three adjacent worksheets in a window—that is, the range B2..F6 in worksheets A, B, and C (see Figure 3.12).

When you choose a menu command that operates over a range, the command's dialog box typically includes a text box in which you specify the target range. The Range box in the Edit Clear Special dialog box (shown in Figure 3.5) is an

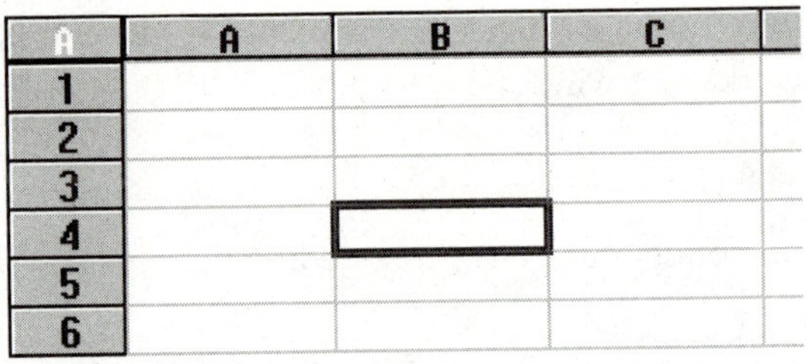

FIGURE 3.8:

A range consisting of a single cell, B4..B4

example. As you learned in Chapter 1, you can select a range for a menu command either before or after you actually choose the command. If you choose the command first, 1-2-3 provides special mouse and keyboard pointing techniques for entering a range into a text box.

Selecting a range before you choose a menu command is sometimes referred to as *preselecting* a range. Preselection is often a convenience, and sometimes a requirement. In particular, some of the tools in the 1-2-3 icon palette require that you preselect a range before clicking the icon.

There are three ways to preselect a range in 1-2-3, one with the mouse and two with the keyboard. In each case, 1-2-3 switches from the READY mode to the POINT mode, indicating that you are in the process of pointing to a range of cells. As you point to the cells, 1-2-3 highlights your selection by displaying a double-line border around the range. In addition, the corresponding range notation appears in the contents box at the top of the 1-2-3 window.

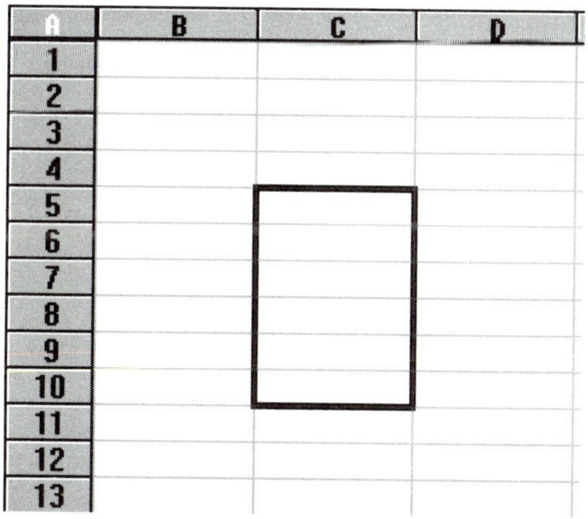

FIGURE 3.9:

A column range, C5..C10

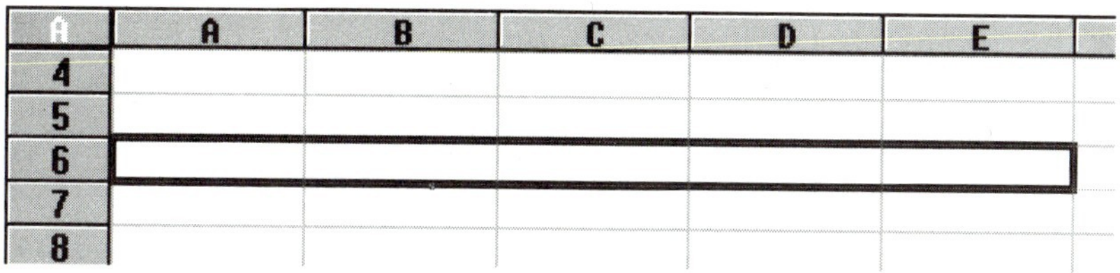

FIGURE 3.10:

A row range, A6..E6

Here are the steps for preselecting a worksheet range with the mouse:

1. Position the mouse pointer over the first cell in the range.
2. Hold down the left mouse button and drag the pointer down and/or across to the last cell in the range.
3. Release the mouse button when the target range is highlighted.

With the keyboard, the F4 function key switches 1-2-3 from the READY mode to the POINT mode. Here are the steps for preselecting a range with the keyboard:

1. Select the cell that is to become the first cell in the range.
2. Press the F4 function key. This anchors the current cell as the starting point of the range, and switches 1-2-3 into the POINT mode.

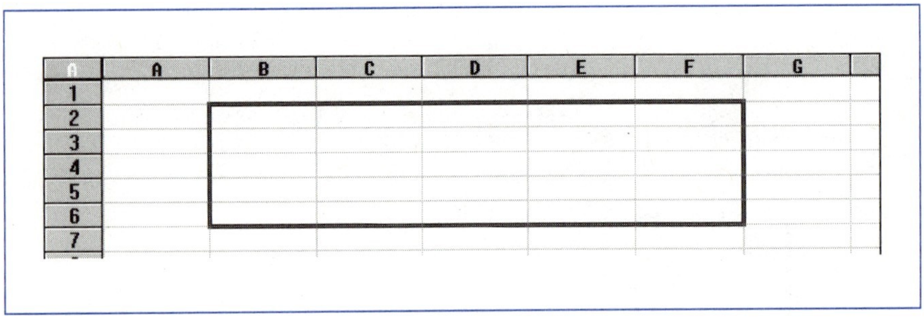

FIGURE 3.11:

A two-dimensional range, B2..F6

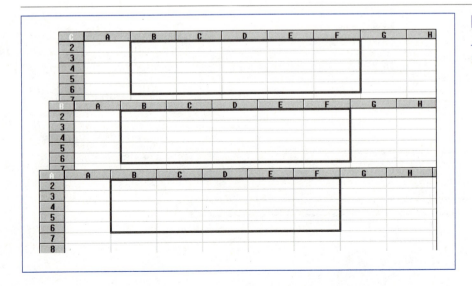

FIGURE 3.12:

A three-dimensional range, A:B2..C:F6

3. Press arrow keys to highlight the target range. For example, use ↓ for a column range and/or → for a row range.

4. To select a three-dimensional range over adjacent worksheets in a window, press Ctrl-PgUp or Ctrl-PgDn while you are in the POINT mode. (The current window must already contain two or more worksheets. You'll recall that you use the Worksheet Insert command to add worksheets to a window.)

5. Press ↵ to complete the range selection. This final step switches you back into the READY mode, but leaves the selected range in its highlighted state.

Here is a second keyboard technique for preselecting a range:

1. Select the first cell of the range.

2. Hold down the Shift key as you press →, ←, ↑, or ↓ to define a range on the active worksheet.

3. Hold down the Shift key and press Ctrl-PgUp or Ctrl-PgDn to select a three-dimensional range over multiple worksheets in the active window.

You'll have opportunities to practice these techniques as you continue developing the conference worksheet.

FINDING TOTALS

The summation icon is one of the tools that requires a preselected range. The icon is located near the middle of the default icon palette (see Figure 3.13). Using this tool takes two simple steps:

1. Preselect the target range of values, plus a final cell in which 1-2-3 will store the summation formula. This final cell in the range must be blank. For a *column* of numbers, select the range of values in the column and a blank cell at the bottom of the column. For a *row* of numbers, select the row plus a blank cell at the right of the numbers.

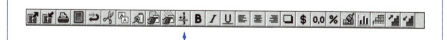

FIGURE 3.13:

The summation icon

2. Click the summation icon. In response, 1-2-3 finds the sum of the values in the selected range and enters the value into the blank cell at the end of the range.

In the conference worksheet, cell D12 is reserved for the total of the fixed expenses. Follow these steps to produce this total:

1. Use a mouse or the keyboard technique to preselect the range D8..D12.

2. Click the summation icon in the icon palette. The value *6800* appears in cell D12. This number represents the total fixed expenses.

3. To view the formula that 1-2-3 has created, select cell D12. (Click the cell with the mouse or press ↓ four times.) In the contents box, you see the following formula:

@SUM(D8..D11)

@SUM is one of the tools in 1-2-3's large library of *built-in functions*. In this case, 1-2-3 has entered a formula that finds the sum of the numeric values stored in the range D8..D11. You'll study this and other functions in Chapter 5. Of course, you can enter the @SUM function into cell D12 directly from the keyboard if you prefer. To try this exercise, select D12 and press Delete to erase the cell's current contents. Then follow these steps:

1. Begin the summation formula by entering **@SUM(** from the keyboard. When you do so, 1-2-3 switches into the VALUE mode.

2. You could now type the target range directly from the keyboard, but the pointing technique is easier: Press ↑ four times, selecting cell D8. The program switches into the POINT mode and automatically enters the cell address into the summation formula in the contents box.

3. Type a period (.) to anchor the range. In this case, D8 is the starting point for the range.

4. Press ↓ three times. As you do so, 1-2-3 highlights the range D8..D11, and the range notation appears in the summation formula in the contents box. At this point, the screen looks like Figure 3.14.

5. Type **)**, the close parenthesis character, to complete the summation formula.

6. Press ↵ to complete the entry.

The end result is identical to that of the first technique. After trying both techniques, you can see how much time you can save by employing the tools of 1-2-3's icon palette.

As you begin entering formulas and functions like @SUM into your worksheet, you can sometimes simplify your work by assigning names to specific ranges of data. You'll look briefly at this technique in the next section.

CREATING RANGE NAMES

Formulas that contain the addresses of cells and ranges are sometimes difficult to read and understand. For example, consider the summation formula you just entered into the conference worksheet. If you return to this worksheet some weeks or months from now, you may not immediately see the significance of the formula **@SUM(D8..D11)**. But suppose the range notation D8..D11 were replaced with a meaningful name, such as EXPENSES; you would have an easier time recognizing the purpose of a formula that read **@SUM(EXPENSES)**.

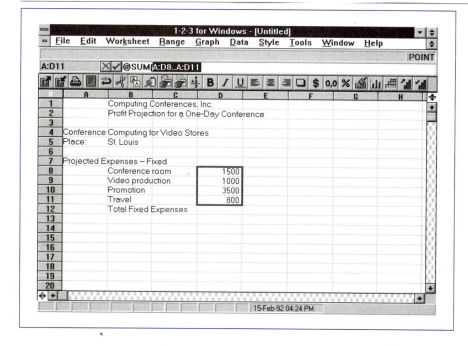

FIGURE 3.14:

Entering a summation formula

For this reason, 1-2-3 gives you the option of assigning names to individual cells or to ranges of cells on a worksheet. The command that you use to assign names is called Range Name Create. To find this command, follow these steps:

1. Pull down the Range menu and choose the Name command. This command results in a cascade menu containing a list of commands related to range names.

2. Choose the Create command from the cascade menu. The dialog box shown in Figure 3.15 appears on the screen. (For now, click the Cancel button after you have examined the dialog box.)

You use the Range Name Create dialog box to assign a name to a particular range. A range name that you create may contain as many as 15 characters; 1-2-3 automatically converts a range name entry to all uppercase letters. As a first exercise with range names, try assigning the name EXPENSES to the range of fixed expenses on the conference worksheet:

1. Preselect the range of expense values, D8..D11.

2. Choose the Create command from the Range Name menu.

3. In the Range name text box, enter the name **EXPENSES**.

4. Click the OK button or press ↵ to confirm your entry.

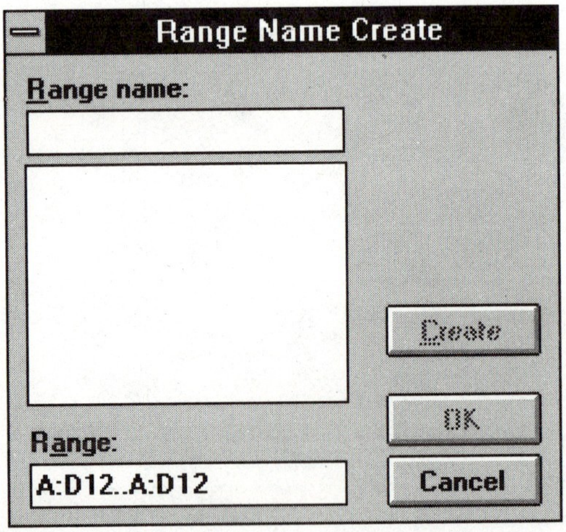

FIGURE 3.15:
The Range Name Create dialog box

This new definition does not change the appearance of your worksheet in any way. But the next time you need to write a formula involving the column of fixed expenses, you can use the name EXPENSES to represent the range. In fact, while you are in the process of entering a formula, 1-2-3 can provide a convenient list of all the existing range names defined for the current worksheet. To view this list, you press the F3 function key in the VALUE mode. For example, in the following exercise you'll reenter the summation formula into cell D12, this time using the new range name you have defined:

1. Select cell D12 and press the Delete key to erase the formula currently in the cell.

2. Begin reentering the summation formula: **@SUM(**.

3. After you type the open parenthesis, press the F3 function key. A new dialog box called Range Names appears on the screen (see Figure 3.16). A list in this box displays the name you have defined for the column of expense figures.

4. Double-click the name EXPENSES in the list. The Range Names dialog box disappears, and the name EXPENSES appears in the formula: *@SUM(EXPENSES*.

5. Complete the formula by typing the close parenthesis character and pressing ↵.

You'll work with other range names later in this chapter.

Next, you'll copy the fixed expense figures from column D to column E in the conference worksheet. Looking back at Figure 3.1, you can see that the fixed

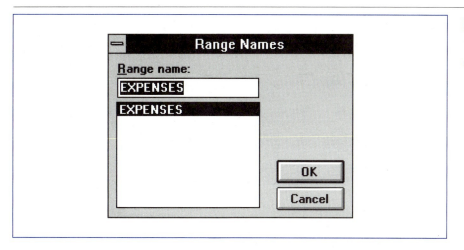

FIGURE 3.16:

The Range Names dialog box

expenses are almost the same in the two columns. Rather than reenter the figures in the second column, you can quickly copy them and then revise the data in column E as necessary.

COPYING A RANGE OF VALUES

There are three techniques for copying a range of data from one place to another in the worksheet. The first and simplest technique is to use the range-copy icon in the icon palette. This icon appears as a hand pointing to the right with a pair of pages in the background (see Figure 3.17). Move the mouse pointer to this icon and press the right mouse button. The following description appears in the 1-2-3 title bar:

Select the range to copy to

The other copy techniques use commands from the Edit menu: the Quick Copy command and the Copy and Paste commands. In the following exercises, you'll try all three techniques, which produce identical results on the worksheet itself. After each of the first two exercises you'll delete the copy so you can try the next technique. In each copy procedure, you begin your work by preselecting the range of cells that you want to copy. Make this range selection using either the mouse or the F4 function key.

Using the Range-Copy Icon

Here is how you use the range-copy icon:

1. Select the range D8..D12.

2. Click the range-copy icon.

3. Position the mouse pointer over cell E8, at the top of the range to which you want to copy the data. (When you move the mouse

FIGURE 3.17:
The range-copy icon

pointer over the worksheet, the mouse pointer changes to a hand icon pointing to the right.) Click the left mouse button. In response, 1-2-3 copies the column of data into the range E8..E12.

Clicking a single cell—E8 in this case—is sufficient to indicate the range that is the destination of the copy. Because the source of the copy is a column of cells, 1-2-3 assumes that you want to copy the same column to the destination range, starting at E8.

There is another very important point to notice in the result of this copy operation. Move the cell pointer down to E12 and look at the contents box to examine the formula that 1-2-3 has copied to the cell, @SUM(E8..E11). This formula was copied from the equivalent formula in cell D12. In the copy, 1-2-3 has adjusted the range of the @SUM function to E8..E11. Thanks to this adjustment, the formula in cell E12 produces the total of the expense figures in column E. Furthermore, this formula will be recalculated if you make any changes in those figures. To see that this is true, move the cell pointer to E8 now and enter the new value **2000**. In response to this new entry, 1-2-3 instantly recalculates the formula in cell E12, giving the new result, 7300. Later in this chapter, you'll learn much more about the adjustments that 1-2-3 makes in formulas that you copy from one location to another in a worksheet.

To prepare for the next copy exercise, delete the copy you have just made. Select the range E8..E12 and press the Delete key at the keyboard. Delete has the same effect on a range of cells as it does on a single cell: All the data is cleared away.

Using the Quick Copy Command from the Edit Menu

If you prefer to use the keyboard to copy a range of cells, the Quick Copy command is a good approach. Here are the steps for using this command to copy the column of expense data:

1. Preselect the range D8..D12.

2. Pull down the Edit menu and choose the Quick Copy command. In the resulting dialog box (shown in Figure 3.18), the preselected range appears in the From text box. The To text box has the focus. (The From box defines the source of the copy operation and the To box defines the destination.)

3. Press → from the keyboard to point to a range for the To box. The Edit Quick Copy dialog box temporarily disappears from the screen, and cell E8 is selected. Pointing to E8 is sufficient to indicate the destination of the copy.

4. Press ↵ to confirm the destination range. The Edit Quick Copy dialog box reappears, and the notation *A:E8* is displayed inside the To box. This is all the information you need to supply.

5. Press ↵ to complete the copy operation. 1-2-3 instantly copies the expense data from column D to column E.

The range-copy icon is a shortcut for the Edit Quick Copy command. Both procedures copy data and formulas, but neither uses the Windows clipboard in the process. By contrast, the last of the three copy techniques employs the clipboard as an intermediate storage place.

Once again, select the range E8..E12 and press the Delete key to erase the data you just copied. In the next exercise, you'll try an operation known as *copy and paste*.

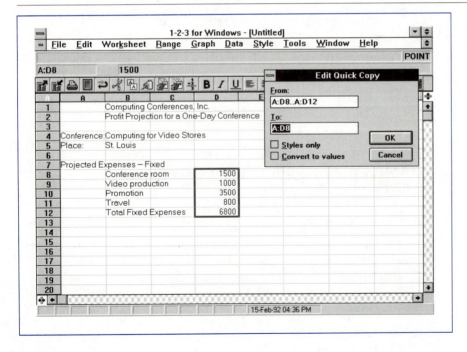

FIGURE 3.18:

Using the Edit Quick Copy command

Performing a Copy-and-Paste Operation

If you are an experienced Windows user, you are probably familiar with the Copy and Paste commands. They appear in the Edit menus of most major Window applications, and they operate in much the same way from one application to the next. The Copy command copies the currently selected data to the Windows clipboard without deleting or otherwise changing the original version of the data. The Paste command copies the current contents of the clipboard to a specified location in the current document. In 1-2-3, you can use these commands as an alternative for the Quick Copy command.

You choose the Copy command by pressing Ctrl-Ins, and Paste by pressing Shift-Ins (look back at Figure 3.4). In addition, 1-2-3 provides icons for both commands. The copy-to-clipboard icon appears as a pair of overlapping squares, each containing the letter A (see Figure 3.19). The paste-from-clipboard icon depicts a jar of paste (see Figure 3.20).

As you have learned, there is one significant difference between Quick Copy and the copy-and-paste operation: Copy and Paste use the clipboard as an intermediate storage area between the steps of the operation. Otherwise, these different approaches produce identical results.

Here are the steps for performing a copy-and-paste operation:

1. Select the range D8..D12.

2. Choose the Copy command by pressing Ctrl-Ins or clicking the copy-to-clipboard icon.

FIGURE 3.19:
The copy-to-clipboard icon

FIGURE 3.20:
The paste-from-clipboard icon

3. Select cell E8.

4. Choose the Paste command by pressing Shift-Ins or clicking the paste-from-clipboard icon.

Once again, examine the formula stored in cell E12 after the copy operation is complete. You'll see the same adjustment as before: The @SUM function applies to the data in column E.

The range-copy icon clearly represents the simplest of these three copy operations. Nonetheless, you might sometimes find yourself using copy and paste if you are familiar with this procedure from your work with other Windows applications. You'll learn much more about copying formulas later in this chapter.

As the final step in this first stage of worksheet development, enter a value of **2000** as the conference room expense in cell E8. At this point, your worksheet appears as shown in Figure 3.21. In the sections ahead, you'll change the worksheet in several ways to make room for additional data. But first, it is time to save the worksheet as a file on disk.

SAVING THE WORKSHEET

As in any other program, you should perform frequent save operations during your work in 1-2-3. If you experience a hardware or software problem, you can lose any data you might have entered since the last save. The correct

	A	B	C	D	E	F	G	H
1		Computing Conferences, Inc.						
2		Profit Projection for a One-Day Conference						
3								
4	Conference:	Computing for Video Stores						
5	Place:	St. Louis						
6								
7	Projected Expenses – Fixed							
8		Conference room		1500	2000			
9		Video production		1000	1000			
10		Promotion		3500	3500			
11		Travel		800	800			
12		Total Fixed Expenses		6800	7300			
13								
14								
15								
16								
17								
18								
19								
20								

FIGURE 3.21:
The first stage of development for the conference worksheet

length of time between save operations therefore depends upon how much data you are willing to risk losing. Fortunately, 1-2-3 saves your worksheet in response to the click of an icon, so it is easy to save worksheets at regular intervals.

The first time you save a given worksheet to disk, use the Save As command in the File menu. This command gives you the opportunity to supply a name for the file. The file name you enter can contain up to eight characters, consisting of letters, digits, underscore characters, and hyphens. (Other characters may be accepted by 1-2-3, but are not advisable.) When you save a worksheet, 1-2-3 supplies a default extension of .WK3 for the worksheet file, and also saves a *format file* with an extension of .FM3. The format file contains information about the formatting options that you have assigned to your worksheet. The Save As command also has a Password protect option that you can select if you want to restrict access to the file.

After the first save operation, you can simply choose the Save command to save new versions of your worksheet to disk under the same file name.

USING THE SAVE AS COMMAND

When you pull down the File menu and choose the Save As command, the dialog box shown in Figure 3.22 appears on the screen. You use the Drives

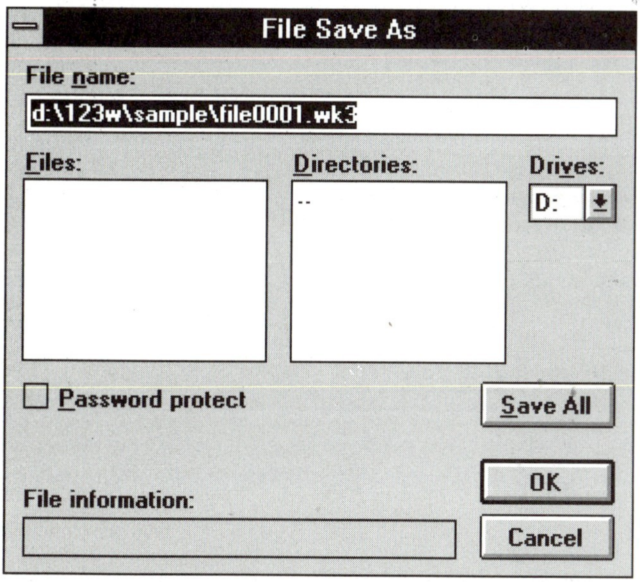

FIGURE 3.22:
The File Save As dialog box

and Directories boxes to navigate to the path location where you want to save your worksheet file. Enter a new file name in the File name text box and click the OK button to complete the save operation.

Follow these steps to save the conference worksheet for the first time:

1. Pull down the File menu and choose the Save As command. You can save your worksheet file in the default directory, or select another location if you wish.

2. Enter the file name CONF into the File name text box.

3. Click OK or press ↵ to save the file.

As a result of these steps, the worksheet is saved as CONF.WK3. In addition, 1-2-3 creates a format file named CONF.FM3.

The File Save As dialog box allows you to enter an existing file name as the name for the current save operation. If you do so, a second dialog box appears on the screen prompting you for specific instructions (see Figure 3.23). The box displays the message *File already exists* and offers you three choices in the form of command buttons:

◆ Click the Replace button to replace the existing file with the new file you are now saving.

◆ Click the Backup button to retain the existing file on disk as a backup for the current worksheet. The worksheet you are saving receives the extension .WK3, and the extension of the existing worksheet on disk is changed to .BAK. (The extension of the existing format file becomes .FMB.)

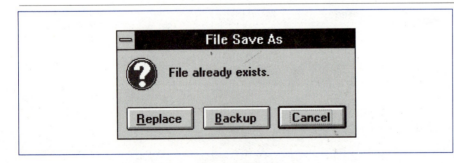

FIGURE 3.23:
Saving a file under an existing file name

- Click the Cancel button to cancel the save operation under the name you have selected.

Assigning a Password to the File

If you wish, you can save your file with password protection to restrict the number of people who are allowed to open the file. In response to a subsequent Open command, 1-2-3 prompts the user to enter the password, and denies access to the file if the user cannot supply the exact password. Keep in mind the possible liability of password protection: If you forget the password you have created, you will not be able to open your own file.

Here are the general steps for saving a file with a password:

1. Choose the Save As command from the File menu.

2. After supplying a file name, click the Password protect option. An *X* appears in the option box.

3. Click the OK button. A new dialog box, shown in Figure 3.24, appears on the screen, prompting you for the password that will be assigned to the file. You must enter the password twice, first in the Password box and then in the Verify box. Asterisks appear in both boxes as you enter the characters of the password. The password may be up to 15 characters long, and alphabetic case *is* significant.

4. Click the OK button in the second dialog box to confirm the password, or click Cancel if you change your mind.

You can change a file's password if you know the original password. First, open the file, supplying the original password when 1-2-3 asks you for it. Then choose File Save As, make sure that Password protect is checked, and click OK. Enter the new password twice in the resulting dialog box.

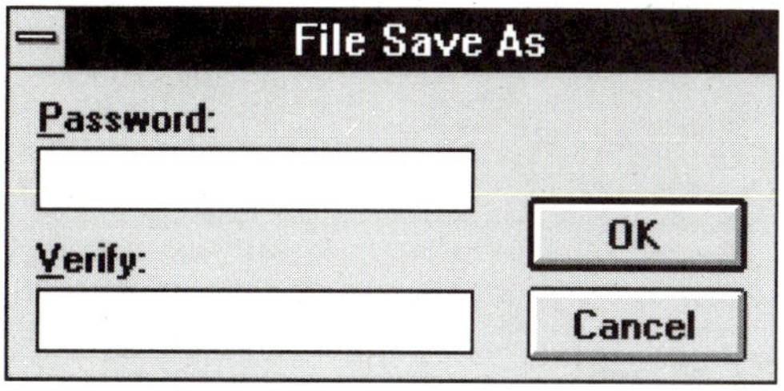

FIGURE 3.24:
Assigning a password to a file

USING THE SAVE COMMAND

After you save a file for the first time, you can *update* the file by choosing the Save command from the File menu. Updating means storing the current version of the worksheet under its existing file name. As you make significant changes in data, format, or organization during the development of a worksheet, you should update your file regularly.

Here are the steps for updating a file:

1. Activate the window containing the worksheet you want to save.

2. Pull down the File menu and choose the Save command, or simply click the save-file icon in the icon palette. (The save-file icon is depicted as a floppy disk with a bold arrow pointing toward its center, as indicated in Figure 3.25. Note that the open-file icon is a disk with an outward-pointing arrow.)

The next step in the development of the conference worksheet is to enter the projected revenues. As you anticipated at the beginning, you'll have to move the range of expense data down several rows below its current position to make room for the revenues data. In the next section of this chapter, you'll learn how to move a range of data and to insert blank columns and rows at specified locations in the worksheet; and you'll continue entering data into the worksheet.

CHANGING THE WORKSHEET

You've already learned about several important commands from the Edit menu, including the Cut, Copy, and Paste commands, the Clear and Clear Special commands, and the Quick Copy command. Several of these are represented by icons in the 1-2-3 icon palette. Now you'll use one additional Edit menu command, which also has an icon equivalent—the Move Cells command. You can use this command to move the data stored in a range of cells to a new location on the worksheet. Interestingly enough, you can achieve

FIGURE 3.25:
The save-file icon

the same effect in some situations by inserting blank rows or columns at selected locations in the worksheet; you perform these operations with the Insert command in the Worksheet menu. In the exercises ahead, you'll work with the Move Cells and Insert commands.

Moving Ranges of Data

When you choose the Move Cells command from the Edit menu, the dialog box shown in Figure 3.26 appears on the screen. The command is easy to use, especially if you preselect the range of cells that you want to move. Here are the general steps:

1. Preselect the source range of cells on your worksheet. (This is the data that you want to move to a new location on the worksheet.)

2. Pull down the Edit menu and choose the Move Cells command. The notation for the preselected range appears in the From text box.

3. In the To text box, enter the upper-left corner address of the range to which you want to move the data. (Alternatively, you can use a mouse or keyboard pointing technique to supply this address.)

4. Click the OK button or press ↵ to complete the operation. In response, 1-2-3 moves the data in the source range to the specified destination.

An even easier approach is to use the range-move icon. This icon depicts a hand pointing right in front of what is apparently a newly repositioned page of data (see Figure 3.27). As with other icons you have studied in this chapter, you must select the source range of data *before* clicking the range-move icon.

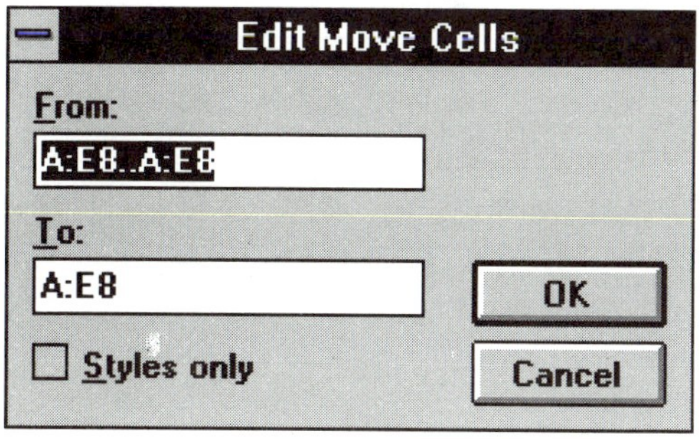

FIGURE 3.26:

The Edit Move Cells dialog box

After you click the icon, you move the mouse pointer to the upper-left corner of the destination range, and click the left mouse button. For example, in the following exercise, you'll move the range of expense data down the worksheet by several rows:

1. Use a mouse or keyboard technique to preselect the range A7..E12 on the conference worksheet.

2. Click the range-move icon.

3. Move the mouse pointer down to cell A15. The mouse pointer becomes a hand pointing right. Click the left mouse button. In response, 1-2-3 moves the range of expense data down by eight rows, as shown in Figure 3.28.

You might wonder what has happened to the two summation formulas that are included in the range of data that you just moved. To find out, select cells D20 and E20 in turn and examine their formulas, as displayed in the contents

FIGURE 3.27:
The range-move icon

FIGURE 3.28:
Moving a range of data on the worksheet

box at the top of the 1-2-3 window. You'll see that 1-2-3 has automatically adjusted the ranges in the cells in response to the move. For example, the formula in cell E20 is now *@SUM(E16..E19)*. In the case of cell D20, 1-2-3 has adjusted the range represented by the name EXPENSES. Accordingly, the values displayed in D20 and E20 still correctly represent the total fixed expenses for the low and high attendance estimates.

In the area that has been opened up by the move, you can now enter the new labels and values that you see in Figure 3.29:

1. Starting in column A, enter the following three labels in cells A6, A8, and A10, respectively:

   Date:

   Price:

   Projected Revenues

2. Enter the following revenue categories into cells B11, B12, and B13, respectively:

   Attendance

   Video Sales

   Total Revenues

FIGURE 3.29:

Entering new data into the conference worksheet

	A	B	C	D	E	F	G	H
1		Computing Conferences, Inc.						
2		Profit Projection for a One-Day Conference						
3								
4	Conference:	Computing for Video Stores						
5	Place:	St. Louis						
6	Date:			Expected attendance:				
7				Minimum	Maximum			
8	Price:	195		80	150			
9								
10	Projected Revenues							
11		Attendance						
12		Video Sales						
13		Total Revenues						
14								
15	Projected Expenses – Fixed							
16		Conference room		1500	2000			
17		Video production		1000	1000			
18		Promotion		3500	3500			
19		Travel		800	800			
20		Total Fixed Expenses		6800	7300			

Notice that Computing Conferences, Inc. earns revenue both from the price of attendance to a conference and from sales of a video that is produced during the conference.

3. Enter a value of **195** in cell B8. This is the per-person attendance price for this particular conference.

4. Enter the label **Expected attendance:** into cell D6, and notice that the label is displayed across two columns of the worksheet.

5. The labels in cells D7 and E7 should be right-aligned in their respective cells, to match the alignment of the numeric values that will appear immediately beneath them. To achieve right-alignment, you can use a simple technique at the time you enter a label into its cell: Start the label with a double quotation mark. Try this technique as you enter these labels into cells D7 and E7, respectively:

   "Minimum

   "Maximum

   As you'll learn in Chapter 4, there are several other ways to control label alignment in 1-2-3.

6. Finally, enter a value of **80** in cell D8 as the low estimate for the number of people who will attend the conference, and a value of **150** in cell E8 as the high estimate.

Now, if you compare Figure 3.29 with Figure 3.1, you'll notice that you need additional space on the worksheet for information that you have not entered yet. Specifically, you need a blank row for column headings, just above the Projected Revenues label; and you need a blank column for the per-person revenue and expense figures, just to the right of column C. One way to open up these ranges would be to use the Move Cells command again. But in this case the task can be accomplished more easily by inserting a blank row and a blank column at appropriate positions on the worksheet. You'll learn how to do this in the next section.

INSERTING ROWS AND COLUMNS

You used the Worksheet Insert command in Chapter 1 to experiment with the process of adding new worksheets to a worksheet window. Other options in this same command are for inserting columns and rows in an individual worksheet. This command produces the dialog box shown in Figure 3.30. To add a single new row or column to the active worksheet, you use this command in the following way:

1. Select a cell that is located in the row or column position where you want to make the insert.

2. Pull down the Worksheet menu and choose the Insert command.

3. Click either the Column or Row option.

4. Click the OK button or press ↵ to complete the insert operation.

To insert more than one row at a time, select a range of consecutive cells in a single column—one cell for each row that you want to insert. Conversely, to insert multiple columns, preselect a range of adjacent cells in a row—one cell for each column you want to insert. Choose the Insert command and click the Row or Column option after you have selected the range.

In the current version of the conference worksheet, you can select cell D9 as the insert position for both the new row and the new column. Follow these steps to make the insertions:

1. Select cell D9 on the worksheet.

2. Pull down the Worksheet menu and choose Insert. The default option selection is Row.

3. Click OK or press ↵ to insert a new row at the current position.

4. Pull down the Worksheet menu and select Insert again.

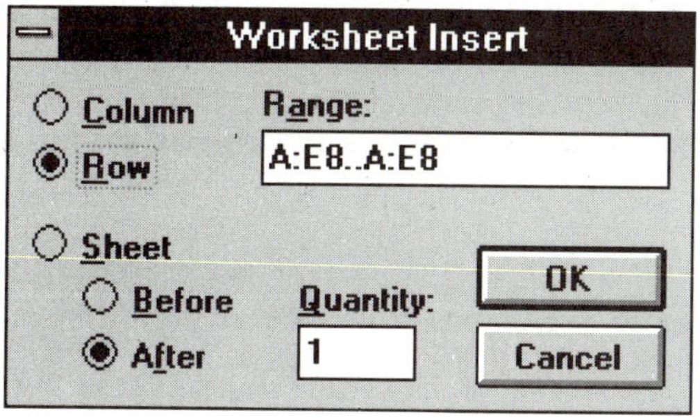

FIGURE 3.30:

The Worksheet Insert dialog box

5. Click the Column option.

6. Click the OK button or press ↵ to insert a new column.

After these insertions, you might once again want to examine the summation formulas, now located in cells E21 and F21. As before, 1-2-3 has adjusted the ranges in these formulas in response to the changes you have made in the worksheet.

Now you are ready to enter column headings in row 10 and the per-unit price of the conference video in column D, completing this second stage of data entry into the worksheet:

1. Enter the following three labels into cells D10, E10, and F10 respectively, again starting each label with a double-quote character to achieve right-alignment:

"Per Person

"Min. Total

"Max. Total

2. Enter a value of **35** into cell D13. This is the retail price of the conference video.

3. Select cell B8 and choose the Range Name Create command to assign the name **PRICE** to this single cell. Click OK or press ↵ to confirm.

4. Likewise, select cell D13 and choose Range Name Create to assign the name **VIDEO** to the cell. Click OK or press ↵.

5. Preselect the range E7..F7, containing the Minimum and Maximum labels. Now pull down the Range menu, select the Name command, and choose the Label Create command from the cascade menu. In the dialog box that appears on the screen, select the Down option and then click the OK command button (see Figure 3.31). The Range Name Label Create command is a way to assign existing column headings or row labels as range names to cells or ranges on the worksheet; using this command, you have just assigned the name MINIMUM to cell E8, and the name MAXIMUM to cell F8. You can now use these two names to represent the two attendance estimates in formulas you will write for the worksheet.

6. Pull down the File menu and choose the Save command, or simply click the save-file icon. This saves your latest version of the conference worksheet to disk, again under the file name CONF.WK3.

When you complete these steps, your worksheet appears as shown in Figure 3.32.

The next step in developing the worksheet is to enter formulas for calculating the minimum and maximum revenue projections, based on expected attendance. When you enter these formulas, you'll use the range names you've created for several individual cells on the worksheet.

WORKING WITH FORMULAS IN THE WORKSHEET

Formulas transform a worksheet from a static collection of data to a dynamic calculation tool. As you first saw in Chapter 1, formulas are made up of a variety of elements, including:

- ◆ Arithmetic operations, such as +, −, *, and /

- ◆ Literal numeric values like 2 or 5280

- ◆ Cell addresses—or alternatively, range names—that represent the values stored in those cells

- ◆ Worksheet functions like @SUM

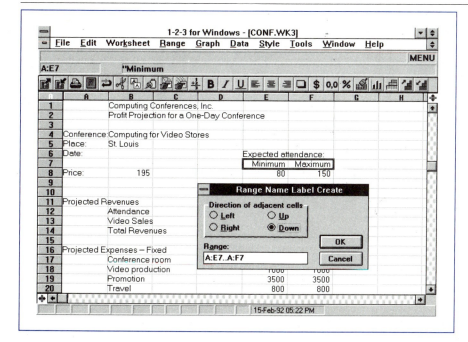

FIGURE 3.31:

Using the Range Name Label Create command

When you enter a formula into a cell, 1-2-3 immediately evaluates it and displays its numeric result in the cell. Furthermore, 1-2-3 *recalculates* a formula whenever you change the value of a cell that is part of the formula. This is what users sometimes refer to as the "what-if" feature of a spreadsheet.

As a quick demonstration of this feature, follow the steps of this exercise:

1. Pull down the File menu and choose the New command to open a new worksheet window.

2. Enter a value of **92** in cell A1.

3. Select cell B1 and enter the formula **2*A1**. For this exercise, you can simply enter the entire formula directly from the keyboard. (Later you'll use the pointing technique to enter a cell address into a formula.) The formula multiplies the value stored in A1 by 2. The result is displayed in B1 as *184*.

4. Now select A1 again and enter a new value into it: **32**. In response, 1-2-3 instantly recalculates the value in B1, displaying the result as *64*.

5. Try several more new values in A1, one at a time: **5**, **3212**, **19**, **543**, and **27**. Each time you enter a new value into A1, 1-2-3 instantly recalculates the value in B1: The values *10*, *6424*, *38*, *1086*, and *54* appear in turn in cell B1 (as shown in Figure 3.33).

6. When you are finished experimenting, pull down the worksheet window's control menu box and choose the Close command. Click No when 1-2-3 asks if you want to save the worksheet.

FIGURE 3.32:

Inserting a row and a column for additional data entries

	A	B	C	D	E	F	G	H
1		Computing Conferences, Inc.						
2		Profit Projection for a One-Day Conference						
3								
4	Conference:	Computing for Video Stores						
5	Place:	St. Louis						
6	Date:				Expected attendance:			
7					Minimum	Maximum		
8	Price:	195			80	150		
9								
10				Per Person	Min. Total	Max. Total		
11	Projected Revenues							
12		Attendance						
13		Video Sales		35				
14		Total Revenues						
15								
16	Projected Expenses – Fixed							
17		Conference room			1500	2000		
18		Video production			1000	1000		
19		Promotion			3500	3500		
20		Travel			800	800		

The idea is the same for complex worksheets designed to perform business calculations: Given a formula containing a cell reference, 1-2-3 recalculates the formula whenever you change the value in the cell.

Return now to the conference worksheet for a more interesting illustration of this feature. In an upcoming exercise, you'll enter formulas into cells E12 and F12 to calculate the projected attendance revenue from the conference.

Entering Formulas

The attendance revenue is calculated by multiplying the price per person by the number of people attending the conference. The price per person is stored in cell B8 and the first of the two attendance estimates is stored in cell E8. Furthermore, you know that multiplication is represented by the asterisk character (*) in 1-2-3. Given all this information, you might expect to enter the following formula into cell E12:

B8*E8

But there is a problem here. If you type B, the first character of this formula, into the cell, 1-2-3 switches into the LABEL mode, whereas the correct mode for entering a formula is VALUE. You clearly need to start the formula with some other character that triggers the VALUE mode.

The general-purpose character for starting a formula in 1-2-3 is the plus sign (+). This character is not needed in all formulas—for example, when a formula begins with a number or with the @ symbol of a function. But when the first element of a formula is a cell address, the plus sign is the way to begin in the VALUE mode. Here, then, is the correct format for the projected revenue formula:

+B8*E8

You can enter a formula like this one directly from the keyboard if you want to. But there is an easier way. As you are entering the formula, you can use

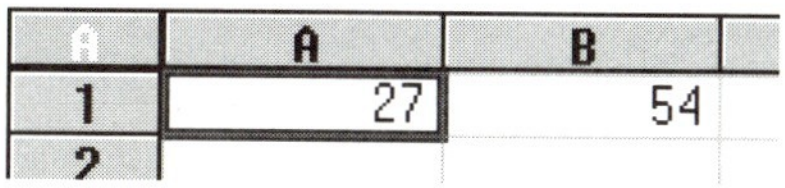

FIGURE 3.33:

An experiment with formula recalculation

arrow keys at the keyboard to *point* to cells that you want to include in the formula. You'll see how this works as you enter the first revenue formula into cell E12:

1. Select cell E12 in the conference worksheet.

2. Type + (the plus sign) to begin the formula. The + appears in the contents box, and 1-2-3 switches into the VALUE mode.

3. Point to the first cell address in the formula, B8. At the keyboard, press ↑ four times and ← three times to select cell B8. The mode switches to POINT while you are pointing to the cell. The contents box now displays the formula as *+A:B8*.

4. Type * (the asterisk character) for multiplication. The cell pointer returns to E12.

5. Point to the second cell address in the formula, E8. Press ↑ four times. When the cell is selected, the formula is displayed as *+A:B8*A:E8* in the contents box.

6. Now press ↵ to complete the formula entry. When you do so, 1-2-3 immediately calculates the result of the formula and displays it in cell E12 as *15600*.

Figure 3.34 shows the 1-2-3 window at this point in your work. Because this formula involves only worksheet A, the contents box now displays the formula in its simpler form:

+B8*E8

You now need to enter a similar formula into cell F12 to calculate the revenue projection from the higher of the two attendance estimates. This time, try expressing the formula with range names. Recall that cell B8 is named PRICE and cell F8 is named MAXIMUM. You can therefore write the formula as:

+PRICE*MAXIMUM

Notice that the formula must still begin with a plus sign to start the entry correctly in the VALUE mode. You can type this formula directly into cell F12 from the keyboard, or you can use the F3 key to display a list of defined names from the worksheet. Here are the steps of the second approach:

1. Select cell F12.

2. Type + from the keyboard to start the formula.

3. Press the F3 function key. The Range Names dialog box appears on the screen, with a list of all the range names you have defined for the worksheet.

4. Double-click the name PRICE in the Range Names list. The name appears in the contents box as the first reference in your formula: +PRICE.

5. Type * for multiplication.

6. Once again, press the F3 function key to view the Range Names list.

7. Double-click the name MAXIMUM in the list. This name appears as the second reference in the contents box: +PRICE*MAXIMUM.

8. Press ↵ to confirm the formula entry.

When you complete these steps, 1-2-3 enters the result of your formula into cell F12. The revenue projection is displayed as *29250*.

Now you have seen two distinct ways of expressing and entering formulas into the conference worksheet. You can identify cells by their addresses or by the range names you have assigned to the cells. Your choice between these two options does not affect the result of the formula.

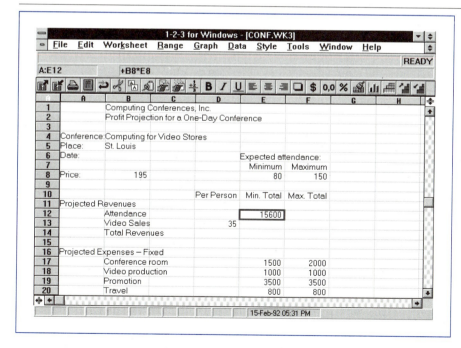

FIGURE 3.34:

Entering the first formula into the worksheet

There are two more formulas to enter into the revenue section of the worksheet. In cells E13 and E14, you must write formulas to calculate projected revenues from sales of the conference video. The planners at Computing Conferences, Inc. know from experience that they can count on approximately half of the participants of a given conference to order and pay for the video tape. (Copies of the video are mailed out a few weeks after the conference.) Given this expectation, the revenue is equal to the retail video price times one-half the number of participants.

You'll recall that you assigned the range name VIDEO to cell D13, where the unit retail price of the video is stored. Here is the formula you can enter into cell E13:

+VIDEO*MINIMUM/2

Likewise, here is the formula for cell F13:

+VIDEO*MAXIMUM/2

Enter these two formulas into their respective cells now. The result is 1400 for the minimum revenue projection (cell E13) and 2625 for the maximum (cell F13).

Finally, you need to enter summation formulas into row 14 to find the two total revenue projections. You may be surprised to learn that you can enter both formulas in a single action. Here are the steps:

1. Preselect the range E12..F14.
2. Click the summation icon in the icon palette.

When you click the icon, 1-2-3 enters the two summation formulas into cells E14 and F14. The results of the formulas are displayed as 17000 and 31875, respectively. Figure 3.35 shows what the worksheet looks like at this stage of your work. Click the save-file icon now to save your work to disk.

You still have two sections of information to enter into the conference worksheet—the variable expenses and the bottom-line profit. As you work on these sections, you'll explore another important worksheet topic—the techniques for copying formulas from one range to another.

Copying Formulas

In many worksheets, you'll find that a formula in one cell is identical in structure to formulas that you need to enter into other cells. Rather than enter these similar formulas one by one, you would like to be able to copy the original formula to other locations on the worksheet. Lotus 1-2-3 for Windows handles this copy operation in a logical manner, taking care to adjust references to cell and range addresses as necessary.

You've already seen an example. Earlier in this chapter, you copied the summation formula for fixed expenses from one column to an adjacent column. At the time of the copy operation, the expense figures were located in column D, and the summation formula in cell D12 was

@SUM(D8..D11)

When you copied this formula to cell E12, 1-2-3 automatically adjusted the range reference, as follows:

@SUM(E8..E11)

The logic that 1-2-3 follows to make this adjustment is simple: In a formula copied from column D to column E, a reference to a range in D becomes a reference to the adjacent range in E. The range address in this copy operation is an example of a *relative reference.* When you copy a formula containing a relative reference, 1-2-3 adjusts the cell or range address *relative to the location of the copy.*

A similar adjustment occurs when you copy a formula from one row to another. For example, imagine that you have entered the formula **+A3+B3** into cell C3. This formula adds the contents of the two cells located to the left of

	A	B	C	D	E	F	G	H
1		Computing Conferences, Inc.						
2		Profit Projection for a One-Day Conference						
3								
4	Conference:	Computing for Video Stores						
5	Place:		St. Louis					
6	Date:				Expected attendance:			
7					Minimum	Maximum		
8	Price:		195		80	150		
9								
10				Per Person	Min. Total	Max. Total		
11	Projected Revenues							
12		Attendance			15600	29250		
13		Video Sales		35	1400	2625		
14		Total Revenues			17000	31875		
15								
16	Projected Expenses – Fixed							
17		Conference room			1500	2000		
18		Video production			1000	1000		
19		Promotion			3500	3500		
20		Travel			800	800		

FIGURE 3.35:

Completing the revenue formulas

C3 in row 3. If you copy this formula down to cell C4, 1-2-3 adjusts the formula to read **+A4+B4**. The logic is the same: A formula copied to row 4 should contain references to the data stored in row 4. Accordingly, 1-2-3 adjusts the address references relative to the row to which the formula is copied.

Unless you specify otherwise, 1-2-3 treats cell and range addresses as relative references whenever you copy a formula from one place to another. In short, relative references are the default in copy operations.

But in some contexts you will want to override this default. A formula may contain a reference to a fixed cell address—that is, an address that you want to remain unchanged when you copy the formula to other locations. In this case, you must express the address as an *absolute reference*. You'll learn how to do this in upcoming exercises.

Understanding Reference Types

The distinction between relative and absolute references is perhaps the single most important concept for you to master now as you continue your work with the 1-2-3 spreadsheet. The concept itself is not difficult or subtle, but it does add a dimension to the process of writing a formula. In effect, you must think carefully about *two* properties of each formula you create:

- ◆ The arithmetic structure of the formula—that is, the specific operations and operands that ultimately produce the correct result in the original formula

- ◆ The types of address references in the formula—that is, the specifications that determine what the formula will look like when you copy it to other locations in the worksheet.

Of course, the second property is relevant only in formulas that you intend to copy. If you write a formula that applies to only one location on a worksheet— a formula that will not be copied elsewhere—then you do not have to worry about relative and absolute references. But as you develop your own worksheets, you may be surprised at how often you find yourself copying formulas.

Absolute and Relative References

Lotus 1-2-3 has a simple notation that you use to distinguish between relative and absolute references, and a simple technique for changing an address from one reference type to another. The default address format that you have been using in all your work up to now is the relative reference format. For example, the following address is a relative reference:

B8

To change this address to an absolute reference, you insert a dollar sign ($) before each element of the address. Here is the absolute reference to this same address:

$B$8

You can also create an absolute reference from a range name. Place a $ character just before the name:

$PRICE

While you are entering a formula, you can create absolute references by typing $ characters at the appropriate locations. But 1-2-3 offers an easier technique for transforming a reference from relative to absolute. In the POINT, EDIT, or VALUE mode you can press the F4 function key to change a reference that currently appears in the contents box. (You'll recall that F4 has an additional use: When you are in the READY mode, pressing F4 switches you into the POINT mode so you can preselect a range.)

In the following exercise, you'll explore the significance of absolute references, and you'll practice the mechanical details of changing an address from relative to absolute. For the purposes of this exercise, you're going to backtrack a little in the conference worksheet, and redo some work that you completed earlier. Specifically, you'll reenter the formula for projected attendance revenues in cell E12; then you'll copy this formula to cell F12. You'll recall that the formulas in these cells are designed to multiply the attendance price per person by the anticipated number of people attending the conference. You'll make no change in the *structure* of these formulas, and the end result will remain the same. What you will change is the reference type that allows you to copy the formula successfully from E12 to F12.

To prepare for this exercise, begin by deleting the current contents of these two cells. Select the range E12..F12 and press the Delete key. Now you have an empty range in which to perform the following steps:

1. Select cell E12 and type a + to begin the formula entry. This switches 1-2-3 into the VALUE mode.

2. Use the keyboard to point to cell B8, which contains the price of attendance. (Press ↑ four times and ← three times.) The mode changes to POINT and the contents box displays the reference +A:B8.

3. Press the F4 function key one time. This transforms the address to an absolute reference, as you can see in the contents box: +$A:$B$8. Notice that 1-2-3 places a $ character in front of all three elements of the address: the worksheet name, the column letter, and the row number.

4. Now type the * sign, representing multiplication. The cell pointer returns to E12 and the mode switches back to VALUE.

5. Use the keyboard to point to cell E8, the low estimate of the number of people expected to attend the conference. (Press ↑ four times.) The contents box now displays +$A:$B$8*A:E8. Do not change the reference type of this second address. It must remain a relative reference for the purposes of copying the formula.

6. Press ↵. The value *15600* appears in cell E12. This is the same as the value produced by the previous version of the formula. But now the formula in the cell reads *+$B$8*E8*. The first address in the formula is in the form of an absolute reference, and the second is a relative reference.

7. Now copy the formula to cell F12: With the cell pointer positioned at E12, click the range-copy icon. Then move the mouse pointer to cell F12 and click the left mouse button. (Alternatively, pull down the Edit menu and choose the Quick Copy command. In the resulting dialog box, a reference to E12 already appears in the From box. Enter a reference to F12 in the To box and click OK to complete the copy operation.) The same value as before appears in cell F12—a projected attendance revenue of 29250.

To see exactly what has happened in this exercise, you should now examine the new formulas in cells E12 and F12. At E12, you see the formula you have entered, with an absolute reference to B8 (the address of the attendance price) and a relative reference to E8 (the address of the minimum expected attendance level):

+$B$8*E8

Then at F12, you find the copied formula:

+$B$8*F8

In copying the formula, 1-2-3 has made no change in the absolute reference, but has adjusted the relative reference appropriately. This is exactly what you wanted to happen: Whereas the original formula in cell E12 calculates the *minimum* expected attendance revenue, the formula copied to cell F12 gives the *maximum* revenue.

In summary, you write absolute and relative references to instruct 1-2-3 exactly how to copy a formula:

◆ An absolute reference is copied without change.

◆ A relative reference is adjusted according to the row or column to which it is copied.

But this is not yet the complete picture. In some worksheets, you might plan to copy a particular formula in *two* directions—both down a column and across a row. To anticipate this double copy operation, you'll find yourself working with a third type of address format—the *mixed reference*. You'll learn about mixed references as you complete the final sections of the conference worksheet.

To prepare for the remaining exercises of this chapter, perform the following data entry tasks:

1. Enter the subtitle **Projected Expenses -- Variable by Attendance** in cell A23.

2. In cells B24 to B27, enter the variable expense categories. These represent the materials and meals given to each participant in the conference:

   Conference materials
   Coffee and pastries
   Box lunch
   Total Variable Expenses

3. Enter the corresponding per-person costs for these items: in cell D24, type **8.25**; in D25, type **3.25**; and in D26, type **4.75**.

4. Finally, enter the profit subtitle in cell A29: **Projected Profit**.

When you complete these entries, your worksheet will appear as shown in Figure 3.36.

Mixed References

A mixed reference instructs 1-2-3 to adjust one part of an address and leave another part unchanged when the address is copied from one cell to another.

In the notation for a mixed reference, a $ character appears to the left of one address element but not the other. For example, in the following reference the column is absolute and the row is relative:

$D24

When you copy a formula containing this address, 1-2-3 retains a fixed reference to column D but adjusts the row reference to match the row of the copy. Conversely, the following example contains a relative column reference and an absolute row reference:

E$8

In copies of this address, 1-2-3 adjusts the column reference to match the column location of the copy, but retains a fixed reference to row 8.

You can use the F4 function key to create mixed references just as you did to create absolute references. In the POINT, VALUE, and EDIT modes, you press F4 *multiple times* to cycle through the various reference types. As you have seen, the first key press gives an absolute reference. The second and third times you press F4, an address switches between forms of the mixed reference. You'll see how this works shortly.

The variable expense section of the conference worksheet (see Figure 3.36) presents a perfect opportunity to experiment with mixed references. In the range E24..F26, you need to enter six instances of essentially the same formula. The

	A	B	C	D	E	F	G	H
11	Projected Revenues							
12		Attendance			15600	29250		
13		Video Sales		35	1400	2625		
14		Total Revenues			17000	31875		
15								
16	Projected Expenses – Fixed							
17		Conference room			1500	2000		
18		Video production			1000	1000		
19		Promotion			3500	3500		
20		Travel			800	800		
21		Total Fixed Expenses			6800	7300		
22								
23	Projected Expenses – Variable by Attendance							
24		Conference materials		8.25				
25		Coffee and pastries		3.25				
26		Box lunch		4.75				
27		Total Variable Expenses						
28								
29	Projected Profit							
30								

FIGURE 3.36:
Preparing the final sections of the worksheet

formula should calculate the total expense amounts for each variable expense category—that is, the per-person expense amount times the number of participants. Using mixed references, you can enter this formula once into cell E24. Then you can copy the formula in two directions: down column E and across rows 24, 25, and 26. Here are the steps:

1. Select cell E24 and type a + character to start the formula.

2. Point to cell D24 (the first of the per-person expense figures) by pressing ← one time.

3. Press the F4 function key three times. Each time you do so, the address displayed in the contents box changes its format: First it becomes an absolute reference, then a mixed reference with a fixed row and variable column, and finally a mixed reference with a fixed column and variable row:

   $A:$D$24

   $A:D$24

   $A:$D24

   This final format is the reference you want. When you later copy the formula to other rows, column D will remain fixed but the row number will change.

4. Type the * character.

5. Point to cell E8 (the low attendance estimate) by pressing the PgUp key once, then ↓ four times.

6. Press the F4 function key two times. The address displayed in the contents box first becomes an absolute reference, then a mixed reference:

   $A:$E$8

   $A:E$8

   This second format is correct. When you copy the formula, the column letter will change, but row 8 will remain fixed.

7. Press ↵ to confirm the formula entry. The value *660* appears in cell E24. The cell's formula appears in the contents box as +*$A:$D24*$A:E$8*.

There is nothing arbitrary about the formula you have just created. It contains the only reference formats that allow you to copy the formula successfully in two directions. Here are the steps for copying the formula:

1. With the cell pointer positioned at cell E24, click the range-copy icon. Then, drag the mouse pointer over the destination column range, E25..E26. (Alternatively, use the Quick Copy command from the Edit menu.) When you are finished, the values *260* and *380* appear in cells E25 and E26. These are projected variable expenses for the minimum attendence.

2. Preselect the range E24..E26 and click the range-copy icon. Then, position the mouse pointer over cell F24 and click the left mouse button. (Or use the Quick Copy command.) The values *1237.5*, *487.5*, and *712.5* appear in cells F24, F25, and F26. These are the projected variable expenses for the maximum attendance.

3. As a final step, produce the total variable expense projections: Preselect the range E24..F27 and click the summation icon. The result of your work appears in Figure 3.37.

The best way to see the effect of mixed references on the copy operations you have just performed is to examine the six formulas in the range E24..F26:

+$A:$D24*$A:E$8   +$A:$D24*$A:F$8
+$A:$D25*$A:E$8   +$A:$D25*$A:F$8
+$A:$D26*$A:E$8   +$A:$D26*$A:F$8

	A	B	C	D	E	F	G	H
11	Projected Revenues							
12		Attendance			15600	29250		
13		Video Sales		35	1400	2625		
14		Total Revenues			17000	31875		
15								
16	Projected Expenses – Fixed							
17		Conference room			1500	2000		
18		Video production			1000	1000		
19		Promotion			3500	3500		
20		Travel			800	800		
21		Total Fixed Expenses			6800	7300		
22								
23	Projected Expenses – Variable by Attendance							
24		Conference materials		8.25	660	1237.5		
25		Coffee and pastries		3.25	260	487.5		
26		Box lunch		4.75	380	712.5		
27		Total Variable Expenses			1300	2437.5		
28								
29	Projected Profit							
30								

FIGURE 3.37:
Copying a formula in two directions

For each row, 1-2-3 has adjusted the row portion of the first reference ($D24, $D25, $D26). Conversely, for each of the two columns, the column portion of the second address reference has been adjusted (E$8, F$8).

Now you are ready to enter the formula for the projected profit. As you do so, you'll learn how to control the order in which operations are performed.

Controlling the Order of Operations

By default, 1-2-3 follows standard mathematical rules for the *order of precedence*—that is, for deciding the order of operations in a formula that contains more than one operation. For example, here are the two rules governing the most common arithmetic operations:

- Multiplication and division are performed before addition and subtraction.
- Given two operations of equal precedence, 1-2-3 performs the operations from left to right.

You can override the precedence rules by inserting pairs of parentheses in a formula. Operations enclosed in parentheses are performed before others. Furthermore, one pair of parentheses can be *nested* inside another pair; in this case, 1-2-3 begins with the operation inside the innermost parentheses.

The formula for calculating the bottom-line profit in the convention worksheet requires parentheses. The profit is calculated as revenues minus expenses. But in this worksheet there are two groups of expenses, fixed and variable. To make sure that the two expense categories are added together before the subtraction is performed, you must enclose the expense references in parentheses. For example, here is the formula that you'll enter into cell E29 for the first profit projection:

+E14–(E21+E27)

Cells E21 and E27 contain the two expense subtotals and cell E14 contains the total revenues. If you were to omit the parentheses from this formula, 1-2-3 would perform the operations from left to right, resulting in an incorrect calculation.

Enter this formula into cell E29, and then copy the formula over to F29:

1. Select cell E29 and type the **+** character to begin the formula.

2. Point to the total revenues figure in cell E14. (Press PgUp and then press ↓ five times.)

3. Type –, the minus sign, and then (, the open parenthesis character. At this point, the formula is displayed as +A:E14–(in the contents box.

4. Point to the total fixed expense figure in cell E21. (Press ↑ eight times.)

5. Type + (the plus sign).

6. Point to the total variable expense figure in cell E27. (Press ↑ twice.)

7. Type), the close parenthesis character. In the contents box, the formula now appears as +A:E14-(A:E21+A:E27). Notice that all the address references are relative. There is no need for absolute or mixed references for the upcoming copy operation.

8. Press ↵ to confirm the formula entry.

9. Use the range copy icon or the Edit Quick Copy command to copy the formula from cell E29 to cell F29.

10. Click the save-file icon or choose the File Save command to save this version of the worksheet to disk.

The final version of the worksheet for this chapter appears in Figure 3.38.

Examining "What-If" Scenarios

The conference worksheet presents many opportunities for "what-if" experiments—changing the original data to view the effect on the calculated values.

	A	B	C	D	E	F	G	H
10				Per Person	Min. Total	Max. Total		
11	Projected Revenues							
12		Attendance			15600	29250		
13		Video Sales		35	1400	2625		
14		Total Revenues			17000	31875		
15								
16	Projected Expenses – Fixed							
17		Conference room			1500	2000		
18		Video production			1000	1000		
19		Promotion			3500	3500		
20		Travel			800	800		
21		Total Fixed Expenses			6800	7300		
22								
23	Projected Expenses – Variable by Attendance							
24		Conference materials		8.25	660	1237.5		
25		Coffee and pastries		3.25	260	487.5		
26		Box lunch		4.75	380	712.5		
27		Total Variable Expenses			1300	2437.5		
28								
29	Projected Profit				8900	22137.5		

FIGURE 3.38:
Calculating the projected profit

For example, imagine that Computing Conferences, Inc. is considering the possibility of increasing the price of attendance from $195 to $225. In so doing, they anticipate a possible 15 percent decrease in attendance. They would like to see what happens to the projected profit under these combined circumstances.

To view the results of this scenario, revise three values in the worksheet:

1. Enter a value of **225** in cell B8.
2. Enter a value of **68** in cell E8.
3. Enter a value of **128** in cell F8.

Each time you enter a new value, 1-2-3 instantly recalculates all the formulas that contain references to the revised cell. The split worksheet in Figure 3.39 shows the three revised values, and the new profit projections. Comparing this worksheet to Figure 3.38, you can see that the range of profits in this scenario is down from the original projection. The company decides against raising the price at this time.

You might want to try other changes in the worksheet to see what happens to profits. For example, make the changes corresponding to each of these situations:

◆ The company is notified of a 10-percent price increase for the use of the conference room.

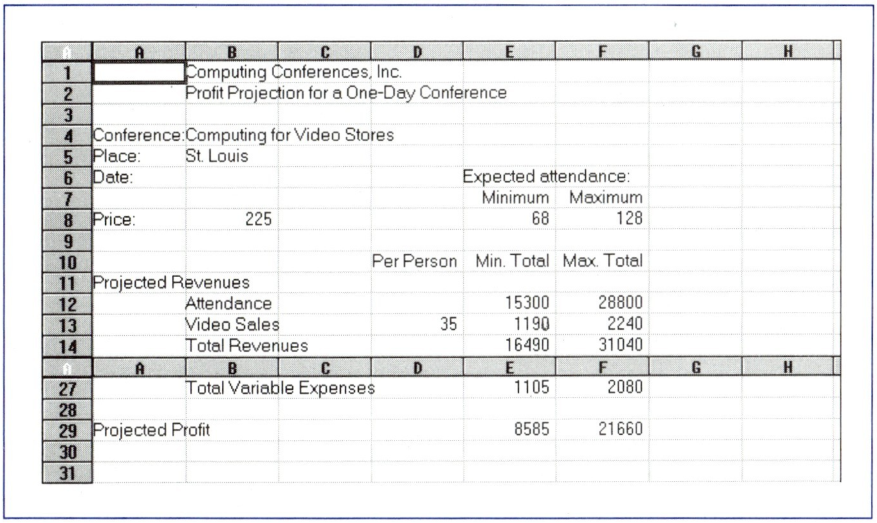

FIGURE 3.39:
Experimenting with changes in the initial data

	A	B	C	D	E	F	G	H
1		Computing Conferences, Inc.						
2		Profit Projection for a One-Day Conference						
3								
4	Conference:	Computing for Video Stores						
5	Place:	St. Louis						
6	Date:				Expected attendance:			
7					Minimum	Maximum		
8	Price:	225			68	128		
9								
10				Per Person	Min. Total	Max. Total		
11	Projected Revenues							
12		Attendance			15300	28800		
13		Video Sales		35	1190	2240		
14		Total Revenues			16490	31040		
	A	B	C	D	E	F	G	H
27		Total Variable Expenses			1105	2080		
28								
29	Projected Profit				8585	21660		
30								
31								

◆ Due to last-minute revisions in the curriculum, some conference materials have to be redone, increasing the cost of materials by five dollars per person.

◆ The company decides to produce a radio commercial promoting the conference. The commercial adds $2,500 to promotion costs, but the company anticipates a possible 25-percent increase in attendance.

These and other experiments demonstrate the flexibility of the worksheet as a tool for exploring the results of "what-if" problems.

When you finish these exercises, exit from 1-2-3 *without* saving the latest revisions to disk. You'll continue working with the conference worksheet in Chapter 4, using the original data that you've already saved in the CONF.WK3 file. Specifically, you'll begin exploring the variety of formatting and style options available in 1-2-3, and you'll see the results of these options on the printed worksheet.

SUMMARY

In the first steps of creating a new worksheet, you are often preoccupied with data entry and organization. To help you with these tasks, 1-2-3 has a variety of tools you can use to move and copy data from one location on the worksheet to another, or to delete entries from a cell or a range. You perform these procedures by choosing menu commands or, more conveniently, by clicking icons.

When a command operates over a range of data, you normally have the choice of *pre*selecting the range before you choose the command, or of pointing to the range after the command's dialog box has appeared on the screen. Preselection often seems like the more natural approach, and is in fact required for successful use of some icons, such as the range-move icon and the range-copy icon.

Once you've begun investing your time in a worksheet, you'll want to save your work to disk without much delay. The Save As command in the File menu gives you the opportunity to name your file and to add password protection if you wish. For subsequent updates of your worksheet file you can simply click the save-file icon.

As you complete sections of numeric data in your worksheet, you can begin adding formulas to produce calculated values. For producing totals at the bottom of a column or at the end of a row, 1-2-3 provides a very convenient summation icon. This tool automatically enters @SUM formulas onto your worksheet to calculate the totals of specified ranges of numbers.

In formulas that you write yourself, the use of range names can often make your work simpler and clearer. When you write a formula that you intend to copy to other locations on your worksheet, you must choose carefully among relative, absolute, and mixed address references. (While you are entering a formula, pressing the F4 function key cycles you through these reference types.) References determine how 1-2-3 ultimately copies your formula to other cells.

A well organized worksheet becomes an ideal tool for investigating "what-if" questions. By making changes in key data items you can find out what happens to totals and other calculated values under new assumptions.

FAST TRACK

**To move the cell pointer quickly to a named cell
or range,** 164
    press the F5 function key and select a range name
    from the list in the Range Go To dialog box.

**To change the width of a column on the
worksheet,** 166
    select a cell in the column and choose the Worksheet
    Column Width command, or use the mouse to drag the
    column's right border.

**To left-align, center, or right-align the labels in a
range of cells,** 173
    preselect the range and click one of the three align-
    ment icons in the icon palette.

To center a label over a horizontal range of cells, ... 175
    preselect the horizontal range, where the first cell in
    the range contains the label that you want to center;
    then choose Style Alignment and click the Center and
    Align over columns options.

**To remove the display of grid lines from the
worksheet window,** 181
    choose the Window Display Options command and
    uncheck the Grid lines check box.

**To apply a format to a selected range on the
worksheet,** 185
    preselect the range, then choose the Range Format com-
    mand and select an entry in the Format list.

To display a date value in a cell, ...**192**
enter the date in a format that begins with a digit (such as 10/15/92 or 15-Oct-92); 1-2-3 translates your entry into a date number. Next, choose the Range Format command and select one of the five available date formats.

To display a time value in a cell, ...**199**
enter the time in a format that begins with a digit (such as 7:00 PM or 19:00); 1-2-3 translates your entry into a decimal time value. Next, choose the Range Format command and select one of the four available time formats.

To establish a protection scheme for a worksheet, ...**205**
choose the Worksheet Global Settings command and check the Protection option. Then use the Range Unprotect command to release selected ranges from the global protection setting.

To see a preview of the printed worksheet, ...**220**
click the preview icon after you select a print range.

To define a print range, ...**222**
choose the File Print command and enter one or more ranges in the Range(s) box. Back on the worksheet, 1-2-3 encloses your selected print range or ranges in a light dashed border. To print the worksheet, click the print icon.

CHAPTER 4

Worksheet Formatting and Printing

After you create a working table of data and formulas, your next task is to refine the appearance of your worksheet. On all important worksheets, you'll want to make the presentation of information as clear and attractive as possible, both for your own benefit as you work with data on the screen and for the benefit of other people who later see your work as a printed document. Lotus 1-2-3 for Windows gives you a wealth of choices for controlling the appearance of values and labels on the worksheet.

In this chapter, you'll concentrate primarily on commands that affect the way your worksheet looks, and to some extent the way it functions. Specifically, you'll learn to accomplish the following tasks:

◆ Change column widths, both for the entire worksheet and for individual columns.

◆ Control the alignment of labels on the worksheet.

- Hide columns and ranges of data.
- Select numeric formats for the whole worksheet and for ranges on the worksheet.
- Enter date and time values in their appropriate formats, then perform arithmetic operations with these values.
- Protect the worksheet from accidental revisions.
- Select styles, fonts, shadings, colors, and borders.
- Print the worksheet.

To practice these procedures, you'll return to the conference worksheet that you began developing in Chapter 3. In its current version, the worksheet is already a functioning tool for projecting the revenues, expenses, and profit of a future business event. Now, you'll transform it into a document that presents this financial data clearly and with the correct emphasis on specific categories of information. The first step is to reopen the CONF.WK3 file from disk.

RESUMING WORK ON AN EXISTING WORKSHEET

In Chapter 2, you practiced opening an existing worksheet file from disk by choosing the Open command from the File menu. You can perform the operation more simply by clicking the open-file icon located at the beginning of the icon palette (see Figure 4.1). Either way you choose the command, the File Open dialog box appears on the screen. Here are the steps for reopening the CONF.WK3 worksheet that you saved at the end of Chapter 3:

1. Click the open-file icon, or choose the Open command.
2. If necessary, navigate to the directory where you saved the file. When you find the correct directory, CONF.WK3 appears in the Files list box (as in Figure 4.2).

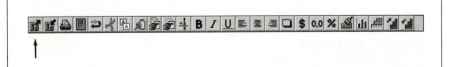

FIGURE 4.1:
The open-file icon

3. Double-click the file name to open the file.

The conference worksheet reappears on the screen, with all the work that you completed in the last chapter. Press the worksheet window's maximize button to expand your work over the available screen area.

SETTING A DEFAULT DIRECTORY

The *default directory* in 1-2-3 is the directory that is first active in the dialog box when you select either the Open command or the Save As command from the File menu. Initially, this default is determined by the 1-2-3 installation program (see Appendix A), but you can change the default by choosing the User Setup command from the Tools menu. This can be a convenient change to make, especially if you intend to save most of your worksheets in a single directory.

Here are the steps for establishing the default directory:

1. Pull down the Tools menu and choose the User Setup command.

2. In the Worksheet directory text box (shown in Figure 4.3), enter the full name of the directory path that you want to specify as the default.

3. If you want to change this default directory for both the current session and future sessions with 1-2-3, click the Update command button or

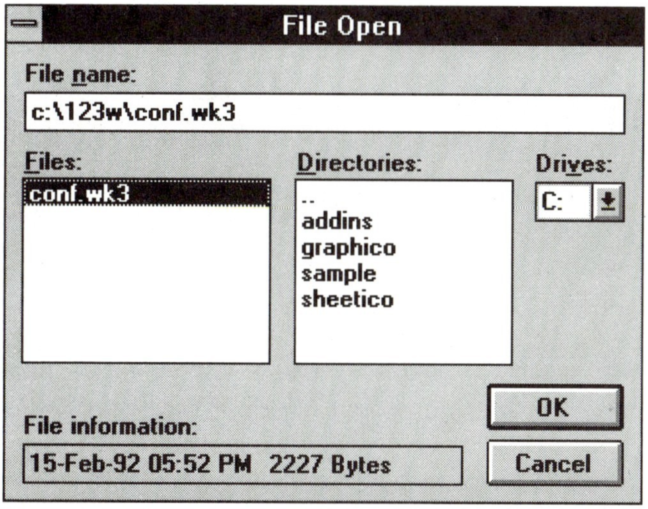

FIGURE 4.2:
The File Open dialog box

press Alt-U. In response, 1-2-3 saves your new default specification in a file named 123W.INI in the Windows directory. On the other hand, if you want this new default directory to apply only to the current session with 1-2-3, do not click Update; in this case, the 123W.INI file remains unchanged.

4. Click the OK button or press ↵ to complete the operation.

The next time you choose the Open or Save As command, the new default directory appears as the initial selection.

The User Setup command offers many other options that allow you to control general aspects of 1-2-3's behavior. You'll examine additional options from this command later in this chapter.

In upcoming exercises, you'll be moving back and forth to specific ranges and cells on the conference worksheet to change formats and styles. A tool that can speed you on your way to a specified location on the worksheet is the Go To command from the Range menu.

USING THE GO TO COMMAND

In response to the Go To command, the cell pointer jumps to a cell or range that you specify. To perform the command, pull down the Range menu and choose Go To, or simply press the F5 function key. Either way, the Range Go To dialog box appears on the screen. In this box you can enter the address of

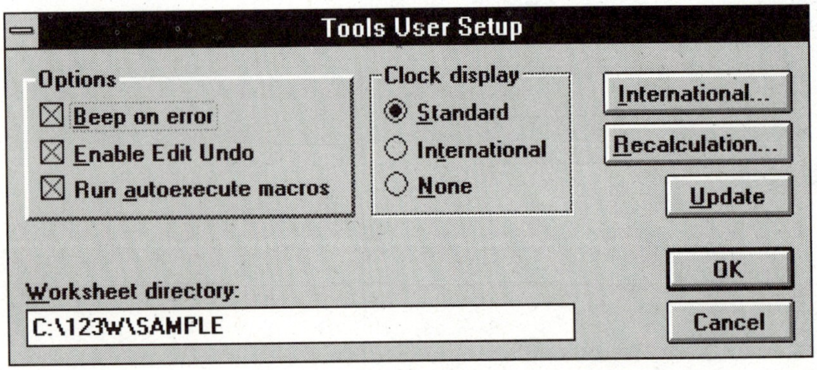

FIGURE 4.3:
The Tools User Setup dialog box

the cell to which you want to move, or you can select a range name from a list box that the command displays.

In Figure 4.4, you can see the list of range names you have defined on the conference worksheet. To jump to the cell or range represented by one of these names, you highlight the name and press ↵, or double-click the selected name in the list. If you select a name that represents a range, the cell pointer jumps to the cell at the upper-left corner of the range.

Now that the conference worksheet is open, try the following exercise with the Go To command:

1. Press the F5 function key to choose the command.

2. Highlight the EXPENSES name in the range name list. (When the Go To dialog box first appears, you can press the Tab key and then ↓ to highlight the first name in the list.)

3. Click the OK button or press ↵.

In response, the pointer jumps to cell E17, the top cell of the range you have named EXPENSES.

As you work through the exercises in this chapter, you'll find that the F5 function key, representing the Go To command, is a quick and convenient tool for moving to a particular location in the current worksheet window. In addition, you might also press F5 if you simply want to review a list of all the range names you have defined for your worksheet.

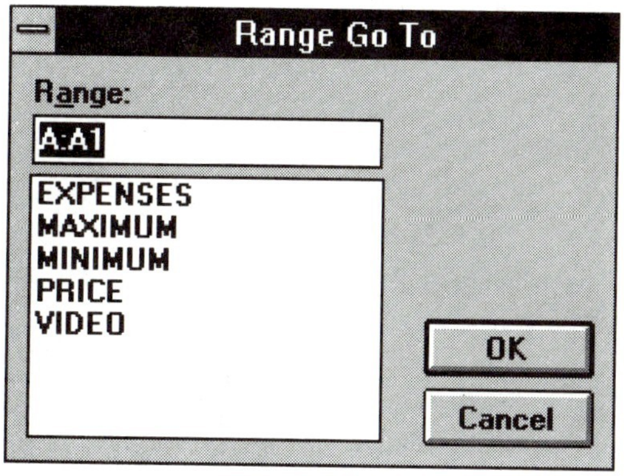

FIGURE 4.4:

The Range Go To dialog box

MAKING ADJUSTMENTS IN THE WORKSHEET

As you refine the appearance of your worksheet, you'll find that some worksheet properties can be changed in two ways:

◆ Globally, for the entire worksheet

◆ Selectively, for one or more ranges on the worksheet

The Worksheet and Range menus offer distinct commands corresponding to these two options.

Column width is an example of a visual property that you can change globally for the whole worksheet or individually for specific columns on the worksheet.

CHANGING COLUMN WIDTHS

To increase or decrease the width of all columns, you use the Global Settings command in the Worksheet menu. In the resulting dialog box, shown in Figure 4.5, the Column width box has a default setting of 9. Under this default, each column in the worksheet is wide enough to display a nine-digit number in the default font. (You'll learn about using fonts later in this chapter.)

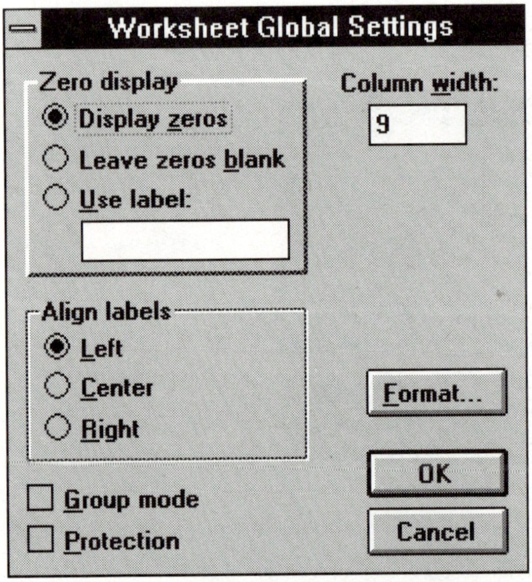

FIGURE 4.5:

The Worksheet Global Settings dialog box

You can enter any value from 1 to 240 in the Column width box for the worksheet's global column width.

Take the following steps now to increase the global column width of the conference worksheet to 11:

1. Pull down the Worksheet menu and choose the Global Settings command.

2. Select the Column width text box and enter a value of 11.

3. Click OK or press ↵.

After you widen the columns, the data on your worksheet spreads out over almost the entire width of the screen area.

The Worksheet menu also has a Column Width command, which you can use to change the width of a single column or a range of columns. This command is useful when you know the exact numeric width you want to assign to a particular column or when you want to restore the column's width to the global width setting. As you can see in Figure 4.6, these choices are represented as a pair of option buttons in the Worksheet Column Width dialog box.

To experiment with the Column Width dialog box, follow these steps to widen columns E and F to a setting of 14:

1. Preselect the range E1:F1.

2. Pull down the Worksheet menu and choose Column Width. In the resulting dialog box, the preselected range appears in the Range text box, as shown in Figure 4.6.

3. Enter a value of **14** in the Set width to text box.

4. Click OK or press ↵ to complete the operation.

FIGURE 4.6:

The Worksheet Column Width dialog box

Now if you select any cell in column E or F, the notation *[W14]* appears on the format line at the top of the 1-2-3 window. This notation appears whenever the width of a column is different from the defined global width. Pay attention to the notations in the format line throughout this chapter as you make specific changes in your worksheet's appearance.

Finally, there is a convenient mouse technique for changing the width of one column at a time: You can drag a column's border to the right to increase the column width, or to the left to decrease it. Unlike the two menu commands you've just worked with, the mouse technique allows you to change a column width by visual judgment rather than by numeric specification.

Try increasing the width of column C with this technique:

1. Position the mouse pointer over the vertical border line between the C and D headings at the top border of the worksheet. The mouse pointer becomes a double-headed arrow icon.

2. Hold down the left mouse button, and drag the border to the right. As you do so, a moving border shows you where the new border will be when you release the mouse button. Move this border to a position just to the left of the D heading.

3. Release the mouse button. Press the Home key to move the cell pointer to A1.

Now if you move the cell pointer to any cell in column C, you'll see that you've increased the width to the setting of 16. Figure 4.7 shows the 1-2-3 window at this point in your work. Part of column F is now out of view because of the increased column widths.

In the conference worksheet, changing the column widths is merely a first step in the process of improving the presentation of your data. In other cases, you may need to increase the widths of columns for a more basic reason—to enable your worksheet to display all of its numeric data. If a number in a cell is too long to fit in the width of the corresponding column, 1-2-3 replaces the numeric display with a string of asterisks. When you see such a string, you know that you must increase the column width in order to display the number itself.

Experiment with this effect in the following exercise:

1. Pull down the File menu and select New to open a new worksheet. The cell pointer starts out in cell A1.

2. Click the $ icon in the icon palette to assign a dollar-and-cent format to cell A1.

3. Type the value **123456789** in the cell. When you press ↵, you'll see the cell fill with a string of asterisks, as shown in Figure 4.8.

4. Now drag the right border of column A to a point that increases the column's width by about half. When you release the mouse button, you'll see the number displayed as *$123,456,789.00* (see Figure 4.9).

5. After you have examined the result of this exercise, close the worksheet window without saving.

In this experiment, the number in A1 could not be displayed until you increased the column width appropriately.

Another interesting adjustment that you can make in a worksheet is to *hide* a column completely.

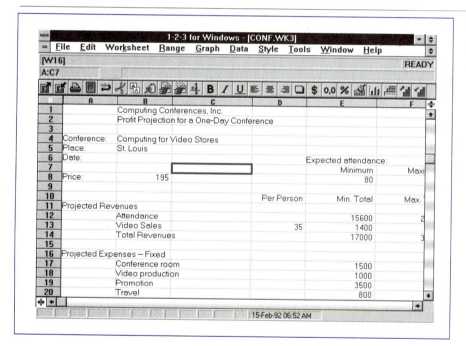

FIGURE 4.7:
Changing column widths on the worksheet

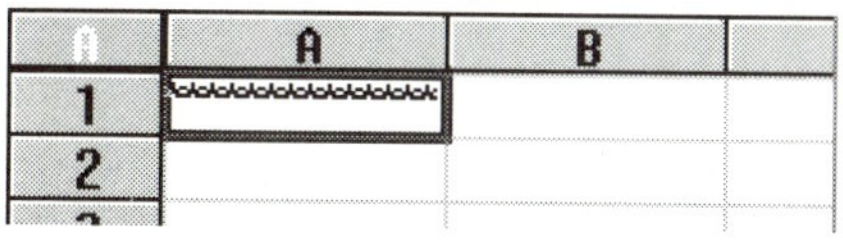

FIGURE 4.8:
A numeric entry that is too long to be displayed in its cell

Hiding Columns

You may want to hide one or more columns temporarily so that you can concentrate on other columns of data on your worksheet. Or, if many people need to view a particular worksheet, you might decide to hide a column of sensitive or private information.

Whatever your reasons, you use the Hide command in the Worksheet menu to hide a column, and the Unhide command to restore it. For example, imagine that you've decided to focus temporarily on the financial projections corresponding to the maximum attendance estimate on your conference worksheet. To do so, you want to hide the column containing the minimum estimate, column E. Here are the steps for accomplishing this:

1. Preselect cell E1 on the worksheet.

2. Pull down the Worksheet menu and select the Hide command. The resulting dialog box contains options for hiding a column or an entire worksheet in a window. The default selection is Column. A reference to the preselected cell E1 appears in the Range text box, as shown in Figure 4.10.

3. Click OK or press ↵ to complete the Hide operation. Press the Home key to move the cell pointer to A1.

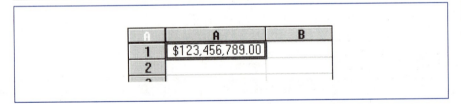

FIGURE 4.9:

Increasing the column width to display the long number

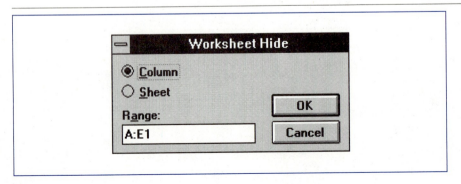

FIGURE 4.10:

The Worksheet Hide dialog box

At the end of these steps, column E disappears from the worksheet, as you can see in Figure 4.11. You can now concentrate on the data in column F.

Interestingly enough, you can also use a mouse technique to hide a column: Drag the column's border to the left until you reach the right border of the previous column. Release the mouse button, and the column disappears. The effect is the same as choosing the Worksheet Hide command.

At some point, you'll want to restore the hidden data in column E. To do so, you choose the Unhide command from the Worksheet menu. You can preselect the hidden column before choosing the command: Position the cell pointer in D1 and drag the pointer to the right; when you do so, column E temporarily reappears and becomes part of the preselected range.

But in this case you might prefer to postpone selecting the range until after you choose the command itself. Here are the steps:

1. Pull down the Worksheet menu and choose the Unhide command. The Worksheet Unhide dialog box appears on the screen, as you see in Figure 4.12.

2. Press the Tab key to activate the Range text box. Press → to point to a range; the Worksheet Unhide dialog box temporarily disappears from the screen. Press → three more times to move the cell pointer to E1. For the purposes of the Unhide operation, 1-2-3 redisplays the hidden column; an asterisk next to the column letter (*E**) indicates that the column is hidden, as shown in Figure 4.13.

	A	B	C	D	F	G
1		Computing Conferences, Inc.				
2		Profit Projection for a One-Day Conference				
3						
4	Conference:	Computing for Video Stores				
5	Place:	St. Louis				
6	Date:					
7					Maximum	
8	Price:		195		150	
9						
10				Per Person	Max. Total	
11	Projected Revenues					
12		Attendance			29250	
13		Video Sales		35	2625	
14		Total Revenues			31875	
15						
16	Projected Expenses – Fixed					
17		Conference room			2000	
18		Video production			1000	
19		Promotion			3500	
20		Travel			800	

FIGURE 4.11:

Hiding a column

3. Press ↵ to complete the pointing operation. The Worksheet Unhide dialog box returns to the screen, with a reference to E1 in the Range text box.

4. Click OK or press ↵ to confirm the Unhide operation.

The worksheet is restored to its original state, with all its columns in view. Column E has the column width setting you assigned it before the Hide operation.

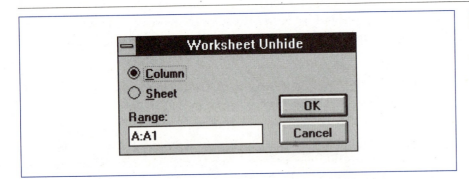

FIGURE 4.12:
The Worksheet Unhide dialog box

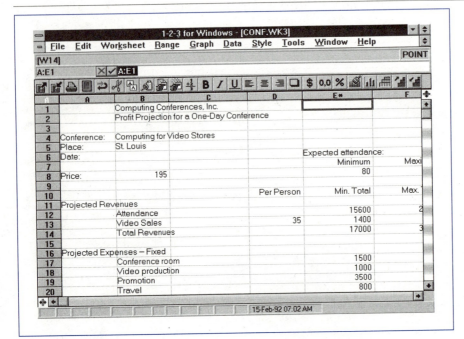

FIGURE 4.13:
Pointing to a hidden column

You can also use the mouse to perform the Unhide operation. To do so, you actually drag the border of the missing column. For example, to restore a hidden column E, you position the mouse pointer on the border between the letter headings for columns D and F and drag the border to the right. Column E reappears when you release the mouse button.

Once you have arranged the column widths the way you want them, you'll start formatting the data in specific ranges on the worksheet. One property that you've already begun to learn about is label alignment. In Chapter 3, you used double quotation mark prefixes to right-align the label entries Maximum and Minimum in their cells. Sometimes it is easier to apply alignment properties to a range of labels *after* you enter the labels into the worksheet.

SELECTING LABEL ALIGNMENTS

There are actually three different prefixes that determine a label's alignment in a worksheet cell:

◆ A single-quotation mark (') produces left-alignment, the default.

◆ A caret symbol (^) centers a label in its cell.

◆ A double-quotation mark (") produces right-alignment.

You can use the Alignment command in the Style menu to change the alignment of labels in a range, or you can simply click one of the three alignment icons in the icon palette, identified in Figure 4.14. Either way, 1-2-3 changes the prefix of each label in the selected range. (You can also select a new default alignment for the entire worksheet by clicking one of the option buttons in the Align labels box of the Worksheet Global Settings command, shown back in Figure 4.5).

As a quick experiment with label alignments, try changing the alignments of the labels in the range A4..A8 on the conference worksheet. This range contains the labels Conference:, Place:, Date:, and Price:, all of which initially have the default left-alignment. Notice that a single quote appears as

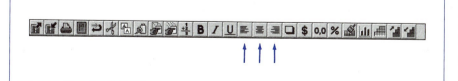

FIGURE 4.14:

The alignment icons—align-left, center, and align-right

the prefix for each label in the contents box, as in '*Conference:*. You can follow these steps to examine the other possible alignments:

1. Preselect the range A4..A8.

2. Click the center icon. The four labels are centered in their cells (see Figure 4.15), and the prefix in the contents box changes to a caret symbol: ^*Conference*.

3. Click the align-right icon. The labels are right-aligned (as in Figure 4.16), and the prefix changes to a double-quote character: "*Conference:*. Right-alignment is a good choice for these labels, but a small adjustment is now necessary.

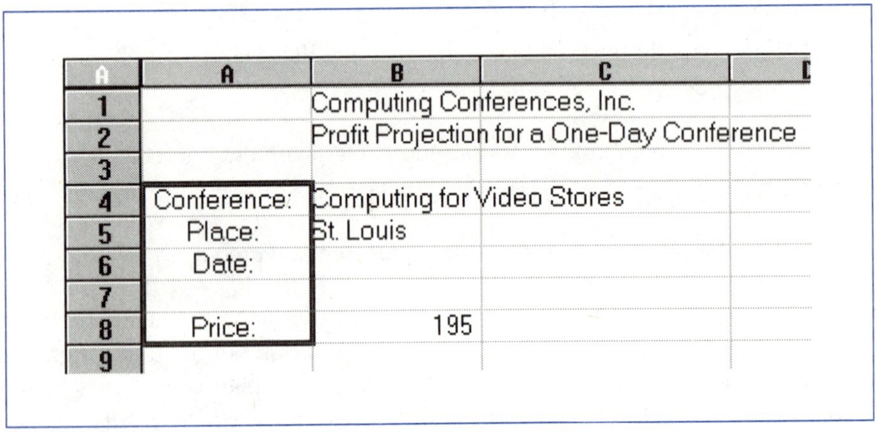

FIGURE 4.15:

Centering a range of labels

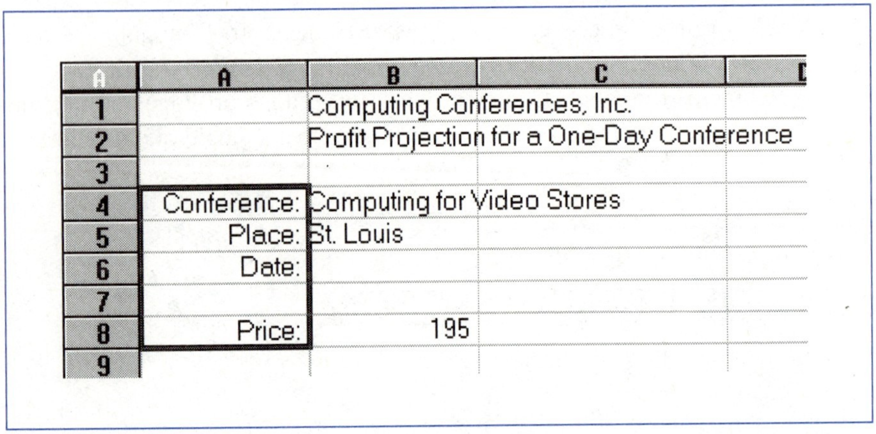

FIGURE 4.16:

Right-aligned labels

4. Use the F2 function key to edit the labels in this range, one label at a time. Insert a blank space after the colon in each label. On the printed worksheet this space will serve to separate the right-aligned labels in column A from the labels in column B.

Alignment in a single cell has no visual effect on a long label that extends beyond the right border of its cell. The label's prefix changes, but the label retains its left-alignment. You can confirm this by selecting cell A11 (which contains the long label Projected Revenues) and clicking the center-alignment and right-alignment icons in turn.

There *is* a way to change the alignment of long labels over a horizontal *range* of adjacent cells. For example, consider the two title lines of the conference worksheet in cells B1 and B2. To center these titles horizontally over the worksheet, you can select a range of columns for the centering operation. In this exercise, you'll have your first look at the Style Alignment dialog box:

1. Preselect the range B1..E2 on the conference worksheet.

2. Pull down the Style menu and choose the Alignment command. The Style Alignment dialog box appears on the screen. The Align label frame starts out with three option buttons, labeled Left, Center, and Right. The Range text box contains a reference to the preselected range.

3. Click the Align over columns check box. (When you do so, a fourth option button, labeled Even, appears inside the Align label frame. You can use this option to stretch the text of a label over the width of a range.)

4. Click the Center option. The Style Alignment dialog box now appears as shown in Figure 4.17.

5. Click OK or press ↵ to complete the centering operation.

When you complete this procedure, 1-2-3 centers the two title labels horizontally within the width of columns B through E. As you can see in Figure 4.18, this approximately centers the titles over the worksheet area. However, the titles themselves are still contained in cells B1 and B2. Selecting each of these cells in turn, you see the following labels in the contents box:

^Computing Conferences, Inc.
^Profit Projection for a One-Day Conference

Notice that 1-2-3 uses the caret prefix for centering within either a single cell or a horizontal range of cells.

Using Other Label Prefixes

Lotus 1-2-3 has two additional label prefixes, not related to alignment. The backslash prefix (\) instructs 1-2-3 to fill a cell with a single repeating character or with a pattern of repeating characters. You can use this feature to create division lines or other visual effects in a cell or a row of cells. Here is an exercise with the backslash prefix:

1. Pull down the File menu and choose the New command to open a new worksheet.

2. Use the mouse to expand the width of column A to a setting of about 50.

3. Enter the following labels, one each into cells A1 through A6:

   \()

   \#!

   \.

   \\

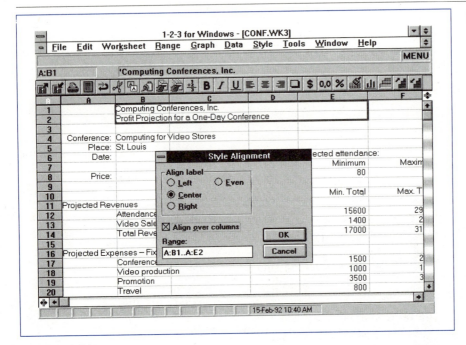

FIGURE 4.17:

The Style Alignment dialog box

\-

\Lotus 1-2-3

Figure 4.19 shows the results of these six entries. (When you have finished examining the results of this experiment, close the worksheet without saving it. The conference worksheet remains open on the screen.)

The fifth label prefix is the vertical bar character (|). Placing this character before the first cell in a row of the current *print range* instructs 1-2-3 *not* to include the row in a printed worksheet. You'll learn how to establish a print range later in this chapter.

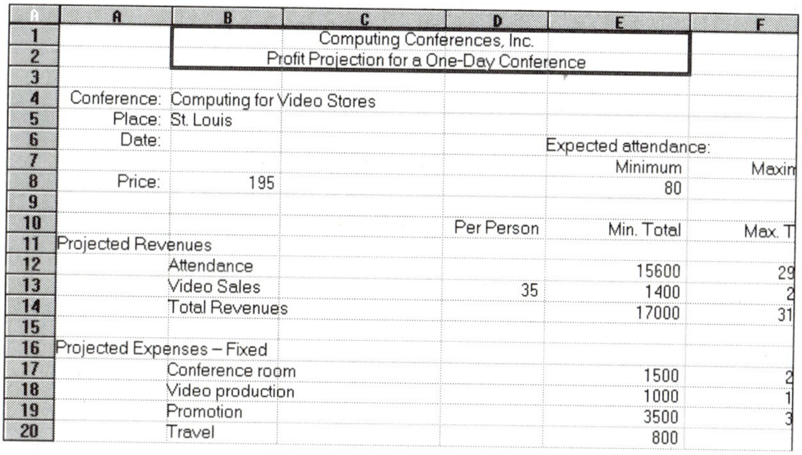

FIGURE 4.18:

Centering titles over a horizontal range of cells

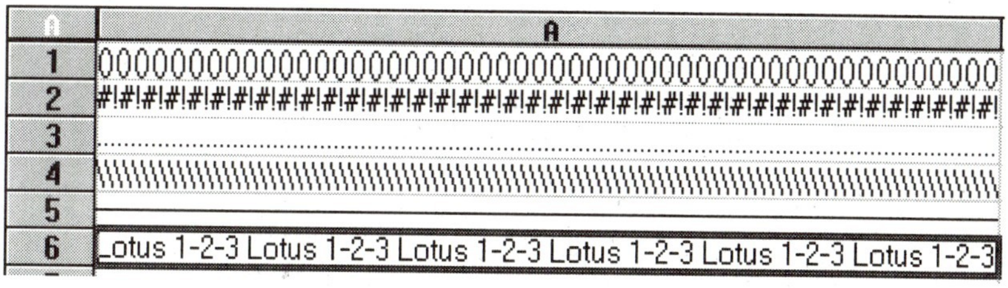

FIGURE 4.19:

An experiment with the backslash prefix

Returning to the conference worksheet, you'll now learn about another operation that affects the display of information located at the top of the worksheet.

HOLDING WORKSHEET TITLES ON THE SCREEN

As you know, you can scroll down the worksheet by pressing the PgDn key at the keyboard or by using the vertical scroll bar. Normally when you scroll down by a window's length, the rows at the top of the worksheet disappear from view. Likewise, when you scroll to the right—by pressing Ctrl-→ or by using the horizontal scroll bar—you normally lose sight of the columns located at the left of your worksheet. Sometimes you might want a way to hold a range of rows or columns on the screen, even when you scroll down or across the worksheet. The Titles command in the Worksheet menu "freezes" beginning rows and/or columns on the worksheet, so that these ranges always remain in view.

For example, on the conference worksheet it would be convenient to freeze the first ten rows in the worksheet—the rows containing the worksheet title, the general information about the planned conference, and the column headings. In other words, you might like to have all this information stay in view as you scroll down the worksheet. Here are the steps for freezing these rows on the worksheet:

1. Move the cell pointer to cell A11. This is the row just *below* the range of rows that you want to freeze onto the screen.

2. Pull down the Worksheet menu and choose the Titles command. The dialog box shown in Figure 4.20 appears on the screen. As you can see, you can freeze a horizontal range (a range of rows at the top of the worksheet), a vertical range (a range of columns at the left side of the worksheet), or both at once. In this case you want the Horizontal option, which is selected by default.

3. Click OK or press ↵ to complete the operation.

Now press the PgDn key to scroll down the worksheet. When you do so, the first ten rows remain in view, and scrolling takes place only in the lower half of the worksheet. For example, in Figure 4.21, the worksheet has been scrolled all the way down to the projected profit line, giving you a juxtaposed view of the summary information in the first ten rows along with the bottom-line profit.

Interestingly enough, you cannot use arrow keys or the mouse to move the cell pointer into a frozen range. When you press the Home key, the cell pointer now jumps to cell A11 instead of A1. Furthermore, clicking the mouse inside the frozen range has no effect. If you need to go into the frozen range to edit information there, you have two choices:

◆ Choose the Worksheet Titles command again, and select the Clear option to "unfreeze" the titles range.

◆ Press the F5 function key to choose the Range Go To command.

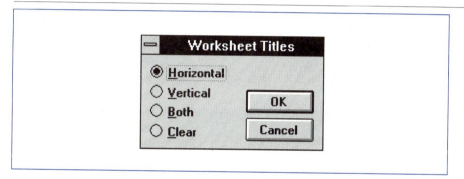

FIGURE 4.20:
The Worksheet Titles dialog box

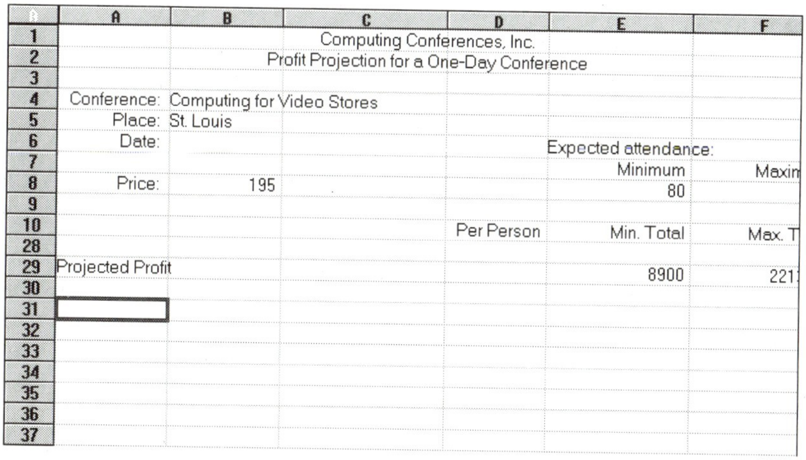

FIGURE 4.21:
A range of frozen rows at the top of the worksheet

Try pressing F5 now, and type a reference to cell A1 in the Range text box. Click OK or press ↵. When you do so, 1-2-3 presents you temporarily with a *second* view of the frozen titles, as shown in Figure 4.22. Inside this second view, you can now edit entries in the range. When you scroll down the worksheet, however, the second view is lost and the top rows remain frozen.

Now use the Titles command to clear the frozen rows:

1. Pull down the Worksheet menu and choose the Titles command.

2. Select the Clear option.

3. Click OK or press ↵.

You can now press the Home key to select cell A1. Before you read on, you might want to try freezing columns at the left side of the worksheet. For example, try establishing columns A and B as a titles range. After you do so, scroll toward the right side of the worksheet. What happens as you do so? What is the advantage of freezing these columns? Clear the frozen columns again when you are finished with this exercise.

REMOVING GRID LINES

Another change you can make in the appearance of the worksheet is the removal of the grid lines. Working with or without grid lines is a matter of personal

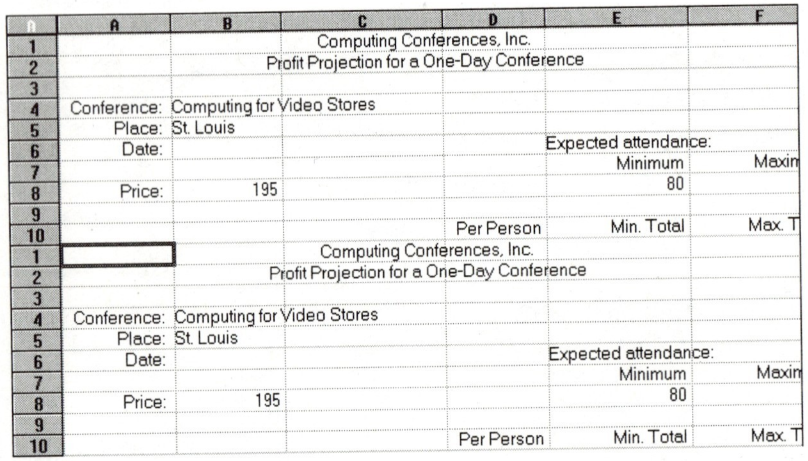

FIGURE 4.22:

Gaining access to the frozen rows by choosing the Range Go To command

preference; this option does not affect any other aspect of operations inside the worksheet.

To remove the grid lines, you deactivate an option in the Window Display Options dialog box. Here are the steps:

1. Pull down the Window menu and choose the Display Options command. The Window Display Options dialog box appears on the screen, as shown in Figure 4.23.

2. Click the Grid lines check box or press Alt-G from the keyboard. This removes the X from the check box.

3. Click OK or press ↵.

In response, 1-2-3 removes the grid lines from the worksheet window, as you can see in Figure 4.24. You can restore them by choosing Display Options again and checking the Grid lines box.

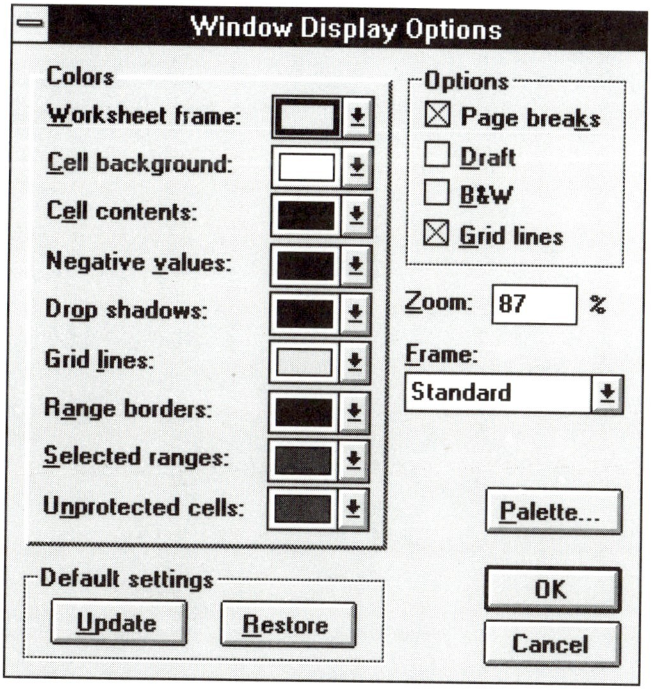

FIGURE 4.23:

The Window Display Options dialog box

Here's a brief look at other options offered in the Window Display Options dialog box:

◆ The Colors frame has pull-down lists containing display colors you can choose for various elements of the 1-2-3 interface.

◆ The Options frame has three check boxes in addition to the Grid lines box that you just used: The Page breaks check box determines whether a selected print range is marked by light dashed lines on your worksheet. The Draft and B&W check boxes represent optional display modes.

◆ The Zoom text box allows you to change the size of cells as they are displayed on the screen; you can increase the size by as much as 400 percent, or decrease it to as little as 25 percent of its original value. Figures 4.25 and 4.26 show two examples of the changes resulting from this option.

◆ The Frame box has a pull-down list containing a variety of measurements you can display around the borders of your worksheet. For example, you can display inches, picas, metric measurements, or character measurements. If you select an option other than Standard, the measurements replace the column letters and the row numbers. (There is also a None option, for removing this border altogether.)

◆ The Palette command button displays a box of colors or shades of gray, as shown in Figure 4.27. You can make selections from this box

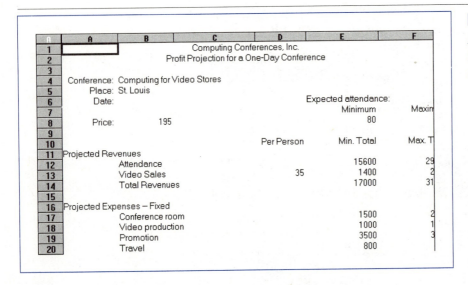

FIGURE 4.24:

Removing the grid lines from the worksheet window

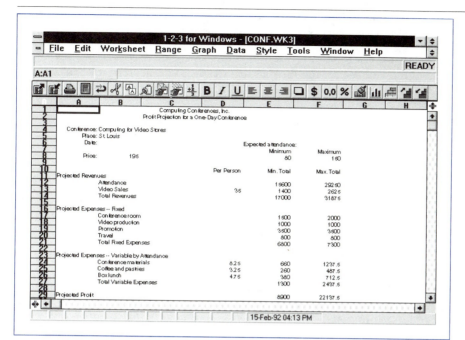

FIGURE 4.25:
Result of setting the Zoom option to 60%

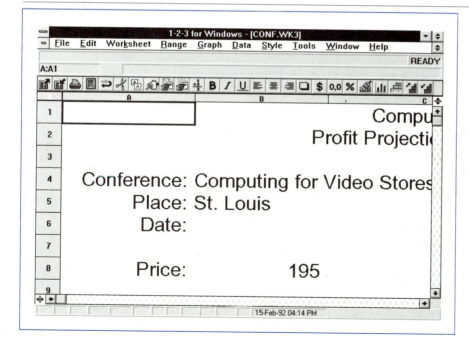

FIGURE 4.26:
Result of setting the Zoom option to 200%

to replace the standard colors displayed in the nine pull-down color lists of the Window Display Options dialog box.

◆ Finally, the Update and Restore command buttons write to or read from 123W.INI, the file that records the 1-2-3 defaults. Update saves the current display selections as the new defaults. Conversely, the Restore button reads the current defaults from the .INI file and restores them as the selections in the Window Display Options dialog box.

FORMATTING VALUES ON THE WORKSHEET

One way to give meaning to a numeric value on your worksheet is to pair the value with a descriptive label. A number and an adjacent label in this way form an item of information, such as the following:

Price: 195

But another important technique for establishing the meaning of numbers—and for improving the general readability of your worksheet—is to apply appropriate *formats* to numeric values:

Price: $195.00

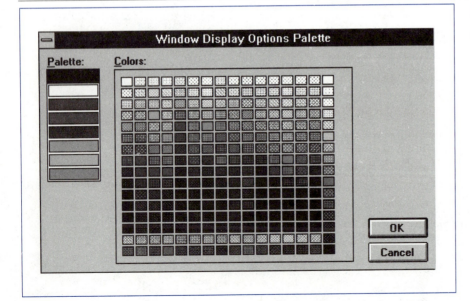

FIGURE 4.27:
The color palette

Lotus 1-2-3 for Windows provides standard numeric formats that you can assign to the numbers on your worksheet. Like other worksheet properties, you can apply formats globally to the entire worksheet, or selectively to particular cells or ranges on your worksheet. A format does not change the numeric value entered into a cell, only the way the number is displayed in the cell.

You can apply most formats either before or after you actually enter values onto your worksheet. The Global Settings command from the Worksheet menu establishes formats for the entire worksheet. Looking back at Figure 4.5, you'll see that the Worksheet Global Settings dialog box contains a Format command button. When you click this button a new dialog box appears on the screen, as shown in Figure 4.28. The dialog box has three main tools: The Format box lists global formats available for the worksheet. The Decimal places text box controls the number of digits displayed after the decimal point. The Parentheses check box gives you the option of displaying numeric values within parentheses.

Lotus 1-2-3 presents a similar dialog box when you select the Format command from the Range menu (shown in Figure 4.29). The main difference is that this second dialog box is designed for applying formats to a selected range on the worksheet rather than the entire worksheet. The list of format settings is the same as in the Global settings dialog box. The Range Format dialog box also has a Reset command button. Clicking this button resets the range format to the current global format.

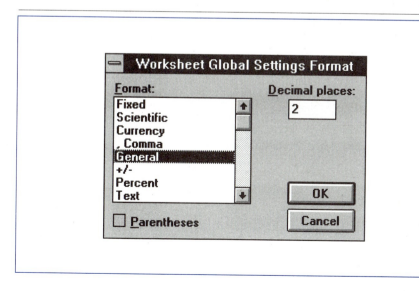

FIGURE 4.28:

The Worksheet Global Settings Format dialog box

The worksheet in Figure 4.30 shows examples of commonly used formats. Column C on this worksheet displays the six available numeric formats:

◆ The Fixed format displays values with a specified number of decimal places, up to 15.

◆ The Scientific format displays numbers in an exponent notation, where the digits after the letter E represent the power of 10 by which the base value is multiplied.

◆ The Currency format displays a dollar sign at the beginning of the number, and a comma before every third digit at the left of the decimal point. (You can apply this format by preselecting a range and then clicking the currency-format icon.)

◆ The Comma format displays a comma before every third digit at the left of the decimal point. (You can select this format by clicking the comma-format icon.)

◆ The General format displays a value without special formatting; this is the default.

◆ The Percent format multiplies the displayed value by 100 and appends a percent sign. (You can select this format by clicking the percent-format icon.)

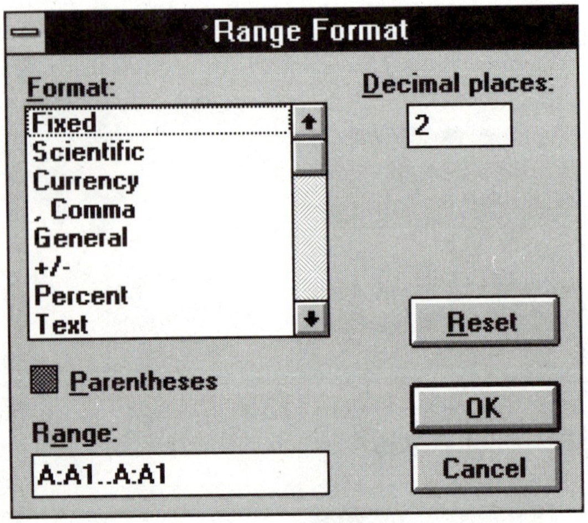

FIGURE 4.29:

The Range Format dialog box

Figure 4.31 identifies the three format icons contained in the default icon palette.

Examples of two other formats appear in Figure 4.30. The +/− format transforms the display of a value into an equivalent number of plus or minus characters. This format is useful for creating simple character-based horizontal bar graphs on a worksheet. (In Figure 4.30, column F contains the same positive numbers that are displayed in column E. Likewise, column I contains the same negative values displayed in column H.)

Finally, the Text format operates on a cell that contains a formula. Under this format, the cell displays the text of the formula itself rather than the formula's numeric result, as you can see in cell D16 of Figure 4.30. If you want to examine all the formulas on your worksheet at once, select Text as the global format.

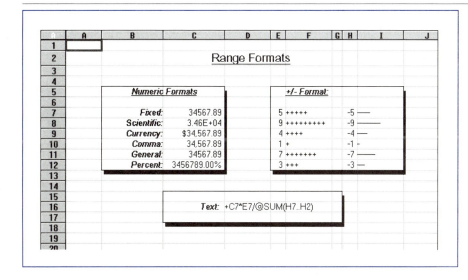

FIGURE 4.30:
Examples of commonly used numeric formats

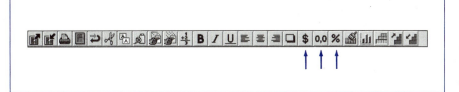

FIGURE 4.31:
The currency-format icon, the comma-format icon, and the percent-format icon

Selecting Global and Range Formats

Because most of the values on the conference worksheet are dollar-and-cent figures, it is convenient to assign a global Currency format to the worksheet. Here are the steps required:

1. Pull down the Worksheet menu and choose the Global Settings command. The Worksheet Global Settings dialog box appears on the screen.

2. Click the Format command button to view the Worksheet Global Settings Format dialog box.

3. Select the Currency format in the Format box. (Do not change the default setting of 2 in the Decimal places box.)

4. Click OK or press ↵ to confirm the global format selection. (The Worksheet Global Settings dialog box remains on the screen.)

5. Click OK to complete the formatting operation.

As a result, all of the values on the worksheet are displayed as dollar-and-cent values. But the worksheet currently contains two values that should be displayed as simple integers: the minimum and maximum attendance estimates in cells E8 and F8. You can use the comma-format icon to change these two values to an appropriate format:

1. Preselect the range E8..F8.

2. Click the comma-format icon.

Figure 4.32 shows part of your worksheet after you complete these formatting operations.

By the way, if you are working with international currencies you may want to change the symbol used for the Currency format and, optionally, reverse the roles of commas and periods, as in some international currency notations. To do so, you can take advantage of a feature that is part of the Tools User Setup command. When you pull down the Tools menu and choose User Setup, the resulting dialog box (shown back in Figure 4.3) has a command button labeled International. When you click this button, the Tools User Setup International dialog box appears, as shown in Figure 4.33. To change the currency symbol, enter a new character in the Symbol for currency box. To change the comma and period punctuation, make a new selection in the pull-down list attached to the Punctuation box.

Changing the Data-Entry Mode

Atypically, Lotus 1-2-3 has two formats that take effect only on entries that you make *after* selecting the format itself. In effect, these two formats represent special data-entry modes:

◆ The Label format accepts all new entries on the worksheet as labels, even if they begin with digits or other characters that would normally trigger the VALUE entry mode. As a result of this format selection, 1-2-3 places a single-quote prefix at the beginning of each new entry you make in the worksheet. This format is useful when you have to enter a series of labels that happen to begin with digits—for example, a column of addresses. Without the Label format, you would have to begin each such label by typing the single-quotation mark, as you learned in Chapter 3.

◆ The Automatic format applies a format to an individual cell according to the way you initially enter a value into the cell. In other words, each new numeric entry you make under this mode has two results: A value is stored in the cell, and the cell is assigned a format. (If you subsequently enter a different value into the same cell, the new value is displayed in the existing format.) The Automatic format is useful

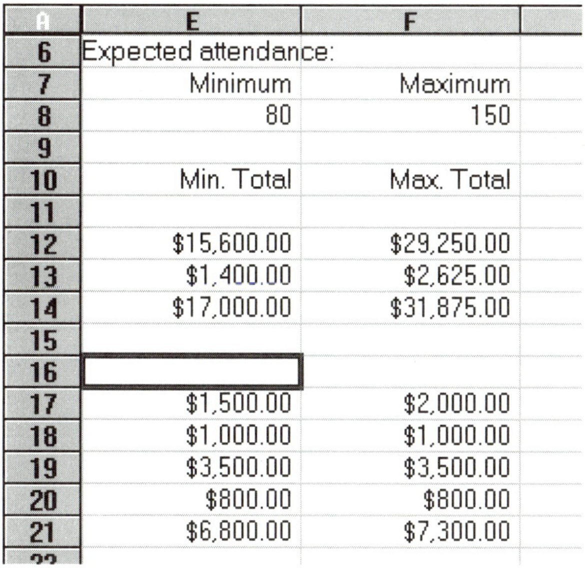

FIGURE 4.32:

Formatting numbers on the worksheet

A	E	F
6	Expected attendance:	
7	Minimum	Maximum
8	80	150
9		
10	Min. Total	Max. Total
11		
12	$15,600.00	$29,250.00
13	$1,400.00	$2,625.00
14	$17,000.00	$31,875.00
15		
16		
17	$1,500.00	$2,000.00
18	$1,000.00	$1,000.00
19	$3,500.00	$3,500.00
20	$800.00	$800.00
21	$6,800.00	$7,300.00

on a worksheet that requires a large variety of different formatting selections; under Automatic, you can set each cell's format at the time of data entry.

In the following exercise, you'll apply these two formats to individual cells on a worksheet, and you'll also experiment with a format that hides the contents of a range of cells:

1. Pull down the File menu and select the New command to create a new worksheet window for use in this exercise.

2. With the cell pointer positioned at address A1, pull down the Range menu and choose the Format command. In the Format list box, select the Label format. (While the Format box is active, you can simply type **L** at the keyboard to jump immediately down to the target format in the list.)

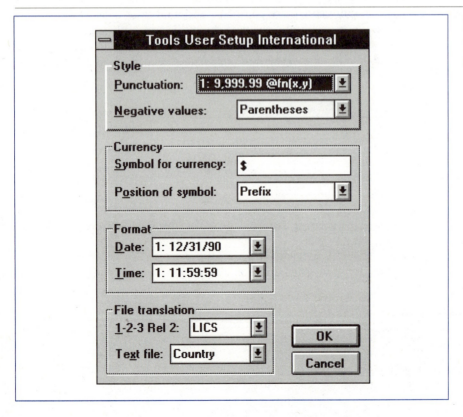

FIGURE 4.33:

The Tools User Setup International dialog box

3. Click OK or press ↵. A1 now operates under the Label format.

4. Type **123 Maple Drive** into cell A1. When you begin the entry, 1-2-3 switches into the VALUE mode—but when you press ↵, the entry is stored as a label. You can confirm this by examining the contents box at the top of the 1-2-3 window; the entry begins with a single-quote character: *'123 Maple Drive.*

5. Now select cell A2 for an experiment with the Automatic format.

6. Pull down the Range menu and choose the Format command again. This time select the Automatic format. (Simply type **A** at the keyboard to jump down to Automatic in the Format list.)

7. Click OK or press ↵. Cell A2 is now under the effect of the Automatic mode.

8. Type **$1234.56** into A2. You have not included a comma in your entry, but the initial dollar sign is enough to assign the currency format to the cell. Press ↵ and note the results. The cell displays the new entry as *$1,234.56*. And the format line displays the cell's format as *(C2)*. This notation represents the Currency format displayed with two decimal places. Finally, notice that the contents box displays the entry simply as *1234.56*.

9. Enter a new numeric value, **6543.21**, into cell A2. The previously assigned format applies to this new entry, which is displayed in the cell as *$6,543.21*.

10. Preselect the range A1..A2. Choose the Range Format command again and select the Hidden option from the Format list. Click OK or press ↵ to confirm the format selection. When you do so, the contents of the two cells disappear. Selecting each cell in turn, you can see in the contents box that the entries have not been deleted, just hidden. The Hidden format is useful when you want to withhold certain sensitive data items from view in a worksheet.

11. When you have finished examining the results of this exercise, close the worksheet window without saving it.

Keep the Label and Automatic formats in mind for special data-entry requirements. In appropriate situations, they can speed up your work considerably. You'll have another opportunity to experiment with the Automatic mode in the next section of this chapter, as you turn to two other kinds of worksheet data—date and time values.

Entering Date Values into a Worksheet

Lotus 1-2-3 includes a versatile collection of tools for working with calendar dates. You can enter a date on your worksheet as a specially-formatted numeric value. Then you can use that date value in important operations known as *date arithmetic*. For example, here are two date-related operations commonly used in business worksheets:

◆ Finding the number of days between any two dates

◆ Finding the date that is a specified number of days forward or backward from either today's date or another date

Performing these two operations is a complicated programming task in some software environments. But in 1-2-3 you can accomplish them with simple arithmetic formulas, as you'll see shortly.

There are two different ways of recording a date in a worksheet. If you only want to *display* a date—but you have no need to perform any special date arithmetic operations—a label entry is the most straightforward way. If you enter the date in a format that starts with the name of a month—for example, October 15, 1992—1-2-3 automatically accepts your entry as a label (the same as it accepts any entry that begins with a letter of the alphabet).

But if you anticipate working with the date entry in any calendar-related calculations, you must enter the date as a number. To do this, you have to understand the system of numeric dates used in Lotus 1-2-3. The system relies on 1-2-3's built-in ability to compute an integer equivalent for every date between January 1, 1900 and December 31, 2099. The first of these dates, January 1, 1900, is established as day 1 in the system, and each date forward is numbered consecutively—that is, one greater than the previous date. Here is a sampling of the date numbers in this system:

January 1, 1900	1
January 2, 1900	2
May 10, 1910	3783
December 1, 1945	16772
March 2, 1976	27821
October 15, 1992	33892
December 31, 2099	73050

When you enter a value in a format that 1-2-3 can recognize as one of the dates within this range, the entry is actually stored in the cell as a date-number equivalent. Therefore, after the date entry, your next task is to reformat the cell in one of five date formats available in the Range Format dialog box. In Figure 4.34, the Format box is scrolled down far enough so that you can view these five special formats. The first three formats use a three-character month abbreviation, along with two digits each for the month and/or year, such as the following:

15-Oct-92

15-Oct

Oct-92

The second two formats, named Long International Date and Short International Date, have defaults corresponding to these examples:

11/15/92

11/15

If you wish, you can select a different setting for these international date formats in the Tools User Setup International dialog box (see Figure 4.33).

In summary, to create a date entry in a worksheet cell, you first enter the date in one of the two complete date formats that begin with a digit, such

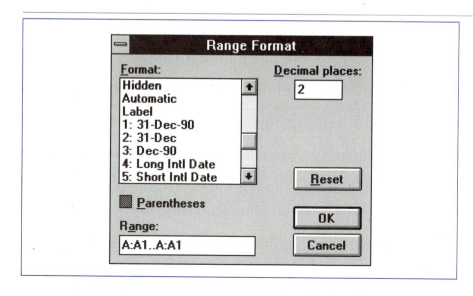

FIGURE 4.34:

Date formats available in the Range Format dialog box

as 15-Oct-92 or 11/15/92. (Alternatively, if you use the incomplete 15-Oct format, 1-2-3 assumes the date is in the current year.) Lotus 1-2-3 converts your entry into the corresponding date number. Next, you choose the Range Format command and select one of the five date formats available in the Format list. To practice this technique, return now to the conference worksheet. Cell B6 is set aside for the date of the conference, but the cell is still empty. Here are the steps for entering this date:

1. Select cell B6 and type **15-Oct-92** as the date of the conference. Press ↵ and then examine the contents box. The corresponding date number is displayed as *33892*. This same value is displayed in the cell itself, but—somewhat incongruously—in the worksheet's global currency format: *$33,892.00*.

2. Pull down the Range menu and choose the Format command. In the Format list box, type **1** to select the first of the five date formats.

3. Click OK or press ↵ to complete the formatting operation.

Now the date is displayed in the format you have selected: *15-Oct-92*. The format line displays the format selection as *(D1)*. This notation represents date format 1.

You can save time in the date-entry process by using the Automatic format. In a range that requires many date entries, consider setting the format to Automatic. Then you can enter a date in one of the formats that 1-2-3 recognizes, and the format will automatically be assigned to the cell. Try this technique in the following exercise.

1. Select B6 and press the Delete key to delete the current date entry. (This action also removes the cell's current format setting.)

2. Pull down the Range menu and choose the Format command.

3. In the Format list, type **A** to select the Automatic option.

4. Click OK or press ↵.

5. In cell B6, reenter the date in the same format as before: **15-Oct-92**. This time the date display has the same format as your date entry. The date number *33892* again appears in the contents box.

6. Click the save-file icon to save the work you have done on the worksheet up to now.

Now that you have learned how to enter and format a date value, the following section will guide you through a brief exercise in date arithmetic. Along the way, you'll learn to use an icon associated with range formatting—the apply-formats icon.

Date Arithmetic

Computing Conferences, Inc, has decided to offer discounts to participants who can enroll and pay in advance for admission to the conference. There will be a 10-percent discount for payments received 45 days in advance, and a 20-percent discount for payments received 90 days in advance. Accordingly, the conference organizers want to develop a small worksheet that formulates and displays the discount schedule.

In the following steps, you will begin developing this schedule by adding a second worksheet to the CONF.WK3 file:

1. Pull down the Worksheet menu and choose the Insert command.

2. On the Worksheet Insert dialog box, select the Sheet option.

3. Click OK or press ↵. Worksheet B is added to the window and becomes the current worksheet.

4. Click the perspective-view icon so that you can view worksheets A and B together in one window.

5. In cell B:A2, enter the title **Discount Schedule for Advance Enrollment**.

6. In worksheet A, preselect the range A:A4..A:B8. (This range contains the basic information about the conference, which you are now going to copy to worksheet B.)

7. Click the copy-to-clipboard icon. In worksheet B, select cell B:A4. Click the paste-from-clipboard icon. A copy of the conference information appears in worksheet B. Click the perspective-view icon again, to toggle back into a view or worksheet B alone. Notice that the range date format in cell B:B6 was copied from worksheet A, but the global currency format was not copied.

8. Select cell B:B8 and click the currency-format icon.

9. Enter the following three column headings in cells B:B10, B:C10, and B:D10, respectively:

   If paid by:

   Discount

   Price

10. Preselect the range B:C10..BD10 and click the align-right icon. The alignment of the column headings in these two cells will now match the alignment of the numeric values that will appear beneath them.

11. Choose the Worksheet Global Settings command and enter **11** as the global column width. Click OK or press ↵.

At this point in the process, worksheet B appears as shown in Figure 4.35.
The next step is to write formulas in cells B:B11 and B:B12 to display the deadline dates for the two discount rates. Because cell B:B6 contains a date number representing the date of the conference, you will create formulas that subtract the appropriate number of days from this date.
Enter the following formula in B:B11:

+B:B6−90

B	A	B	C	D
1				
2	Discount Schedule for Advance Enrollment			
3				
4	Conference:	Computing for Video Stores		
5	Place:	St. Louis		
6	Date:	15-Oct-92		
7				
8	Price:	$195.00		
9				
10		If paid by:	Discount	Price
11				
12				
13				
14				

FIGURE 4.35:
Creating a discount schedule on worksheet B

As you can see, this formula subtracts a value of 90 (representing 90 days) from the date number stored in cell B6. The result initially displayed in cell B6 is 33802. Enter the formula into cell B:B12 to subtract 45 days from the conference date:

+B:B6–45

The initial result is 33847.

Now you have to format these two cells so they will appear as dates. To do so, you can practice using the apply-formats icon, identified in Figure 4.36. This icon copies a *format* from one place in a worksheet to another. Using this icon takes three simple steps:

1. Select cell B:B6, which has the format that you want to apply elsewhere on the worksheet.

2. Click the apply-formats icon. Now when you move the mouse pointer over the worksheet, the pointer takes on the form of a paint brush icon.

3. Drag the mouse pointer over the cells B:B11..B:B12, the range over which you want to apply the specified format.

In response, 1-2-3 applies the format from cell B6 to cells B11 and B12. These latter two cells now display the discount deadline dates, as follows:

17-Jul-92
31-Aug-92

Now follow these steps to complete the discount schedule worksheet:

1. Enter a value of **.2** in cell B:C11 and a value of **.1** in B:C12.

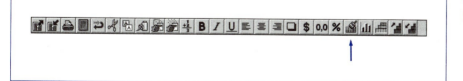

FIGURE 4.36:
The apply-formats icon

2. Preselect the range B:C11..B:C12. Then pull down the Range menu and choose the Format command.

3. In the Format list, select the Percent format.

4. Activate the Decimal places text box and enter a value of **0**.

5. Click OK or press ↵. The values in C11 and C12 now appear as percentages.

6. Select cell B:D11 and enter the following formula:

    +$B:$B$8*(1–B:C11)

    (After typing **+** and pointing to the first address in the formula, press the F4 function key to change the address to an absolute reference. The second address can remain a relative reference.)

7. Use the range-copy icon to copy this formula into cell B:D12. The copied formula—adjusted for its position relative to the original formula—appears as *+$B$8*(1–C12)*.

8. Preselect the range B:D11..B:D12 and click the currency-format icon.

9. Click the save-file icon to save your work to the disk file CONF.WK3.

The result of your work is shown in Figure 4.37.

	A	B	C	D
1				
2	Discount Schedule for Advance Enrollment			
3				
4	Conference:	Computing for Video Stores		
5	Place:	St. Louis		
6	Date:	15-Oct-92		
7				
8	Price:	$195.00		
9				
10		If paid by:	Discount	Price
11		17-Jul-92	20%	$156.00
12		31-Aug-92	10%	$175.50
13				
14				

FIGURE 4.37:
Completing the discount schedule worksheet

ENTERING TIME VALUES INTO A WORKSHEET

Lotus 1-2-3 is equally adept at displaying and manipulating chronological values, or time values during a 24-hour day. Like a date, a time value is stored in a cell as a special kind of number; to display the number as a time, you apply one of 1-2-3's time formats. Then you can perform a variety of *time arithmetic* operations. For example, here are the two most common time arithmetic operations in business worksheets:

◆ Finding the number of minutes between two time values in a 24-hour day

◆ Finding the point in time that is a specified number of minutes forward or backward from either the current time or a specified time

Once again, you have to begin by learning exactly how 1-2-3 translates time values into numbers before you can perform operations like these. A time number is a fractional value, expressed as a decimal. Specifically, the fraction expresses the portion of the 24-hour day that has gone by at a specified time. For example, the time value for 12:00 noon is .5, because one-half of the day has elapsed at noon. Here is a sampling of other time values and their equivalent time numbers, as formulated by 1-2-3:

3:00 AM	.125	(One-eighth of the day)
6:00 AM	.25	(One-fourth of the day)
9:00 AM	.375	(Three-eighths of the day)
6:00 PM	.75	(Three-fourths of the day)
9:00 PM	.875	(Seven-eighths of the day)

To enter and display a time value, you use formats that 1-2-3 recognizes for such entries. In Figure 4.38, you can see the four available time formats, displayed at the bottom of the Format list in the Range Format dialog box. The first two, numbered 6 and 7 in the Format list, are AM/PM formats. The second two, numbered 8 and 9, are 24-hour international formats. Here are examples of these latter two formats:

23:59:59

23:59

(You can select a new international time format in the Tools User Setup International dialog box, shown back in Figure 4.33.)

When you enter a value in any one of these four formats, 1-2-3 recognizes your entry as a time and automatically translates the entry into a decimal time number. Your next step is to pull down the Range menu, choose the Format command, and select a time format for displaying your entry. Alternatively, you can select the Automatic format for your worksheet; in this case, 1-2-3 applies a time format corresponding to the format of your entry. As you can see, the process of entering time values is precisely parallel to that of entering date values.

In your first exercise with time values, you'll insert yet another worksheet into the CONF.WK3 file—this time, the worksheet named C. You'll begin by entering one time value onto this worksheet, but then you'll use the sheet to build another document for Computing Conferences, Inc. Here are the beginning steps:

1. With worksheet B as the current worksheet, pull down the Worksheet menu and choose the Insert command. Select the Sheet option and press ↵ to insert the third worksheet into the file. When you complete this operation, worksheet C becomes the current worksheet.

2. Select cell C:D8 for this first entry. (You'll see why shortly.) In the cell, enter the following time value:

   7:00 AM

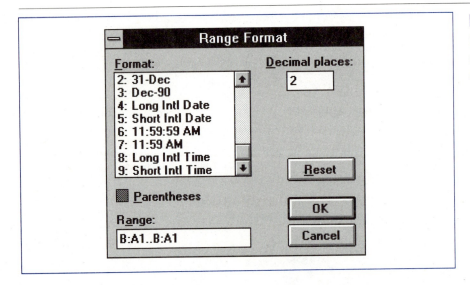

FIGURE 4.38:

Time formats in the Range Format dialog box

In response, 1-2-3 displays the time number equivalent of this value: *0.291667*. In the contents box, the value is expanded to a greater number of decimal places.

3. Pull down the Range menu and choose the Format command. Scroll down to format 7 in the Format box and click the format, or simply type **7** at the keyboard to select the format.

4. Click OK or press ↵.

The time entry is now displayed in cell D8 as *07:00 AM*. The notation *(D7)* represents this format selection on the format line. In the next section, you'll use this time entry as the starting point for an exercise in time arithmetic.

Time Arithmetic

The conference organizers at Computing Conferences, Inc., are ready to begin planning the schedule for the one-day conference in St. Louis. During the course of the conference day there will be four major presentations, each lasting between one and two hours. In addition, there will be other miscellaneous activities, including an introduction, an hour of hands-on demonstrations, coffee breaks, and lunch. The planners therefore want to develop a worksheet that calculates the day's schedule, given the length of each event. They also want to be able to adjust the length of time allotted to a given activity, and immediately see the effect on the whole schedule.

You'll develop this schedule on worksheet C. Begin with the following formatting and data-entry tasks:

1. Use the apply-formats icon to duplicate the format of cell D8 in the cells below it in column D. With the cell pointer located at D8, click the apply-formats icon with the mouse. Then drag the paint brush mouse pointer over the range C:D9..C:D18. When you release the mouse button, 1-2-3 applies the time format to each cell in this range, although no visible change takes place in the worksheet window.

2. Press the Home key to select cell A1, and enter the title **Conference Schedule** into the cell.

3. Copy the range containing the conference name, the place, and the date from worksheet B to worksheet C. Press Ctrl-PgDn to move the cell pointer to worksheet B. Preselect the range B:A4..B:B6 and click the copy-to-clipboard icon. Press Ctrl-PgUp to move the cell pointer to worksheet C. Select cell C:A3 and click the paste-from-clipboard

icon. Next, choose the Worksheet Global Settings command, and change the global column width to **11**.

4. Enter the following column headings into cells C:A7, C:D7, and C:E7, respectively:

   Event

   Start time

   Minutes

   Select the range C:D7..C:E7 and click the align-right icon to align these two column headings with the numeric entries that will eventually appear below them. Then select the range C:A7..C:E7 and click the bold icon.

5. Enter the following list of event descriptions into column A, from C:A8 to C:A18:

   Coffee and pastries
   Introduction
   Managing a Video Database
   Coffee break
   Managing a Customer Database
   Hands-on demonstrations
   Lunch and discussion
   Setting Up a Computer System
   Coffee break
   Software Options
   No-host cocktail hour

6. In column E, from C:E8 to C:E18, enter values representing the planned length in minutes of each event:

   45
   30
   90
   15
   120
   60
   60
   120
   30
   60
   60

7. Select cell C:D9 to prepare for the upcoming formula entry.

The result of your work appears in Figure 4.39. You now need to write a formula in D9 that calculates the starting time of the second event. The formula should be simple: Add the length in minutes of the first event (in C:E8) to the starting time of the first event (in C:D8). But there is one complication—the worksheet expresses these two values in incompatible terms. The starting time is stored as a decimal time number, and the length of the event is expressed in minutes. To add the two values you must first find a way to convert them into common terms.

In this worksheet, the best approach is to convert the minutes to a decimal time value. The following expression calculates the fraction of a 24-hour day represented by the minutes in cell C:E8:

+C:E8/(60*24)

Multiplying 60 by 24 gives the number of minutes in a day. Dividing the value in cell E8 by this number results in the appropriate decimal time value. Given this expression, here is the formula that calculates the starting time of the second event:

+C:D8+C:E8/(60*24)

C	A	B	C	D	E
1	Conference Schedule				
2					
3	Conference:	Computing for Video Stores			
4	Place:	St. Louis			
5	Date:	15-Oct-92			
6					
7	Event			Start time	Minutes
8	Coffee and pastries			07:00 AM	45
9	Introduction				30
10	Managing a Video Database				90
11	Coffee break				15
12	Managing a Customer Database				120
13	Hands-on demonstrations				60
14	Lunch and discussion				60
15	Setting Up a Computer System				120
16	Coffee break				30
17	Software Options				60
18	No-host cocktail hour				60

FIGURE 4.39:
Building a worksheet for the conference schedule

In the following steps, you'll use the pointing technique to enter this formula into cell D9. Then, you'll copy the formula down the appropriate range in column D:

1. With the cell pointer positioned at D9, type **+** to start the formula entry.

2. Press ↑ once to point to the starting time in D8. Then type **+** again.

3. Press ↑ and → once each to point to the value in cell E8. Then complete the formula by typing **/(60*24)**. Press ↵ to confirm the formula entry. Cell D9 displays *07:45 AM* as the formatted time value.

4. Click the range-copy icon. Drag the mouse pointer (now in the form of a pointing-hand icon) over the range C:D10..C:D18. When you release the mouse button, 1-2-3 copies the formula down column D.

Figure 4.40 shows the schedule worksheet. Examine the formulas that 1-2-3 has copied into cells D9 through D18. Do you see why relative references were appropriate for the addresses in this copy operation?

Now the conference planners want to adjust the schedule for the morning events. They want lunch to take place one-half hour earlier than its currently scheduled time at 1:00 in the afternoon. To accomplish this, they decide to reduce the time for the second presentation—Managing a Customer Database, in row 12—by 30 minutes.

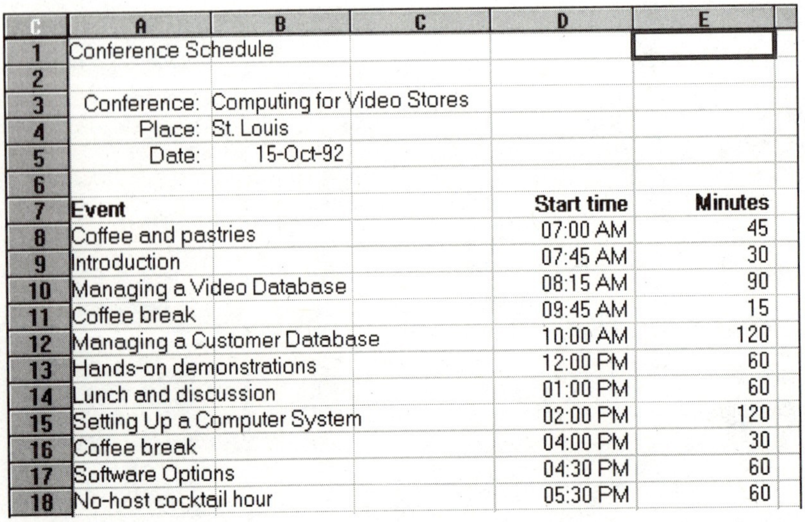

FIGURE 4.40:

Entering and copying a formula to calculate the time schedule

	A	B	C	D	E
1	Conference Schedule				
2					
3	Conference:	Computing for Video Stores			
4	Place:	St. Louis			
5	Date:	15-Oct-92			
6					
7	Event			Start time	Minutes
8	Coffee and pastries			07:00 AM	45
9	Introduction			07:45 AM	30
10	Managing a Video Database			08:15 AM	90
11	Coffee break			09:45 AM	15
12	Managing a Customer Database			10:00 AM	120
13	Hands-on demonstrations			12:00 PM	60
14	Lunch and discussion			01:00 PM	60
15	Setting Up a Computer System			02:00 PM	120
16	Coffee break			04:00 PM	30
17	Software Options			04:30 PM	60
18	No-host cocktail hour			05:30 PM	60

Enter a new value of 90 in cell C:E12, and watch what happens to the schedule. All the starting times from C:D13 down are adjusted for the half-hour change, as shown in Figure 4.41. The schedule worksheet is working according to design.

Click the save-file icon now to update the CONF.WK3 file on disk. Then click the previous-worksheet icon twice to move the cell pointer to worksheet A. In the next section, you'll learn to protect the conference worksheet from inadvertent revisions or deletions.

PROTECTING THE WORKSHEET

The conference worksheet is designed to be reused for planning other conferences. Entering new data values in the worksheet's "input" ranges, you can quickly produce financial projections for any conference in the future. When you create a tool like this one, you may find yourself distributing copies of the worksheet file to other people who need to perform similar tasks in 1-2-3. But other users may not be aware of your worksheet's carefully designed structure. In particular, a user may fail to distinguish between cells that contain simple data entries and cells that contain formulas. The structure of the worksheet can easily be ruined if a user inadvertently makes a new entry in a formula cell.

C	A	B	C	D	E
1	Conference Schedule				
2					
3	Conference:	Computing for Video Stores			
4	Place:	St. Louis			
5	Date:	15-Oct-92			
6					
7	Event			Start time	Minutes
8	Coffee and pastries			07:00 AM	45
9	Introduction			07:45 AM	30
10	Managing a Video Database			08:15 AM	90
11	Coffee break			09:45 AM	15
12	Managing a Customer Database			10:00 AM	90
13	Hands-on demonstrations			11:30 AM	60
14	Lunch and discussion			12:30 PM	60
15	Setting Up a Computer System			01:30 PM	120
16	Coffee break			03:30 PM	30
17	Software Options			04:00 PM	60
18	No-host cocktail hour			05:00 PM	60

FIGURE 4.41:

Making a change in the schedule worksheet

To prevent this from happening, you can establish a protection scheme for the worksheet. The purpose of worksheet protection is to prohibit new entries in cells that contain formulas, allowing entries only in appropriate "input" cells. Two commands are involved in establishing this protection scheme. First, you use the Global Settings command from the Worksheet menu to protect your worksheet globally. Then you use the Unprotect command from the Range menu to release selected ranges of cells from the global protection setting.

Look back at Figure 4.5 to reexamine the Worksheet Global Settings dialog box. At the lower-left corner of the box you can see two check boxes, both unchecked by default:

◆ The Group mode option allows you to apply the formatting patterns of the current worksheet to all other worksheets in the same file. For CONF.WK3, this option remains unchecked, because worksheets A, B, and C all have distinct formatting requirements.

◆ The Protection option determines whether a worksheet is protected globally, prohibiting new data entries. Checking this option is the first step in establishing a protection scheme for the conference worksheet.

In the following exercise, you'll set the global protection mode and then you'll unprotect the first of several input ranges on the worksheet:

1. Pull down the Worksheet menu and choose the Global Settings command. In the resulting dialog box, click the Protection check box or type **P** from the keyboard. An X appears inside the box. Click OK or press ↵ to confirm the selection.

2. Now that the worksheet is protected, try entering a new value into any cell. In response, 1-2-3 beeps and displays an error message. No new entry is accepted. In addition, you cannot preselect a range on the protected worksheet. An attempt to drag the mouse pointer over a range of cells results in a beep and an error message. Also notice that the format line displays *PR* for all cells in the protected worksheet.

3. Move the cell pointer to B4, the first cell in the range of general information about the conference, A:B4..A:B8. This is the first input range that you want to release from the protection mode.

4. Pull down the Range menu and choose the Unprotect command. The Range Unprotect dialog box appears on the screen, as shown in Figure 4.42. Because you were not able to preselect the range for this operation, you'll now use the pointing technique to enter a range into the Range box.

5. Press ↓ once. The Range Unprotect dialog box temporarily disappears from the screen. Press ↓ three more times to select the range A:B4..A:B8. Then press ↵ to confirm the range selection. When the dialog box reappears, the notation for this selection is displayed in the Range box.

6. Click OK or press ↵ to complete the Unprotect operation.

Now the range of general conference information is unprotected again. Two significant visual changes have taken place on the worksheet. First, the unprotected range is now displayed in blue (or gray on a black-and-white display). This is 1-2-3's way of highlighting an unprotected range on a protected worksheet. Second, the format line now displays *U* for each of the unprotected cells in the range. You can now try entering a new value into this range. Select cell B8 and enter a new price of $225.00. When you do so, 1-2-3 accepts your new entry and instantly recalculates all the worksheet formulas that depend on this value, just as it did before you established protection. (Change the value in B8 back to $195.00 before you move on to the next step.)

There are four more ranges of input data to release from protection; they are

A:E8..A:F8	The minimum and maximum attendance estimates
A:D13	The retail price of the conference video
A:E17..A:F20	The fixed expenses
A:D24..A:D26	The per-person variable expenses

These ranges all contain data entries that may need to be changed in a worksheet for a new conference. Use the Range Unprotect command now on each of these ranges in turn. When you complete these steps, the conference worksheet appears as shown in Figure 4.43.

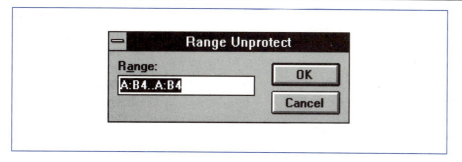

FIGURE 4.42:

The Range Unprotect dialog box

In summary, protection makes your worksheet a safer and more valuable tool for distribution to other users. By restricting new input to appropriate cells, a protection scheme insures the continued reliability of your formulas.

For now, deactivate the protection mode so that you can perform some additional tasks on the conference worksheet. Choose the Worksheet Global Settings command and uncheck the Protection option, then press ↵. When you do so, notice that the unprotected ranges are still displayed in blue (or gray), even though protection is off. If you later decide to restore the global protection mode, these unprotected ranges will resume their role as the worksheet's input cells.

USING COMMANDS IN THE STYLE MENU

Now it's time to put the finishing touches on the conference worksheet in preparation for printing a finished document. In this section, you'll examine 1-2-3's options for displaying, and ultimately printing, fonts, type styles, borders, lines, and shadings on your worksheet. All of these options are presented in the Style menu, although several of them also appear as tools in the default icon palette. Figure 4.44 identifies the bold, italics, underline, and outline icons. In the upcoming exercises, you'll practice using these icons and their equivalent commands in the Style menu itself.

FIGURE 4.43:

Unprotected ranges on the protected worksheet

	A	B	C	D	E	F
1			Computing Conferences, Inc.			
2			Profit Projection for a One-Day Conference			
3						
4	Conference:	Computing for Video Stores				
5	Place:	St. Louis				
6	Date:	15-Oct-92			Expected attendance:	
7					Minimum	Maxim
8	Price:	$195.00			80	
9						
10				Per Person	Min. Total	Max. T
11	Projected Revenues					
12		Attendance			$15,600.00	$29,25
13		Video Sales		$35.00	$1,400.00	$2,62
14		Total Revenues			$17,000.00	$31,87
15						
16	Projected Expenses – Fixed					
17		Conference room			$1,500.00	$2,00
18		Video production			$1,000.00	$1,00
19		Promotion			$3,500.00	$3,50
20		Travel			$800.00	$80

As you work with these effects, you may also want to insert new blank rows into your worksheet to improve the overall visual impact. This is the case in the conference worksheet. Before beginning your work with the commands in the Style menu, use the Insert command in the Worksheet menu to insert an additional blank row at each of the following five locations; at some of these places there will now be two blank rows:

◆ Below the worksheet's two-line title

◆ Below the row that contains the attendance price and the minimum and maximum attendance estimates

◆ Above the Total Revenues line

◆ Between the Total Revenues line and the fixed expenses subtitle

◆ Above the Projected Profit line

When you complete these five row insertions, your worksheet appears as in Figure 4.45. Figure 4.46 shows the changes you're going to make in this worksheet in the exercises ahead.

FONTS, TYPE STYLES, SHADINGS, AND BORDERS

Begin with the title lines at the top of the worksheet. To place emphasis on these two lines, you'll select a larger font size, display the text in combinations of bold and italics, apply a dark shading to the range, and add a shadowed border called a drop-shadow. Here are the steps you should follow:

1. Preselect the range A:B1..A:E2.

2. Pull down the Style menu and choose the Font command. The resulting dialog box, shown in Figure 4.47, contains two main groups of options—the Fonts list and a column of check boxes representing type styles. The Range box displays the notation for the range you have preselected.

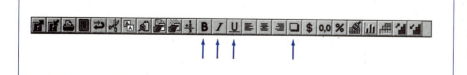

FIGURE 4.44:

The bold, italics, underline, and outline icons

3. Select the next larger font, down one entry from the current selection in the Fonts list. (The new selection is shown as Ariel MT 14 in Figure 4.46. This selection is four points larger than the default font.)

4. Check the Bold option.

5. Click the OK button or press ↵ to confirm your selections in the dialog box. Back on the worksheet, the display type of the titles is larger than before. To accommodate this larger point size, 1-2-3 has automatically increased the height of rows 1 and 2.

6. Without changing the range selection, pull down the Style menu and choose the Shading command. As you can see in Figure 4.48, a group of four option buttons appears in the dialog box, representing light, dark, and solid shading and a Clear instruction. Select the Dark option.

7. Click OK or press ↵ to confirm your shading selection.

	A	B	C	D	E	F
1			Computing Conferences, Inc.			
2			Profit Projection for a One-Day Conference			
3						
4						
5	Conference:	Computing for Video Stores				
6	Place:	St. Louis				
7	Date:	15-Oct-92		Expected attendance:		
8					Minimum	Maximum
9	Price:	$195.00			80	150
10						
11						
12				Per Person	Min. Total	Max. Total
13	Projected Revenues					
14		Attendance			$15,600.00	$29,250.00
15		Video Sales		$35.00	$1,400.00	$2,625.00
16						
17		Total Revenues			$17,000.00	$31,875.00
18						
19						
20	Projected Expenses -- Fixed					
21		Conference room			$1,500.00	$2,000.00
22		Video production			$1,000.00	$1,000.00
23		Promotion			$3,500.00	$3,500.00
24		Travel			$800.00	$800.00
25		Total Fixed Expenses			$6,800.00	$7,300.00
26						
27	Projected Expenses -- Variable by Attendance					
28		Conference materials		$8.25	$660.00	$1,237.50
29		Coffee and pastries		$3.25	$260.00	$487.50
30		Box lunch		$4.75	$380.00	$712.50
31		Total Variable Expenses			$1,300.00	$2,437.50
32						
33						
34	Projected Profit				$8,900.00	$22,137.50

FIGURE 4.45:

Inserting blank rows in the worksheet

8. Now click the outline icon in the icon palette. This puts a thin border around the selected range, and places a drop shadow behind the border.

9. Finally, select cell B2 and click the italics icon. (Keep in mind that the two title lines are actually stored in cells B1 and B2.)

After all these steps, the titles appear as in Figure 4.46.

Here are a few additional notes about the Style Font and Style Shading commands:

- Associated with the Underline check box in the Style Font dialog box, there is a drop-down list that offers three different underlining styles—thin line, double line, or bold line. To activate one of these choices, click the down-arrow icon to pull down the list (as in Figure 4.49) and then make your selection. Click the Underline option to place an X inside the check box.

FIGURE 4.46:

Changes in the worksheet's appearance

	A	B	C	D	E	F
1		Computing Conferences, Inc.				
2		Profit Projection for a One-Day Conference				
3						
4						
5	Conference:	Computing for Video Stores				
6	Place:	St. Louis				
7	Date:	15-Oct-92		Expected attendance:		
8					Minimum	Maximum
9	Price:	$195.00			80	150
10						
11						
12				Per Person	Min. Total	Max. Total
13	Projected Revenues					
14		Attendance			$15,600.00	$29,250.00
15		Video Sales		$35.00	$1,400.00	$2,625.00
16						
17		Total Revenues			$17,000.00	$31,875.00
18						
19						
20	Projected Expenses -- Fixed					
21		Conference room			$1,500.00	$2,000.00
22		Video production			$1,000.00	$1,000.00
23		Promotion			$3,500.00	$3,500.00
24		Travel			$800.00	$800.00
25		Total Fixed Expenses			$6,800.00	$7,300.00
26						
27	Projected Expenses -- Variable by Attendance					
28		Conference materials		$8.25	$660.00	$1,237.50
29		Coffee and pastries		$3.25	$260.00	$487.50
30		Box lunch		$4.75	$380.00	$712.50
31		Total Variable Expenses			$1,300.00	$2,437.50
32						
33						
34	Projected Profit				$8,900.00	$22,137.50

- The Style Font dialog box also has a Replace button for changing the current list of fonts in the Fonts list box. When you click Replace, the Style Font Replace dialog box appears on the screen. As you see in Figure 4.50, this dialog box displays the Current fonts list next to a longer, scrollable list of all the Windows and 1-2-3 fonts available on *your* system. To replace a font, click a font in the Current fonts list and then click the replacement font in the Available fonts list. Click a size for the new font in the Size list. Finally, click the Replace button to confirm the replacement. Clicking the Update button updates the *default font set* with your current font selection. Clicking the Restore button restores the current font selection from the default font list. Finally, the Save and Retrieve buttons allow you to create and read special-purpose font list files that you build yourself and store on disk with extension names of .AF3.

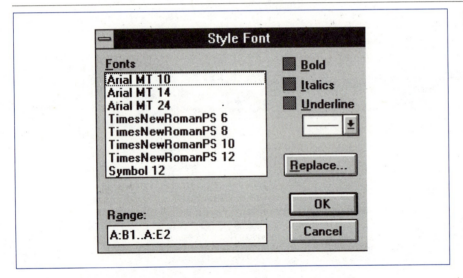

FIGURE 4.47:
The Style Font dialog box

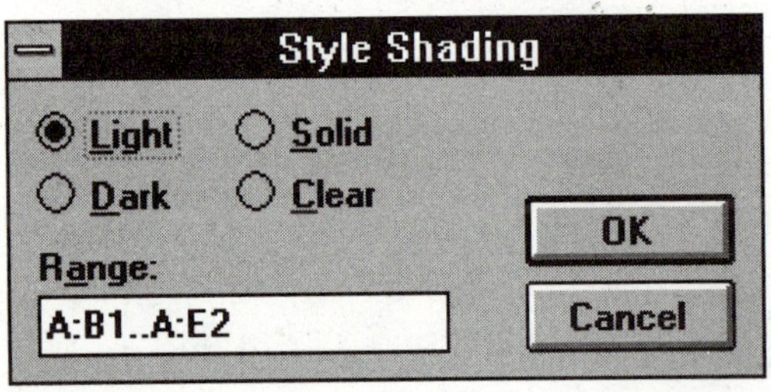

FIGURE 4.48:
The Style Shading dialog box

◆ As you have seen, 1-2-3 automatically increases the row height when you select a larger font than the current size. Alternatively, you can change the row height manually by choosing the Worksheet Row Height command, which produces the dialog box shown in Figure 4.51. Notice that the height of a row is measured in points, the same as the measurement for font sizes. You can also change the height of a row by dragging the row's lower border up or down with the mouse (in the left side of the worksheet frame).

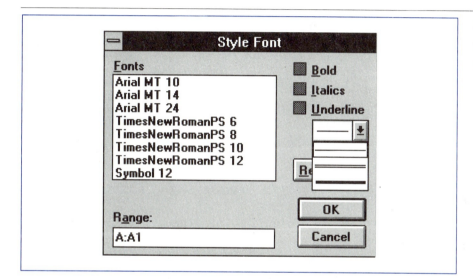

FIGURE 4.49:
The underline options in the Style Font dialog box

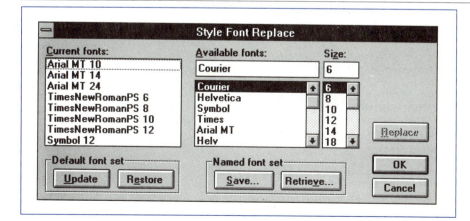

FIGURE 4.50:
The Style Font Replace dialog box

♦ The Style Shading command applies a shaded or solid color that matches the current Cell contents setting in the Window Display Options dialog box (see Figure 4.23). The default setting is black, which produces gray shadings or a solid black background.

Continue your work on the conference worksheet by applying the larger font, the bold style, the dark shading, and the drop-shadow border to the Projected Profit line in row 34, just as you did to the titles at the top of the worksheet. Then practice using the bold and italics icons in the following exercise:

1. Preselect the range A:A5..A:A27.

2. Click the bold icon. In response, 1-2-3 applies the boldface style to all the labels in the selected range.

3. Select cell B5. Click the bold icon, then click the italics icon. As a result, the conference name is displayed in boldface italics.

4. Following the styles displayed back in Figure 4.46, apply patterns of bold and italics to the appropriate ranges of cells throughout the worksheet.

Next, you'll use the Style Border command to draw horizontal lines between sections of the worksheet. As you can see in Figure 4.52, the command's dialog box contains a group of check boxes, each with its own drop-down box of line styles. To apply a line as a border on the worksheet, check the position where you want the line to appear within the current range selection, and then select the type of line—thin line, double line, or bold line—from the drop-down box. By the way, checking the Outline and Drop shadow options together on the Style Border dialog box is equivalent to clicking the outline icon.

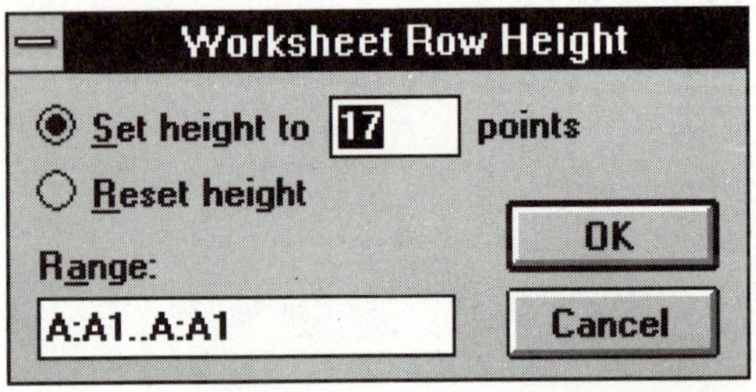

FIGURE 4.51:
The Worksheet Row Height dialog box

Here are the steps for drawing lines on the conference worksheet:

1. Preselect the row range A:A11..A:F11.
2. Pull down the Style menu and choose the Border command.
3. Select the Top option, and keep the default single-line selection.
4. Click OK or press ↵. Back on the worksheet, a horizontal line now separates the general conference information from the revenues section.
5. Now preselect A:A19..A:F19.
6. Once again, choose the Style Border command and click the Top option. After you confirm your selection by clicking OK, a second horizontal line appears on the worksheet, this time separating the revenues and expense sections.

As a final exercise with the tools of the Style menu, you'll next learn how to create a name—and a convenient selection method—for any frequently used style or combination of styles on your worksheet.

DEFINING STYLE NAMES

Using the Style Name command, you can add your own style names to the style menu itself. Each style name you add to the menu can represent a single

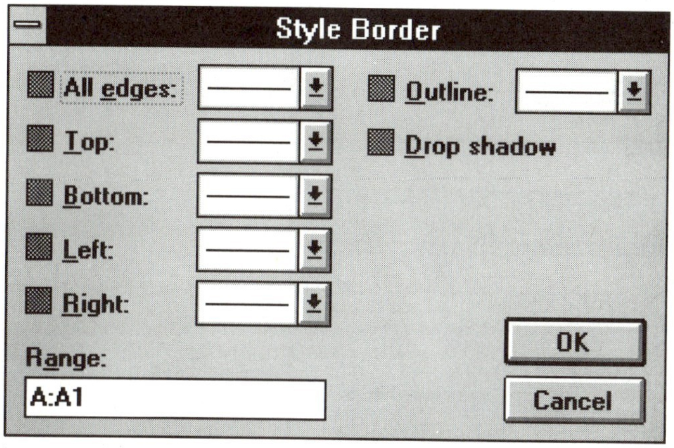

FIGURE 4.52:
The Style Border dialog box

style option, or a combination of style effects. The Style Name dialog box has room for as many as eight style names and descriptions. Here are the general steps for creating a new style name:

1. Using any combination of style icons or commands from the Style menu, apply one or more styles to a range on the worksheet.

2. Retaining this range as the current selection, pull down the Style menu and select the Name command. In the Style Name dialog box, shown in Figure 4.53, enter a name and description for the style you are defining. The name can contain up to six characters, and the description up to 36 characters.

3. Click OK or press ↵.

When you next pull down the Style menu, the style name you have defined appears as one of the numbered entries beneath the Name command. When you highlight the name of your style, the description you entered into the Description box on the Style Name dialog box appears on the title bar of the 1-2-3 window.

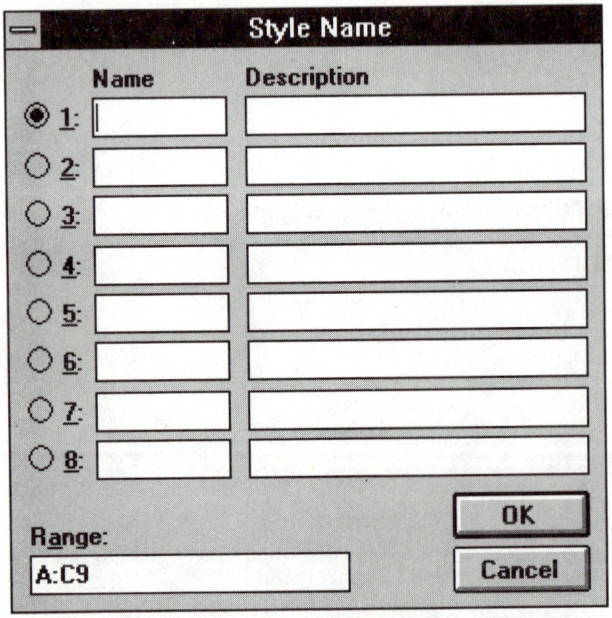

FIGURE 4.53:
The Style Name dialog box

Style names are defined independently for each worksheet file. You can therefore define the style names that are most useful for a given worksheet. As a simple example of a style name, try the following exercise on the conference worksheet:

1. Preselect the range A:B5..A:C9.

2. Pull down the Style menu and choose the Shading command. The Light option is selected by default; do not change this selection.

3. Click OK or press ↵. In response, 1-2-3 applies a light gray shading to the selected range, as shown back in Figure 4.46.

4. Now select cell C9, the bottom-right corner of this shaded range. (In this case, you are going to define a name to represent light shading alone. You therefore want to make sure that the cell you select does not have any other styles currently applied to it.)

5. Pull down the Style menu and choose the Name command.

6. In the first Name box of the Style Name dialog box, enter the name **LShade**. In the corresponding Description box, enter the text **Light shading**.

7. Click OK or press ↵ to confirm this definition.

8. Now preselect A:E9..A:F9, another range to which you want to apply the style shading.

9. Pull down the Style menu. Notice that your custom-defined style, LShade, is listed as entry 1 after the Name command (see Figure 4.54). Press ↓ until LShade is highlighted. In the 1-2-3 title bar, you will see the words *Light shading*, the text description you defined for your custom style.

10. Now press ↵ to choose LShade. The light shading effect is applied to the preselected range on the worksheet.

Now use this same technique to apply light shading to the other shaded areas shown in Figure 4.46—cell A:D15, and the ranges A:E21..A:F24 and A:D28..A:D30.

This completes your current work on the conference worksheet. As a further exercise with the commands of the Style menu, you might want to try applying a variety of styles and alignments to the discount and schedule worksheets (B and C). When you complete your work, click the save-file icon to update the CONF.WK3 file. In the next section, you'll learn about one further command in the Style menu—the Color command.

Applying Colors to the Worksheet

The Style Color command gives you the opportunity to display different sections of your worksheet in different colors. On a worksheet that is organized into sections, you can use colors to distinguish among the different sections. In the Style Color dialog box, shown in Figure 4.55, you can make a color selection for the labels or values displayed in a range (the Cell contents box) and another selection for the background. In addition, a check box labeled *Negative values in red* allows you to use color to distinguish between positive and negative values in a table of numbers.

The best way to gain an appreciation for the Color command is simply to experiment with it in a worksheet. Try the following exercise:

1. Pull down the File menu and choose the New command to open a new worksheet window for this exercise.

2. In cell A1, enter your name. In cell A2, enter your age as a numeric value. In cell A3, enter the negative value **–100**.

3. Preselect the range A1..B3.

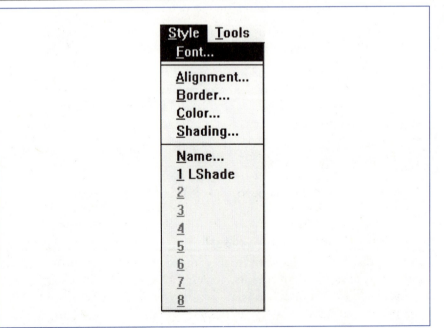

FIGURE 4.54:
The Style menu with a custom style name

4. Pull down the Style menu and choose the Color command. Click the down-arrow icon next to the Cell contents box. In the resulting drop-down list of colors (see Figure 4.56), click the dark blue box.

5. Click the down-arrow icon next to the Background box and select the light blue box in the resulting drop-down list. (This color is known as cyan.)

6. Click the Negative values in red option. An X appears in the check box.

7. Click OK or press ↵ to confirm your selections. On the worksheet, the entire selected range now has a light blue background. Your name

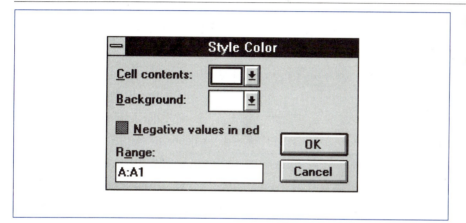

FIGURE 4.55:

The Style Color dialog box

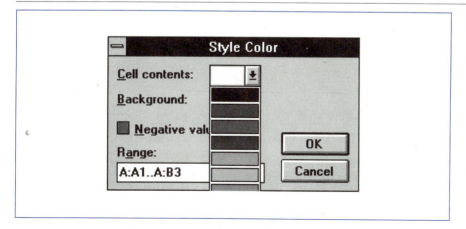

FIGURE 4.56:

Pulling down a color list

and age are displayed in dark blue, but the negative number in cell A3 is displayed in red.

8. Click the bold icon and then click the italics icon. As you can see, these options have the same effect on color text as they do on black text against a white background. The notation now displayed on the format line reads {*Bold Italics Dark-Blue / Cyan −*}. The minus sign at the end of this notation indicates that you have activated the Negative values in red option.

9. Use the Style Color command to experiment with other foreground and background color combinations.

10. When you complete this exercise, close the worksheet window without saving it.

It's easy to overdo colors on a worksheet. But with a little restraint, you can often use color to your advantage, clarifying the organization of your work and placing emphasis on particular ranges of labels and values.

In the final sections of this chapter, you'll study the commands that deal with printing the worksheet.

PRINTING THE WORKSHEET

All the special visual effects that you've created in this chapter can be printed on paper, assuming your printer has the appropriate capabilities. Before sending your worksheet to the printer, however, you'll want to take advantage of several options that affect the layout and content of the printed page. Once you've made selections among these options, printing the worksheet is as simple as clicking the print icon. Alternatively, you can see a screen *preview* of the printed page by clicking the preview icon first. When you take this intermediate step, 1-2-3 displays a preview like the one shown in Figure 4.57. Examining this screen, you can see the details of the document's layout without actually using paper.

The two icons related to the printing process—the print-range icon and the preview icon—are identified in Figure 4.58. In addition to these two convenient tools, there are four commands in the File menu and one in the Worksheet menu that deal directly with printing. In the final exercises of this chapter you'll learn the significance of these tools:

◆ The Printer Setup command (from the File menu) identifies the printer or printers you have installed in Windows, as shown in Figure 4.59. You can select the printer you want to use if two or more are shown in the Printers list box. In addition, clicking the Setup command button produces a Windows dialog box in which you can redefine the characteristics of the active printer. If you have only one printer attached to your computer and you have already successfully installed it for use in Windows, you will probably seldom need to use the File Printer Setup command.

◆ The Page Setup command produces the dialog box shown in Figure 4.60. In this box, you'll find several important groups of options that control the features of your printed worksheet.

◆ The Page Break command in the Worksheet menu allows you to specify exactly where the division will take place from one page to the next of your printed worksheet. As you can see in the Worksheet Page Break dialog box, displayed in Figure 4.61, you can add horizontal and/or vertical page breaks, or you can clear previously established page breaks. This command is useful in printing a long single worksheet, or in printing two or more sheets stored in a single worksheet file.

◆ The Preview command in the File menu displays a preview of the page or pages that will be printed from your worksheet. Choosing this command is the same as clicking the preview icon.

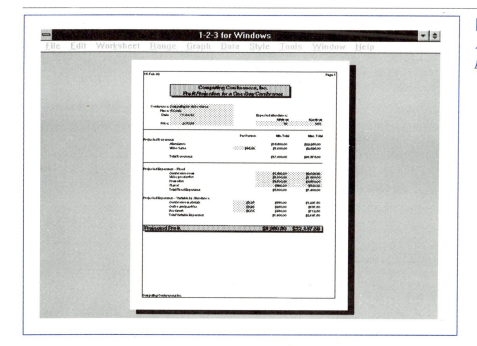

FIGURE 4.57:
A preview of the printed page

◆ Finally, the Print command produces the dialog box shown in Figure 4.62. In the Range(s) text box you can define one or more *print ranges*. These are the portions of your worksheet that will be included in the printed output. Back on the worksheet itself, 1-2-3 encloses these print ranges within a border of light dashed lines. File Print is one of a few 1-2-3 commands in which you can specify multiple worksheet ranges for a single operation. In addition, you can identify the range of pages that you want to print, and the page number to be printed on the first page of the print run.

These commands are intuitive and easy to use. However, the options of the Page Setup command require some additional explanation.

USING THE PAGE SETUP COMMAND

The File Page Setup dialog box (shown back in Figure 4.60) includes the tools you use to accomplish each of the following tasks in preparation for printing

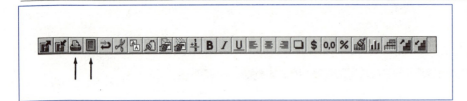

FIGURE 4.58:
The print-range icon and the preview icon

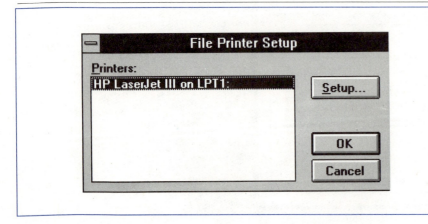

FIGURE 4.59:
The File Printer Setup dialog box

your worksheet:

- Creating a header and/or a footer
- Changing the page margins
- Specifying rows or columns of headings that will be printed on every page
- Compressing the print size so the worksheet will fit on a page, or expanding the size so the worksheet will fill up a page
- Optionally displaying the worksheet's column letters, row numbers, and grid lines
- Selecting a horizontal or vertical orientation on the page for the worksheet

You'll learn about each of these tasks in turn in the sections ahead.

Creating a Header and Footer

A header is a line of text that 1-2-3 prints at the top of each page of the worksheet. A footer is a line of text printed at the bottom. You enter the text of these elements into the Header and Footer boxes on the File Page Setup

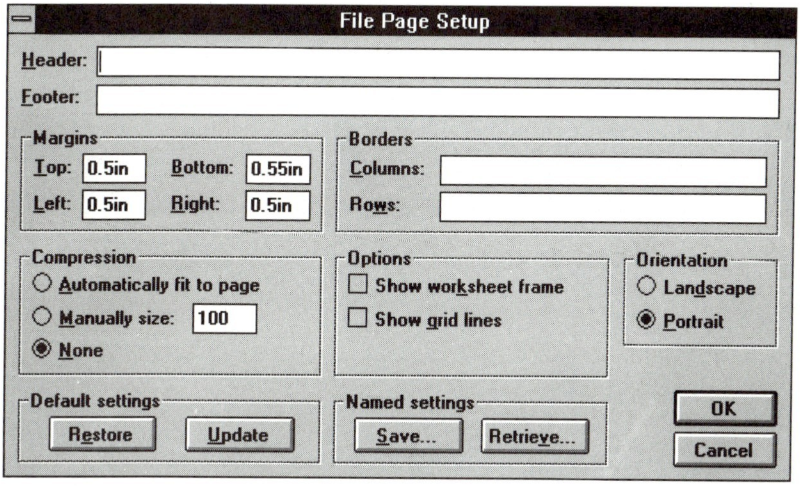

FIGURE 4.60:

The File Page Setup dialog box

dialog box. In addition to text, you can include three special code characters: the "at" character, @; the pound sign, #; and the backslash character, \. These characters represent items of information that 1-2-3 can supply in the header or footer:

- ◆ @ represents the current date.
- ◆ # represents the current page number. For example, you might include the following entry in either the Header or Footer box:

    Page #

- ◆ \ instructs 1-2-3 to print the contents of a specified cell on each printed page. Immediately following the backslash, you enter a reference to the cell address containing the information you want to print. For

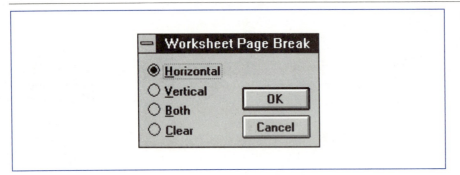

FIGURE 4.61:
The Worksheet Page Break dialog box

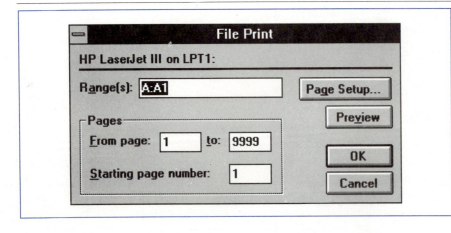

FIGURE 4.62:
The File Print dialog box

example, the following entry in the Header or Footer box instructs 1-2-3 to print the contents of cell B2 on each page:

\B2

The \ code cannot be combined with any other text or code in the Header or Footer box.

A fourth code that you can include in the Header or Footer text box is the vertical bar character, |. You use this character to separate the contents of the header or footer into three sections—left-aligned text, centered text, and right-aligned text. For example, the following header code displays a left-aligned date, a centered title, and a right-aligned page number:

@|Conference Planner|Page #

The resulting header might appear as:

> 11-Aug-92   Conference Planner   Page 5

To include centered text only, use one vertical bar character, as in this example:

|Conference Planner

To include right-aligned text only, use two vertical bar characters:

||Page #

Specifying Margins

The Margins frame in the File Page Setup dialog box contains four text boxes, labeled Top, Bottom, Left, and Right. Into these boxes you enter specific numeric measurements for the four margins of the printed page. By default, 1-2-3 assumes your entries are in inches. For example, if you enter **.75** into a box, 1-2-3 converts the entry into *0.75in*.

Alternatively, you can use metric measurements, expressed in millimeters or centimeters. To do so, include an abbreviation of **mm** or **cm** immediately after the number. However, 1-2-3 converts centimeter measurements into millimeters. For example, if you enter **.8cm** in all four margin boxes, 1-2-3 converts the entries to *8mm*.

Printing Headings on Every Page

When you print a long worksheet, you might want to include column headings or row labels from your worksheet on each page of the printout. For example, imagine a worksheet that has 500 rows of data, with column headings displayed in row 1. In the multiple-page printout of this worksheet, you would want the column headings from row 1 to appear at the top of each page. Conversely, imagine a worksheet containing dozens of columns, with row labels in column A. You would want the row labels to be repeated on each page of the printed worksheet.

To accomplish these effects, you enter references into the Columns and Rows boxes in the File Page Setup dialog box. (These two text boxes are enclosed in a frame labeled Borders.) If you want to specify one row or one column to be printed on each page, you enter a reference to a single cell located in the row or column. For example, a reference to A1 could serve to identify column A in the Columns box or row 1 in the Rows box. Enter a range if you want to print headings from multiple rows or columns. For example, if the column headings in your worksheet are displayed in rows 1 and 2, enter the range A1..A2.

Compressing or Expanding the Printed Worksheet

The Compression frame in the File Page Setup dialog box contains three option buttons that control a special printing feature. If you have a worksheet that doesn't quite fit on one printed page, you can instruct 1-2-3 to compress the printout to attempt to create a single page of output. Conversely, if a worksheet is too small for a page, you can instruct 1-2-3 to expand the printout by a percentage to attempt to fill the page.

The three option buttons are labeled Automatically fit to page, Manually size, and None. The default option, None, results in no compression or expansion. Select the first option, Automatically fit to page, if you want 1-2-3 to try to compress the printout down to a page.

Alternatively, select the Manually size option if you want to supply a specific percentage for compression or expansion. In this case, you supply a percentage in the corresponding text box. The default value of 100 produces no compression or expansion. A value below 100 compresses the printout. For example, enter a value of 50 to compress the worksheet size by half. (You can enter compression values from 15 to 99.) Enter a value of 200 to expand by a factor of 2. (You can enter expansion percentages from 101 to 1000.) Use the

File Preview command to view compressed or expanded worksheets before you send them to the printer. Finding just the right percentage usually takes some experimentation.

Printing Other Worksheet Elements

In some printouts you might want to include the column letters, row numbers, and grid lines from the worksheet. To do so, select one or both of the check boxes displayed in the Options frame of the File Page Setup dialog box. The first of these check boxes, labeled Show worksheet frame, refers to the column letters and row numbers. The second is labeled Show grid lines.

Look back at Figures 4.45 and 4.46 for examples of these options. For these printouts, both Show worksheet frame and Show grid lines were checked.

Selecting an Orientation for the Printout

By default, 1-2-3 prints the rows of your worksheet one by one down the length of the page, in a mode called Portrait orientation. An example of this default orientation appears in the preview screen back in Figure 4.57. In a table that contains many columns, you might prefer to print the rows of the worksheet sideways, across the length of the paper; this option is called the Landscape orientation.

The File Page Setup dialog box contains two option buttons, labeled Landscape and Portrait. These options control the orientation of your printout. Figure 4.63 shows a preview of the conference worksheet under the Landscape option.

After entering new settings into the File Page Setup dialog box, you can click the Update button to make your settings the default. Or, click the Restore button to restore the current defaults back to the dialog box. You can also use the Save and Retrieve buttons to create or read page setup files, containing specific layout settings. Lotus 1-2-3 saves such files with a default extension name of .AL3.

PRINTING THE CONFERENCE WORKSHEET

Figures 4.64 and 4.65 show the conference worksheet, the discount worksheet, and the schedule worksheet, printed together on two pages. These pages illustrate many of the options 1-2-3 offers you for controlling the layout of printed worksheets. In this chapter's final exercise, you'll follow through the steps of creating this printout yourself:

1. On worksheet A, use the mouse to reduce the width of column G to 2. (Because the drop shadow in the profit line intrudes slightly into column G, you'll include this narrowed column in the print range.)

2. Use the Range Name Create command to assign the name CONFERENCE to the range A:A1..A:G34.

3. Press Ctrl-PgUp to move the cell pointer to worksheet B, and select cell B:A1. Pull down the Worksheet menu and choose the Page Break command. Keeping the default Horizontal option selection, press ↵ to insert a page break at the top of worksheet B.

4. Use the Range Name Create command to assign the name DISCOUNT to the range B:A1..B:D17.

5. Press Ctrl-PgUp to move the cell pointer to worksheet C. Use the Range Name Create command to assign the name SCHEDULE to the range C:A1..C:E19. These three new range names—CONFERENCE, DISCOUNT, and SCHEDULE—will simplify the process of specifying a multiple print range, as you'll see in the next step.

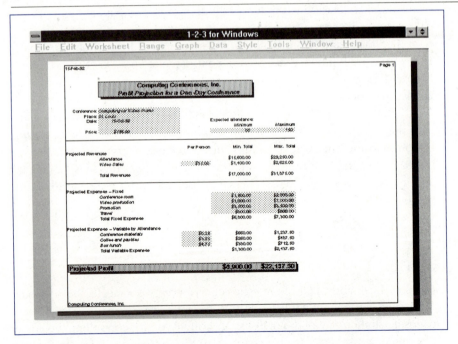

FIGURE 4.63:
The Landscape orientation option

6. Pull down the File menu and choose the Print command. In the Range(s) text box, enter the following three names as the multiple print range: **CONFERENCE;DISCOUNT;SCHEDULE**. Notice the use of the semicolon to separate one range reference from the next.

7. Now click the Page Setup command button in the File Print dialog box. The File Page Setup dialog box appears on the screen.

8. In the Header text box, enter the following coded information:

@||Page #

In the Footer text box, enter the code for printing the contents of a cell:

\A:B1

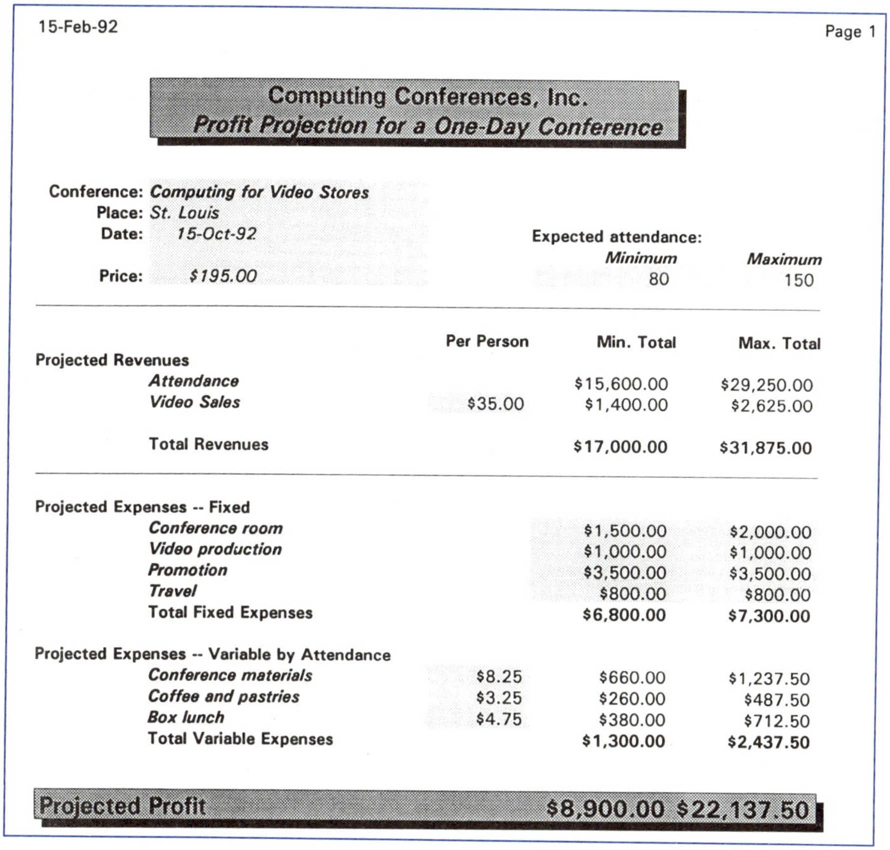

15-Feb-92 Page 1

Computing Conferences, Inc.
Profit Projection for a One-Day Conference

Conference: ***Computing for Video Stores***
Place: *St. Louis*
Date: *15-Oct-92*
Price: *$195.00*

Expected attendance:

	Minimum	*Maximum*
	80	150

	Per Person	Min. Total	Max. Total
Projected Revenues			
Attendance		$15,600.00	$29,250.00
Video Sales	$35.00	$1,400.00	$2,625.00
Total Revenues		**$17,000.00**	**$31,875.00**
Projected Expenses -- Fixed			
Conference room		$1,500.00	$2,000.00
Video production		$1,000.00	$1,000.00
Promotion		$3,500.00	$3,500.00
Travel		$800.00	$800.00
Total Fixed Expenses		**$6,800.00**	**$7,300.00**
Projected Expenses -- Variable by Attendance			
Conference materials	$8.25	$660.00	$1,237.50
Coffee and pastries	$3.25	$260.00	$487.50
Box lunch	$4.75	$380.00	$712.50
Total Variable Expenses		**$1,300.00**	**$2,437.50**
Projected Profit		**$8,900.00**	**$22,137.50**

FIGURE 4.64:
The Landscape orientation option

9. Click the Manually size option, and enter a value of **110** into the corresponding text box. This setting results in a slightly enlarged printed worksheet.

10. Click OK or press ↵ to complete the Page Setup operation.

11. Back in the File Print dialog box, click the Preview button. When the preview screen appears, examine the page layout you are about to print. Press the PgDn key to view page 2 of the upcoming printout.

12. Press Escape to close the preview. Then click the print icon to print the worksheet. The results are shown in Figure 4.64 and 4.65.

When you print your worksheet for the first time, you may find that the output is not exactly what you expected it to be—even if the display

FIGURE 4.65:

The printed worksheet, page 2

15-Feb-92

Discount Schedule for Advance Enrollment

Conference: *Computing for Video Stores*
Place: *St. Louis*
Date: *15-Oct-92*

Price: *$195.00*

If paid by:	Discount	Price
17-Jul-92	20%	$156.00
31-Aug-92	10%	$175.50

Conference Schedule

Conference: *Computing for Video Stores*
Place: *St. Louis*
Date: *15-Oct-92*

Event	Start time	Minutes
Coffee and pastries	07:00 AM	45
Introduction	07:45 AM	30
Managing a Video Database	08:15 AM	90
Coffee break	09:45 AM	15
Managing a Customer Database	10:00 AM	90
Hands-on demonstrations	11:30 AM	60
Lunch and discussion	12:30 PM	60
Setting Up a Computer System	01:30 PM	120
Coffee break	03:30 PM	30
Software Options	04:00 PM	60
No-host cocktail hour	05:00 PM	60

from the File Preview command seemed correct. You may have to experiment with small adjustments in various settings to achieve the results you want. For example, you might need to make some changes in the File Page Setup dialog box, specifically in the margin settings and the Manually size value. Furthermore, if some values do not print out properly, you might need to increase selected column widths on your worksheet. In the end, the best approach to refining the appearance of the printed page is to experiment with the commands and options you've learned about in this chapter.

SUMMARY

In this chapter, you've worked extensively with commands in four different menus—Worksheet, Range, Style, and File.

The Worksheet menu contains commands that you use to apply global property settings to the current worksheet. In particular, the Worksheet Global Settings dialog box contains tools for setting the width of all columns on the worksheet, selecting a global alignment, protecting the entire worksheet from inadvertent data entries, and determining whether multiple worksheets in a file will all share the same formatting characteristics (the Group mode option). In addition, the Worksheet Global Settings Format dialog box allows you to select a default format for all numeric values on a worksheet.

The Worksheet menu also has commands that apply to selected rows and columns on the worksheet. These include the Hide command, which hides one or more columns from view, and the Unhide command, which brings hidden columns back into view. The Column Width and Row Height commands allow you to adjust the dimensions of columns and rows. And, the Titles command can be used to freeze a range of rows or columns on the screen so that they remain in view even when you scroll the worksheet.

The Range menu contains important commands that change the properties of selected ranges on the worksheet. The Format command contains a list of formats available for displaying not only numeric values, but also date and time values. The Range command also has two options that represent unique data-entry modes—Label and Automatic. These two formats affect only values that you enter *after* you select the format. Under the Label format, 1-2-3 accepts new numeric entries as labels. In the Automatic mode, 1-2-3 applies a format to a cell, corresponding to the format of your actual value entry.

The Range menu's Unprotect command releases selected ranges from the global protection mode. The Range Go To command is a useful tool for moving the cell pointer to any cell address or named range on the worksheet.

The Style menu contains commands that dramatically change the visual properties of a worksheet. In the Style Font dialog box, you can select a display font and choose combinations of bold, italic, and underlined type styles. The Alignment command offers left-alignment, centering, and right-alignment, which can be applied over a single cell or a horizontal range of cells. The Border command creates lines, borders, and drop-shadow effects on the worksheet. The Color and Shading commands allow you to highlight sections of your worksheet with distinct background and foreground effects.

When you have established all these properties to your own satisfaction, it is time to print the worksheet. The File menu contains four commands involved in printing: The Printer Setup command provides a list of Windows-installed printers; in the File Print dialog box you establish one or more print ranges; the Page Setup command offers tools for creating headers and footers, setting margins, printing headings on every page, and compressing or expanding the worksheet to fit a page; finally, the Preview command allows you to view the layout of your worksheet on the screen before you actually send the document to the printer.

FAST TRACK

To fill a worksheet range with a sequential series of numbers, ... 239

preselect a range on the worksheet and choose the Data Fill command. Enter appropriate values into the Start, Step, and Stop boxes to define the numeric sequence.

To find the number of days between two dates, ... 244

enter the dates in two different cells, using one of the date formats that 1-2-3 recognizes. Then write a formula that subtracts one of the resulting date numbers from the other.

To write a logical formula or expression, ... 246

use the relational operators =, <>, <, >, <=, and >=, and/or the logical operators #NOT#, #AND#, and #OR#.

To join two strings or labels in a text formula, ... 249

use the & text operator.

To view a list of all the 1-2-3 functions, ... 254

select a cell where you want to enter a function and type the @ character. Then press the F3 function key to view the @Function Names dialog box.

To view the Help topic for a particular function, ... 254

press the F1 function key after entering the function's name into the Edit box.

To convert a formula to its current value before completing the formula entry, ... 276

press the F9 function key while the formula is still in the Edit box.

**To convert a range of existing formulas into their
current values,** 276

    preselect the range, and choose the Edit Quick Copy command. Check the option labeled Convert to values.

To find the day of the week for a date number, ...280

    use the formula @MOD(*date*,7). This formula produces an integer from 0 to 6 for the days from Saturday to Friday.

To convert the alphabetic case of a string, ...293

    use the @PROPER, @UPPER, and @LOWER functions.

To convert a number to a string, ...296

    use the @STRING function.

To convert a string of digits to a number, ...297

    use the @VALUE function.

**To generate a three-character abbreviation for
the day of the week,** 298

    use the following formula on a date number:

        @CHOOSE(@MOD(*date*,7),"Sat","Sun","Mon","Tue", "Wed","Thu","Fri")&"."

**To find a value in a lookup table on your
worksheet,** 300

    use the @HLOOKUP and @VLOOKUP functions.

CHAPTER 5

Worksheet Formulas and Functions

riting formulas is the creative part of your work with the 1-2-3 spreadsheet. Without your precise and detailed instructions—which you express in formulas—a worksheet can do nothing. Formulas are responsible for establishing the relationships among data items, supplying the steps of operations, producing new values and labels, and defining the structure of your worksheet.

Depending upon the tasks you want the worksheet to accomplish, the formulas you write can be succinct and straightforward, or painstakingly complex. To simplify the task of writing formulas, Lotus 1-2-3 has a library of over a hundred *functions* that you can use within formulas—or, in many cases, as substitutes for formulas. A function is a predefined calculation or operation, represented by a specific name that denotes the function's role in the worksheet. All function names in 1-2-3 begin with @, the "at" character.

Up to now you've seen a single function example—the @SUM function, which you entered into the conference worksheet to find the total of a column of numbers. Like @SUM, many of the 1-2-3 functions are designed to replace formulas that you would otherwise have to write yourself. For instance, imagine that you want to calculate the monthly payment for a fixed-rate bank loan, for which you know the principal, interest rate, and term in years. You enter these three loan parameters into a column of your worksheet, and you assign the range names PRINCIPAL, RATE, and TERM to the three cells that contain the data. Next, you need to enter the formula for calculating the monthly payment on the loan.

Few people can produce the formula for this loan calculation from memory. But you could look it up in a business mathematics book, and then carefully enter the formula into a cell of your worksheet. The entry would look something like this:

(PRINCIPAL*RATE/12)/(1−(1+RATE/12)^(−TERM*12))

This formula successfully calculates the monthly payment, but at a considerable cost of time and effort on your part. Fortunately, 1-2-3 offers a much simpler approach for this commonly performed calculation. The formula for finding a monthly loan payment is available as the function named @PMT. Using this function, you can calculate the loan payment without having to concern yourself with the details of the formula itself. Here is how you would enter the @PMT function:

@PMT(PRINCIPAL,RATE/12,TERM*12)

The three loan parameters appear as the *arguments* of the @PMT function. An argument is a value you supply for a function to work with. In order to calculate the *monthly* payment amount, you express the rate and the term as monthly values; for this reason, two of the arguments you send to the @PMT function appear as calculated values. As you can see, this use of the @PMT function is a lot simpler than the equivalent loan-payment formula.

Other functions are designed to perform specific data operations. The effect of these functions is to give you broader options and greater flexibility for the design of your worksheet. For example, you can use the @HLOOKUP function to select values from a *look-up table,* a collection of numeric data items organized like an income tax table. Using this function, a formula can read appropriate data items from a two-dimensional data table that you've entered in a range of the worksheet.

In short, functions simplify your work and expand the range of tasks you can perform on a worksheet. In this chapter, you'll see examples of @PMT and @HLOOKUP, along with dozens of other functions in several categories.

As you proceed through this chapter, you'll find many individiual exercises designed to help you understand specific formulas and functions. As a quick technique for supplying sample data in some of these exercises, you'll use a special command called Fill from the Data menu. The Data Fill command enters a sequence of numbers into a selected range on your worksheet. Following your specifications, each number in a Data Fill sequence is a fixed amount greater than or less than the number before it. Here is an introductory exercise with the Data Fill command:

1. On a blank worksheet, preselect the range A1..A10.

2. Pull down the Data menu and choose the Fill command. The dialog box shown in Figure 5.1 appears on the screen. Notice the four text boxes: The Range box displays the notation for your preselected range. The Start box displays the first value in the sequence of numbers that Data Fill will enter into the range; this value is 0 by default. The Step box shows the increment for each subsequent value in the sequence; it is 1 by default. The Stop box shows the maximum value in the sequence. This last value is relevant only if the preselected range is large enough to display the entire sequence, up to the maximum value. Otherwise, Data Fill stops the sequence when the preselected range is full.

3. Click OK or press ↵ to accept all the defaults. The Data Fill command enters a sequence of integers from 0 to 9 in the preselected range, as you can see in Figure 5.2.

4. Preselect the two-dimensional range C2..E6, and then choose the Data Fill command again. Type a value of **5** in the Step box. Click OK or press ↵. In this case, Data Fill enters a sequence of values from 0 to 70, incremented by 5, into the three columns of your preselected range (see Figure 5.2).

5. Preselect the horizontal range A12..F12. Choose the Data Fill command one more time and enter a value of **-.75** into the Step box. Then insert a minus sign before the number in the Stop box. Click OK or press ↵. Each value in the resulting sequence is a fractional amount less than the previous value.

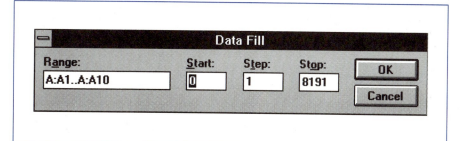

FIGURE 5.1:

The Data Fill dialog box

6. When you have examined the result of your work, close the worksheet without saving.

As you can see by studying all three examples in Figure 5.2, the Data Fill command is a simple but versatile way of entering an evenly incremented or decremented sequence of numbers into a range on your worksheet. You'll use this command in several of the exercises in this chapter.

WRITING FORMULAS

As you've learned, formulas contain a variety of elements, including:

- Literal data values such as 3.14 or 1000
- Operators such as + or −
- Functions such as @SUM or @PMT
- References to cell or range addresses such as A1, $C$5, or $B$3..$K$7; or range names that you have defined to represent particular cells or ranges on your worksheet

Lotus 1-2-3 recognizes any one of several characters as the beginning of a formula entry. For example, the plus sign (+) often begins a formula that starts with a reference to a cell address, as you saw in Chapters 3 and 4. Here are

	A	B	C	D	E	F
1	0					
2	1		0	25	50	
3	2		5	30	55	
4	3		10	35	60	
5	4		15	40	65	
6	5		20	45	70	
7	6					
8	7					
9	8					
10	9					
11						
12	0	-0.75	-1.5	-2.25	-3	-3.75
13						

FIGURE 5.2:
Entering sequences of numbers into selected ranges on the worksheet

the most common ways to begin formulas in 1-2-3:

- When the first element of a formula is a number, the formula can begin with a digit from 0 to 9, an optional plus sign (+), a minus sign (−), or a decimal point (.). If the first element is a positive numeric value, you can begin the formula with the first digit of the number, from 0 to 9. For example, the formula 365*A5 multiplies a positive number by the value stored in cell A5. You can begin this same formula with an optional plus sign, but 1-2-3 drops the + from the formula after you press ↵. When a formula begins with a negative number, you type a minus sign to start the formula, as in −19*C2. If the first element is a decimal value, you can begin the formula with a decimal point, but 1-2-3 makes some changes in the format of your entry after you press ↵. For example, you can enter a formula as .123*B1. But once you complete the entry, the formula appears in the contents box as *0.123*B1*. If the decimal value is very small, 1-2-3 converts the number to scientific format. For example, consider the formula .0000123*B1. After you press ↵ to complete this entry, 1-2-3 changes the format of this number to *1.23E-05*B1*.

- A plus sign or a minus sign is required as the first character of a formula that begins with an address reference. For example, the formula +E19*10 instructs 1-2-3 to multiply the value in cell E19 by 10. The formula −E19*10 multiplies the result by −1. After you type either the plus sign or the minus sign, you can type the address reference directly from the keyboard or you can use a pointing technique to enter the address.

- An initial @ character indicates that a formula begins with one of 1-2-3's built-in functions. A function can appear by itself as the complete entry in a cell, or a function name can be one of several elements in a formula. For example, the following function finds the sum of a range of values:

@SUM(C5..C10)

The following formula multiplies the sum by 25:

@SUM(C5..C10)*25

In both cases, the result of the function or the calculation appears in the cell where you enter the formula.

- Any formula can begin with an open parenthesis character. As you learned in Chapter 3, you can use parentheses to enclose operations in a formula when you want to override 1-2-3's default order of operations. For example, the formula (A1+A2)*5 adds two numbers together and then multiplies the sum by 5.

Here are two more important facts to keep in mind as you write formulas: First, a formula entry should contain no spaces. (The exception to this rule is for *string* values that appear within quotation marks; you'll learn about strings later in this chapter.) Usually, 1-2-3 eliminates any spaces from a formula when you complete the entry. But to be safe you should learn to avoid pressing the Spacebar while you are typing the elements of a formula.

Second, you can include a short note or comment at the end of a formula to help you remember what the formula does. To place a note at the end of a formula, type a semicolon (;) immediately after the formula itself and then type your note; for example, you might type

@PMT(PRINCIPAL,RATE/12,TERM*12); The monthly payment.

When you later examine the formula, your note appears along with the formula in the contents box at the top of the 1-2-3 window. This is an important feature, especially in a complicated worksheet that contains many formulas. Writing notes and comments is a simple way to *document* the structure of the worksheet, so that you can later review how you've organized your work. Ultimately, this kind of documentation makes it easier to revise a worksheet if you ever want to change the way your formulas operate.

By the way, a formula entry—along with a note or comment—can be as long as 512 characters. You are unlikely ever to reach this maximum, even if you write extensive comments along with your formulas.

Understanding Categories of Formulas

A formula in 1-2-3 can perform several types of operations:

- Calculate a numeric value.
- Perform date or time arithmetic.
- Evaluate a logical condition—that is, an expression that is either true or false.
- Build a label or a text display.

You've already written formulas that perform some of these operations. In the upcoming sections, you'll further examine each kind of formula.

Numeric Formulas

You've seen examples of the four most common numeric *operations*—addition, subtraction, multiplication, and division—and the *operators* that represent them: +, −, *, and /. (Note the distinction between these two terms: An operation is a calculation that 1-2-3 performs; an operator is a character or symbol that represents the operation in a formula.) You've also seen the use of plus and minus signs to represent positive and negative values or references.

Lotus 1-2-3 has another numeric operation known as *exponentiation*. Given a base value x and an exponent y, this operation finds x to the power of y. In 1-2-3, exponentiation is represented by ^, the caret symbol. For example, consider the formula +A1^3. If A1 contains a value of 5, this formula results in 125, or 5 to the power of 3. The exponent can also be fractional, in which case exponentiation produces a root value; for example, the formula +A1^(1/4) finds the fourth root of the value in A1. To try this formula on your worksheet, enter a value of **2401** in cell A1, then enter **+A1^(1/4)** in cell A2. The result displayed in A2 is 7.

In the order of operations followed by 1-2-3, exponentiation has the highest precedence—that is, exponentiation is performed before any other numeric operation. Here is the complete list of numeric operations, in their order of precedence:

1. Exponentiation (^)

2. Positive and negative signs (+ and −)

3. Multiplication and division (* and /)

4. Addition and subtraction (+ and −)

As you know, parentheses override this order of precedence. For example, given the formula +A1^(1/4), 1-2-3 performs the division before the exponentiation.

In 1-2-3, the operations of date and time arithmetic are treated as numeric formulas, even though the results displayed on the worksheet appear to be very different from numbers. You began exploring the elements of date and time arithmetic in Chapter 4. In the upcoming section of this chapter, you'll see some further examples.

Date and Time Formulas

In the discount worksheet that you developed in Chapter 4, you subtracted 90 days and 45 days from a conference date to calculate two different payment due dates. Similarly, on the schedule worksheet you added the length in minutes of each conference activity to the starting time, to calculate the starting time for the next activity. Review these two operations by looking back at Figures 4.37 and 4.40. Both involve adjusting individual chronological values (dates or times) by a fixed amount of elapsed time (days or minutes) to produce a new chronological value.

Another important operation finds the difference between two chronological values. Specifically, you can subtract one date from another in a worksheet:

+DATE1–DATE2

This formula gives the number of days between the two dates. This result is a positive value if DATE1 is later on the calendar than DATE2, or a negative value if DATE1 is earlier on the calendar. You might want to find the difference between two dates in a variety of business contexts. For example, on a customer billing worksheet you might calculate the number of days a customer takes to pay your invoices—that is, the difference between the billing date and the payment date. On an employee worksheet, you might want to know the number of days that have elapsed since an employee's last evaluation, or the number of days since the employee was hired.

You can also subtract one time value from another, with this formula:

+TIME1–TIME2

This formula gives the elapsed time, expressed as a decimal fraction. You'll recall that a time number in 1-2-3 is a decimal that represents a portion of a 24-hour day. Again, the result of the subtraction is positive if TIME1 is later than TIME2, or negative if TIME1 is earlier than TIME2. One common use for this operation is to determine the length of time spent on a given task or project.

The following exercise helps you experiment with these two important chronological operations:

1. On a blank worksheet, preselect the range A1..B5. Choose the Range Format command, and select the first date format (31-Dec-90) from the Format list. Click OK to confirm.

2. Preselect the range A1..A5. Choose the Data Fill command. Enter **33800** in the Start box, **7** in the Step box, and **34000** in the Stop box. Click OK or press ↵. As a result, a sequence of dates from 15-Jul-92 to 12-Aug-92 appears in the selected range on the worksheet.

3. Enter today's date in cell B1. Use the 31-Dec-90 date format for the entry. Then use the range-copy icon to copy the date down column B, to the range B2..B5.

4. Enter the formula **+A1-B1** into cell C1. The result displayed in C1 is the number of days between the dates in A1 and B1. Use the range-copy icon again to copy this formula down column C, to the range C2..C5. The upper half of the worksheet in Figure 5.3 shows the result. Of course, the number of days displayed in column C on your own worksheet depends upon the date you enter in column B.

5. Preselect the range A8..B12 on the same worksheet. Choose the Range Format command and select the second time format (11:59 AM) from the Format list. Click OK.

6. Preselect the range A8..A12. Choose the Data Fill command. Type **.25** in the Start box, **.125** in the Step box, and **1** in the Stop box. Click OK or press ↵. As a result, a sequence of time values from *6:00 AM* to *6:00 PM* appears in the selected range.

7. Enter the current time in cell B8, and then use the range-copy icon to copy this time value down column B, to the range B8..B12.

8. Enter the formula **(A8–B8)*24** into cell C8. The result displayed in C8 is the number of hours elapsed between the two time values in A8 and B8. (Do you see why the formula multiplies the difference by 24 in order to calculate the elapsed time in hours?) Copy this formula down column C, to the range C9..C12. The lower half of the worksheet in Figure 5.3 shows the result. Again, your own worksheet will differ according to the time value you entered in column B.

9. Close the worksheet without saving after you have completed the exercise.

Study Figure 5.3 carefully and make sure you understand the two operations represented in the worksheet. Later in this chapter you'll examine other chronological operations, represented by 1-2-3's built-in date and time functions.

Logical Formulas

The purpose of a *logical formula* is to determine whether a particular condition is true or false. A condition is typically expressed as a relationship between two or more data values on a worksheet. As the result of a logical formula, 1-2-3 generates a numeric value:

◆ A value of 1 represents *true*.

◆ A value of 0 represents *false*.

To build logical formulas, you use 1-2-3's *relational* and *logical operators*. The six relational operators express relationships of equality or inequality between pairs of numbers. These operators are as follows:

= means "is equal to"

<> means "is not equal to"

< means "is less than"

> means "is greater than"

<= means "is less than or equal to"

>= means "is greater than or equal to"

	A	B	C
1	15-Jul-92	15-Feb-92	151
2	22-Jul-92	15-Feb-92	158
3	29-Jul-92	15-Feb-92	165
4	05-Aug-92	15-Feb-92	172
5	12-Aug-92	15-Feb-92	179
6			
7			
8	06:00 AM	07:15 AM	-1.25
9	09:00 AM	07:15 AM	1.75
10	12:00 PM	07:15 AM	4.75
11	03:00 PM	07:15 AM	7.75
12	06:00 PM	07:15 AM	10.75
13			

FIGURE 5.3:
Experiments with date and time arithmetic

Here is an example of a logical formula that compares the values stored in cells A1 and B1:

+A1<B1

This formula results in a value of 1 (true) if the number stored in A1 is less than the number stored in B1; or a value of 0 (false) if the number in A1 is greater than or equal to the number in B1.

The three logical operators available in 1-2-3 are represented as #NOT#, #AND#, and #OR#. Note that each of these operators is always enclosed within a pair of number signs. The #AND# and #OR# operators are *binary,* meaning that they are each designed to work with two logical values. The #NOT# operator is *unary;* its role is to modify the result of a single logical value. In the following descriptions, VAL1 and VAL2 are names of cells containing logical values of true or false:

- The expression #NOT#VAL1 results in the opposite value of VAL1. If VAL1 is true, #NOT#VAL1 is false; if VAL1 is false, #NOT#VAL1 is true. (Note that you can begin the entry of a logical formula with the # character if the formula begins with the #NOT# operator.)

- The expression +VAL1#AND#VAL2 is true if both VAL1 and VAL2 are true. If either VAL1 or VAL2 is false—or if both are false—the #AND# expression is also false.

- +VAL1#OR#VAL2 is true if either VAL1 or VAL2 is true, or if both are true. If both VAL1 and VAL2 are false, the #OR# expression is also false.

Here is an example of a logical formula that uses the #AND# operator:

+B1>A1#AND#B2>A2

This formula results in a value of 1 (true) if both of the relations are true—that is, if the value in B1 is greater than the value in A1 *and* the value in B2 is greater than the value in A2. If one or both of the two relations are false, the formula itself results in a value of 0 (false). You'll see additional examples in the upcoming exercise.

Logical formulas are often useful as entries in a worksheet, especially in a database application. In addition, logical expressions appear as arguments in a 1-2-3 function named @IF. As you'll learn later in this chapter, the @IF function chooses between two values, depending upon the result of a logical expression.

Here is an exercise that demonstrates the results of logical formulas:

1. On a blank worksheet, enter the following six integers in the range A1..B3: **73** in A1, **53** in A2, **1** in A3, **0** in B1, **94** in B2, and **32** in B3. In addition, enter the following labels in column A, from A5 through A10:

   A1 less than B1.
   A2 greater than or equal to B2.
   Opposite of B1.
   Opposite of A3.
   All values in B greater than values in A.
   Any value in B greater than value in A.

2. Preselect the range A5..D10. Click the bold icon to display the six labels in boldface. Choose the Style Alignment command, check the Align over columns option, and click the Right option. Click OK or press ↵.

3. Enter the following logical formulas into column E, from E5 to E10:

   +A1<B1
   +A2>=B2
   #NOT#B1
   #NOT#A3
   +B1>A1#AND#B2>A2#AND#B3>A3
   +B1>A1#OR#B2>A2#OR#B3>A3

Figure 5.4 shows the results. You can see that each of these six logical formulas has produced a value of 1 or 0, representing true or false. For comparison, Figure 5.5 shows the same worksheet with the range E5..E10 displayed in the Text format, so you can see the formulas themselves. Study each formula, and make sure you understand why it produces the value it does.

You'll learn more about logical values when you study 1-2-3's built-in logical functions later in this chapter.

All the formulas you've written up to now have resulted in numeric values. Even though the date, time, and logical formulas produce results that have special nonnumeric *meanings,* the results are numeric nonetheless. In the next section, you'll learn that 1-2-3 also recognizes formulas that produce labels, or *text* values.

Text Formulas

A text formula combines two or more labels to produce a new text value. Lotus 1-2-3 has one text operation, represented by the & (ampersand) character. The & operator joins two text values. The 1-2-3 documentation refers to & as the *text operator,* but in other software packages you may know of this operation as *concatenation.*

The text data items joined together in a text formula may include any of the following:

- References to cells that contain labels. As always, a cell reference can appear as an address or a range name.

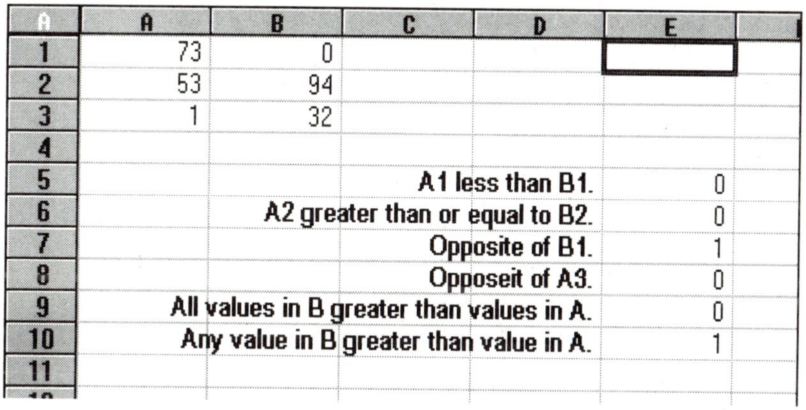

FIGURE 5.4:
An exercise with logical formulas

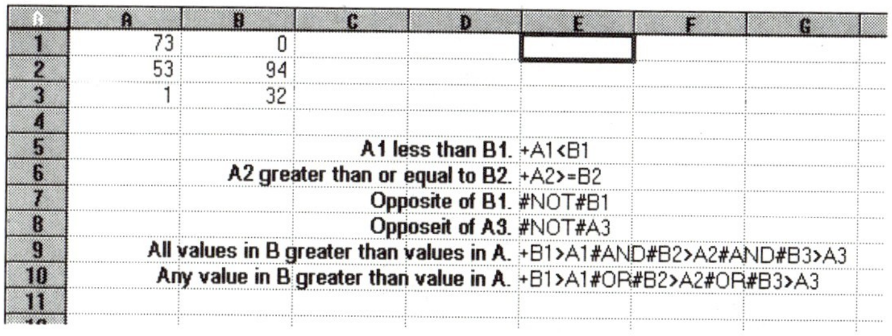

	A	B	C	D	E
1	73	0			
2	53	94			
3	1	32			
4					
5				A1 less than B1.	0
6			A2 greater than or equal to B2.		0
7				Opposite of B1.	1
8				Opposeit of A3.	0
9		All values in B greater than values in A.			0
10		Any value in B greater than value in A.			1
11					

FIGURE 5.5:
A display of the formulas themselves

	A	B	C	D	E	F	G
1	73	0					
2	53	94					
3	1	32					
4							
5				A1 less than B1.	+A1<B1		
6				A2 greater than or equal to B2.	+A2>=B2		
7				Opposite of B1.	#NOT#B1		
8				Opposeit of A3.	#NOT#A3		
9			All values in B greater than values in A.		+B1>A1#AND#B2>A2#AND#B3>A3		
10			Any value in B greater than value in A.		+B1>A1#OR#B2>A2#OR#B3>A3		
11							

- *Literal strings*—that is, sequences of characters enclosed in double quotation marks
- Built-in 1-2-3 functions that produce text values

Each data item in a text formula is joined to the previous item by the & operator. For example, the following formula joins labels stored in cells A1 and A2 with a literal string value:

+A1&" and "&A2

Note that the formula begins with a plus sign, just like a numeric formula. Also notice the blank spaces enclosed within the quotation marks; this is the one place where spaces are legal in a 1-2-3 formula.

Here is a brief exercise with a text formula:

1. On a blank worksheet, enter the labels from the first several lines of the conference worksheet, as shown in rows 1 through 5 of Figure 5.6.

2. In cell A7, enter the following text formula:

   +B1&", invites you to attend "&B4&" in "&B5&"."

   As usual, you can use the pointing technique to enter the cell references into the formula. Figure 5.6 shows the result of this formula—a sentence displayed across row 7.

3. Change the label in cell B4 to **Computing for Lawyers**. Then change the label in cell B5 to **New York**. After each one of these changes, 1-2-3 recalculates the value of the text formula in cell A7. The result is shown in Figure 5.7.

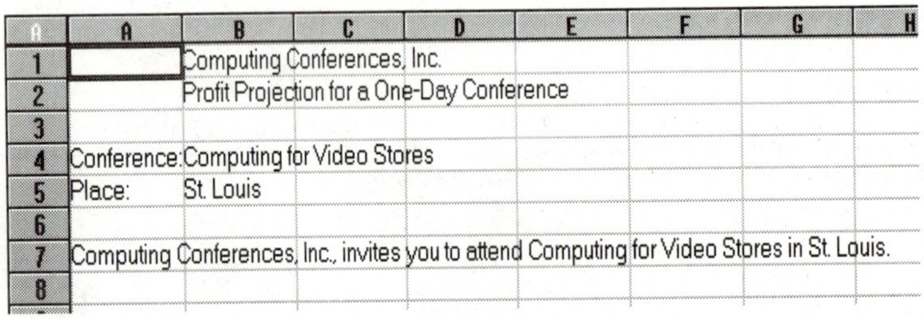

FIGURE 5.6:
Entering a text formula

	A	B	C	D	E	F	G	H
1		Computing Conferences, Inc.						
2		Profit Projection for a One-Day Conference						
3								
4	Conference:	Computing for Video Stores						
5	Place:	St. Louis						
6								
7	Computing Conferences, Inc., invites you to attend Computing for Video Stores in St. Louis.							
8								

You'll learn much more about text formulas when you examine 1-2-3's built-in string functions later in this chapter.

FINDING ERRORS IN FORMULAS

Occasionally, 1-2-3 responds to a new formula entry by displaying *ERR* in the formula's cell. As you can guess, the ERR message means that there is an error in your formula. Because of the error, 1-2-3 cannot calculate the formula's result. Sometimes the error's location is in the formula itself, and sometimes it is a problem in the data that the formula reads from other cells. In either event, the appearance of the ERR value in a cell means that you need to go back and investigate the formula and perhaps other entries in your worksheet.

A number of problems can cause the ERR message. Here are three of the most common:

- ◆ A reference to an undefined range name
- ◆ An inappropriate mixture of data types in a formula—for instance, a numeric data value in a text formula or a text value in a numeric formula
- ◆ An attempt to divide by zero in a numeric formula. (Division by zero is undefined in 1-2-3)

In the following exercise, you'll simulate these three error conditions by entering formulas that are devised to produce the ERR value. Then you'll go through the steps to correct the errors by changing values on the worksheet:

1. On a blank worksheet, widen column A to a setting of 12, and then enter the following data values: the label **Lotus 1-2-3 for** in cell A1, the label **Windows** in cell A2, the numeric value **3** in cell A3, and the value **0** in A4. (See cells A1 to A4 in Figure 5.8.)

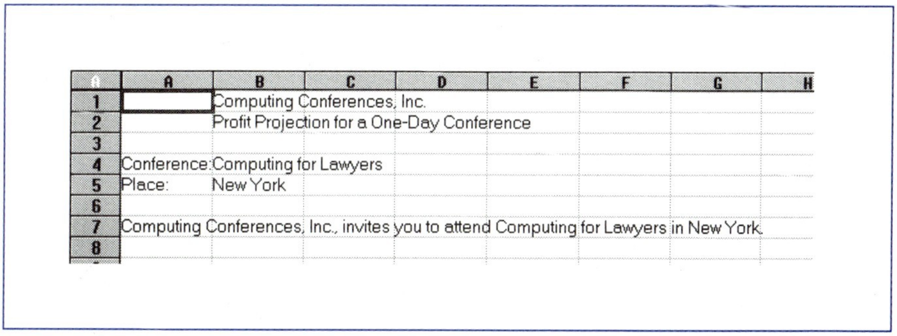

FIGURE 5.7:

Recalculation in a text formula

2. Preselect cell A1 and choose the Range Name Create command. Enter **TITLE1** as the range name for this cell. Click OK or press ↵.

3. Enter the following text formula into cell A6:

   TITLE1&" "&TITLE2

   Lotus 1-2-3 responds by displaying *ERR* in the cell. Can you identify the problem in the formula?

4. Enter the text formula **+A2&A3** into cell A7. The response is the same—another ERR message. Once again, examine the worksheet's data and try to find the error in the formula.

5. Finally, enter the numeric formula **365/A4** into cell A8. A third ERR message appears in column A, as shown in Figure 5.8. Figure 5.9 shows the worksheet's three formulas, displayed in the Text format.

6. Now begin correcting the conditions that produce the three ERR values. First, preselect cell A2 and choose the Range Name Create command. Enter **TITLE2** as the range name for the cell. As soon as you complete this operation, 1-2-3 recalculates the formula in cell A6, which previously contained a reference to an undefined range name. Now the formula's result appears as a text value.

7. Select cell A3 and enter 3 as a label rather than a value: Begin the entry by pressing the Spacebar; 1-2-3 switches into the LABEL mode. Next, type **3** and press ↵. Now 1-2-3 recalculates the text formula in cell A7, which previously contained an unusable reference to a numeric value.

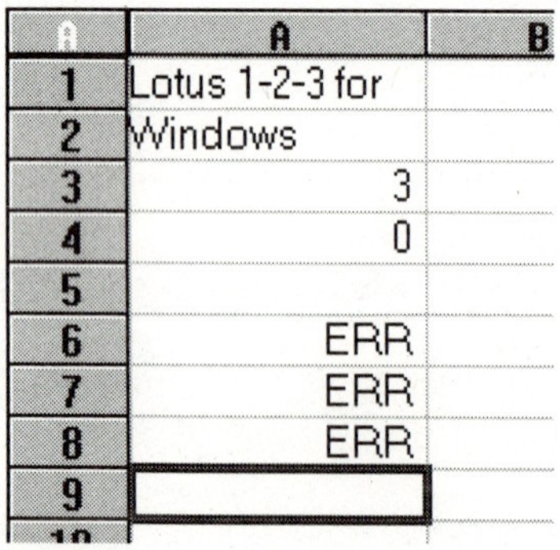

FIGURE 5.8:
The ERR value

A	A	B
1	Lotus 1-2-3 for	
2	Windows	
3	3	
4	0	
5		
6	ERR	
7	ERR	
8	ERR	
9		

8. Finally, select cell A4 and enter a value of **5**. In response, 1-2-3 recalculates the numeric formula in cell A8. Because the denominator is no longer zero, 1-2-3 successfully calculates the numeric result of the formula.

Figure 5.10 shows the results of all three formulas after you complete these corrections.

As you know from your experience with the conference worksheet, formulas are often interconnected in a complex system of calculations. If 1-2-3 detects an error in one formula, all dependent formulas are also evaluated as ERR. As a result, a single error condition can produce ERR messages all over your worksheet. Conversely, a single correction can take away all of the ERR messages.

USING FUNCTIONS

Lotus 1-2-3's function library is one of the program's most important features. The library includes groups of special-purpose functions that are designed for particular fields of work, such as accounting, engineering, and statistics. Other functions are designed for much more general use. Functions will be among the tools you use most frequently in the 1-2-3 spreadsheet.

A library of over one hundred functions seems dauntingly hard to master. But over time you'll identify the dozen or so functions that are most useful to you in your own worksheets; these are the ones you'll become most adept at using. You can learn about other functions when occasions arise that call for their use.

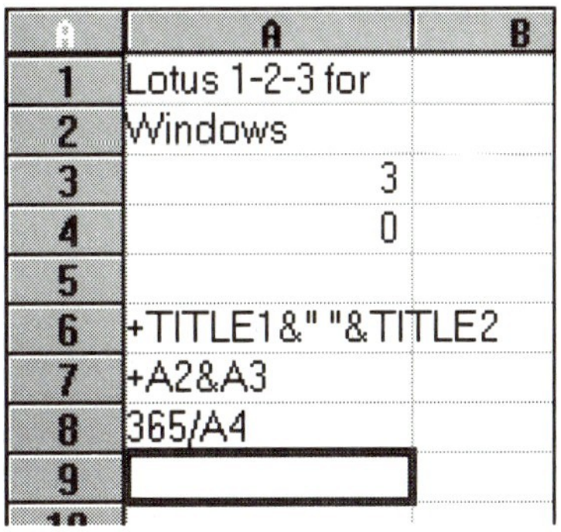

FIGURE 5.9:
The formulas producing ERR values

	A	B
1	Lotus 1-2-3 for	
2	Windows	
3		3
4		0
5		
6	+TITLE1&" "&TITLE2	
7	+A2&A3	
8	365/A4	
9		

ENTERING A FUNCTION INTO A CELL

Fortunately, 1-2-3 offers you detailed and substantial help when you need to learn how to use a new function. The help comes in two forms:

- After you type the @ character into a cell as the start of a function entry, you can press the F3 function key to view the @Function Names dialog box, which contains a complete list of the tools in 1-2-3's function library. When you select a name from the list, 1-2-3 copies the function directly to the edit line.

- Once a selected function name is displayed in the edit line, you can press the F1 function key to go directly to the help topic for the function.

For example, imagine that you are building a worksheet like the one in Figure 5.11 to calculate the monthly payment on a bank loan. You are ready to enter the formula for the payment in cell A4. You know that 1-2-3 has a function that will do the job, but you can't recall the name of the function or how it is used. Here are the steps you take to get help:

1. With A4 selected as the current cell, type the @ character to begin a function entry.

2. Press the F3 function key. In response, 1-2-3 displays the @Function Names dialog box. Press the Tab key once to activate the list box, and then type **P** to scroll quickly down the alphabetically ordered list of function names. Press ↓ once, and the PMT function is highlighted in the list, as shown in Figure 5.11.

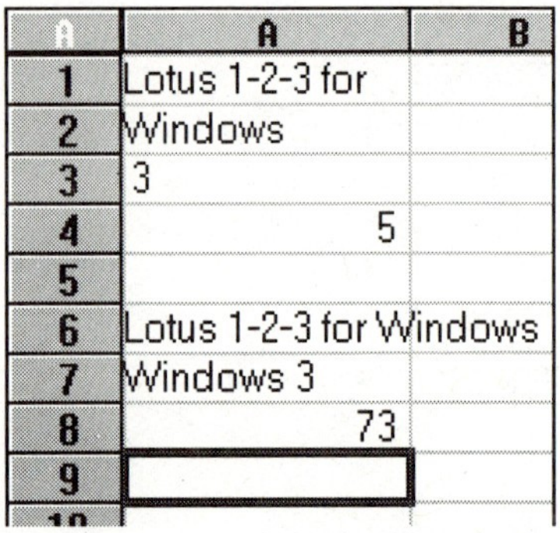

FIGURE 5.10:
Correcting the ERR conditions

A	A	B
1	Lotus 1-2-3 for	
2	Windows	
3	3	
4		5
5		
6	Lotus 1-2-3 for Windows	
7	Windows 3	
8		73
9		

3. Press ↵ to select this function. In response, 1-2-3 enters the function's name into the Edit box. Now press the F1 function key to view the help topic for this function. The Help window appears on the screen, as shown in Figure 5.12. This Help topic describes the PMT function in detail, giving you all the information you need to use the function successfully.

4. After you have read the information, click the Help window's minimize button. Then continue entering the function into the cell.

Of course, if you already know exactly how a function works, you can enter the function's name and arguments directly from the keyboard without using either of these help features. But even experienced spreadsheet users rely on the 1-2-3 Help system for reviewing the details of functions.

The Elements of a Function

Functions conform to a standard format, with only a few variations. To examine the elements of this format, take another look at the function discussed at the beginning of this chapter:

@PMT(PRINCIPAL,RATE/12,TERM*12)

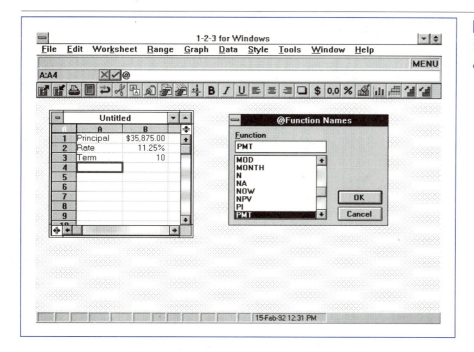

FIGURE 5.11:

The @Function Names dialog box

This @PMT function illustrates the general features you need to understand in order to use any function:

◆ A function name consists of the @ character, followed by the predefined name for the function itself. If you misspell a function name, 1-2-3 will not recognize your entry. (To avoid this problem, use the F3 function key to select a function from the @Function Names dialog box.)

◆ Immediately following the function name, you type an open parenthesis character, to mark the beginning of the argument list. A close parenthesis character goes at the end of the list.

◆ Between the parentheses, you enter the function's required arguments. Each argument is separated from the next with a comma or a semicolon, but no spaces. (You can change the default argument separator in the Tools User Setup International dialog box.) A given argument can be expressed in any form that produces the required type of data. For example, an argument can appear as a cell reference, a range name, an expression, or even as another function name.

◆ The correct number and type of arguments are defined for each function in the 1-2-3 library. A few functions take no argument. Do not

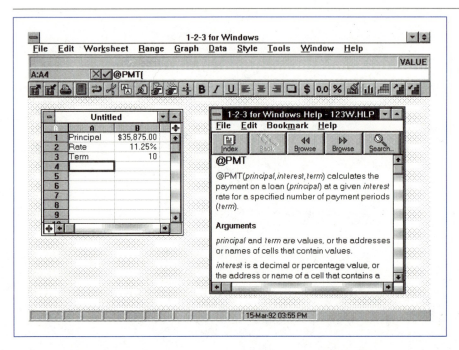

FIGURE 5.12:
Viewing the Help topic for a function

enter the parentheses after the names of these functions. A few other functions have optional arguments, or varying lists of arguments.

You'll see many examples of this function format and its variations in upcoming exercises.

UNDERSTANDING CATEGORIES OF FUNCTIONS

The 1-2-3 documentation divides the function library into eight categories: statistical, financial, mathematical, date and time, logical, string, database, and special functions. There is nothing absolute about these categories. You are likely to find useful tools in unexpected places among them. You will also find yourself mixing functions from different categories to solve individual problems on a worksheet.

The following sections present a selective survey of the most commonly used worksheet functions. You'll study additional functions in other chapters. For example, you'll look at database functions in Chapter 8.

Statistical Functions

The statistical functions are tools for investigating groups of numbers. You can use these tools to count the number of entries in a list; to find the sum, the average, the largest value, and the smallest value of the list; and to calculate the more esoteric statistics known as *variance* and *standard deviation*. Here are brief descriptions of the ten statistical functions:

- The @COUNT function counts the number of cells that contain entries in a range.

- The @SUM function finds the total of a list of numbers.

- The @AVG function calculates the average value of a list of numbers.

- The @MIN and @MAX functions find the smallest and largest numeric values in a list.

- The @VAR and @VARS functions represent two different ways of calculating the variance, a measure of how the numbers in a list diverge from the average. A large variance means great divergence, and a small variance means little divergence. The @VAR function performs the calculation known as the *population* variance, or the *n* method, a technique used to analyze a complete list of values from a given application. The @VARS function performs the *sample* variance, or the *n-1* method, a technique designed for calculating the variance when the list is only a sample of all the values in an application. @VARS produces a larger variance than @VAR.

◆ The @STD and @STDS functions give the standard deviation, calculated as the square root of the variance. @STD supplies the standard deviation for a population—that is, the square root of @VAR. @STDS produces the result for a sample, or the square root of @VARS.

◆ The @SUMPRODUCT function, as its name indicates, performs two operations in one efficient step: First, the function multiplies corresponding values in a list of ranges, and then it finds the sum of all the multiplication products.

The statistical functions accept lists of numeric arguments that can include ranges, individual cell references, literal numeric values, calculated values, and range names. The exception is @SUMPRODUCT, which accepts only ranges as arguments. Statistical functions accept three-dimensional ranges, or ranges across multiple worksheets in a file.

When you use a range reference as an argument in a statistical function, you'll normally want to make sure that all the cells in the range contain numeric entries. If a cell contains a label instead of a number, the statistical functions treat the entry as a value of zero. Because this value is then included in the statistical calculation, the result may be inaccurate.

The worksheet in Figure 5.13 illustrates the statistical functions. The conference organizers at Computing Conferences, Inc. have compiled a list of conferences conducted in 1991, along with the number of people who attended each conference. As you can see, column A on the worksheet displays the city in which each conference was held, column B gives the date, and column C the number of participants. Columns D and E supply a variety of statistics about the conferences and the attendance records, including the number of conferences, the total attendance for all conferences, the average attendance (rounded to an integer), and the largest and smallest attendance records. In addition, the worksheet shows the variance and the standard deviation calculations, produced with both the *n* and *n-1* methods and rounded to the nearest hundredth. In Figure 5.14, you can see the functions that produce all these statistics. Notice that the column of attendance records, C6..C19, has the range name ATTENDANCE.

Finally, Figure 5.15 provides an example of the @SUMPRODUCT function. Column D in this worksheet shows the individual attendance prices for

FIGURE 5.13:
Using the statistical functions

	A	B	C	D	E	F
1			Computing Conferences, Inc.			
2			Attendance at Conferences Conducted in 1991			
3			Computing for Video Stores			
4						
5	Place	Date	Attendance	Statistics		
6	Chicago	09-Jan-91	154			
7	St. Louis	21-Jan-91	119	Number of conferences:	14	
8	Indianapolis	15-Feb-91	174	Total attendance:	1,994	
9	New York	07-Mar-91	201	Average attendance:	142	
10	Boston	25-Mar-91	136	Largest attendance:	235	
11	Washington, D.C.	03-Apr-91	172	Smallest attendance:	86	
12	Atlanta	11-May-91	112			
13	Miami	28-May-91	97	Variance (n):	1632.53	
14	Dallas	03-Jun-91	86	Standard deviation (n):	40.40	
15	Albuquerque	29-Jun-91	104	Variance (n-1):	1758.11	
16	Las Vegas	05-Sep-91	235	Standard deviation (n-1):	41.93	
17	Los Angeles	11-Oct-91	119			
18	San Francisco	29-Oct-91	137			
19	Seattle	05-Nov-91	148			
20						

FIGURE 5.14:
Viewing the statistical functions on the worksheet

	A	B	C	D	E	F
1			Computing Conferences, Inc.			
2			Attendance at Conferences Conducted in 1991			
3			Computing for Video Stores			
4						
5	Place	Date	Attendance	Statistics		
6	Chicago	09-Jan-91	154			
7	St. Louis	21-Jan-91	119	Number of conferences:	@COUNT(ATTENDANCE)	
8	Indianapolis	15-Feb-91	174	Total attendance:	@SUM(ATTENDANCE)	
9	New York	07-Mar-91	201	Average attendance:	@AVG(ATTENDANCE)	
10	Boston	25-Mar-91	136	Largest attendance:	@MAX(ATTENDANCE)	
11	Washington, D.C.	03-Apr-91	172	Smallest attendance:	@MIN(ATTENDANCE)	
12	Atlanta	11-May-91	112			
13	Miami	28-May-91	97	Variance (n):	@VAR(ATTENDANCE)	
14	Dallas	03-Jun-91	86	Standard deviation (n):	@STD(ATTENDANCE)	
15	Albuquerque	29-Jun-91	104	Variance (n-1):	@VARS(ATTENDANCE)	
16	Las Vegas	05-Sep-91	235	Standard deviation (n-1):	@STDS(ATTENDANCE)	
17	Los Angeles	11-Oct-91	119			
18	San Francisco	29-Oct-91	137			
19	Seattle	05-Nov-91	148			
20						

each of the conferences held in 1991. The following @SUMPRODUCT function appears in cell F11:

@SUMPRODUCT(C6..C19,D6..D19)

The first range argument in this function represents the attendance records, and the second argument contains the prices. The function multiplies each attendance record by the corresponding price, and finds the sum of all the products. The result is displayed as $434,920.00.

Financial Functions

The financial functions represent the formulas for several kinds of calculations, including depreciation, loan payments, present value and future value, and investment analysis.

Depreciation Functions

Depreciation refers to any one of several standard methods for allocating the expense of a large purchase over the useful life of the asset. Because depreciation has an important impact on taxes, businesses are always concerned with

	A	B	C	D	E	F	G
1			Computing Conferences, Inc.				
2			Attendance at Conferences Conducted in 1991				
3			Computing for Video Stores				
4							
5	Place		Date	Attendance	Price		
6	Chicago		09-Jan-91	154	$195.00		
7	St. Louis		21-Jan-91	119	$195.00		
8	Indianapolis		15-Feb-91	174	$195.00	Total Attendance	
9	New York		07-Mar-91	201	$225.00	Revenues:	
10	Boston		25-Mar-91	136	$225.00		
11	Washington, D.C.		03-Apr-91	172	$225.00	$434,920.00	
12	Atlanta		11-May-91	112	$225.00		
13	Miami		28-May-91	97	$225.00		
14	Dallas		03-Jun-91	86	$195.00		
15	Albuquerque		29-Jun-91	104	$195.00		
16	Las Vegas		05-Sep-91	235	$245.00		
17	Los Angeles		11-Oct-91	119	$245.00		
18	San Francisco		29-Oct-91	137	$245.00		
19	Seattle		05-Nov-91	148	$195.00		
20							

FIGURE 5.15:

Using the @SUMPRODUCT function

finding the most advantageous way to calculate this expense among the allowed methods.

Four depreciation methods are available as functions in 1-2-3. The straight-line method, represented by the function named @SLN, is the simplest. It assigns equal portions of the asset's cost to each year of useful life. The other three methods represent various approaches to *accelerated depreciation*—the process of assigning greater portions of the expense to the earlier years of useful life, and lesser portions to later years. These three methods are:

- The sum-of-the-years'-digits method, calculated by the @SYD function
- The double-declining-balance method, calculated by the @DDB function
- The variable-rate declining-balance method, calculated by the @VDB function

These functions have common arguments, which can be represented as *cost, salvage, life,* and *period:*

- *Cost* is the original purchase price of the asset.
- *Life* is the defined useful life of the asset, in years.
- *Salvage* is the remaining value of the asset at the end of the useful life.
- *Period* is the target year for which you want to calculate the depreciation.

The @SLN function takes only the first three arguments, because the result of straight-line depreciation is the same for each year of useful life:

@SLN(cost,salvage,life)

The @SYD and @DDB functions calculate different amounts for each year of useful life. The target year therefore appears as the fourth argument, *period:*

@SYD(*cost,salvage,life,period*)

@DDB(*cost,salvage,life,period*)

The @VDB function is the most complex of all. It takes two *period* arguments, representing the start and the end of the target period; this allows you to calculate the depreciation expense for a portion of a year. In addition, @VDB takes two optional arguments, *factor* and *switch*:

@VDB(*cost,salvage,life,period1,period2,factor,switch*)

The *factor* argument is the percentage by which the remaining value of the asset is multiplied to calculate the accelerated depreciation for a given period. For example, you might enter a value of 150% or 175% for this argument. If you omit *factor,* the default is 200%; in this case, @VDB produces the same result as @DDB. In the *switch* argument, you specify whether you want @VDB to switch to straight-line depreciation at the point when it is advantageous to do so. Supplying a *switch* value of 0 (or omitting the argument altogether) instructs 1-2-3 to make the switch; a value of 1 prevents the switch.

Figure 5.16 shows examples of all four depreciation methods, calculated for an asset with a four-year useful life. Here are the steps for producing this sample worksheet on your own computer:

1. Enter the labels **Asset**, **Cost**, **Life**, and **Salvage** in cells A1 to A4, and the data items **Computer system**, **9600**, **4**, and **1600** in cells B1 to B4. Enter the label **years** in cell C3, and the labels **Depreciation** and **factor** in cells E2 and E3, respectively. Enter the @VDB depreciation factor, **1.75**, in cell E4.

2. Enter the column headings **Year**, **SLN**, **SYD**, **DDB**, and **VDB** in cells A6 to E6, and the year numbers **1**, **2**, **3**, and **4** in cells A7 to A10.

3. Format all these entries as you see them displayed in Figure 5.16. Preselect the range B7..E10, and click the currency icon.

	A	B	C	D	E
1	Asset	Computer system			
2	Cost	$9,600.00			Depreciation
3	Life		4 years		factor
4	Salvage	$1,600.00			175%
5					
6	Year	SLN	SYD	DDB	VDB
7	1	$2,000.00	$3,200.00	$4,800.00	$4,200.00
8	2	$2,000.00	$2,400.00	$2,400.00	$2,362.50
9	3	$2,000.00	$1,600.00	$800.00	$1,328.91
10	4	$2,000.00	$800.00	$0.00	$108.59
11					

FIGURE 5.16:
The four depreciation methods

4. Preselect the range A2..A4 and choose the Range Name Label Create command. Keep the default selection, the Right option. Click OK to confirm. This action assigns the range names COST, LIFE, and SALVAGE to the appropriate cells in column B. Select the cell E3, and choose Range Name Label Create again. This time, select the Down option and click OK to confirm. This action assigns the name FACTOR to cell E4.

5. In cell B7, enter the formula for the straight-line depreciation method:

   @SLN($COST,$SALVAGE,$LIFE)

   Notice the absolute references to range names. This format is necessary for the upcoming copy operation.

6. In cell C7, enter the formula for the sum-of-the-years'-digits method:

   @SYD($COST,$SALVAGE,$LIFE,A7)

7. In cell D7, enter the formula for the double-declining-balance method:

   @DDB($COST,$SALVAGE,$LIFE,A7)

8. In cell E7, enter the formula for the variable-rate declining-balance method:

   @VDB($COST,$SALVAGE,$LIFE,A7–1,A7,$FACTOR)

9. Use the range-copy icon to copy the four depreciation formulas down their respective columns: Preselect the range B7..E7, click the range-copy icon, and then drag the mouse pointer (in the form of a pointing-hand icon) over the range B8..B10. When you release the mouse button, the formulas are copied and your work is complete.

Try making changes in the basic data—the cost, the salvage value, and the depreciation factor—and watch as 1-2-3 recalculates the depreciation schedules. If you increase the useful life value, you also have to add a new row to the depreciation table for each year's increase.

Using 1-2-3's Other Financial Functions

The eight other financial functions available in 1-2-3 are as follows:

- @PV, the present value function
- @NPV, the net present value function

- @FV, the future value function
- @PMT, the payment function
- @CTERM and @TERM, the investment term functions
- @RATE, the interest rate function
- @IRR, the internal rate of return function

Most of these functions take an interest rate as one of several arguments. You can supply this argument as a decimal value such as .085, or as a percentage such as 8.5%. Either way, 1-2-3 stores the argument in its decimal format. Of course, you can also provide the rate argument as a reference to a cell that contains the interest rate. If you enter 8.5% into a cell, 1-2-3 accepts the entry as 0.085. You can then format the entry as a percentage if you wish. Alternatively, you can enter the rate as 8.5 in a worksheet cell, and then divide the rate argument by 100 in the function itself:

RATE/100

If a financial function gives a value that you know is incorrect, you should double-check the interest rate argument. Make sure you have not inadvertently supplied a rate argument that is off by a factor of 100.

The @PV and @NPV Functions

The @PV function finds the *present value* of a series of future periodic income amounts, where each amount is the same. The present value calculation takes into account the time-value of money at a given interest rate. @PV takes three arguments:

@PV(*payment,rate,term*)

The *payment* argument is the income amount that will be received at the end of each period in the *term*. The *rate* argument is the periodic rate of return. The periods of *rate* and *term* must be the same.

The @NPV function finds the *net present value* of a series of future periodic cash flow amounts, positive or negative. @NPV takes two arguments, a rate and a range of cash flow amounts:

@NPV(rate,cashflows)

The worksheet in Figure 5.17 uses the @PV and @NPV functions to compare the following two five-year investments: Investment #1 provides five annual income amounts of $10,000 at the end of each year. Investment #2 provides an initial amount of $5,000 at the end of the first year, and then a final amount of $50,000 at the end of the fifth year. Using a rate of 8.5 percent for the comparison, which is the better investment?

The @PV function in cell B8, @PV(B5,B7,B6), gives the present value of the first investment. The @NPV function in cell E13, @NPV(B7,E6..E10), gives the present value of the second investment. As you can see, the first investment has a greater present value, even though the net income of the second investment is $5,000 more than the first.

The @FV Function

The @FV function finds the *future value* of a series of equal periodic payments at a fixed periodic interest rate. @FV takes three arguments:

@FV(*payment,rate,term*)

The future value is equal to the amount of the periodic payments, plus the accumulated interest over the specified term.

Figure 5.18 illustrates the use of @FV for the following application: The parents of a new baby girl have decided to deposit $1,500 in a bank account at the end of each year until their child is ready to go to college. How much will the account be worth at the end of 18 years if the interest rate is 8 percent, compounded annually?

The @FV function in cell B7 is @FV(B3,B4,B5). As Figure 5.18 shows, there will be $56,175.37 in the account at the end of the 18-year term.

	A	B	C	D	E
1	Comparing Investments				
2					
3	Investment #1			Investment #2	
4					
5	Payment	$10,000.00		Year	
6	Years	5		1	$5,000.00
7	Rate	8.50%		2	$0.00
8	Present Value	$39,406.42		3	$0.00
9				4	$0.00
10				5	$50,000.00
11					
12				Net Present	
13				Value	$37,860.57

FIGURE 5.17:

The @PV and @NPV functions

The @PMT Function

The @PMT function finds the fixed periodic payment amount required to pay back a loan. @PMT takes three arguments:

@PMT(*principal,rate,term*)

When you use @PMT to find the monthly payment for a bank loan, you must supply the monthly interest rate, and the term in months.

Figure 5.19 shows an example of the @PMT function. The principal of the loan in this example is $35,825. The rate is 11.25 percent (entered into the worksheet as .1125) and the term is 10 years. The formula in cell B6 is @PMT(B3,B4/12,B5*12). Notice that the annual rate is divided by 12 to produce the monthly rate, and the term in years is multiplied by 12 to find the term in months. The rounded monthly payment is $498.57.

FIGURE 5.18:
The @FV function

	A	B	C
1	College Education Fund		
2			
3	Payment	$1,500.00	per year
4	Rate	8.00%	annually
5	Term	18	years
6			
7	Future Value	$56,175.37	
8			

FIGURE 5.19:
The @PMT function

	A	B	C
1	Monthly Payment		
2			
3	Principal	$35,825.00	
4	Rate	11.25%	
5	Term	10	years
6	Payment	$498.57	
7			
8			

The @CTERM and @TERM functions

The @CTERM function finds the number of compounding periods required to reach a specified future value from a one-time investment amount, given a fixed interest rate. This function takes three arguments:

@CTERM(*rate,futurevalue,presentvalue*)

The @TERM function finds the number of equal payments required to reach a specified future value, given a fixed interest rate. @TERM also takes three arguments, but in a different order:

@TERM(*payment,rate,futurevalue*)

The worksheet in Figure 5.20 compares these two functions, analyzing two different scenarios for attaining a future value of $25,000. Under the first scenario, a one-time amount of $15,000 is deposited in a bank account at the beginning of the period. Under the second scenario, $1,000 is deposited in an account at the end of each year. In both cases, the accounts yield 8 percent interest annually. How long will it take each investment to reach the goal of $25,000?

The following @CTERM function is stored in cell B8:

@CTERM(B6,B7,B5)

In this case, the required term is approximately seven years. (The value in B8 has been rounded by formatting.) The following @TERM function is stored

A	B	C	D	E	F
Time Needed to Save $25,000					
Single Deposit			Annual Deposits		
Deposit	$15,000.00		Payment	$1,000.00	annually
Rate	8.00%		Rate	8.00%	
Goal	$25,000.00		Goal	$25,000.00	
Term	7	years	Term	14	years

FIGURE 5.20:
The @CTERM and @TERM functions

in cell E8:

@TERM(E5,E6,E7)

Given annual deposits of $1,000, the account balance would reach $25,000 in approximately 14 years. (The value in E8 is also rounded.)

The @RATE Function

The @RATE function calculates the interest rate corresponding to a fixed future return from a current investment amount. The function takes three arguments:

@RATE(*futurevalue,presentvalue,term*)

Figure 5.21 illustrates the @RATE function for the following situation: A friend asks to borrow $15,000 from you now, and promises to pay you $25,000 at the end of four years. What will be the annual interest rate that you will earn from the loan?

The @RATE function @RATE(B4,B3,B5) is entered into cell B6. The resulting annual interest rate (displayed in the Percent format, with two decimal places) is *13.62%*.

The @IRR Function

Finally, the @IRR function gives the *internal rate of return* from a series of positive and negative cash flow amounts. The internal rate of return is defined as the interest rate that gives a net present value of zero. @IRR takes

	A	B	C
1	Calculating the Interest Rate		
2			
3	Present value	$15,000.00	
4	Future value	$25,000.00	
5	Term	4 years	
6	Rate	13.62%	
7			
8			

FIGURE 5.21:
The @RATE function

two arguments, a rate and a range of cash flow amounts:

@IRR(*guess,cashflows*)

In the first argument, you supply a reasonable guess for the internal rate of return. Lotus 1-2-3 uses this guess as a starting point for the iterative process that calculates the internal rate of return. The second argument is a worksheet range that contains the positive and negative cash flow amounts.

Figure 5.22 contains an illustration of the @IRR function that finds the internal rate of return for a six-year investment project. In the first year, an output of $80,000 is required to start the investment. The five subsequent years produce various income amounts: $15,000 at the end of the second year; $20,000 at the end of the third and fourth years; and $25,000 at the end of the fifth and sixth years. What is the calculated IRR for this sequence of cash flow amounts?

The @IRR function @IRR(0.1,B4..B9) is stored in cell B11. The guess supplied as the first argument is 10 percent. The range of cash flow amounts is B4..B9. @IRR calculates the internal rate of return as 9 percent. (The value in cell B11 is displayed in the Percent format.) To confirm that this figure matches the IRR definition, the formula @NPV(B11,B4..B9) appears in cell B12. Given the calculated IRR, the @NPV function gives an approximate result of zero.

	A	B
1	Internal Rate of Return	
2		
3	Year	Cash Flow
4	1	($80,000.00)
5	2	$15,000.00
6	3	$20,000.00
7	4	$20,000.00
8	5	$25,000.00
9	6	$25,000.00
10		
11	IRR	9.00%
12	NPV	($0.00)
13		
14		
15		

FIGURE 5.22:
The @IRR function

Mathematical Functions

Lotus 1-2-3 has a standard set of mathematical functions, many of which are used in scientific and engineering applications. These include the trigonometric, logarithmic, and exponential functions. In addition, several of the mathematical functions have important roles in everyday business worksheets; for example,

- The @RAND function produces random numbers, which you can use to supply random data for testing worksheet formulas, or to rearrange data in a random order.

- The @INT and @ROUND functions are useful for converting real numbers to integers, or for rounding numbers to a specified decimal place.

- The @ABS (absolute value) and @MOD (modulus) functions have special uses in date arithmetic.

In the sections ahead, you'll see examples of all these functions.

Trigonometric, Logarithmic, and Exponential Functions

Lotus 1-2-3 has three trigonometric functions, @SIN, @COS, and @TAN; and four inverse trigonometric functions, @ASIN, @ACOS, @ATAN, and @ATAN2. The trigonometric functions take arguments expressed in *radians*. The inverse functions produce radian values. A radian measurement is a multiple of the value π, where the range 0 to $2*\pi$ is equivalent to 0 to 360 degrees. Here are some sample radian equivalents:

0*PI	0 degrees
PI/4	45 degrees
PI/2	90 degrees
PI	180 degrees
3*PI/2	270 degrees
2*PI	360 degrees

To simplify the task of supplying arguments in radians, 1-2-3 has a built-in @PI function; this function gives the value of π, accurate to 17 digits:

3.14159265358979324

Figure 5.23 shows @SIN, @COS, and @TAN values for a range of radian arguments from $-\pi/2$ to $+\pi/2$. The sine and cosine values move through their familiar wave patterns in this range: Sine goes from −1 to 0 to 1, and cosine goes from 0 to 1 to 0. The result of the tangent function approaches infinity for arguments approaching $+\pi/2$, and negative infinity for arguments approaching $-\pi/2$.

The following exercise guides you through the steps of producing the sine and cosine table on your own worksheet:

1. On a blank worksheet, preselect the range A4..A20. Choose the Data Fill command and enter **−.5** as the Start value and **.0625** as the Step value. Click OK or press ↵ to confirm, and 1-2-3 fills the preselected range with decimal values from −0.5 to 0.5.

2. Choose the Worksheet Global Settings Format command and select the Fixed format. Enter **4** in the Decimal places box and click OK twice.

3. Enter **@PI*A4** in cell B4, **@SIN(B4)** in C4, and **@COS(B4)** in D4.

4. Use the range-copy icon to copy these formulas down their respective columns in the range B5..D20. Enter the column headings as you see them in Figure 5.23.

	A	B	C	D	E F	G	H	I
1			Trigonometric Functions					
2								
3		Radians	Sine	Cosine				
4	-0.5000	-1.5708	-1.0000	0.0000		Radians	Tangent	
5	-0.4375	-1.3744	-0.9808	0.1951	-0.4375	-1.3744	-5.0273	
6	-0.3750	-1.1781	-0.9239	0.3827	-0.3750	-1.1781	-2.4142	
7	-0.3125	-0.9817	-0.8315	0.5556	-0.3125	-0.9817	-1.4966	
8	-0.2500	-0.7854	-0.7071	0.7071	-0.2500	-0.7854	-1.0000	
9	-0.1875	-0.5890	-0.5556	0.8315	-0.1875	-0.5890	-0.6682	
10	-0.1250	-0.3927	-0.3827	0.9239	-0.1250	-0.3927	-0.4142	
11	-0.0625	-0.1963	-0.1951	0.9808	-0.0625	-0.1963	-0.1989	
12	0.0000	0.0000	0.0000	1.0000	0.0000	0.0000	0.0000	
13	0.0625	0.1963	0.1951	0.9808	0.0625	0.1963	0.1989	
14	0.1250	0.3927	0.3827	0.9239	0.1250	0.3927	0.4142	
15	0.1875	0.5890	0.5556	0.8315	0.1875	0.5890	0.6682	
16	0.2500	0.7854	0.7071	0.7071	0.2500	0.7854	1.0000	
17	0.3125	0.9817	0.8315	0.5556	0.3125	0.9817	1.4966	
18	0.3750	1.1781	0.9239	0.3827	0.3750	1.1781	2.4142	
19	0.4375	1.3744	0.9808	0.1951	0.4375	1.3744	5.0273	
20	0.5000	1.5708	1.0000	0.0000				

FIGURE 5.23:
The @SIN, @COS, and @TAN functions

The inverse trigonometric functions @ASIN, @ACOS, and @ATAN take single numeric arguments. @ASIN gives the angle (in radians) corresponding to a sine argument. Likewise, @ACOS gives the angle for a cosine argument, and @ATAN gives the angle for a tangent argument. Figure 5.24 shows the arcsine and arccosine values for a range of decimal arguments between −1 and 1. The arcsine value goes from $-\pi/2$ to $\pi/2$ for this range of arguments, and the arccosine value goes from π down to zero. (@ASIN and @ACOS return ERR for arguments greater than 1 or less than −1.) The function @ASIN(A4) is entered into cell B4, and @ACOS(A4) is entered into C4. To produce the table, these functions were copied down columns B and C.

Figure 5.24 also shows a range of arctangent functions. As you can see, the arctangent approaches $-\pi/2$ for large negative arguments, and $+\pi/2$ for large positive arguments. The formula stored in cell F4 is @ATAN(E4).

Finally, the @ATAN2 function supplies radian angles in a four-quadrant x-y coordinate system. This function takes two numeric arguments, forming a coordinate pair:

@ATAN2(x,y)

FIGURE 5.24:
The inverse trigonometric functions

	A	B	C	D	E	F	G	H	I	J	K
1					Trigonometric Functions						
2											
3	Argument	ASIN	ACOS		Argument	ATAN		x	y	ATAN2	
4	-1.000	-1.5708	3.1416		-100000	-1.5708		-0.5	-1.0	-2.0344	
5	-0.875	-1.0654	2.6362		-10000	-1.5707		-1.0	-1.0	-2.3562	
6	-0.750	-0.8481	2.4189		-1000	-1.5698		-1.0	-0.5	-2.6779	
7	-0.625	-0.6751	2.2459		-100	-1.5608		-1.0	0.0	3.1416	
8	-0.500	-0.5236	2.0944		-10	-1.4711		-1.0	0.5	2.6779	
9	-0.375	-0.3844	1.9552		-1	-0.7854		-1.0	1.0	2.3562	
10	-0.250	-0.2527	1.8235		-0.1	-0.0997		-0.5	1.0	2.0344	
11	-0.125	-0.1253	1.6961		0	0.0000		0.0	1.0	1.5708	
12	0.000	0.0000	1.5708		0.1	0.0997		0.5	1.0	1.1071	
13	0.125	0.1253	1.4455		1	0.7854		1.0	1.0	0.7854	
14	0.250	0.2527	1.3181		10	1.4711		1.0	0.5	0.4636	
15	0.375	0.3844	1.1864		100	1.5608		1.0	0.0	0.0000	
16	0.500	0.5236	1.0472		1000	1.5698		1.0	-0.5	-0.4636	
17	0.625	0.6751	0.8957		10000	1.5707		1.0	-1.0	-0.7854	
18	0.750	0.8481	0.7227		100000	1.5708		0.5	-1.0	-1.1071	
19	0.875	1.0654	0.5054					0.0	-1.0	-1.5708	
20	1.000	1.5708	0.0000								

The result of @ATAN2 is the angle formed by two lines in the coordinate system: the x-axis extending horizontally to the right from the origin, and the line from (0,0) to (*x,y*). Figure 5.24 shows a range of examples. The formula in cell J4 is as follows:

@ATAN2(H4,I4)

The exponential and logarithmic functions are @EXP and @LN, both based on the natural constant e; and @LOG, based on 10. The @EXP function calculates exponents of e, where the value of e is represented as

2.71828182845904524

@EXP takes one numeric argument, *x*, and supplies the value of e to the *x* power. The @LN function finds the natural logarithm of its argument. @LN takes one argument, *x*, and supplies the power of e that produces *x*. The @LOG function gives the base-10 logarithm. @LOG takes one numeric argument, *x*, and returns the power of 10 that gives *x*. Figure 5.25 shows a range of examples for all three of these functions.

Finally, the @SQRT function gives the square root of its numeric argument. The argument must be greater than or equal to zero. The last column of the worksheet in Figure 5.25 shows examples of @SQRT.

	A	B	C	D	E	F	G	H	I
1				The Exponential, Logarithmic, and Square Root Functions					
2									
3		x	EXP(x)		x	LN(x)	LOG(x)	x	SQRT(x)
4		-1.00	0.3679		0.50	-0.6931	-0.3010	0.25	0.5000
5		-0.75	0.4724		1.00	0.0000	0.0000	0.50	0.7071
6		-0.50	0.6065		1.50	0.4055	0.1761	0.75	0.8660
7		-0.25	0.7788		2.00	0.6931	0.3010	1.00	1.0000
8		0.00	1.0000		2.50	0.9163	0.3979	1.25	1.1180
9		0.25	1.2840		3.00	1.0986	0.4771	1.50	1.2247
10		0.50	1.6487		3.50	1.2528	0.5441	1.75	1.3229
11		0.75	2.1170		4.00	1.3863	0.6021	2.00	1.4142
12		1.00	2.7183		4.50	1.5041	0.6532	2.25	1.5000
13		1.25	3.4903		5.00	1.6094	0.6990	2.50	1.5811

FIGURE 5.25:

The @EXP, @LN, @LOG, and @SQRT functions

The @RAND Function

The @RAND function produces random numbers. The function takes no argument, and supplies a random decimal value between 0 and 1. If you want to generate random numbers in another range, you can multiply @RAND by the maximum value in the range. For example, the following formula produces random numbers between 0 and 100:

@RAND*100

To produce random integers, you can use 1-2-3's built-in @INT function with @RAND. @INT eliminates the decimal portion of a real number, and supplies the integer portion. For instance, the following formula gives random integers between 0 and 100:

@INT(@RAND*100)

This is an example of a formula in which one function appears as the argument of another function. You'll see other examples as you continue in this chapter.

Figure 5.26 shows four columns of random numbers, generated using the @RAND and @INT functions. Column A contains random decimal values between 0 and 1; column B, random numbers from 0 to 100; column C, random integers from 0 to 10; and column D, random integers from 0 to 1000.

	A	B	C	D
1		The @RAND Function		
2				
3	@RAND	@RAND*100	@INT(@RAND*10)	@INT(@RAND*1000)
4	0.940756065	28.718129652	6	242
5	0.76168877	70.315207946	8	731
6	0.070106278	27.620998643	2	693
7	0.646600351	41.209208053	0	59
8	0.557460089	23.17081323	3	367
9	0.797966321	41.996327481	3	623
10	0.531511828	11.929462763	9	642
11	0.224484612	91.287957268	7	598
12	0.241365147	62.403237337	1	50
13	0.195128969	53.2574286	9	49
14	0.057559983	41.063260539	5	455
15				

FIGURE 5.26:

Generating random numbers

To produce these numbers, the four formulas shown in row 3 were copied down their respective columns. (The Text format was then applied to row 3.)

The @RAND function is commonly used for producing random test data and for arranging records in random order. But before you use @RAND for these applications, you should be aware of a peculiar characteristic resulting from 1-2-3's automatic recalculation mode. As you know, 1-2-3 recalculates formulas in a worksheet whenever a change occurs in the data that the formulas depend on. The @RAND function takes no argument, and is therefore independent of any particular data value on the worksheet. However, whenever 1-2-3 recalculates any formula on the worksheet, it also recalculates all cells that contain @RAND entries. For this reason, the random values on the worksheet appear to be unstable: They change whenever the worksheet is recalculated. This can be a problem if you are trying to perform a test with a fixed set of random numbers.

There are two different ways of solving this problem. One way is to switch 1-2-3 out of its automatic recalculation mode while you use the @RAND function. You do this by choosing the Tools User Setup Recalculation command, and clicking the Manual option in the resulting dialog box, as shown in Figure 5.27. In the manual recalculation mode, 1-2-3 recalculates formulas on the worksheet only when you instruct it to do so: You force a recalculation by pressing the F9 function key. Whenever formulas need to be recalculated—normally after a change in the worksheet's data—1-2-3 displays the word *CALC* in the first panel of the status line at the bottom of the 1-2-3 window. Ignore the CALC message if you are working with a particular set of random

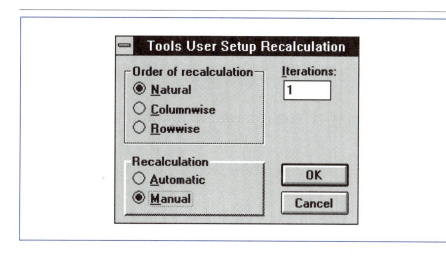

FIGURE 5.27:

The Tools User Setup Recalculation dialog box

numbers that you want to keep. Press F9 only when you want to *change* the set of random numbers on your worksheet.

Try this exercise with @RAND in the manual recalculation mode:

1. On a blank worksheet, enter **@RAND** into cell A1. A random number between 0 and 1 appears in the cell.

2. Now select cell A2 and enter a value of **1**. Even though this new entry has no relationship to the formula in cell A1—or to any other formula, since none other currently appears in the worksheet—1-2-3 recalculates the @RAND function anyway. A new random number appears in cell A1. This change could be disconcerting if you were using random numbers as test data on your worksheet. You would prefer to have the opportunity to examine the results of one random scenario before suddenly jumping to a new one.

3. Choose the Tools User Setup command and click the Recalculation button on the resulting dialog box. In the Tools User Setup Recalculation dialog box, click the Manual option to switch into the manual recalculation mode. Click OK on both dialog boxes to confirm the change.

4. Now enter a value of **2** into cell A2. In the manual mode, 1-2-3 does *not* automatically recalculate any formula on the worksheet. The random number displayed in cell A1 does not change.

5. Notice the word CALC at the left side of the status line. This tells you that 1-2-3 has not recalculated the worksheet, because of the manual recalculation mode. Press the F9 function key to force a recalculation. A new random number appears in cell A1, and the word CALC disappears from the status line.

6. Continue experimenting with this worksheet in the manual mode, if you wish. Then close this worksheet without saving.

By the way, the Recalculation settings apply to all worksheets that are open at the time you select a setting.

The second way to prevent 1-2-3 from recalculating random numbers is to convert a @RAND function entry into a simple numeric value entry. As a result of this conversion, a worksheet cell will contain a random number that was generated by @RAND, but the @RAND function itself will not be present in the cell. You can accomplish this conversion either before or after you complete the @RAND entry. To convert a function or formula to a value during the entry process, you simply press the F9 function key before pressing ↵. After a function or formula is already entered into a cell, you can make the same conversion by choosing the Edit Quick Copy command. You'll experiment with both of these techniques in the following exercise:

1. Select cell A1 on a blank worksheet, and type **@RAND** as a formula entry. Do not press ↵.

2. Press the F9 function key. In response, 1-2-3 converts the @RAND function into a numeric value entry—specifically, the first random number that the function would have produced if you had entered the function into the cell.

3. Now press ↵. The random number in A1 is now static, because the entry is a value rather than a formula.

4. Select cell A2 and type the **@RAND** function into the cell. Press ↵ to complete the entry. (Do not press F9 this time.)

5. Use the range-copy icon to copy the formula from cell A2 down to the range A3..A10. When you complete the copy operation, a different random number appears in each of the cells in the range.

6. Preselect the range A2..A10. Pull down the Edit menu and choose the Quick Copy command. In the resulting dialog box, shown in Figure 5.28, click the check box labeled Convert to values. An X appears inside the box.

7. Click OK or press ↵ to confirm the new selection. Back on your worksheet, the entries in the preselected range are now numeric value entries, not functions. You can confirm this by selecting any cell in the range and examining the contents box. You will see a long decimal number in the box, not a @RAND entry.

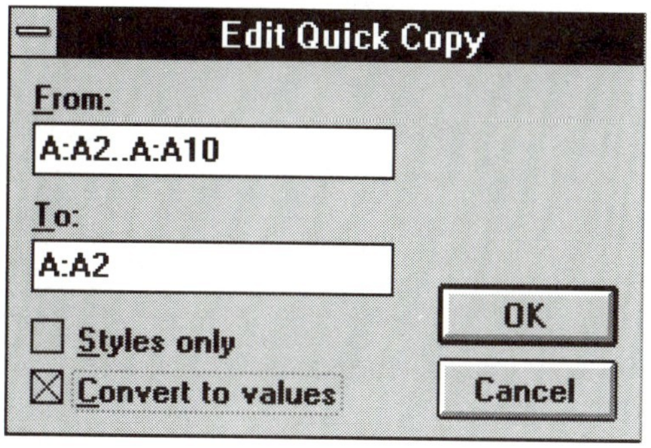

FIGURE 5.28:
The Edit Quick Copy dialog box

Now consider a situation in which you might use the @RAND function in a worksheet. Imagine that you have a group of employees whom you evaluate formally once a year. You hold individual evaluation meetings in September. To avoid conducting these meetings in the same alphabetical order each year, you need a way to rearrange the list of employees in random order.

The list of employee names appears in columns B and C in the worksheet shown in Figure 5.29. The list is currently in alphabetical order. Here are the steps you take to rearrange the list randomly:

1. Enter the formula **@INT(@RAND*50)** in cell A1. Next, use the range-copy icon to copy the formula down column A to each cell in the range A2..A15. A random integer between 0 and 50 appears in each cell, as in Figure 5.29 (although the random numbers on your worksheet will be different from the ones in this figure).

2. Preselect the range A1..A15, then choose the Edit Quick Copy command. Click the Convert to values option. An X appears in the check box. Click OK or press ↵ to confirm. Back on the worksheet, the random numbers in column A are now simple value entries rather than function entries.

3. Preselect the range A1..C15. Pull down the Data menu and choose the Sort command. The Data Sort dialog box appears on the

	A	B	C
1	36	Alcott	M.
2	27	Burton	C.
3	4	Calloway	D.
4	47	Dalton	R.
5	16	Everett	V.
6	13	Fine	M.
7	38	Graves	A.
8	37	Hines	D.
9	35	Jackson	N.
10	44	Kelley	N.
11	10	Larson	W.
12	9	Madson	I.
13	4	Nelson	P.
14	25	Oliver	A.
15	47	Parker	H.
16			

FIGURE 5.29:
Using random numbers to rearrange a list of names

screen. Click the Ascending option in the Primary key frame (as shown in Figure 5.30), then click OK or press ↵ to confirm. Back on the worksheet, the list of employee names is now rearranged randomly according to the random numbers you entered into column A (see Figure 5.31).

Once you have completed your employee evaluation, you can use the Data Sort command to realphabetize the list of employees. (You'll learn more about the Data Sort command in Chapter 7.)

Additional Mathematical Functions

Three miscellaneous but important mathematical functions remain for you to examine. They are @ROUND, @MOD, and @ABS.

The @ROUND function takes two numeric arguments. The first argument, x, is the real number that you want to round, and the second, n, is an integer representing the decimal place at which you want the rounding to occur:

@ROUND(x,n)

If n is positive, rounding takes place at the right side of the decimal point. For example, if you enter a value of 2 for n, the function rounds the value x to the nearest hundredth. If n is negative, rounding occurs at the left side of the decimal point. For example, if you enter −1 for n, the function rounds x to the nearest multiple of ten. Finally, a value of zero for n results in rounding to the nearest whole integer.

The worksheet in Figure 5.32 shows examples of the @ROUND function. Column A in this worksheet contains a series of random numbers between

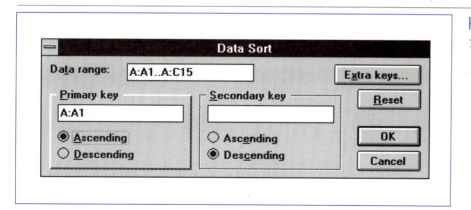

FIGURE 5.30:

The Data Sort dialog box

0 and 100. In columns B through E, these numbers are rounded to the nearest thousandth, the nearest hundredth, the nearest integer, and the nearest multiple of ten, respectively. Here are the formulas in cells A4, B4, C4, D4, and E4, respectively:

@RAND*100
@ROUND(A4,3)
@ROUND(A4,2)
@ROUND(A4,0)
@ROUND(A4,–1)

These formulas are copied down the worksheet, to the range A5..E13.
    The @MOD function performs division between two integers, but unlike the division operator, @MOD supplies the *remainder* from the division, not the quotient. @MOD is known as the *modulus* function. It takes two arguments, the numerator and the denominator of the division operation:

@MOD(x,y)

If y divides evenly into x with no remainder, @MOD supplies a value of zero. Otherwise, @MOD returns the remainder from the division. For example, try

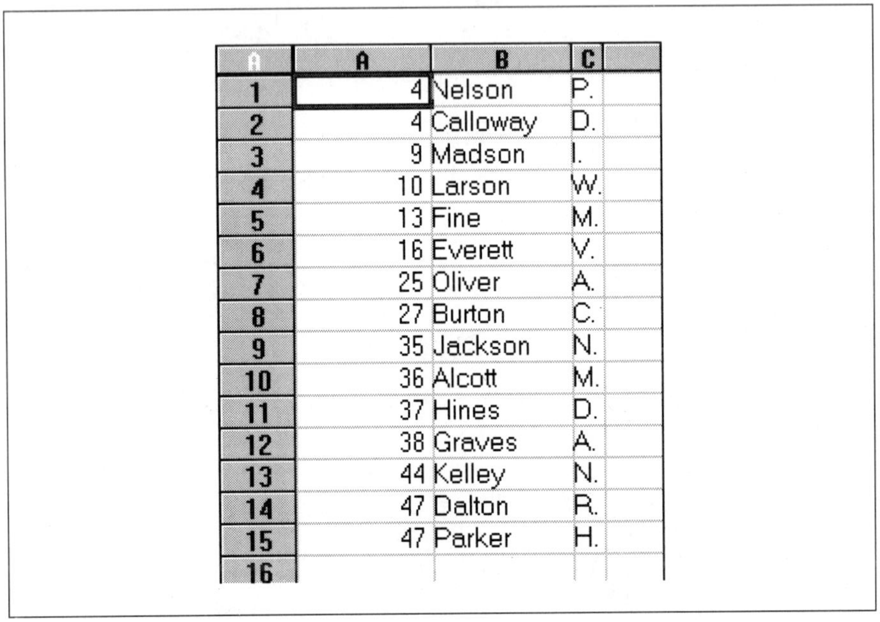

FIGURE 5.31:

The randomly arranged employee list

	A	B	C
1	4	Nelson	P.
2	4	Calloway	D.
3	9	Madson	I.
4	10	Larson	W.
5	13	Fine	M.
6	16	Everett	V.
7	25	Oliver	A.
8	27	Burton	C.
9	35	Jackson	N.
10	36	Alcott	M.
11	37	Hines	D.
12	38	Graves	A.
13	44	Kelley	N.
14	47	Dalton	R.
15	47	Parker	H.
16			

entering **@MOD(25,9)** into a cell. The result is 7. The division of 9 into 25 gives a quotient of 2 with a remainder of 7.

One of the important applications of the @MOD function is finding the day of the week (Sunday, Monday, Tuesday, and so on) for a date. Given a date number in the format of 1-2-3's date system, here is the formula for determining the day of the week:

@MOD(*date*,7)

This formula yields an integer from 0 to 6, representing a day of the week from Saturday to Friday (0 is Saturday, 1 is Sunday, 2 is Monday, and so on). For example, the worksheet in Figure 5.33 shows a series of dates in column C. The following formula in cell B6 finds the day-of-the-week integer for the first of these dates:

@MOD(C6,7)

This formula is copied down column B, to determine the day of the week for each date in the list. You'll work further with this list later in this chapter.

Finally, the @ABS function gives the *absolute value* of a number. @ABS takes one numeric argument, *x*:

@ABS(*x*)

A	B	C	D	E
	The @ROUND Function			
RAND	n=3	n=2	n=0	n=-1
63.12912	63.129	63.13	63	60
11.11789	11.118	11.12	11	10
58.33212	58.332	58.33	58	60
87.90175	87.902	87.9	88	90
64.68746	64.687	64.69	65	60
2.115833	2.116	2.12	2	0
60.81018	60.81	60.81	61	60
36.74362	36.744	36.74	37	40
49.99018	49.99	49.99	50	50
84.93287	84.933	84.93	85	80

FIGURE 5.32:
Examples of the @ROUND function

Whether *x* is positive or negative, @ABS returns the unsigned (positive) equivalent of the argument.

Use this function when the sign of a numeric value is not relevant to your worksheet. For example, when you subtract one number from another, the result may be positive or negative, depending upon which number is larger; applying @ABS to the subtraction guarantees a positive result. In the worksheet shown in Figure 5.34, cell B4 contains a formula for finding the number of days between the two dates:

@ABS(A2–A1)

This formula gives a positive number of days, regardless of which day is later in time.

Date and Time Functions

Lotus 1-2-3 has a useful set of functions that work with date and time values. These tools fall into four categories: functions that supply the current date and time; functions that give information about existing date and time values; functions that convert other types of data into date and time values; and functions that perform date arithmetic.

	A	B	C
5	Place		Date
6	Chicago	4	09-Jan-91
7	St. Louis	2	21-Jan-91
8	Indianapolis	6	15-Feb-91
9	New York	5	07-Mar-91
10	Boston	2	25-Mar-91
11	Washington, D.C.	4	03-Apr-91
12	Atlanta	0	11-May-91
13	Miami	3	28-May-91
14	Dallas	2	03-Jun-91
15	Albuquerque	0	29-Jun-91
16	Las Vegas	5	05-Sep-91
17	Los Angeles	6	11-Oct-91
18	San Francisco	3	29-Oct-91
19	Seattle	3	05-Nov-91

FIGURE 5.33:
Determining the day of the week for a list of dates

Two important functions read the system clock and calendar, and supply values representing the current date and the current time:

- @TODAY returns a date number representing the current date. For example, @TODAY gives the integer value 33835 for the date 19-Aug-92. The @TODAY function takes no argument.

- @NOW returns a combined date-and-time number representing both the current date and the current time. For example, @NOW supplies the combined value 33835.25 for the date 19-Aug-92 at 6:00 AM. @NOW takes no argument.

Six functions supply information about a date value or a time value:

- @DAY takes a date number as its argument—@DAY(*datenumber*)—and returns an integer from 1 to 31, representing the day of the month.

- @MONTH takes a date number argument—@MONTH(*datenumber*)—and returns an integer from 1 to 12, representing the month.

- @YEAR takes a date number argument—@YEAR(*datenumber*)—and returns an integer representing the year.

- @HOUR takes a decimal time number as its argument—@HOUR(*timenumber*)—and returns an integer from 0 to 23, representing the hour.

- @MINUTE takes a time number argument—@MINUTE(*timenumber*)—and returns an integer from 0 to 59, representing the minutes.

- @SECOND takes a time number argument—@SECOND(*timenumber*)—and returns an integer from 0 to 59, representing the seconds.

These six functions also accept combined date-and-time arguments, in the form supplied by the @NOW function.

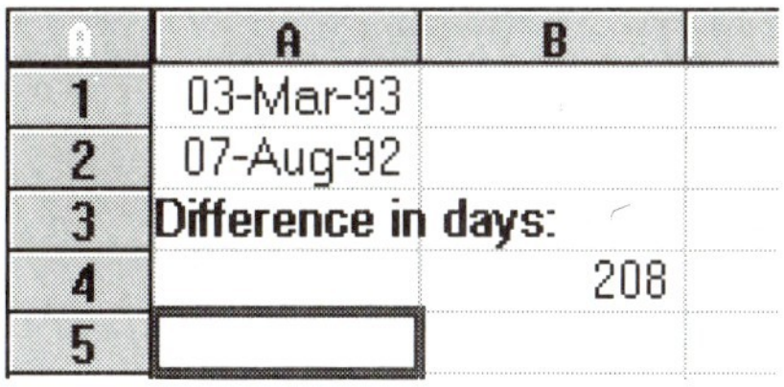

FIGURE 5.34:
Using the @ABS function

	A	B
1	03-Mar-93	
2	07-Aug-92	
3	Difference in days:	
4		208
5		

Four functions convert numeric values or strings into 1-2-3 date numbers or time numbers:

- The @DATE function takes three integer arguments representing the year, the month, and the day—@DATE(*year,month,day*). The function returns the corresponding date number. For example, @DATE(92,8,19) gives the date number 33835.

- The @DATEVALUE function takes a string argument in a format that 1-2-3 can recognize as a date—@DATEVALUE(*string*). The function returns the corresponding date number. For example, @DATEVALUE("19-Aug-92") supplies the number 33835.

- The @TIME function takes three numeric arguments representing the hour, the minutes, and the seconds—TIME(*hour,minutes,seconds*). The function returns the corresponding decimal time number. For example, @TIME(4,30,0) gives the value 0.1875.

- The @TIMEVALUE function takes a string argument in a format that 1-2-3 can recognize as a time—@TIMEVALUE(*string*). The function returns the corresponding time number. For example, @TIMEVALUE("4:30 AM") gives the value 0.1875.

Finally, two functions perform special date arithmetic operations:

- The @DAYS360 function takes two date numbers as arguments—@DAYS360(*date1,date2*). The function calculates the number of days between the two dates, using a standard algorithm based on a 360-day year.

- The @D360 function also takes two date numbers as arguments—@D360(*date1,date2*). This function calculates the number of days between the two dates, based on a year of 12 months with 30 days each.

In the upcoming exercises, you'll see worksheet examples of these functions. To start, here is a simple experiment with the @NOW function and the six functions that supply information about date-and-time values: @DAY, @MONTH, @YEAR, @HOUR, @MINUTE, and @SECOND.

1. On a new blank worksheet, type the **@NOW** function into cell B1. (Recall that the function takes no argument.) To convert the function to a value, press the F9 key before you press ↵. A number representing the current date and time appears in B1. Choose the Range Name Create command and assign the name DATETIME to this cell.

2. In cells B2 through B7, enter the following six functions:

@DAY(DATETIME)
@MONTH(DATETIME)
@YEAR(DATETIME)
@HOUR(DATETIME)
@MINUTE(DATETIME)
@SECOND(DATETIME)

These six functions give the components of the date-and-time value displayed in cell B1.

The worksheet in Figure 5.35 shows an example of this experiment. (Of course, the date-and-time value in this figure will be different from the value you have entered on your worksheet. Figure 5.35 also includes labels in column A to identify the numbers in column B.)

In the worksheet shown in Figure 5.36, you'll see a practical use of the @MONTH and @DAY functions, along with an example of the @TODAY function in a formula. The worksheet shows a list of employees. The employees' names are displayed in column A, and their birth dates are in column B. Column C contains a formula that calculates each employee's age. The following formula is entered in cell C4—for the first employee—and then copied down the column:

@INT((@TODAY−B4)/365)

Examine this formula carefully. The expression inside the inner parentheses finds an employee's age in days by subtracting the employee's birth date from today's date (@TODAY−B4). Dividing this number of days by 365 gives the

	A	B
1	Now	33835.19
2	Day	19
3	Month	8
4	Year	92
5	Hour	4
6	Minute	30
7	Second	14
8		

FIGURE 5.35:
Experimenting with @NOW and the date-and-time functions

employee's age in years. Finally, the @INT function eliminates the fractional portion from the result of this division operation.

You can see the result of the formula in column C of Figure 5.36. Notice that this list is arranged by the employees' ages, in descending order—that is, from the oldest employee to the youngest, or from the earliest birth date to the most recent. Imagine the following situation: The company that these employees work for has a policy of giving each employee an extra vacation day per year on the employee's birthday. To monitor these vacation days, the employees' manager would like to rearrange the employee list in calendar order of birthdays—from the first birthday in January to the last birthday in December. Accomplishing this requires the use of the @MONTH and @DAY functions:

1. Enter the function **@MONTH(B4)** in cell D4, and the function **@DAY(B4)** in cell E4. Use the range-copy icon to copy these two formulas down their respective columns, to the range D5..E18. Together, these two functions give the month and day of each employee's birthday, as shown in Figure 5.36.

2. Preselect the range A4..E18 and choose the Data Sort command. In the resulting dialog box, enter **D4** in the Primary key box and **E4** in the Secondary key box. Click Ascending for both keys. Then click OK or

FIGURE 5.36:

Using the @TODAY function to calculate the age of each employee

	A	B	C	D	E
1	Employees' Birthdays				
2					
3	Name	Date of Birth	Age	Mo	Day
4	Graves, A.	23-Jun-35	56	6	23
5	Alcott, M.	05-Aug-39	52	8	5
6	Parker, H.	08-May-45	46	5	8
7	Dalton, R.	06-Jul-47	44	7	6
8	Hines, D.	27-Oct-51	40	10	27
9	Oliver, A.	03-Sep-54	37	9	3
10	Jackson, N.	19-Jun-59	32	6	19
11	Everett, V.	02-Dec-59	32	12	2
12	Larson, W.	07-Aug-65	26	8	7
13	Nelson, P.	02-Jan-67	25	1	2
14	Madson, I.	07-Apr-68	23	4	7
15	Burton, C.	05-Aug-69	22	8	5
16	Fine, M.	01-Feb-70	22	2	1
17	Kelley, N.	08-Nov-71	20	11	8
18	Calloway, D.	03-Mar-72	19	3	3

press ↵ to complete the operation. As a result, 1-2-3 sorts the list by employees' birthdays, from January to December.

As you can see in Figure 5.37, columns D and E show the month and the day of each birthday through the course of the calendar year. The manager can now use this worksheet to anticipate each employee's extra vacation day.

In some worksheet applications, you might prefer to enter the day, month, and year components of dates in three separate columns, as shown in columns A, B, and C of Figure 5.38. Some spreadsheet users find this arrangement to be more efficient for input purposes, especially when dates have to be read from handwritten forms and entered manually into a worksheet. Given a list of dates in this three-column format, you can use 1-2-3's @DATE function to convert the date components into date numbers, so that you can ultimately perform date arithmetic operations on the worksheet. For example, here is the formula entered into cell D2 in Figure 5.38:

@DATE(C2,B2,A2)

After copying this formula down column D, you can choose the Range Format command and select an appropriate date display format.

You'll need to perform another kind of data conversion on a worksheet that contains date or time values that have been entered as labels. In particular,

FIGURE 5.37:
Using @MONTH and @DAY to sort the employee list by birthdays

	A	B	C	D	E
1		Employees' Birthdays			
2					
3	Name	Date of Birth	Age	Mo	Day
4	Nelson, P.	02-Jan-67	25	1	2
5	Fine, M.	01-Feb-70	22	2	1
6	Calloway, D	03-Mar-72	19	3	3
7	Madson, I.	07-Apr-68	23	4	7
8	Parker, H.	08-May-45	46	5	8
9	Jackson, N.	19-Jun-59	32	6	19
10	Graves, A.	23-Jun-35	56	6	23
11	Dalton, R.	06-Jul-47	44	7	6
12	Alcott, M.	05-Aug-39	52	8	5
13	Burton, C.	05-Aug-69	22	8	5
14	Larson, W.	07-Aug-65	26	8	7
15	Oliver, A.	03-Sep-54	37	9	3
16	Hines, D.	27-Oct-51	40	10	27
17	Kelley, N.	08-Nov-71	20	11	8
18	Everett, V.	02-Dec-59	32	12	2

you might find yourself in this situation if you load data into a 1-2-3 worksheet from a different software environment. Figure 5.39 shows the date and time label formats that 1-2-3 can successfully convert into date and time numbers. Column A of this worksheet contains examples of the five date formats that 1-2-3 recognizes. The @DATEVALUE function converts these labels into date numbers. The following formula has been entered into cell B5 and copied down column B:

@DATEVALUE(A5)

	A	B	C	D
1	Day	Month	Year	Date
2	31	1	63	31-Jan-63
3	28	2	61	28-Feb-61
4	21	3	93	21-Mar-93
5	5	4	71	05-Apr-71
6	9	5	88	09-May-88
7	30	6	55	30-Jun-55
8	24	7	88	24-Jul-88
9	17	8	76	17-Aug-76
10				

FIGURE 5.38:
Using the @DATE function

	A	B	C	D	E
1		String to Number Conversion			
2		for Date and Time Values			
3					
4	Date String	Date Number		Time String	Time Number
5	1-Dec-91	33573		4:30:00 PM	0.6875
6	1-Dec	33939		4:30 PM	0.6875
7	Dec-91	33573		16:30:00	0.6875
8	12/1/91	33573		16:30	0.6875
9	12/1	33939			
10					

FIGURE 5.39:
Using @DATEVALUE and @TIMEVALUE

Column D of the same worksheet shows examples of the four time formats that 1-2-3 recognizes. In this case, the @TIMEVALUE function converts these labels into decimal time numbers. The following formula in cell E5 has been copied down column E:

@TIMEVALUE(D5)

Finally, the @DAYS360 and @D360 functions are available for special financial contexts in which date arithmetic is based on a 360-day year. The worksheet in Figure 5.40 shows examples of these tools. Columns A and B in this worksheet show two lists of dates. Columns C, D, and E display the results of the three techniques for finding the difference in days between pairs of dates. Here are the three formulas in cells C4, D4, and E4:

+B4–A4
@DAYS360(A4,B4)
@D360(A4,B4)

Of course, only the first of these formulas finds the exact number of days between two dates. The @DAYS360 and @D360 functions find approximations of the difference for the convenience of particular financial applications. As you can see, the three formulas produce different results.

	A	B	C	D	E
1		Difference between Two Dates			
2					
3	Date1	Date2	ABS	DAYS360	D360
4	15-Jan-85	22-May-86	492	487	487
5	04-Sep-86	31-Aug-83	-1100	-1083	-1084
6	31-Oct-92	28-Feb-94	485	478	478
7	07-Jul-91	02-Nov-86	-1708	-1685	-1685
8	31-Oct-93	30-Oct-93	-1	0	0
9	11-Dec-85	27-Feb-82	-1383	-1364	-1364
10	18-Feb-89	06-Mar-87	-715	-702	-702
11	18-Feb-86	31-Aug-95	3481	3433	3432
12	30-Apr-95	30-Jun-93	-669	-660	-660
13	21-Jan-86	05-Jan-94	2906	2864	2864
14					

FIGURE 5.40:
Comparing date arithmetic tools

Logical Functions

Lotus 1-2-3 has an interesting assortment of logical functions that supply information about a worksheet. Like logical formulas, these functions give values of 1 or 0, representing true or false. For example, the @ISNUMBER function takes a cell address as its argument, and returns a value of 1 (true) if the cell contains a numeric value or is blank. @ISNUMBER returns a value of Ø (false) if the cell contains a label. You are more likely to use functions like this one in macros than in everyday worksheet applications.

But there is one tool in the category of logical functions that is very important in worksheets—the @IF function. This function evaluates a logical expression, and chooses between one of two values, depending on whether the expression is true or false. The @IF function takes three arguments:

@IF(*expression,value1,value2*)

The first argument is the logical expression that @IF evaluates. You can use operators that you studied earlier in this chapter to build a logical expression for the @IF function: the relational operators =, <>, <, >, <=, and >=; and the logical operators #NOT#, #AND#, and #OR#.

The second and third arguments of the @IF function are the data items that the function chooses between. If the logical expression in the first argument is evaluated as true, @IF returns *value1*. If the logical expression is false, @IF gives *value2*. In other words, when you enter the @IF function into a worksheet cell, you can expect the function to display either *value1* or *value2* in the cell.

Try the following simple example:

1. Enter a value of **0** in cell A1 of a blank worksheet.

2. Enter the following formula in cell A2:

    @IF(A1=0,"zero","not zero")

    The word *zero* appears in cell A2.

3. Now select cell A1 again and enter a value of **10**. The display in cell A2 changes to *not zero*.

The @IF function evaluates the expression *A1=0* to decide which label to display in cell A2.

The *value1* and *value2* arguments in the @IF function can be strings enclosed in quotes, as in the previous example, or they can appear as values or calculations. For a more interesting example of the @IF function, consider the worksheet in Figure 5.41. This worksheet shows part of a billing application. Column A in this worksheet contains a list of dates on which a company has sent bills to its customers. Normally, each invoice is payable in 30 days, as shown in column B. However, if a 30-day due date falls on a Sunday, the formula in column B adds an additional day, to produce a Monday due date. Here is the @IF function that performs this calculation in cell B2:

@IF(@MOD(A2+30,7)=1,A2+31,A2+30)

This formula is copied down column B, to the range B3..B11. The first argument in the @IF function is an expression that determines whether the 30-day due date falls on a Sunday:

@MOD(A2+30,7)=1

The @MOD function adds 30 to the date in column A, and performs the modulus 7 operation on the result. If this @MOD function gives a value of 1, representing Sunday, the @IF function chooses the *value1* argument, a 31-day due date:

A2+31

	A	B
1	Billing Date	Due Date
2	15-Jan-92	14-Feb-92
3	17-Jan-92	17-Feb-92
4	27-Jan-92	26-Feb-92
5	03-Feb-92	04-Mar-92
6	10-Feb-92	11-Mar-92
7	13-Feb-92	14-Mar-92
8	17-Feb-92	18-Mar-92
9	26-Feb-92	27-Mar-92
10	06-Mar-92	06-Apr-92
11	18-Mar-92	17-Apr-92
12		

FIGURE 5.41:
Using the @IF function

But if the @MOD function shows that the 30-day due date is not a Sunday, the *value2* argument is chosen:

A2+30

The use of the @IF function can become even more complex than this example. In some applications, you might write additional "nested" @IF functions in the positions of the *value1* and *value2* arguments of an initial @IF function. This can result in multifaceted decision-making processes for a worksheet.

String Functions

A large library of string functions gives you the power to manipulate the contents of labels and strings in your worksheets. Like the logical functions, many of the string functions are more likely to be used in macros than in worksheets. String-related tasks require careful attention to detail, and are more often the concern of programmers than everyday spreadsheet users. But some of the string functions prove to be useful worksheet tools, as you'll see in upcoming exercises.

The categories of string functions include *substring* functions, which work with sequences of characters from within existing strings or labels; alphabetic case functions, which change letters to uppercase or lowercase; conversion functions, which produce strings from numeric values, or numbers from strings; and a miscellaneous variety of other string functions.

Examples of all but a few of these functions appear in the worksheet you see in Figure 5.42. This worksheet is organized as follows: Cell A1 contains the label *Lotus 1-2-3 for   windows*. Each function example in the worksheet uses this label to illustrate a particular string operation. (Notice two odd details about the string in cell A1: There are four spaces between *for* and *windows*, and the word *windows* is not capitalized as it should be. Some functions in the worksheet illustrate ways to correct these details.) The results of the function examples appear in column B. In addition, column G shows complete text copies of the functions in column B.

The first five examples in the worksheet show the substring functions:

- ◆ @LEFT supplies a copy of a substring from the beginning of a string. @LEFT takes two arguments, a string and an integer: @LEFT(*string,n*). The function supplies the first *n* characters of *string*. For example, @LEFT(A1,5) displays the string "Lotus" in cell B3 of the worksheet.

- ◆ @RIGHT supplies a copy of a substring from the end of a string. @RIGHT also takes two arguments: @RIGHT(*string,n*). The function supplies the last *n* characters of *string*. For example, @RIGHT(A1,7) displays the string "windows" in cell B4 of the worksheet.

◆ @MID supplies a copy of a substring from a position inside a string. @MID takes three arguments, a string and two integers: @MID(*string,pos,n*). The function copies *n* characters from *string*, starting from the position identified as *pos*. For example, @MID(A1,6,5) displays the string "1-2-3" in cell B5. Note that the first character in a string has a *pos* value of 0; this value is sometimes called the *offset number*. The offset number for a character in a string is one less than the character's actual position in the string. For example, the seventh character in a string has a *pos* value of 6.

◆ @FIND identifies the position of a substring inside a larger string. @FIND takes three arguments: @FIND(*substring,string,pos*). The function searches for *substring* inside *string*, starting the search at the *pos* character in *string*. If the search is successful, @FIND returns the offset location of the substring. For example, @FIND("1-2-3",A1,0) searches for the string "1-2-3" in the label stored in cell A1. The search begins at the beginning of the label. It results in a value of 6, the offset where the substring is found.

◆ @REPLACE writes a sequence of characters over existing characters in a string. @REPLACE takes four arguments: @REPLACE(*string,pos,n, substring*). The function replaces *n* characters of *string*, starting from *pos*.

	A	B	C	D	E	F	G	H	I
1	Lotus 1-2-3 for	windows							
2									
3	Left	Lotus					@LEFT(A1,5)		
4	Right	windows					@RIGHT(A1,7)		
5	Mid	1-2-3					@MID(A1,6,5)		
6	Find	6					@FIND("1-2-3",A1,0)		
7	Replace	Lotus 1-2-3 for Windows					@REPLACE(A1,16,10,"Windows")		
8									
9	Proper	Lotus 1-2-3 For Windows					@PROPER(A1)		
10	Upper	LOTUS 1-2-3 FOR WINDOWS					@UPPER(A1)		
11	Lower	lotus 1-2-3 for windows					@LOWER(A1)		
12									
13	Length	26					@LENGTH(A1)		
14	Exact	0					@EXACT(A1,G9)		
15	Repeat	Lotus 1-2-3 for windowsLotus 1-2-3 for windows					@REPEAT(A1,2)		
16									
17	Trim	Lotus 1-2-3 for windows					@TRIM(A1)		
18									
19	S	Lotus 1-2-3 for windows					@S(A1..A1)		
20	N	0					@N(A1..A1)		

FIGURE 5.42:

Illustrations of string functions

The *substring* argument supplies the replacement characters. For example, @REPLACE(A1,16,10,"Windows") replaces the final characters of the string.

The next three examples in Figure 5.42 show the alphabetic case functions, @PROPER, @UPPER, and @LOWER. Each of these three functions takes a single string argument, and returns a copy of the same string with specified changes in the alphabetic case:

- The @PROPER function capitalizes the first letter in each word of its string argument. An example appears in cell B9.

- The @UPPER function capitalizes all the letters in the string, as shown in cell B10.

- The @LOWER function changes all the letters in the string to lowercase, as in cell B11.

The remaining six functions illustrated in Figure 5.42, in cells B13 to B20, perform a variety of string operations:

- The @LENGTH function supplies the length, in characters, of a string. @LENGTH takes one string argument. For example, @LENGTH(A1) displays 26 as the length of the string.

- The @EXACT function compares two strings and determines whether or not they are the same. @EXACT returns a value of 1 (true) if its two string arguments are identical, or a value of 0 (false) if they are not. For example, @EXACT(A1,B9) returns a value of 0.

- The @REPEAT function generates a new string consisting of multiple copies of a string argument. The function takes two arguments: @REPEAT(*string,n*). The first argument is the string to be repeated, and the second argument is an integer that specifies the number of repetitions. For example, @REPEAT(A1,2) produces the display shown in cell B15.

- The @TRIM function removes extraneous spaces from a string—that is, spaces at the beginning and the end of the string, and multiple consecutive spaces inside the string. For example, @TRIM(A1) in cell B17 removes the extra three spaces between "for" and "windows."

- The @S function returns the label located in the first cell of a range. If this cell does not contain a label, @S returns an empty string. For example, the function @S(A1..A1) in B19 copies the label from cell A1.

◆ The @N function returns the numeric value located in the first cell of a range. If this cell does not contain a value, @N returns a value of zero. For example, the function @N(A1..A1) in B20 returns a value of zero.

Figure 5.43 contains an interesting application of the @MID function. The following formula has been entered into cell B6 and copied down column B to display the day of the week of each date in column C:

@MID("SatSunMonTueWedThuFri",@MOD(C6,7)*3,3)&"."

The first argument is a string containing three-character abbreviations for the days of the week. The second argument calculates a starting point in this string, to extract the abbreviation for a particular day. As you saw back in Figure 5.33, the function @MOD(C6,7) supplies an integer from 0 to 6 representing the day of the week of the date in cell C6. Multiplying this value by 3 gives the correct starting point in the string. Finally, the third @MID argument is the value 3, the length of each day name. To complete the abbreviation, the formula joins the selected name with a period.

The remaining four string functions perform conversions from one data type to another, and give you access to the character code used in Lotus 1-2-3

	A	B	C
5	Place		Date
6	Chicago	Wed.	09-Jan-91
7	St. Louis	Mon.	21-Jan-91
8	Indianapolis	Fri.	15-Feb-91
9	New York	Thu.	07-Mar-91
10	Boston	Mon.	25-Mar-91
11	Washington, D.C.	Wed.	03-Apr-91
12	Atlanta	Sat.	11-May-91
13	Miami	Tue.	28-May-91
14	Dallas	Mon.	03-Jun-91
15	Albuquerque	Sat.	29-Jun-91
16	Las Vegas	Thu.	05-Sep-91
17	Los Angeles	Fri.	11-Oct-91
18	San Francisco	Tue.	29-Oct-91
19	Seattle	Tue.	05-Nov-91

FIGURE 5.43:
Using the @MID and @MOD functions to display a day-of-the-week string

for Windows:

- The @CHAR function takes an integer as its argument, and supplies the corresponding character from the *Lotus Multibyte Character Set*. This character code, known by its abbreviation LMBCS, represents all the characters that can be produced and displayed from Lotus 1-2-3. Figure 5.44 shows an excerpt from the LMBCS code.

- The @CODE function supplies the LMBCS code number of a given character. @CODE takes one string argument, and gives the code number of the first character in the string.

- The @STRING function produces a string from a numeric value. @STRING takes two arguments: @STRING(*value,n*). The *value* argument is the number to be converted to a string, and the *n* argument specifies the number of decimal places that will be displayed in the result. For example, @STRING(123.456,1) produces the string "123.5" as its result.

- The @VALUE function performs the opposite conversion, producing a number from a string of digits. The single argument of @VALUE must be a string that 1-2-3 can read as a number. For example, @VALUE("9876") produces the number 9876.

FIGURE 5.44:

An excerpt from the LMBCS code

	A		B		C		D		E		F	G		H	I	J
1	33	!	52	4	71	G	90	Z	109	m
2	34	"	53	5	72	H	91	[	110	n
3	35	#	54	6	73	I	92	\	111	o
4	36	$	55	7	74	J	93	]	112	p
5	37	%	56	8	75	K	94	^	113	q
6	38	&	57	9	76	L	95	_	114	r
7	39	'	58	:	77	M	96	`	115	s
8	40	(	59	;	78	N	97	a	116	t
9	41	)	60	<	79	O	98	b	117	u
10	42	*	61	=	80	P	99	c	118	v
11	43	+	62	>	81	Q	100	d	119	w
12	44	,	63	?	82	R	101	e	120	x
13	45	-	64	@	83	S	102	f	121	y
14	46	.	65	A	84	T	103	g	122	z
15	47	/	66	B	85	U	104	h	123	{
16	48	0	67	C	86	V	105	i	124	|
17	49	1	68	D	87	W	106	j	125	}
18	50	2	69	E	88	X	107	k	126	~
19	51	3	70	F	89	Y	108	l		

The worksheet in Figure 5.45 shows two short experiments with the @STRING and @VALUE functions. The @STRING function is important in situations where you need to incorporate a numeric value into a string. The & operation will not join a string and a number; before you can perform the concatenation, you must convert the number into a string. This is the job of the @STRING function. For example, cell A4 in Figure 5.45 contains the calculated number of days between today's date and December 25; the following string formula combines this number with two strings to form the sentence displayed in cell A5:

+"There are "&@STRING(A4,0)&" shopping days 'til Christmas."

Conversely, you may sometimes need to convert a string of digits into a number so you can perform arithmetic operations on the value. The @VALUE function does this. For example, consider the sentence displayed in cell A9 of Figure 5.45: *We received 107 units @ $1.25 per unit.* In order to perform arithmetic operations on the two numbers in this string, you have to extract the strings of digits and convert them into numeric values. The formulas in cells A11 and A12 illustrate the technique:

@VALUE(@MID(A9,12,3))
@VALUE(@MID(A9,25,4))

	A	B	C	D
1	Experiments with @STRING and @VALUE			
2				
3				
4	81			
5	There are 81 shopping days 'til Christmas.			
6				
7				
8				
9	We received 107 units @ $1.25 per unit.			
10				
11	107	units		
12	$1.25	per unit		
13	$133.75	total cost		
14				
15				

FIGURE 5.45:
Using the @STRING and @VALUE functions

The argument in each of these @VALUE functions is a @MID function that extracts a string of digits from the sentence in cell A9. @VALUE then makes the conversion from string to number. After this conversion, the numbers can be formatted and used in numeric formulas; for example, cell A13 contains the formula +A11*A12.

Special Functions

Like the logical and string functions, the *special functions* include several tools that are more relevant to macros than to the spreadsheet. But there is a group of very important worksheet functions in this category, known as *lookup functions*. They are called @CHOOSE, @INDEX, @HLOOKUP, and @VLOOKUP. These functions allow you to select a data item from a table that you enter into a range of your worksheet—or, in the case of @CHOOSE, from a list that is contained within the arguments of the function itself. Using these functions requires some careful planning on your part, because you have to begin by developing the list or table of data. But once you have organized your worksheet appropriately, these functions prove to be very powerful tools, as you'll see in this chapter's final exercises.

The @CHOOSE Function

@CHOOSE is the easiest function to use in the group. This function takes one numeric argument, *n*, followed by a list of data values or references to cells:

@CHOOSE(*n*,*datalist*)

The purpose of *n* is to select one of the values in *datalist*. The elements of the list are separated by commas. The value of *n* must be within the range from 0 up to the number of entries in the list minus 1. Using *n* as an offset number, @CHOOSE returns the *n*th value in the list.

@CHOOSE provides an interesting alternative to the formula used in Figure 5.43 to produce the days of the week. You can generate exactly the same day names by entering the following @CHOOSE formula into cell B6 and then copying the formula down column B:

@CHOOSE(@MOD(C6,7),"Sat","Sun","Mon","Tue","Wed","Thu","Fri")&"."

In this function, @MOD(C6,7) produces the value from 0 to 6 that serves as a selector value for the list of names. For example, if the @MOD function returns a value of 3, the @CHOOSE function returns "Tue" as its string result.

The @INDEX Function

By contrast, the @INDEX function selects a label or value from a table on your worksheet. @INDEX takes three required arguments and one optional argument. Here is its format with three arguments:

@INDEX(*range,column,row*)

The *range* argument is the location of the table where @INDEX reads a data item. The *column* and *row* arguments identify column and row offsets within *range*. The *column* argument ranges from 0 up to the number of columns in the table minus 1. Likewise, the *row* argument ranges from 0 up to the number of rows in the table minus 1. The fourth optional argument is an integer representing the worksheet that contains the lookup table:

@INDEX(*range,column,row,worksheet*)

This argument allows you to build the lookup table in a different worksheet location from the function itself.

An example of the @INDEX function appears in Figure 5.46. This worksheet illustrates a technique for producing a complete date string from the date numbers that appear in column A. As you can see in the lower

	A	B	C	D
1	32946	Wednesday, March 14, 1990		
2	34132	Saturday, June 12, 1993		
3	32129	Friday, December 18, 1987		
4	16705	Tuesday, September 25, 1945		
5				
6		DOW	MO	
7		Saturday	January	
8		Sunday	February	
9		Monday	March	
10		Tuesday	April	
11		Wednesday	May	
12		Thursday	June	
13		Friday	July	
14			August	
15			September	
16			October	
17			November	
18			December	

FIGURE 5.46:
Using the @INDEX function to create date strings

part of the worksheet, columns B and C contain lists of day names and month names. The worksheet reads these as one-column @INDEX tables. The column of day names, B7..B13, is assigned the range name DOW; and the column of month names, C7..C18, is named MO.

Formulas in cells B1 to B4 use the @INDEX function to read names from the DOW and MO ranges. Here is the formula in cell B1:

```
@INDEX($DOW,0,@MOD(A1,7))&", "&
  @INDEX($MO,0,@MONTH(A1)-1)&" "&
  @STRING(@DAY(A1),0)&", 19"&
  @STRING(@YEAR(A1),0)
```

This is the most detailed formula you've seen yet, but it's easy to understand if you study it one part at a time. The first @INDEX function uses the expression @MOD(A1,7) as a row offset in the DOW range to select the day of the week. The second uses the expression @MONTH(A1)−1 as a row offset in the MO range to select the name of the month. In both @INDEX functions, the column offset is 0, because both tables have only one column. Then two @STRING functions are used to convert the results of @DAY and @YEAR to strings. When all of these substrings are joined together, the result is a full date display:

Wednesday, March 14, 1990

The formula in cell B1 is copied down to the range B2..B4. (Notice the use of absolute references to make this copy procedure possible.)

The @HLOOKUP and @VLOOKUP Functions

Finally, the @HLOOKUP and @VLOOKUP functions read values from specially organized lookup tables. The first row or column of a lookup table contains a range of reference values that are central to the process of searching for a target data item in the table.

For example, look at the Conference Room Price Table, shown in the lower part of the worksheet in Figure 5.47. The conference planners at Computing Conferences, Inc. use this table to determine the price of a downtown conference room for a one-day event. As you can see, the price of a conference room varies according to the number of people attending and to the date of the event. To find the correct price for an expected attendance size *n*, you begin by looking across the first row of the table, which contains a range of attendance figures from 1 to 300. Find the *largest* value in this row that is less than or equal to *n*. This value heads the column in which you will find the price for the conference room. Next, look down the column to the row containing the date of the conference. The correct price is found in the cell at the intersection of the attendance column and date row.

The @HLOOKUP function automates this search. The function takes three arguments—a lookup value, a table range, and a row offset:

@HLOOKUP(*n,table,row*)

The first argument, *n,* is the value that the function looks for in the first row of the lookup table. The second argument, *table,* is the range of the lookup table itself, and the third argument, *row,* is the target row offset in the table.

In Figure 5.47, the @HLOOKUP function is used in cells E11 and F11 to find the conference room costs corresponding to the minimum and maximum attendance estimates. The table in the range B16..H19 is assigned the name ROOM. The two attendance estimates are in E8 and F8. Here is the function in cell E11:

@HLOOKUP(E8,$ROOM,2)

	A	B	C	D	E	F	G	H
1		Computing Conferences, Inc.						
2		Conference Room Expense						
3								
4	Conference:	Computing for Video Stores						
5	Place:	St. Louis						
6	Date:	15-Oct-92						
7					Expected attendance:			
8	Price:	$195.00			Minimum	Maximum		
9					80	150		
10								
11				Conference room cost	$1,750.00	$2,300.00		
12								
13								
14								
15	Conference Room Price Table							
16	Attendance	1	35	75	100	150	200	300
17	1991 price	$400.00	$600.00	$1,500.00	$1,750.00	$2,000.00	$3,000.00	$3,500.00
18	1992 price	$450.00	$700.00	$1,750.00	$1,900.00	$2,300.00	$3,400.00	$3,700.00
19	1993 price	$500.00	$750.00	$1,900.00	$2,000.00	$2,500.00	$3,500.00	$3,850.00
20								

FIGURE 5.47:

Using the @HLOOKUP function

In this example, E8 is the attendance estimate that the function looks for in the first row of the ROOM range. A row offset of 2 gives the correct row for a 1992 conference date. In short, the @HLOOKUP function finds the conference room price corresponding to an estimated attendance of 80 people: In the first row of the lookup table, the largest value that is less than or equal to 80 is the attendance figure of 75 in cell D16. Searching down column D to the 1992 row, the function finds the correct price for the conference room, $1,750.00, in cell D18.

The @VLOOKUP function performs an equivalent data search, but in a vertically organized lookup table:

@VLOOKUP(*n,table,column*)

This function searches for *n* in the first column of *table*. The third argument, *column,* gives the column offset in the lookup table.

You can also enter labels rather than numbers in the first row or column of a lookup table. In this case, the first argument in the @HLOOKUP and @VLOOKUP functions is a string:

@HLOOKUP(*string,table,row*)

@VLOOKUP(*string,table,column*)

The @HLOOKUP function looks for a label that exactly matches *string* in the first row of the lookup table. Likewise, the @VLOOKUP function looks for a match for *string* in the first column of the table.

The @HLOOKUP and @VLOOKUP functions are versatile and powerful, especially in applications that require very large lookup tables. Of course, the classic example is an income tax table, in which the first column contains a range of income levels, and the first row contains taxpayer categories. The @VLOOKUP function is ideally suited to reading tax amounts from such a table.

SUMMARY

Each of the three major categories of formulas in 1-2-3—numeric, logical, and text—has its own set of operators:

◆ Numeric formulas use the familiar operators *, /, +, and −, along with the ^ operator for exponentiation.

- Logical formulas produce values of true or false, represented numerically by 1 and 0. There are two groups of logical operators: Relational operators determine equality or inequality; they are =, <>, <, >, <=, and >=. The three logical operators modify or combine logical expressions; they are #NOT#, #AND#, and #OR#.

- Finally, 1-2-3 has one text operator, &, which joins two labels or strings.

The 1-2-3 function library includes over one hundred tools that can be entered into cells by themselves or used in formulas. Here is a brief summary of the function categories you have studied in this chapter:

- The statistical functions include tools designed to calculate totals, averages, counts, and maximum and minimum values, along with the more advanced statistical calculations known as variance and standard deviation.

- The financial functions include calculations for depreciation methods; present value and future value; payment, term, and rate values; and the internal rate of return.

- Mathematical functions include built-in formulas for trigonometric, logarithmic, and exponential values, plus an assortment of other important tools: a random number generator, integer and rounding functions, and the absolute value and modulus operations.

- The date and time functions include tools that supply the current date and time; functions that give information about date-and-time values; conversion functions; and date arithmetic functions.

- The most important logical function for spreadsheet use is @IF, which evaluates a logical expression and returns one of two values as its result.

- The string functions include tools that work with substrings; alphabetic case functions; and functions that convert between numeric and string values.

- The special functions include four important lookup tools that read values from tables and lists on the worksheet.

FAST TRACK

To create a graph and assign a name of your own choosing to the graph window, ... 313

preselect the appropriate data ranges and choose the Graph New command. Enter the name into the Graph name text box.

To create a graph from a table of worksheet data, ... 315

preselect the appropriate data ranges and click the create-graph icon. Lotus 1-2-3 supplies a default name such as GRAPH1 for the graph window.

To delete a graph definition from your worksheet, ... 315

choose the Graph Name Delete command. Select the target graph from the list of names, and click the Delete button. Then click OK to confirm.

To change the graph type displayed in the current graph window, ... 319

choose the Chart Type command. Select a type from the Types list, and then click one of the format pictures displayed to the right of the list.

To change the current graph to a rowwise graph, ... 322

choose the Chart Ranges command and click the Group Range button. In the resulting Chart Ranges Group Range dialog box, select the Rowwise option. Click OK for both dialog boxes.

To add a legend to a graph, ... 326

preselect the legend range on the source worksheet, then activate the graph. Choose the Chart Legend command and click the Group Range button.

To add titles and footnotes to the curent graph, ...327
> choose the Chart Headings command and enter text values into any combination of the Title, Subtitle, Note, and 2nd note text boxes. To use a label from the source worksheet as a title or footnote, enter a backslash character followed by a reference to the cell that contains the label.

To add an arrow, line, ellipse, polygon, rectangle, or drawing to a graph, ...330
> pull down the Draw menu and choose the desired object, or click the corresponding icon in the graph window's icon palette. Use the mouse to position and size the object.

To add a line of text as an object to a graph, ...331
> choose the Draw Text command and enter the text into the New text box. Then use the mouse to position the text.

To add a graph to the worksheet, ...336
> activate the worksheet and preselect the range in which you want to display the graph. Choose the Graph Add to Sheet command. Select the target graph from the Graph name list.

To print a graph, ...337
> add the graph to the linked worksheet (using the worksheet's Graph Add to Sheet command). Preselect the print range and choose the worksheet's File Print command; or click the worksheet's print-range icon.

To display a title along the x-axis or y-axis, ...345
> choose the Chart Axis X or Chart Axis Y command and click the Options button. Enter the title into the Axis title text box.

CHAPTER 6

Graphs

In business, technology, and everyday life, graphs have a universal appeal. People often prefer to look at pictorial representations of numbers rather than the numbers themselves. Grasping the sense of a table of numbers requires time, effort, and concentration, but a graph has an instant impact. When you look at a graph, you can answer many questions about the data, almost before you can even ask the questions: Which data item is the smallest and which is the largest? Is there a downward or upward trend over time? Are there any atypical values that don't conform to the trends of the other data? How significant is a given value in relation to the total? The answers to these and many other questions are visibly clear in a graph of numeric data.

Producing a graph in 1-2-3 is simple, yet you can create an extraordinary variety of visual effects. There are seven major graph types to choose from.

The most familiar are bar graphs, line graphs, area graphs, and pie charts; these four are available in both two-dimensional and three-dimensional versions. In addition, you can create XY graphs, mixed graphs, and high-low-open-close graphs for special kinds of data. Once you have chosen a graph type, you use 1-2-3's powerful collection of graphics tools to refine and clarify the message contained in a graph.

You work on a graph inside a distinct *graph window*. As you can see in Figure 6.1, Lotus 1-2-3 displays a special set of pull-down menus, along with a new icon palette, when a graph window is active. In this chapter, you'll learn to use the tools of the graph window. You'll also get used to switching from the graph window back to the familiar worksheet window, where you find all the menus and commands you've worked with in previous chapters. In fact, the menu bar for the worksheet window includes a Graph menu (shown in Figure 6.2), which contains commands for creating, identifying, viewing, and managing the graphs associated with a given worksheet. After you have finished designing a graph, you use tools in this menu to incorporate the graph into the worksheet from which it was originally created. As you'll learn in an exercise near the end of this chapter, this step allows you to print the graph along with the worksheet.

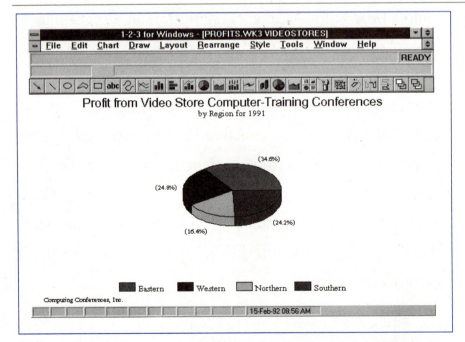

FIGURE 6.1:
The graph window

CREATING A GRAPH FROM WORKSHEET DATA

A graph is linked to a worksheet in 1-2-3, and is saved to disk as part of the worksheet file. A worksheet can have multiple linked graphs, each identified by a unique name.

To create a graph, you begin by developing the table of worksheet data that the graph will ultimately represent. Once the worksheet is ready, you follow a general pattern of steps to develop your graph:

1. Preselect the range of data from which the graph will be created.

2. Choose the spreadsheet's Graph New command to create the graph. Enter a name for the graph in the Graph New dialog box.

3. Use the menu commands and the icons of the graph window to add objects to your graph, and to refine the graph's appearance. For example, you can add titles and footnotes, arrows and shapes, free-floating text, and a legend.

4. When your graph is complete, return to the spreadsheet and choose the Graph Add to Sheet command to incorporate the graph into the original worksheet.

5. Print the worksheet with the graph.

In this chapter, you'll create several different graphs from one fairly simple worksheet example. The worksheet, shown in Figure 6.3, is a one-year profit summary from Computing Conferences, Inc. The worksheet's columns show the profits from each of the company's four regions—Eastern, Western,

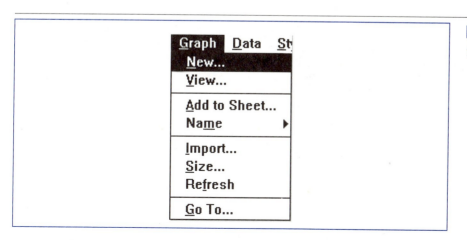

FIGURE 6.2:
The Graph menu

Northern, and Southern. The rows represent the various types of computer-training conferences that the company conducts in each region, including conferences designed for accountants, doctors, lawyers, retail businesses, and video stores. In the worksheet's title, these are referred to as the conference "topics."

To prepare for the exercises ahead, your first job is to enter this table of data into your own worksheet. Here are the steps:

1. On a blank worksheet (default size, not maximized), enter the following titles into cells A1, A2, and A3:

   Computing Conferences, Inc.
   Conference Profits by Region and Topic
   1991

   Remember to begin the entry in cell A3 (1991) with a single-quotation mark, so that 1-2-3 will accept the entry as a label rather than a value.

2. Preselect the range A1..F3. To center the titles horizontally over this range, choose the Style Alignment command and select the Center and Align over borders options. Click OK to confirm. Then click the bold and italics icons to set the display style for the titles.

3. Choose the Worksheet Global Settings command and click the Format button on the resulting dialog box. Select the Currency format in the Worksheet Global Settings Format dialog box, and enter a value of **0** into the Decimals box. Click OK on both dialog boxes to confirm.

4. Enter the labels **Accountants**, **Doctors**, **Lawyers**, **Retail Business**, **Video Stores**, and **Total** into cells A6 to A11. Drag the border of

FIGURE 6.3:
The conference profits worksheet

	A	B	C	D	E	F	G
1		*Computing Conferences, Inc.*					
2		*Conference Profits by Region and Topic*					
3		*1991*					
4							
5		Eastern	Western	Northern	Southern	Total	
6	Accountants	$111,200	$79,300	$59,500	$64,200	$314,200	
7	Doctors	$131,900	$116,900	$77,500	$96,700	$423,000	
8	Lawyers	$63,500	$81,500	$54,000	$88,400	$287,400	
9	Retail Business	$92,800	$88,600	$57,900	$78,400	$317,700	
10	Video Stores	$88,300	$63,200	$41,900	$61,900	$255,300	
11	Total	$487,700	$429,500	$290,800	$389,600	$1,597,600	
12							

column A to the right to increase the column width to 13. Then enter the column headings **Eastern**, **Western**, **Northern**, **Southern**, and **Total** into cells B5 to F5. Right-align each of these headings in its respective cell. Finally, enter the numeric profit values into the range B6..E10, as shown in Figure 6.3.

5. Preselect the range B6..F11 and click the summation icon once. In response, 1-2-3 enters all the appropriate @SUM functions into column F and row 11.

6. To complete your work, apply the boldface style to columns A and F and rows 5 and 11, as shown in Figure 6.3.

7. Choose the File Save As command and save the worksheet as PROFITS.WK3.

You're now ready to create a graph from this worksheet.

Understanding Data Ranges for Graphs

The first step is to preselect the data range from which 1-2-3 will create a graph. By default, 1-2-3 reads your data range selection in a *columnwise* mode. This means that each column of the range has a specific role in the graph that 1-2-3 creates:

◆ The first column in the data range is known as the *X data range*. For most graph types, 1-2-3 expects to find labels in this range to identify the numeric data in the columns to the right. Where appropriate, 1-2-3 displays these labels along the *x-axis* of the graph. (The x-axis is the horizontal line at the bottom border of a graph.)

◆ As many as six adjacent columns are known as the *A* through *F data ranges*. In these columns, 1-2-3 generally expects to find the numeric data that will be represented in the graph.

This description of the data range applies to area graphs, line graphs, and bar graphs. Other graph types impose additional requirements on the selected data range, as you'll learn later in this chapter.

On the profits worksheet, the data range for your first graph is A6..E10. The first column in this range, A6..A10, is the X data range. As you'll see shortly, these labels will appear along the x-axis of the graph.

The four adjacent columns are the A, B, C, and D data ranges. These columns contain the one-year profit figures for the four regions in which the company does business.

Select the range A6..E10 on your worksheet now. Notice what this range does *not* contain: You are not including the column of topic totals (column F), or the row of regional totals (row 11); doing so would make no sense in the resulting graph. Furthermore, you have omitted the row of column headings (row 5) from the data range. Eventually, you'll want to use these headings to create a legend for your graph; but adding this feature is a separate step in 1-2-3, performed after the graph has been created.

Once you have selected an appropriate data range, there are two ways to create the graph: Select the Graph New command or click the create-graph icon. You'll try both of these approaches in the next exercises.

Choosing Commands from the Graph Menu

When you pull down the Graph menu from the spreadsheet's menu bar, you see a list of eight commands, as shown back in Figure 6.2. Here are brief descriptions of these commands:

- ◆ The Graph New command creates a new graph from a data range that you select. This command also gives you the opportunity to assign a name to the graph. Once you confirm this command, 1-2-3 switches you to the graph window, with its distinct menu bar and icon palette.

- ◆ The Graph View command presents a list of all the graphs defined for the current worksheet. Each existing graph is identified by name. You can view any graph by selecting a name from the list. Again, 1-2-3 switches to the graph window after you make a selection.

- ◆ Graph Add to Sheet is the command you choose when you are ready to incorporate your finished graph into the worksheet. You specify the worksheet range in which you want to display the graph, and you select the target graph from a list of all the graphs defined for the worksheet.

- ◆ The Graph Name command presents a cascade menu containing two secondary commands: Graph Name Delete and Graph Name Paste Table. You can use the Delete command to remove the definition of one or more graphs from the current worksheet. The Paste Table command creates a reference list of the graphs defined for a worksheet, and pastes the list into a selected range on the worksheet itself.

- ◆ The Graph Import command reads a picture file created by a program other than 1-2-3.

- ◆ The Graph Size command gives you the opportunity to change the size of a graph that you have added to a range on your worksheet.

- ◆ The Graph Refresh command redraws all graphs linked to the current worksheet, adjusting them to any changes that have been made in the corresponding data ranges. You need to use this command only when 1-2-3 is in the manual recalculation mode. In the default automatic recalculation mode, 1-2-3 redraws a graph whenever you change the data upon which the graph depends.

- ◆ Finally, the Graph Go To command moves the cell pointer to the range containing a graph that you have added to your worksheet.

Graph New is the first command you should learn to use in this menu.

Using the Graph New Command

When you choose the Graph New command, the dialog box shown in Figure 6.4 appears on the screen. This dialog box contains two text boxes, labeled Graph name and Range. The Range box displays the notation for the data range you have already selected on your worksheet, in this case *A:A6..A:E10*. The Graph name box displays the default name for your first graph, *GRAPH1*. You can accept this default if you wish, or you can enter a more descriptive name to identify the graph. A graph name can be as long as 15 characters. Use letters of the alphabet for this name; avoid any special characters (such as +, –, or &) that would make the name look like a formula or a range address. You can enter the graph name in uppercase or lowercase letters, but 1-2-3 converts your entry to all uppercase.

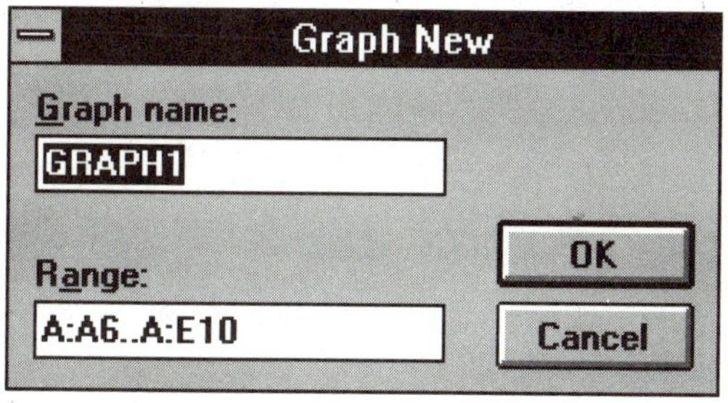

FIGURE 6.4:
The Graph New dialog box

The graph you are about to create will eventually appear as a bar graph depicting the relative profit levels generated by the five different conference topics. Consequently, you'll assign the name TOPICBARS to this graph:

1. With the range A6..E10 still preselected on your worksheet, pull down the spreadsheet's Graph menu and choose the New command.

2. Enter the name TOPICBARS into the Graph name box.

3. Click OK or press ↵ to confirm the command.

When you complete your work in the Graph New dialog box, 1-2-3 immediately creates a new graph window and draws a graph of your selected data range. As you can see in Figure 6.5, the new window displays the name *PROFITS.WK3 TOPICBARS* in its title bar. This name identifies both the graph and the worksheet to which the graph is linked. As long as the graph window is active, the graph menu bar and the graph icon palette appear at the top of the 1-2-3 window, as shown back in Figure 6.1.

By default, the line graph is the initial type for any new graph you create. As you can see in Figure 6.5, the profit data is represented in this graph by a set of four lines. Each line represents one of the four regions, and the points along a line represent the profit level for a given conference topic in the region. The line graph type is not particularly appropriate for this data. Usually, line graphs are reserved for data sets that show specific changes over time. In a moment, you'll transform this graph into a bar graph.

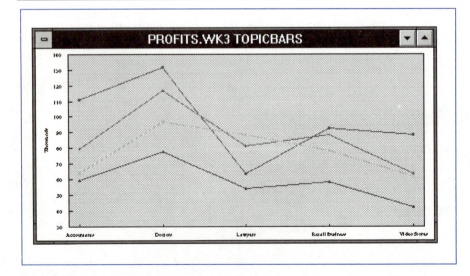

FIGURE 6.5:

The initial line graph created from the profit data

But first, return to the spreadsheet now for an experiment with the other tool available for creating a graph—the create-graph icon. To reactivate the profits worksheet, you can simply click the worksheet window with the mouse. Or, if the worksheet window is hidden from view behind the graph window (which will happen later when you maximize the graph window), you can pull down the Window command and choose PROFITS.WK3 from the list of window names displayed in the menu. Either way, when the worksheet window is active again, the spreadsheet menu bar reappears at the top of the 1-2-3 window, along with the familiar spreadsheet icon palette. While working with graphs, you'll find yourself switching frequently between the graph menu and the spreadsheet menu.

Using the Create-Graph Icon

The create-graph icon is located toward the right side of the spreadsheet icon palette, as shown in Figure 6.6. To use this icon, you begin by preselecting a data range; then you just click the icon. The create-graph icon bypasses the Graph New dialog box, and assigns a default name to the new graph that 1-2-3 creates. In the following exercise, you'll create a new graph using this icon, and then you'll delete the graph using the Graph Name Delete command:

1. Preselect the range A6..E10 on the profit worksheet once again.

2. Click the create-graph icon. In response, 1-2-3 creates a line graph like the one in Figure 6.5. The only difference is that the title bar of the graph window displays the default title assigned to the new graph, *PROFITS.WK3 GRAPH1*. Clearly, the advantage of the create-graph icon is its one-step efficiency. The disadvantage is the default name assigned to the graph; you have no opportunity to provide a name of your own choice. Furthermore, 1-2-3 offers no direct technique for changing the name of an existing graph. An indirect approach is to delete the graph, and then create it again via the Graph New command.

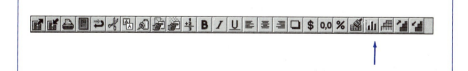

FIGURE 6.6:
The create-graph icon

3. To delete the GRAPH1 window that you just created, begin by activating the profits worksheet. Click the worksheet with the mouse, or select PROFITS.WK3 from the Window menu.

4. In the spreadsheet menu, choose the Graph Name command. On the resulting cascade menu, choose the Delete command. The Graph Name Delete dialog box contains a list of all the graphs currently linked to the profit worksheet. The list currently contains two names, GRAPH1 and TOPICBARS. Select GRAPH1 and 1-2-3 copies the name to the Graph name text box, as shown in Figure 6.7.

5. Click the Delete button. GRAPH1 disappears from the list and from the Graph name text box. The graph now no longer exists. Click OK to complete your work on the Graph Name Delete dialog box.

In summary, you should use the Graph New command to create a graph when you prefer to assign a name of your choice to the resulting graph window. Click the create-graph icon when you are prepared to accept the default name that 1-2-3 assigns to the graph window.

After the Graph Name Delete operations, only one graph is linked to the profits worksheet. Activate the graph now by pulling down the Window menu and selecting PROFITS.WK3 TOPICBARS from the name list. Then click the maximize button on the graph window to expand the window over the available screen area. In the next exercise, you'll select a bar graph type as the new format for the graph.

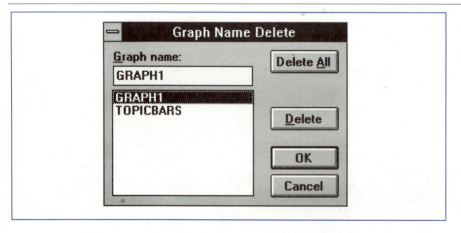

FIGURE 6.7:
The Graph Name Delete dialog box

Using the Graph Window's Menu Bar and Icon Palette

Looking back at Figure 6.1, you can see that the menu bar for the graph window contains ten commands, representing the pull-down menus for graphs. Here are brief summaries of the commands contained in these menus:

- The File menu contains only two commands: The File Close command closes the current graph window; the File Exit command terminates the current 1-2-3 session.

- The Edit menu contains commands for selecting and working with objects in a graph, and for copying graph images to the Windows clipboard.

- The Chart menu contains the commands you'll probably use the most often as you develop graphs. Specifically, the Chart Ranges command allows you to adjust the data ranges for a graph. The Chart Type command gives you choices among the available graph types. Other commands in this menu add new elements to the graph, such as titles and a legend, and offer varieties of display options for the graph.

- The Draw menu includes seven tools for adding *objects* to your graph, including text, arrows, lines, ellipses, polygons, rectangles, and drawings. (The seven commands in the Draw menu are represented by the first seven icons in the graph window's icon palette.)

- The next three menus, Layout, Rearrange, and Style, contain tools you can use to change the position, orientation, and style of objects that you add to your graph. Several of these options are also represented as icons in the graph window's icon palette.

- The Tools menu contains one command, Tools SmartIcons. Like the equivalent command in the spreadsheet menu, this command gives you options for changing the position and the content of the icon palette. You can remove existing icons from the default palette and replace them with other predefined icons that relate to graph operations.

- The Window menu contains commands that allow you to focus on an enlarged, or zoomed, portion of the current graph. In addition, the

Window Tile and Window Cascade commands change the size and orientation of the current worksheet and graph windows, as do the equivalent commands in the spreadsheet menu. Finally, the Window menu contains a list of windows that are currently open; as you've seen, you can select a name from this list to activate a given worksheet or graph window.

◆ Finally, the Help menu gives you the familiar access routes into the 1-2-3 Help system.

The graph window's icon palette contains 26 new icons for you to use. Learning their various jobs is not difficult. As with the spreadsheet icons, you can click any icon in the palette with the *right* mouse button to view a brief description of the icon. This description appears temporarily in the 1-2-3 window's title bar.

Furthermore, this new icon palette is conveniently arranged in groups of tools that are easy to distinguish. For example, Figure 6.8 identifies the dozen icons that produce the most immediate and dramatic results on the current graph. Clicking one of these icons changes the graph type displayed in the graph window. For example, clicking the bar-graph icon (the second icon in the group) changes the current graph to a two-dimensional bar graph. These icons represent options available in the Chart Type command, which you'll be examining shortly. The last icon in this group actually displays the Chart Type dialog box on the screen.

Figure 6.9 shows the seven icons that are equivalent to the commands in the Draw menu. Each of these icons allows you to place a new object on

FIGURE 6.8:

The chart-type icons in the graph icon palette

FIGURE 6.9:

The draw icons, equivalent to the commands in the Draw menu

your graph: an arrrow, a line, an ellipse, a polygon, a rectangle, a text item, or a freehand drawing. Figures 6.10 and 6.11 identify the remaining icons in the graph window's default icon palette. Each of these performs a specific task on a selected graph object—deleting, duplicating, or changing the orientation or position of an object. These icons are equivalent to commands in the Edit, Rearrange, and Layout menus. You'll experiment with these icons and the objects they work with later in this chapter.

Selecting a Graph Type

For now, the TOPICBARS graph is the active window. Your next step is to transform this display into a bar graph. Take this opportunity to examine the Chart Type dialog box:

1. Pull down the Chart menu and choose the Type command. The resulting dialog box contains a complete list of 1-2-3's graph types, represented as a column of option buttons. When you click one of these buttons, the dialog box displays pictures of the formats available in the selected graph type.

2. Click the option labeled 3D Bar (for "three-dimensional bar graph"). The Chart Type dialog box appears, as shown in Figure 6.12. As you can see, there are three formats available for the three-dimensional bar graph: one in which bars in a given category are grouped together in adjacent positions; another in which bars are clustered and visually overlapped; and a third in which bars are stacked one

FIGURE 6.10:

The delete icon and the duplicate icon, equivalent to commands in the Edit menu

FIGURE 6.11:

The object icons, equivalent to commands in the Rearrange and Layout menus

on top of another. The default selection is the first of these three.

3. Click OK or press ↵ to accept the default 3D Bar format. In response, 1-2-3 redraws the current graph, as shown in Figure 6.13.

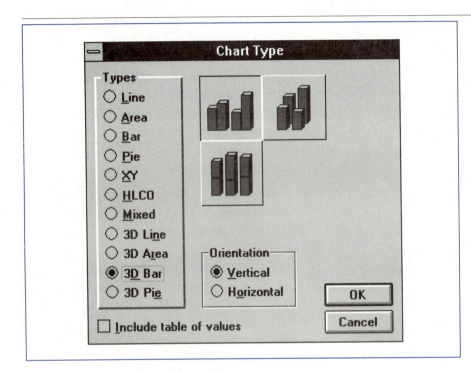

FIGURE 6.12:
The Chart Type dialog box

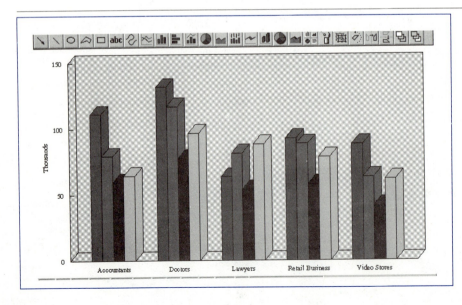

FIGURE 6.13:
A three-dimensional bar graph

In this new graph format, each group of vertical bars represents the profit figures from one of the five training-conference topics. Within a given topic, each of the four bars represents one of the four regions. This begins to be a good visual representation of the data. You can see which conference topic brings in the largest profits and which region is generally the strongest for most topics.

Interestingly, 1-2-3 gives you a way of viewing a data table along with the graph. You activate this feature by clicking the option labeled *Include table of values* in the Chart Type dialog box. To see what this option produces, try the following exercise:

1. Pull down the Chart menu again and choose the Type command.
2. Click the Include table of values option. An X appears inside the check box.
3. Click OK or press ↵.

As a result, the graph window shown in Figure 6.14 appears on the screen. Beneath each group of bars, you can now read the exact data values that the bars represent.

Now, to get ready for the next exercise, pull down the Window menu and choose the PROFITS.WK3 worksheet window in the list of names. When the worksheet is displayed on the screen again, click the save-file icon to save

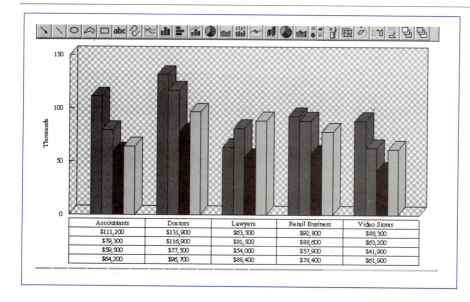

FIGURE 6.14:
A bar chart with the corresponding table of values

your work to disk. Keep in mind that 1-2-3 saves any linked graph definitions along with the worksheet itself.

You learned earlier in this chapter that the *columnwise* method is 1-2-3's default way of translating a table of data into a graph. In the TOPIC-BARS graph, this means that each group of bars on the graph contains one bar representing a data value from each column of the worksheet. The focus of the resulting graph is on the conference topics, and on the profits generated from each topic category. But what if you want to create a graph that focuses instead on the regions? Because you know that *columnwise* graphs are the default, you might consider reorganizing the worksheet itself, entering the regional data values into rows and the topic profits into columns.

Fortunately, 1-2-3 offers a simpler approach. You can select a series of rows as the data range for a graph; then, once the graph is displayed, you can use the Chart Range command to instruct 1-2-3 to reorganize the graph in a *rowwise* format. In the next section of this chapter, you'll work through the steps of this technique.

CREATING A GRAPH IN THE ROWWISE FORMAT

Here is your task in the next exercise: Create a stacked bar graph in which you can compare the total profits from each of the four regions. Each regional bar will consist of five stacked components representing the five conference topics. The labels along the x-axis—that is, the X data range—will identify the four regions. The A, B, C, D, and E data ranges will be the profit figures from each of the five topics.

Looking at the profits worksheet (back in Figure 6.3), it's easy to see that this arrangement requires a *rowwise* graph. Here are the steps for creating it:

1. Preselect the range B5..E10 on the profits worksheet. Ultimately, you will want 1-2-3 to read row 5 as the X data range, and rows 6 through 10 as the A, B, C, D, and E data ranges.

2. Pull down the Graph menu and choose the New command. Enter REGIONBARS as the name for this new graph. Click OK or press ↵ to confirm. In response, 1-2-3 creates a new graph window in which the selected data range is represented as a line graph in the default columnwise format. The result makes little sense.

3. In the graph window menu bar, pull down the Chart menu and choose the Ranges command. This command gives you control over the data ranges of the current graph. Examining the Chart Ranges dialog box, shown in Figure 6.15, you can confirm that 1-2-3 has created the current graph in the columnwise mode. Column B on the worksheet has been selected as the X data range, and columns C, D, and E have been selected as the remaining data ranges. This is not the arrangement you want for this graph.

4. To change the ranges, begin by clicking the Group Range button, located at the upper-right corner of the Chart Ranges dialog box. The resulting Chart Ranges Group Range dialog box is where you instruct 1-2-3 to change the range orientation of the graph. In a frame labeled *Divide into data ranges*, there are two option buttons, labeled Columnwise and Rowwise. The default selection, as you have guessed, is Columnwise. Click the Rowwise button now, as shown in Figure 6.16. Then click OK or press ↵. The Chart Ranges dialog box regains the focus.

5. Now 1-2-3 has correctly reorgnized the data ranges, as you can see in Figure 6.17. The labels in row 5 are identified as the X data range, and the five rows of profit figures beneath these labels are identified as data ranges A through E. Click OK or press ↵ to confirm.

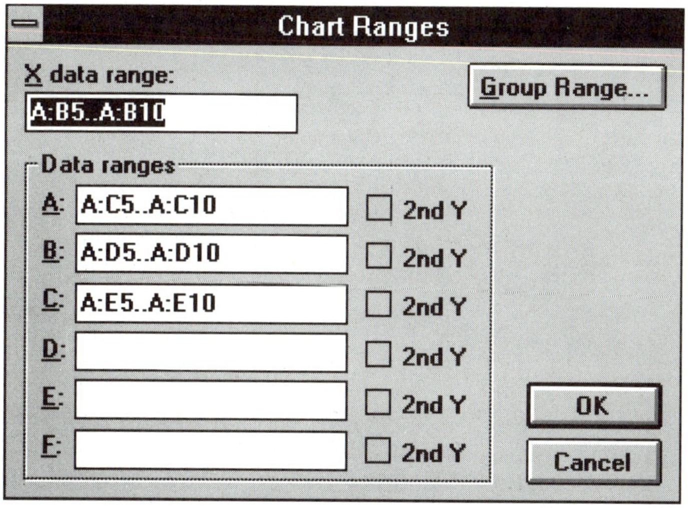

FIGURE 6.15:
The Chart Ranges dialog box

6. Pull down the Chart menu again and choose the Type command. Select the 3D Bar option, and click the picture of the stacked bar graph. Then click OK or press ↵ to confirm your selections.

The resulting stacked bar graph appears in Figure 6.18. You have achieved the effect that you wanted: Each stacked bar represents one of the four regions, and each portion of a given bar represents one of the conference topics. This presentation makes it easy to compare the profits of the four regions.

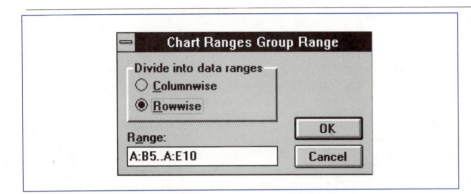

FIGURE 6.16:
The Chart Ranges Group Range dialog box

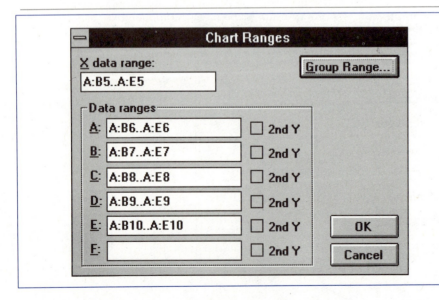

FIGURE 6.17:
Changing the range orientation

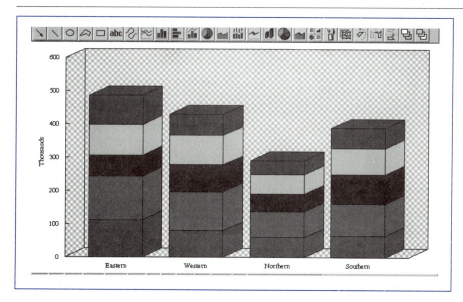

FIGURE 6.18:

A rowwise stacked bar graph

PERFORMING "WHAT-IF" EXPERIMENTS WITH A GRAPH

What happens now if you make a change in the original data on the worksheet to which the graphs are linked? For example, imagine this situation: After creating these graphs, one of the managers at Computing Conferences, Inc. has discovered an unfortunate clerical error. The profit amount for Video Stores training conferences in the Southern region has been underreported by $100,000. Instead of the current $61,900, the figure should be $161,900. What will the graphs look like when this figure is corrected? To find out, follow these steps:

1. Pull down the Window menu and choose the PROFITS.WK3 worksheet window.

2. When the worksheet reappears on the screen, select cell E10 and enter the corrected profit value, **$161,900**.

3. Pull down the Window menu and choose the REGIONBARS graph window. As shown in Figure 6.19, 1-2-3 has redrawn the graph in response to the correction on the worksheet. Now the Southern region has the highest profits of the four regions.

4. Choose the TOPICBARS graph from the Window menu. You'll see that this graph has also been redrawn appropriately.

5. Activate the worksheet window again, and click the save-file icon to save the profits worksheet to disk, along with its linked graphs.

ADDING FEATURES TO THE GRAPH

Your next job is to improve the presentation of your graph by adding a variety of new elements, starting with titles and a legend. The commands for adding these first two features are in the graph window's Chart menu.

ADDING TITLES AND A LEGEND

The Chart Headings and Chart Legend commands create new elements at fixed positions on your graph. Specifically, the Chart Headings dialog box contains text boxes for a title and a subtitle, to be displayed at the top of the graph; and for one or two lines of "footnotes," to be displayed at the lower-left corner of the graph. The Chart Legend dialog box has six text boxes, labeled A through F. In these boxes, you enter labels for the legend that 1-2-3 displays beneath your graph.

In many cases, you will want to copy titles and labels directly from your worksheet to the graph. For example, the titles for the REGIONBARS graph are in cells A1, A2, and A3 of the profits worksheet; and the labels for the legend are the conference topics, in cells A6 through A10. Fortunately, 1-2-3 supplies a special notation you can use to select a worksheet cell as the source

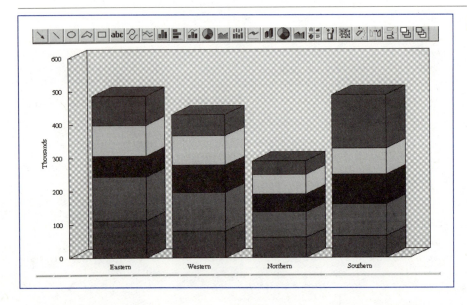

FIGURE 6.19:
The stacked bar graph, redrawn in response to new data

for one of these text items. In this notation, you simply enter a backslash character before the cell reference. The entry \A1 tells 1-2-3 to copy text from cell A1. In the next exercise, you'll supply entries like this one in the Chart Headings dialog box to identify the text for headings and footnotes.

The Chart Legend dialog box has an additional feature. Because the text entries for the graph's legend are likely to be arranged in a row or column of your worksheet, Chart Legend allows you to identify a *group range* for these items. Here are the steps for adding the legend, titles, and footnotes to the REGIONBARS graph:

1. Activate the profits worksheet if it is not already active. Select the range A6..A10, containing the five labels describing the conference topics. These are the labels that you want to display in the legend.

2. Pull down the Window menu and select REGIONBARS to activate the graph window. In the graph menu bar, pull down the Chart menu and choose the Legend command. On the resulting Chart Legend dialog box, click the Group Range button. Normally this button produces a new dialog box in which you can enter the data range containing the legend labels. But because you have preselected the correct range on the profits worksheet, 1-2-3 enters the correct cell references into the Legend text boxes. As you can see in Figure 6.20, the five individual cell references containing legend labels have been entered into the text boxes labeled A through E.

3. Click OK or press ↵. The legend appears at the bottom of the REGIONBARS graph. For this graph, the legend consists of the five

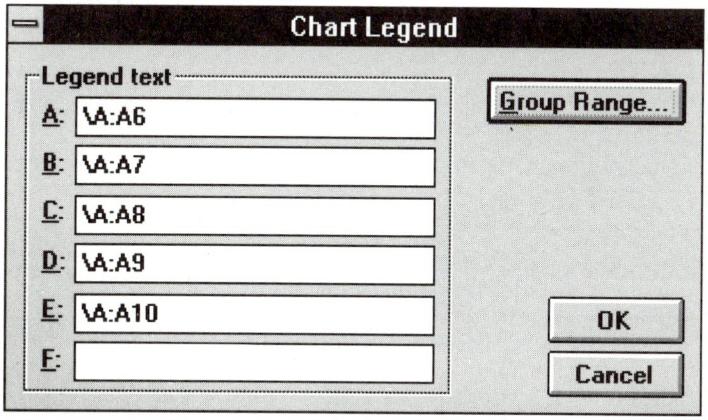

FIGURE 6.20:
Using the Group Range button in the Chart Legend dialog box

topic labels, each paired with a small rectangle that identifies the corresponding color in the stacked bar graph.

4. Now, to add titles and a footnote to the graph, pull down the Chart menu and choose the Headings command. In the Chart Headings dialog box, enter **A2** into the Title text box, **A3** into the Subtitle text box, and **A1** into the Note text box, as shown in Figure 6.21. (Leave the 2nd note text box empty.)

5. Click OK or press ⏎. A title and subtitle now appear at the top of the graph, and *Computing Conferences, Inc.* appears as a footnote at the lower-left corner of the graph. Unfortunately, the title and the legend labels are displayed in a font size that seems out of proportion to the rest of the graph. You'll correct this problem next, using the Chart Options Fonts command.

6. Pull down the Chart menu and choose the Options command. On the resulting cascade menu, choose the Fonts command. The Chart Options Fonts dialog box appears on the screen, as shown in Figure 6.22. This command gives you a selection of fonts for the chart title, the legend, and other text that appears at fixed positions on the graph. (The fonts that appear on your screen may not be the same as those in Figure 6.22.) Pull down the Chart title list, and choose the next smaller font size, located above the current selection in the list. Likewise, pull down the list labeled *Subtitle, axis titles, legend*, and select the next smaller font size in the list.

7. Click OK or press ⏎. The REGIONBARS graph now appears as shown in Figure 6.23.

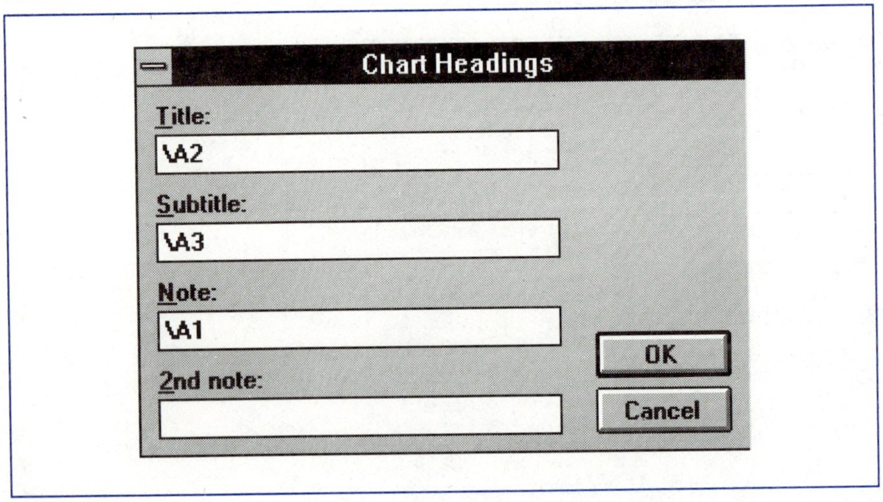

FIGURE 6.21:
Entering references into the Chart Headings dialog box

These new entries make your graph much more complete. The legend clarifies the meaning of the five data ranges, and the titles and footnote supply general information about the graph. As a formal presentation of the data, this graph is nearly ready to be printed and distributed.

But for more informal documents, such as memos to staff members or notes to colleagues, you may want to add other elements to your graph. For example, to focus attention on a particular value in the graph, you might want

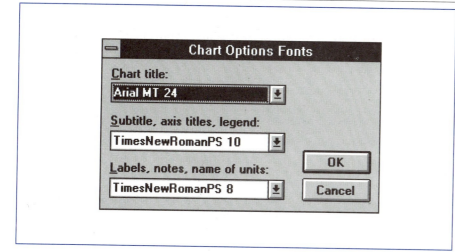

FIGURE 6.22:
The Chart Options Fonts dialog box

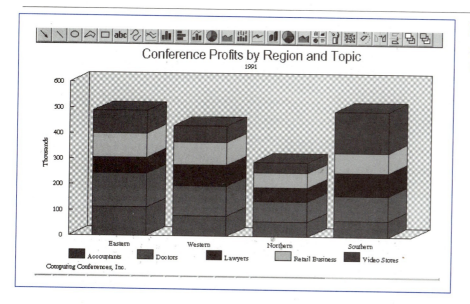

FIGURE 6.23:
Adding titles and a legend to the graph

to add a line of text, along with an arrow pointing from the text to the appropriate section of the graph. These are examples of graph *objects*. Unlike titles and the legend, objects can be placed anywhere on the graph. You choose commands from the Draw menu to add objects to your graph, or you click the corresponding icons shown back in Figure 6.9. In the next section, you'll try your hand at adding a few objects to the REGIONBARS graph.

ADDING OBJECTS TO THE GRAPH

Because objects can be displayed in any size and at any position in the graph, you may need to experiment for a while before you'll be satisified with the results of your work in the upcoming exercise. You'll begin by drawing a rectangle on the graph. Then you'll place a line of text inside the rectangle, and you'll point an arrow from the rectangle to the graph. The purpose of these additions is to draw attention to the unusually high profits for the Video Stores conferences in the Southern region:

1. Pull down the Draw menu and choose the Rectangle command, or click the add-rectangle icon (the fifth icon from the left in the graph icon palette). The mouse pointer becomes a small cross.

2. Take a look at Figure 6.24 to see the position and size of the rectangle you'll be drawing. Position the pointer just above and to the left of the fourth stacked bar in the graph area. Hold down the left mouse

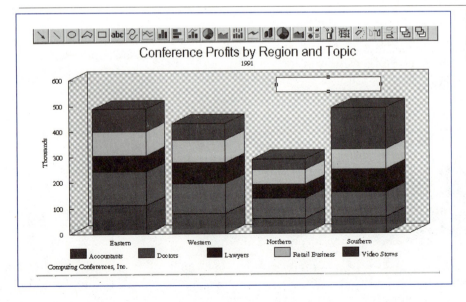

FIGURE 6.24:

Drawing a rectangle on the graph

button and drag the mouse down and to the right. As you do so, an outline of the rectangle appears over the graph. When the outline is the correct size and shape, release the mouse button. The four small black squares that appear around the perimeter of the rectangle are called *handles*. These handles indicate that the rectangle is the selected object in the graph. A number of commands in the Edit, Layout, Rearrange, and Style menus operate on the currently selected object.

3. Pull down the Style menu and choose the Color command. The Style Color dialog box, shown in Figure 6.25, allows you to change the color of the selected object in the graph. Pull down the list labeled *Interior fill*. When you do, a color palette appears on the screen. Click the white selection, at the upper-left corner of the palette. Then click OK or press ↵. Back on the graph, the inside of the rectangle is now white, as in Figure 6.24.

4. Pull down the Draw menu and choose the Text command, or click the add-text icon (the sixth icon in the palette, labeled *abc*). The Draw Text dialog box appears on the screen. In the New text box, enter **Congratulations, Video Group!**, as shown in Figure 6.26. Click OK or press ↵ to confirm. The mouse pointer is transformed into a dotted

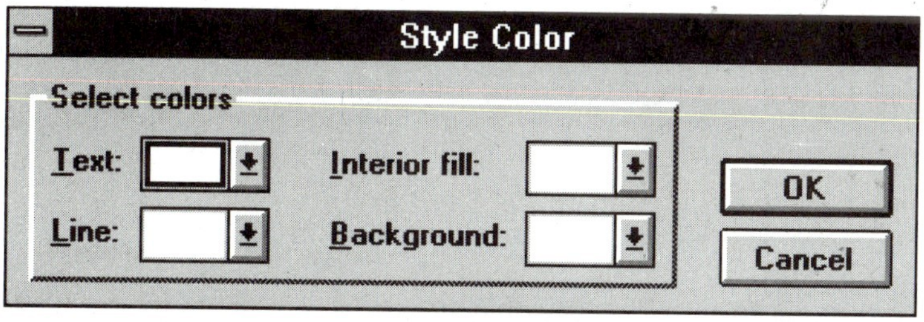

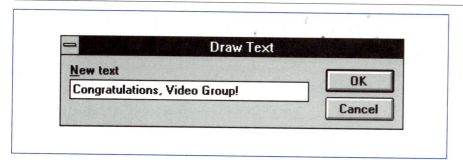

FIGURE 6.25:
The Style Color dialog box

FIGURE 6.26:
The Draw Text dialog box

rectangle. For now, move this object to a position near the upper-right corner of the graph, and click the left mouse button. The text that you entered into the Draw Text dialog box appears inside the dotted rectangle. Handles appear around the perimeter of the rectangle, indicating that the text is now the selected object.

5. The default font size of this text object is too large for the graph. To change the font, pull down the Style menu and select the Font command. The Style Font dialog box, shown in Figure 6.27, contains a list of the available fonts. (The list on your screen may not be the same as the one in Figure 6.27.) Select a font that is smaller than the current font. Click OK or press ↵ to confirm. You may have to repeat this step one or more times until you find an appropriate font size.

6. Position the mouse pointer over the text, and hold down the left mouse button. The mouse pointer becomes a white hand as soon as you begin moving the mouse. Drag the text into the white rectangle that you placed on the graph earlier. Then click the mouse at some other position inside the graph to deselect the text.

7. Pull down the Draw menu and choose the Arrow command. (Or click the add-arrow icon, the first icon in the palette.) The mouse pointer becomes a small cross. Position the pointer along the lower border of the white rectangle. Hold down the left mouse button and drag the mouse down and to the right, into the top stacked bar portion for the Southern region. Double-click the mouse pointer to finish drawing the arrow. Then click the mouse once in some other area of the graph to deselect the arrow. The new objects that you've created appear approximately as shown in Figure 6.28.

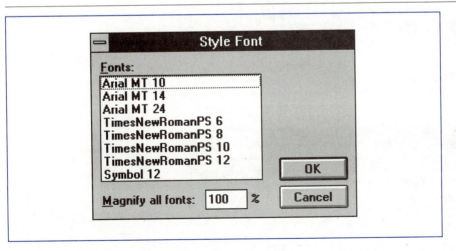

FIGURE 6.27:
The Style Font dialog box

Sometimes you'll add an object to a graph, only to decide that you liked your graph better without the object. Lotus 1-2-3 conveniently allows you to change your mind about any detail of your graph's presentation. In an upcoming exercise, you'll delete the arrow, the text, and the rectangle from the REGIONBARS graph. But before you do so, you might want to experiment briefly with some of the commands in the Rearrange menu. These commands change the size and orientation of a selected object in the graph:

1. Click the arrow object with the mouse. A handle reappears on the arrow, indicating that this is once again the selected object. The Rearrange commands all operate on the currently selected object.

2. Choose the Rearrange Flip command, and then choose the Horizontal command from the resulting cascade menu. This action repoints the arrow toward the lower-left corner of the graph.

3. Choose the Rearrange Turn command. A dotted box appears around the arrow. Any subsequent movement of the mouse results in a rotation of the arrow around a central point. Click the mouse when you have reached the desired rotation.

4. Choose the Rearrange Clear command. The arrow returns to its original position on the graph.

5. Now position the mouse pointer above and to the left of the rectangle object. Hold down the left mouse button and drag the

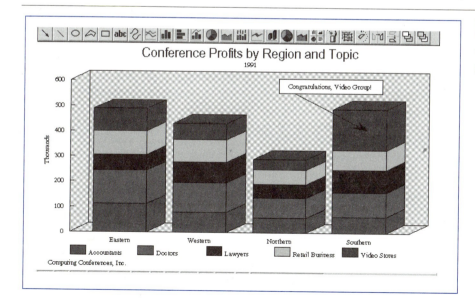

FIGURE 6.28:
Adding objects to the graph

mouse pointer down and to the right, forming a solid rectangle around the three objects you have added to your graph. Release the mouse button. The result of this action is that the three objects—rectangle, text, and arrow—are all selected at once. Handles appear over all three.

6. To delete the three objects, you can take any one of these actions: Pull down the Edit menu and choose the Delete command; click the Delete icon (identified back in Figure 6.10); or press the Delete key on the keyboard. When you take one of these actions, the three objects disappear from the graph.

7. Now as an experiment, choose the Edit Undelete command. The three objects reappear. Delete them once again.

MAKING OTHER CHANGES IN THE GRAPH

The graph menu contains many other options for controlling the appearance of your graph. In particular, the Chart menu contains options for changing the scales and appearance of the axes (the Chart Axis commands), for adding borders and grid lines to the graph (the Chart Borders/Grids command), and for selecting new colors, patterns, and fonts for the graph (the Chart Options commands). In the following exercise, you'll change the format of the numbers displayed along the y-axis, and you'll add horizontal grid lines to the graph:

1. Pull down the Chart menu and choose the Axis command. On the resulting cascade menu, choose the Y command. In the Chart Axis Y dialog box, click the Format button. In the Chart Axis Y Format dialog box, select the Currency option and enter a value of 0 in the Decimal places text box, as shown in Figure 6.29.

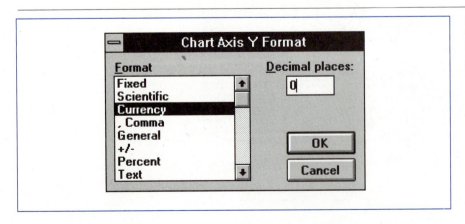

FIGURE 6.29:
The Chart Axis Y Format dialog box

Click OK on both dialog boxes. Back on the graph, the values along the y-axis are now displayed as dollar amounts.

2. Pull down the Chart menu again and choose the Borders/Grids command. On the resulting dialog box, click the Y-axis option in the Grid lines frame, as in Figure 6.30. Click OK or press ↵. This action displays horizontal grid lines across the width of the graph, as shown in Figure 6.31.

3. Activate the profits worksheet and click the save-file icon to update your worksheet and graph on disk.

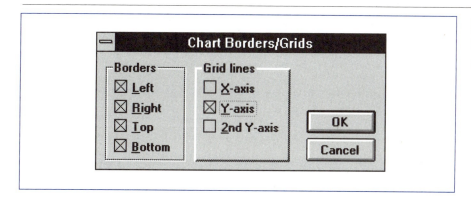

FIGURE 6.30:
The Chart Borders/Grids dialog box

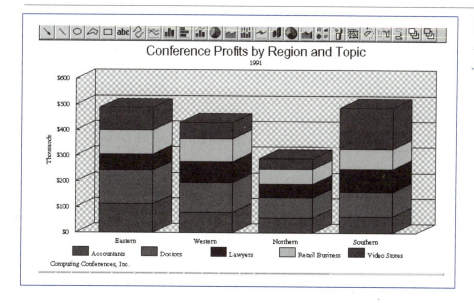

FIGURE 6.31:
Adding grid lines and formatting to the graph

In the final stage of your work with this application, you'll add the REGIONBARS graph to the profits worksheet.

ADDING THE GRAPH TO THE WORKSHEET

You've seen that the graph window's File menu has no Print command. To print a graph in 1-2-3, you first add the graph to its linked worksheet, and then you print the worksheet. You perform the first of these steps by choosing the Add to Sheet command in the spreadsheet's Graph menu:

1. Preselect the range A14..F33 on the profits worksheet.

2. Pull down the Graph menu and choose the Add to Sheet command. The Graph Add to Sheet dialog box contains a list of the graphs currently linked to the worksheet. The REGIONBARS graph is selected, and 1-2-3 has copied the name to the Graph name text box, as shown in Figure 6.32.

3. Click OK or press ↵. In response, 1-2-3 adds the graph to the selected range.

4. To prepare for printing the worksheet and graph, preselect the range A1..F33. Click the preview icon to see approximately how the printed document will look. Press Escape to return to the worksheet.

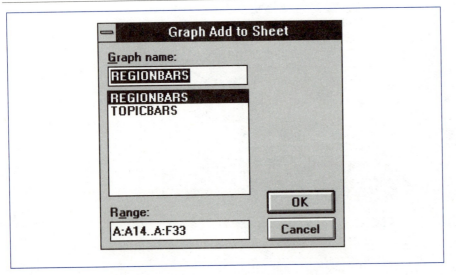

FIGURE 6.32:

The Graph Add to Sheet dialog box

5. If the graph does not immediately appear the way you want it, there are several simple ways to change its shape and size. Experiment with any combination of the following techniques: Increase the width of column F on the worksheet; when you do so, 1-2-3 widens the graph over the new width of the range. Choose the File Page Setup command and enter a value greater than 100% in the Manually size text box; this increases the overall dimensions of the spreadsheet and graph on the printed page. Finally, choose the Graph Size command and enter a new range for the graph in the Range text box, shown in Figure 6.33; in response, 1-2-3 changes the size of the graph to fit the new range you specify. (Don't forget to adjust the print range accordingly before you print the worksheet.)

6. Click the print-range icon to print a copy of the worksheet and graph. If you are not immediately satisfied with the results, keep making adjustments in the worksheet until you get what you want. Figure 6.34 shows one version of the worksheet, printed after several such adjustments.

7. Click the save-file icon to save your work to disk.

WORKING WITH OTHER GRAPH TYPES

To complete your introduction to the 1-2-3 graph component, you'll now take a brief look at other available graph types. As you learned earlier in

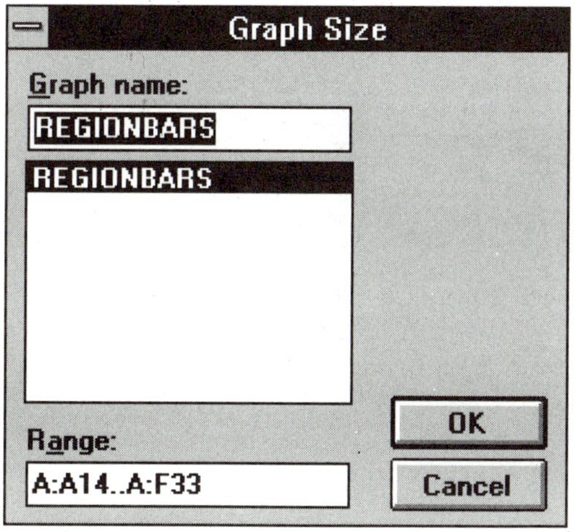

FIGURE 6.33:
The Graph Size dialog box

this chapter, 1-2-3 uses the X, A, B, C, D, E, and F data ranges in a variety of ways for different graph types. To create a given graph type successfully, you generally need to plan your worksheet according to the appropriate data range requirements.

Fortunately, the graph window's Chart Range command gives you some leeway: You can begin by creating a graph in one way, and then use Chart Range to make adjustments in 1-2-3's initial interpretation of the data ranges. You've already seen this command's usefulness in transforming the REGION-BARS graph from a columnwise to a rowwise organization scheme. You'll see other examples of its usefulness in this chapter's final exercises.

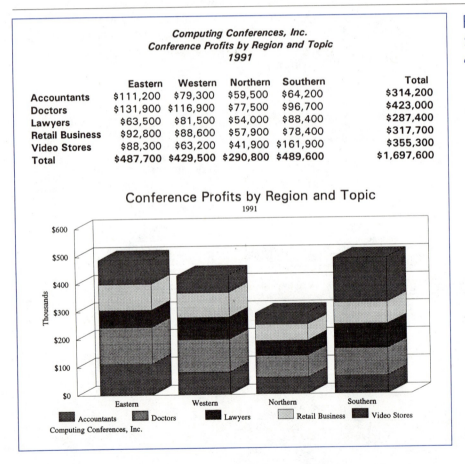

FIGURE 6.34:
The printed worksheet and graph

CREATING LINE GRAPHS AND AREA GRAPHS

Line and area graphs are appropriate for illustrating the downward or upward trends in data over time. Both graph types come in two-dimensional and three-dimensional formats, and in unstacked and stacked versions. In an unstacked graph, each point on a line represents an actual value from the corresponding data range. In a stacked graph, the values of each data range are added to the accumulated values of previous data ranges, so that the top line of the graph represents the totals of all the data ranges.

Both of these graph types use the standard data range definitions: The X data range contains the labels displayed along the x-axis, and the A through F ranges contain the numeric data. For example, Figure 6.35 shows a table of yearly regional profit figures over a five-year period, and Figure 6.36 shows a line graph created from this data. Each line in the graph represents the variations in a region's profit over the five-year period. Notice that some of the lines cross each other one or more times; this is typical of an unstacked line graph.

By contrast, Figure 6.37 shows a stacked area graph created from the same data. An area graph is the same as a line graph, except that the areas beneath the lines are filled in with shades or colors. In this stacked area graph, the area between one line and the next represents the variations in profit for a given region. But the area between the x-axis and the top line of the graph represents the *total* profit for all four regions in a given year.

	A	B	C	D	E
1		Computing Conferences, Inc.			
2		Five-Year Profits by Region			
3		1988 to 1992			
4					
5					
6		Eastern	Western	Northern	Southern
7	1988	$195,000	$187,000	$86,300	$105,700
8	1989	$175,000	$215,000	$66,000	$42,300
9	1990	$229,600	$355,300	$142,300	$244,100
10	1991	$487,700	$389,700	$290,800	$389,600
11	1992	$510,000	$455,000	$375,000	$475,000
12					

FIGURE 6.35:
Yearly regional profits over a five-year period

Creating Pie Charts

A pie chart depicts one range of numeric data. The wedges (or "slices") of the pie show how each individual data value relates to the total, and how each value compares in importance with all the other values. Pie charts are available in two-dimensional and three-dimensional formats. (You saw a three-dimensional pie chart back in Figure 6.1.)

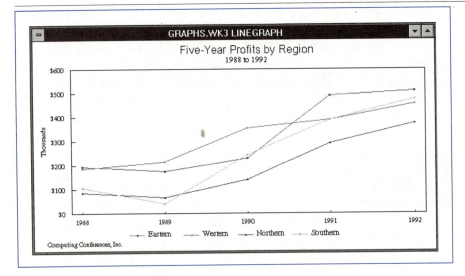

FIGURE 6.36:
A line graph from the five-year profit table

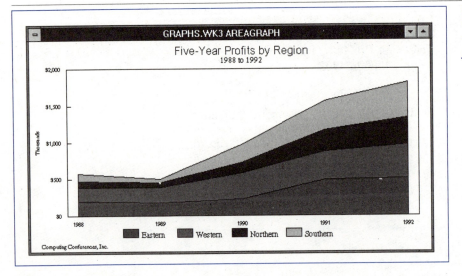

FIGURE 6.37:
An area graph from the five-year profit table

In its simplest organizational scheme, a pie chart uses only two columns of data—an X range and an A range. The X range contains the labels that are displayed alongside the wedges of the pie, and the A range contains the numeric data depicted in the chart. For example, Figure 6.38 shows a column of profit figures for a single region during a one-year period. The pie chart created from this data appears in Figure 6.39. By default, 1-2-3 displays two items of information next to each wedge of the pie: The appropriate label from

	A	B
1	Computing Conferences, Inc.	
2	1991 Profits	
3	*Eastern Region*	
4		
5		Eastern
6	Accountants	$111,200
7	Doctors	$131,900
8	Lawyers	$63,500
9	Retail Business	$92,800
10	Video Stores	$88,300
11	Total	**$487,700**
12		

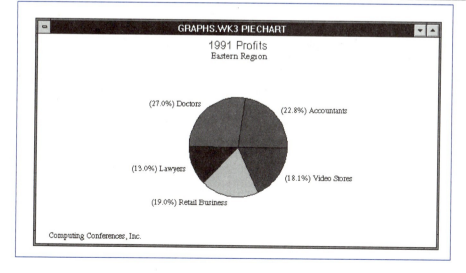

FIGURE 6.38:
Profits for one region

FIGURE 6.39:
A pie chart

the A data range, and the percentage represented by a given wedge. For example, you can see in Figure 6.39 that Video Stores conferences represent 18.1 percent of annual profit in the Eastern region.

You can supply two additional data ranges for defining the appearance of a pie chart. The B and C ranges do not represent numeric data, but rather codes that 1-2-3 reads as instructions for creating the chart. The B range, also known as the *color range,* gives three kinds of information:

- A color code ranging from 1 to 14 represents the color that 1-2-3 will display inside a given wedge.

- A negative color code is an instruction to hide the wedge—that is, to leave a blank space where the wedge belongs.

- A value of 100 added to the color code is an instruction to "explode" the wedge—that is, to display the wedge slightly outside the circumference of the pie.

The C range, also known as the *percent-labels* range, is much simpler. You can enter a value of 0 (false) in each cell of this range as an instruction to omit the percentage that 1-2-3 normally displays with the label. A value of 1 (true) instructs 1-2-3 to include the percentage.

For example, Figure 6.40 shows an expanded worksheet table that includes appropriate instructions for modifying the pie chart. The column of color codes includes a value of 105 in cell C10—an instruction to explode the Video Stores wedge. The percent-labels range contains values of 0 in each cell,

	A	B	C	D
1	Computing Conferences, Inc.			
2	1991 Profits			
3	Eastern Region			
4				
5		Eastern	colors	percents
6	Accountants	$111,200	1	0
7	Doctors	$131,900	2	0
8	Lawyers	$63,500	3	0
9	Retail Business	$92,800	4	0
10	Video Stores	$88,300	105	0
11	Total	$487,700		
12				

FIGURE 6.40:
Supplying additional information for the pie chart

instructions to omit the percentage figures. Figure 6.41 shows the pie chart created from this worksheet. As you can see, the Video Stores wedge is slightly removed from the pie, and there are no percentages.

CREATING XY GRAPHS AND MIXED GRAPHS

The XY and mixed graphs are perhaps the most complex of the available graph types. An XY graph plots points in a true x-y coordinate system. This graph type is the only one that does not use the X data range as labels for the graph. Instead, the X data range supplies the x-coordinate of each plotted point in the graph, and the A through F data ranges supply y-coordinates.

For example, the worksheet in Figure 6.42 is an attempt to discover a correlation between conference attendance and advertising. Column C in the worksheet shows the amount that Computing Conferences, Inc. spent on advertising in advance of a given conference, and column D shows the number of people who attended each computer-training conference in the list. The XY graph in Figure 6.43 was created using the advertising figures as the X data range, and the attendance data as the A data range. Each point on the graph therefore represents an advertising amount and the corresponding attendance figure as an ordered pair (x,y) of values in the coordinate system.

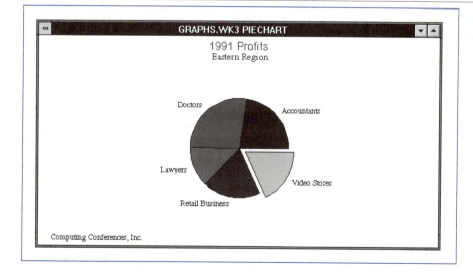

FIGURE 6.41:
A modified pie chart

	A	B	C	D
1	Computing Conferences, Inc.			
2	Attendance and Advertising			
3	Computing for Video Stores			
4				
5	Place	Date	Advertising	Attendance
6	Chicago	09-Jan-91	$5,000.00	154
7	St. Louis	21-Jan-91	$3,500.00	119
8	Indianapolis	15-Feb-91	$6,000.00	174
9	New York	07-Mar-91	$6,000.00	201
10	Boston	25-Mar-91	$3,500.00	136
11	Washington, D.C.	03-Apr-91	$5,000.00	172
12	Atlanta	11-May-91	$3,500.00	112
13	Miami	28-May-91	$1,000.00	97
14	Dallas	03-Jun-91	$1,000.00	86
15	Albuquerque	29-Jun-91	$1,000.00	104
16	Las Vegas	05-Sep-91	$7,500.00	235
17	Los Angeles	11-Oct-91	$1,500.00	119
18	San Francisco	29-Oct-91	$2,500.00	137
19	Seattle	05-Nov-91	$3,500.00	148

FIGURE 6.42:
A worksheet containing attendance and advertising data

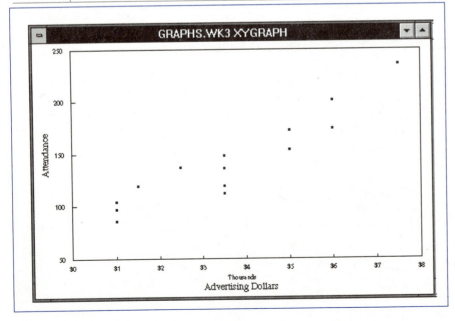

FIGURE 6.43:
An XY graph correlating conference attendance with advertising dollars

By the way, you'll notice that this graph displays titles along the x-axis and y-axis. Here are the general steps for creating these titles:

1. Pull down the Chart menu and choose the Axis command.

2. In the resulting cascade menu, choose the X or the Y command.

3. In the Chart Axis X or Chart Axis Y dialog box, click the Options button.

4. In the resulting dialog box, enter a title into the Axis title text box. Click OK for both dialog boxes to confirm your entry.

Figure 6.44 shows a mixed graph, also created from the attendance-advertising worksheet in Figure 6.42. A mixed graph superimposes a line graph, representing one or more numeric data ranges, over a bar graph, representing another set of numeric data ranges. This graph type uses data ranges in a unique way:

◆ The X range supplies labels for the x-axis, as usual.

◆ The A, B, and C ranges become bars in the bar graph.

◆ The D, E, and F ranges become lines in the superimposed line graph.

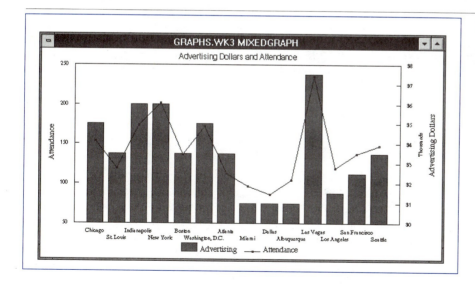

FIGURE 6.44:
A mixed graph

Here are the initial steps for creating the mixed graph in Figure 6.44 from the worksheet data in Figure 6.42:

1. Preselect the range A6..D19 on the attendance-advertising worksheet, and click the create-graph icon. The initial graph needs several adjustments in its data range definitions.

2. Pull down the Chart menu and choose the Ranges command. In the Chart Ranges dialog box, the range A6..A19 is displayed as the X data range. Keep this entry as it is. Enter **C6..C19** for the A data range, and **D6..D19** for the D data range. Delete the entries in all the other data range boxes.

3. Click the 2nd Y check box located next to the A data range box. This option displays a second y-axis at the right side of the graph. Because a mixed graph represents two different data sets, the two vertical axes are often necessary.

4. The Chart Ranges dialog box appears as shown in Figure 6.45. Click OK or press ↵.

5. Click the mixed-graph icon, identified in Figure 6.46.

In the resulting mixed graph (Figure 6.44), the y-axis on the left contains a scale of values for the line chart, which represents attendance. The y-axis

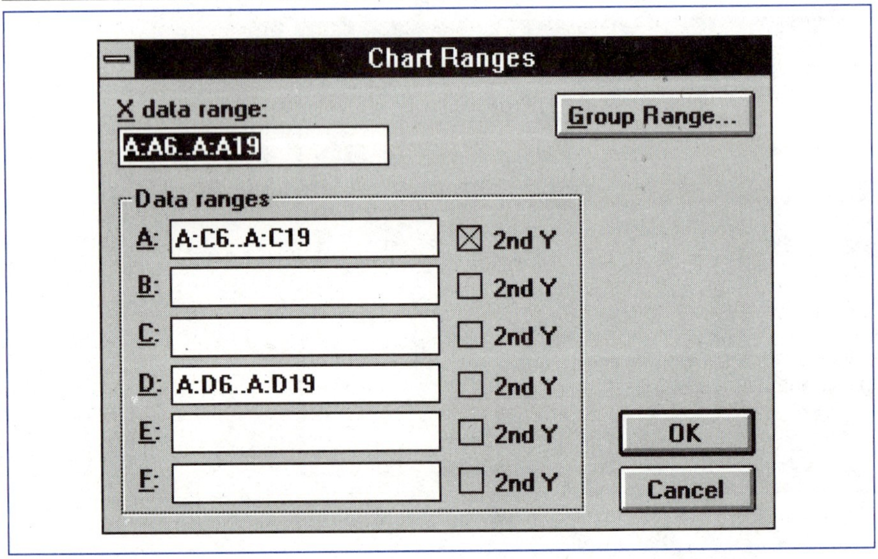

FIGURE 6.45:

Using the Chart Ranges dialog box to prepare for a mixed graph

FIGURE 6.46:

The mixed-graph icon

on the right contains a scale of values for the bar chart, which represents advertising dollars.

CREATING HLCO GRAPHS

A high-low-close-open graph is also known as a stock market graph. This graph type displays vertical lines representing pairs of high and low values. In addition, special markings along each vertical line represent opening and closing values. The HLCO graph is a special form of the mixed graph type; it uses data ranges as follows:

- ◆ The X data range supplies labels along the x-axis.
- ◆ The A and B data ranges represent high and low values, respectively.
- ◆ The C and D data ranges represent closing and opening values, respectively.
- ◆ The E data range becomes an additional bar graph, located beneath the high-low lines.
- ◆ The F data range becomes a horizontally-oriented line graph, which runs through the high-low lines.

All of these ranges have typical uses for reporting stock market data: The high-low lines represent stock prices, as do the opening and closing values; the bar graph beneath the lines represents trading volume; and the horizontal line graph represents stock averages.

However, you may find other uses for the HLCO graph. For example, consider the weather worksheet shown in Figure 6.47. This worksheet contains data ranges displaying daily high and low temperatures; morning and evening readings; daily rainfall; and average temperatures. Using these six columns as the A through F data ranges, 1-2-3 creates the HLCO graph shown in Figure 6.48.

	A	B	C	D	E	F	G
1			One Week of February Weather				
2			San Francisco				
3							
4		High	Low	6:00 A.M.	6:00 P.M.	Rainfall (in.)	Avg. Temp.
5	Mon.	53	32	43	50	0.75	41
6	Tue.	67	35	51	62	1.25	49
7	Wed.	71	38	59	67	1.25	54
8	Thu.	55	30	39	50	2.00	40
9	Fri.	50	28	39	50	1.25	38
10	Sat.	59	29	43	55	2.25	43
11	Sun.	68	37	49	60	2.00	49

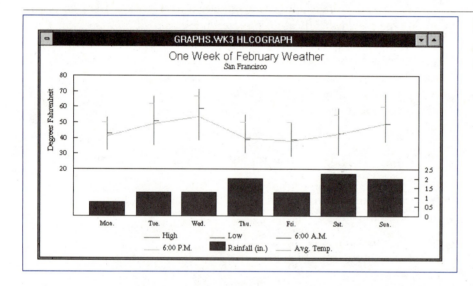

FIGURE 6.47: *Weather data*

FIGURE 6.48: *An HLCO graph from the weather data*

SUMMARY

A graph is linked to a worksheet in 1-2-3, and is saved on disk as part of the worksheet file. You can produce a graph from as many as six columns of numbers, known as the A, B, C, D, E, and F data ranges, plus a column of labels, known as the X data range. After preselecting the range containing these columns, you use the Graph New command to create the graph.

You work with a graph inside a graph window. When a graph window is active, 1-2-3 displays a distinct menu bar and icon palette, offering an abundance of tools for modifying, refining, and enhancing the elements of a graph.

In particular, the Chart Type command offers variations on seven different graph types: bar graphs, line graphs, area graphs, pie charts, XY graphs, mixed graphs, and HLCO graphs.

By default, 1-2-3 produces a columnwise graph, meaning that each of the selected data ranges is a column. But once a graph is created, you can choose the graph window's Chart Ranges command to redraw the current graph in a rowwise organization. For a given table of data, the choice between columnwise and rowwise often determines the focus and emphasis of the graph.

Typically, the first elements you will want to add to a new graph are titles and a legend. You use the Chart Headings and Chart Legend commands to enter text for these elements. These commands also allow you to copy labels to the graph directly from the worksheet. You can then use the Chart Options Fonts command to change the display fonts and point sizes of these elements.

You use the commands of the Draw menu to add geometric shapes to a graph. The available shapes include arrows, lines, ellipses, polygons, rectangles, and free-hand drawings. These shapes are known as *objects*. After choosing an object from the Draw menu (or clicking the corresponding icon), you use the mouse to form the shape in a particular size and to place it at an appropriate location in the graph. Commands in the Edit, Layout, Rearrange, and Style menus give you control over the appearance of objects. You can also enter lines of text as objects in a graph. A line of text with an arrow is a way of drawing attention to a particular element of the graph itself.

Each of the seven graph types is suited to a particular variety of data, and each uses the X, A, B, C, D, E, and F data ranges in its own way. For example, line and area graphs typically depict data values that change over time. Pie charts show the importance of individual data items in relation to the total of all the data. In an XY graph, sets of paired data values are plotted as points against an x-y coordinate system. A mixed graph shows the A, B, and C data ranges as bar graphs and the D, E, and F ranges as superimposed line graphs. Finally, the HLCO graph displays high and low values as vertical lines, with closing and opening points marked along the length of each line.

FAST TRACK

To create a database table, ... 355
    enter a row of field names at the top of the table range, and then enter the records in consecutive rows immediately after the field names.

To create a calculated field, ... 359
    enter the formula as the field entry in the first record, then copy the formula down to all the records in the database table.

To sort a database, ... 364
    preselect the range containing all the records in the database, *but do not include the field names.* Then choose the Data Sort command. In the Primary and Secondary key boxes, enter references to cells contained in the fields you have chosen as keys to the sort. Click Ascending or Descending for each key.

To prepare for database queries, ... 373
    create a criteria range containing a row of field names from the database table followed by one or more rows of criteria. For the Extract and Modify commands, create an output range, also containing a row of field names from the database table. For convenience, assign range names to the criteria range, the output range, and the database table itself.

To find records that match the stated criteria, ... 374
    choose the Data Query command. Enter the database table range in the Input range box. Enter the criteria range reference or range name into the Criteria range box. Then click the Find command button. In the FIND mode, press ↓ to move to the next matching record, or ↑ to move to the previous matching record.

To write multiple criteria that 1-2-3 will read as an <u>and</u> condition, ...378

enter the criteria in a single row of the criteria range.

To repeat the previous query operation, ...379

press the F7 function key.

To extract records that match the stated criteria, ...379

choose the Data Query command, enter ranges or range names in the Input, Criteria, and Output range boxes, and click the Extract command button.

To delete records that match the stated criteria, ...382

choose the Data Query command, enter ranges in the Input and Criteria range boxes, and click the Delete command button. A message box appears, asking you to confirm the operation. Click Delete or Cancel.

To create criteria that 1-2-3 will read as an <u>or</u> condition, ...384

enter the criteria on consecutive rows in the criteria range.

To revise records that match the stated criteria, ...386

choose the Data Query command, enter ranges into the Input, Criteria, and Output range boxes, and click the Modify command button. In the Data Query Modify dialog box, click the Extract command button, then click Cancel to close the dialog box. In the output range, make revisions in the extracted records. Then press F7 to view the Data Query Modify dialog box again, and click the Replace command button.

CHAPTER 7

Database Essentials

A database is a collection of information, systematically organized to provide convenient access to individual records. Business databases are created for a great variety of subjects, such as inventory, product lines, sales transactions, business assets, employees, customers, regional divisions, salespeople, and so on.

The 1-2-3 database component is an ideal tool for building small to medium-sized databases that you manage at your own desk. The main power of this component lies in the options of 1-2-3's Data Query command. To examine these options, pull down the Data menu and choose Query. The resulting dialog box, shown in Figure 7.1, will be the focus of your attention throughout much of this chapter.

The commands in the Data Query dialog box help you perform a variety of operations on your database, including:

◆ Finding records that match stated conditions (Data Query Find)

◆ Deleting records that you no longer need (Data Query Delete)

◆ Listing selected portions of the database (Data Query Extract)

◆ Selecting records for the purpose of revision (Data Query Modify)

Using the 1-2-3 database component, you can perform queries on one or more tables of information. You'll begin your work in this chapter by learning how to organize a 1-2-3 database. Then you'll study the essential database operations available in 1-2-3.

DEFINING A DATABASE

The basic structural components of a database are known as *records* and *fields*. A record consists of all the information describing a single item or person in the database—for example, a product, transaction, property, customer, employee, regional office, or salesperson. A field is one category of information for each record in the database—for example, the product name, transaction date, property address, customer credit rating, employee's salary, office manager, or sales region.

In 1-2-3, you store a database in the rows and columns of a worksheet. Specifically, this is how a database appears in a 1-2-3 worksheet:

◆ Records are stored in consecutive rows of the worksheet. All the information for a given record is displayed in one row.

◆ Fields appear side by side in adjacent columns of the worksheet. Each entry in a given column belongs to the same field and the same data type. At the top of each field column, just above the first record in the database, is a *field name*. The field name is a label that identifies the field.

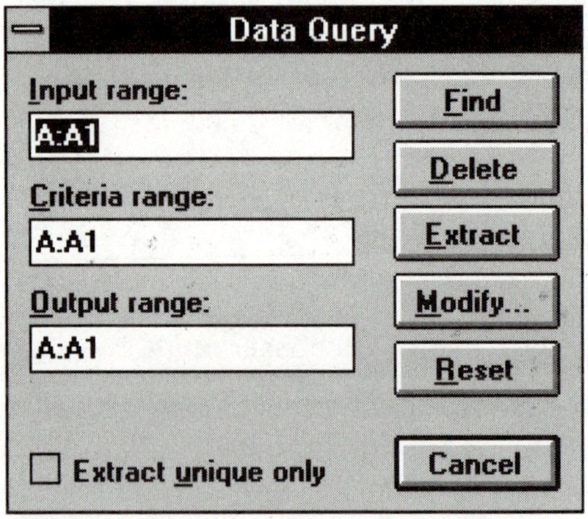

FIGURE 7.1:

The Data Query dialog box

A *database table* is a collection of records, organized into distinct fields of information and stored in a single worksheet. Every database table begins with a row of field names. For successful query operations, a consistent data type within each field is an essential part of database design.

The best way to clarify these terms and concepts is to consider an example. In the exercises of this chapter, you'll once again look into the business files of Computing Conferences, Inc. This time you'll examine the company's database of conference instructors. This database table contains information about computer specialists who have signed contracts with Computing Conferences, Inc. to present specific topics at conferences.

In Figure 7.2, you see the beginning of the database, displayed inside a worksheet window. Each record in the database is stored in a row of the worksheet, and contains all the information about one instructor. The first record is in row 4. There are eleven fields, displayed across the worksheet in columns A through K. The field names are in row 3. As you can see, a complete record consists of one entry for each of the eleven fields. Here are descriptions of the fields:

- The ID field is an identification number, assigned to an instructor at the time of the initial contract with Computing Conferences, Inc.

- The Last field is the instructor's last name.

- The First field is the initial of the instructor's first name.

- The City field is the major city in which the instructor prefers to work.

	A	B	C	D	E	F	G	H	I	J	K
1					Instructor Database						
2											
3	ID	Last	First	City	Region	Specialty	Rate	Hrs	Contract	Yrs	Ok
4	D-140	Abrams	P.	Atlanta	S	Database	$125	29	20-Oct-90	1.3	B
5	W-154	Alexander	E.	Los Angeles	W	WP	$150	10	14-Jun-91	0.6	New
6	S-125	Ashford	W.	Washington, D.C.	E	Spreadsheet	$150	145	10-May-87	4.7	A
7	S-126	Ballinger	I.	Boston	E	Spreadsheet	$150	40	12-Feb-87	5.0	C
8	W-145	Banks	S.	St. Louis	S	WP	$150	55	10-Jun-90	1.6	A
9	W-130	Burke	C.	Miami	S	WP	$100	41	22-May-88	3.7	B
10	D-141	Cheung	F.	Las Vegas	W	Database	$125	61	15-May-90	1.7	A
11	D-143	Cody	L.	Los Angeles	W	Database	$75	43	20-Jun-90	1.6	B
12	A-146	Daniels	A.	Atlanta	S	Accounting	$125	24	09-May-91	0.7	New
13	W-119	Davis	G.	San Francisco	W	WP	$150	139	09-Jul-87	4.6	A
14	N-115	Dixon	G.	Las Vegas	W	Networks	$150	59	09-May-86	5.7	B
15	S-120	Edmonds	R.	Indianapolis	N	Spreadsheet	$75	35	27-Sep-87	4.3	C
16	T-128	Eng	R.	Albuquerque	S	Telecomm	$75	75	11-Oct-87	4.3	B
17	D-105	Fitzpatrick	P.	New York	E	Database	$125	164	07-Nov-86	5.2	A
18	S-131	Garcia	A.	Seattle	N	Spreadsheet	$100	17	02-Jul-88	3.6	C
19	W-114	Garrison	V.	Boston	E	WP	$125	207	06-May-86	5.7	A
20	S-127	Gill	P.	Los Angeles	W	Spreadsheet	$100	25	22-Jun-87	4.6	C

FIGURE 7.2:
The beginning of the instructor database, displayed in a worksheet window

- The Region field contains a single letter—N, S, E, or W—designating one of the company's four regions. This is the instructor's home region.

- The Specialty field is the instructor's primary area of expertise. The entry in this field is one of the following six categories: Spreadsheet, Database, WP (for word processing), Accounting, Networks, or Telecomm (for telecommunications).

- The Rate field is the instructor's current hourly rate of pay for making presentations at conferences. This amount is established individually for each instructor, in negotiation with the company. As you can see, the numeric entries in this field range from $75 to $150.

- The Hrs field is the total number of conference hours the instructor has worked for the company since the initial contract.

- The Contract field is the date of the instructor's initial contract with the company.

- The Yrs field is the number of years since the instructor's initial contract.

- The Ok field is a rating of A, B, or C, indicating the instructor's level of experience. If the instructor has worked for Computing Conferences, Inc. for less than a year, the entry in this field is New.

As you'll see later in this chapter, field names play an important role in query operations on the database. For this reason, 1-2-3 establishes specific rules that you must follow when you create field names for a database. Write each field name as a one-word label with no spaces. Do not use characters or formats that would make a field name look like a formula or a cell address. Most important of all, create a unique name for each field in a database table. You'll be using field names in formulas and operations; for your own convenience, write field names that are clear, reasonably short, and easy to remember.

Figure 7.3 shows the complete database table, describing all the instructors who work for Computing Conferences, Inc. in the four regions. There are over fifty records. In this particular listing, the records are arranged in alphabetical order by the instructors' last names. Notice that the entries in a given column all belong to the same data type, and are formatted consistently. The first six fields, in columns A through F, are labels. The next four are numeric fields—the rate, formatted as a dollar amount; the hours, formatted as an integer; the contract date, a date number formatted in a date display format; and the years, formatted as a numeric value with one decimal place. The last field, Ok, is a label.

FIGURE 7.3:
The complete instructor database table

Instructor Database

ID	Last	First	City	Region	Specialty	Rate	Hrs	Contract	Yrs	Ok
D-140	Abrams	P.	Atlanta	S	Database	$125	29	20-Oct-90	1.3	B
W-154	Alexander	E.	Los Angeles	W	WP	$150	10	14-Jun-91	0.6	New
S-125	Ashford	W.	Washington, D.C	E	Spreadsheet	$150	145	10-May-87	4.7	A
S-126	Ballinger	I.	Boston	E	Spreadsheet	$150	40	12-Feb-87	5.0	C
W-145	Banks	S.	St. Louis	S	WP	$150	55	10-Jun-90	1.6	A
W-130	Burke	C.	Miami	S	WP	$100	41	22-May-88	3.7	B
D-141	Cheung	F.	Las Vegas	W	Database	$125	61	15-May-90	1.7	A
D-143	Cody	L.	Los Angeles	W	Database	$75	43	20-Jun-90	1.6	B
A-146	Daniels	A.	Atlanta	S	Accounting	$125	24	09-May-91	0.7	New
W-119	Davis	G.	San Francisco	W	WP	$150	139	09-Jul-87	4.6	A
N-115	Dixon	G.	Las Vegas	W	Networks	$150	59	09-May-86	5.7	B
S-120	Edmonds	R.	Indianapolis	N	Spreadsheet	$75	35	27-Sep-87	4.3	C
T-128	Eng	R.	Albuquerque	S	Telecomm	$75	75	11-Oct-87	4.3	B
D-105	Fitzpatrick	P.	New York	E	Database	$125	164	07-Nov-86	5.2	A
S-131	Garcia	A.	Seattle	N	Spreadsheet	$100	17	02-Jul-88	3.6	C
W-114	Garrison	V.	Boston	E	WP	$125	207	06-May-86	5.7	A
S-127	Gill	P.	Los Angeles	W	Spreadsheet	$100	25	22-Jun-87	4.6	C
S-156	Hale	S.	San Francisco	W	Spreadsheet	$75	28	09-Jun-91	0.6	New
S-149	Harris	P.	Dallas	S	Spreadsheet	$150	17	12-Feb-91	1.0	New
D-109	Hayes	S.	San Francisco	W	Database	$75	95	07-Feb-86	6.0	B
T-138	Hermann	J.	Los Angeles	W	Telecomm	$125	74	24-May-89	2.7	B
S-132	Jones	L.	Atlanta	S	Spreadsheet	$125	5	10-Feb-88	4.0	C
W-116	Jordan	E.	Dallas	S	WP	$100	17	06-Oct-86	5.3	C
W-117	Kim	E.	Washington, D.C	E	WP	$100	137	11-Oct-86	5.3	B
N-144	King	T.	New York	E	Networks	$75	13	06-Jan-90	2.1	C
D-136	Koenig	O.	Albuquerque	S	Database	$125	20	02-Jun-89	2.7	C
S-111	Kwan	O.	New York	E	Spreadsheet	$100	71	21-Jun-86	5.6	B
D-123	Lambert	S.	Dallas	S	Database	$150	145	26-Jun-87	4.6	A
D-134	Lee	H.	Seattle	N	Database	$150	21	17-Dec-88	3.1	C
W-150	Leung	M.	Chicago	N	WP	$100	16	26-Mar-91	0.9	New
W-112	Manning	P.	Atlanta	S	WP	$75	71	09-Nov-86	5.2	B
W-107	Martinez	G.	Las Vegas	W	WP	$150	178	15-Mar-86	5.9	A
N-129	McKay	J.	Washington, D.C	E	Networks	$150	35	09-May-87	4.7	C
W-124	Meyer	J.	New York	E	WP	$150	85	05-May-87	4.7	B
A-135	Meyer	L.	New York	E	Accounting	$100	57	17-Aug-88	3.5	B
T-148	Miranda	O.	Las Vegas	W	Telecomm	$75	9	04-Jan-91	1.1	C
S-153	Nichols	B.	Albuquerque	S	Spreadsheet	$150	19	28-Feb-91	0.9	New
N-118	O'Neil	P.	Atlanta	S	Networks	$75	5	01-May-87	4.8	C
A-103	Perez	D.	Las Vegas	W	Accounting	$100	5	11-Jul-86	5.6	C
W-113	Porter	D.	Seattle	N	WP	$125	59	02-Aug-86	5.5	B
D-139	Porter	M.	Washington, D.C	E	Database	$150	26	28-Mar-89	2.8	B
T-133	Ramirez	F.	Boston	E	Telecomm	$150	73	08-Feb-88	4.0	B
S-155	Roberts	P.	Chicago	N	Spreadsheet	$100	10	21-Aug-91	0.4	New
D-137	Sanchez	W.	Indianapolis	N	Database	$100	47	16-Apr-89	2.8	B
N-101	Schwartz	B.	Boston	E	Networks	$150	178	02-Mar-86	5.9	A
W-151	Schwartz	P.	Indianapolis	N	WP	$150	23	10-May-91	0.7	New
D-104	Taylor	F.	Boston	E	Database	$100	17	24-Oct-86	5.3	C
D-142	Thomas	T.	St. Louis	S	Database	$150	35	23-Dec-90	1.1	A
S-108	Tong	C.	St. Louis	S	Spreadsheet	$150	35	12-Nov-86	5.2	C
N-152	Tong	P.	San Francisco	W	Networks	$150	23	13-May-91	0.7	New
N-110	Tong	W.	Los Angeles	W	Networks	$150	83	09-May-86	5.7	B
S-122	Vasquez	T.	Las Vegas	W	Spreadsheet	$75	5	27-Apr-87	4.8	C
T-102	Vaughn	A.	Washington, D.C	E	Telecomm	$75	53	11-Sep-86	5.4	B
T-147	Webb	F.	New York	E	Telecomm	$125	32	27-Jan-91	1.0	A
D-106	Weinberg	P.	Miami	S	Database	$75	59	18-Jan-86	6.0	B
D-121	Williams	C.	Chicago	N	Database	$150	30	02-Oct-87	4.3	C

ENTERING THE DATABASE

For the exercises of this chapter, you'll need a copy of the instructor database table in a worksheet of your own; but to avoid spending too much time creating this example, you can enter a shortened form of the database. The short version, shown in Figure 7.4, contains a selection of 17 record entries in rows 4 through 20.

To create the shortened database, start with a new blank worksheet, and follow these steps:

1. Choose the Worksheet Insert command and click the Sheet option to insert worksheet B into the window. Click OK or press ↵ to complete the Insert operation. You'll enter the instructor database into worksheet B, saving worksheet A for a later exercise.

2. Use the Worksheet Column Width command to adjust columns A through K to the following widths: A, **6**; B, **8**; C, **4**; D, **13**; E, **6**; F, **10**; G, **5**; H, **4**; I, **9**; J, **4**; K, **4**.

3. Enter the title **Instructor Database** into cell A1, and use the Style Alignment command to center the title horizontally over columns A through K. Click the bold and underline icons to apply these styles to the title.

4. Enter the field names into row 3, cells A3 through K3. Copy these names from Figure 7.4, then select the range A3..K3 and click the

FIGURE 7.4:
The short version of the instructor database table

	A	B	C	D	E	F	G	H	I	J	K
1					Instructor Database						
2											
3	ID	Last	First	City	Region	Specialty	Rate	Hrs	Contract	Yrs	Ok
4	S-149	Harris	P.	Dallas	S	Spreadsheet	$150	17	12-Feb-91		
5	A-146	Daniels	A.	Atlanta	S	Accounting	$125	24	09-May-91		
6	A-103	Perez	D.	Las Vegas	W	Accounting	$100	5	11-Jul-86		
7	W-113	Porter	D.	Seattle	N	WP	$125	59	02-Aug-86		
8	N-101	Schwartz	B.	Boston	E	Networks	$150	178	02-Mar-86		
9	S-155	Roberts	P.	Chicago	N	Spreadsheet	$100	10	21-Aug-91		
10	S-125	Ashford	W.	Washington, D.C.	E	Spreadsheet	$150	145	10-May-87		
11	D-106	Weinberg	P.	Miami	S	Database	$75	59	18-Jan-86		
12	W-119	Davis	G.	San Francisco	W	WP	$150	139	09-Jul-87		
13	W-124	Meyer	J.	New York	E	WP	$150	85	05-May-87		
14	W-145	Banks	S.	St. Louis	S	WP	$150	55	10-Jun-90		
15	D-137	Sanchez	W.	Indianapolis	N	Database	$100	47	16-Apr-89		
16	D-139	Porter	M.	Washington, D.C.	E	Database	$150	26	28-Mar-89		
17	T-133	Ramirez	F.	Boston	E	Telecomm	$150	73	08-Feb-88		
18	D-143	Cody	L.	Los Angeles	W	Database	$75	43	20-Jun-90		
19	S-127	Gill	P.	Los Angeles	W	Spreadsheet	$100	25	22-Jun-87		
20	T-128	Eng	R.	Albuquerque	S	Telecomm	$75	75	11-Oct-87		

bold icon. Right-align the Rate, Hrs, and Yrs field names, and center the Contract field name.

5. Enter the label data of the first six fields into columns A, B, C, D, E, and F. Copy each entry exactly as you see it in Figure 7.4. Center the entries of the Region field in column E.

6. Enter the numeric data of the next two fields, Rate and Hrs, into columns G and H. Format the entries of column G in the Currency format, with no decimal places.

7. Before entering the dates into column I, select the range I4..I20 and choose the Range Format command. Select the 31-Dec-90 date format and click OK. Now enter the dates into column I just as they appear in Figure 7.4. As you know, 1-2-3 converts these entries into date numbers, which you can use in date arithmetic operations.

8. Choose the File Save As command, and save this file to disk as INSTRUCT.WK3.

The Yrs and Ok fields, in columns J and K, remain blank in Figure 7.4. Yrs and Ok are *calculated fields* in the instructor database.

Calculated Fields

You can write a formula to calculate the data for any field in a database table. To create a calculated field, you enter the formula as the field entry for the first record in the database, then you copy the formula down the field column—just as you would do in an ordinary worksheet application. The formulas for calculated fields often contain references to values in other fields of the database table. As you would expect, 1-2-3 recalculates a field formula whenever you make a change in the data that the formula uses.

The Yrs field in the instructor database table is the number of years since an instructor's initial contract with Computing Conferences, Inc. This number is calculated as the difference between today's date and the date in the Contract field. Normally, you would enter the following formula for the first record in this field:

(@TODAY−I4)/365

This formula finds the difference, in days, between today's date (@TODAY) and the contract date (I4); then the result is divided by 365 to calculate the difference in years. The advantage of this formula in a database is that 1-2-3 can recalculate the Yrs field each time the value of @TODAY changes—that is, every day. This means that the values in the Yrs field are always up to date. However, for the exercises in this chapter, you'll replace this formula with one that supplies a fixed date instead of @TODAY:

(@DATE(92,1,31)–I4)/365

By making this small adjustment, you will be able to duplicate the database examples exactly as you see them in this chapter.

The value in the Ok field for a given instructor is based on the instructor's experience level—specifically, the average number of conference hours the instructor has worked per year, since the initial contract:

- An instructor who has worked an average of 30 hours or more per year receives an Ok rating of A.
- An instructor who has worked fewer than 30 hours but at least 9 hours per year receives a rating of B.
- An instructor who has worked fewer than 9 hours per year receives a rating of C.

Here are the steps for entering these two formulas into the first record of the database table and copying them down their respective field columns:

1. Enter the following formula into cell J4, to calculate the number of years since the initial contract:

   (@DATE(92,1,31)–I4)/365

2. Enter this formula carefully into cell K4:

   @IF(J4<1,"New",@IF(H4/J4>=30,"A",@IF(H4/J4<9,"C","B")))

   This formula uses a sequence of "nested" @IF functions to select a label of New, A, B, or C for the Ok field. (You may want to turn briefly back to Chapter 5 to review the structure and use of 1-2-3's built-in @IF function.) The outermost @IF function enters a label of New if the value of the Yrs field is less than 1. Otherwise, the middle @IF function enters A if the average yearly work hour amount (H4/J4) is greater than or equal to 30. Finally, if neither of these first two conditions is true, the innermost @IF function chooses between labels of C or B, depending upon whether the average work hour figure is less than or greater than 9.

3. To copy these two formulas down columns J and K, respectively, preselect the range J4..K4, and click the range-copy icon. Drag the

mouse over the range J5..J20. When you release the mouse button, 1-2-3 copies the formulas.

4. Preselect the range J4..J20 and choose the Range Format command. Select the Fixed format and then enter a value of **1** in the Decimals box. When you complete this step, the two calculated fields, Yrs and Ok, appear as shown in Figure 7.5.

5. Click the save-file icon to update the file on disk.

Multiple Tables in a Database

In 1-2-3 there is an important distinction between a *database table* and a *database*. A database table, as you've seen, is a collection of records stored in consecutive rows in a single worksheet. A database is defined as a collection of one or more database tables.

The 1-2-3 database component gives you the power to perform special query operations on multiple database tables. In this sense, 1-2-3 is a *relational* database system: Given two database tables that have a field in common, 1-2-3 can match records from the two tables and build new tables that combine data from each of the original tables.

In the next exercise, you'll enter a short new database table in worksheet A, which you've left empty up to now. This new table, shown in Figure 7.6, contains information about the regional offices for Computing Conferences, Inc. The office database table has only four records, one for

B	A	B	C	D	E	F	G	H	I	J	K
1				Instructor Database							
2											
3	ID	Last	First	City	Region	Specialty	Rate	Hrs	Contract	Yrs	Ok
4	S-149	Harris	P.	Dallas	S	Spreadsheet	$150	17	12-Feb-91	1.0	New
5	A-146	Daniels	A.	Atlanta	S	Accounting	$125	24	09-May-91	0.7	New
6	A-103	Perez	D.	Las Vegas	W	Accounting	$100	5	11-Jul-86	5.6	C
7	W-113	Porter	D.	Seattle	N	WP	$125	59	02-Aug-86	5.5	B
8	N-101	Schwartz	B.	Boston	E	Networks	$150	178	02-Mar-86	5.9	A
9	S-155	Roberts	P.	Chicago	N	Spreadsheet	$100	10	21-Aug-91	0.4	New
10	S-125	Ashford	W.	Washington, D.C.	E	Spreadsheet	$150	145	10-May-87	4.7	A
11	D-106	Weinberg	P.	Miami	S	Database	$75	59	18-Jan-86	6.0	B
12	W-119	Davis	G.	San Francisco	W	WP	$150	139	09-Jul-87	4.6	A
13	W-124	Meyer	J.	New York	E	WP	$150	85	05-May-87	4.7	B
14	W-145	Banks	S.	St. Louis	S	WP	$150	55	10-Jun-90	1.6	A
15	D-137	Sanchez	W.	Indianapolis	N	Database	$100	47	16-Apr-89	2.8	B
16	D-139	Porter	M.	Washington, D.C.	E	Database	$150	26	28-Mar-89	2.8	B
17	T-133	Ramirez	F.	Boston	E	Telecomm	$150	73	08-Feb-88	4.0	B
18	D-143	Cody	L.	Los Angeles	W	Database	$75	43	20-Jun-90	1.6	B
19	S-127	Gill	P.	Los Angeles	W	Spreadsheet	$100	25	22-Jun-87	4.6	C
20	T-128	Eng	R.	Albuquerque	S	Telecomm	$75	75	11-Oct-87	4.3	B

FIGURE 7.5:

Calculated fields in the database table

each of the four regional offices. There are seven fields in the database:

- The Region field contains an entry of N, S, E, or W.
- The Address, City, State, and Zip fields provide the complete address of each office, and the Phone field gives the phone number.
- The Manager field gives the name of the regional manager in charge of operations at each office.

Notice that this new table has one field in common with the instructor table—the Region field. This field allows you to correlate records in the two tables. For example, imagine the steps you might take to find the name of the regional manager who is in charge of a particular instructor: You would begin by searching for the instructor's name in the instructor database table. After locating the correct record, you would take note of the instructor's region. Then you would switch over to the office database, look up the office record corresponding to the same region, and find the manager's name in the Manager field. In Chapter 8, you'll learn how 1-2-3 automates this sequence of steps, in a special kind of query operation that *joins* data from multiple database tables.

For now, take the following steps to enter the office database table into worksheet A:

1. Click the previous-worksheet icon (or click Ctrl-PgDn) to move the cell pointer to worksheet A.

2. Use the Worksheet Column Width command to set the correct widths of columns A through G: A, **6**; B, **17**; C, **11**; D, **4**; E, **7**; F, **12**; G, **12**.

3. Enter the title **Regional Offices** into cell A1. Click the bold and underline icons to apply these two styles to the title.

	A	B	C	D	E	F	G
1	Regional Offices						
2							
3	Region	Address	City	State	Zip	Phone	Manager
4	E	222 Allen Street	New York	NY	10103	(212) 555-4678	Campbell, R.
5	N	Mills Tower, Suite 992	Chicago	IL	60605	(312) 555-8803	Logan, C.
6	S	11 Maple Street	Dallas	TX	75210	(214) 555-6754	Harvey, J.
7	W	432 Market Avenue	Los Angeles	CA	90028	(213) 555-9974	Garcia, M.

FIGURE 7.6:

The office database table

4. Enter the seven field names into row 3, as shown in Figure 7.6. Then preselect the range A3..G3 and click the bold icon. Center the Address and Zip field names.

5. Choose the Worksheet Global Settings command and click the Format button. In the Worksheet Global Settings Format dialog box, type **L** to select the Label format. Click OK on both dialog boxes to confirm the selection. Recall that the Label format gives you a convenient way to enter labels into a worksheet, even when an entry begins with a digit or some other character that 1-2-3 would normally read as the beginning of a value entry. Note that all seven of the fields in the office database table are label fields.

6. Enter the four regional office records into rows 4 through 7 of the worksheet. Thanks to the global Label format, you don't have to worry about starting addresses, zip codes, and phone numbers with special label prefixes.

7. Center the Region and Zip field values in their respective columns.

Now the INSTRUCT.WK3 database file consists of two database tables—the office table in worksheet A, and the instructor table in worksheet B. Adding range names to the file will simplify your work in upcoming exercises with these two tables. In the following steps, you'll assign two range names to each table:

1. On worksheet A, preselect the range A:A3..A:G7. This range contains the entire database table, including the field names. Choose the Range Name Create command and assign the name OFFICEDB (for "office database") to this range.

2. Now preselect the range A:A4..A:G7. This range contains the four regional office records, without the field names. Choose Range Name Create and enter OFFICERECS (for "office records") as the name for this range.

3. Click the next-worksheet icon (or press Ctrl-PgUp) to move the cell pointer to worksheet B. Preselect the range B:A3..B:K20. This range contains the entire instructor database table, including the field names. Choose Range Name Create and assign the name INSTRUCTDB (for "instructors database") to this range.

4. Next, preselect the range B:A4..BK20. This range contains the instructor records, without the field names. Choose Range Name Create and enter INSTRUCTRECS (for "instructor records") as the name for this range. Press Home to deselect the range.

5. Click the save-file icon to update the database file to disk.

You'll use the OFFICEDB and INSTRUCTDB range names in query operations that require references to the entire database tables, including field names. In contrast, the OFFICERECS and INSTRUCTRECS names will prove convenient in procedures for *sorting* the database records.

SORTING THE DATABASE

Once you create a database, you may want to rearrange its records in an order other than the way you originally entered them. This operation is called *sorting;* you accomplish it by choosing the Data Sort command. As you learned in Chapter 5, Data Sort is not exclusively for use in databases. You can use this command to sort the data in any range of rows, whether or not they form a database.

You can probably imagine several useful new arrangements for the records in the instructor database. For example, you might decide to sort the database in alphabetical order by instructors' ID numbers; in numerical order by their hourly rates; or in chronological order by their contract dates. In each of these examples, the specified field—ID, Rate, or Contract—is called the *key* to the sort.

Given a sorting key and a database range to be sorted, the Data Sort command can arrange the records in *ascending* or *descending* order. The difference between these two sorting directions depends on the type of data stored in the key field:

◆ If the key field contains labels, an ascending sort arranges the records in alphabetical order, from A to Z. A descending sort produces the reverse alphabetical order, from Z to A. By default, 1-2-3 ignores uppercase and lowercase distinctions during a sort operation.

◆ If the key field contains numeric values, an ascending sort arranges the records from the smallest value to the largest; and a descending sort arranges the records from the largest to the smallest.

◆ If the key contains dates that have been entered as 1-2-3 date numbers, an ascending sort arranges the database from the earliest to the latest date; and a descending sort arranges the records from the latest to the earliest date.

USING THE DATA SORT COMMAND

The Data Sort dialog box appears in Figure 7.7. For a one-key sort, you need to specify three items of information: In the Data range box, you enter the range of records that you want to sort. In the Primary key box, you enter a reference to a cell inside the selected key field. Finally, you make a selection between the Ascending and Descending options in the Primary key frame.

There is one important rule to keep in mind when you sort a database: Do not include the row of field names in the range to be sorted. If you do, the field names will leave their correct position at the top of the database, and end up somewhere within the range of records. If you inadvertently sort the field names into the range of records, click the undo icon to correct the error. In response, 1-2-3 restores your database to its original order. (For this corrective action to work, the Undo option must be enabled in your system, and you must click the icon immediately after the sort—before you choose any other menu command.)

In the following exercise, you'll sort the instructor database in ascending chronological order by contract dates:

1. Select worksheet B if it is not already current. Pull down the Data menu and choose the Sort command. The initial focus is on the Data range box.

2. Press the F3 function key. In response, 1-2-3 displays the Range Names dialog box on the screen, with a list of all the range names you have defined up to now for your database (shown in Figure 7.8). Double-click the name INSTRUCTRECS. Recall that this name represents the range of records, *without* the row of field names. The Range Names box disappears and 1-2-3 enters the name into the Data range box.

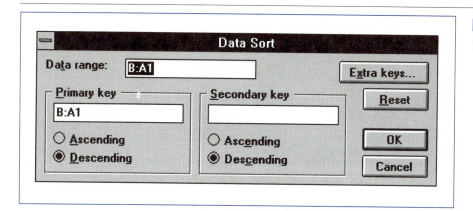

FIGURE 7.7:
The Data Sort dialog box

3. Use the mouse to drag the dialog box window further down the screen from its original position, so you can see the field names and the first few records in the instructor database. Then activate the Primary key text box. Click cell I4 in the instructor database. This cell contains the contract date for the first record in the database. In response to your mouse click, 1-2-3 enters a reference to this cell in the Primary key box. This reference is sufficient to select the Contract field as the key to the sort.

4. Click the Ascending option button, located just beneath the Primary key box. At this point in your work, the Data Sort dialog box appears as shown in Figure 7.9. Click OK or press ↵ to complete the sort operation.

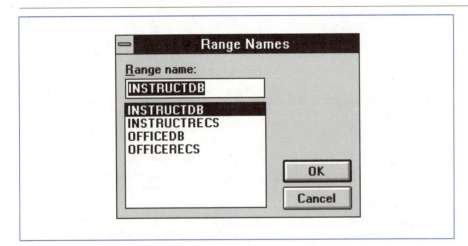

FIGURE 7.8:

The Range Names dialog box, with a list of database range names

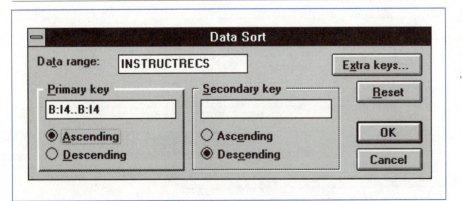

FIGURE 7.9:

The Data Sort dialog box, with instructions for a chronological sort

The sorted database appears in Figure 7.10. As you can see, 1-2-3 has rearranged the instructor records in order of contract dates, from the earliest to the most recent.

Sometimes a single key is not enough to produce a complete or useful sort. When two or more records have the same entry in the primary key field, you need to choose a secondary key to decide the order of these matching records. One simple example of this occurs in the instructor database: There are two instructors with the last name of Porter. When you sort the records alphabetically by instructors' names, you should select the First field as the secondary key to make sure that these two names appear in the correct order. Figure 7.11 shows the Data Sort dialog box with instructions for primary and secondary sorting keys. Notice the reference to cell C4—the first record entry in the First field—in the Secondary key box. In addition, the Ascending option is selected for both keys. You can see the resulting sort in Figure 7.12. The records are now arranged by the Last and First fields. In particular, notice that the two Porters are in the correct order: first D. Porter of Seattle, then M. Porter of Washington, D.C.

Extra Sort Keys

The Data Sort command allows you to select more than just two key fields. For example, imagine that you have sorted the database by the Region field as the primary key and the City field as the secondary key.

	A	B	C	D	E	F	G	H	I	J	K
1				Instructor Database							
2											
3	ID	Last	First	City	Region	Specialty	Rate	Hrs	Contract	Yrs	Ok
4	D-106	Weinberg	P.	Miami	S	Database	$75	59	18-Jan-86	6.0	B
5	N-101	Schwartz	B.	Boston	E	Networks	$150	178	02-Mar-86	5.9	A
6	A-103	Perez	D.	Las Vegas	W	Accounting	$100	5	11-Jul-86	5.6	C
7	W-113	Porter	D.	Seattle	N	WP	$125	59	02-Aug-86	5.5	B
8	W-124	Meyer	J.	New York	E	WP	$150	85	05-May-87	4.7	B
9	S-125	Ashford	W.	Washington, D.C.	E	Spreadsheet	$150	145	10-May-87	4.7	A
10	S-127	Gill	P.	Los Angeles	W	Spreadsheet	$100	25	22-Jun-87	4.6	C
11	W-119	Davis	G.	San Francisco	W	WP	$150	139	09-Jul-87	4.6	A
12	T-128	Eng	R.	Albuquerque	S	Telecomm	$75	75	11-Oct-87	4.3	B
13	T-133	Ramirez	F.	Boston	E	Telecomm	$150	73	08-Feb-88	4.0	B
14	D-139	Porter	M.	Washington, D.C.	E	Database	$150	26	28-Mar-89	2.8	B
15	D-137	Sanchez	W.	Indianapolis	N	Database	$100	47	16-Apr-89	2.8	B
16	W-145	Banks	S.	St. Louis	S	WP	$150	55	10-Jun-90	1.6	A
17	D-143	Cody	L.	Los Angeles	W	Database	$75	43	20-Jun-90	1.6	B
18	S-149	Harris	P.	Dallas	S	Spreadsheet	$150	17	12-Feb-91	1.0	New
19	A-146	Daniels	A.	Atlanta	S	Accounting	$125	24	09-May-91	0.7	New
20	S-155	Roberts	P.	Chicago	N	Spreadsheet	$100	10	21-Aug-91	0.4	New

FIGURE 7.10:

The chronologically sorted instructor database

Examining the result of this sort (shown in Figure 7.13), you realize that you would like to be able to sort the records within each city in alphabetical order by the Specialty field. In other words, your goal is three sorting keys: First the Region field, then the City field, and finally the Specialty field.

To sort by more than two keys, you begin by entering references for the primary and secondary keys, then you click the Extra keys command button on the Data Sort dialog box. As a result, 1-2-3 displays the Data Sort Extra Keys dialog box on the screen, as you can see in Figure 7.14. In this box, you can develop a list of additional sorting keys. For example, here are the steps for

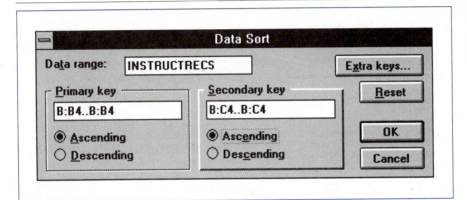

FIGURE 7.11:

Sorting the database by two keys

FIGURE 7.12:

An alphabetical sort by the Last and First fields

	A	B	C	D	E	F	G	H	I	J	K
1				Instructor Database							
2											
3	ID	Last	First	City	Region	Specialty	Rate	Hrs	Contract	Yrs	Ok
4	S-125	Ashford	W.	Washington, D.C.	E	Spreadsheet	$150	145	10-May-87	4.7	A
5	W-145	Banks	S.	St. Louis	S	WP	$150	55	10-Jun-90	1.6	A
6	D-143	Cody	L.	Los Angeles	W	Database	$75	43	20-Jun-90	1.6	B
7	A-146	Daniels	A.	Atlanta	S	Accounting	$125	24	09-May-91	0.7	New
8	W-119	Davis	G.	San Francisco	W	WP	$150	139	09-Jul-87	4.6	A
9	T-128	Eng	R.	Albuquerque	S	Telecomm	$75	75	11-Oct-87	4.3	B
10	S-127	Gill	P.	Los Angeles	W	Spreadsheet	$100	25	22-Jun-87	4.6	C
11	S-149	Harris	P.	Dallas	S	Spreadsheet	$150	17	12-Feb-91	1.0	New
12	W-124	Meyer	J.	New York	E	WP	$150	85	05-May-87	4.7	B
13	A-103	Perez	D.	Las Vegas	W	Accounting	$100	5	11-Jul-86	5.6	C
14	W-113	Porter	D.	Seattle	N	WP	$125	59	02-Aug-86	5.5	B
15	D-139	Porter	M.	Washington, D.C.	E	Database	$150	26	28-Mar-89	2.8	B
16	T-133	Ramirez	F.	Boston	E	Telecomm	$150	73	08-Feb-88	4.0	B
17	S-155	Roberts	P.	Chicago	N	Spreadsheet	$100	10	21-Aug-91	0.4	New
18	D-137	Sanchez	W.	Indianapolis	N	Database	$100	47	16-Apr-89	2.8	B
19	N-101	Schwartz	B.	Boston	E	Networks	$150	178	02-Mar-86	5.9	A
20	D-106	Weinberg	P.	Miami	S	Database	$75	59	18-Jan-86	6.0	B

achieving the three-key sort by the Region, City, and Specialty fields:

1. Choose the Data Sort command. If necessary, use the F3 function key to enter the INSTRUCTRECS range name into the Data range box. Enter a reference to cell E4 into the Primary key box and click the

	A	B	C	D	E	F	G	H	I	J	K
1					Instructor Database						
2											
3	ID	Last	First	City	Region	Specialty	Rate	Hrs	Contract	Yrs	Ok
4	T-133	Ramirez	F.	Boston	E	Telecomm	$150	73	08-Feb-88	4.0	B
5	N-101	Schwartz	B.	Boston	E	Networks	$150	178	02-Mar-86	5.9	A
6	W-124	Meyer	J.	New York	E	WP	$150	85	05-May-87	4.7	B
7	S-125	Ashford	W.	Washington, D.C.	E	Spreadsheet	$150	145	10-May-87	4.7	A
8	D-139	Porter	M.	Washington, D.C.	E	Database	$150	26	28-Mar-89	2.8	B
9	S-155	Roberts	P.	Chicago	N	Spreadsheet	$100	10	21-Aug-91	0.4	New
10	D-137	Sanchez	W.	Indianapolis	N	Database	$100	47	16-Apr-89	2.8	B
11	W-113	Porter	D.	Seattle	N	WP	$125	59	02-Aug-86	5.5	B
12	T-128	Eng	R.	Albuquerque	S	Telecomm	$75	75	11-Oct-87	4.3	B
13	A-146	Daniels	A.	Atlanta	S	Accounting	$125	24	09-May-91	0.7	New
14	S-149	Harris	P.	Dallas	S	Spreadsheet	$150	17	12-Feb-91	1.0	New
15	D-106	Weinberg	P.	Miami	S	Database	$75	59	18-Jan-86	6.0	B
16	W-145	Banks	S.	St. Louis	S	WP	$150	55	10-Jun-90	1.6	A
17	A-103	Perez	D.	Las Vegas	W	Accounting	$100	5	11-Jul-86	5.6	C
18	D-143	Cody	L.	Los Angeles	W	Database	$75	43	20-Jun-90	1.6	B
19	S-127	Gill	P.	Los Angeles	W	Spreadsheet	$100	25	22-Jun-87	4.6	C
20	W-119	Davis	G.	San Francisco	W	WP	$150	139	09-Jul-87	4.6	A

FIGURE 7.13:
The Region field as the primary key and the City field as the secondary key

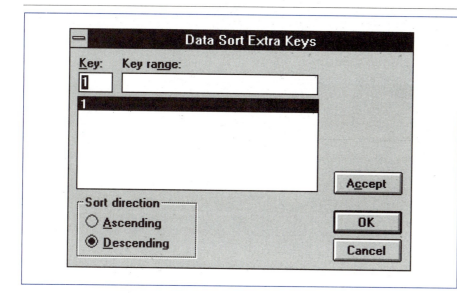

FIGURE 7.14:
The Data Sort Extra Keys dialog box

Ascending option. Then enter a reference to cell D4 into the Secondary key box and click Ascending again. Use the mouse to drag the Data Sort dialog box window down the screen, creating a clear view of the field names and the first few records in the database.

2. Click the Extra keys command button. The Data Sort Extra Keys dialog box appears on the screen. Again, drag the dialog box window out of the way of the top rows of the database.

3. Activate the Key range box. Click cell F4—the first entry in the Specialty field—on the database worksheet. A reference to this cell appears in the Key range box.

4. Click the Ascending option in the Sort direction box at the bottom of the dialog box.

5. Click the Accept command button, located at the right side of the dialog box. When you do so, the reference to F4 becomes the first entry in the Extra Keys list, as shown in Figure 7.15.

6. Because you have no more keys to create, click the OK button to close the Data Sort Extra Keys dialog box. Click OK again on the remaining Data Sort dialog box. In response, 1-2-3 carries out your instructions for the database sort.

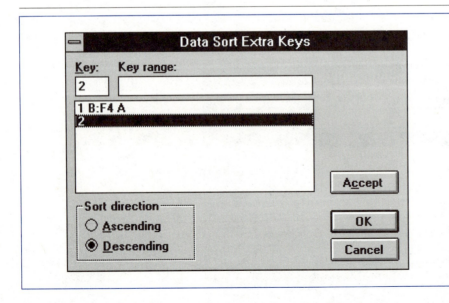

FIGURE 7.15:
Creating an extra key

The sorted database appears in Figure 7.16. You can see that the database has indeed been sorted by three keys: First the records are arranged by region. Then, within each region, they are arranged by city. And where there are duplicate city entries—specifically, Boston, Washington, D.C., and Los Angeles—the records are arranged by the instructors' specialties.

According to the 1-2-3 documentation, the Data Sort Extra Keys dialog box allows you to create a list of as many as 253 extra sorting keys. It may be hard to imagine a 1-2-3 database in which you would need more than, say, half a dozen extra sorting keys; but in effect, 1-2-3 supports as many keys as your database requires.

Each time you choose the Data Sort and Data Sort Extra Keys commands, 1-2-3 retains your sorting instructions from the previous sort. If you want to start over again with a fresh set of sorting instructions, simply click the Reset button on the Data Sort dialog box. This clears all the instructions from both dialog boxes. To see how this works, and to sort the database by instructors' names in preparation for upcoming exercises, follow these steps:

1. Choose the Data Sort command and click the Reset button on the resulting dialog box. This clears the current entries from the Data Sort dialog box and from the Extra Keys box. (Click the Extra keys button if you want to confirm this. Then click Cancel after you have examined the Data Sort Extra Keys dialog box.)

	A	B	C	D	E	F	G	H	I	J	K
1				Instructor Database							
2											
3	ID	Last	First	City	Region	Specialty	Rate	Hrs	Contract	Yrs	Ok
4	N-101	Schwartz	B.	Boston	E	Networks	$150	178	02-Mar-86	5.9	A
5	T-133	Ramirez	F.	Boston	E	Telecomm	$150	73	08-Feb-88	4.0	B
6	W-124	Meyer	J.	New York	E	WP	$150	85	05-May-87	4.7	B
7	D-139	Porter	M.	Washington, D.C.	E	Database	$150	26	28-Mar-89	2.8	B
8	S-125	Ashford	W.	Washington, D.C.	E	Spreadsheet	$150	145	10-May-87	4.7	A
9	S-155	Roberts	P.	Chicago	N	Spreadsheet	$100	10	21-Aug-91	0.4	New
10	D-137	Sanchez	W.	Indianapolis	N	Database	$100	47	16-Apr-89	2.8	B
11	W-113	Porter	D.	Seattle	N	WP	$125	59	02-Aug-86	5.5	B
12	T-128	Eng	R.	Albuquerque	S	Telecomm	$75	75	11-Oct-87	4.3	B
13	A-146	Daniels	A.	Atlanta	S	Accounting	$125	24	09-May-91	0.7	New
14	S-149	Harris	P.	Dallas	S	Spreadsheet	$150	17	12-Feb-91	1.0	New
15	D-106	Weinberg	P.	Miami	S	Database	$75	59	18-Jan-86	6.0	B
16	W-145	Banks	S.	St. Louis	S	WP	$150	55	10-Jun-90	1.6	A
17	A-103	Perez	D.	Las Vegas	W	Accounting	$100	5	11-Jul-86	5.6	C
18	D-143	Cody	L.	Los Angeles	W	Database	$75	43	20-Jun-90	1.6	B
19	S-127	Gill	P.	Los Angeles	W	Spreadsheet	$100	25	22-Jun-87	4.6	C
20	W-119	Davis	G.	San Francisco	W	WP	$150	139	09-Jul-87	4.6	A

FIGURE 7.16:

Sorting the database by three key fields—Region, City, and Specialty

2. Enter **INSTRUCTRECS** in the Data range box, **B4** in the Primary key box, and **C4** in the Secondary key box. Click Ascending for both keys. Then click OK or press ↵.

3. Click the save-file icon to update the INSTRUCT.WK3 worksheet on disk.

The Sort Order

The *sort order* refers to 1-2-3's default technique for sorting the database when a key field contains some label entries that begin with digits and others that begin with letters of the alphabet. You can see an example of this problem by looking back at the office database table in Figure 7.6. The Address field contains three labels that begin with digits, and one that begins with a letter. If you were to sort this table by the Address field, what would be the resulting order?

By default, 1-2-3 uses the *numbers first* sort order. To demonstrate that this is so, try the following brief exercise:

1. Click the previous-worksheet icon (or click Ctrl-PgDn) to move the cell pointer to worksheet A.

2. Choose the Data Sort command and click the Reset button to clear all the previous sorting instructions.

3. Enter the range name OFFICERECS into the Data range box. Then enter a reference to cell A:B4 into the Primary key box. Click the Ascending option, then click OK.

Figure 7.17 shows the office database, sorted by the Address field. You can see the result of 1-2-3's default sort order: The addresses that begin with digits come first, followed by the address that begins with a letter.

A	B	C	D	E	F	G
1	Regional Offices					
2						
3	Region	Address	City	State	Zip	Phone	Manager
4	S	11 Maple Street	Dallas	TX	75210	(214) 555-6754	Harvey, J.
5	E	222 Allen Street	New York	NY	10103	(212) 555-4678	Campbell, R.
6	W	432 Market Avenue	Los Angeles	CA	90028	(213) 555-9974	Garcia, M.
7	N	Mills Tower, Suite 992	Chicago	IL	60605	(312) 555-8803	Logan, C.

FIGURE 7.17:

A demonstration of the numbers first sort order

Except for the purposes of this experimental exercise, it is a little unlikely that you would actually want to sort the office database by the Address field, because the four addresses in the table are all in different cities. This sort is more realistic in a database containing many addresses in the same city, in which case you may want to control the default sort order. To change this order, you must rerun the 1-2-3 Install program. (See Appendix A for information about this program.) When you run Install, the Main Menu appears on the screen, as shown in Figure 7.18. To change the sort order, click the option labeled Choose international options. In the resulting dialog box, which appears in Figure 7.19, you can select from a list of 1-2-3's sort orders, including Numbers First, Numbers Last, and ASCII.

PERFORMING QUERY OPERATIONS

As you learned at the beginning of this chapter, you use the Data Query commands when you want to find, list, delete, or revise records that match certain conditions in your database. The conditions for selecting records in a query operation are known as *criteria*. The expressions for criteria can be simple or complex. For example, in the instructor database, you might want to perform query operations to find any of the following combinations of records:

◆ Instructors in the Southern region

◆ Instructors who specialize in word processing

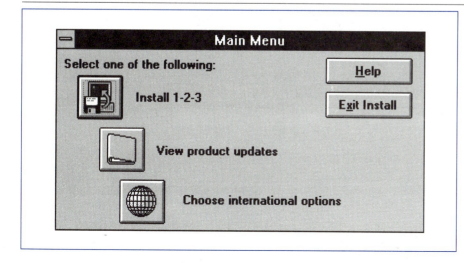

FIGURE 7.18:
The Main Menu of the 1-2-3 Install program

- A Los Angeles instructor who specializes in spreadsheets
- Cities that have telecommunications or networking experts
- Western region instructors whose hourly rate is less than or equal to $100
- Spreadsheet experts who have an A rating in the Ok field
- Southern or Eastern database experts who have an A or B rating and work for less than $100 per hour
- Eastern region instructors who signed their first contracts with Computing Conferences, Inc. at least four years ago and have an A or B rating.

To perform each of these queries, you write a single criterion or a combination of criteria. You store these expressions in a specially organized worksheet range that you designate as the *criteria range*. A criteria range consists of a row of field names from your database, plus one or more rows of criteria that 1-2-3 can use to select records from the database.

Actually, the Data Query commands require you to identify as many as three special worksheet ranges. In addition to the criteria range, you must specify an *input range* that contains the database table from which you want to select records; and, in some operations, an *output range,* where 1-2-3 can copy records that match your criteria. The output range also contains a row

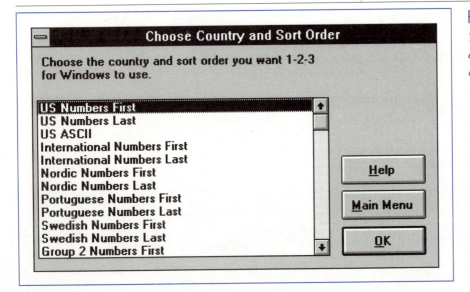

FIGURE 7.19:
The Choose Country and Sort Order dialog box

of field names; 1-2-3 uses this row of names to determine which fields to copy from the database. One convenient way to organize queries in a 1-2-3 worksheet window is to create separate worksheets for the input range, the criteria range, and the output range. In the next section, you'll begin developing these ranges for the instructor database.

Preparing the Input, Criteria, and Output Ranges

As you know, the INSTRUCT.WK3 file already contains two worksheets, for the office database table and the instructor database table. In this chapter's query exercises, you'll identify the instructor database table as the input range. You have already assigned this table a range name of INSTRUCTDB. In the following steps, you'll insert two more worksheets into the file, for the criteria range and the output range:

1. Click the next-worksheet icon (or press Ctrl-PgUp) to move to worksheet B.

2. Choose the Worksheet Global Settings command. Click the Group mode option to place an X in the check box. Click OK to confirm.

3. Choose the Worksheet Insert command. Click the Sheet option and enter a value of **2** in the Quantity box. Click OK or press ↵. In response, 1-2-3 inserts worksheets C and D into the file. Worksheet C is active initially. Thanks to the Group mode option, 1-2-3 has duplicated the column widths from worksheet B in the two new worksheets.

4. Click the previous-worksheet icon twice to view worksheet A. Unfortunately, the column widths from worksheet B have also been imposed on worksheet A. Choose the Worksheet Global Settings command again, and disable the Group mode option. (The X disappears from the check box.) Click OK to confirm. Now you'll have to take the time to reestablish the correct column widths for the office worksheet: A, **6**; B, **17**; C, **11**; D, **4**; E, **7**; F, **12**; G, **12**. In exchange for this repeated effort on worksheet A, you saved time on the new worksheets C and D.

5. Click the next-worksheet icon (or press Ctrl-PgUp) to move to worksheet B. Now choose the Window Split command and select the Perspective option button. Click the Synchronize option, removing the X from the check box. (Disabling the Synchronize option allows you to scroll each of the worksheets independently.) Click OK or

press ↵ to confirm. Now you have a perspective view of worksheets B, C, and D.

6. On worksheet B, select the range of field names, B:A3..B:K3. Click the copy-to-clipboard icon, or press Ctrl-Insert.

7. Move to worksheet C and select cell C:A3. Click the paste-from-clipboard icon, or press Shift-Insert. The row of field names appears in row 3 of worksheet C. Now move to worksheet D, select cell D:A3, and perform the same paste operation. A copy of the field names appears in worksheet D.

8. Move the cell pointer to worksheet C again. Enter the name **Criteria Range** in cell C:A1. Now preselect the two-row range C:A3..C:K4. Choose the Range Name Create command and enter the name **CRITERIA1** for this range. Click OK to confirm.

9. Move to worksheet D. Enter the name **Output Range** in cell D:A1 of worksheet D. Now preselect the one-row range D:A3..D:K3. Choose the Range Name Create command and enter the name **OUTPUT1** for this range. Click OK to confirm. Click elsewhere on the worksheet to deselect the range.

10. Click the save-file icon to update INSTRUCT.WK3 on disk.

When you complete all these steps, your worksheet window appears as shown in Figure 7.20. You are now ready to begin experimenting with the Data Query commands.

FIGURE 7.20:
Preparing the criteria range and the output range

	A	B	C	D	E	F	G	H	I	J	K
1	Output Range										
2											
3	ID	Last		First	City		Region	Specialty	Rate	Hrs	Contract	Yrs

	A	B	C	D	E	F	G	H	I	J	K
1	Criteria Range										
2											
3	ID	Last		First	City		Region	Specialty	Rate	Hrs	Contract	Yrs

	A	B	C	D	E	F	G	H	I	J	K
1					Instructor Database						
2											
3	ID	Last		First	City		Region	Specialty	Rate	Hrs	Contract	Yrs	Ok
4	S-125	Ashford	W.	Washington, D.C.	E	Spreadsheet	$150	145	10-May-87	4.7	A
5	W-145	Banks	S.	St. Louis	S	WP	$150	55	10-Jun-90	1.6	A
6	D-143	Cody	L.	Los Angeles	W	Database	$75	43	20-Jun-90	1.6	B
7	A-146	Daniels	A.	Atlanta	S	Accounting	$125	24	09-May-91	0.7	New

Using the Data Query Commands

In worksheet C, you have established a criteria range that includes the row of field names copied from the database, plus the row just beneath the names. When you perform your first query operations, and you identify CRITERIA1 as the criteria range, 1-2-3 will look in this range for values or expressions representing criteria. There are several kinds of criteria you can use for queries. The simplest kind is a label or a value that you enter below a particular field name in the criteria range. This kind of criterion instructs 1-2-3 to find all the records that contain the same label or value in the specified field. For example, if you enter the label E under the name Region in the criteria range, 1-2-3 searches for all records that have a Region entry of E.

The Data Query Find Command

As your first database query, try this Find operation:

1. Move the cell pointer to worksheet C, and enter the label **E** in cell E4, just beneath the Region field.

2. Pull down the Data menu and choose the Query command. As shown back in Figure 7.1, the Data Query dialog box contains three text boxes, labeled Input range, Criteria range, and Output range. At the right is a column of command buttons representing 1-2-3's query operations, Find, Delete, Extract, and Modify.

3. The Input range box initially has the focus. Press the F3 function key to view the Range Names box. Double-click the name INSTRUCTDB. In response, 1-2-3 copies this name into the Input range box.

4. Press Tab to activate the Criteria range box. Press F3 to view the Range Names box again. Double-click the name CRITERIA1 to enter this name as the criteria range. Alternatively, you can skip the Range Names dialog box, and simply enter the name **CRITERIA1** directly from the keyboard. Your first query operation will be a Find command; this command does not use an output range, so you can leave the Output range box unchanged. At this point in your work, the Data Query dialog box appears as shown in Figure 7.21.

5. Click the Find button, instructing 1-2-3 to find records that match the single criterion currently expressed in the criteria range. In response, 1-2-3 places a frame around the first record in the instructor database that matches the criterion. (The word *FIND* appears as mode indicator at the upper-right corner of the 1-2-3 window.)

6. Now press the ↓ key to view the next record that matches the criterion. In response, 1-2-3 jumps past several records, down to the next instructor in the Eastern region, as shown in Figure 7.22. Press ↓ three more times. Each time, 1-2-3 highlights a new matching record.

7. Press ↓ one more time; 1-2-3 beeps to let you know that you have arrived at the last record that matches the criterion. Now press ↑ four times. Each time, 1-2-3 jumps up the database to the previous matching record.

8. To exit from the Data Query Find operation, press the Escape key or ↵. The Data Query dialog box reappears on the screen. Click the Cancel button to close the dialog box.

To further define the conditions for selecting records, you can place more than one label or value in a row of the criteria range. If you enter two criteria in a given row, 1-2-3 reads the entries as *and* conditions. In other words, a record must match both criteria to be selected. For example, if you now enter an A beneath the Ok field in the CRITERIA1 range, 1-2-3 combines this new entry with the E that is already beneath the Region field. As a result, the Data Query Find operation selects all Eastern region instructors who have a rating of A.

You'll try this combination of criteria in the next exercise. At the same time, you'll learn to use the F7 function key to repeat a Query operation:

1. Move to worksheet C and select cell C:K4. Enter the label **A** in the cell.

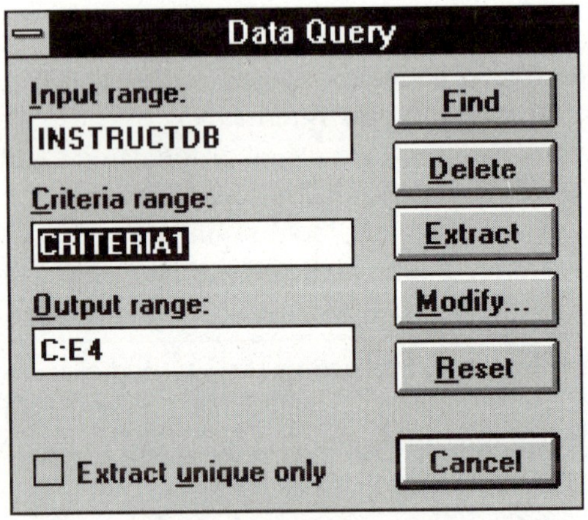

FIGURE 7.21:
Entering Range Names into the Data Query dialog box

2. Press the F7 function key. F7 is known as the Query key; it repeats or resumes the previous query operation. In this instance, 1-2-3 switches back into the FIND mode, using the same input range and criteria range that you specified for the previous Find operation. The difference now is that you have entered a second selection criterion into the criteria range. To begin, 1-2-3 places a frame highlight around the first record in the database that meets both criteria—an E in the Region field and an A in the Ok field.

3. Press the ↓ key once. The highlight jumps down to the second record that meets the criteria. Press ↓ again, and 1-2-3 beeps; there are only two records in the database that meet the criteria.

4. Press ↵ or the Escape key to exit from the FIND mode. This time, the Data Query dialog box does *not* automatically reappear on the screen, because you entered the FIND mode by pressing the F7 function key rather than by choosing Data Query.

The Data Query Extract Command

Unlike the Find command, which merely highlights selected records, the Extract command actually makes a copy of the records that meet the selection criteria. Extract copies the selected records to the location that you designate as the output range. To perform an extract operation, you therefore need to return to the Data Query dialog box and enter a range name in the Output range box.

FIGURE 7.22:
Performing a Find operation

	A	B	C	D	E	F	G	H	I	J	K
	Output Range										
	ID	Last	First	City	Region	Specialty	Rate	Hrs	Contract	Yrs	
	Criteria Range										
	ID	Last	First	City	Region	Specialty	Rate	Hrs	Contract	Yrs	
					E						
9	T-128	Eng	R.	Albuquerque	S	Telecomm	$75	75	11-Oct-87	4.3	B
10	S-127	Gill	P.	Los Angeles	W	Spreadsheet	$100	25	22-Jun-87	4.6	C
11	S-149	Harris	P.	Dallas	S	Spreadsheet	$150	17	12-Feb-91	1.0	New
12	W-124	Meyer	J.	New York	E	WP	$150	85	05-May-87	4.7	B
13	A-103	Perez	D.	Las Vegas	W	Accounting	$100	5	11-Jul-86	5.6	C
14	W-113	Porter	D.	Seattle	N	WP	$125	59	02-Aug-86	5.5	B
15	D-139	Porter	M.	Washington, D.C.	E	Database	$150	26	28-Mar-89	2.8	B

In the following steps, you'll use the current criteria to create an output list of all Eastern region instructors with A ratings:

1. Choose the Data Query command, and activate the Output range box. Press the F3 function key to view the Range Names box and double click the name OUTPUT1. In response, 1-2-3 copies this name to the Output range box, as shown in Figure 7.23.

2. Click the Extract button. The extract operation is performed, but the Data Query dialog box remains on the screen. Click the Cancel button to close the dialog box.

3. Move the cell pointer to worksheet D and scroll the worksheet horizontally so that you can see columns B though K.

When you complete these steps, the worksheet file appears as in Figure 7.24. In the output range of worksheet D, 1-2-3 has selected and copied the two matching records.

Now you can use the F7 function key to perform additional Extract commands. In other words, you can change the selection criteria and then press F7. In response, 1-2-3 copies a new selection of records into the output range, replacing the records currently displayed in the range.

In the next exercise, you'll experiment with a new kind of criterion expression. You can enter relational expressions into the criteria range—that is, expressions beginning with one of the relational operators, such as <, >, <=, or >=. You enter these expressions as labels. For example, if you enter the expression >100 as the criterion for a numeric field, 1-2-3 selects all the records

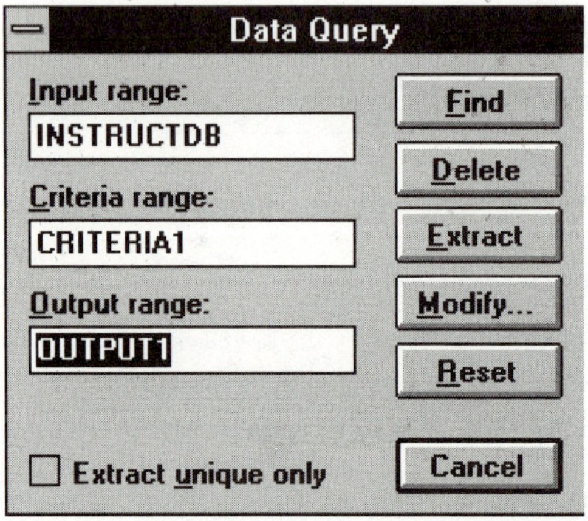

FIGURE 7.23:

Entering a name for the output range

that have a value greater than 100 in that field. This kind of criterion also works with date fields. For example, the criterion expression <=15-Jun-86 prompts 1-2-3 to search for records that have date values on or before June 15, 1986.

There is one problem with entering a label expression that begins with <, the less-than character. This key normally opens the 1-2-3 Classic window, as you learned in Chapter 1. To avoid this response, you must begin the label with a label prefix such as the single-quotation mark.

Follow these steps to try using these criteria in a sequence of extract operations:

1. Delete the two criteria currently displayed in the criteria range: Select cell C:E4, and press the Delete key. Then select C:K4 and press Delete again.

2. Select cell C:H4 in the Hrs field and enter the criterion **>100**. This criterion instructs 1-2-3 to find all the instructors who have worked for more than 100 hours.

3. Press the F7 function key. Examining the output range in worksheet D, you can see that 1-2-3 has found three records that match this criterion. Select worksheet D and scroll the worksheet vertically so you can see all three selected records. When you do so, your worksheet will look like Figure 7.25.

4. Now delete the criterion from cell C:H4, and then select cell C:I4 in the Contract field. Enter the expression **'<=15-Jun-86** into this cell.

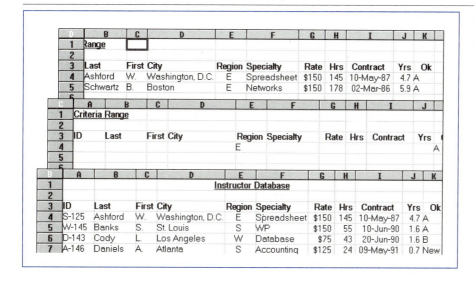

FIGURE 7.24:
An extract operation

5. Press the F7 function key. In response, 1-2-3 searches for instructors who signed contracts on or before June 15, 1986. As you can see in Figure 7.26, there are two such records.

Label criteria can appear in additional forms. For example, you can use "wildcard" characters to search for labels that contain certain combinations of characters. The ? character represents any single character in a label, and the * character represents an unspecified number of characters. For example, imagine that you are searching for an instructor whose name begins with P, but you can't recall the rest of the name. To find all the names that begin with P, enter P* as a criterion under the Last field in the criteria range. Delete the criterion from cell C:I4. Then press F7. Figure 7.27 shows the response; 1-2-3 finds the three instructors whose names begin with P, and copies the records to the output range.

In addition to the ? and * characters, you can also use ~, the tilde character, to identify a value that you want to *exclude* from the selected records. For example, an entry of ~E in the Region field of the criteria range instructs 1-2-3 to select all the records *except* those of the Eastern region.

The Data Query Delete Command

The Data Query Delete command removes selected records from your database. Like delete operations in any software environment, this command requires some care. Accidental or incorrect use of the Delete command can result in large losses of data. For this reason, you should take one or more of

FIGURE 7.25:

Using a relational expression as a criterion

	B	C	D	E	F	G	H	I	J	K
3	Last	First	City	Region	Specialty	Rate	Hrs	Contract	Yrs	Ok
4	Ashford	W.	Washington, D.C.	E	Spreadsheet	$150	145	10-May-87	4.7	A
5	Davis	G.	San Francisco	W	WP	$150	139	09-Jul-87	4.6	A
6	Schwartz	B.	Boston	E	Networks	$150	178	02-Mar-86	5.9	A
7										

	A	B	C	D	E	F	G	H	I	J
1	Criteria Range									
2										
3	ID	Last	First	City	Region	Specialty	Rate	Hrs	Contract	Yrs
4								>100		
5										

	A	B	C	D	E	F	G	H	I	J	K
1					Instructor Database						
2											
3	ID	Last	First	City	Region	Specialty	Rate	Hrs	Contract	Yrs	Ok
4	S-125	Ashford	W.	Washington, D.C.	E	Spreadsheet	$150	145	10-May-87	4.7	A
5	W-145	Banks	S.	St. Louis	S	WP	$150	55	10-Jun-90	1.6	A
6	D-143	Cody	L.	Los Angeles	W	Database	$75	43	20-Jun-90	1.6	B
7	A-146	Daniels	A.	Atlanta	S	Accounting	$125	24	09-May-91	0.7	New

the following precautions before you use this command:

1. Save your database just *before* you perform the Delete command. If Delete produces results that you did not expect, you can close the current worksheet window without saving it, and then reopen the original version from disk.

2. Perform a Find operation before Delete. The Find command allows you to examine the records that will be removed from your database if you go through with the Delete operation.

3. Click the undo icon immediately after a Delete operation if you decide you want to bring back the deleted records. (If the Undo feature is currently disabled, choose the Tools User Setup command now and check the Enable Edit Undo option. Click OK to confirm.) You lose the undo option as soon as you perform some other command; for this reason, you should examine your database carefully just after the Delete command.

As an experiment with the Data Query Delete command, imagine that you have decided to drop instructors who have Ok ratings of C. Here are the steps for accomplishing this:

1. Delete any previous entries in the criteria range. Select cell C:K4 and enter the label **C**.

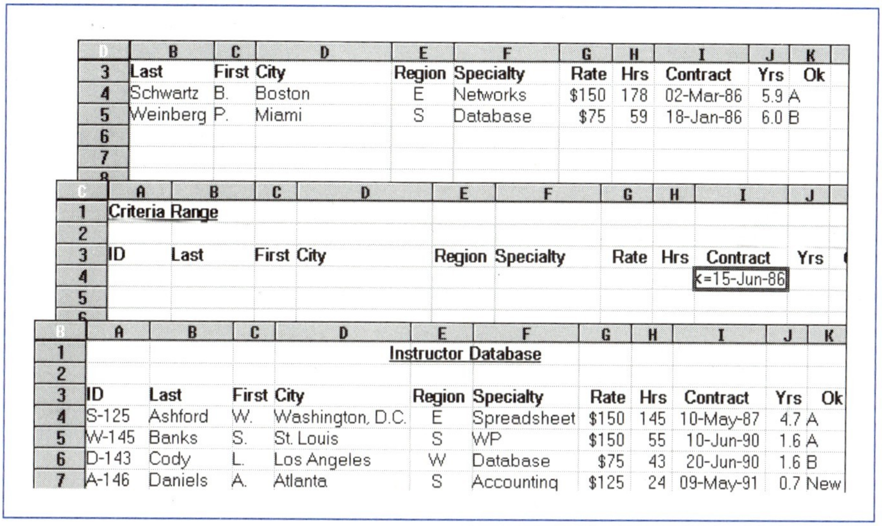

FIGURE 7.26:
A date criterion

2. Move the cell pointer to worksheet B and click the perspective-view icon so that you can see the entire instructor database at once.

3. Choose the Data Query command and click Find on the resulting dialog box. Use the ↓ and ↑ keys to examine the records that match the criterion. You'll find two instructors with ratings of C.

4. Press Escape or ↵. The Data Query dialog box reappears on the screen.

5. Click the Delete button. The message box shown in Figure 7.28 appears on the screen. Notice that you can abandon the Delete operation by clicking Cancel.

6. Click the Delete button in the message box, then click Cancel in the Data Query box. When you examine the resulting database, shown in Figure 7.29, you'll see that the two instructors with C ratings are no longer part of the database.

7. Now click the undo icon. The two deleted records reappear in the database.

If the undo command did not work for some reason, close your worksheet without saving it. Then reopen INSTRUCT.WK3 from disk.

In the upcoming exercise with the Data Query Modify command, you'll work with yet another variation in the criteria range. Up to now, you've entered each criterion in a single row, just beneath the field names in the criteria range. You've seen that 1-2-3 treats multiple criteria in a row as *and*

FIGURE 7.27:

Using wildcard characters in criteria

	A	B	C	D	E	F	G	H	I	J
3	ID	Last	First	City	Region	Specialty	Rate	Hrs	Contract	Yrs
4	A-103	Perez	D.	Las Vegas	W	Accounting	$100	5	11-Jul-86	5.6
5	W-113	Porter	D.	Seattle	N	WP	$125	59	02-Aug-86	5.5
6	D-139	Porter	M.	Washington, D.C.	E	Database	$150	26	28-Mar-89	2.8

	A	B	C	D	E	F	G	H	I	J
1	Criteria Range									
2										
3	ID	Last	First	City	Region	Specialty	Rate	Hrs	Contract	Yrs
4		P*								

	A	B	C	D	E	F	G	H	I	J	K
1					Instructor Database						
2											
3	ID	Last	First	City	Region	Specialty	Rate	Hrs	Contract	Yrs	Ok
4	S-125	Ashford	W.	Washington, D.C.	E	Spreadsheet	$150	145	10-May-87	4.7	A
5	W-145	Banks	S.	St. Louis	S	WP	$150	55	10-Jun-90	1.6	A
6	D-143	Cody	L.	Los Angeles	W	Database	$75	43	20-Jun-90	1.6	B
7	A-146	Daniels	A.	Atlanta	S	Accounting	$125	24	09-May-91	0.7	New

conditions; to be selected, a record must match all the criteria. In contrast, expressions entered on different rows of the criteria range are treated as *or* conditions. This means that a given record from the database will be selected if it matches *any one* of the criteria.

For example, imagine that you want to examine the records for all Western region instructors who specialize in either spreadsheets or word processing. Figure 7.30 shows the criteria range that you will prepare for this query. In the Specialty field, one row has an entry of Spreadsheet and the other WP. In addition, an entry of W appears in both rows beneath the Region field. (If you were to omit the W from the second row, 1-2-3 would select Western region spreadsheet specialists, along with word processing instructors from *all* regions.)

FIGURE 7.28:

The Data Query Delete box

FIGURE 7.29:

Deleting records from the database

	A	B	C	D	E	F	G	H	I	J	K
1					Instructor Database						
2											
3	ID	Last	First	City	Region	Specialty	Rate	Hrs	Contract	Yrs	Ok
4	S-125	Ashford	W.	Washington, D.C.	E	Spreadsheet	$150	145	10-May-87	4.7	A
5	W-145	Banks	S.	St. Louis	S	WP	$150	55	10-Jun-90	1.6	A
6	D-143	Cody	L.	Los Angeles	W	Database	$75	43	20-Jun-90	1.6	B
7	A-146	Daniels	A.	Atlanta	S	Accounting	$125	24	09-May-91	0.7	New
8	W-119	Davis	G.	San Francisco	W	WP	$150	139	09-Jul-87	4.6	A
9	T-128	Eng	R.	Albuquerque	S	Telecomm	$75	75	11-Oct-87	4.3	B
10	S-149	Harris	P.	Dallas	S	Spreadsheet	$150	17	12-Feb-91	1.0	New
11	W-124	Meyer	J.	New York	E	WP	$150	85	05-May-87	4.7	B
12	W-113	Porter	D.	Seattle	N	WP	$125	59	02-Aug-86	5.5	B
13	D-139	Porter	M.	Washington, D.C.	E	Database	$150	26	28-Mar-89	2.8	B
14	T-133	Ramirez	F.	Boston	E	Telecomm	$150	73	08-Feb-88	4.0	B
15	S-155	Roberts	P.	Chicago	N	Spreadsheet	$100	10	21-Aug-91	0.4	New
16	D-137	Sanchez	W.	Indianapolis	N	Database	$100	47	16-Apr-89	2.8	B
17	N-101	Schwartz	B.	Boston	E	Networks	$150	178	02-Mar-86	5.9	A
18	D-106	Weinberg	P.	Miami	S	Database	$75	59	18-Jan-86	6.0	B
19											
20											

One additional step is required to establish this as the criteria range. You can no longer use the name CRITERIA1 to identify the range. CRITERIA1 represents the row of field names, along with only one row of criteria. You'll want to create a new range name for the expanded criteria range.

Here are the steps for creating this criteria range on your worksheet:

1. Click the perspective icon, if necessary, to view three worksheets at once. Select cell C:K4. Press the Delete key to delete the criterion from the previous exercise.

2. Select cell C:E4 and enter a label of **W**. Enter the same label in cell C:E5. Then enter the labels **Spreadsheet** and **WP** in cells C:F4 and C:F5, respectively.

3. Preselect the range C:A3..C:K5. Choose the Range Name Create command and enter the name **CRITERIA2** for this new criteria range. Click OK or press ↵ to confirm.

4. Click the save-file icon to save your work to disk.

You'll make use of this new criteria range in the next section, as you explore the use of the Modify command.

The Data Query Modify Command

The last of the four query operations, Data Query Modify, gives you a convenient way to revise selected records in your database. This command represents a multistep procedure. You begin by using Modify to extract records that match a given set of criteria. The records appear in your output range. Then you activate this range and revise the records in any way necessary. Finally, you choose Data Query Modify again and instruct 1-2-3 to copy the revised records back to the database. When you use the Modify command, 1-2-3 keeps track of the original locations of the extracted records.

C	A	B	C	D	E	F	G	H	I	J	K
1	Criteria Range										
2											
3	ID	Last	First	City	Region	Specialty	Rate	Hrs	Contract	Yrs	Ok
4					W	Spreadsheet					
5					W	WP					
6											

FIGURE 7.30:
Two rows of criteria

Clicking the Modify button in the Data Query dialog box produces the Data Query Modify dialog box on the screen. As you can see in Figure 7.31, this box contains its own column of command buttons: The Extract command copies the selected records to the output range. After you have revised the records, the Replace command copies them back to their correct places in the database. The Insert command copies new records from the output range to the end of the database. The Finish command ends the Modify procedure without replacing any records.

Here is a situation for testing the Modify command. The Western region has just completed a series of conferences focusing on spreadsheets and word processing. The regional instructors specializing in these fields each worked for ten hours. Your job is to locate the records for these instructors and increase the entries in their Hrs fields.

You have already entered the correct criteria into worksheet C for accomplishing this task, and you have assigned the name CRITERIA2 to the new criteria range. This is what you do next:

1. Choose the Data Query command. Activate the Criteria range box and press F3 to view the Range Names list. Double-click CRITERIA2 to enter this name as the criteria range. (The input and output ranges should remain the same as for previous queries. Enter them as INSTRUCTDB and OUTPUT1 if necessary.)

2. Click the Modify command button. The Data Query Modify dialog box appears on the screen, as shown back in Figure 7.31. Click the Extract button. In response, 1-2-3 copies the selected records into the output range. Click Cancel to close the Data Query dialog box. Your worksheet appears as shown in Figure 7.32.

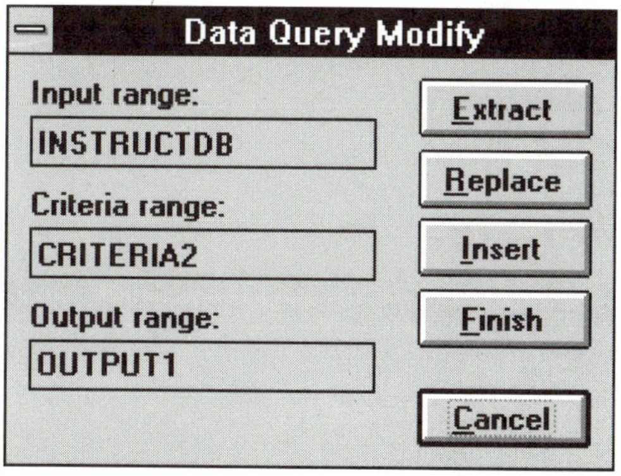

FIGURE 7.31:

The Data Query Modify dialog box

3. Select cell D:H4. Enter a new value of **149**, ten hours more than the previous entry. Next, select cell D:H5 and enter a new value of **35**.

4. Press the F7 function key. The Data Query Modify dialog box returns to the screen. Click the Replace button. In response, 1-2-3 copies your revised records from the output range back to the database.

5. Preselect the range D:A3..D:K3 and choose the Range Name Create command. Enter **OUTPUT1** in the Range Name box and click OK. (Renaming this range is necessary after the Data Query Modify command.)

6. Click the save-file icon to save your work to disk.

Figure 7.33 shows your database after the Modify operation is complete. By scrolling vertically down the database in worksheet B, you can see the two records that have been revised in rows 8 and 10. They contain the correct new entries for the Hrs field.

WRITING FORMULAS AS CRITERIA

In some database applications, you may not be able to express all your selection criteria as simple labels, values, or relations. For more complex queries, 1-2-3 allows you to write logical formulas as criteria. As you'll recall from Chapter 5, a logical formula is an expression that results in a value of true or

FIGURE 7.32:
Extracting data for a Modify operation

	A	B	C	D	E	F	G	H	I	J
3	ID	Last	First	City	Region	Specialty	Rate	Hrs	Contract	Yrs
4	W-119	Davis	G.	San Francisco	W	WP	$150	139	09-Jul-87	4.6
5	S-127	Gill	P.	Los Angeles	W	Spreadsheet	$100	25	22-Jun-87	4.6
6										
7										

	A	B	C	D	E	F	G	H	I	J
1	Criteria Range									
2										
3	ID	Last	First	City	Region	Specialty	Rate	Hrs	Contract	Yrs
4					W	Spreadsheet				
5					W	WP				

	A	B	C	D	E	F	G	H	I	J	K
1					Instructor Database						
2											
3	ID	Last	First	City	Region	Specialty	Rate	Hrs	Contract	Yrs	Ok
4	S-125	Ashford	W.	Washington, D.C.	E	Spreadsheet	$150	145	10-May-87	4.7	A
5	W-145	Banks	S.	St. Louis	S	WP	$150	55	10-Jun-90	1.6	A
6	D-143	Cody	L.	Los Angeles	W	Database	$75	43	20-Jun-90	1.6	B
7	A-146	Daniels	A.	Atlanta	S	Accounting	$125	24	09-May-91	0.7	New

false. You build logical formulas with the relational operators, =, <>, <, >, <=, and >=, along with the logical operators, #NOT#, #AND#, and #OR#.

In a formula criterion, you use field names as the operands. For example, suppose you want to find all the instructors who charge hourly rates that are greater than $75 but less than $150. To do so, you could enter the following formula in the Rate field of the criteria range:

+RATE>75#AND#RATE<150

Figure 7.34 shows how this formula works as a criterion in an extract operation. As you can see in worksheet D, 1-2-3 has copied the records of instructors who charge $100 or $125. Notice that the formula in the criteria range (in cell C:G4) is displayed in the Text format. When you enter a formula like this one into the criteria range, 1-2-3 may respond by displaying *ERR* in the cell. This does not mean that there is anything wrong with the formula as a criterion. To clarify your worksheet—and to avoid displaying *ERR*—you will probably want to choose Range Format and select Text format for the cell.

Here is another example. Imagine that you want to review all the contracts that were signed during the last half of 1987 and all of 1988. To find the names of instructors who signed contracts in this period, you enter the following formula below the Contract field name in the criteria range:

+CONTRACT>@DATE(87,6,30)#AND#CONTRACT<=@DATE(88,12,31)

FIGURE 7.33:
Completing the Modify operation

D

	A	B	C	D	E	F	G	H	I	J
1	Output Range									
2										
3	ID	Last	First	City	Region	Specialty	Rate	Hrs	Contract	Yrs
4	W-119	Davis	G.	San Francisco	W	WP	$150	149	09-Jul-87	4.6
5	S-127	Gill	P.	Los Angeles	W	Spreadsheet	$100	35	22-Jun-87	4.6

C

	A	B	C	D	E	F	G	H	I	J
1	Criteria Range									
2										
3	ID	Last	First	City	Region	Specialty	Rate	Hrs	Contract	Yrs
4					W	Spreadsheet				
5					W	WP				

B

	A	B	C	D	E	F	G	H	I	J	K
8	W-119	Davis	G.	San Francisco	W	WP	$150	149	09-Jul-87	4.6	A
9	T-128	Eng	R.	Albuquerque	S	Telecomm	$75	75	11-Oct-87	4.3	B
10	S-127	Gill	P.	Los Angeles	W	Spreadsheet	$100	35	22-Jun-87	4.6	C
11	S-149	Harris	P.	Dallas	S	Spreadsheet	$150	17	12-Feb-91	1.0	New
12	W-124	Meyer	J.	New York	E	WP	$150	85	05-May-87	4.7	B
13	A-103	Perez	D.	Las Vegas	W	Accounting	$100	5	11-Jul-86	5.6	C
14	W-113	Porter	D.	Seattle	N	WP	$125	59	02-Aug-86	5.5	B

Figure 7.35 shows how this formula works in an Extract operation. Three records match the criterion expressed in the formula.

SUMMARY

A 1-2-3 database table is a collection of records that you enter into consecutive rows of a worksheet. Each database table begins with a row of field names. The entries within a field all belong to the same data type.

You use the Data Sort command to rearrange the records of a database table in alphabetical, numeric, or chronological order. The Data Sort dialog box allows entries for primary and secondary sorting keys, and options for ascending or descending sorts. To define additional key fields, you click the Extra keys command button.

The Data Query command is the central feature of the 1-2-3 database component. You use options in this command to perform any of four major query operations:

- ◆ The Find command highlights records that match specific criteria.

- ◆ The Extract command copies matching records to an output range that you specify.

- ◆ The Delete command removes matching records from the database.

FIGURE 7.34:

Using a formula as a criterion

	A	B	C	D	E	F	G	H	I	J	K
1						Instructor Database					
2											
3		ID	Last	First	City	Region	Specialty	Rate	Hrs	Contract	Yrs Ok
4		S-125	Ashford	W.	Washington, D.C.	E	Spreadsheet	$150	145	10-May-87	4.7 A
5		W-145	Banks	S.	St. Louis	S	WP	$150	55	10-Jun-90	1.6 A
6		D-143	Cody	L.	Los Angeles	W	Database	$75	43	20-Jun-90	1.6 B
7		A-146	Daniels	A.	Atlanta	S	Accounting	$125	24	09-May-91	0.7 New

	A	B	C	D	E	F	G	H	I	J
1	Criteria Range									
2										
3	ID	Last	First	City	Region	Specialty	Rate	Hrs	Contract	Yrs
4									+RATE>75#AND#RATE<150	
5										

	B	C	D	E	F	G	H	I	J	K
4	Daniels	A.	Atlanta	S	Accounting	$125	24	09-May-91	0.7	New
5	Gill	P.	Los Angeles	W	Spreadsheet	$100	35	22-Jun-87	4.6	C
6	Perez	D.	Las Vegas	W	Accounting	$100	5	11-Jul-86	5.6	C
7	Porter	D.	Seattle	N	WP	$125	59	02-Aug-86	5.5	B
8	Roberts	P.	Chicago	N	Spreadsheet	$100	10	21-Aug-91	0.4	New
9	Sanchez	W.	Indianapolis	N	Database	$100	47	16-Apr-89	2.8	B

- The Modify command copies matching records to the output range, but keeps track of their original positions in the database. After you have revised the records in the output range, you can then choose the Modify command again to copy the records back to the database.

To prepare for these query operations, you create a criteria range containing a row of field names and one or more rows of criteria. In addition, the Extract and Modify commands require an output range containing a row of field names.

In the criteria range, 1-2-3 reads a group of criteria arranged in a single row as an *and* condition; to be selected, a record must match all of the criteria. Criteria in separate rows of the range are taken as an *or* condition; to be selected, a record need match only one of the criteria. The 1-2-3 database component recognizes a variety of criteria formats. You can enter simple labels or values in the criteria range to find records that contain matching entries. Or, you can use relational operators (<, >, <=, >=) with labels or values to find records that contain a range of field entries. To express more complex criteria, you can enter complete logical formulas into the criteria range.

A database in 1-2-3 consists of one or more database tables. The database component can perform special query operations on multiple tables in a database; in this sense, 1-2-3 is a relational database system. You'll learn more about this in Chapter 8.

FIGURE 7.35:

A criterion formula that works with dates

	B	C	D	E	F	G	H	I	J	K
3	Last	First	City	Region	Specialty	Rate	Hrs	Contract	Yrs	Ok
4	Davis	G.	San Francisco	W	WP	$150	149	09-Jul-87	4.6	A
5	Eng	R.	Albuquerque	S	Telecomm	$75	75	11-Oct-87	4.3	B
6	Ramirez	F.	Boston	E	Telecomm	$150	73	08-Feb-88	4.0	B
7										

	G	H	I	J	K	L	M	N	O	P
1										
2										
3	Rate	Hrs	Contract	Yrs	Ok					
4			+CONTRACT>@DATE(87,6,30)#AND#CONTRACT<=@DATE(88,12,31)							
5										

	A	B	C	D	E	F	G	H	I	J	K
1					Instructor Database						
2											
3	ID	Last	First	City	Region	Specialty	Rate	Hrs	Contract	Yrs	Ok
4	S-125	Ashford	W.	Washington, D.C.	E	Spreadsheet	$150	145	10-May-87	4.7	A
5	W-145	Banks	S.	St. Louis	S	WP	$150	55	10-Jun-90	1.6	A
6	D-143	Cody	L.	Los Angeles	W	Database	$75	43	20-Jun-90	1.6	B
7	A-146	Daniels	A.	Atlanta	S	Accounting	$125	24	09-May-91	0.7	New

FAST TRACK

**To use a statistical database function such as
@DSUM or @DAVG,** 397
   supply three arguments: the database range, the
   target field name enclosed in quotation marks, and
   the criteria range.

**To create a computed column from a Data Query
Extract operation,** 402
   enter a formula in the top row of the output range.
   The formula for a computed column typically uses one
   or more field names as its operands.

**To create an aggregate column from a Data
Query Extract operation,** 406
   enter a statistical function such as @SUM, @AVG,
   @MIN, or @MAX in the top row of the output range.
   Also include a field name in the output range, to indicate the category of records you want grouped
   together in the aggregate column. (For example, include the Region field in the output range to find ag-
   gregates by region.) In the Data Query dialog box,
   check the option labeled Extract unique only.

**To perform a Data Query Extract operation on
two database tables,** 409
   select two tables that have a field in common. The two
   fields do not necessarily need to have the same name,
   but they must contain the same data entries. One of
   the database tables should contain only unique data
   entries in the field; the other can have multiple entries
   of the same data. In the top row of the criteria range,
   enter a compound field name in the form *Table-
   Name.FieldName*. Beneath this field name, enter a *join*

formula in the form *+TableName1.FieldName1=TableName2.FieldName2*. This formula identifies the common field in the two database tables. In the top row of the output range, enter compound field names to select output fields from either database table. In the Data Query dialog box, enter the names of both database tables (separated by a comma) into the Input range box. Enter ranges or range names in the Criteria range and Output range boxes; then click the Extract button.

To establish a connection to an external database, ... 416
choose the Data Connect to External command. In the Connect to driver text box, type three items of information separated by spaces: the name of the DataLens driver, the name of the directory where the external database is stored, and the name of the database file. Press ↵. In response to the next prompt, *Enter range name for table*, enter a range name to represent the external table, or press ↵ to accept the default range name. Click OK to complete the connection.

**To perform a Data Query Extract operation on an
external database, ... 417**
choose Data Connect to External to establish the connection and to define a range name for the database. Create a criteria range to select records from the external database, and an output range where 1-2-3 can copy records from the database. Choose the Data Query command. In the Input range box, enter the range name defined for the external database. Enter ranges or range names in the Criteria range and Output range boxes, then click the Extract command button.

CHAPTER 8

Database Calculations and Operations

In addition to the query operations you learned about in Chapter 7, Lotus 1-2-3 has several other important features designed to help you extract information from a database. Using a variety of tools, you can:

- Calculate statistical values and other numeric data from selected groups of records.
- Join data from two database tables.
- Perform queries on an *external database,* a file created in a database management program such as dBASE IV, dBASE III Plus, or Paradox.

These operations make use of the same three kinds of database ranges you've prepared for other queries: The input range contains the database itself; the criteria range expresses conditions for selecting records; and the output range displays the information that 1-2-3 copies from your database.

To explore these operations in this chapter, you'll continue working with the instructor database you've developed for Computing Conferences, Inc. Open the INSTRUCT.WK3 file from disk now, and briefly review its current contents: Worksheets A and B contain the office and instructor database tables, respectively; and worksheets C and D contain the current criteria and output ranges. You have defined several range names for use in query operations: OFFICEDB is the name of the office database table; INSTRUCTDB is the instructor database table; CRITERIA1 and CRITERIA2 are the criteria ranges; and OUTPUT1 is the output range. In upcoming exercises, you'll reuse these same ranges, and you'll also add new worksheets to the file for additional criteria and output ranges.

PERFORMING CALCULATIONS ON DATABASE RECORDS

Given a database table containing one or more numeric fields, you may want to perform a variety of numeric and statistical calculations. For example, suppose you are focusing on one of the four regions in the instructor database; you might need to find answers to questions like these:

- What is the average number of hours an instructor has worked in this region?
- How much has each instructor in the region earned from working at conferences?
- What is the average hourly rate for instructors in the region? What are the highest and lowest rates?

There are several general approaches to answering questions like these. First, 1-2-3 has a useful group of statistical functions that operate on database records. You use these tools along with a criteria range to perform statistical calculations on selected groups of records. In addition, you can perform calculations as part of a Data Query Extract procedure. To do so, you write special formulas in the output range for this procedure. You'll study these tools and techniques in the upcoming sections of this chapter.

USING THE DATABASE FUNCTIONS

Lotus 1-2-3 supplies the following special functions for calculating statistical values on selected records in a database:

- @DSUM totals the numeric entries of a particular field for a selected group of records.
- @DCOUNT counts the entries in the field.
- @DAVG computes the average of the values in the field.

- @DMAX finds the largest value in the field, and @DMIN finds the smallest.

- @DVAR and @DSTD compute the variance and standard deviation using the population method; @DVARS and @DSTDS calculate the variance and standard deviation using the sample method. (Turn back to Chapter 5 if you wish to review the distinction between these methods.)

These database functions represent the same statistical formulas as the equivalent worksheet functions, @SUM, @COUNT, @AVG, and so on. The difference is that the database functions perform their calculations on a *selection* of records in the database. You define this selection by writing specific criteria in a criteria range associated with the database.

In simplest usage, each of the statistical database functions takes three arguments:

- The first argument is the input range—that is, the range of the database itself.

- The second argument identifies the field that is the target of the calculation. This argument can appear either as a field name, enclosed in quotation marks; or an offset number, from 0 to $n–1$, where n is the number of fields in the database.

- The third argument is the criteria range you have created to select records from the database.

For example, consider the following @DSUM function:

@DSUM(INSTRUCTDB,"Hrs",CRITERIA1)

This function selects all the records in the instructor database that match a criterion expressed in the CRITERIA1 range. Then, within this selection of records, the function finds the sum of all the entries in the Hrs field.

Figure 8.1 shows the result of this @DSUM function, along with the results of five other database functions—@DCOUNT, @DAVG, @DMIN, @DMAX, and @DSTD. Worksheet E, at the top of the worksheet window, contains the function entries; the calculations focus on the work hours recorded for the instructors in the Southern region. As you can see, this worksheet shows the number of instructors in the region (5), the average number of conference hours these instructors worked (46), the total hours they have worked (230), the smallest number of hours worked by an individual instructor (17), the largest number of hours worked (75), and the standard deviation calculated for this set of data (displayed as *21.98*). The six database functions that produce these calculations all use the CRITERIA1 range to select records; notice that this range contains a single criterion, an S in the Region field.

To create this example for yourself in the upcoming exercise, you'll begin by adding the E worksheet to the INSTRUCT.WK3 file. Then, to see worksheets B, C, and E together in the perspective view, you'll use the Worksheet Hide command to hide worksheet D. (When you later want to view worksheet D again, choose the Worksheet Unhide command.) Here are the steps for producing this worksheet:

1. Use the perspective-view and next-worksheet icons, if necessary, to view worksheets B, C, and D in the worksheet window.

2. In worksheet C, the criteria range, delete any expressions currently displayed in rows 4 and 5. Enter the label **S** in cell C:E4, under the Region field.

3. Move to worksheet D and choose the Worksheet Insert command. Choose the Sheet option. Click OK or press ↵ to add the new worksheet to the file.

4. Move to worksheet D again and choose the Worksheet Hide command. Choose the Sheet option. Click OK or press ↵ to hide worksheet D. Click the previous-worksheet icon twice. Now you can see worksheets B, C, and E in the worksheet window.

FIGURE 8.1:
Using the database functions

Worksheet E:

	A	B	C	D	E	F	G	H
1	Conference Hours in Region:		S					
2								
3	Number of instructors		5		Lowest instructor hours		17	
4	Average instructor hours		46.00		Higest instructor hours		75	
5	Total instructor hours		230		Standard deviation		21.98	

Worksheet C:

	A	B	C	D	E	F	G	H	I	J
1	Criteria Range									
2										
3	ID	Last	First	City	Region	Specialty	Rate	Hrs	Contract	Yrs
4					S					
5										

Worksheet B:

	A	B	C	D	E	F	G	H	I	J	K
1					Instructor Database						
2											
3	ID	Last	First	City	Region	Specialty	Rate	Hrs	Contract	Yrs	Ok
4	S-125	Ashford	W.	Washington, D.C.	E	Spreadsheet	$150	145	10-May-87	4.7	A
5	W-145	Banks	S.	St. Louis	S	WP	$150	55	10-Jun-90	1.6	A
6	D-143	Cody	L.	Los Angeles	W	Database	$75	43	20-Jun-90	1.6	B
7	A-146	Daniels	A.	Atlanta	S	Accounting	$125	24	09-May-91	0.7	New

5. Enter the title **Conference Hours in Region:** in cell E:A1. Then enter the formula **+C:E4** in cell E:D1; this formula copies the label representing the selected region from the criteria range. Preselect the range E:A1..E:D1 and click the bold and underline icons.

6. Enter the following three labels into the range E:A3..E:A5:

    Number of instructors
    Average instructor hours
    Total instructor hours

    Enter these three labels in the range E:E3..E:E5:

    Lowest instructor hours
    Highest instructor hours
    Standard deviation

7. Enter these six functions into the worksheet, the first three in the range E:C3..E:C5, and the remaining three in the range E:G3..E:G5:

    @DCOUNT(INSTRUCTDB,"Hrs",CRITERIA1)
    @DAVG(INSTRUCTDB,"Hrs",CRITERIA1)
    @DSUM(INSTRUCTDB,"Hrs",CRITERIA1)

    @DMIN(INSTRUCTDB,"Hrs",CRITERIA1)
    @DMAX(INSTRUCTDB,"Hrs",CRITERIA1)
    @DSTD(INSTRUCTDB,"Hrs",CRITERIA1)

8. With the cell pointer at E:G5, choose the Range Format command and select the Fixed format. Keep the default value of 2 in the Decimal places box. Click OK or press ↵. Apply the same format to cell E:C4.

9. Move to worksheet B and press the Home key. Click the save-file icon to save your work to disk.

Now your worksheet appears as shown back in Figure 8.1.

In a sense, the database functions perform individual queries. They use the criteria range to select records from the database and they read data from a specific field. But there are a couple of important differences between a database function and a query: First, you don't have to choose the Data Query command to make the function work; and second, 1-2-3 automatically recalculates the function if you make any change in the criteria range.

To see how this recalculation works, enter the new label **E** in cell C:E4. Then, examine the result in worksheet E; the worksheet now contains statistical data about the instructors in the Eastern region, as shown in Figure 8.2.

Try other selection criteria on this application if you wish. For example, try selecting records from each of the remaining two regions, Northern and Western. Then try entering a second criterion, **Spreadsheet**, in cell C:F4. Given the combined criteria of W in the Region field and Spreadsheet in the Specialty field, 1-2-3 selects only one record. Notice what happens to the results of the statistical functions in this case: The @DAVG, @DSUM, @DMIN, and @DMAX functions all produce the same value, and the @DSTD returns a value of 0.

There are two more tools available in 1-2-3's collection of database functions. One of the two, named @DQUERY, is for use only on external databases, a subject you'll study in the final sections of this chapter. The other, named @DGET, reads and returns individual field entries from a database; this function is useful when you need to build a worksheet that lists values from a single record.

The @DGET Function

The @DGET function takes the same three types of arguments as the other database functions you've examined—an input range, a field name, and a criteria range. However, for successful use of the @DGET function, the expressions in the criteria range must select a single record from the database. @DGET returns a label or a value from a specified field in this selected record. However, if two or more records match the criteria, @DGET returns an ERR value.

FIGURE 8.2:

Applying the database functions to a different selection of records

	A	B	C	D	E	F	G	H
1	Conference Hours in Region:				E			
2								
3	Number of instructors			5		Lowest instructor hours		26
4	Average instructor hours			101.40		Higest instructor hours		178
5	Total instructor hours			507		Standard deviation		53.91

	A	B	C	D	E	F	G	H	I	J
1	Criteria Range									
2										
3	ID	Last	First	City		Region	Specialty	Rate	Hrs	Contract	Yrs
4						E					
5											

	A	B	C	D	E	F	G	H	I	J	K
1					Instructor Database						
2											
3	ID	Last	First	City	Region	Specialty	Rate	Hrs	Contract	Yrs	Ok
4	S-125	Ashford	W.	Washington, D.C.	E	Spreadsheet	$150	145	10-May-87	4.7	A
5	W-145	Banks	S.	St. Louis	S	WP	$150	55	10-Jun-90	1.6	A
6	D-143	Cody	L.	Los Angeles	W	Database	$75	43	20-Jun-90	1.6	B
7	A-146	Daniels	A.	Atlanta	S	Accounting	$125	24	09-May-91	0.7	New

The worksheet window in Figure 8.3 shows a simple exercise with the @DGET function. The criteria range in worksheet C contains one criterion: A name in the Last field selects one instructor's record from the database. The @DGET functions entered into worksheet E read labels and values from this selected record. Here are the steps for setting up this example on your own worksheet:

1. In worksheet C, delete any existing criteria from row 4 of the criteria range. Enter the name **Cody** in cell C:B4, under the Last field.

2. Move to worksheet E and scroll down the worksheet by several rows, so that row 6 is displayed at the top of the worksheet window. Enter the labels **Name:**, **City:**, **Specialty:**, and **Rate:** in cells E:C7, E:C8, E:C9, and E:C10, respectively. Preselect this range of cells and click the bold icon. Then enter the formula **+C:B4** in cell E:D7; this formula copies the selected instructor's name from the criteria range.

3. Enter the following three @DGET functions in cells E:D8, E:D9, and E:D10:

    @DGET(INSTRUCTDB,"City",CRITERIA1)
    @DGET(INSTRUCTDB,"Specialty",CRITERIA1)
    @DGET(INSTRUCTDB,"Rate",CRITERIA1)

4. Use the Range Format command to apply the currency format with no decimal places to cell E:D10.

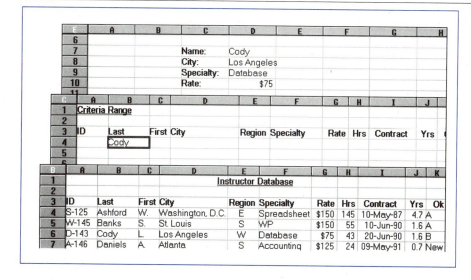

FIGURE 8.3:

An experiment with the @DGET function

5. Click the save-file icon to save your work to disk.

When you complete these steps, your worksheet appears as shown back in Figure 8.3.

Now try changing the criterion in worksheet C to select a new record from the database. Enter the new name **Daniels** in cell C:B4. As shown in Figure 8.4, 1-2-3 immediately recalculates the @DGET functions in worksheet E, to display entries from the record for the instructor named Daniels.

Finally, try one more experiment with this worksheet: Enter the name **Porter** as the criterion in C:B4. As you may recall, the database contains two instructors named Porter. Because this criterion selects more than one record, the three @DGET functions in worksheet E all return values of ERR, as you can see in Figure 8.5. Whenever you use the @DGET function you have to keep in mind this unique characteristic: The function operates successfully only on a single selected record.

The database functions are not the only tools available for producing calculations from a database table. For some applications, you'll prefer to use the Data Query Extract command to create output tables that include calculations. In the following two sections, you'll learn about two varieties of calculated output fields, known as *computed columns* and *aggregate columns*.

CREATING COMPUTED COLUMNS

Worksheet D, currently hidden from view, contains the output range that you used for the query exercises in Chapter 7. To reexamine this output range

FIGURE 8.4:
Selecting a new record for the @DGET function

E	A	B	C	D	E	F	G	H
6								
7			Name:	Daniels				
8			City:	Atlanta				
9			Specialty:	Accounting				
10			Rate:	$125				

C	A	B	C	D	E	F	G	H	I	J
1	Criteria Range									
2										
3	ID	Last	First	City		Region	Specialty	Rate	Hrs	Contract	Yrs
4		Daniels								
5										

B	A	B	C	D	E	F	G	H	I	J	K
1					Instructor Database						
2											
3	ID	Last	First	City		Region	Specialty	Rate	Hrs	Contract	Yrs	Ok
4	S-125	Ashford	W.	Washington, D.C.		E	Spreadsheet	$150	145	10-May-87	4.7	A
5	W-145	Banks	S.	St. Louis		S	WP	$150	55	10-Jun-90	1.6	A
6	D-143	Cody	L.	Los Angeles		W	Database	$75	43	20-Jun-90	1.6	B
7	A-146	Daniels	A.	Atlanta		S	Accounting	$125	24	09-May-91	0.7	New

now, follow these steps to bring the worksheet back into view:

1. Choose the Worksheet Unhide command. In the resulting dialog box, click the Sheet option.

2. Enter **D:A1** into the Range box. Click OK or press ↵ to confirm. Move the cell pointer to worksheet D and press the Home key.

Row 3 in this worksheet displays a complete group of field names from the instructor database. As you know, this particular output range prompts 1-2-3 to copy all of the fields from each record selected in a query operation. This is not the only way to design an output range. If you want to extract information from a smaller group of fields, you enter the corresponding selection of field names in the output range; 1-2-3 copies a column of data for each field you include.

You can also enter formulas in place of simple field names in the output range. A typical formula contains one or more references to fields in the database. In response to such a formula, 1-2-3 creates a computed column in the output range. In the following exercise, you'll create a new output range, OUTPUT2, with a computed column that displays the total amount each instructor has earned from conference jobs:

1. Move the cell pointer to worksheet E. Choose the Worksheet Insert command and select the Sheet option. Click OK or press ↵. A new worksheet named F appears in the worksheet window.

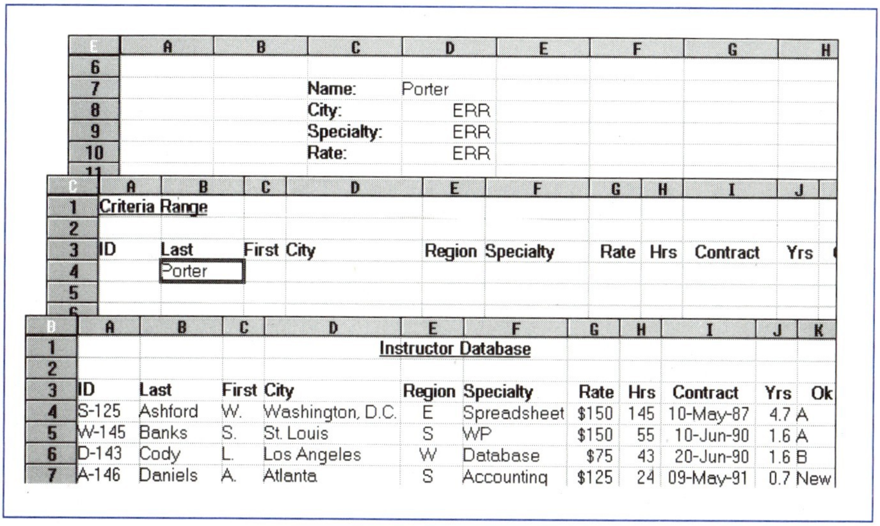

FIGURE 8.5:

@DGET returns ERR when multiple records are selected.

2. Choose the Worksheet Hide command. Select the Sheet option and enter D:A1..E:A1 in the Range box. Click OK or press ↵. Sheets D and E disappear from view. Click the previous-worksheet icon twice so you can see worksheets B, C, and F in the worksheet window.

3. In worksheet C, delete any existing criteria from row 4. Enter **W** into cell C:E4, beneath the Region field.

4. Move to worksheet F. In row 2 of the worksheet, cells F:A2 through F:E2, enter the field names **ID**, **Last**, **Specialty**, **Rate**, and **Hrs**. In cell F:F1, enter the label **Total Paid**. Click the align-right icon for this label. Then preselect the range F:A1..F:F2 and click the bold icon. Preselect F:D2..F:E2 and click the align-right icon again. Adjust the widths of columns C through F to the following settings: C, **11**; D, **6**; E, **5**; F, **11**.

5. Enter the following formula into cell F:F2:

    +RATE*HRS

    Ignore the ERR value that this formula generates. While the cell pointer is still at F:F2, choose the Range Format command and select the Text format. As a result of this action, the text of the formula itself is displayed in the cell.

6. Preselect the range F:F3..F:F6. This is the column in which 1-2-3 will enter computed values corresponding to the formula you have entered into cell F:F2. Use the Range Format command to apply the Currency format, with no decimal places, to the range.

7. Preselect the range of field names, F:A2..F:F2. Choose the Range Name Create command and enter **OUTPUT2** as the new name for this range. Click OK or press ↵. Then press the Home key to move the cell pointer to F:A1.

8. Choose the Data Query command. As shown in Figure 8.6, enter **IN-STRUCTDB** in the Input range box, **CRITERIA1** in the Criteria range box, and **OUTPUT2** in the Output range box. (You can enter these names directly from the keyboard, or you can press F3 to select each name in turn from the Range Names list.)

9. Click the Extract command button. Then click Cancel to close the Data Query dialog box.

When you complete these steps, your worksheet appears as shown in Figure 8.7. In worksheet F, 1-2-3 has copied records from the Western region, with an entry for each field in the output range. In addition, column F in this output range now displays the calculated total earnings of each instructor in the region.

You can now perform additional Data Query Extract operations to view the same computed column for other selections of records. When you change the selection criterion and press the F7 function key, 1-2-3 copies new records to the output range and recalculates the formula in the computed column. For example, try entering **N** as the new criterion

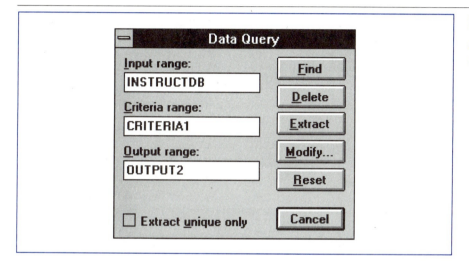

FIGURE 8.6:

A query using the new output range

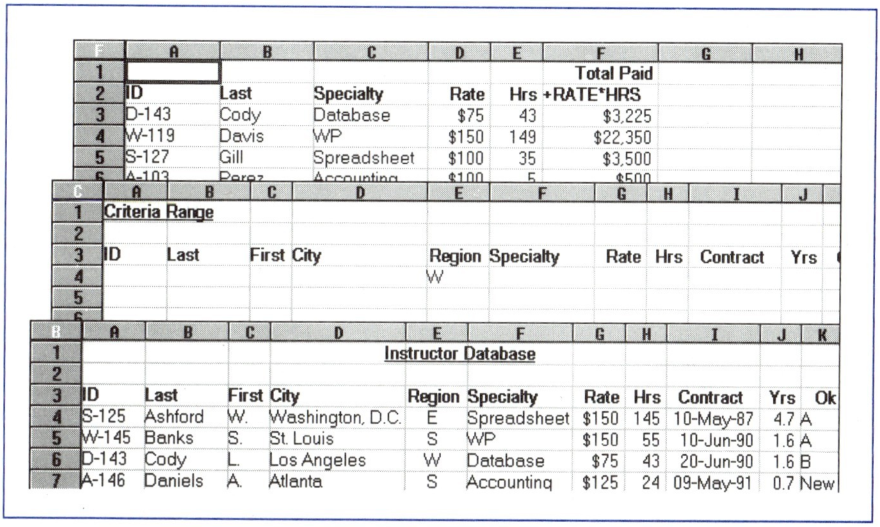

FIGURE 8.7:

A computed column in the output range

in cell C:E4. Then press F7 to repeat the Extract operation. In response, 1-2-3 creates the output in Figure 8.8, showing the total earnings of the three instructors in the Northern region.

CREATING AGGREGATE COLUMNS

An aggregate column displays a statistic that describes or summarizes a group of records in the database. You create an aggregate column by entering a statistical function, such as @SUM, @AVG, @MAX, or @MIN, at the top of a column in the output range. (Notice that these are worksheet functions, not database functions.) In response, 1-2-3 calculates the statistic for a specified group of records.

For example, suppose you want to create a table containing the average, maximum, and minimum hourly rates charged by instructors in each of the four regions. The easiest way to produce this table is with aggregate columns in a new output range. Here are the steps:

1. Move to worksheet F and choose the Worksheet Insert command. Select the Sheet option. Click OK or press ↵. Worksheet G appears in the window.

2. Move to worksheet F again and choose the Worksheet Hide command. Select the Sheet option. Click OK or press ↵. Click the previous-worksheet icon twice. You can now see worksheets B, C, and G in the worksheet window.

FIGURE 8.8: *Repeating the Extract operation with a computed column*

F worksheet:

	A	B	C	D	E	F	G	H
1						Total Paid		
2	ID	Last	Specialty	Rate	Hrs	+RATE*HRS		
3	W-113	Porter	WP	$125	59	$7,375		
4	S-155	Roberts	Spreadsheet	$100	10	$1,000		
5	D-137	Sanchez	Database	$100	47	$4,700		

C worksheet:

	A	B	C	D	E	F	G	H	I	J
1	Criteria Range									
2										
3	ID	Last	First	City	Region	Specialty	Rate	Hrs	Contract	Yrs
4					N					
5										

B worksheet:

	A	B	C	D	E	F	G	H	I	J	K
1					Instructor Database						
2											
3	ID	Last	First	City	Region	Specialty	Rate	Hrs	Contract	Yrs	Ok
4	S-125	Ashford	W.	Washington, D.C.	E	Spreadsheet	$150	145	10-May-87	4.7	A
5	W-145	Banks	S.	St. Louis	S	WP	$150	55	10-Jun-90	1.6	A
6	D-143	Cody	L.	Los Angeles	W	Database	$75	43	20-Jun-90	1.6	B
7	A-146	Daniels	A.	Atlanta	S	Accounting	$125	24	09-May-91	0.7	New

3. Enter the label **Region** in cell G:A1. Then enter the following functions in cells G:B1, G:C1, and G:D1:

   @AVG(RATE)
   @MAX(RATE)
   @MIN(RATE)

   Again, ignore the ERR values displayed in response to these entries.

4. Preselect the range G:B1..G:D1. Choose the Range Format command and select the Text option. Click OK or press ↵. The three functions are displayed as text in their cells. Now increase the widths of columns B, C, and D to 12.

5. Preselect the range G:B2..G:D5 and click the currency icon. Next, preselect the range G:A1..GD1 and click the bold icon. Then, without changing the range selection, choose the Range Name Create command and enter a new range name of OUTPUT3. Click OK or press ↵.

6. In worksheet C, delete the criterion from the previous exercise. Leave row 4 of the criteria range completely blank.

7. Choose the Data Query command and enter the names **INSTRUCTDB**, **CRITERIA1**, and **OUTPUT3** into the three text boxes. Click the Extract unique only option; an X appears in the check box, as shown in Figure 8.9. Next, click the Extract command button. Click Cancel to close the Data Query dialog box.

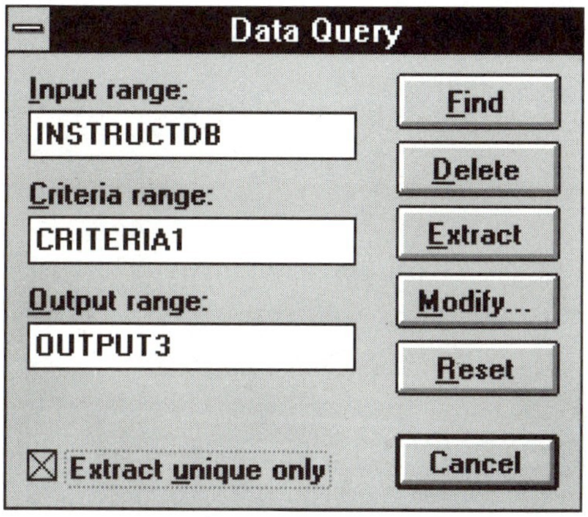

FIGURE 8.9:
Using the Extract unique only option

8. Click the save-file icon to save your work to disk.

Figure 8.10 shows the result of your work. As you can see, the output range displays average, maximum, and minimum hourly rates for each of the four regions. Because the second row of the criteria range is empty, 1-2-3 has selected all the records in the database. But thanks to the Extract unique only option, the output range contains exactly one aggregate record for each region.

Continue experimenting with this output range. Try changing the first output field in worksheet G to **Specialty**. Then press the F7 function key. In response, 1-2-3 creates an aggregate table of rate statistics for the six specialty areas, as shown in Figure 8.11. (The currency format has been applied to rows 6 through 8 of this table.) As you can see, creating an aggregate table is a very efficient way to generate statistical information about specific groups of records in the database.

JOINING MULTIPLE DATABASES

Up to this point, you've been working with the instructor table as though it were the sole component of the database. But as you know, worksheet A contains a second table, with information about the company's four regional offices. You can use the Data Query Extract command to produce combinations of data from both database tables.

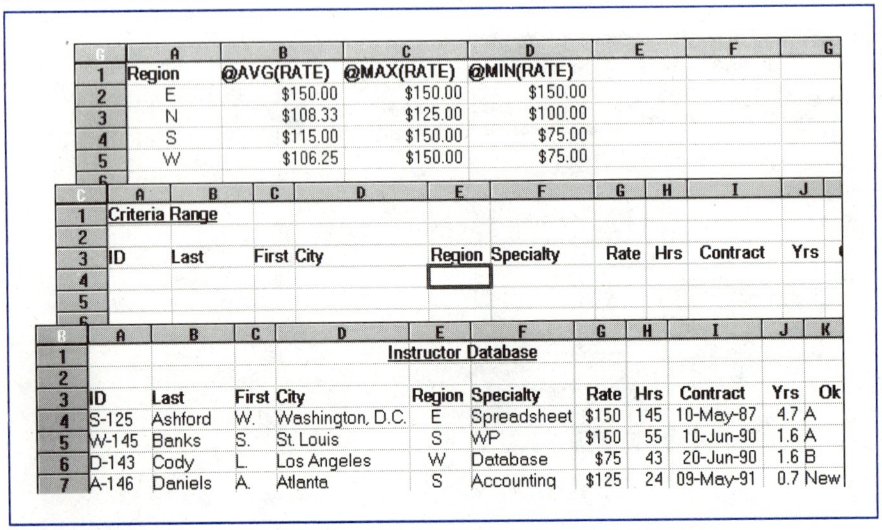

FIGURE 8.10:
Creating aggregate columns

Region	@AVG(RATE)	@MAX(RATE)	@MIN(RATE)
E	$150.00	$150.00	$150.00
N	$108.33	$125.00	$100.00
S	$115.00	$150.00	$75.00
W	$106.25	$150.00	$75.00

Criteria Range

ID	Last	First	City	Region	Specialty	Rate	Hrs	Contract	Yrs

Instructor Database

ID	Last	First	City	Region	Specialty	Rate	Hrs	Contract	Yrs	Ok
S-125	Ashford	W.	Washington, D.C.	E	Spreadsheet	$150	145	10-May-87	4.7	A
W-145	Banks	S.	St. Louis	S	WP	$150	55	10-Jun-90	1.6	A
D-143	Cody	L.	Los Angeles	W	Database	$75	43	20-Jun-90	1.6	B
A-146	Daniels	A.	Atlanta	S	Accounting	$125	24	09-May-91	0.7	New

For example, suppose you need to compile a list of the records that fall into either of two categories: the instructors who signed their initial contract within the last year; and the instructors who have worked the fewest hours per year with the company. The records in these two groups display entries of either New or C in the Ok field. On your list you want the names, ratings, and regions of the instructors in these two groups; but you also want your list to include fields for the names of the regional managers and for the phone numbers of the regional offices.

Anticipating the need for a list like this one, you might have considered organizing your original database differently. The instructor database table itself could have included fields for the regional manager's name and the office phone number, as shown in Figure 8.12. But this wider database structure has some distinct disadvantages. First, the additional fields make the database table awkward to handle inside a worksheet window; you can no longer view the entire width of the table at once. In addition, these two fields considerably enlarge the job of entering data into the table. You would have to enter each of the manager's names and phone numbers repeatedly to complete the list of records.

Dividing the database into two separate tables—as you have done—is the ideal way to avoid these problems. But within the context of this structure, you now need an efficient way to combine data from both tables.

PREPARING THE RANGES FOR A TWO-TABLE QUERY

Lotus 1-2-3 imposes some special requirements on the input range, the criteria range, and the output range for queries on multiple database tables. Here is

FIGURE 8.11:
Aggregate columns for the six specialty areas

	A	B	C	D
1	Specialty	@AVG(RATE)	@MAX(RATE)	@MIN(RATE)
2	Accounting	$112.50	$125.00	$100.00
3	Database	$100.00	$150.00	$75.00
4	Networks	$150.00	$150.00	$150.00
5	Spreadsheet	$125.00	$150.00	$100.00
6	Telecomm	$112.50	$150.00	$75.00
7	WP	$143.75	$150.00	$125.00
8				

how you organize your work for a two-table query operation:

- ◆ The two database tables that make up the input range must have a field in common. The field may or may not have the same name in both databases, but the two tables must contain matching data entries in this common field. In addition, one of the databases should contain only unique entries in the field; the other database may contain duplicate entries. For example, the Region field in the office database table has four unique entries, N, S, E, and W; but the same field in the instructor database contains three or more entries for each region.

- ◆ In the top row of the criteria range, you enter a compound field name in the form *TableName.FieldName,* where *TableName* is the range name for one of the two tables, and *FieldName* is the name of the common field. Beneath this name, you enter a *join formula* in the format *+TableName1.FieldName1=TableName2.FieldName2*. This formula establishes a relationship between the common fields in the two tables. For example, here is the compound field name and the join formula you could enter into the criteria range to prepare for a query operation on the instructor and office tables:

Instructdb.Region
+INSTRUCTDB.REGION=OFFICEDB.REGION

Note that you can use any combination of uppercase or lowercase letters for these entries.

- ◆ In the top row of the output range, you enter compound field names, also in the format *TableName.FieldName*. In this case, *FieldName* identifies any field in *TableName;* for example, Instructdb.Last or Officedb.Manager.

ID	Last	First	City	Region	Specialty	Rate	Hrs	Contract	Yrs	Ok	Manager	Phone
S-125	Ashford	W.	Washington, D.C	E	Spreadsheet	$150	145	10-May-87	4.7	A	Campbell, R.	(212) 555-4678
W-145	Banks	S.	St. Louis	S	WP	$150	55	10-Jun-90	1.6	A	Harvey, J.	(214) 555-6754
D-143	Cody	L.	Los Angeles	W	Database	$75	43	20-Jun-90	1.6	B	Garcia, M.	(213) 555-9974
A-146	Daniels	A.	Atlanta	S	Accounting	$125	24	09-May-91	0.7	New	Harvey, J.	(214) 555-6754
W-119	Davis	G.	San Francisco	W	WP	$150	149	09-Jul-87	4.6	A	Garcia, M.	(213) 555-9974
T-128	Eng	R.	Albuquerque	S	Telecomm	$75	75	11-Oct-87	4.3	B	Harvey, J.	(214) 555-6754
S-127	Gill	P.	Los Angeles	W	Spreadsheet	$100	35	22-Jun-87	4.6	C	Garcia, M.	(213) 555-9974
S-149	Harris	P.	Dallas	S	Spreadsheet	$150	17	12-Feb-91	1.0	New	Harvey, J.	(214) 555-6754
W-124	Meyer	J.	New York	E	WP	$150	85	05-May-87	4.7	B	Campbell, R.	(212) 555-4678
A-103	Perez	D.	Las Vegas	W	Accounting	$100	5	11-Jul-86	5.6	C	Garcia, M.	(213) 555-9974
W-113	Porter	D.	Seattle	N	WP	$125	59	02-Aug-86	5.5	B	Logan, C.	(312) 555-8803
D-139	Porter	M.	Washington, D.C	E	Database	$150	26	28-Mar-89	2.8	B	Campbell, R.	(212) 555-4678
T-133	Ramirez	F.	Boston	E	Telecomm	$150	73	08-Feb-88	4.0	B	Campbell, R.	(212) 555-4678
S-155	Roberts	P.	Chicago	N	Spreadsheet	$100	10	21-Aug-91	0.4	New	Logan, C.	(312) 555-8803
D-137	Sanchez	W.	Indianapolis	N	Database	$100	47	16-Apr-89	2.8	B	Logan, C.	(312) 555-8803
N-101	Schwartz	B.	Boston	E	Networks	$150	178	02-Mar-86	5.9	A	Campbell, R.	(212) 555-4678
D-106	Weinberg	P.	Miami	S	Database	$75	59	18-Jan-86	6.0	B	Harvey, J.	(214) 555-6754

FIGURE 8.12:

An alternative design for the database

Once you have created input, criteria, and output ranges to meet these requirements, you are ready to choose the Data Query Extract command.

Performing the Two-Table Query Operation

In the following exercise, you'll create the criteria range and the output range for the two-table query. To simplify this procedure, you'll enter both ranges on a single worksheet:

1. Move to worksheet G and choose the Worksheet Insert command. Select the Sheet option, and click OK or press ↵. Worksheet H appears in the worksheet window. Click the perspective-view icon to gain a full-window view of worksheet H.

2. Enter the criteria range into the top three lines of worksheet H: Enter the two field names, **Ok** and **Instructdb.Region** into cells H:A1 and H:B1. Use the bold icon to display these two names in boldface. Under the Ok field, enter the criteria **New** and **C** into cells H:A2 and H:A3. In each of the cells H:B2 and H:B3, enter the join formula, **+Instructdb.Region=Officedb.Region**. Ignore the resulting ERR values; use the Range Format command to apply the Text format to the formulas in the two cells.

3. Preselect the range H:A1..H:B3 and choose the Range Name Create command. Enter the name **CRITERIA3** for this range, and click OK or press ↵.

4. In row 5 of the worksheet, enter the following compound field names into cells from H:A5 to H:E5: **Instructdb.Last**, **Instructdb.Ok**, **Officedb.Region**, **Officedb.Manager**, and **Officedb.Phone**. Increase the widths of columns A through E to 14. Apply the Bold style to these labels, and center the labels in H:B5 and H:C5.

5. Preselect the range H:A5..H:E5 and choose the Range Name Create command. Enter the name **OUTPUT4** for this range. Click OK or press ↵ to confirm.

6. Choose the Data Query command. In the Input range box, enter the names of the two database tables, separated by a comma: **INSTRUCTDB,OFFICEDB**. Enter **CRITERIA3** in the Criteria range box and **OUTPUT4** in the Output range box, as shown in Figure 8.13.

7. Click the Extract command button, then click Cancel to close the Data Query dialog box. The resulting output table is shown in Figure 8.14.

As you can see, 1-2-3 has found five instructors with Ok ratings of either New or C; the output list includes the name, rating, region, manager, and phone number for each instructor.

8. Now suppose you want to create a similar phone directory for the instructors who have Ok ratings of A or B. To do so, change the selection criteria by entering **A** into cell H:A2, and **B** into cell H:A3. Then press the F7 function key. The resulting output table appears in Figure 8.15.

9. Click the save-file icon to save your work to disk.

Of course, this kind of query operation is not limited to two database tables. You can combine data from any number of tables, as long as each table

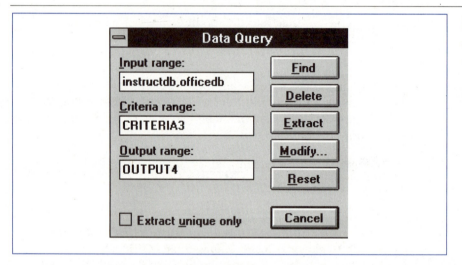

FIGURE 8.13:
A two-table query operation

FIGURE 8.14:
Extracting data from both database tables

is related to another in the group through a common field. The capacity for relational database queries is clearly one of the most powerful features of the 1-2-3 database component.

WORKING WITH EXTERNAL DATABASES

Finally, you can use the 1-2-3 database component to gain access to external databases created in programs like dBASE IV, dBASE III Plus, Paradox, or SQL Server. To work with an external database, you begin by establishing a connection between the database on disk and the current worksheet. At the time that you create this connection, you also define the equivalent of a 1-2-3 range name for the external database. This range name represents the database as long as the connection is active. Using this range name, you can perform a variety of operations on the external database file, as though the database were stored in an open worksheet file. For example, you can use the 1-2-3 database functions to perform statistical calculations on selected records of the external database; and you can perform any variety of Data Query Extract operations to copy records from the external database to an output range.

The software that makes this kind of connection possible is called a DataLens driver. Lotus 1-2-3 for Windows comes with three DataLens drivers, for dBASE, Paradox, and SQL Server. You can include one or more of these in your system at the time you install 1-2-3. The appropriate driver must be available on your hard disk if you want to use 1-2-3 to access an external

	A	B	C	D	E
1	Ok	Instructdb.Region			
2	A	+INSTRUCTDB.REGION=OFFICEDB.REGION			
3	B	+INSTRUCTDB.REGION=OFFICEDB.REGION			
4					
5	Instructdb.Last	Instructdb.Ok	Officedb.Region	Officedb.Manager	Officedb.Phone
6	Ashford	A	E	Campbell, R.	(212) 555-4678
7	Banks	A	S	Harvey, J.	(214) 555-6754
8	Cody	B	W	Garcia, M.	(213) 555-9974
9	Davis	A	W	Garcia, M.	(213) 555-9974
10	Eng	B	S	Harvey, J.	(214) 555-6754
11	Meyer	B	E	Campbell, R.	(212) 555-4678
12	Porter	B	N	Logan, C.	(312) 555-8803
13	Porter	B	E	Campbell, R.	(212) 555-4678
14	Ramirez	B	E	Campbell, R.	(212) 555-4678
15	Sanchez	B	N	Logan, C.	(312) 555-8803
16	Schwartz	A	E	Campbell, R.	(212) 555-4678
17	Weinberg	B	S	Harvey, J.	(214) 555-6754
18					

FIGURE 8.15:
Repeating the two-table query operation with new criteria

database. For complete information about the three DataLens drivers, read the document called *DataLens Drivers for 1-2-3*, included in your 1-2-3 package.

In the final sections of this chapter, you'll look at a few examples of external database queries. For these exercises, imagine that the original instructor database from Computing Conferences, Inc. is a dBASE III Plus database file, stored on disk as INSTRUCT.DBF in a directory named C:\DBASE. Figure 8.16 shows the complete database listing, printed from the dBASE program. In the

FIGURE 8.16:

A dBASE database

ID	LAST	FIRST	CITY	REGION	SPECIALTY	RATE	HRS	CONTRACT
D-140	Abrams	P.	Atlanta	S	Database	125	29	10/20/90
W-154	Alexander	E.	Los Angeles	W	WP	150	10	06/14/91
S-125	Ashford	W.	Washington, D.C	E	Spreadsheet	150	145	05/10/87
S-126	Ballinger	I.	Boston	E	Spreadsheet	150	40	02/12/87
W-145	Banks	S.	St. Louis	S	WP	150	55	06/10/90
W-130	Burke	C.	Miami	S	WP	100	41	05/22/88
D-141	Cheung	F.	Las Vegas	W	Database	125	61	05/15/90
D-143	Cody	L.	Los Angeles	W	Database	75	43	06/20/90
A-146	Daniels	A.	Atlanta	S	Accounting	125	24	05/09/91
W-119	Davis	G.	San Francisco	W	WP	150	139	07/09/87
N-115	Dixon	G.	Las Vegas	W	Networks	150	59	05/09/86
S-120	Edmonds	R.	Indianapolis	N	Spreadsheet	75	35	09/27/87
T-128	Eng	R.	Albuquerque	S	Telecomm	75	75	10/11/87
D-105	Fitzpatrick	P.	New York	E	Database	125	164	11/07/86
S-131	Garcia	A.	Seattle	N	Spreadsheet	100	17	07/02/88
W-114	Garrison	V.	Boston	E	WP	125	207	05/06/86
S-127	Gill	P.	Los Angeles	W	Spreadsheet	100	25	06/22/87
S-156	Hale	S.	San Francisco	W	Spreadsheet	75	28	06/09/91
S-149	Harris	P.	Dallas	S	Spreadsheet	150	17	02/12/91
D-109	Hayes	S.	San Francisco	W	Database	75	95	02/07/86
T-138	Hermann	J.	Los Angeles	W	Telecomm	125	74	05/24/89
S-132	Jones	L.	Atlanta	S	Spreadsheet	125	5	02/10/88
W-116	Jordan	E.	Dallas	S	WP	100	17	10/06/86
W-117	Kim	E.	Washington, D.C	E	WP	100	137	10/11/86
N-144	King	T.	New York	E	Networks	75	13	01/06/90
D-136	Koenig	O.	Albuquerque	S	Database	125	20	06/02/89
S-111	Kwan	O.	New York	E	Spreadsheet	100	71	06/21/86
D-123	Lambert	S.	Dallas	S	Database	150	145	06/26/87
D-134	Lee	H.	Seattle	N	Database	150	21	12/17/88
W-150	Leung	M.	Chicago	N	WP	100	16	03/26/91
W-112	Manning	P.	Atlanta	S	WP	75	71	11/09/86
W-107	Martinez	G.	Las Vegas	W	WP	150	178	03/15/86
N-129	McKay	J.	Washington, D.C	E	Networks	150	35	05/09/87
W-124	Meyer	J.	New York	E	WP	150	85	05/05/87
A-135	Meyer	L.	New York	E	Accounting	100	57	08/17/88
T-148	Miranda	O.	Las Vegas	W	Telecomm	75	9	01/04/91
S-153	Nichols	B.	Albuquerque	S	Spreadsheet	150	19	02/28/91
N-118	O'Neil	P.	Atlanta	S	Networks	75	5	05/01/87
A-103	Perez	D.	Las Vegas	W	Accounting	100	5	07/11/86
W-113	Porter	D.	Seattle	N	WP	125	59	08/02/86
D-139	Porter	M.	Washington, D.C	E	Database	150	26	03/28/89
T-133	Ramirez	F.	Boston	E	Telecomm	150	73	02/08/88
S-155	Roberts	P.	Chicago	N	Spreadsheet	100	10	08/21/91
D-137	Sanchez	W.	Indianapolis	N	Database	100	47	04/16/89
N-101	Schwartz	B.	Boston	E	Networks	150	178	03/02/86
W-151	Schwartz	P.	Indianapolis	N	WP	150	23	05/10/91
D-104	Taylor	F.	Boston	E	Database	100	17	10/24/86
D-142	Thomas	T.	St. Louis	S	Database	150	35	12/23/90
S-108	Tong	C.	St. Louis	S	Spreadsheet	150	35	11/12/86
N-152	Tong	P.	San Francisco	W	Networks	150	23	05/13/91
N-110	Tong	W.	Los Angeles	W	Networks	150	83	05/09/86
S-122	Vasquez	T.	Las Vegas	W	Spreadsheet	75	5	04/27/87
T-102	Vaughn	A.	Washington, D.C	E	Telecomm	75	53	09/11/86
T-147	Webb	F.	New York	E	Telecomm	125	32	01/27/91
D-106	Weinberg	P.	Miami	S	Database	75	59	01/18/86
D-121	Williams	C.	Chicago	N	Database	150	30	10/02/87

upcoming sections, you'll learn how to connect a file like this one to a 1-2-3 worksheet, and how to perform a variety of queries on the database.

USING THE DATA CONNECT TO EXTERNAL COMMAND

The starting point for your work with an external database is the Connect to External command in the Data menu. When you choose this command, the Data Connect to External dialog box appears on the screen, as shown in Figure 8.17. This box contains a list of the DataLens drivers that you have installed in your system. To establish a connection with an external database, you have to supply four items of information:

◆ The name of the appropriate DataLens driver

◆ The directory location of the database file. In the context of the Data Connect to External command, this directory is known as the database.

◆ The database file name. This file is known as the external table.

◆ The 1-2-3 range name that you will use to represent the external database table

As an illustration of the Data Connect to External command, the following steps show you how to establish a connection to the dBASE file C:\DBASE\INSTRUCT.DBF. You can use these same steps on an external

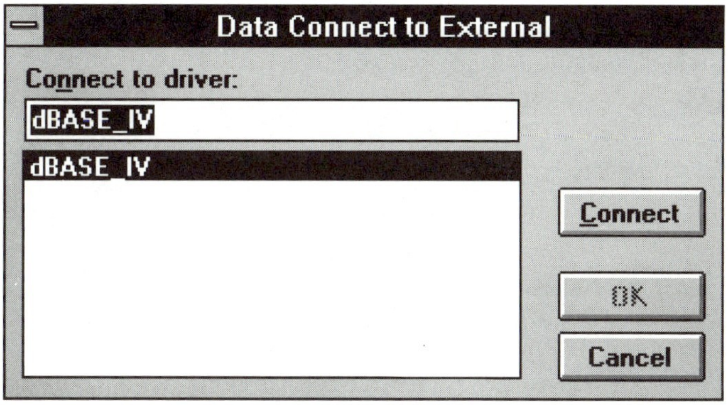

FIGURE 8.17:
The Data Connect to External dialog box

database file of your own by substituting the appropriate driver, directory, file, and range name:

1. Open the 1-2-3 worksheet file to which you want to connect the database. (Even if the worksheet file was formerly connected to an external database, you must reestablish the connection every time you reopen the file.)

2. Choose the Data Connect to External command. Type the driver, directory, and file names into the Connect to driver text box, as follows:

   dBASE_IV C:\DBASE INSTRUCT

   (The driver named dBASE_IV also handles database files originating from dBASE III Plus.)

3. Press ↵. The dialog box next displays the prompt *Enter range name for table:*, as shown in Figure 8.18. The text box beneath this prompt contains the external file name INSTRUCT as the default range name. Press ↵ again to accept this default as the range name.

4. The *Connect to table:* prompt appears, along with the name of the external database, as shown in Figure 8.19. Click the OK key to complete the connection.

After these steps are complete, the range name INSTRUCT represents the external dBASE file in a variety of 1-2-3 database operations. For example, this name can appear as the first argument in a database function, as you'll learn in the next section of this chapter.

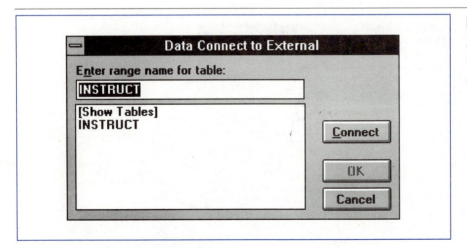

FIGURE 8.18:

Selecting a range name to represent the external database

USING DATABASE FUNCTIONS WITH AN EXTERNAL DATABASE

To use database functions on an external table, you begin by preparing a criteria range to select records from the connected database. In the first row of the criteria range, you enter one or more field names from the external database. For example, in Figure 8.20, the worksheet range A3..A4 expresses a single criterion for selecting data from the INSTRUCT database. This criterion, named EXTCRIT1, selects instructor records from the Southern region.

Column C in the same worksheet contains a set of database functions that compute statistics from the external database. Figure 8.21 displays the functions in the text format. As you can see, each function uses the external database name INSTRUCT as the input range, the field name Hrs as the target field, and EXTCRIT1 as the criteria range. For example, the following function computes the total work hours recorded in the external database for the selected region:

@DSUM(INSTRUCT,"Hrs",EXTCRIT1)

If you revise the criterion for selecting data, 1-2-3 reads a new selection of records from the external file, and recalculates the database functions accordingly. For example, in Figure 8.22 a new criterion, N, appears in cell A4 of the criteria range. The new results in column C are the statistics for the Northern region. As you might expect, 1-2-3 takes a little more

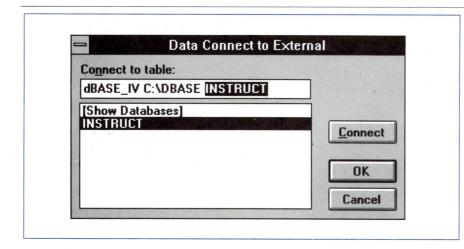

FIGURE 8.19:
Completing the connection to the external database

time to recalculate these functions for an external table than it would for a database in an open worksheet.

If you close this worksheet, 1-2-3 disconnects the external database. When you later reopen the worksheet, the database functions return values of ERR, because the range name INSTRUCT is no longer defined. To reestablish the connection with the external database, choose the Data Connect to External command again. When you complete the connection, 1-2-3 correctly recalculates the database functions.

Performing Queries on an External Database

To extract records from an external database, you use the Data Query command. Once again, you begin the procedure by establishing the connection with the external database. Except for this initial task, the general steps for performing a query on an external database are the same as for a 1-2-3 database:

1. Choose the Data Connect to External command. Establish the connection with the external database, and define a range name to represent the database.

2. Prepare a criteria range to select records from the database. The range must contain field names from the external database.

	A	B	C	D	E
1	Connection to External Database:			INSTRUCT.DBF	
2				(dBASE III Plus)	
3	Region				
4	S				
5					
6	Statistical Database Functions:				
7					
8	Number of instructors		16		
9	Average instructor hours		40.75		
10	Total instructor hours		652		
11	Lowest instructor hours		5		
12	Highest instructor hours		145		
13	Standard deviation		34.06		
14					
15					

FIGURE 8.20:
Setting up a criteria range for the external database

3. Prepare an output range to which 1-2-3 can copy records from the external database. Again, the field names are from the external database.

4. Choose the Data Query command. In the Input range box, enter the range name that represents the external database. Enter the names for the criteria and output ranges.

5. Click the Extract command button.

Figure 8.23 displays a worksheet in which a criteria range and output range have been prepared for the external database INSTRUCT.DBF. The criteria range, A3..C4, is named EXTCRIT2. As you can see, it contains expressions for selecting Southern-region word processing instructors who signed contracts before January 1, 1990. The output range is defined by the three field names in row 6. The range A6..C6 is named EXTOUTPUT. In Figure 8.24, these three range names, INSTRUCT, EXTCRIT2, and EXTOUTPUT, appear in the Data Query dialog box. In response to a click of the Extract command button, 1-2-3 finds the matching records in the external database and copies the appropriate fields to the output range, as shown in Figure 8.23.

You can use the F7 function key to repeat the previous query operation on an external database. For example, Figure 8.25 shows a revision in the criteria for the external database; now the selection is for *Northern*-region word processing instructors who signed contracts before January 1, 1990. After you make a change like this one, you press F7 to perform the extract operation again. In response, 1-2-3 reads matching records from the external database

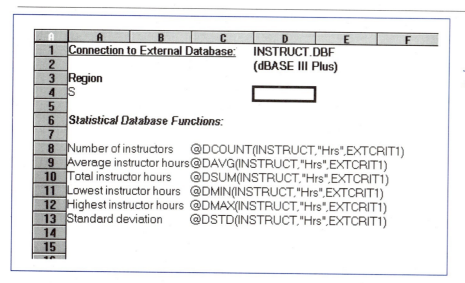

FIGURE 8.21:

Using database functions with the external database

and displays them in the output range. In this case, only one record matches the criteria, as you can see in Figure 8.25.

Performing Other External Database Operations

Most of the database operations that you've learned to perform on 1-2-3 databases are also available for external databases. For example, you can use Data Query Delete to remove matching records from an external database, and Data Query Modify to revise or insert records. Only the Data Query Find command is unavailable for external databases; this command requires a 1-2-3 database in an open worksheet.

The Data External Options command displays a cascade menu of additional commands that apply to external databases. As shown in Figure 8.26, this cascade menu contains four commands. Here are brief summaries of these four commands:

◆ The Data External Options Paste Fields command produces a table describing the structure of an external database. When you choose this command, a dialog box displays a list of all external databases that are currently connected, as shown in Figure 8.27. To produce a

	A	B	C	D
1	Connection to External Database:			INSTRUCT.DBF
2				(dBASE III Plus)
3	Region			
4	N			
5				
6	Statistical Database Functions:			
7				
8	Number of instructors		9	
9	Average instructor hours		28.67	
10	Total instructor hours		258	
11	Lowest instructor hours		10	
12	Highest instructor hours		59	
13	Standard deviation		15.03	
14				
15				

FIGURE 8.22:
Revising the selection criterion for the external database

structure table, you select a target database, and you supply a worksheet range in which 1-2-3 can create the table. The resulting table has six columns and one row for each field in the external database, plus one blank row. (Be careful to specify an empty worksheet range for this table; 1-2-3 overwrites any existing data in the worksheet.) For example, Figure 8.28 shows the structure table that 1-2-3 creates for the dBASE database INSTRUCT.DBF. The first column displays the field names, and the second and third columns

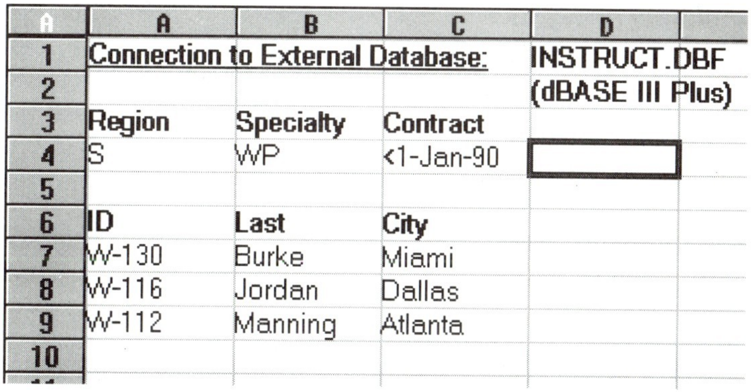

	A	B	C	D
1	Connection to External Database:			INSTRUCT.DBF
2				(dBASE III Plus)
3	Region	Specialty	Contract	
4	S	WP	<1-Jan-90	
5				
6	ID	Last	City	
7	W-130	Burke	Miami	
8	W-116	Jordan	Dallas	
9	W-112	Manning	Atlanta	
10				

FIGURE 8.23:
Performing a query on an external database

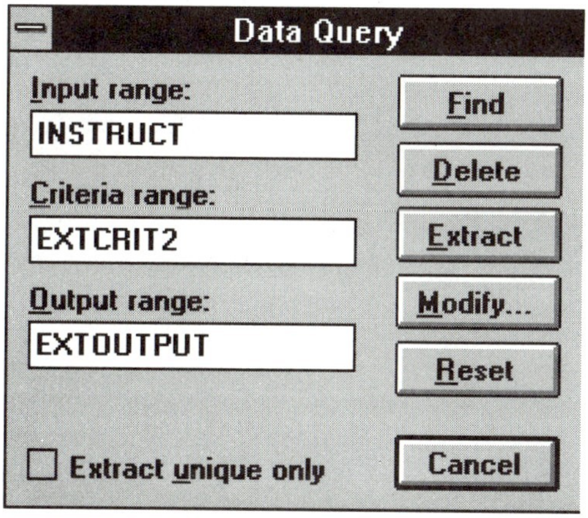

Data Query

Input range: INSTRUCT
Criteria range: EXTCRIT2
Output range: EXTOUTPUT

☐ Extract unique only

[Find] [Delete] [Extract] [Modify...] [Reset] [Cancel]

FIGURE 8.24:
Entering the external database range name in the Input range box

give the data type and width of each field. The fourth, fifth, and sixth columns are unused in this dBASE example, but still take up space in the worksheet range specified for the table.

- ◆ Data External Options Send Command is a tool for sending program-specific commands to the external database. The commands available for this option depend upon the DataLens driver you are using. See *DataLens Drivers for 1-2-3* for complete information.

- ◆ The Data External Options Create Table command creates a new external database table in the file format used by a particular database management program, such as dBASE, Paradox, or SQL Server. You can use this command to create an external database from an existing 1-2-3 database table. Figure 8.29 shows the Data External Options

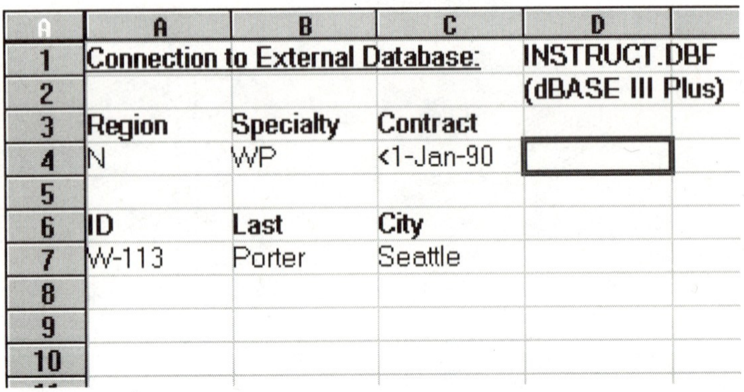

FIGURE 8.25:

Repeating the query on the external database

	A	B	C	D
1	Connection to External Database:			INSTRUCT.DBF
2				(dBASE III Plus)
3	Region	Specialty	Contract	
4	N	WP	<1-Jan-90	
5				
6	ID	Last	City	
7	W-113	Porter	Seattle	
8				
9				
10				

FIGURE 8.26:

The Data External Options cascade menu

```
Paste Fields...
Send Command...
Create Table...
Disconnect...
```

Create Table dialog box. You use the Connect to driver box to establish the connection with the database. In the Model range box, you supply the range name of the 1-2-3 database you want to use as the "model" for the new external database. In the Output range box, you supply an empty worksheet range where 1-2-3 can create a table to define the structure of the new database. (This table is like the one produced by the Paste Fields command for an existing external

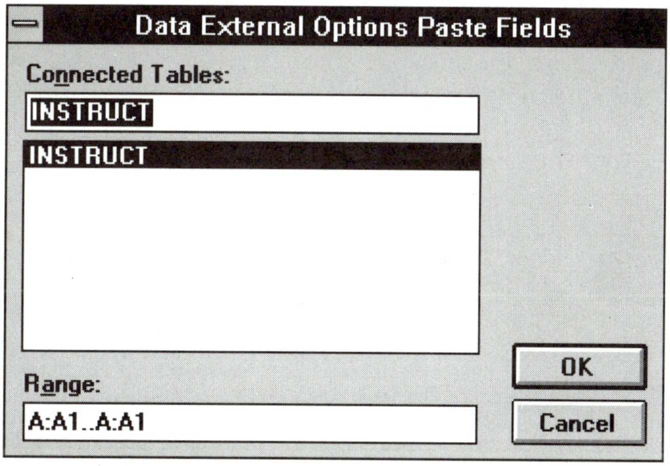

FIGURE 8.27:

The Data External Options Paste Fields dialog box

FIGURE 8.28:

A table describing the structure of an external database

	A	B	C	D	E	F
1	ID	Character	5	NA	NA	NA
2	LAST	Character	11	NA	NA	NA
3	FIRST	Character	2	NA	NA	NA
4	CITY	Character	15	NA	NA	NA
5	REGION	Character	1	NA	NA	NA
6	SPECIALTY	Character	11	NA	NA	NA
7	RATE	Numeric	3,0	NA	NA	NA
8	HRS	Numeric	3,0	NA	NA	NA
9	CONTRACT	Date	8	NA	NA	NA
10						
11						

database.) After you create a new external database, you use the Data Query Modify Insert command to copy records from your 1-2-3 database table (the output range) to the new external table (the input range).

◆ The Data External Options Disconnect command closes the connection between 1-2-3 and an external database. The resulting dialog box displays a list of all current database connections, as shown in Figure 8.30. To disconnect, you select a name from this list.

Finally, with the SQL Server DataLens you can use the @DQUERY function to call functions available in SQL Server. @DQUERY takes a string argument representing the name of the external function, followed by any arguments required by the external function itself:

@DQUERY("*FunctionName*",*ArgumentList*)

SUMMARY

To calculate statistics from a database, you can use database functions such as @DSUM, @DAVG, @DCOUNT, @DMIN, and @DMAX. These functions

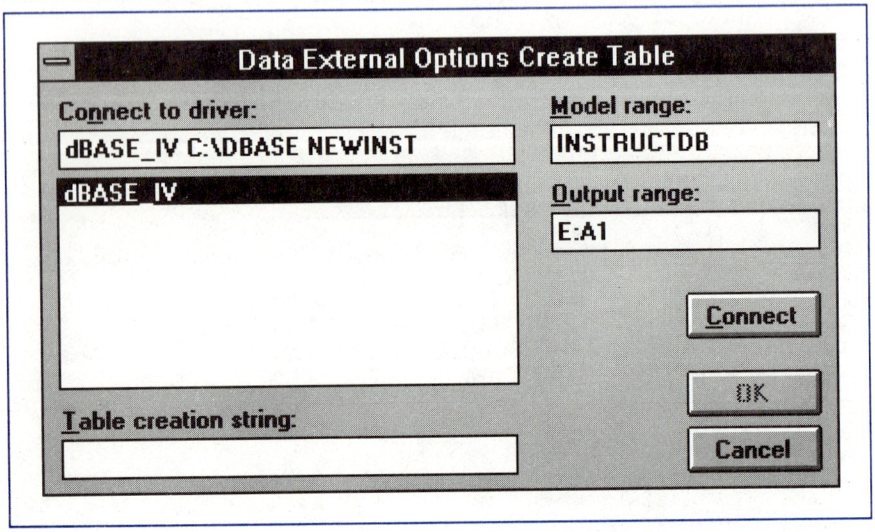

FIGURE 8.29:
The Data External Options Create Table dialog box

calculate totals, averages, or other statistical values from numeric field entries in selected database records. Each of the statistical database functions takes three arguments: an input range, a field name or offset number, and a criteria range.

Two other kinds of database calculations, known as computed and aggregate columns, result from the Data Query Extract operation. To produce a computed column, you enter a formula in the first row of the output range. The formula typically expresses an arithmetic operation on one or more fields in the database. An aggregate column uses a worksheet function such as @SUM or @AVG to calculate a statistical value for a selected category of records.

In a query operation involving two or more database tables, the tables are related by common fields of data. To prepare for this kind of query, you enter a join formula in the criteria range, and a series of compound field names in the first row of the output range. The result of the query is a combination of data from the multiple tables.

An external database is a file that originates from a database management program such as dBASE IV, dBASE III Plus, or Paradox. To establish a connection between an external database and a 1-2-3 worksheet, you use the Data Connect to External command. As long as the connection is active, you can apply 1-2-3 database functions to the external database, and you can use the Data Query commands to read or modify the database.

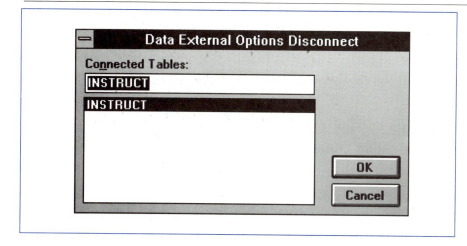

FIGURE 8.30:
The Data External Options Disconnect dialog box

FAST TRACK

CHAPTER 9

To create a macro that you can run directly from the keyboard, ... 430

assign the macro's first cell a special range name, consisting of the backslash plus a single letter from A to Z. You can then press Ctrl-*letter* from the keyboard to run the macro. For example, to run a macro named \M, press Ctrl-M.

To represent a nonprinting keystroke in a macro, ... 431

use a macro key name, enclosed in braces. For example, {Home}, {Alt}, and {Down}, are common macro key names. Use the tilde character, ~, to represent ↵.

To represent a function key from F1 to F10 in a macro, ... 432

use one of the following macro key names: {Help}, {Edit}, {Name}, {Anchor}, {Abs}, {Goto}, {Window}, {Query}, {Table}, {Calc}, and {MenuBar}.

To run a macro that has an ordinary range name, ... 436

choose the Tools Macro Run command, or press Alt-F3. Double-click the name of the appropriate macro library, then select the name of the macro you want to run.

To call one macro as a subroutine from within another macro, ... 438

enter the macro's range name within braces.

To write a macro instruction that chooses a menu command, ... 440

use the macro key name {Alt} followed by the letters that represent the menu and command names. For example, {Alt}RNL~ chooses the Range Name Label Create command; the final tilde is equivalent to clicking OK in the resulting dialog box.

To write a macro instruction that selects an option from a dialog box, ... 443

include the option's letter in the {Alt} instruction. For example, {Alt}KI{Alt "S"}~ chooses Worksheet Insert and selects the Sheet option in the resulting dialog box.

To create a keystroke macro from the steps of an activity you have just completed, ... 445

choose the Tools Macro Show Transcript command to view the Transcript window. Then use a copy-and-paste operation to copy some or all of the window's contents to your macro library worksheet.

To attach a macro to an icon in 1-2-3's icon palette, ... 449

start the Windows Paintbrush program and create your own icon from the pattern file named SAMPLE.BMP; save the new icon file in the directory \123W\SHEETICO. Back in 1-2-3, select the worksheet range containing the macro you want to attach to the new icon, and then choose the Tools SmartIcons Customize command. Select your new icon in the Custom icons box, and click the Assign macro button. In the resulting dialog box, click the Get macro button. The text of your pre-selected macro appears in the Macro box; click OK to assign the macro to the icon. Select the final position in the Current palette box and click the Add button to add your new icon to the icon palette.

To create an autoexecute macro, ... 459

assign the macro the special name \0 (backslash, zero).

CHAPTER 9

Introduction to Macros

acros are tools you create to streamline your activities in 1-2-3, and to customize your working environment. You can design macros to perform any variety of tasks, from simple keystroke repetitions to sophisticated programming procedures. Your use of macros is a matter of individual choice and preference. While some users employ macros as an integral part of their daily operations, others work effectively in 1-2-3 without macros. The best way to begin formulating the role of macros in your own work is to experiment with a variety of macro tools, and to choose the ones that seem useful to you.

At the simplest level, a macro is a record of a particular sequence of commonly used keystrokes. When you *run* the macro, 1-2-3 repeats the keystrokes as though you had typed them directly from the keyboard. The keystrokes can include individual data entries along with instructions for choosing menu commands. For example, you might write one macro to enter your company's name and address into consecutive cells of a worksheet column, and another macro to choose formatting options from the Range or Style menus. Or, you might write a single macro to enter and format the data in one step.

To choose commands and perform worksheet operations from within a macro, you use 1-2-3's special *macro key names*. As you'll learn in this chapter, these names represent the keys and the key combinations that you press at the keyboard to carry out particular actions.

You can also create macros that accomplish more complex jobs. Along with macro key names, 1-2-3 supplies a complete set of *macro commands* that represent specific programming tasks. For example, you can design macro programs that make decisions, perform repetitive actions, read or write worksheet data, or elicit data from the user at the keyboard. In effect, the macro commands provide a complete programming language that operates within the 1-2-3 environment.

In this chapter, you'll create and run a dozen or so small macros. Along the way, you'll become familiar with many of 1-2-3's macro tools, including the macro key names and some examples of macro commands. If you want to learn more, Chapter 12 of this book is an introduction to the concepts and techniques of macro programming.

CREATING KEYSTROKE MACROS

Macros are created and saved in 1-2-3 worksheet files. A worksheet can contain any number of macros; all are available for you to use when you open the worksheet that contains them. Conveniently, you can store a collection of your favorite general-purpose macros in a single worksheet. Opening this one worksheet then gives you access to the entire collection.

A worksheet that contains a collection of macros is sometimes known as a *macro library*. Because 1-2-3 allows you to open multiple worksheet files concurrently, your macro library can be open at the same time that you are working on one or more other open worksheets. In general, a keystroke macro is designed to accomplish its task on the worksheet that is current at the time you run the macro.

You enter the instructions of a macro into consecutive cells of a worksheet column. There are two basic steps necessary for creating a macro:

1. Enter macro instructions into a column of cells.

2. Assign a range name to the first cell of the macro.

The range name is the key to running a macro. For convenience, 1-2-3 allows you to create a special kind of macro name consisting of two characters: a backslash followed by a letter from A to Z. For example, \C, \N, and \H are all macro names. When you assign a name like this to a macro, you can then run the macro by pressing the Ctrl key along with the designated letter key. For example, you press Ctrl-C to run the macro that has the range name \C.

In the following brief exercise, you'll create your first macro and assign it a name; then you'll try running it. This first macro performs the simple job of entering a company's name into a selected cell on a worksheet:

1. Select cell B2 on a new blank worksheet. Enter the following label into the cell:

   Computing Conferences, Inc.~

   The last character of this entry is called a *tilde*. In a macro, a tilde represents ↵, the Enter key.

2. With the cell pointer still at B2, choose the Range Name Create command. Enter **\C** as the two-character range name. Click OK to confirm.

3. Choose the File Save As command and save the worksheet file as COMPANY.WK3. Now pull down the worksheet window's control menu and choose the Minimize command or simply click the window's minimize button to reduce the worksheet to an icon. (Macros in a minimized worksheet are still available for use.)

4. Choose the File New command to open a second new worksheet.

5. With the cell pointer positioned at cell A1 of the new worksheet, hold down the Ctrl key and type **C**. In response, the macro you've created enters the company name as a label in the current cell.

6. Now select a new cell, say D8, and press Ctrl-C again. As you can see in Figure 9.1, the macro repeats its task: It enters the company name as a label in the selected cell.

In this first exercise, you have created a simple example of a keystroke macro. Except for the final tilde character, the entire example consists of characters that are entered into the current cell when you run the macro. The tilde character represents the action of completing the entry, the equivalent of pressing ↵ when you finish typing a label onto the edit line.

USING MACRO KEY NAMES

Other keys and commands in a macro are represented by names enclosed within *braces,* { and }. The macro key names are generally easy to recognize and remember, because many of them match the names that appear directly on your keyboard. For example, the macro key names {Home}, {End}, {PgUp}, {PgDn}, {Ins}, and {Del} correspond to the keys located on the number pad at the side of your keyboard. Other readily identifiable macro key names include {Backspace}, {Esc}, and {Tab}. In addition, four of the most commonly used macro key names represent the arrow keys on your keyboard: {Up}, {Down}, {Right}, and {Left}.

Some variations are allowed in the representation of keys in a 1-2-3 macro. For instance, you can enter the macro key names in any combination of uppercase or lowercase letters: {Down}, {DOWN}, and {down} all represent the ↓ key. In addition, some of the keys have abbreviated or alternate forms—for example, {Ins} and {Insert}; {Del} and {Delete}; {BS} and {Backspace}; and {U}, {D}, {R}, and {L} for the four arrow keys.

The ten function keys, F1 to F10, are represented by the tasks they perform in 1-2-3:

- {Help} represents F1, the command to open the 1-2-3 help system.

- {Edit} represents F2, the command to edit the contents of the current cell.

- {Name} represents F3, the command to request a list of range names, function names, graph names, and so on.

- {Anchor} represents F4 in the READY mode; this is the command for preselecting a range on the worksheet. In contrast, {Abs} represents F4 in the EDIT, POINT, and VALUE modes; in these modes, F4 is the command for creating an absolute, relative, or mixed reference.

- {Goto} represents F5, the command for moving the cell pointer to a selected location.

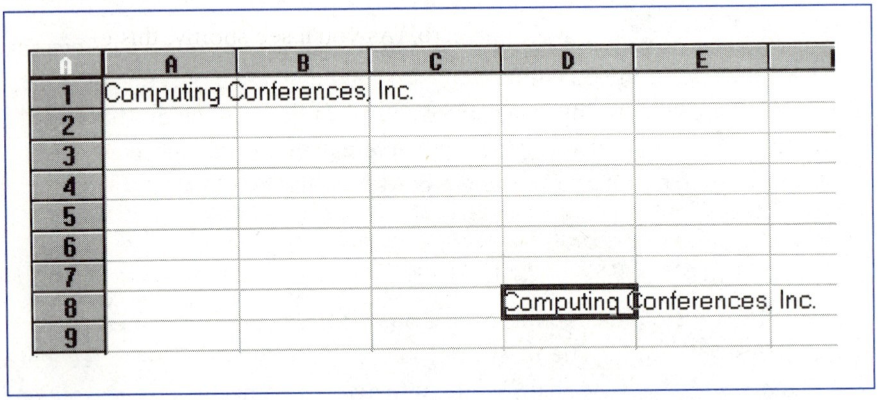

FIGURE 9.1:
Running your first macro

- {Window} represents F6, the command for moving the cell pointer between panes and worksheets.

- {Query} represents F7, the command to repeat the previous Data Query command.

- {Table} represents F8, a command for repeating an operation from the Data What-if Table command. (You'll learn about this command in Chapter 10.)

- {Calc} represents F9, the command to recalculate the current worksheet.

- {MenuBar} or {MB} represents F10, the key that activates the 1-2-3 menu bar.

As you know, pressing the Alt key is equivalent to pressing F10. The macro key name {Alt} is used more commonly than {MenuBar} to represent this action.

Other macro key names represent key combinations. For example, the Ctrl-→ and Ctrl-← combinations are represented by the names {BigRight} and {BigLeft}, respectively. (You'll find a complete list of all the macro key names on the back endpapers of this book.)

With some of the key names, 1-2-3 allows you to include an integer to represent repetitions of the keystroke. For example, the instruction {Down 3} is equivalent to {Down}{Down}{Down}. You'll see an example of this in an upcoming exercise.

Entering Macros into a Worksheet

Because macros can become complex and difficult to read, it's a good idea to make room for brief comments and explanations on macro worksheets. One common way of organizing macros is in the following three-column format:

- In the first column, enter the name of each macro in the cell just to the left of the first line of the macro. (As you'll see shortly, this entry allows you to use the Range Name Label Create command to assign names to your macros.)

- In the second column, enter the macro instructions themselves. Each entry in a macro is a label, consisting of keystrokes, macro key names, and macro commands. While a macro is running, 1-2-3 reads down the column from one instruction to the next. A blank cell, or a cell with a numeric value rather than a label, marks the end of a macro. For this reason, you should be careful not to include blank cells or cells with value entries inside the range of a given macro.

- In the third column, enter brief comments that explain the lines and instructions of the macro. Lotus 1-2-3 does not read these comments as part of your macro; rather, the third column is for your own benefit or the benefit of any other person who is trying to understand what your macro does. In short macros, you can write a single comment to describe the macro; in longer and more complex macros, you may want to write individual comments for each row of instructions.

In addition, each macro presented in this chapter begins with a title, displayed in boldface type and located just above the first line of macro instructions. This title is inside the macro column, but is not part of the macro. The first named cell of the macro is the line immediately beneath the title.

Figure 9.2 illustrates this three-column macro format in the COMPANY.WK3 worksheet. The first macro, Company Name, now displays the following new elements: a title in cell B1; a range name in cell A2; and a brief explanation in cell C2. A second macro, entitled **Address of Northern Office**, is located beneath the first one. Notice that a blank cell separates the two macros. This second macro performs another simple data-entry task: It displays a two-line address in consecutive cells of a worksheet column.

Maximize your own copy of the COMPANY.WK3 worksheet now, so you can complete the first macro and enter the second one. Here are some tips to guide you as you enter the macros into the worksheet:

- Begin by adjusting the widths of the three columns appropriately. In Figure 9.2, the width settings are as follows: A, 3; B, 23; and C, 19.

- When you enter the macro range names into column A, begin each entry with a double-quotation mark, to right-justify the label in its cell. (Otherwise, 1-2-3 reads the backslash character as a label prefix, resulting in a repeating character.) Make sure you enter these names in their correct cells, just to the left of the first line of instructions in each macro—*not* next to the boldfaced title.

A	B	C
1	**Company Name**	
2	\C Computing Conferences, Inc.~	Enter the company name.
3		
4	**Address of Northern Office**	Enter the address
5	\N Mills Tower, Suite 992{Down}	of the northern
6	Chicago, IL 60605~	regional office.
7		

FIGURE 9.2:
Macros in the three-column format

- Don't enter any extraneous spaces or other characters in the macro instructions. For example, notice that there is no space between the end of the address and the {Down} instruction in cell B5. When you run a macro, 1-2-3 assumes that every letter, character, and space in the macro is significant.

- In column C, initially enter the comment for each macro as a long label in a single cell. Then use the Justify command in the Range menu to break the long label into smaller portions displayed down the column. For example, type the entire comment for the second macro into cell C4 as follows:

    Enter the address of the northern regional office.

    Then, while C4 is still the current cell, pull down the Range menu and choose the Justify command. Click OK on the resulting dialog box. In response, 1-2-3 rearranges the command down column C, as shown in Figure 9.2.

When you finish entering the macros, your next task is to apply the range names displayed in column A to the adjacent cells in column B. (Actually, you have already named the first macro, but for the purpose of the upcoming exercise you'll proceed as though you hadn't done so yet.) Here are the steps:

1. Preselect the range A2..A5.

2. Choose the Range Name Label Create command. In the resulting dialog box, Right is the default selection; click the OK button to accept this selection.

3. Click the save-file icon to update COMPANY.WK3 on disk.

As a result of the Range Name Label Create command, the name \C is assigned (or reassigned in this case) to the first cell of the Company Name macro, and \N is assigned to the first cell of the Address of Northern Office macro.

Now you can try running the macros. Activate the other open worksheet, on which you have already been experimenting with the first macro. Select cell A3 and press Ctrl-C to make sure the first macro still works properly. Then select cell A4 and press Ctrl-N to run the second macro. Press Home and examine the result, shown in Figure 9.3. Notice that the second macro enters two labels into consecutive cells of the column. The {Down} instruction performs two tasks in the first line of this macro: First, it completes the entry of the street address; and second, it moves the cell pointer down by one row for the city, state, and zip code entry. (You use the ↓ key for this same purpose when you are entering a sequence of data values into a column.)

USING THE TOOLS MACRO RUN COMMAND

You can choose the Tools Macro Run command to view a list of the macros currently available in all open worksheets and to select a macro to run. For a macro that has a name consisting of a backslash character and a letter, the use of the Tools Macro Run command is normally unnecessary; it's easier to press the Ctrl-*letter* keyboard sequence to run the macro. But 1-2-3 also allows you to assign any ordinary range name to a macro. If the name is not a backslash with a letter, you must use the Tools Macro Run command to run the macro.

With the worksheet on which you have been testing the macros still current, try the following exercise with the Tools Macro Run command:

1. Pull down the Tools menu and choose the Macro command. A cascade menu appears on the screen. Choose the Run command. The Tools Macro Run dialog box appears on the screen, as in Figure 9.4. The list box displays the name of the worksheet file that is currently serving as your macro library: <<COMPANY.WK3>>. The double angle brackets, << and >>, are 1-2-3's notation for a file reference when more than one file is open in the spreadsheet environment.

2. Double-click the file name in the list box. When you do so, 1-2-3 displays a list of all the macros stored in this file, as you can see in Figure 9.5. You can now run any macro in the list by selecting the macro's name.

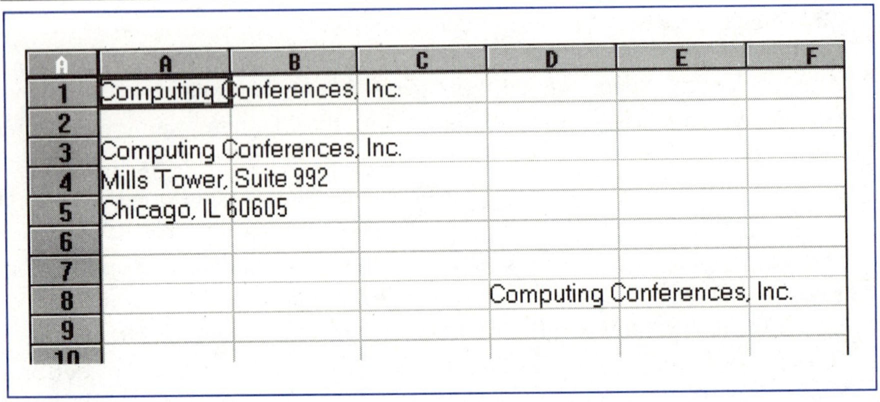

FIGURE 9.3:

Trying the second macro

A	A	B	C	D	E	F
1	Computing Conferences, Inc.					
2						
3	Computing Conferences, Inc.					
4	Mills Tower, Suite 992					
5	Chicago, IL 60605					
6						
7						
8				Computing Conferences, Inc.		
9						
10						

3. Select the \N macro and click OK. Back on the worksheet, the macro once again enters the two lines of the address. After you have examined the results, close this worksheet without saving it; the macro library worksheet, COMPANY.WK3, remains open.

So now you have seen two ways to run a macro: If the macro has a name consisting of a backslash and a letter, press the designated Ctrl-*letter* key combination. Alternatively, choose the Tools Macro Run command to run any macro, regardless of its range name. By the way, the keyboard shortcut for the Tools Macro Run command is Alt-F3.

Interestingly enough, you can also run one macro from within another macro. In programming terms, this is known as *calling* a macro as a *subroutine*.

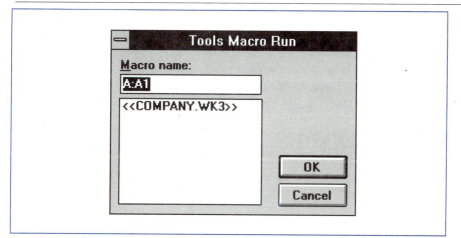

FIGURE 9.4:
The Tools Macro Run dialog box

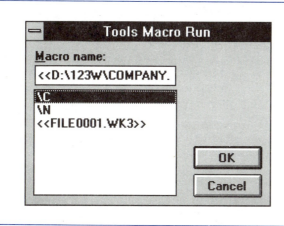

FIGURE 9.5:
The list of macros in the selected macro library

USING MACROS AS SUBROUTINES

When one macro calls another, 1-2-3 performs all the instructions of the called macro and then returns control to the original macro. To write a call instruction, you simply enclose the range name of the macro within braces. For example, the instruction {\C} calls the macro named \C.

A call instruction works successfully regardless of the format of the macro name. For instance, suppose you assign the range name SCHEDULE to a macro you have written; the instruction {Schedule} represents a call to this macro. (Alphabetic case is not significant in a call instruction.) Organizing a macro into small subroutines is an effective way to avoid entering duplicate instructions for the same task in a long macro.

Figure 9.6 displays a third macro in the COMPANY.WK3 worksheet. This new macro contains three lines of instructions. The first line calls the macro named \C, and then moves the cell pointer down by one row:

{\C}{Down}

The second line enters a label into the current cell and then moves the cell pointer down again:

Northern Region{Down}

	A	B	C
1		Company Name	
2	\C	Computing Conferences, Inc.~	Enter the company name.
3			
4		Address of Northern Office	Enter the address
5	\N	Mills Tower, Suite 992{Down}	of the northern
6		Chicago, IL 60605~	regional office.
7			
8		Heading for Northern Office	Enter a complete
9	\H	{\C}{Down}	heading for the
10		Northern Region{Down}	northern region.
11		{\N}{Down 3}	
12			

FIGURE 9.6:
Calling macros as subroutines

Finally, the third line calls the macro named \N, and moves the cell pointer down by three rows:

{\N}{Down 3}

Enter this macro into your own copy of the COMPANY.WK3 worksheet. Also enter the macro name, \H, in column A, and the comment in column C. (Once again, use the Range Justify command to arrange the comment down column C.) Select cell A9, and choose the Range Name Label Create command to designate \H as the name of the macro. Click the save-file icon to update COMPANY.WK3 on disk. Then choose the File New command to open a new blank worksheet, and press Ctrl-H to run the new macro. Figure 9.7 shows the result, a four-line heading that contains the company name, the region name, and the regional office address. As you can see, the output from the \H macro includes labels produced by calls to the \C and \N macros.

Take a moment to reexamine this third macro before you move on. The instructions of the macro are divided into three parts, which you entered into three consecutive cells of column B. But this division is actually arbitrary. Lotus 1-2-3 runs the macro in exactly the same way if you divide its instructions into only two parts, such as

{\C}{Down}Northern Region
{Down}{\N}{Down 3}

or even if you enter the entire macro into a single cell:

{\C}{Down}Northern Region{Down}{\N}{Down 3}

	A	B	C
1	Computing Conferences, Inc.		
2	Northern Region		
3	Mills Tower, Suite 992		
4	Chicago, IL 60605		
5			
6			
7			
8			
9			

FIGURE 9.7:

Running the \H macro

The purpose of dividing the instructions into smaller sections is to make the macro easy for *people* to read. For 1-2-3, this division is irrelevant, as long as you follow the few simple rules you have learned for entering a macro: Enclose macro key names within braces; don't enter any extraneous spaces or characters in the macro instructions; and use a blank cell to mark the end of the macro.

In preparation for this chapter's next exercises, you can now close both the COMPANY.WK3 file and the worksheet you have used to test the third macro. In the new Untitled worksheet that 1-2-3 opens you'll develop a second library of macros.

WRITING MACROS AS MENU SHORTCUTS

You can create a useful variety of menu-shortcut macros—that is, macros that choose commands from the 1-2-3 menu system. Like the tools in the icon palette, a menu-shortcut macro streamlines the multistep process of pulling down a menu, choosing a command, and selecting options from a dialog box. Instead of going through these steps, you can simply press the Ctrl-*letter* keyboard combination that runs your macro.

A macro that chooses a command from a pull-down menu consists of the following elements:

◆ The macro key name {Alt}, which is the equivalent of activating the menu bar

◆ A sequence of letters that represent a menu choice and one or more commands

The characters you include after {Alt} in a menu-shortcut macro are the letters that you see underlined in the commands of the menu system. For example, consider the following macro:

{Alt}RNL~

In this sequence, {Alt} activates the menu bar, R chooses the Range menu, N chooses the Name command, and L chooses the Label Create command from the cascade menu. This macro includes a final tilde character to respond to the options of the Range Name Label Create command. In this case, the tilde is equivalent to clicking the OK button to accept the default options.

The default selection in the Range Name Label Create dialog box is the Right option. The effect of the macro {Alt}RNL~ is therefore to define a label in the current cell as a range name for the adjacent cell at the right. As you'll see shortly, this macro is an ideal tool to use while you are developing other macros in the three-column macro library format. To assign a name to a macro, you move the cell pointer to the cell in the first column that contains the name, and run this macro.

Here is another example of a menu-shortcut macro, also useful in the development of other macros:

{Alt}RJ~

This macro chooses the Range Justify command, and accepts the default entry in the resulting dialog box. You can use this command to rearrange a long label that you have entered as a comment in an adjacent cell at the right of a macro. Select the cell that contains the comment, and run this macro; in response, 1-2-3 divides the long label into shorter one-cell sections.

Figure 9.8 shows these two menu-shortcut macros in a worksheet. In the following exercise, you'll enter them into a worksheet of your own, as the first two tools of a new macro library that you'll save on disk as MACROLIB.WK3:

1. Adjust the widths of the first three columns of the Untitled worksheet as follows: A, **2**; B, **17**; and C, **17**.

2. Enter the macro names **\R** and **\J** in cells A2 and A6; click the bold icon for each cell. Then enter the titles and the macro instructions themselves in column B, exactly as you see them in Figure 9.8.

	A	B	C
1		Right Label	
2	\R	{Alt}RNL~	
3			
4			
5		Justify in Column	
6	\J	{Alt}RJ~	
7			
8			

FIGURE 9.8:

Two menu-shortcut macros

3. Select cell A2 and choose the Range Name Label Create command. Click OK to assign the name \R to the macro. The Right Label macro is now ready to use.

4. Select cell A6, and press Ctrl-R to run the Right Label macro. As a result, 1-2-3 assigns the name \J to the Justify in Column macro. To confirm that this has actually happened, press Alt-F3 to choose the Tools Macro Run command; examine the list of defined macro names in the current worksheet. The two macro names have both been defined successfully.

5. Enter the following long label as a comment in cell C1: **Assign a label name to the cell on the right.** Initially, the label is displayed across the width of three columns, as shown in Figure 9.9.

6. With the cell pointer still positioned at C1, press Ctrl-J. The macro breaks the long label up into three parts, as in Figure 9.10.

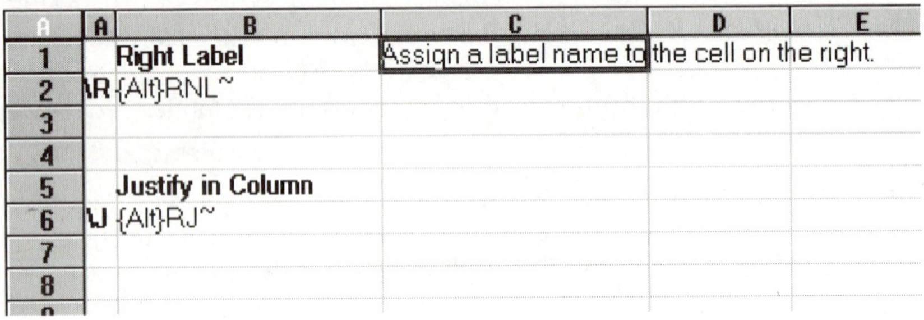

FIGURE 9.9:
Entering a long label as a comment

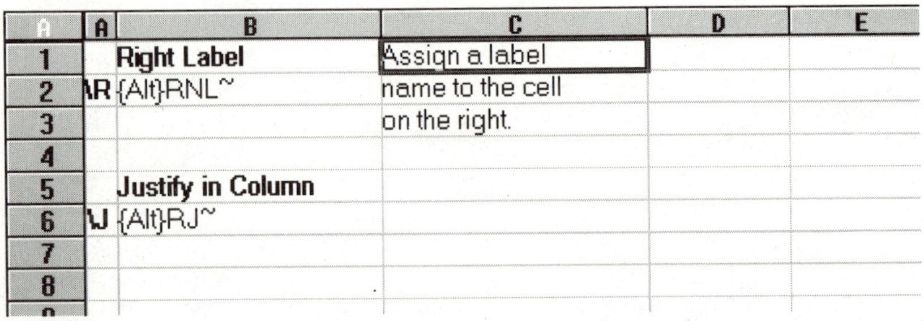

A	B	C	D	E
1	Right Label	Assign a label name to	the cell on the right.	
2	\R {Alt}RNL~			
3				
4				
5	Justify in Column			
6	\J {Alt}RJ~			
7				
8				

FIGURE 9.10:
Using the Justify in Column macro

A	B	C	D	E
1	Right Label	Assign a label		
2	\R {Alt}RNL~	name to the cell		
3		on the right.		
4				
5	Justify in Column			
6	\J {Alt}RJ~			
7				
8				

7. Enter the following long label into cell C5: **Justify a long label within the current column.** With the cell pointer at C5, press Ctrl-J again.

8. Choose the File Save As command and save this worksheet on disk as MACROLIB.WK3.

Using {Alt} to Select Options from Dialog Boxes

To write a macro that selects an option from a dialog box, you use {Alt} in a different format: Inside the braces, after the word Alt, you include the letter that represents the option you wish to select. Enclose the letter in double-quotation marks. For example, {Alt "S"} selects an option that is represented by the letter S. (In the label identifying this option in the corresponding dialog box, S is the underlined letter.)

You can use this second {Alt} format only after your macro has chosen an appropriate menu command. Consider this example:

{Alt}KI
{Alt "S"}~

The first line in this macro chooses the Worksheet Insert command. The second line is the equivalent of selecting the Sheet option in the Worksheet Insert dialog box. Again, the final tilde is the same as clicking the OK command button. The effect of the macro is to insert a new worksheet in the current worksheet window.

When a macro selects a text box inside a dialog box, you may want to clear the current entry from the text box before making a new entry. A special macro instruction named {ClearEntry}, or simply {CE}, performs this task. For example, here is a macro that makes selections from the Range Format dialog box:

{Alt}RFC
{Alt "D"}{CE}
0~

The first line in this macro selects the Currency format from the Range Format list. The second line activates the Decimal places box and clears the current entry from the box. Finally, the third line enters 0 (zero) into the Decimal places box, and confirms the selections. The effect of this macro is to apply the currency format (with no decimal places) to values in a current range selection.

Figure 9.11 shows these two new macros in the MACROLIB.WK3 file, along with a half-dozen other useful menu-shortcut macros. Take the time now to enter all these macros into your own worksheet. Use the Right Label macro to assign a name to each of the new macros you enter, and use the Justify in Column macro to arrange the corresponding comment in column C or column F. When you finish entering the macros, click the save-file icon to update your MACROLIB.WK3 file on disk.

When you create a macro library like this one, you should test each of the macros it contains to make sure you haven't made any mistakes. Here are some suggestions for testing some of the macros in the MACROLIB.WK3 library:

1. Choose File New to open a new worksheet window. Press Ctrl-I to test the Insert Sheet macro. A new worksheet is added to the window.

2. Enter the value **12345** in a cell on the worksheet. Without moving the cell pointer, press Ctrl-C to test the Currency macro. The entry is displayed as *$12,345*.

3. Enter the **@RAND** function in another cell. Without moving the cell pointer, press Ctrl-F to test the Formula as Text macro. The cell displays the function name rather than the result of the function. Now press Ctrl-V to test the Value Conversion macro. The cell now contains a fixed random value rather than an entry of the @RAND function.

A	B	C	D	E	F
1	Right Label	Assign a label		Formula as Text	Display the
2	\R {Alt}RNL~	name to the cell		\F {Alt}RFT~	selected
3		on the right.			formulas as text.
4					
5	Justify in Column	Justify a long		Date Format	Display current
6	\J {Alt}RJ~	label within the		\D {Alt}RF1~	value as a date.
7		current column.			
8				Time Format	Display current
9	Insert Sheet	Add a new sheet		\T {Alt}RF7~	decimal value in
10	\I {Alt}KI	to the current			time format.
11	{Alt "S"}~	worksheet window.			
12				Macro Transcript	Show the
13	Currency	Apply the		\M {Alt}TMS	transcript
14	\C {Alt}RFC	currency format,			window.
15	{Alt "D"}{CE}	with no decimal			
16	0~	places.			
17				Exit from 1-2-3	Close the 1-2-3
18	Value Conversion	Convert selected		\X {Alt}FX	window, and exit
19	\V {Alt}EQ	formulas to			from the program.
20	{Alt "C"}~	values.			

FIGURE 9.11:

A library of menu-shortcut macros

4. Enter @NOW into another cell on the worksheet. Without moving the cell pointer, press Ctrl-D to test the Date Format function. The cell displays today's date in the format 31-Dec-90. Now press Ctrl-T to test the Time Format function. The cell displays the current time in the format 11:59 AM.

If any of the macros do not perform as expected, turn back to MACROLIB.WK3 and make corrections as necessary. (Refer to Figure 9.11 to find the correct macros.) After making any corrections, save the final version of the library to disk.

USING THE TRANSCRIPT WINDOW TO DEVELOP MACROS

You have now created two separate libraries of macros—COMPANY.WK3 and MACROLIB.WK3—by entering instructions directly from the keyboard. After this much experience, you may be happy to learn that 1-2-3 offers an alternate method that sometimes simplifies the process of planning and writing macros. The central tool in this method is called the Transcript window.

The Transcript window records the most recent keystrokes you've typed during the current session with 1-2-3. This recording feature is always on, as long as the 1-2-3 window itself is active. The Transcript window holds up to 512 bytes of information. When the window reaches its maximum capacity, it releases characters from the beginning of its current recording, and continues appending new characters at the end. All recordings are made as macro entries, using the macro key names you've been working with in this chapter.

You can view the Transcript window at any time by choosing the Tools Macro Show Transcript command. When the Transcript window is active, a simplified menu bar appears at the top of the 1-2-3 window. Using commands from this menu bar, you can perform several important operations with the Transcript window, including the following three:

◆ Clear the entire current recording from the window, so you can start afresh with a new recording.

◆ Rerun a selection of keystrokes in the current recording, to examine the actions they represent.

◆ Copy a selection of entries from the current recording to the clipboard. Then you can paste this selection to a worksheet to create a new macro.

A macro you create by copying a selection from the Transcript window may not always be identical to an equivalent macro that you write yourself. There are almost always several different ways to structure a macro for a particular task, and the Transcript window has its own way of recording events.

The following exercise serves as a brief introduction to the Transcript window. In the course of this exercise, you'll create a new version of the Insert Sheet macro, and you'll confirm that this Transcript-recorded version has the same effect as the version displayed back in Figure 9.11:

1. Close both the MACROLIB.WK3 worksheet and the other worksheet on which you were testing the macros. In response, 1-2-3 opens a new blank Untitled worksheet.

2. Choose the Tools Macro Show Transcript command. The Transcript macro initially appears as a small window located at the lower-left corner of the screen; it contains the recording of your most recent activities. The Untitled worksheet is still the current window, and the spreadsheet menu bar is still displayed at the top of the 1-2-3 window.

3. Activate the Transcript window by pressing Ctrl-F6 or by clicking the window's title bar with the mouse. Some interesting changes occur in the 1-2-3 window when you do so. The Transcript menu bar appears, displaying the names of only five pull-down menus: File, Edit, Macro, Window, and Help. In addition, the icon palette disappears from the window; no icons are available when the Transcript window is active.

4. Pull down the Window menu and choose the Tile command. The Transcript and Untitled windows are resized, to take up equal halves of the worksheet area.

5. Pull down the Edit menu and choose the Clear All command. The current contents of the Transcript window are deleted.

6. Activate the Untitled worksheet window by pressing Ctrl-F6 or by clicking the window's title bar with the mouse. The icon palette and the familiar Main Menu return to view.

7. Using the mouse or the keyboard, choose the Worksheet Insert command and select the Sheet option. Click OK or press ↵ to confirm. When you complete the operation, worksheet B is added to the Untitled window, and a sequence of macro instructions appears in the Transcript window.

8. Activate the Transcript window. Use the mouse or the keyboard to select the entire current recording in the window: Drag the mouse

pointer over the contents, from beginning to end; or press Home and then Shift-End at the keyboard. Next, pull down the Macro menu, as shown in Figure 9.12. The first command in this menu, Run, reads the highlighted recording and runs the selection as a macro.

9. Choose the Run command. In response, 1-2-3 activates the Untitled worksheet window, and inserts worksheet C into the window. As this action demonstrates, you can use the Transcript menu's Macro Run command to test a selected portion of the current recording.

10. Now activate the Transcript window again; the recording is still highlighted. Choose the Edit Copy command, or press Ctrl-Insert from the keyboard. This copies the selected recording to the clipboard. Notice that no changes take place in the contents of the Transcript window; 1-2-3 does not record your actions while the Transcript window itself is active.

11. Activate the Untitled window. The cell pointer is currently located at cell C:A1. Click the paste-from-clipboard icon; in response, 1-2-3 pastes the selected recording into column A as a macro. (However, 1-2-3 does not record any keystrokes for the paste operation; the Transcript window never records mouse clicks in the icon palette.)

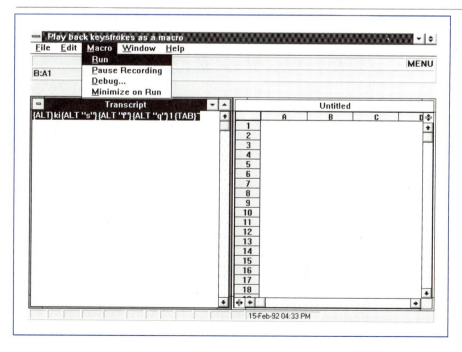

FIGURE 9.12:

Running the recording as a macro

12. Choose the Range Name Create command and enter **\W** as the name for this new macro. Click OK or press ⏎ to complete the operation. This action is duly recorded in the Transcript window.

13. Press Ctrl-W twice. Worksheets D and E are added to the Untitled window. In the Transcript window, the two macro calls are recorded as {\W}{\W}, as shown in Figure 9.13.

14. Continue experimenting with the Transcript window if you wish: Perform other worksheet commands and note how 1-2-3 records them, or create additional macros from selected portions of the recording. When you are finished experimenting, close the Transcript window by pulling down its control menu and choosing the Close command. Also close the Untitled worksheet window without saving it.

Of course, you are free to edit and modify any recording that you paste from the Transcript window. You can also combine recorded passages from the window with macro instructions that you write yourself; this is a common way to build a large macro project.

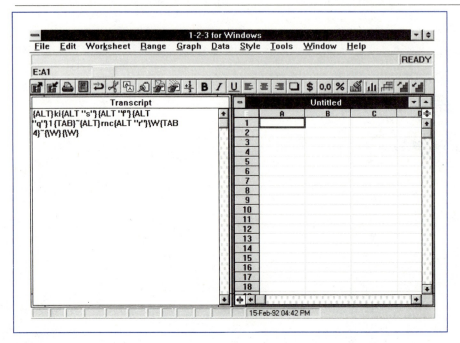

FIGURE 9.13:
The Transcript window continues to record keystrokes

ATTACHING A MACRO TO AN ICON

Perhaps the ultimate step in customizing 1-2-3 is to create a new tool in the icon palette to represent a macro that you've written yourself. Any macro that you use during most sessions with 1-2-3 is a good candidate for this step. So is a macro that performs a task that you find inconvenient to perform or difficult to remember. For example, in the upcoming exercise, you'll create a new icon to represent the Value Conversion macro shown back in Figure 9.11. When you complete this process, the value-conversion icon will appear at the right side of the icon palette, as shown in Figure 9.14. You'll be able to click this new icon to convert any formulas into their current calculated values.

Developing an icon for a macro is a detailed, multistep process, but not really very difficult. You start out by temporarily leaving 1-2-3 and starting up the Windows Paintbrush program to create the icon itself. You save this new icon as a .BMP file in a directory named \123W\SHEETICO. (Or, if you are creating a new icon for the graph icon palette, you save the .BMP file in the directory \123W\GRAPHICO.) When you return to 1-2-3, you open your macro library and select the macro you want to assign to this new icon. Then you choose the Tools SmartIcons command and click the Customize button; the icon you've created shows up in the dialog box. You select the icon, assign the macro, and add the icon to the icon palette. You may also have to delete an existing icon from the current palette, to make room for the new one.

Here are the steps for creating the value-conversion icon as a new tool in the icon palette:

1. Minimize the 1-2-3 window, and start up the Paintbrush program from the Windows Program Manager. (Paintbrush is a Microsoft program that comes packaged with Windows 3. It is part of the Accessories program group by default.)

FIGURE 9.14:
The value-conversion icon

2. In Paintbrush, choose the File Open command, and navigate to the \123W\SHEETICO directory. This is the directory from which 1-2-3 reads customizable icon files for the icon palette. Open the file named SAMPLE.BMP. A small blank icon with a gray background appears in the upper-left corner of the Paintbrush work area.

3. As a simple way of developing a graphic to represent the Value Conversion macro, you can simply enter a large bold V inside the blank icon: Click the Paintbrush abc icon. Select a suitable font from the Font menu. Choose the Style Bold command. Select a point size from the Size menu. Then click inside the blank icon button, and enter an uppercase **V**, as shown in Figure 9.15. (The font for the V displayed in this figure is 26-point Helvetica bold.)

4. Choose the File Save As command, and save the new icon as VALUE.BMP in the \123W\SHEETICO directory. Exit from Paintbrush. Maximize the 1-2-3 window to return to your work in the spreadsheet program.

5. Open the MACROLIB.WK3 worksheet and preselect the range B19..B20, which contains the instructions of the Value Conversion macro.

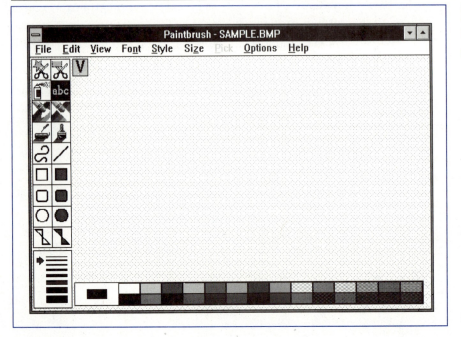

FIGURE 9.15:

Creating a .BMP file for a new icon

6. Choose the Tools SmartIcons command and click the Customize command button. Your new V icon appears in the Custom icons box, as shown in Figure 9.16.

7. Click the V icon to select it. Then click the Assign macro command button. In the resulting Tools SmartIcons Customize Assign Macro dialog box, click the Get macro button. In response, 1-2-3 copies your pre-selected macro from the MACROLIB.WK3 file to the Macro box, as in Figure 9.17. Click OK to assign this sequence of macro instructions to the icon. The Tools SmartIcons Customize dialog box becomes active again.

8. In the Current palette box, select the cut-to-clipboard icon, which displays a pair of scissors as its graphic. Click the Remove button to delete this icon from the Current palette box. (Or, if you prefer, you can remove some other standard icon that you seldom use.)

9. Scroll horizontally to the end of the Current palette box, and click the empty dotted square located after the last icon. Click the V icon again in the Custom icons dialog box, and then click the Add command button. The new value-conversion icon is now part of the Current palette collection, as you can see in Figure 9.18.

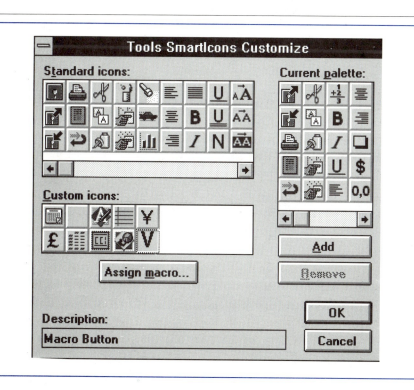

FIGURE 9.16:
The new icon appears in the Tools SmartIcons Customize dialog box.

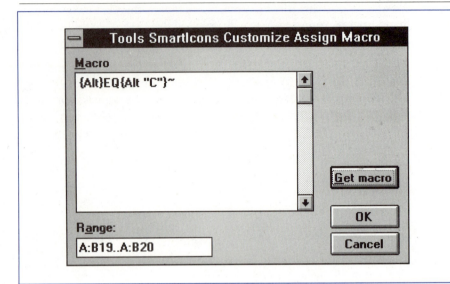

FIGURE 9.17:
Assigning a macro to the new icon

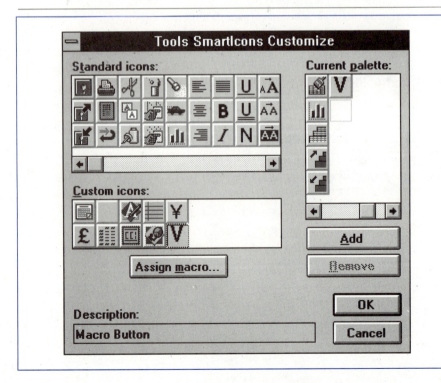

FIGURE 9.18:
Adding the icon to the Current palette box

10. Click OK in the Tools SmartIcons Customize dialog box, and then on the Tools SmartIcons box. When you complete this procedure, the value-conversion icon appears in the icon palette, as shown back in Figure 9.14.

In this exercise, you've assigned a simple menu-shortcut macro to the new icon. This icon reappears in the icon palette each time you start a new session with 1-2-3. To restore the original selection of icons to the icon palette, return to the Tools SmartIcons Customize dialog box, delete the V icon, and reinsert the cut-to-clipboard icon.

WRITING MACRO PROGRAMS

As you examine advanced macro programs, you'll begin learning about 1-2-3's significant vocabulary of macro commands. These commands perform programmed operations such as decision making, repetition, and interaction with the user during the program run. Like a macro key name, a macro command appears within braces, { and }. But a macro command represents a predefined action rather than a simple keystroke. Most macro commands require *arguments,* which you supply inside the braces after the command itself. Depending upon the requirement of a particular macro command, arguments may appear as values or labels; arithmetic, string, or logical expressions; functions; cell or range references; or range names.

One interesting example of a macro command is {GetLabel}. This command is a central element in an *interactive* macro, a program that pauses one or more times during the run, to get input from the user at the keyboard. The {GetLabel} command displays the 1-2-3 Classic window at the top of the screen; but instead of a menu bar, the window contains a *prompt,* asking the user for a particular item of information. After the user types the information and presses ↵, {GetLabel} copies the input as a label to a specified worksheet cell.

As you might expect, {GetLabel} takes two arguments:

{GetLabel *string,reference*}

The *string* argument is the prompt that {GetLabel} displays in the 1-2-3 Classic window; and the *reference* argument is the cell location where {GetLabel} copies the input. Notice that there is one space between the command itself and the first argument; by contrast, the two arguments are separated by a comma but no spaces. The entire command, with its arguments and braces, must appear within a single cell of the macro column. You cannot break up a macro command into multiple cells.

You'll see examples of {GetLabel} in the sample macro presented in the next section of this chapter.

THE MEMO MACRO

The Memo macro, shown in Figure 9.19, is a useful office tool for writing quick memos to business associates and coworkers. The program asks you to enter three strings of information from the keyboard, one at a time: the name of the person who is to receive the memo, the name of the sender, and the text of the message itself. Given this information, the macro organizes the memo neatly on a worksheet, along with entries for the current date and time. It then defines the memo as a print range, and displays a preview of the printed memo. When the macro run is over, you can simply click the print-range icon to print the memo.

The Memo macro is designed to be saved on disk as a self-contained program file. The file contains two worksheets: Worksheet A is reserved for the text of the memo created during a program run, and worksheet B contains the Memo macro itself. The contents of worksheet A change each time you

FIGURE 9.19:

The Memo macro

	A	B	C
1		Memo Macro	
2	\M	{Goto}MEMO~{Blank MEMO}	Delete the previous memo.
3		{Home}Memorandum~{Down 2}To:~{Right}	Enter the title and "To" labels.
4		{GetLabel "To? ",@CELLPOINTER("address")}	Get the recipient's name.
5		{Left}{Down}From:~{Right}	Enter the "From" label.
6		{GetLabel "From? ",@CELLPOINTER("address")}	Get the sender's name.
7		{Left}{Down 2}Date:~	Enter the "Date" label.
8		{Home}{Anchor}{Down 5}~{Alt}SF{Alt "B"}~	Display the labels in boldface.
9		{Right}{Down 5}	Select a cell for the date.
10		@TODAY{Calc}~{Alt}RF1~{Right}	Enter and format the date.
11		@NOW{Calc}~{Alt}RF7~{Left 2}{Down 3}	Enter and format the time.
12		{GetLabel "Message: ",@CELLPOINTER("address")}	Get the text of the memo.
13		{Anchor}{Right 6}~{Alt}RJ{Down 15}\-~	Justify the text over a range.
14		{Home}{Anchor}{Down 8}{End}{Down}{Right 6}~	Preselect the print range.
15		{Alt}RNCmemo~	Assign a range name.
16		{Alt}FP{Alt "V"}	Preview the printed memo.
17			
18			
19			
20			

run the macro. Follow these steps to create your own copy of this macro:

1. On a blank worksheet, use the Range Name Create command to assign the range name MEMO to cell A:A1.

2. Choose the Worksheet Insert command and add worksheet B to the window. Carefully enter the three columns of the Memo macro into worksheet B. (Copy the macro from Figure 9.19.) Remember to start the entries in cells B10 and B11 with single quotation marks so that 1-2-3 will accept them as labels.

3. Select cell B:A2, where the macro name \M is displayed. Choose the Range Name Label Create command and click OK to assign this name to B:B2, the first cell of the macro.

4. Select cell B:B2, and choose the Range Name Create command. Assign the second range name \0 (backslash, zero) to the cell. You'll learn the purpose of this second range name later in this chapter.

5. Save the file as MEMO.WK3.

Now you can try running the macro. Press Ctrl-M to start. The macro moves to worksheet A, and displays the 1-2-3 Classic window at the top of the screen. The window contains a one-word prompt, *To?*, along with an underscore cursor. At this point, you enter the name of the person to whom you are sending a memo, as shown in the example in Figure 9.20. When you press ↵, the macro enters the name onto the memo worksheet. Then the 1-2-3 Classic window reappears with a new prompt, *From?*. Here, you enter your own name. The macro does some more work on the memo worksheet, and then displays a third prompt in the 1-2-3 Classic window, *Message:*. To complete your memo, you enter the text of your message in the input window. The message can be as long as 511 characters, or approximately 100 words.

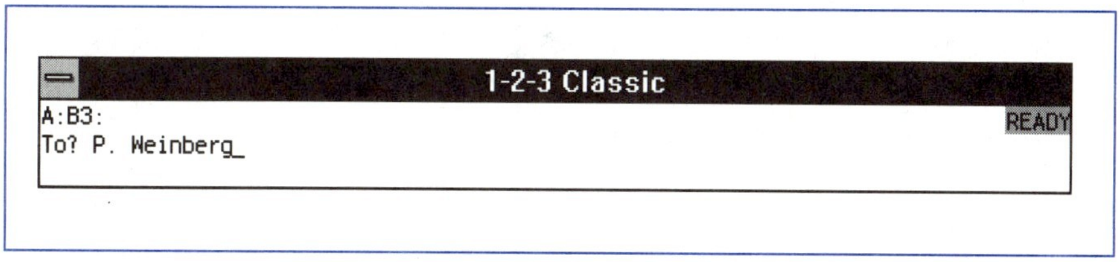

FIGURE 9.20:

Responding to an input prompt in the 1-2-3 Classic window

When you press ↵ at the end of the message text, the Memo macro enters and formats the message text in the rows below the heading. Then the Print Preview window appears on the screen, showing you what your memo will look like when you print it. This is the end of the macro run. Press the Escape key to return to the memo worksheet. Figure 9.21 shows an example of the memo worksheet that the macro creates. As you can see, the heading includes the names of the recipient and the sender, and the date and time when the memo was written. To print the memo, click the print-range icon. An example of the printed output appears in Figure 9.22.

Although the memo macro is longer than the macros you created earlier in this chapter, it is really not much more complicated. Its major new element is the {GetLabel} command. Here are brief line-by-line explanations of the program instructions, identified by their cell locations in worksheet B, shown back in Figure 9.19:

◆ B2: First a {Goto} instruction moves the cell pointer to the beginning of the MEMO range. This instruction is included in case worksheet B is current at the time the macro run begins. Then the macro command {Blank MEMO} erases the former contents of the memo worksheet, stored in the range MEMO. (As you'll see later, an instruction at the end of the macro reassigns the range name MEMO to the entire text of the current memo.)

FIGURE 9.21:

A memo created by the Memo macro

	A	B	C	D	E	F	G	H
1	Memorandum							
2								
3	To:	P. Weinberg						
4	From:	J. Harvey						
5								
6	Date:	17-Feb-92	04:36 PM					
7								
8								
9	Please examine the enclosed schedule for our upcoming						
10	conference on Computers for Lawyers. You will be teaching two						
11	seminars for intermediate spreadsheet users, and one general						
12	introduction to database management. I'm allowing extra time						
13	for you to prepare the spreadsheet course, because I know this						
14	is not your usual topic. I know you'll do a great job. Thanks.						
15	P.W.							
16								
17								
18								
19								
20								

- B3: The labels *Memorandum* and *To:* are entered into their respective cells in the memo worksheet.

- B4: A {GetLabel} instruction elicits the name of the person who is to receive the memo. Notice the format of the command:

{GetLabel "To? ",@CELLPOINTER("address")}

The first agument, "To? ", is the prompt displayed in the 1-2-3 Classic window. The second argument is a call to the special function @CELLPOINTER. Given an argument of "address", this function supplies a reference to the address of the current cell. Once the input is complete, the {GetLabel} command copies the input to the current location of the cell pointer.

- B5: The label *From:* is entered onto the worksheet macro.

- B6: Another {GetLabel} command elicits the name of the person who is writing the memo.

- B7: The label *Date:* is entered onto the memo worksheet.

- B8: The macro applies the boldface style to the range of labels in column A. The following sequence of instructions preselects the range:

{Home}{Anchor}{Down 5}~

Memorandum

To: P. Weinberg
From: J. Harvey

Date: 17-Feb-92   04:36 PM

Please examine the enclosed schedule for our upcoming conference on Computers for Lawyers. You will be teaching two seminars for intermediate spreadsheet users, and one general introduction to database management. I'm allowing extra time for you to prepare the spreadsheet course, because I know this is not your usual topic. I know you'll do a great job. Thanks.
P.W.

FIGURE 9.22:
The printed memo

Then these instructions select the Bold option from the Style Font command:

{Alt}SF{Alt "B"}~

- B9: The cell pointer is moved to the location for today's date.
- B10: The value of the @TODAY function is entered into the current cell:

  @TODAY{Calc}~

  This instruction is equivalent to pressing the F9 function key while @TODAY is still displayed on the Edit line. The next instruction chooses the Range Format command and selects the first date display format:

  {Alt}RF1~

  A {Right} instruction then moves the cell pointer one cell to the right, for the time entry.

- B11: The current value of the @NOW function is entered into the cell, and then the cell is formatted for time display. Then the cell pointer is repositioned for the message text.
- B12: A third {GetLabel} command elicits the text of the message, and then enters the entire long label into the current cell.
- B13: The {Anchor}{Right 6}~ instruction preselects a range of columns for displaying the message. Then the {Alt}RJ instruction chooses the Range Justify command to display the message down a range of consecutive rows. (No ~ is necessary in this instruction; the Range Justify command does not display a dialog box when the current range selection consists of more than one cell.) Next, {Down 15}\-~ enters a row of hyphens in a cell located below the text of the message. This entry serves as a marker for the end of the print range; it is used only if the memo message consists of a single row of text.
- B14: The macro preselects the entire range of the memo; this will become the print range.
- B15: The range name MEMO is assigned to this preselected range. As you've seen, the *next* run of the macro will begin by deleting all the labels and values currently displayed in this range.
- B16: The macro chooses the File Print command, which establishes the preselected range as the print range; and finally, the macro selects the Preview option.

An Autoexecute Macro

You'll recall that you assigned two different range names to the first cell in the Memo macro: \M and \0. You've seen the purpose of the first of these names; you pressed Ctrl-M to run the macro for the first time.

The second name has a different purpose. Assigning \0 to a macro in a worksheet file creates an *autoexecute* macro. When you open a file from disk, 1-2-3 looks to see if the range name \0 exists anywhere in the worksheet. If it does, the macro with this name is automatically run as the first event on the newly opened worksheet.

You can see how this works with the MEMO.WK3 file. Close the file now, without saving the current changes. Then choose the File Open command and reopen the file. As soon as you do so, 1-2-3 runs the Memo macro. As you've seen, the macro begins by clearing the previous memo from worksheet A and displaying the 1-2-3 Classic window at the top of the screen to elicit the first input label. (If you don't want to complete the macro run, you can stop it prematurely by pressing Ctrl-Break; then click OK in the resulting message box.)

To open a file like MEMO.WK3 without performing the autoexecute macro that it contains, choose the Tools User Setup command and remove the X from the Run autoexecute macros option. When you next open the file, the macro will not be performed automatically.

Another way to automate macros is to create a library file named AUTO123.WK3 in the default directory. You'll recall that the default directory is defined in the Worksheet directory box of the Tools User Setup dialog box. If a worksheet file named AUTO123.WK3 exists in this directory, 1-2-3 automatically opens the file at the beginning of each session. Furthermore, if the file contains an autoexecute macro named \0, the macro is run as the first action in the new session.

SUMMARY

A macro is a program that records and performs a particular operation in the 1-2-3 environment. Macros can include literal keystrokes, specific menu commands, or detailed sequences of programmed activities. Lotus 1-2-3 has two categories of special reserved words that you can use in macros: macro key names and macro commands. The macro key names represent nonprinting keyboard operations, such as {Right}, {Alt}, {Home}, and {Anchor}. The tilde character, ~, represents ↵. Macro commands perform specific programming activities; for example, {GetLabel} elicits input from the user during a macro performance. (You'll learn more about macro commands in Chapter 12.)

You enter the instructions of a macro as labels in consecutive cells of a worksheet column. Assign a range name to the first cell of every macro, using either the Range Name Create command or the Range Name Label Create command. It is also a good idea to document a macro inside the worksheet: Include a column of range names at the left side of the macro, and a column of explanatory comments at the right. A worksheet that contains a collection of macros is sometimes known as a macro library. When you open such a worksheet, all the macros in the library are available for use.

There are two ways to run a macro, depending upon the macro's range name. For convenience, you can assign a special two-character range name consisting of the backslash character followed by a letter from A to Z; this name allows you to run the macro directly from the keyboard. For example, you press Ctrl-M to run a macro named \M. Alternatively, if a macro has an ordinary range name (not the backslash and a letter), you must use the Tools Macro Run command to run it.

Macros can be automated and integrated into the 1-2-3 environment. A macro with the name \0 (backslash, zero) is an autoexecute macro; 1-2-3 starts a run of this macro as soon as you open the worksheet that contains it. A macro library stored in the default 1-2-3 directory with the file name AUTO123.WK3 is automatically opened at the beginning of each session with 1-2-3. In addition, you can use the Tools SmartIcons Customize command to assign a macro to a custom icon, and then to add the icon to the 1-2-3 icon palette. Create an icon for your macro in the Windows Paintbrush program.

The Transcript window can help you develop certain kinds of macros. This window records your activities during a given session with 1-2-3; the recordings appear in macro format. To view the Transcript window, choose the Tools Macro Show Transcript command. Then use a copy-and-paste operation to copy a selection of instructions from the Transcript window to a macro worksheet.

PART THREE

FAST TRACK

To solve simultaneous equations on a worksheet, ... 470
enter the coefficients of the variables as a square matrix on the worksheet. Then enter the constant values from the right side of each equation as a one-column matrix. Use the Data Matrix Invert command to create the inverse of the coefficient matrix. Then use the Data Matrix Multiply command to perform matrix multiplication between the inverse matrix and the constant matrix. The result of the multiplication is the solution matrix.

To insert a graphic object into a worksheet, ... 474
choose the Range Annotate command. Create the object (such as an arrow, a circle, or a box) in the resulting graph window.

To count the number of values that belong to specified numeric categories, ... 482
create a bin range that defines the categories. Then preselect the values range, and choose the Data Distribution command. Enter a reference to the bin range and click OK.

To analyze the mathematical correlation between two or more columns of values, ... 484
choose Data Regression. Enter the X-range, Y-range, and ouput range, and click OK.

To create a one-way what-if table, ... 491
enter a column of input values at the left side of the table range, and enter one or more formulas at the top of each column in the table range. Preselect the table range, and choose the Data What-if Table 1-Way command. Specify the input cell and click OK.

To recalculate a defined what-if table, ... 494
press the F8 function key.

To create a two-way what-if table, ... 495
enter a column of values at the left side of the table range for the first input cell; and a row of values at the top of the table range for the second input cell. Enter the target formula into the upper-left corner of the table range. Preselect the table range, and choose the Data What-if Table 2-Way command. In the dialog box, enter references for Input cell 1 and Input cell 2, and click OK.

To create a three-way what-if table, ... 497
enter a column and a row of input values, for the first and second input cells, into each worksheet in a three-dimensional range. At the upper-left corner of the table range in each worksheet, enter a value for the third input cell. Preselect the three-dimensional range, and choose the Data What-if Table 3-Way command. In the dialog box, enter references to the formula cell and the three input cells, and click OK.

**To find the input value that yields a target result
from a worksheet formula,** 499
choose the Tools Backsolver command. Specify the formula location, the target result, and the adjustable cell, and click OK.

**To analyze a complex data problem on a
worksheet,** 502
create a range of logical formulas to represent the constraints. Then choose the Tools Solver command. Specify the adjustable cells, the constraint cells, and the optimum formula cell, and click OK.

CHAPTER 10

Advanced Worksheet Tools

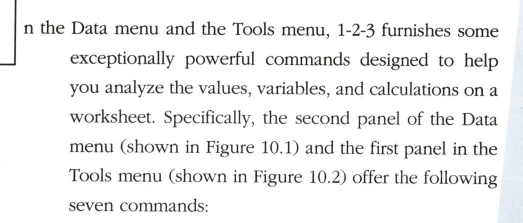

In the Data menu and the Tools menu, 1-2-3 furnishes some exceptionally powerful commands designed to help you analyze the values, variables, and calculations on a worksheet. Specifically, the second panel of the Data menu (shown in Figure 10.1) and the first panel in the Tools menu (shown in Figure 10.2) offer the following seven commands:

- Data What-if Table calculates worksheet formulas multiple times while varying the data in one, two, or three input cells.

- Data Distribution counts the number of entries that belong to specified numeric categories.

- The Data Matrix cascade menu offers two important *matrix arithmetic* operations: Data Matrix Invert produces the *inverse* of a square matrix, and Data Matrix Multiply performs *matrix multiplication* between two matrices. You can use these two operations together to find solutions for *simultaneous equations*.

- Data Regression examines the correlations between sets of numeric data, in a series of calculations known as *regression analysis*.

- Data Parse converts the lines of an imported text file into a table of individual value and label entries on a worksheet.

- Tools Backsolver finds the numeric input value that produces a desired result in a selected worksheet formula.

- Tools Solver, the most sophisticated of all these commands, produces worksheet scenarios from a system of variables, formulas, and constraints that you specify.

You'll explore these important features through the examples and exercises presented in this chapter. Along the way, you'll also learn about several commands in the Range and File menus:

- The Range Transpose command changes the orientation of a table, exchanging rows for columns and columns for rows.

- The Range Annotate command gives you the opportunity to insert a graphic shape such as an arrow, a rectangle, or an oval into a worksheet range.

- The File Import From Text command reads the rows of a text file and displays them as entries in a worksheet column.

- The File Combine From command reads data from a worksheet file, and incorporates it into the current worksheet window.

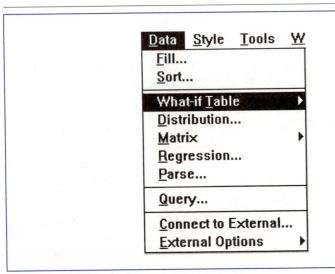

FIGURE 10.1:

The Data menu

Starting with a discussion of the Data Matrix commands, this chapter presents an independent topic in each of its main sections. The topics are arranged in an order that accommodates the development of particular exercises presented in the chapter. However, you can read individual topics in any order that suits your own needs.

USING THE DATA MATRIX COMMANDS

A group of numbers arranged in rows and columns is called a *matrix*. In mathematics books, a matrix is represented as a rectangular array of numbers enclosed within a large pair of parentheses. However, in a 1-2-3 worksheet, a matrix is an ordinary table of numbers in an application in which you can successfully apply the Data Matrix commands.

You use these commands to solve simultaneous equations in business, financial, or technical applications. A set of simultaneous equations has a common group of unknown values, known as *variables*. In typical examples, each equation has the same number of variables, and the number of equations is equal to the number of variables. For instance, in a set of four simultaneous equations, each equation has the same four variables. To *solve* these equations, you must find a set of four numeric values that satisfy all four equations.

Consider the example shown in Figure 10.3: The central office of Computing Conferences, Inc. has incurred expenses for curriculum development in each of four topic areas: computer training courses for accountants, doctors, lawyers, and video store owners. These expenses will be shared among the company's four regions in proportion to each region's profits. The table of

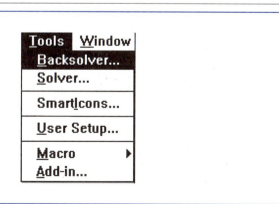

FIGURE 10.2:
The Tools menu

numbers in the range B5..E8 represents the profits earned from regional conferences in the four topic areas. Column F shows the expenses for curriculum development. The problem of this worksheet is to find the percentage of each region's profits to charge for curriculum costs.

This problem can be expressed as a group of four simultaneous equations with four unknowns. In this case, the unknowns are the percentages to charge the four regions—that is, the amount by which each profit figure in B5..E8 should be multiplied to find the correct share of the curriculum expense. In the following equations, these unknowns are represented as *E, W, N,* and *S*:

$$111200*E + 79300*W + 59500*N + 64200*S = 8058.76$$

$$131900*E + 116900*W + 77500*N + 96700*S = 10852.33$$

$$63500*E + 81500*W + 54000*N + 88400*S = 7376.34$$

$$88300*E + 63200*W + 41900*N + 161900*S = 9619.99$$

Accordingly, the goal of the worksheet in Figure 10.3 is to find values for *E, W, N,* and *S* that satisfy all four equations.

To prepare for the upcoming exercise, enter the values and labels of the curriculum expense worksheet onto a new blank worksheet of your own, and format the data as shown in Figure 10.3. Save the worksheet as CURREXP.WK3.

	A	B	C	D	E	F	G
1	Distributing the Cost of Curriculum Development						
2						Cost of	
3		Profits by Region				Curriculum	
4	Topic	Eastern	Western	Northern	Southern	Development	
5	Accountants	$111,200	$79,300	$59,500	$64,200	$8,058.76	
6	Doctors	$131,900	$116,900	$77,500	$96,700	$10,852.33	
7	Lawyers	$63,500	$81,500	$54,000	$88,400	$7,376.34	
8	Video Stores	$88,300	$63,200	$41,900	$161,900	$9,619.99	
9							
10							
11							
12							
13							
14							
15							
16	Region	% of Profit					
17	Eastern						
18	Western						
19	Northern						
20	Southern						

FIGURE 10.3:
Setting up the curriculum expense worksheet

UNDERSTANDING MATRIX ARITHMETIC

Before you start using the Data Matrix commands, you may find it helpful to review briefly the mathematics of matrices. The worksheet in Figure 10.4 displays a group of matrices generated from the curriculum expense problem. In the range A2..D5, the *coefficient matrix* is the table of regional profits, the numbers by which the four variables are multiplied in the simultaneous equations. The *constant matrix,* shown in the range F2..F5, is the column of values from the right side of each equation, the expense amounts for curriculum development.

Here is a summary of the two operations you can perform on matrices using the Data Matrix commands:

- ◆ The Data Matrix Invert operation can be performed only on a *square matrix*—that is, any matrix that contains an equal number of rows and columns. The result of this operation is a second matrix that has the same dimensions as the first. For example, the inverse of the coefficient matrix appears in the range A8..D11.

- ◆ The Data Matrix Multiply operation is performed between two matrices and results in a third matrix. The number of columns in the first matrix must be the same as the number of rows in the second matrix. In this operation, 1-2-3 multiplies values in each

FIGURE 10.4:
Matrices and matrix arithmetic

	A	B	C	D	E	F
1	Coefficient Matrix					Constant Matrix
2	111200	79300	59500	64200		8058.76
3	131900	116900	77500	96700		10852.33
4	63500	81500	54000	88400		7376.34
5	88300	63200	41900	161900		9619.99
6						
7	Inverse Matrix					
8	-1.4E-07	0.000019	-3.2E-05	6.1E-06		
9	-9.6E-05	0.000099	-3.5E-05	-2.1E-06		
10	0.000145	-0.00016	0.0001	-1.7E-05		
11	2.1E-08	-7.9E-06	4.9E-06	8.2E-06		
12						
13	Identity Matrix					Solution Matrix
14	1	(0)	0	0		0.028618
15	(0)	1	(0)	0		0.024705
16	(0)	(0)	1	0		0.016878
17	(0)	(0)	0	1		0.029799
18						

row of the first matrix by the corresponding values in each column of the second matrix; the sums of these products become the elements of the third matrix. If the first matrix in the operation has *r1* rows and *c1* columns, and the second matrix has *r2* rows and *c2* columns, the resulting matrix will have *r1* rows and *c2* columns.

By definition, the result of multiplying a matrix by its own inverse matrix is the *identity matrix*. As you can see in the range A14..D17 of Figure 10.4, an identity matrix consists of values of 0 and 1, where the values of 1 are arranged in a diagonal from the upper-left to the lower-right corners of the matrix. (Due to the limits of precision in the matrix operations, the values displayed as zero are actually very small positive or negative numbers. Notice that 1-2-3 encloses the small negative numbers in parentheses.)

The identity matrix suggests an approach to solving the simultaneous equations. If the four equations can be rearranged so that one variable in each equation has a coefficient of 1 and the remaining variables have coefficients of 0, the resulting constants on the right sides of the equations are the solutions to the problem. Keep in mind that the identity matrix is the result of multiplying the coefficient matrix by its own inverse. This implies the basic rule that you use to solve simultaneous equations: The one-column *solution matrix* is found by multiplying the *inverse of the coefficient matrix* by the *constant matrix*, the column of values from the right sides of the original equations.

For example, consider the solution matrix displayed in the range F14..F17 of Figure 10.4. This column of values is the result of using the Data Matrix Multiply command to multiply the inverse matrix in the range A8..D11 by the constant matrix in F2..F5. Each element in the solution matrix is the value for one of the four variables, *E, W, N,* or *S*.

SOLVING THE SIMULTANEOUS EQUATIONS

Returning now to the original curriculum expense worksheet, CURREXP.WK3 (shown back in Figure 10.3), here are the steps for finding the correct percentage for each region:

1. Preselect the range of profit figures in B5..E8.

2. Pull down the Data menu and choose the Matrix command. In the Data Matrix cascade menu, choose the Invert command. In the resulting dialog box, the preselected range is displayed in the From text box. In the To text box, enter a reference to cell A:B11, as shown in Figure 10.5. This is the upper-left corner of the range where 1-2-3 will generate the inverse matrix. Click OK, and the inverse matrix appears on the worksheet, as shown in Figure 10.6.

3. Now preselect the inverse matrix, in the range B11..E14. Choose the Data Matrix Multiply command. In the resulting dialog box, the preselected range (of the inverse matrix) appears in the First matrix text box. Enter the range of the constant matrix, A:F5..A:F8, in the Second matrix text box. Then enter A:B17 in the Output matrix text box, as shown in Figure 10.7. Click OK to complete the operation.

4. Preselect the range of the solution matrix, B17..B20, and click the percent icon to format these figures as percentages. Your worksheet now appears as shown in Figure 10.8.

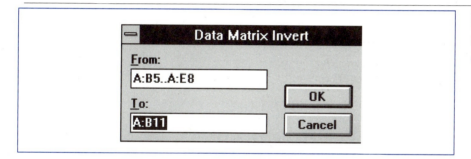

FIGURE 10.5:

The Data Matrix Invert dialog box

FIGURE 10.6:

Generating the inverse matrix

5. Click the save-file icon to save your work to disk.

In effect, you have now solved the four simultaneous equations. The values in the range B17..B20 show the percentage to take from each region's profits to cover the shared expense of curriculum development.

Now suppose that you would like to produce a table that shows the actual curriculum expense amount to be charged against the earnings for each conference topic in each region. For this table, you need to display the four percentages across a row, rather than down a column as they currently appear. The Range Transpose command is a convenient tool for accomplishing this task.

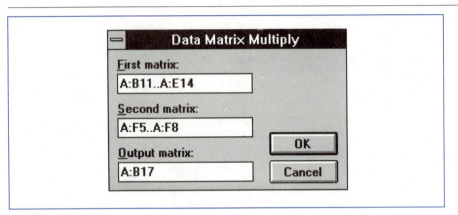

FIGURE 10.7:

The Data Matrix Multiply dialog box

	A	B	C	D	E	F	G
1	Distributing the Cost of Curriculum Development						
2							
3		Profits by Region				Cost of Curriculum	
4	Topic	Eastern	Western	Northern	Southern	Development	
5	Accountants	$111,200	$79,300	$59,500	$64,200	$8,058.76	
6	Doctors	$131,900	$116,900	$77,500	$96,700	$10,852.33	
7	Lawyers	$63,500	$81,500	$54,000	$88,400	$7,376.34	
8	Video Stores	$88,300	$63,200	$41,900	$161,900	$9,619.99	
9							
10							
11		-1.4E-07	0.000019	-3.2E-05	6.1E-06		
12		-9.6E-05	0.000099	-3.5E-05	-2.1E-06		
13		0.000145	-0.00016	0.0001	-1.7E-05		
14		2.1E-08	-7.9E-06	4.9E-06	8.2E-06		
15							
16	Region	% of Profit					
17	Eastern	2.86%					
18	Western	2.47%					
19	Northern	1.69%					
20	Southern	2.98%					

FIGURE 10.8:

Producing the solution matrix

USING THE
RANGE TRANSPOSE COMMAND

The Range Transpose command copies the row entries of a source range to the columns of a destination range, or, conversely, the column entries of a source to the rows of a destination. If the source range contains formulas, the Transpose command replaces those formulas with their current values in the destination range. (The original formulas in the source range are not affected.) This command also copies formats and display styles from the source to the destination range.

To produce the detailed table of curriculum expenses, you want to copy the percentages currently displayed in the column range B17..B20 to the row range B10..E10. (Note that these entries are simple values, not formulas.) Because you have no further use for the inverse matrix in the curriculum expense worksheet, you'll begin this next exercise by deleting the matrix:

1. Preselect the range B11..E14. Press the Delete key on your keyboard to erase the entries in this entire range.

2. Preselect the range of labels in A5..A8 and click the range-copy icon. Then click cell A11 to copy these labels to the range A11..A14.

3. Preselect the range of percentages in B17..B20. Pull down the Range menu and choose the Transpose command. The preselected range appears in the From text box. Enter A:B10 into the To text box, as shown in Figure 10.9. Click OK to complete the operation.

4. Enter the formula **+B5*B$10** into cell B11. With the cell pointer still located at B11, click the range-copy icon. Then drag the mouse pointer over the range B12..B14 to copy the formula to the cells in this range. Next, preselect the range B11..B14 and click the range-copy icon again. Drag the mouse pointer over the range C11..E11 to copy the formula to the appropriate cells in columns C, D, and E.

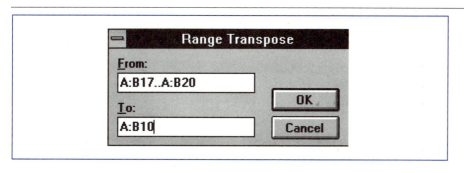

FIGURE 10.9:

The Range Transpose dialog box

5. Preselect the range B11..F14. Click the summation icon to enter @SUM formulas into column F; then click the currency icon to apply this format to the entire range. Move the cell pointer to E1, out of the way of any data. Your worksheet now appears as shown in Figure 10.10.

6. Click the save-file icon to save your work to disk.

Notice that the expense totals that you've produced in the range F11..F14 are the same as the original curriculum costs that you entered into F5..F8. These matching values confirm your solution for the simultaneous equations.

Now that you've created this worksheet, imagine that you want to send copies of it to each of the regional managers, highlighting the appropriate column of figures in each copy. One simple but effective way to draw attention to a particular range of data on a worksheet is to use the Range Annotate command.

USING THE RANGE ANNOTATE COMMAND

Range Annotate inserts a graph window into your worksheet file, and allows you to draw one or more objects in the window for subsequent display in a selected worksheet range. The objects you can add to your worksheet with this command include arrows, lines, circles, ellipses, polygons, squares, rectangles, text, and freehand drawings.

FIGURE 10.10:
Producing the curriculum expense table

	A	B	C	D	E	F	G
1	Distributing the Cost of Curriculum Development						
2						Cost of	
3		Profits by Region				Curriculum	
4	Topic	Eastern	Western	Northern	Southern	Development	
5	Accountants	$111,200	$79,300	$59,500	$64,200	$8,058.76	
6	Doctors	$131,900	$116,900	$77,500	$96,700	$10,852.33	
7	Lawyers	$63,500	$81,500	$54,000	$88,400	$7,376.34	
8	Video Stores	$88,300	$63,200	$41,900	$161,900	$9,619.99	
9							
10		2.86%	2.47%	1.69%	2.98%		
11	Accountants	$3,182.33	$1,959.10	$1,004.22	$1,913.11	$8,058.76	
12	Doctors	$3,774.73	$2,888.00	$1,308.02	$2,881.58	$10,852.33	
13	Lawyers	$1,817.25	$2,013.45	$911.39	$2,634.25	$7,376.34	
14	Video Stores	$2,526.98	$1,561.35	$707.17	$4,824.49	$9,619.99	
15							
16	Region	% of Profit					
17	Eastern	2.86%					
18	Western	2.47%					
19	Northern	1.69%					
20	Southern	2.98%					

For example, in the following exercise you'll use Range Annotate to draw an ellipse around the curriculum expense figures for the Northern region:

1. Preselect the range C9..E15 on the curricum expense worksheet.

2. Pull down the Range menu and choose the Annotate command. In the graph window that appears on the screen, you see an enlarged view of the grid for the selected range of cells. Notice that the graph menu and the graph icon palette now appear at the top of the 1-2-3 window. Also note that 1-2-3 has assigned the name <Blank> to this graph window.

3. Click the add-ellipse icon. Produce an approximation of the ellipse shown in Figure 10.11: Move the mouse pointer to the upper-left corner of the middle column in the grid, and hold down the mouse button while you drag the mouse to the lower-left corner of the third column. A rectangle appears around the perimeter of the area that will contain the resulting ellipse. Release the mouse button and the ellipse appears.

4. Pull down the Window menu and choose CURREXP.WK3 from the list of open windows. The worksheet now appears as shown in Figure 10.12. The ellipse you have drawn is displayed around the expense column for the Northern region.

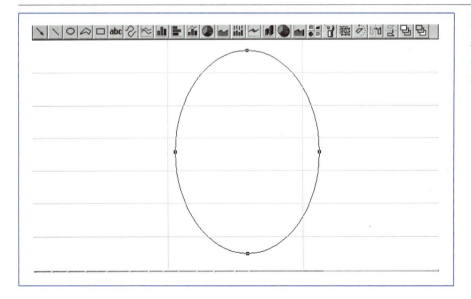

FIGURE 10.11:

Drawing an ellipse around a range of worksheet cells

5. Click the save-file icon to save your work to disk.

As you can see, this ellipse successfully highlights the target range of figures on your worksheet. If you want to include additional objects, you can draw an arrow pointing to the column, and then add a unit of text to the worksheet.

To revise a graphic object produced by the Range Annotate command, simply double-click any cell inside the range. In response, 1-2-3 redisplays the graph window on the screen. To delete a graphic object from the worksheet, choose the Graph Name Delete command while the worksheet window is current, select the name of the graph window you want to delete, and click the Delete button.

USING THE DATA PARSE COMMAND

The Data Parse command is a tool you use in the process of *importing* data into a 1-2-3 worksheet from a text file. A text file, also known as a print file, is made up of letters, digits, and printable symbols from the ASCII character code; typical file extensions for text files are .TXT or .PRN. Given a text file of column-oriented information, you might want a simple way to transfer the data to a 1-2-3 worksheet.

The File Import From Text command is the first step in this process; it reads a text file from disk, and copies it line by line into a worksheet. As a result of this command, each line of the text file is stored as a long label entry

	A	B	C	D	E	F	G
1	Distributing the Cost of Curriculum Development						
2						Cost of	
3		Profits by Region				Curriculum	
4	Topic	Eastern	Western	Northern	Southern	Development	
5	Accountants	$111,200	$79,300	$59,500	$64,200	$8,058.76	
6	Doctors	$131,900	$116,900	$77,500	$96,700	$10,852.33	
7	Lawyers	$63,500	$81,500	$54,000	$88,400	$7,376.34	
8	Video Stores	$88,300	$63,200	$41,900	$161,900	$9,619.99	
9							
10		2.86%	2.47%	1.69%	2.98%		
11	Accountants	$3,182.33	$1,959.10	$1,004.22	$1,913.11	$8,058.76	
12	Doctors	$3,774.73	$2,888.00	$1,308.02	$2,881.58	$10,852.33	
13	Lawyers	$1,817.25	$2,013.45	$911.39	$2,634.25	$7,376.34	
14	Video Stores	$2,526.98	$1,561.35	$707.17	$4,824.49	$9,619.99	
15							
16	Region	% of Profit					
17	Eastern	2.86%					
18	Western	2.47%					
19	Northern	1.69%					
20	Southern	2.98%					

FIGURE 10.12:

The result of the Range Annotate command

in a single cell of the worksheet. Once you have imported such a file into 1-2-3, you can then use the Data Parse command to separate these long labels into individual label and value entries.

For the upcoming exercises, imagine that the INSTRUCT.WK3 database was initially developed as a text file in a word-processing program. Figure 10.13 shows the contents of the file. As you can see, the data values in each row of the file are separated by spaces to align the columns. Keep in mind that this file was saved to disk in ASCII format; string and numeric fields alike are made up of sequences of ASCII characters.

Here are the initial steps for converting a file like this one into the 1-2-3 worksheet format:

1. Use the File New command to open a new blank worksheet into which you can import the text file.

2. Pull down the File menu and choose the Import From command. Choose Text from the resulting cascade menu. In the File Import From Text dialog box, use the Drives and Directories boxes to navigate to the directory location of the existing text file. When you activate the correct directory, the name of the text file appears in the Files list box, as shown in Figure 10.14. (By default, this command looks for text files that have an extension name of .PRN. If you are searching instead for a text file that has a .TXT extension, you can enter *.TXT into the File name box to display lists of files with this extension.)

3. When you find the target file name in the Files list box, double-click the name with the mouse. In response, 1-2-3 enters the file into the current worksheet, starting from the location of the cell pointer. Each line of the text file becomes a long entry in a cell of the current column.

```
S-149   Harris     P.   Dallas              S   Spreadsheet   $150    17   12-Feb-91
A-146   Daniels    A.   Atlanta             S   Accounting    $125    24   09-May-91
A-103   Perez      D.   Las Vegas           W   Accounting    $100     5   11-Jul-86
W-113   Porter     D.   Seattle             N   WP            $125    59   02-Aug-86
N-101   Schwartz   B.   Boston              E   Networks      $150   178   02-Mar-86
S-155   Roberts    P.   Chicago             N   Spreadsheet   $100    10   21-Aug-91
S-125   Ashford    W.   Washington, D.C.    E   Spreadsheet   $150   145   10-May-87
D-106   Weinberg   P.   Miami               S   Database       $75    59   18-Jan-86
W-119   Davis      G.   San Francisco       W   WP            $150   139   09-Jul-87
W-124   Meyer      J.   New York            E   WP            $150    85   05-May-87
W-145   Banks      S.   St. Louis           S   WP            $150    55   10-Jun-90
D-137   Sanchez    W.   Indianapolis        N   Database      $100    47   16-Apr-89
D-139   Porter     M.   Washington, D.C.    E   Database      $150    26   28-Mar-89
T-133   Ramirez    F.   Boston              E   Telecomm      $150    73   08-Feb-88
D-143   Cody       L.   Los Angeles         W   Database       $75    43   20-Jun-90
S-127   Gill       P.   Los Angeles         W   Spreadsheet   $100    25   22-Jun-87
T-128   Eng        R.   Albuquerque         S   Telecomm       $75    75   11-Oct-87
```

FIGURE 10.13:

The instructor database as a text file

For example, Figure 10.15 displays a worksheet containing the instructor database, as imported from the text file shown in Figure 10.13. In the contents box, just above the icon palette, you can see that the entire first line of the text file is stored in cell A1. The worksheet is of little use to you in this format; accordingly, the next step is to *parse* these long labels into individual data entries. The Data Parse command accomplishes this step by developing a special *format line* to represent the actual data structure of each row of data. Here are the steps for using this command on the imported data shown in Figure 10.15:

1. Preselect the long data labels in column A, in the range A1..A17.

2. Pull down the Data menu and choose the Parse command. In the Data Parse dialog box, begin by clicking the Create button, to instruct 1-2-3 to develop a format line for the file. When you do so, the dialog box appears as shown in Figure 10.16. The format line contains three types of characters: A single letter represents the type of data in a given column, known as a *data block;* a sequence of > symbols represents the width of a data block; and a sequence of * symbols represents spaces between data blocks, or extra space for entries that extend beyond the data block width. Beneath the format line, the dialog box displays a sample of the data as it will appear after parsing.

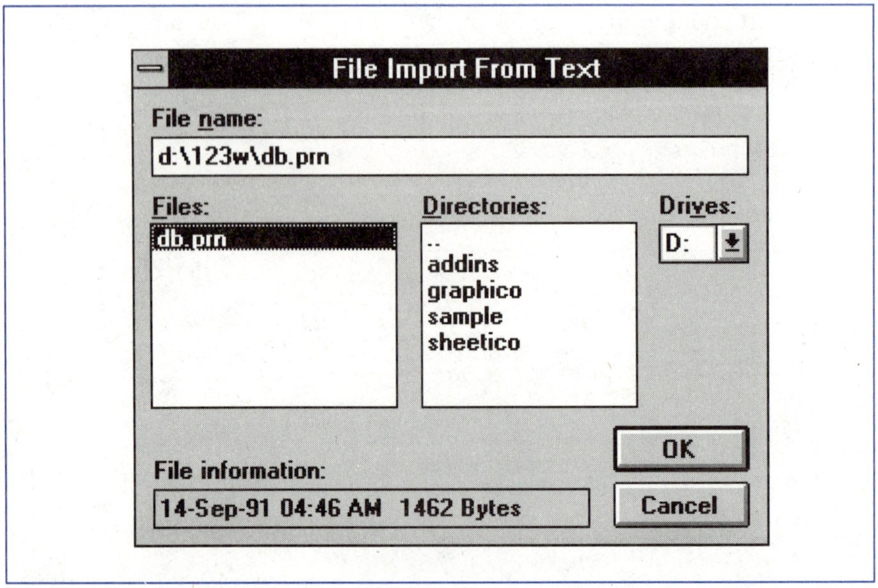

FIGURE 10.14:

The File Import From Text dialog box

3. Use the scroll bar to scroll horizontally through the format line. As you can see in Figure 10.17, the letters L, V, and D represent data blocks containing labels, values, and dates, respectively. (In addition, 1-2-3 uses the letter T in a format line to represent time values.) If the format line that 1-2-3 has developed does not match your expectations for the parse, you can activate the line and edit it. For example, you can change the data type or increase the width of a data block. In addition, you can use the letter S to instruct 1-2-3 to ignore a given data block.

4. When you are satisfied with the data structure represented by the format line, click the OK button to perform the parse. In response, 1-2-3 enters the data blocks into individual columns of the current worksheet. After you adjust the column widths of the worksheet appropriately, the database appears as shown in Figure 10.18. (In the parsing process, 1-2-3 may generate an extraneous copy of a long label at the bottom of the database. Select the cell containing this label and press the Delete key to eliminate it.) The first six columns of data have been entered as labels, and the final three as values. Notice in particular that 1-2-3 has converted the date strings from the text file into date numbers. You can now format these numbers as dates.

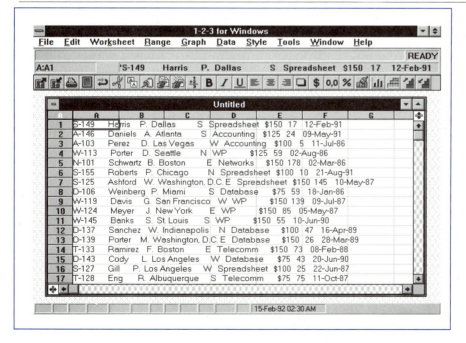

FIGURE 10.15:
The instructor database imported from a text file

By the way, the File Import From cascade menu contains two additional commands: Numbers and Styles. The File Import From Styles command reads styles and graphics from a variety of 1-2-3 format files, and applies those elements to the current worksheet. In contrast, the File Import From Numbers command reads data from a *delimited file*. A delimited file is a text file in which individual data values are separated by recognized delimiter characters, typically commas; and string values are enclosed in double quotation marks.

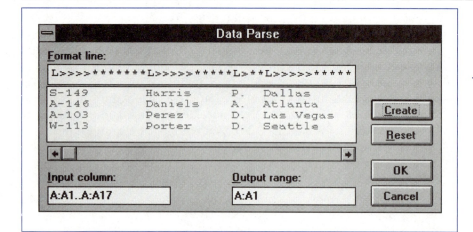

FIGURE 10.16:
The Data Parse dialog box, displaying a format line for the imported file

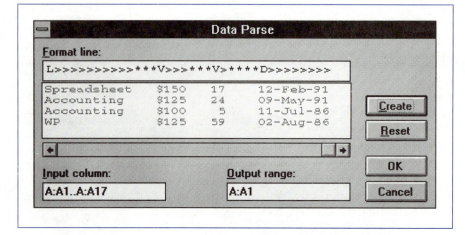

FIGURE 10.17:
Examining the format line

Figure 10.19 shows the instructor database as a delimited file. Data files in this format are created from a variety of software environments; in particular, this is a common way for a BASIC program to save information to disk when the data is meant to be read sequentially. The File Import From Numbers command reads a delimited file into the current worksheet, and enters the data values into individual cells. You do not need to use the Data Parse command after File Import From Numbers. However, if the delimited file includes date strings, 1-2-3 copies them to the worksheet as labels, as shown in Figure 10.20; no automatic conversion to date numbers takes place. You can use the @DATEVALUE command to perform this data conversion, as described back in Chapter 5.

	A	B	C	D	E	F	G	H	I
1	S-149	Harris	P.	Dallas	S	Spreadsheet	150	17	33281
2	A-146	Daniels	A.	Atlanta	S	Accounting	125	24	33367
3	A-103	Perez	D.	Las Vegas	W	Accounting	100	5	31604
4	W-113	Porter	D.	Seattle	N	WP	125	59	31626
5	N-101	Schwartz	B.	Boston	E	Networks	150	178	31473
6	S-155	Roberts	P.	Chicago	N	Spreadsheet	100	10	33471
7	S-125	Ashford	W.	Washington, D.C.	E	Spreadsheet	150	145	31907
8	D-106	Weinberg	P.	Miami	S	Database	75	59	31430
9	W-119	Davis	G.	San Francisco	W	WP	150	139	31967
10	W-124	Meyer	J.	New York	E	WP	150	85	31902
11	W-145	Banks	S.	St. Louis	S	WP	150	55	33034
12	D-137	Sanchez	W.	Indianapolis	N	Database	100	47	32614
13	D-139	Porter	M.	Washington, D.C.	E	Database	150	26	32595
14	T-133	Ramirez	F.	Boston	E	Telecomm	150	73	32181
15	D-143	Cody	L.	Los Angeles	W	Database	75	43	33044
16	S-127	Gill	P.	Los Angeles	W	Spreadsheet	100	25	31950
17	T-128	Eng	R.	Albuquerque	S	Telecomm	75	75	32061

FIGURE 10.18:
The parsed database

```
"S-149","Harris","P.","Dallas","S","Spreadsheet",150,17,"12-Feb-91"
"A-146","Daniels","A.","Atlanta","S","Accounting",125,24,"09-May-91"
"A-103","Perez","D.","Las Vegas","W","Accounting",100,5,"11-Jul-86"
"W-113","Porter","D.","Seattle","N","WP",125,59,"02-Aug-86"
"N-101","Schwartz","B.","Boston","E","Networks",150,178,"02-Mar-86"
"S-155","Roberts","P.","Chicago","N","Spreadsheet",100,10,"21-Aug-91"
"S-125","Ashford","W.","Washington, D.C.","E","Spreadsheet",150,145,"10-May-87"
"D-106","Weinberg","P.","Miami","S","Database",75,59,"18-Jan-86"
"W-119","Davis","G.","San Francisco","W","WP",150,139,"09-Jul-87"
"W-124","Meyer","J.","New York","E","WP",150,85,"05-May-87"
"W-145","Banks","S.","St. Louis","S","WP",150,55,"10-Jun-90"
"D-137","Sanchez","W.","Indianapolis","N","Database",100,47,"16-Apr-89"
"D-139","Porter","M.","Washington, D.C.","E","Database",150,26,"28-Mar-89"
"T-133","Ramirez","F.","Boston","E","Telecomm",150,73,"08-Feb-88"
"D-143","Cody","L.","Los Angeles","W","Database",75,43,"20-Jun-90"
"S-127","Gill","P.","Los Angeles","W","Spreadsheet",100,25,"22-Jun-87"
"T-128","Eng","R.","Albuquerque","S","Telecomm",75,75,"11-Oct-87"
```

FIGURE 10.19:
The database as a delimited file

USING THE
DATA DISTRIBUTION COMMAND

The Data Distribution command counts the number of worksheet entries that fall within specified numeric categories. To prepare for this command, you begin by entering a progression of numbers into a column of the worksheet; these numbers, known as the *bin range,* express the numeric intervals into which you want to distribute the worksheet values. Then you select the *values range,* or the range of worksheet values that are to be the subject of the frequency distribution. Given these two ranges, the Data Distribution command creates a new column of numbers representing the frequency count.

For example, Figure 10.21 shows a use of this command in the instructor database. Several fields in the database have been temporarily hidden from view (using the Worksheet Hide command), and the Yrs field has been reformatted to display two places after the decimal point. In addition, the instructor database appears in Worksheet A in this example. As you'll recall, Yrs is a calculated field that shows the number of years each instructor has been working for Computing Conferences, Inc. The purpose of this particular worksheet is to count the number of instructors whose length of employment falls within each of several categories: one year or less; two years or less, but more than a year; three years or less, but more than two years; and so on. The bin range representing these categories appears in M7..M12.

	A	B	C	D	E	F	G	H	I
1	S-149	Harris	P.	Dallas	S	Spreadsheet	150	17	12-Feb-91
2	A-146	Daniels	A.	Atlanta	S	Accounting	125	24	09-May-91
3	A-103	Perez	D.	Las Vegas	W	Accounting	100	5	11-Jul-86
4	W-113	Porter	D.	Seattle	N	WP	125	59	02-Aug-86
5	N-101	Schwartz	B.	Boston	E	Networks	150	178	02-Mar-86
6	S-155	Roberts	P.	Chicago	N	Spreadsheet	100	10	21-Aug-91
7	S-125	Ashford	W.	Washington, D.C.	E	Spreadsheet	150	145	10-May-87
8	D-106	Weinberg	P.	Miami	S	Database	75	59	18-Jan-86
9	W-119	Davis	G.	San Francisco	W	WP	150	139	09-Jul-87
10	W-124	Meyer	J.	New York	E	WP	150	85	05-May-87
11	W-145	Banks	S.	St. Louis	S	WP	150	55	10-Jun-90
12	D-137	Sanchez	W.	Indianapolis	N	Database	100	47	16-Apr-89
13	D-139	Porter	M.	Washington, D.C.	E	Database	150	26	28-Mar-89
14	T-133	Ramirez	F.	Boston	E	Telecomm	150	73	08-Feb-88
15	D-143	Cody	L.	Los Angeles	W	Database	75	43	20-Jun-90
16	S-127	Gill	P.	Los Angeles	W	Spreadsheet	100	25	22-Jun-87
17	T-128	Eng	R.	Albuquerque	S	Telecomm	75	75	11-Oct-87

FIGURE 10.20:

The database imported from a delimited file

Once you have established the bin range, using the Data Distribution command is simple. Here are the steps to produce the frequency distribution shown in N7..N13:

1. Preselect the values range, in this case the data in the Yrs field, J4..J20.

2. Pull down the Data menu and choose the Distribution command. The preselected values range appears in the Values text box.

3. Enter the bin range as A:M7..A:M12 in the Bin text box, as shown in Figure 10.22.

4. Click OK to complete the operation.

This command enters the frequency distribution into the column located immediately to the right of the bin range. In Figure 10.21, you can see that there are three instructors who have worked for one year or less; two instructors who have worked between one and two years; and so on. In addition, you'll notice that the frequency distribution range contains one more entry than the bin range. The final entry shows the number of value-range entries found to be greater than the last entry in the bin range. In this example, there is one instructor who has worked for more than six years.

FIGURE 10.21:

Using the Data Distribution command

	A	B	C	J	L	M	N	O	P
1		Instructor Database							
2									
3	ID	Last	First	Yrs		Frequency Distribution:			
4	S-149	Harris	P.	0.97					
5	A-146	Daniels	A.	0.73		Years as	Number of		
6	A-103	Perez	D.	5.56		Instructor	Instructors		
7	W-113	Porter	D.	5.50		1	3		
8	N-101	Schwartz	B.	5.92		2	2		
9	S-155	Roberts	P.	0.45		3	2		
10	S-125	Ashford	W.	4.73		4	1		
11	D-106	Weinberg	P.	6.04		5	5		
12	W-119	Davis	G.	4.57		6	3		
13	W-124	Meyer	J.	4.75			1		
14	W-145	Banks	S.	1.64					
15	D-137	Sanchez	W.	2.79					
16	D-139	Porter	M.	2.85					
17	T-133	Ramirez	F.	3.98					
18	D-143	Cody	L.	1.62					
19	S-127	Gill	P.	4.61					
20	T-128	Eng	R.	4.31					

USING THE DATA REGRESSION COMMAND

Regression analysis is an attempt to discover the strength of the mathematical correlation between two or more sets of data. For example, column B of the worksheet in Figure 10.23 shows the amount that Computing Conferences, Inc. has spent on advertising for several recent computer-training conferences; and column C shows the attendance at those same conferences. The general question posed by this worksheet is clear: Does attendance go up when the company spends more money on advertising? Or, in other words, is there a correlation between advertising and attendance? In an analysis of this particular example, attendance is referred to as the *dependent variable,* because the goal of the analysis will be to discover the extent to which attendance depends on advertising. Accordingly, advertising is called the *independent variable*.

You might recall working with this same data in Chapter 6, while you were studying the variety of 1-2-3 graph types. Specifically, Figure 6.43 displays an XY graph in which advertising dollars are plotted against attendance in an x-y coordinate system. This graph seems to show a relationship between the two data sets. In effect, an XY graph is a pictorial form of regression analysis. Suppose you were to draw a straight diagonal line somewhere through the middle of the plotted points in Figure 6.43; you might then formulate an approximate equation describing the relationship between advertising and attendance. The general equation for a straight line is

$$y = mx + b$$

where y is the dependent variable; x is the independent variable; m is the slope of the straight line that represents the relationship; and b is the y-intercept, or the value of y when x is zero. To the extent that the equation you

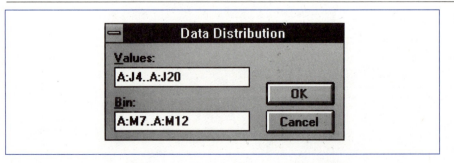

FIGURE 10.22:

The Data Distribution dialog box

develop is a reliable description of the relationship between the two variables, you can use this equation to make predictions about the dependent variable.

The Data Regression command performs this same kind of analysis, but produces specific mathematical results rather than graphic approximations. Data Regression allows you to select a range containing one or more independent variables (known as the X-range) and one dependent variable (known as the Y-range). In addition, you specify an output range on your worksheet, where the command can display the results of its analysis.

Figure 10.24 shows the Data Regression dialog box, filled in with appropriate ranges for an analysis of the advertising and attendance worksheet. The X-range text box displays a reference to the range of advertising data in column B; and the Y-range text box displays a reference to the range of attendance data in column C. Cell A:E5 is specified as the upper-left corner of the output range. In addition, the Y-intercept box presents two option buttons, giving you a choice between calculating the actual y-intercept (the Compute button) or hypothesizing a value of zero for the y-intercept (the Set to zero button). For the advertising and attendance data, you want 1-2-3 to calculate the actual y intercept; in theory, this value represents the expected attendance level when no money is spent on advertising.

FIGURE 10.23:
Advertising and attendance data

	A	B	C
1	Computing Conferences, Inc.		
2	Attendance and Advertising		
3	Computing for Video Stores		
4			
5	Date	Advertising	Attendance
6	09-Jan-91	$5,000.00	154
7	21-Jan-91	$3,500.00	119
8	15-Feb-91	$6,000.00	174
9	07-Mar-91	$6,000.00	201
10	25-Mar-91	$3,500.00	136
11	03-Apr-91	$5,000.00	172
12	11-May-91	$3,500.00	112
13	28-May-91	$1,000.00	97
14	03-Jun-91	$1,000.00	86
15	29-Jun-91	$1,000.00	104
16	05-Sep-91	$7,500.00	235
17	11-Oct-91	$1,500.00	119
18	29-Oct-91	$2,500.00	137
19	05-Nov-91	$3,500.00	148

In Figure 10.25, you see the results of the regression analysis. At the top of the output table, the Constant value (displayed as *74.83875* in cell H6) is the y-intercept. Near the bottom of the table, the X Coefficient(s) value (displayed as *0.018738* in cell G12) is the slope of the line that theoretically describes the relationship between the two variables. Rounding these two values, you can formulate the equation for the line as

$$y = 0.019x + 75$$

or as

$$\text{attendance} = 0.019 * \text{advertising} + 75$$

You can substitute actual advertising amounts into this equation to calculate the corresponding attendance projection. For example, according to this equation, attendance should be at a level of 75 people when no money is spent on advertising, or approximately 150 people when $4,000 is spent.

The Data Regression command also displays output values that tell you the extent to which you can rely on this particular regression analysis as a tool for predicting the behavior of the dependent variable:

◆ The R Squared value is a general measurement of the reliability of the analysis. For a strong correlation between the dependent and

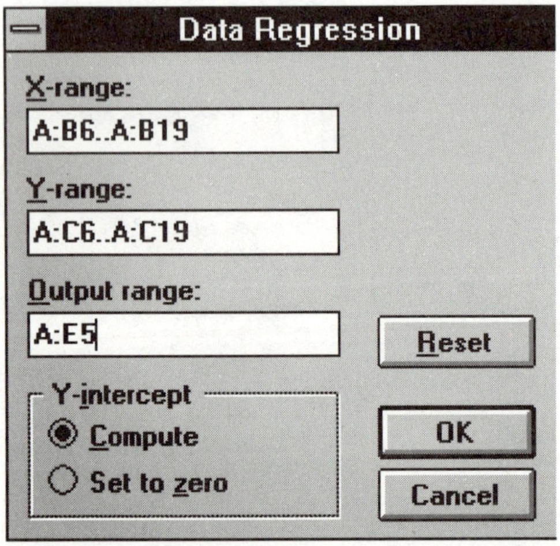

FIGURE 10.24:

The Data Regression dialog box

independent variables, the *R Squared* value is close to 1; for a weak correlation, the value is close to zero.

◆ The value labeled Std Err of Y Est (standard error of the *y* estimate) indicates the range of accuracy for calculated values of *y*. In Figure 10.25, the Std Err of Y Est value is approximately 16. This implies that any attendance value you calculate from the equation is accurate within a range of plus or minus 16.

◆ The value labeled Std Err of Coef. (standard error of the *x* coefficient) indicates the reliability of the slope calculation. The smaller this value is in relation to the X Coefficient(s), the better the reliability.

USING THE DATA WHAT-IF TABLE COMMANDS

The Data What-if Table commands are a group of remarkably efficient tools for exploring multiple "what-if" scenarios on a worksheet. For example, consider the worksheet shown in Figure 10.26, an abbreviated form of the conference worksheet that you developed in Chapters 3 and 4. As you may recall, most of the formulas on this worksheet depend directly or indirectly on the values entered for the attendance level and the per-person attendance price. In Figure 10.26, these two key values appear in cells B4 and B5, respectively. By changing the values in one or both of these cells, you

	A	B	C	D	E	F	G	H
1	Computing Conferences, Inc.							
2	Attendance and Advertising							
3	Computing for Video Stores							
4								
5		Date	Advertising	Attendance		Regression Output:		
6		09-Jan-91	$5,000.00	154	Constant			74.83875
7		21-Jan-91	$3,500.00	119	Std Err of Y Est			15.7763
8		15-Feb-91	$6,000.00	174	R Squared			0.869322
9		07-Mar-91	$6,000.00	201	No. of Observations			14
10		25-Mar-91	$3,500.00	136	Degrees of Freedom			12
11		03-Apr-91	$5,000.00	172				
12		11-May-91	$3,500.00	112	X Coefficient(s)		0.018738	
13		28-May-91	$1,000.00	97	Std Err of Coef.		0.002097	
14		03-Jun-91	$1,000.00	86				
15		29-Jun-91	$1,000.00	104				
16		05-Sep-91	$7,500.00	235				
17		11-Oct-91	$1,500.00	119				
18		29-Oct-91	$2,500.00	137				
19		05-Nov-91	$3,500.00	148				
20								

FIGURE 10.25:

The output from the Data Regression command

can explore individual changes in the bottom-line profit (cell H19) under different projections for attendance and price.

But in some applications you may want to build an entire table of what-if projections. For example, in the conference worksheet you might want to examine a table of profit calculations for a range of attendance and price levels, as shown in Figure 10.27. To create this table manually, you would have to enter many different values into cells B4 and B5 of the worksheet, and then copy each of the resulting profit calculations from cell H19 to your table. Fortunately, this is exactly the kind of task that the Data What-if Table commands are designed to automate. Pull down the Data menu now and choose the What-if Table command; on the resulting cascade menu (shown in Figure 10.28), you can see the three types of what-if tables that are available: 1-Way, 2-Way, and 3-Way. The profit table in Figure 10.27 is an example of a two-way what-if table, which you'll learn to create shortly.

For several of the remaining exercises in this chapter, you'll need your own copy of the shortened conference worksheet. If you wish, you can create this new version by reentering all the data and formulas into a new worksheet; if you choose this approach, Figure 10.29 shows the formulas you should enter into column H. Save this new file as CONF2.WK3.

Alternatively, you can copy a range of data from the original CONF.WK3 file, and then reformat and reorganize the worksheet to match Figure 10.26. The File Combine From command is a useful tool in this task. The command

FIGURE 10.26:

A shortened version of the conference worksheet

	A	B	C	D	E	F	G	H
1	Computing for Video Stores			Projected Revenues				
2	Place:	St. Louis			Attendance			$12,675.00
3	Date:	15-Oct-92			Video Sales		$35.00	$1,137.50
4	Attendance:	65			Total Revenues			$13,812.50
5	Price:	$195.00						
6				Projected Expenses -- Fixed				
7					Conference room			$1,500.00
8					Video production			$1,000.00
9					Promotion			$3,500.00
10					Travel			$800.00
11					Total Fixed Expenses			$6,800.00
12								
13				Projected Expenses -- Variable by Attendance				
14					Conference materials		$8.25	$536.25
15					Coffee and pastries		$3.25	$211.25
16					Box lunch		$4.75	$308.75
17					Total Variable Expenses			$1,056.25
18								
19				Projected Profit				$5,956.25
20								

copies data to the current worksheet window from a worksheet file stored on disk. Here is an outline of this approach:

1. If necessary, choose the File New command to open a new blank worksheet.

2. Pull down the File menu and choose the Combine From command. Use the Drives and Directories boxes to find the directory location of the CONF.WK3 file, and then select the file in the Files list box. In the Action box, keep the default Copy option. (This option simply copies data from the file on disk. The File Combine From command can also perform arithmetic operations that combine data read from disk with data in the current worksheet.)

3. In the Source box, select the Range option, and enter **A5..F34** as the CONF.WK3 range from which to copy data. At this point, the File Combine From dialog box is similar to Figure 10.30; click OK to

FIGURE 10.27:
A profit table, with varying price and attendance projections

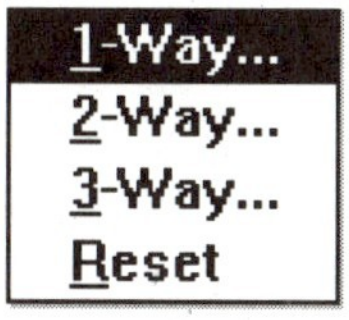

	A	B	C	D	E
1	Profits		Price		
2			$145.00	$170.00	$195.00
3	Attendance	65	$2,706.25	$4,331.25	$5,956.25
4		75	$4,168.75	$6,043.75	$7,918.75
5		85	$5,631.25	$7,756.25	$9,881.25
6		95	$7,093.75	$9,468.75	$11,843.75
7		105	$8,556.25	$11,181.25	$13,806.25
8		115	$10,018.75	$12,893.75	$15,768.75
9		125	$11,481.25	$14,606.25	$17,731.25
10					

FIGURE 10.28:
The Data What-if Table cascade menu

1-Way...
2-Way...
3-Way...
Reset

complete the operation. In response, 1-2-3 copies the data from CONF.WK3 to your current worksheet.

4. Use the Worksheet Delete command to delete the final column of data and to delete extra blank rows from the worksheet. Enter the label **Attendance:** in cell A4. Then use the range-move icon to move ranges of data to their new positions on the worksheet, as shown in Figure 10.26. In particular, when you move the minimum attendance amount to its new position in cell B4, 1-2-3 makes the appropriate adjustments in all the worksheet's formulas. Confirm that these adjustments have been made correctly by entering a new attendance projection of **65** in cell B4; in response, 1-2-3 recalculates the worksheet formulas that depend on this value, including the bottom-line profit. (In the end, the formulas in column H should be essentially the same as those shown in Figure 10.29, although you might see some variations in the reference formats.)

5. To complete your work, apply the appropriate formats and styles to the worksheet. Then choose the File Save As command and save the file on disk as CONF2.WK3.

Now you are ready to begin experimenting with the Data What-if Table commands.

FIGURE 10.29:

The formulas on the shortened conference worksheet

A	D	E	F	G	H	I
1	Projected Revenues:					
2		Attendance			+B4*B5	
3		Video Sales		$35.00	+G3*B4/2	
4		Total Revenues			@SUM(H2..H3)	
5						
6	Projected Expenses -- Fixed					
7		Conference room			1500	
8		Video production			1000	
9		Promotion			3500	
10		Travel			800	
11		Total Fixed Expenses			@SUM(H7..H10)	
12						
13	Projected Expenses -- Variable by Attendance					
14		Conference materials		$8.25	+$G14*$B$4	
15		Coffee and pastries		$3.25	+$G15*$B$4	
16		Box lunch		$4.75	+$G16*$B$4	
17		Total Variable Expenses			@SUM(H14..H16)	
18						
19	Projected Profit				+H4-(H11+H17)	

CREATING A ONE-WAY WHAT-IF TABLE

To create a one-way what-if table, you must be prepared to supply 1-2-3 with three kinds of information:

- A column of input values that 1-2-3 can insert one at a time into the worksheet calculations
- The input location where these values should be entered
- The formula that 1-2-3 should recalculate after each new input entry

For example, Figure 10.31 shows a range of attendance projections in A10..A18. The goal of the upcoming operation is to display the profit amounts corresponding to each of these attendance values. To produce this information, 1-2-3 needs to insert each of the attendance figures into the input cell, B4, and then recalculate the formula that gives the profit. Accordingly, cell B9 contains a copy of the profit formula: +H4−(H11+H17), or the total revenues minus the sum of the fixed and variable expenses.

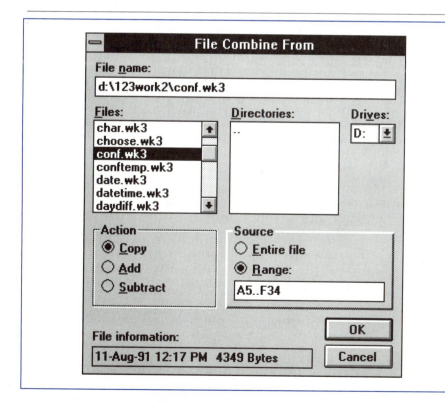

FIGURE 10.30:
The File Combine From dialog box

You can use the Data What-if Table 1-Way command successfully only after you enter the column of input values and the target formula. Here are the steps for producing the table:

1. Use the Data Fill command to enter integer values from **45** to **125** in step increments of **10** into the range A10..A18. Enter the formula **+H4−(H11+H17)** into cell B9. Choose the Range Format command and select the Text format for this cell, so you can see the formula itself. Enter the labels **Attendance** and **Profit** into cells A8 and B8, respectively. Right-justify the label in B8, and apply the Bold style to cells A8, B8, and B9. Preselect the range B10..B18 and click the currency icon.

2. Preselect the range A9..B18. Then pull down the Data menu and choose the What-if Table command. In the resulting cascade menu, choose the 1-Way command. The Data What-if Table 1-Way dialog box appears on the screen.

3. Enter a reference to cell **B4** in the Input cell text box. The dialog box now appears as shown in Figure 10.32. Click OK to confirm. Back on the worksheet, move the cell pointer to A7, out of the way of the what-if table.

4. Choose the File Save As command and save this worksheet as TABLES.WK3. (The original file, named CONF2.WK3, remains unchanged on disk for upcoming exercises.)

	A	B	C	D	E	F	G	H
1	Computing for Video Stores			Projected Revenues				
2	Place:	St. Louis			Attendance			$12,675.00
3	Date:	15-Oct-92			Video Sales		$35.00	$1,137.50
4	Attendance:	65			Total Revenues			$13,812.50
5	Price:	$195.00						
6					Projected Expenses -- Fixed			
7					Conference room			$1,500.00
8	Attendance	Profit			Video production			$1,000.00
9		+H4-(H11+H17)			Promotion			$3,500.00
10	45				Travel			$800.00
11	55				Total Fixed Expenses			$6,800.00
12	65							
13	75				Projected Expenses -- Variable by Attendance			
14	85				Conference materials		$8.25	$536.25
15	95				Coffee and pastries		$3.25	$211.25
16	105				Box lunch		$4.75	$308.75
17	115				Total Variable Expenses			$1,056.25
18	125							
19					Projected Profit			$5,956.25
20								

FIGURE 10.31:
Preparing for the Data What-if Table 1-Way command

As a result of these steps, 1-2-3 fills in the what-if table with a range of profit calculations in B10..B18, as you can see in Figure 10.33. Each of these figures represents the value that would appear in cell H19 of the worksheet if you were to enter the corresponding attendance value into cell B4. The Data What-if Table 1-Way command has generated the entire column of figures in a single operation.

This command also allows you to create what-if tables for more than one formula at a time. For example, suppose you want to add a column to display the variable expenses corresponding to each of the projected attendance levels. As shown in Figure 10.34, you enter the formula **@SUM(H14..H16)** into cell C9 to accomplish this. Then preselect the range A9..C18, and choose the

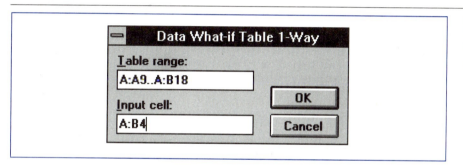

FIGURE 10.32:

The Data What-if Table 1-Way dialog box

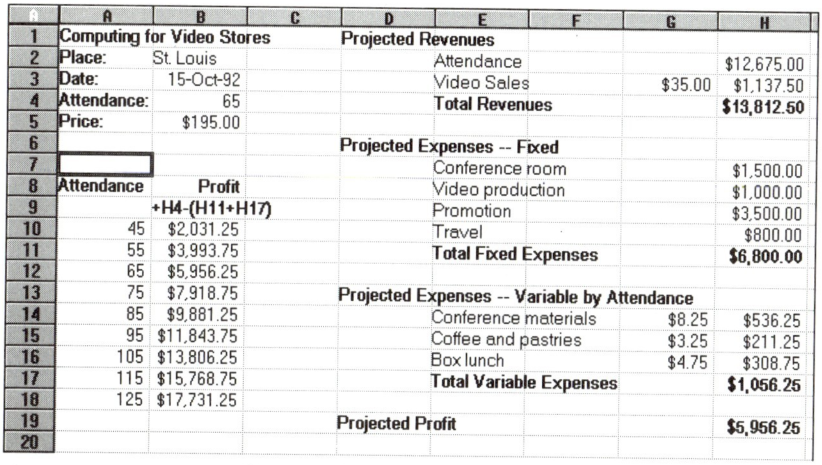

FIGURE 10.33:

Creating the what-if table

Data What-if Table 1-Way command again. Specify **B4** as the input cell, and click OK. The formatted results of this second formula appear in the range C10..C18.

Using the F8 Function Key to Recalculate a What-If Table

The entries that 1-2-3 places in the what-if table are values, not formulas; they are therefore not subject to automatic recalculation when you make changes on the worksheet. However, 1-2-3 gives you a convenient way to repeat the last Data What-if Table command: Simply press the F8 function key. For example, suppose you make some changes in the column of input values in A10..A18. After you revise the entries in this range, you can press F8 to produce a new version of the what-if table.

Try this exercise with the F8 key:

1. Use the Data Fill command to enter a new range of attendance projections into A10..A18—values from **60** to **220** in increments of **20**.

	A	B	C
1	Computing for Video Stores		Proje
2	Place:	St. Louis	
3	Date:	15-Oct-92	
4	Attendance:	65	
5	Price:	$195.00	
6			Proje
7			
8	Attendance	Profit	Var. Exp.
9		+H4-(H11+H17)	@SUM(H14..H16)
10	45	$2,031.25	$731.25
11	55	$3,993.75	$893.75
12	65	$5,956.25	$1,056.25
13	75	$7,918.75	$1,218.75 Proje
14	85	$9,881.25	$1,381.25
15	95	$11,843.75	$1,543.75
16	105	$13,806.25	$1,706.25
17	115	$15,768.75	$1,868.75
18	125	$17,731.25	$2,031.25

FIGURE 10.34:

A one-way what-if table with two formulas

2. Press the F8 function key. The new what-if table appears as shown in Figure 10.35.

You can disable the F8 function key by choosing the Data What-if Table Reset command. Use this command to clear the Data What-if Table 1-Way dialog box when you have produced the final version of the current what-if table.

CREATING TWO-WAY AND THREE-WAY WHAT-IF TABLES

You can also produce what-if tables that calculate formulas in response to changes in two or three input cells. The 2-Way and 3-Way commands in the Data What-if Table cascade menu are the tools you use for these tasks.

To prepare a two-way table, you begin by entering a column of values for the first input cell, and a row of values for the second input cell. For example, suppose you want to generate a profit table for a range of attendance projections and a range of prices. To do so, you enter the attendance values down a column, just as you did for the one-way table. Then you enter the

	A	B	C
1	Computing for Video Stores		Proje
2	Place:	St. Louis	
3	Date:	15-Oct-92	
4	Attendance:	65	
5	Price:	$195.00	
6			Proje
7			
8	Attendance	Profit	Var. Exp.
9		+H4-(H11+H17)	@SUM(H14..H16)
10	60	$4,975.00	$975.00
11	80	$8,900.00	$1,300.00
12	100	$12,825.00	$1,625.00
13	120	$16,750.00	$1,950.00 Proje
14	140	$20,675.00	$2,275.00
15	160	$24,600.00	$2,600.00
16	180	$28,525.00	$2,925.00
17	200	$32,450.00	$3,250.00
18	220	$36,375.00	$3,575.00

FIGURE 10.35:
Using the F8 function key

range of prices across a row at the top of the table range. In the upper-left corner cell of the table range, you enter the formula that 1-2-3 will use for calculating the what-if table.

In the following exercise, you'll generate a two-way what-if table in worksheet B of TABLES.WK3:

1. Choose the Worksheet Insert command and select the Sheet option. Click OK to add worksheet B to TABLES.WK3.

2. In cell B:B2, enter the formula **+A:H4−(A:H11+A:H17)**. Choose the Range Format command, select the Text option, and click OK to display the formula itself in the cell. Apply the bold style to the cell, and widen column B so that the entire formula is displayed within the width of the column.

3. Enter **Prices** as a right-aligned label in B:C1. Then enter **Attendance** into cell B:A3. Apply the boldface style to both labels.

4. Use the Data Fill command to enter a column of attendance projections into the range B:B3..B:B12—values from **45** to **135** in increments of **10**. Then use Data Fill again to enter a row of prices in the range B:C2..B:G2—values from **145** to **245** in increments of **25**. Preselect the range B:C2..B:G12 and click the currency icon.

5. Preselect the range B:B2..B:G12. Pull down the Data menu and choose the What-if Table command. Then choose the 2-Way command from the resulting cascade menu. The preselected range appears in the Table range text box. Enter **A:B4** as the reference for Input cell 1, and **A:B5** as the reference for Input cell 2, as shown in Figure 10.36. Click OK to confirm.

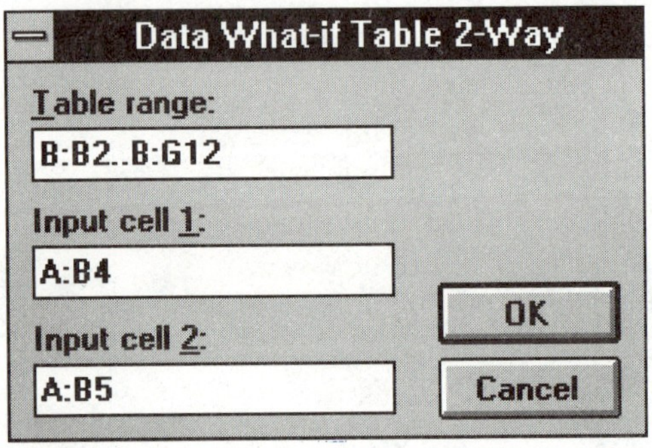

FIGURE 10.36:

The Data What-if Table 2-Way dialog box

Figure 10.37 shows the resulting two-way what-if table. As you can see, 1-2-3 has calculated 50 different what-if scenarios in the conference worksheet. The profit figures resulting from these scenarios are displayed in the range B:C3..B:G12.

A three-way what-if table is organized over a three-dimensional worksheet range. Each worksheet in the range contains a column of entries for the first input cell and a row of entries for the second input cell, just as in a two-way table. But instead of entering a formula in the upper-left corner of the table, you enter a value for the third input cell. Each worksheet in the three-dimensional range displays a different value in this cell. You then specify the formula for the what-if table in the Data What-if Table 3-Way dialog box rather than in the table range itself.

For example, worksheets C, D, and E in Figure 10.38 are prepared for a three-way what-if table. The purpose of this example is to generate profit scenarios by varying the values in three input cells: the attendance estimate (A:B4), the per-person admission price (A:B5), and the cost of renting a conference room (A:H7). The range B3..B7 on each of the three worksheets displays the same column of attendance projections, and the range C2..G2 displays the same row of conference prices. But cell B2 in each worksheet contains a different dollar amount for the conference room rental.

Here are the steps for creating this three-way what-if table in your own copy of the TABLES.WK3 worksheet:

1. With the cell pointer located in worksheet B, choose the Worksheet Insert command and select the Sheet option. Enter **3** in the Quantity box, and click OK. Click the perspective-view icon to view worksheets C, D, and E together in a single window.

B	A	B	C	D	E	F	G
1			Prices				
2		+A:H4-(A:H11+A:H17)	$145.00	$170.00	$195.00	$220.00	$245.00
3	Attendance	45	($218.75)	$906.25	$2,031.25	$3,156.25	$4,281.25
4		55	$1,243.75	$2,618.75	$3,993.75	$5,368.75	$6,743.75
5		65	$2,706.25	$4,331.25	$5,956.25	$7,581.25	$9,206.25
6		75	$4,168.75	$6,043.75	$7,918.75	$9,793.75	$11,668.75
7		85	$5,631.25	$7,756.25	$9,881.25	$12,006.25	$14,131.25
8		95	$7,093.75	$9,468.75	$11,843.75	$14,218.75	$16,593.75
9		105	$8,556.25	$11,181.25	$13,806.25	$16,431.25	$19,056.25
10		115	$10,018.75	$12,893.75	$15,768.75	$18,643.75	$21,518.75
11		125	$11,481.25	$14,606.25	$17,731.25	$20,856.25	$23,981.25
12		135	$12,943.75	$16,318.75	$19,693.75	$23,068.75	$26,443.75
13							

FIGURE 10.37:

A two-way what-if table

2. Enter the labels and values into worksheet C, and format them as they appear in Figure 10.38. Then use the copy-to-clipboard and paste-from-clipboard icons to copy the contents of worksheet C to worksheets D and E. Enter a new value of **$2,000.00** into cell D:B2 and a new value of **$2,500.00** into cell E:B2.

3. Preselect the three-dimensional range C:B2..E:G7. To do so, begin by selecting the two-dimensional range C:B2..C:G7 on worksheet C; then hold down the Shift and Ctrl keys while you press the PgUp key twice. When you release all the keys, the selection appears as in Figure 10.39.

4. Pull down the Data menu and choose the What-if Table command. On the resulting cascade menu, choose the 3-Way command. The preselected three-dimensional range appears in the Table range text box. Enter **A:H19** into the Formula cell text box; this is a reference to the profit formula in worksheet A. Then enter **A:B4** in the Input cell 1 box, **A:B5** in the Input cell 2 box, and **A:H7** in the Input cell 3 box. These are references to the attendance projection, the per-person admission price, and the conference room cost, respectively. When you finish all these entries, the Data What-if Table 3-Way dialog box appears as shown in Figure 10.40.

5. Click OK to confirm the entries in the dialog box. Back in the worksheet, preselect the three-dimensional range C:C3..E:G7 and click the currency icon. Then press the Home key to position the cell pointer at C:A1.

FIGURE 10.38:
Preparing for a three-way what-if table

	A	B	C	D	E	F	G	H
1		Room:						
2		$2,500.00	$145.00	$170.00	$195.00	$220.00	$245.00	
3	Attendance	65						
4		85						
5		105						
6		125						

	A	B	C	D	E	F	G	H
1		Room:						
2		$2,000.00	$145.00	$170.00	$195.00	$220.00	$245.00	
3	Attendance	65						
4		85						
5		105						
6		125						

	A	B	C	D	E	F	G	H
1		Room:						
2		$1,500.00	$145.00	$170.00	$195.00	$220.00	$245.00	
3	Attendance	65						
4		85						
5		105						
6		125						
7		145						

6. Click the save-file icon to update the TABLES.WK3 file on disk.

Figure 10.41 shows the three-way what-if table that 1-2-3 creates in response to these steps. In this example, 1-2-3 has calculated 75 different scenarios of the conference worksheet, and has copied the profit figure from each scenario to the three-way what-if table.

In the final sections of this chapter, you'll look at examples of two powerful commands in the Tools menu: Tools Backsolver and Tools Solver.

USING THE TOOLS BACKSOLVER COMMAND

The Backsolver is a simple but valuable tool to use when you want to work backward through a worksheet scenario—specifically, when you have determined a bottom-line figure as your projection or goal, and you want to discover the input value necessary to achieve this goal. For example, suppose you want to find the attendance level necessary to yield a total profit of $10,000 on the CONF2.WK3 worksheet. One way to find the correct attendance value would be to experiment with new entries in cell B4 until you find the value that gives a profit of $10,000. But this trial-and-error approach could be time consuming.

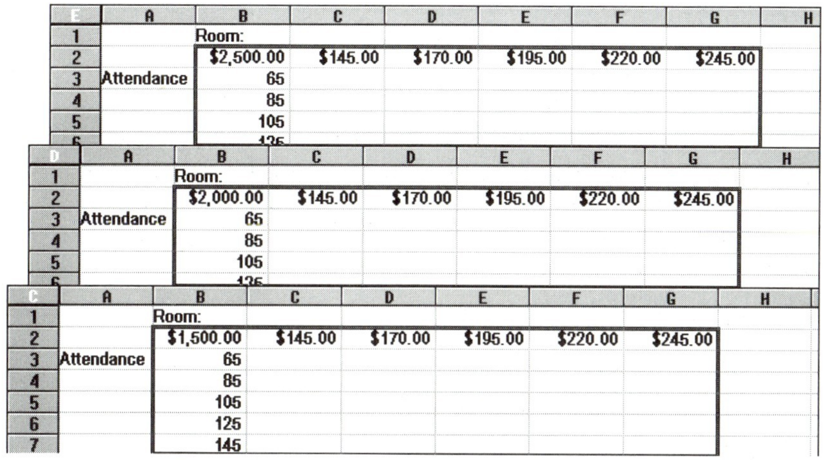

FIGURE 10.39:
Preselecting the three-dimensional range

The 1-2-3 Backsolver performs this task for you much more efficiently. To use this command successfully, you supply three items of information:

- ◆ A worksheet cell that contains the target formula for the Backsolver operation
- ◆ The projected value that you want this formula to yield
- ◆ The cell containing the input value that 1-2-3 will adjust in order to achieve the specified result from the target formula

In the following exercise, you'll experiment with the Backsolver on the CONF2.WK3 worksheet:

1. Close the TABLES.WK3 worksheet, and reopen the CONF2.WK3 worksheet from disk.

2. Pull down the Tools menu and choose the Backsolver command.

3. In the Make cell text box, enter a reference to **A:H19**, the cell that contains the profit formula. Then enter **10000** in the Equal to value text box; this is the value that you want the profit formula to yield. Finally, in the By changing cell text box, enter a reference to cell **A:B4**, which contains the current attendance projection; this is

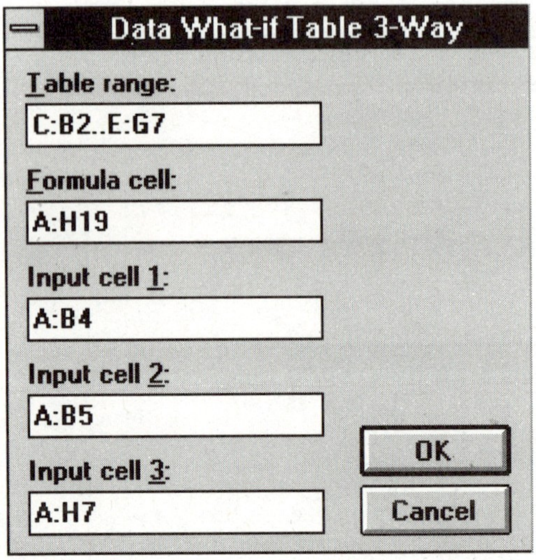

FIGURE 10.40:
The Data What-if Table 3-Way dialog box

the cell that you want 1-2-3 to adjust, in order to achieve the desired profit projection. When you complete these three entries, the Backsolver dialog box appears as shown in Figure 10.42.

4. Click Solve to perform the Backsolver operation. Back on the worksheet, select cell B4 and click the comma-format icon to display the contents of the cell as an integer if this is not already its format.

When you complete this operation, the worksheet looks like Figure 10.43. As you can see, an attendance level of about 86 people is necessary to achieve a profit of $10,000.

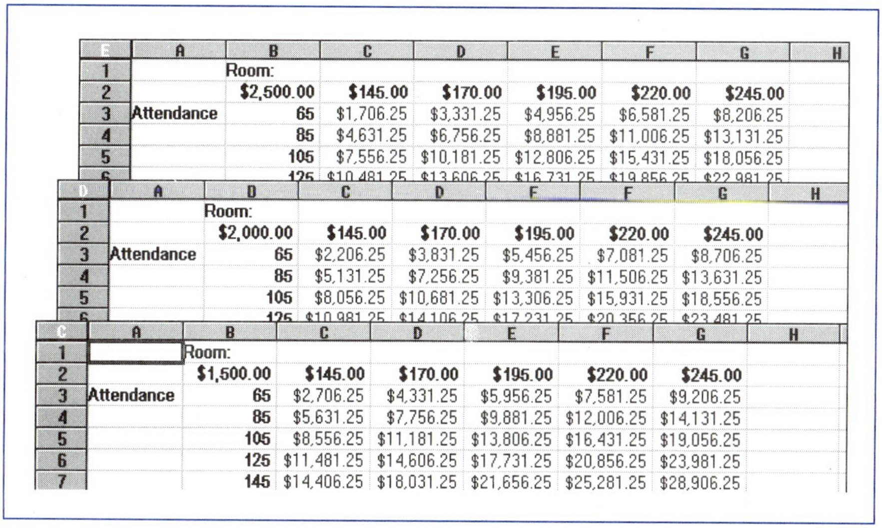

E	A	B	C	D	E	F	G	H
1		Room:						
2		$2,500.00	$145.00	$170.00	$195.00	$220.00	$245.00	
3	Attendance	65	$1,706.25	$3,331.25	$4,956.25	$6,581.25	$8,206.25	
4		85	$4,631.25	$6,756.25	$8,881.25	$11,006.25	$13,131.25	
5		105	$7,556.25	$10,181.25	$12,806.25	$15,431.25	$18,056.25	
6		125	$10,481.25	$13,606.25	$16,731.25	$19,856.25	$22,981.25	

D	A	B	C	D	E	F	G	H
1		Room:						
2		$2,000.00	$145.00	$170.00	$195.00	$220.00	$245.00	
3	Attendance	65	$2,206.25	$3,831.25	$5,456.25	$7,081.25	$8,706.25	
4		85	$5,131.25	$7,256.25	$9,381.25	$11,506.25	$13,631.25	
5		105	$8,056.25	$10,681.25	$13,306.25	$15,931.25	$18,556.25	
6		125	$10,981.25	$14,106.25	$17,231.25	$20,356.25	$23,481.25	

C	A	B	C	D	E	F	G	H
1		Room:						
2		$1,500.00	$145.00	$170.00	$195.00	$220.00	$245.00	
3	Attendance	65	$2,706.25	$4,331.25	$5,956.25	$7,581.25	$9,206.25	
4		85	$5,631.25	$7,756.25	$9,881.25	$12,006.25	$14,131.25	
5		105	$8,556.25	$11,181.25	$13,806.25	$16,431.25	$19,056.25	
6		125	$11,481.25	$14,606.25	$17,731.25	$20,856.25	$23,981.25	
7		145	$14,406.25	$18,031.25	$21,656.25	$25,281.25	$28,906.25	

FIGURE 10.41:
A three-way what-if table

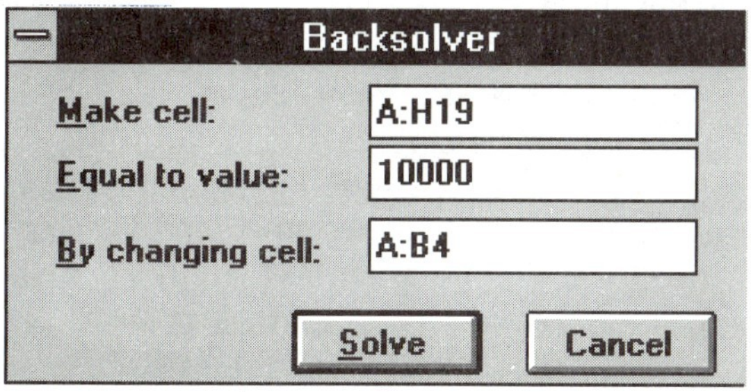

FIGURE 10.42:
The Backsolver dialog box

USING THE SOLVER

The Tools Solver command is designed to calculate meaningful variations in a worksheet, in response to specific patterns that you formulate. You typically use this command on worksheets that contain interrelated formulas of some complexity. To set up a successful problem for the solver, you identify the following elements in your worksheet:

- Cells containing numeric values that you want the Solver to modify. These are called the *adjustable cells*.

- A range of cells containing logical formulas. You write these formulas to impose limits on the changes that the Solver can make in the adjustable values. The cells containing these logical formulas are known as the *constraint cells*.

- Optionally, a formula for which you want to find the optimum result within the constraints defined on your worksheet. The cell containing this formula is known as the *optimal cell*.

For example, consider Figure 10.44, a worksheet from one of the regional offices of Computing Conferences, Inc. To conduct its computer-training conferences, this office uses instructors who are full-time employees of the company, along with other instructors who work for the company on a short-term contractual basis. This worksheet analyzes the costs related to these two

FIGURE 10.43:
Using the Backsolver

	A	B	C	D	E	F	G	H
1	Computing for Video Stores			Projected Revenues:				
2	Place:	St. Louis			Attendance			$16,692.99
3	Date:	15-Oct-92			Video Sales		$35.00	$1,498.09
4	Attendance:	86			Total Revenues			$18,191.08
5	Price:	$195.00						
6				Projected Expenses -- Fixed				
7					Conference room			$1,500.00
8					Video production			$1,000.00
9					Promotion			$3,500.00
10					Travel			$800.00
11					Total Fixed Expenses			$6,800.00
12								
13				Projected Expenses -- Variable by Attendance				
14					Conference materials		$8.25	$706.24
15					Coffee and pastries		$3.25	$278.22
16					Box lunch		$4.75	$406.62
17					Total Variable Expenses			$1,391.08
18								
19				Projected Profit				$10,000.00
20								

groups of workers. The goal of applying the Solver to this worksheet is to determine the most cost-effective mix of employee instructors and contract instructors.

At the present time, the regional office has four employee instructors along with a group of six contract instructors. Here is how the information about these two groups is organized:

- The top section of the worksheet shows the costs related to the four employees: Their individual salaries, benefits, and support costs appear in E3..E5, and the totals for the four employees are calculated in F3..F5. In addition, cell B4 displays the current number of employee instructors, 4.

- Rows 7, 8, and 9 display information about the number of hours of instruction: the total number of instruction hours planned for a given year (E7); the number of hours assigned per year to each individual employee (E8); and a calculation of the number of remaining hours that must be assigned to contract instructors (E9).

- The next section down the worksheet shows information about the contract instructors. Cell B12 shows the current number of contract instructors, 6. The average hourly rate paid to these instructors appears in cell E11, and the corresponding total cost of this hourly instruction for the year is in F11. Rows 12 and 13 show the support and supervision costs related to these contract instructors.

- The total costs for both groups of instructors is calculated in cell F15.

FIGURE 10.44:

Analyzing the mix of instructors

	A	B	C	D	E	F	G
1	Best Mix of Employee and Contract Instructors						
2					Per person	Total	
3	Employee Instructors			Salaries	$32,500.00	$130,000.00	
4		4		Benefits	$9,750.00	$39,000.00	
5				Support	$5,500.00	$22,000.00	
6							
7			Total annual hours of instruction:		2,496		
8			Annual teaching hours per employee:		360		
9			Hours remaining:		1,056		
10							
11	Contract Instructors			Hourly expense	$132.50	$139,920.00	
12		6		Support	$1,000.00	$6,000.00	
13				Supervision	$2,750.00	$16,500.00	
14							
15				Total Instructor Expense		$353,420.00	
16							
17	Constraints						
18			A minimum of 2 employees		1		
19			A maximum of 6 employees		1		
20			A total of 10 instructors		1		

◆ Finally, rows 18, 19, and 20 describe the constraints that will apply to the Solver's calculations on this worksheet: There should be a minimum of two employee instructors, and a maximum of six. The combined number of employee and contract instructors is fixed at ten. The logical formulas expressing these constraints are in the range E18..E20; as you can see, all three formulas yield values of true for the current data.

Figure 10.45 displays the formulas that calculate the data and the constraints on this worksheet. In the range F3..F5, the total employee expenses are calculated by multiplying individual expenses by the number of employees. Cell E9 computes the number of instruction hours assigned to contract instructors—the difference between the total annual hours and the total hours taught by employees. The range F11..F13 calculates the expenses related to contract instructors, and the @SUM function in cell F15 finds the total costs for all instructors. Finally, the constraint formulas appear in E18..E20.

When you choose the Tools Solver command, a dialog box titled Solver Definition appears on the screen. In this dialog box, you identify the worksheet locations of the adjustable values, the constraints, and the optimal formula in your Solver problem. For example, Figure 10.46 shows the Solver Definition box with the correct references and ranges for the instructor-mix worksheet. The adjustable cells are B4 (the number of employee instructors) and B12 (the number of contract instructors). The constraint cells are in the range E18..E20. And the optimal cell is F15—the location of the formula that calculates the total cost of instructors. The Solver can find the minimum or

	A	B	C	D	E	F	G
1	Best Mix of Employee and Contract Instructors						
2					Per person	Total	
3	Employee Instructors			Salaries	$32,500.00	+$B$4*E3	
4		4		Benefits	$9,750.00	+$B$4*E4	
5				Support	$5,500.00	+$B$4*E5	
6							
7			Total annual hours of instruction:		2,496		
8			Annual teaching hours per employee:		360		
9			Hours remaining:		+E7-B4*E8		
10							
11	Contract Instructors			Hourly expense	$132.50	+E9*E11	
12		6		Support	$1,000.00	+$B$12*E12	
13				Supervision	$2,750.00	+$B$12*E13	
14							
15				Total Instructor Expense		@SUM(F3..F13)	
16							
17	Constraints						
18			A minimum of 2 employees		+B4>=2		
19			A maximum of 6 employees		+B4<=6		
20			A total of 10 instructors		+B4+B12=10		

FIGURE 10.45:

Formulas behind the instructor-mix worksheet

maximum value for the optimal formula. In this example, the option button labeled Min has been selected, because the goal of this analysis is to find the instructor mix that results in the least cost.

Once you have defined a problem by making the appropriate entries in the Solver Definition dialog box, you are ready to begin the analysis. To do so, you click the Solve button. Depending upon the number of adjustable cells and the complexity of the formulas on your worksheet, the Solver can take some time to complete its task. Accordingly, a box titled Solver Progress appears on the screen to keep you informed while the Solver completes the various steps of this procedure. First, this box displays the label *Analyzing problem...*, as shown in Figure 10.47; then you will see labels such as *Searching for answer #1*, as in Figure 10.48.

When the analysis is finished, some important changes occur on the screen. First, a new dialog box named Solver Answer takes the place of the Solver

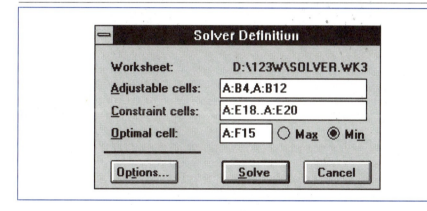

FIGURE 10.46:
The Solver Definition dialog box

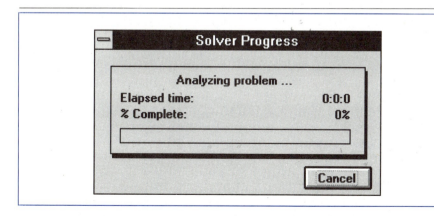

FIGURE 10.47:
The Solver Progress box: Analyzing the problem

Progress box. At the top of this box is a message that tells you how many answers the Solver has found for your problem definition; for example, in Figure 10.49 you see the message *3 answers found*. Because the solver has found an optimal result from the target formula, you also see the label *Optimal answer (#1)* in this box.

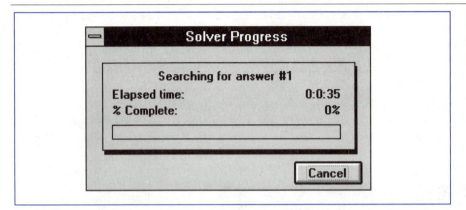

FIGURE 10.48:

The Solver Progress box: Searching for an answer

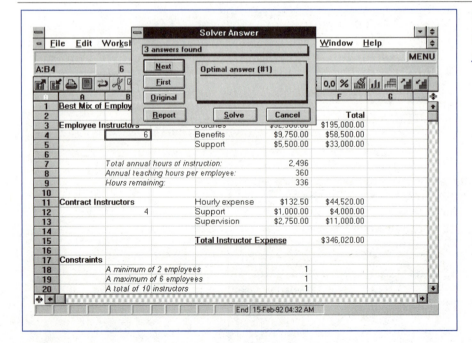

FIGURE 10.49:

The optimal answer from the Solver analysis

At the same time, you'll notice that the Solver has actually made changes in the worksheet locations that you designated as the adjustable cells. For example, in Figure 10.49, the Solver has entered a new value of *6* in cell B4, as the optimal number of employee instructors; and a new value of *4* in cell B12 as the optimal number of contract instructors. The total expense associated with this optimal instructor mix is $346,020, as shown in cell F15.

The Solver Answer dialog box contains an assortment of command buttons you can use to examine other results from the analysis:

◆ Click the Next button to see the next-best answer the solver has found for your problem.

◆ Click First to go back to the optimal answer.

◆ Click Original to display the data values as they were displayed before the Solver analysis.

◆ Click Report to view the Solver Report dialog box, shown in Figure 10.50. This dialog box offers a number of special-purpose reports from the analysis. The Solver generates each report individually; you request a report by selecting a report type from the dialog box and clicking OK. The reports are displayed in specially created worksheet files if you select the Table option, or in dialog boxes on the screen if you select the Cell option.

◆ Click Cancel on each of the Solver dialog boxes to end the Solver operations.

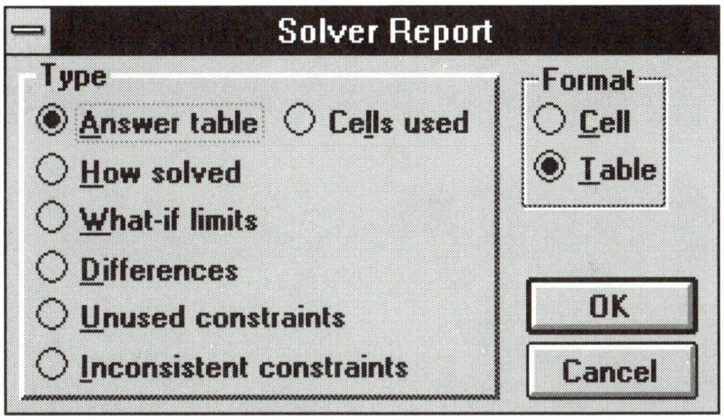

FIGURE 10.50:
The Solver Report dialog box

SUMMARY

The Data menu contains a variety of commands and groups of commands that perform advanced mathematical calculations in appropriately organized worksheets. The Data Matrix Inverse and Data Matrix Multiply commands are the tools to use for solving simultaneous equations, represented as matrix tables in a worksheet. The Data Distribution command counts the worksheet entries that fit into numerical categories in a bin range. The Data Regression command analyzes the correlation between a dependent variable and one or more independent variables. The Data What-if commands produce one-, two-, and three-dimensional what-if tables representing multiple worksheet scenarios. In addition to all of these, the Data Parse command is an essential tool in the process of translating a column-oriented text file into the 1-2-3 worksheet format.

The Tools menu contains two unique commands that perform analyses of worksheet data. The Tools Backsolver command finds the input value that produces a specified bottom-line result from a formula on your worksheet. Finally, in complex systems of worksheet formulas, the Tools Solver facility can find data solutions that fit within specifically formulated constraints.

FAST TRACK

To create a link between the current worksheet and a second worksheet, ...516

enter a formula that has a file reference to the second worksheet. The complete notation for a file reference contains the drive name, directory path, file name, and extension of the second worksheet, all enclosed in pairs of angle brackets, << and >>. The file reference is followed by an ordinary range reference, in the form <<*file*>>*range*. The purpose of the link is to copy data from the second worksheet to the current worksheet, and to update the current worksheet whenever the data changes on the second worksheet.

To create a link to a disk file that is not currently open, ...517

type the complete file reference and range reference directly from the keyboard. No pointing technique is available.

To use the keyboard pointing technique to create a reference to an open file, ...517

begin the formula entry with an appropriate operator, then press Ctrl-End to toggle into the File mode. (The word *File* appears in one of the panels of the status line.) Then use Ctrl-PgUp or Ctrl-PgDn to select the next or previous open file.

To use the Range Names list box to create a reference to an open file, ...518

begin the formula entry with an appropriate operator, then press the F3 function key to view the Range Names list box. Double-click the name of a selected file reference to view the range names defined in the file. Select the name that you want to include in the reference. In response, 1-2-3 enters a complete file reference and range name into the formula.

To update a destination file if the linked source file is not currently open, ... 522

open the destination file from disk, and choose the File Administration Update Links command.

To create a DDE link in which a 1-2-3 worksheet is the source (or server) file, ... 529

select a range of data in the worksheet and click the copy-to-clipboard icon. Then move to the second application and select the location where you want to transfer the data. In the second application, choose the Edit Paste Link command.

To create a DDE link in which a 1-2-3 worksheet is the destination (or client) file, ... 532

move to the source application and select the data that is to be transferred to the 1-2-3 worksheet. In the source application, choose the Edit Copy command. Move to the 1-2-3 window and preselect a worksheet range that is large enough to receive the data that will be transferred. Then choose the Edit Paste Link command.

To view the characteristics of a DDE link in which a 1-2-3 worksheet is the client, ... 534

choose the Edit Link Options command and select the name of the link you want to view. The characteristics of the link are displayed in the Format information boxes.

CHAPTER 11

Links between Files

ajor categories of business data are often organized into multiple files on disk. Consider the following typical examples:

- ◆ Accounting figures and calculations for a given year can be stored in twelve monthly worksheet files.
- ◆ Business information for a particular company might initially be accumulated in individual regional files.
- ◆ Financial worksheets can appear in separate files for revenues, expenses, depreciations, deductions, and so on.
- ◆ Inventory data might be separated into files for individual product categories or inventory locations.

Because you can open multiple worksheet files into the 1-2-3 environment, you may often be able to view all the parts of these applications on the screen at once. Furthermore, 1-2-3 has a very important feature that allows you to integrate and coordinate the parts of a multifile application: You can establish *links* between worksheets, resulting in automatic exchange of information between the corresponding files.

Worksheet links are expressed as special formulas that include *file references* along with the familiar forms of range references. In response to such a formula, 1-2-3 transfers data to the current worksheet from the worksheet named in the file reference. The worksheet that contains such a formula is therefore the *destination file,* and the worksheet that is named in the file reference is the *source file*.

In an application consisting of multiple files, you can use links to create a master worksheet file that consolidates information from several other files. For example, each of the following worksheets presents an overview of the data stored in a specific group of files:

◆ A year-end file that displays totals from twelve monthly files

◆ A corporate file that brings together data from all regions

◆ A profit worksheet that calculates the bottom line from data stored in various financial files

◆ A master inventory worksheet that consolidates information about several categories of products, or summarizes the status of several inventory locations.

To develop these worksheets, you write formulas to link the individual source files with the current destination worksheet. If you later make changes in the data stored in one of the source files, 1-2-3 can automatically update the destination file by transferring the new data to the cell that contains the link formula. In this chapter, you'll learn to write formulas to integrate the parts of a multifile worksheet application.

An analogous feature in the Windows environment is known as Dynamic Data Exchange, or simply DDE. With programs that support DDE, you can establish links between documents that you create in different Windows applications. The primary purpose of a DDE link is to send data from a source file to a destination file, and to update the destination file whenever a change occurs in the source file. Lotus 1-2-3 for Windows supports DDE in two directions: A 1-2-3 worksheet can be the source file or the destination file in the link established between two applications. Dynamic Data Exchange is the second main topic of this chapter. As an example of DDE, you'll see a link between a 1-2-3 worksheet and a document file created in a Windows word-processing program.

In the exercises presented in this chapter, you'll be working with a group of files from the four regions of Computing Conferences, Inc. In this example, the company's central office has asked each of the regional managers to prepare a monthly business summary worksheet. As you can see in Figure 11.1, each of these sample worksheets contains five items of information about a given region's business activities for the month of February 1992:

◆ The number of computer-training conferences conducted in the region

◆ The total number of people who attended these conferences

- The dollar revenues from the conferences
- The total expenses associated with conducting the conferences
- The total profit for the month

The sample files in Figure 11.1 have been sized and positioned so that the contents of all four files can be seen at once. To prepare for your work in this chapter, begin by creating copies of these four files on your own computer. Here is an outline of the steps to follow to create each of the files:

1. If necessary, use the File New command to open a new worksheet window.

2. Enter the appropriate labels into column A of the new worksheet, and apply the boldface, italic, and underlining styles shown in Figure 11.1.

3. Preselect the range A4..A8 and choose the Range Name Label Create command. Without changing the default Right option, click OK to assign these five labels as range names to the adjacent cells in column B.

4. Enter the first four numeric data items into column B: the number of conferences, the attendance, the revenue amount, and the expenses.

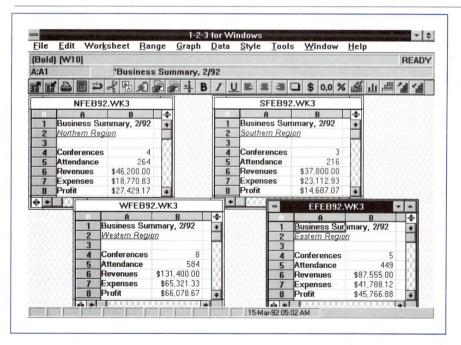

FIGURE 11.1:

Monthly business summaries from the four regions

5. Enter the formula **+REVENUES–EXPENSES** into cell B8. This calculates the region's total profit for the month.

6. Apply the currency format to the range B6..B8. Increase the widths of columns A and B so that the labels and values in the range A4..B8 can be viewed within their respective cells.

7. Choose the File Save As command and save the file under its appropriate name: NFEB92.WK3, SFEB92.WK3, WFEB92.WK3, and EFEB92.WK3 for the Northern, Southern, Western, and Eastern regions, respectively.

8. Resize and reposition each worksheet window so that you can view all four files at once, in an arrangement similar to what you see in Figure 11.1.

With these sample files displayed on your screen, you are ready to begin experimenting with 1-2-3 worksheet links.

CREATING LINKS BETWEEN WORKSHEETS

A reference to a cell or range on another worksheet consists of two parts: a file reference and a range reference. If the source file is currently open, an adequate file reference is simply the name of the file, enclosed within two pairs of angle brackets:

<<file>>

The range appears immediately after the file reference:

<<file>>range

For example, the following formula copies the entry from cell A:A1 in an open file named SUMMARY:

+<<SUMMARY>>A:A1..A:A1

When you enter this formula into a cell in the current worksheet, the contents of cell A1 in the SUMMARY worksheet appear in the destination cell.

In the special case of an unsaved worksheet named Untitled, a file reference appears as two pairs of angle brackets with no name between them. For example, here is a reference to cell A1 in the Untitled worksheet:

+<<>>A:A1..A:A1

If the source worksheet is saved on disk but not currently open, the file reference must include a complete path name and file name, including the extension. For example, the following formula copies an entry from cell A1 of SUMMARY.WK3, a file that is stored in the \123W directory on drive D:

+<<D:\123W\SUMMARY.WK3>>A:A1..A:A1

To enter a reference to a file that is not open, you must type the complete reference directly from the keyboard. But if the source file is open, you can use mouse or keyboard pointing techniques to create the reference. If you have arranged your worksheets so that the source and destination files are both in view, the mouse pointing technique is the simplest: Select a cell on the destination worksheet, and begin your formula with an operator (+, for example). Then click the mouse at the target location of the source worksheet. In response, 1-2-3 provides a complete file reference and range reference. Press ↵ to enter this reference into the current cell in the destination worksheet.

The keyboard pointing technique is more detailed:

1. Type a character such as + to begin the formula.

2. Press Ctrl-End to toggle 1-2-3 into the file-pointing mode. The word *File* appears in one of the panels of the status line. (This step is unnecessary if the current destination file contains only one worksheet. However, if you are working with a multiple worksheet file, you must toggle into the File mode to point to another file rather than to another worksheet in the current file.)

3. Press Ctrl-PgUp to move the cell pointer to the next open file, or Ctrl-PgDn to point to the previous open file. When the cell pointer is in the source file, use the arrow keys to point to the correct location in the file.

4. Continue your formula by pressing another operation, such as +, or press ↵ to complete the formula entry.

If the target cell has a range name in the source file, you can use the F3 function key to select a range name while you are building a formula. This is probably the clearest and simplest way to establish a link between two open files. Because you've taken the trouble to define range names in the regional business summary files currently displayed on your screen, you can use this technique in the upcoming exercise.

BUILDING A TOTALS WORKSHEET FROM THE FOUR SOURCE WORKSHEETS

Your goal in this exercise is to create a new worksheet file that displays the total of the numeric figures in these four regional files. Here are the steps:

1. Preselect the range A1..A8 in any one of the four files, and then click the copy-to-clipboard icon.

2. Click the minimize icon button on each of the four worksheets in turn to reduce the files to icons in the 1-2-3 window.

3. Choose the File New command to create a new worksheet file. With the cell pointer at A:A1, click the paste-from-clipboard icon to paste the labels into column A of the new worksheet. Enter the new label **Totals for Four Regions** in cell A2.

4. Resize the new worksheet to approximately the same dimensions as the other four worksheets, and reposition the worksheet near the center of the screen. Increase the widths of columns A and B.

5. Choose File Save As, and save the file to disk as TOTFEB92.WK3. Then select cell B4.

6. Type the + key and press the F3 function key to view the Range Names list. As shown in Figure 11.2, the list contains file references to the other four open worksheet files. In the list box, double-click the reference to <<EFEB92.WK3>>. When you do so, the Range Names list box displays a list of the range names defined in this file, as shown in Figure 11.3.

7. Select the range name CONFERENCES. A complete reference to the cell appears as follows in the Range name text box:

   +<<D:\123W\EFEB92.WK3>>CONFERENCES

   To view the whole name, you can select the text box and press the → key repeatedly to scroll to the right. (In this example, the four files are saved in the \123W directory on drive D. The file references in your formula may be different, depending upon the path location in which you have saved your files.) Press ↵ to accept this as the first reference in your formula.

8. Now repeat steps 6 and 7 three times, each time selecting a different file reference from the Range Names list box: first <<NFEB92.WK3>>, then <<SFEB92.WK3>>, and finally <<WFEB92.WK3>>. When you are finished with these steps, the following formula appears in the contents box:

+<<D:\123W\EFEB92.WK3>>CONFERENCES+
<<D:\123W\NFEB92.WK3>>CONFERENCES+
<<D:\123W\SFEB92.WK3>>CONFERENCES+
<<D:\123W\WFEB92.WK3>>CONFERENCES

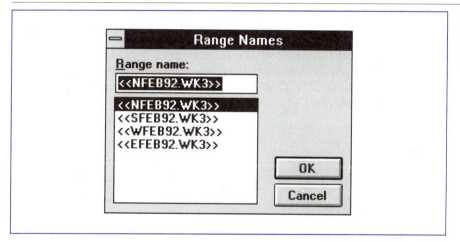

FIGURE 11.2:
File references in the Range Names dialog box

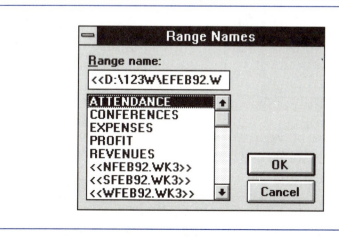

FIGURE 11.3:
The range names in a selected file

This formula finds the sum of the values stored in the cells named CONFERENCES in the four source worksheets.

9. Press ↵ to complete the formula entry. When you do so, the TOT-FEB92.WK3 worksheet appears as shown in Figure 11.4. As you can see, a total of 20 conferences were conducted in the four regions during the month of Feburary 1992.

10. With the cell pointer still at B4, click the range-copy icon. Hold down the mouse button while you drag the mouse pointer over the range B5..B8, then release the mouse button. In response, 1-2-3 copies the formula from cell B4, down to the cells in the range B5..B8. Because the original formula contains relative references to cells in the source worksheets, the references in the new copied formulas are automatically adjusted according to their positions in the column. For example, here is the formula that 1-2-3 copies into cell B8 to calculate the total profit from the four regional files:

+<<D:\123W\EFEB92.WK3>>A:B8..A:B8+
<<D:\123W\WFEB92.WK3>>A:B8..A:B8+
<<D:\123W\SFEB92.WK3>>A:B8..A:B8+
<<D:\123W\NFEB92.WK3>>A:B8..A:B8

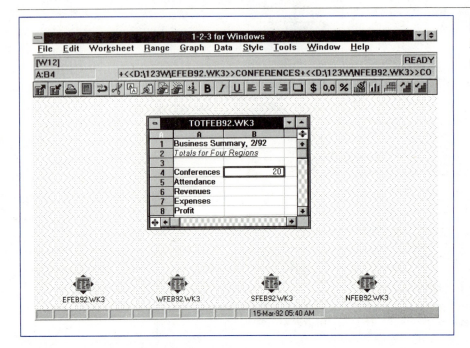

FIGURE 11.4:

Linking the worksheets with a formula

11. Select cell B5 and click the comma-format icon. Then preselect the range B6..B8, and click the currency icon.

12. Click the save-file icon to save your work to disk.

When you complete these steps, the TOTFEB92.WK3 worksheet appears as in Figure 11.5. A quick look back at the worksheets in Figure 11.1 confirms that 1-2-3 has successfully found the totals of the data in the four source worksheets: the total number of conferences in the four regions; the total attendance; and the total revenues, expenses, and profit.

REVISING A SOURCE WORKSHEET

Now if you revise the data in any one of the source worksheets, 1-2-3 automatically updates the corresponding formulas in TOTFEB92.WK3. For example, suppose you reach this point in your work, only to discover that one of the conferences conducted in the Southern region was inadvertently omitted from SFEB92.WK3. The corrected worksheet appears in Figure 11.6.

FIGURE 11.5:
The results of the five formulas in the destination worksheet

	A	B
1	Business Summary, 2/92	
2	Totals for Four Regions	
3		
4	Conferences	20
5	Attendance	1,513
6	Revenues	$302,955.00
7	Expenses	$148,993.21
8	Profit	$153,961.79

FIGURE 11.6:
Revisions in one of the source worksheets

	A	B
1	Business Summary, 2/92	
2	Southern Region	
3		
4	Conferences	4
5	Attendance	281
6	Revenues	$49,175.00
7	Expenses	$30,972.12
8	Profit	$18,202.88

As you can see, the entries in cells B4, B5, B6, and B7 have been changed, and 1-2-3 has recalculated the formula in cell B8. Make these changes now in your own copy of SFEB92.WK3:

1. Double-click the icon representing the file to view the open file once again on the screen.

2. Make the four new entries in the range B4..B7, as shown in Figure 11.6. Notice that the value in B8 is recalculated.

3. Click the save-file icon to save the new version of the file to disk. Then click the minimize button on the SFEB92.WK3 window to reduce the file once again to an icon.

Now look at what has happened to TOTFEB92.WK3 (shown in Figure 11.7). All the values in the range B4..B8 have been revised to reflect the changes in the source file. This demonstrates the advantage of linked worksheets: The destination file is updated when you revise the data in one or more source files.

To prepare for the next exercise, save the current version of TOTFEB92.WK3 and then close the file. Also close all the source files except the worksheet for the Northern region, NFEB92.WK3.

REVISING A SOURCE FILE WHEN THE DESTINATION FILE IS CLOSED

Sometimes you might find yourself making revisions on a source worksheet at a time when the linked destination worksheet is not currently open in the 1-2-3 window. Conversely, you might later open the destination file when the source files are not open. The destination file can still be updated to reflect new data in the source, but the updating is not automatic. To ensure that the

FIGURE 11.7:
The updated TOTFEB92.WK3 file

	A	B
1	Business Summary, 2/92	
2	Totals for Four Regions	
3		
4	Conferences	21
5	Attendance	1,578
6	Revenues	$314,330.00
7	Expenses	$156,852.40
8	Profit	$157,477.60

destination file accurately reflects the data in the source files, you use the Update Links command from the File Administration cascade menu, shown in Figure 11.8. This menu actually contains two commands that are relevant to linked files: Undate Links and Paste Table. (The other two commands in the menu, Network Reserve and Seal File, are for use in a network version of 1-2-3 for Windows.)

In the following exercise, you'll make a single revision in the data contained in NFEB92.WK3, and then you'll close the file. Upon reopening the TOTFEB92.WK3 file, you'll have the opportunity to experiment with commands from the File Administration menu:

- Double-click the icon representing NFEB92.WK3 to view the open worksheet file.

- Enter the new value **56200** in cell B6. The entry is displayed in the currency format, as *$56,200.00.* In addition, 1-2-3 recalculates the profit formula in cell B8; the new version of the worksheet appears in Figure 11.9.

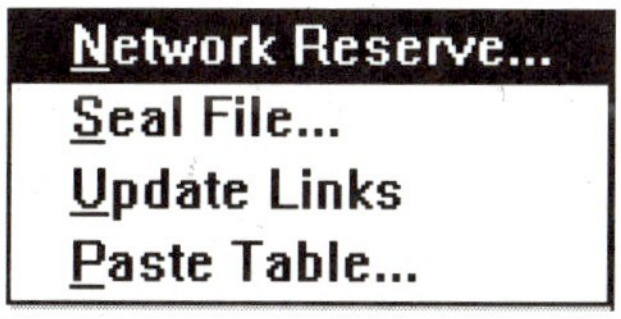

FIGURE 11.8:
The File Administration cascade menu

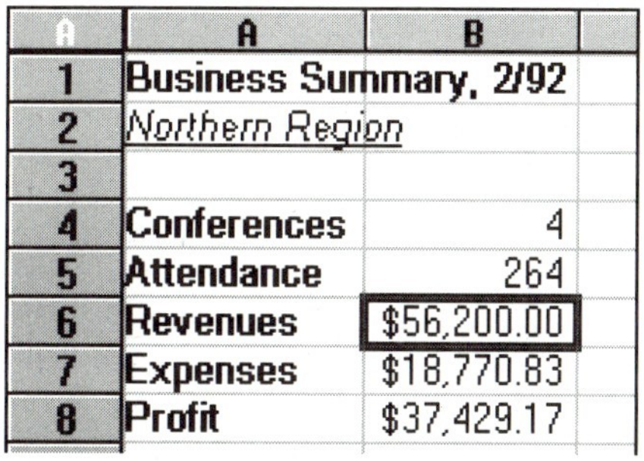

FIGURE 11.9:
Revising a source file while the destination file is closed

3. Click the save-file icon to update this file to disk, then close the file.

4. Open TOTFEB92.WK3 from disk. Notice that the file's contents are still the same as shown in Figure 11.7. The worksheet has not yet been updated to reflect the latest changes you made in NFEB92.WK3.

5. Pull down the File menu and choose Administration. In the resulting cascade menu, choose the Update Links command. In response, 1-2-3 rereads the source files on disk, and makes the revisions necessary in the current destination file. The TOTFEB92.WK3 file now appears as in Figure 11.10.

6. Now resize the worksheet window so that columns A through G and rows 1 through 15 come into view, and then increase the width of column B to about twice its current setting. Move the cell pointer to B11, and then choose the File Administration command again, but this time choose the Paste Table command from the resulting cascade menu.

7. In the File Administration Paste Table dialog box, click the Linked files option, as shown in Figure 11.11; then click OK. The resulting table

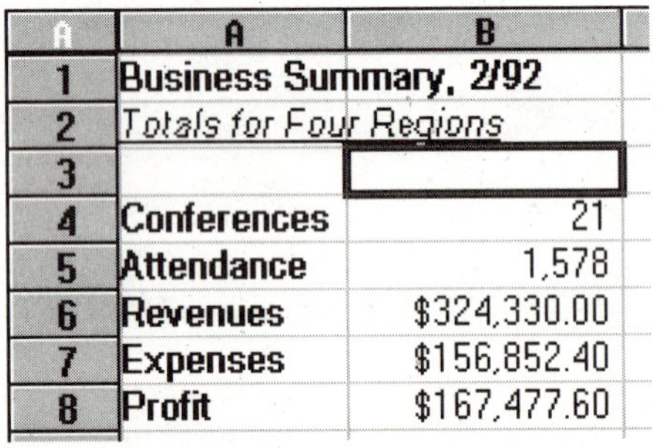

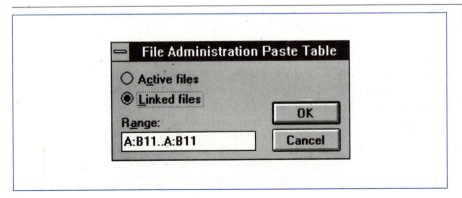

FIGURE 11.10:
Using the File Administration Update Links command

FIGURE 11.11:
The File Administration Paste Table dialog box

is a list of all the files linked to the current destination file. Apply the 31-Dec-90 date format to the four entries in the range C11..C14, and apply the 11:59 AM time format to the entries in D11..D14.

8. Move the cell pointer to C1, and then click the save-file icon to save the new version of this file to disk.

The TOTFEB92.WK3 worksheet now appears as in Figure 11.12. The table created by the File Administration Paste Table command gives you a list of the four source files for this linked worksheet, along with the dates and times when they were last updated, and the number of bytes in each file. This table is useful when you are analyzing the contents of a linked file and you are trying to determine whether it needs to be updated.

Now you have seen the full significance of the linked worksheet file TOTFEB92.WK3. It consolidates the data from the four regional source files, and can be updated whenever the data in one of these source files changes. Another way to create a totals worksheet that is similar *in appearance* to this file is with the File Combine From command.

USING THE FILE COMBINE FROM COMMAND

File Combine From reads data from a worksheet file on disk, and incorporates the data into the current worksheet. This command does not create a link between the current file and the file on disk; it merely transfers data statically,

	A	B	C	D	E
1	Business Summary, 2/92				
2	Totals for Four Regions				
3					
4	Conferences	21			
5	Attendance	1,578			
6	Revenues	$324,330.00			
7	Expenses	$156,852.40			
8	Profit	$167,477.60			
9					
10					
11		D:\123W\EFEB92.WK3	07-Mar-92	12:54 PM	941
12		D:\123W\NFEB92.WK3	07-Mar-92	04:31 PM	940
13		D:\123W\SFEB92.WK3	07-Mar-92	04:21 PM	942
14		D:\123W\WFEB92.WK3	07-Mar-92	12:55 PM	972
15					

FIGURE 11.12:

A table created by the File Administration Paste Table command

and enters the data onto the current worksheet. You had some experience with this command in Chapter 10, when you used it to copy part of the CONF.WK3 worksheet to a new file.

File Combine From can also *add* data to values contained in specified cells of the current worksheet. This process requires some careful planning to make sure the data values from disk are added to the correct locations on the current worksheet. But the Add option is useful when you want to create a totals worksheet without establishing links between source and destination worksheets.

Here is a brief exercise with this command:

1. On the TOTFEB92.WK3 file, preselect the range A1..A8, and click the copy-to-clipboard icon. Then close the TOTFEB92.WK3 file.

2. With the cell pointer located at A1 on the Untitled worksheet, click the paste-from-clipboard icon to copy the labels to column A of the worksheet. Increase the widths of columns A and B. Then move the cell pointer to B4.

3. Pull down the File menu and choose the Combine From command. Using the Drives, Directories, and Files boxes, find and select the file EFEB92.WK3. Click the Add button in the Action box. (Alternatively, you can retain the default Copy option for this very first Combine From operation, because the worksheet range does not yet contain any values. But for the next three files you must select the Add option.)

4. Click the Range button in the Source box. Enter the range **B4..B8** into the Range text box. The dialog box now appears as shown in Figure 11.13. Click OK to complete the first Combine From operation.

5. Repeat steps 3 and 4 for the remaining three source files, NFEB92.WK3, SFEB92.WK3, and WFEB92.WK3. Each operation adds the data from one of these files to the current worksheet.

When you are finished, the data displayed in the worksheet is the same as in Figure 11.10. However, the difference between this worksheet and TOTFEB92.WK3 is essential: The original worksheet contains formulas that link it to the source worksheets; but this new worksheet contains only data, with no formulas and no links. (You can now close this worksheet without saving it.)

CREATING LINKS BETWEEN DOCUMENTS IN DIFFERENT APPLICATIONS

In the Windows environment, you can easily copy data values from 1-2-3 worksheets to documents you create in other applications. The clipboard is the key to this procedure:

1. Select a range of data in a 1-2-3 worksheet.
2. Choose the Edit Copy command. This copies the data to the clipboard.
3. Activate the other Windows application, and move to the location where you want to copy the data.
4. Choose the Edit Paste command. This command pastes the data from the clipboard to the selected location in the second application.

The Edit Paste Command simply makes a copy of the data itself in the new location.

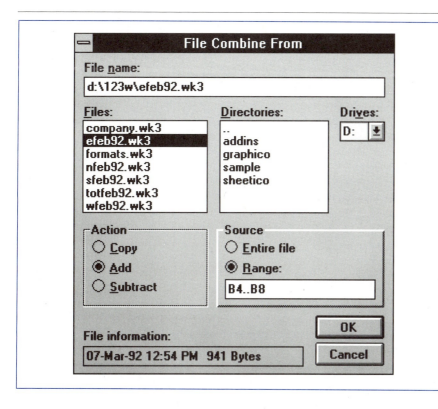

FIGURE 11.13:
Using File Combine From to consolidate data

A more powerful command, available in 1-2-3 and in many other Windows applications, is Edit Paste Link. This command uses the Dynamic Data Exchange facility to establish a link between documents created in two different applications. In a DDE link, the source document is known as the *server* and the destination document is known as the *client*. In other words, the server document belongs to the application where you choose the Edit Copy command; and the client document belongs to the application where you subsequently choose the Edit Paste Link command. While a DDE link is active in the *automatic update* mode, any data changes that take place in the server are automatically sent to the client.

Transferring Data from a Worksheet to Another Document

Figure 11.14 displays the 1-2-3 application alongside Microsoft Word for Windows, a popular Windows word-processing program. The two application windows have been resized so that each takes up about half the screen. In the 1-2-3 window, you can see the TOTFEB92.WK3 worksheet. In the Word document window, you see the beginning of a memo directed to the regional

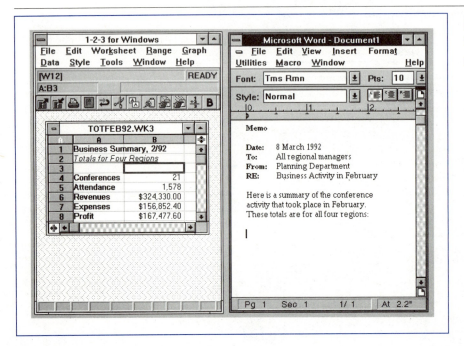

FIGURE 11.14:
Working with two applications in Windows

managers of Computing Conferences, Inc. Imagine that you are writing this memo, and you have reached the point where you want to insert the data from the TOTFEB92.WK3 worksheet into the word-processed document. Because you are anticipating possible changes in the worksheet data, you want to establish a DDE link between the worksheet and the document. Here are the steps you take:

1. Activate the worksheet window, and preselect the range A4..B8.

2. Pull down the 1-2-3 Edit menu and choose the Copy command, or simply click the copy-to-clipboard icon.

3. Activate the Word document window, and move the cursor to the end of the memo text.

4. Pull down the Edit menu in the Word window, and choose the Paste Link command. Word for Windows displays the dialog box shown in Figure 11.15. At the bottom of the dialog box is the notation that Word uses to represent the DDE link that you are about to establish. At the upper-left corner of the dialog box is a check box labeled Auto Update. Click this box so that the link will be established in the automatic update mode.

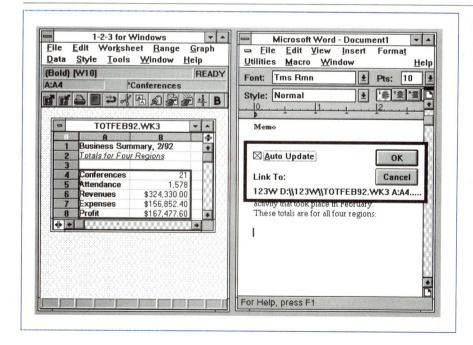

FIGURE 11.15:

Creating a DDE link in which 1-2-3 is the server

Click OK to create the link. As a result, the data from the 1-2-3 worksheet appears as a table at the bottom of the Word document. (You can use the Format Table command in Word for Windows to establish an appropriate column width for displaying this table in the memo.) You next reactivate the 1-2-3 window; at this point, the Windows desktop appears as shown in Figure 11.16. Serendipitously, your phone rings and it is Mary Garcia, the manager of the Western region. She's calling to let you know that she inadvertently omitted a $7,000 expense item for advertising in her February worksheet. No problem, you tell her; you can fix the error right away.

Open the WFEB92.WK3 worksheet in the 1-2-3 window, and select cell B7. As you can see in Figure 11.17, the current expense amount displayed in the cell is *$65,321.33*. Enter the revised figure into the cell, **$72,321.33**. When you do so, several changes take place on the screen, almost at once: First, a new profit figure is calculated in cell B8 of WFEB92.WK3. Then the new expense and profit figures are passed to the TOTFEB92.WK3 worksheet, which is linked to WFEB92.WK3 through formulas. And finally, the newly revised data is automatically sent to the memo document in Word, thanks to the DDE link between the document and the TOTFEB92.WK3 worksheet. The Windows desktop now appears as shown in Figure 11.18.

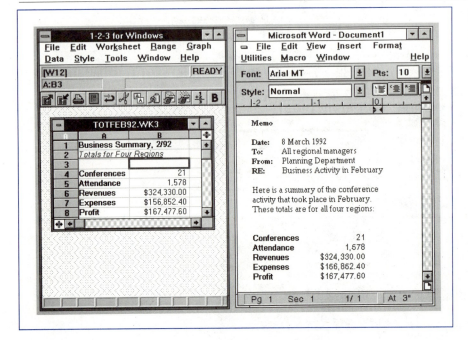

FIGURE 11.16:

The result of the DDE link

531 UNDERSTANDING 1-2-3 FOR WINDOWS   CH. 11

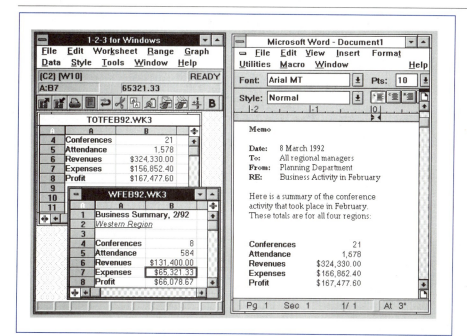

FIGURE 11.17:
Changing data in the DDE link

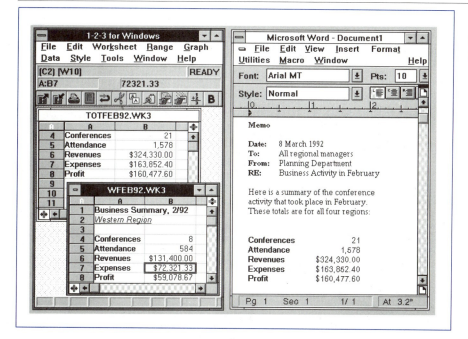

The new data is sent to the client

7. Save the revised worksheets in the 1-2-3 window. Then save and print the memo document in the Word window.

A DDE link is saved to disk with a document, but the link is active only when both the source and destination documents are open in the Windows desktop.

Transferring Data from Another Document to a 1-2-3 Worksheet

In the previous example, the 1-2-3 worksheet was the source of the data in the DDE link. A worksheet can also act as the client, or the destination in the link. The steps for establishing the link are essentially the same, but reversed:

1. In the other application, select the data that you want to transfer to the 1-2-3 worksheet, and then choose the Edit Copy command to copy the data to the clipboard.

2. Activate 1-2-3, and open the worksheet that is to be the client in the link.

3. Preselect the entire worksheet range to which you want to copy the data.

4. Pull down the Edit menu in the 1-2-3 window and choose the Paste Link command. (This 1-2-3 command is available only when the clipboard contains data from an application that can act as the server in a DDE link; otherwise, Paste Link appears as a grayed command in the Edit menu.)

As a result of these steps, the data is copied from the source document, and a link is established in which the 1-2-3 worksheet is the client.

When 1-2-3 is the client, you can use the Edit Link Options command to examine and modify the characteristics of the link. For example, Figure 11.19 shows the Edit Link Options dialog box, with a description of an active link between a Microsoft Excel worksheet and the current 1-2-3 worksheet. The selected link has a default name of LINK1. In the Format frame, a column of information boxes describes the characteristics of the link. As you can see, the server in a DDE link is described by three elements:

◆ The *application* is the name of the Windows program that is supplying the data.

- The *topic* is the name of the document or worksheet that is the actual source of the data.

- The *item* identifies the exact location of the target data in the source document or worksheet.

You can use the command buttons displayed at the right side of the Edit Link Options dialog box to perform specific actions related to this link or to modify the characteristics of the link. For example, the Deactivate button switches the link into an inactive mode, while retaining the link definition. In contrast, the Delete button removes the link between the two Windows documents, and deletes the link definition altogether.

The Update button in the Edit Link Options dialog box forces an update on a DDE link that is in the *manual update* mode. You might sometimes prefer

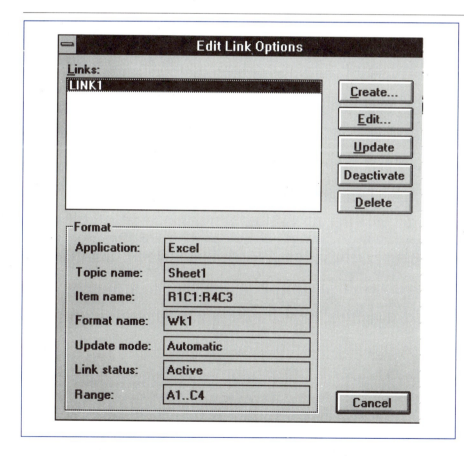

FIGURE 11.19:

The Edit Link Options dialog box

to work in this mode if you need to make many changes in the source document before updating the destination worksheet in 1-2-3. To switch a link to the manual update mode, follow these steps:

1. Choose the Edit Link Options command. In the resulting dialog box, select the name of the link that you want to change.

2. Click the Edit button. The Edit Link Options Edit dialog box appears on the screen. As in the example shown in Figure 11.20, this dialog box contains text boxes and option buttons representing the link characteristics that you can modify.

3. Click the Manual button in the Update mode frame. Click OK in the Edit Link Options Edit dialog box. Then click Cancel to close the Edit Link Options dialog box. Now the destination worksheet is no longer updated automatically in response to changes in the source document.

4. To force an update of the destination worksheet, choose the Edit Link Options command, select the name of the target link, and click the Update button. Click Cancel to close the dialog box.

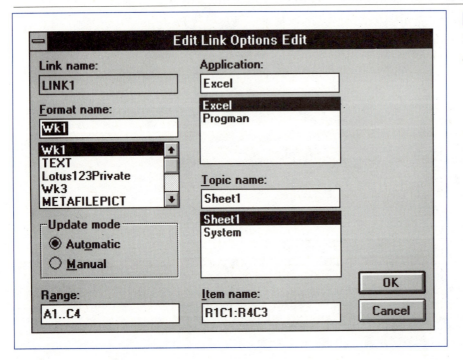

FIGURE 11.20:
The Edit Link Options Edit dialog box

SUMMARY

The purpose of establishing a link between two files is to exchange data between the files and to ensure that the destination file will be updated when there is a change in the source file.

A link between two worksheets is expressed as a formula that includes both a file reference and a range reference. The worksheet containing the formula is the destination file, and the worksheet named in the file reference is the source file. If the source and destination worksheets are both open, 1-2-3 automatically updates the destination file to reflect changes in the source file. However, if you open the destination file at a time when the source file is closed, you must choose the File Administration Update Links command to update the destination file.

Thanks to the Windows feature known as Dynamic Data Exchange, you can also establish links between documents that are created in different Windows applications. To create such a link, you choose the Edit Copy command to copy data from the source document to the clipboard. Then you move to the destination document and choose the Edit Paste Link command from the main menu of the second application. For example, you can use Dynamic Data Exchange to create a link between a source worksheet and a destination document in a word-processing program. While the link is active, the word-processed document is updated whenever you make changes in the worksheet data. When a 1-2-3 worksheet is the destination file in a DDE link, you can use the Edit Link Options command to view or modify the characteristics of the link.

FAST TRACK

To view a help topic for any macro command, ... 540

type an open brace, {, into a worksheet cell and then press the F1 function key; the Macro Command Index appears in the Help window. Click any command name in the index list to view the corresponding help topic.

To create a custom menu for use in a macro performance, ... 548

enter a menu definition in a range of columns in the macro worksheet. Each column in the range describes one of the commands in your custom menu. Within a column, the first cell gives the command name, the second cell provides a description of the command, and subsequent cells contain the macro instructions that 1-2-3 will perform if the user selects this command from your menu. In the main part of the macro, use a {MenuCall} or {MenuBranch} command to display the custom menu on the screen. The menu appears in the 1-2-3 Classic window.

To elicit a numeric data entry from the user during a macro performance, ... 550

use the {GetNumber} command. The command takes two arguments, a string and a reference: The string is an input prompt, and the reference identifies the worksheet cell where the input value will be copied.

To determine the correct format for a reference argument in a macro command, ... 551

keep in mind the rules that 1-2-3 follows for evaluating references in macros: By default, references that represent subroutines or branches of control are assumed to be located within the macro worksheet itself. All other references are assumed to be located within the worksheet that is current at the time of the macro run. To override these rules, you must include a file reference along with a cell or range reference as the argument in a macro command.

To create a repetition loop in a macro, ... 552

use the {For} command. {For} takes five arguments: The first argument is a reference to the cell that serves as the counter for the loop; the second, third, and fourth arguments are numbers or expressions representing the start, stop, and step values, respectively; and the fifth argument is a reference to a subroutine that will be called once for each repetition of the loop.

To create a conditional branch in a macro, ... 559

use an {If} instruction to express the condition of the branch. The {If} command takes a single argument, a logical expression. Immediately following the {If} instruction, in the same cell of the macro worksheet, write a {Branch} command that identifies the destination of the branch. {Branch} also takes a single argument, a reference to the macro location that receives control of the program if the branch is performed.

To locate a logical error in a macro, ... 561

choose the Tools Macro Debug command and activate both the Single step and Trace options. Click OK to confirm. Then run the macro and examine the contents of the Macro Trace window as you move step by step through the program performance.

CHAPTER 12

Macro Programming

 programming language is a collection of tools designed to help you plan and perform tasks on your computer. Accordingly, a program is a sequence of steps, expressed in the commands and keywords of a particular language. In the process of writing a program, regardless of the language, you typically focus on several essential categories of activity:

- ◆ Performing operations on specific types of data values, including numbers, strings, and logical values
- ◆ Reading input from a variety of sources, and writing output to a variety of destinations. For example, an interactive program reads the user's input from the keyboard and displays output on the screen. Disk files can be both the source of input and the destination of output.
- ◆ Making decisions based on expressed conditions. A decision results in a choice between different options for the program's next action.
- ◆ Repeating the performance of a command or group of commands a specified number of times. Statements or commands that control repetition in a program are known as *loops*.

◆ Calling subroutines, or otherwise modifying the sequential line-by-line flow of control in a program. A subroutine performs a particular task and then returns control of the program to the location of the original call. In contrast, a *branch* command simply sends control of the program to a new location, with no expectation of a return.

The 1-2-3 macro language includes commands for performing these basic programming activities within the context of worksheets, graphs, and databases. In addition, the macro language has a variety of important tools for utilizing specific 1-2-3 and Windows features such as the clipboard, external database connections, DDE, and window characteristics.

The macro language contains more than eighty different commands, each represented by a unique keyword. As you first learned in Chapter 9, macro commands appear within braces, { and }. Most macro commands require specific arguments, which may include numeric values, strings, logical expressions, or range references. Each argument is separated from the next by a comma (or by a separator character you select with the Tools User Setup International command). For example, in Chapter 9 you worked with an input command named {GetLabel}. This command displays an input prompt in the 1-2-3 Classic window, and waits for the user to enter a string from the keyboard. When the user completes the string and presses ↵, the {GetLabel} command copies the input to a specified cell location as a label entry. Accordingly, {GetLabel} takes two arguments—a string representing the input prompt, and a cell reference representing the eventual destination of the input:

{GetLabel *string,reference*}

You can view an index of all the macro commands and a help topic describing any individual command by following these steps:

1. Type an opening brace character, {, into a worksheet cell.

2. While the Edit line is still active, press the F1 function key. In response, 1-2-3 opens the Help window and displays a list of all available macro commands, as you can see in Figure 12.1.

3. Scroll down the list to a command you want to learn about, and click the command's name with the mouse. The Help window displays complete information about the selected command, including the action it performs and the arguments it requires. For example, Figure 12.2 shows the Help window for the {GetLabel} command.

Another way to access information about macros and macro programming is to choose the Macros command from the Help menu. This command displays a topic named Macro Basics, which in turn includes a list of all the major macro topics available in the 1-2-3 Help system.

Macro programming is a broad and detailed subject; in fact, you'll find entire books devoted to the techniques of writing macros. This chapter is a short introduction to macros and the basic concepts of macro programming. In the course of this introduction, you'll see examples of a dozen of the most commonly used macro commands. You'll also work with two complete examples of macro programs:

- ◆ A schedule macro, which creates worksheets for keeping track of business appointments. You'll see three versions of this programming exercise, each illustrating different macro commands.

- ◆ A mailing list macro, which reads an address database and creates a text file of address labels from the database. This particular example is designed to work with the instructor database from Computing Conferences, Inc., but you can easily revise the program to create labels from any other address database that you use.

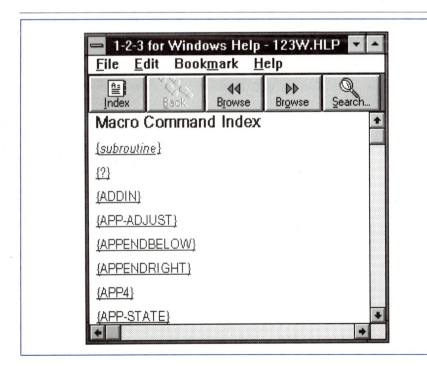

FIGURE 12.1:
The Macro Command Index in the 1-2-3 Help window

These examples illustrate general categories of programming tasks: data operations, input and output, decisions, loops, subroutine calls, and branches of control.

WRITING PROGRAMS THAT INTERACT WITH THE USER

The schedule macro creates worksheets in which you can record daily business activities. For example, the schedule worksheet in Figure 12.3 displays hourly time slots from 6:00 AM to 6:00 PM. To create it, the program begins by choosing the File New command to open a new blank worksheet, and then proceeds to elicit your instructions for the format and contents of the worksheet. Specifically, the program offers these variations:

◆ You can choose between one-hour, half-hour, or quarter-hour increments for the worksheet.

◆ You can create a schedule worksheet for today, tomorrow, the next day, or for a date that you enter yourself.

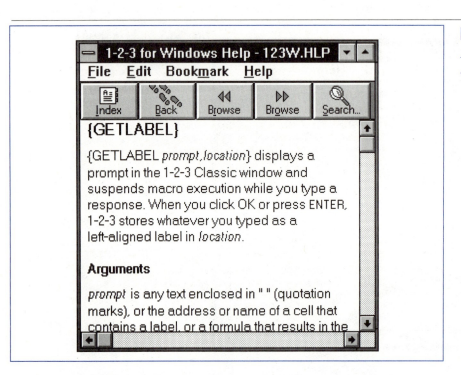

FIGURE 12.2:
Help for the {GetLabel} command

To elicit your instructions, the program displays two menus on the screen, one for the choice of time increments and another for the choice of dates. These menus appear inside the 1-2-3 Classic window, as shown in Figures 12.4 and 12.5. To make a selection in either menu, you press → or ← to move the highlight to the option of your choice, and then you press ↵. Alternatively, you can press the first letter of an option: S, T, or F to choose one of the options in the time menu in Figure 12.4; and 1, 2, 3, or 4 to choose one of the options in the date menu in Figure 12.5.

If you choose the fourth option in the date menu, 4-Date-entry, an input window appears on the screen, as shown in Figure 12.6. This window accepts a date entry from you at the keyboard; the program then copies this date to

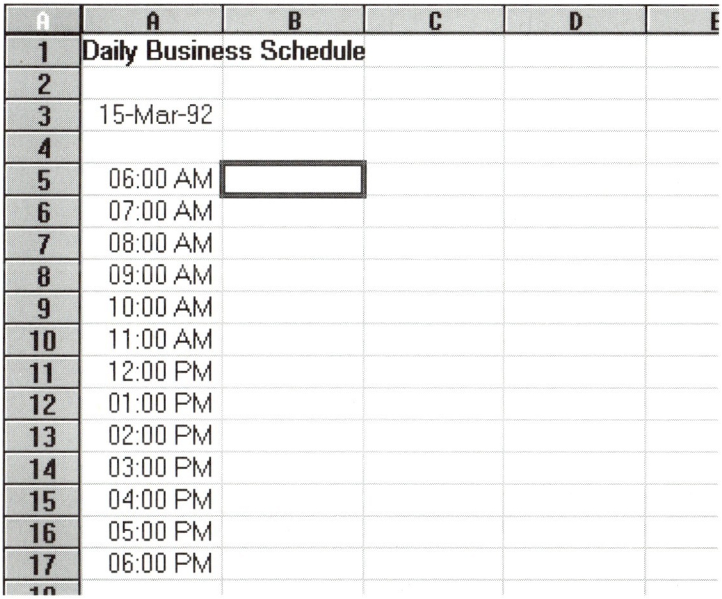

FIGURE 12.3:
A schedule worksheet with one-hour increments

FIGURE 12.4:
The time menu from the first version of the schedule macro

the top of the resulting schedule worksheet. Figures 12.7 and 12.8 show two additional examples of the program's output; the first of these worksheets displays time slots in half-hour increments, and the second in quarter-hour increments. After creating a schedule worksheet, the program moves the cell pointer to the first time slot, 6:00 AM. Then the program run is complete, and you can begin entering your appointments and activities onto the worksheet.

The schedule macro itself appears in columns A through H of a worksheet that is stored on disk as C:\S1.WK3. The main part of the worksheet, in columns A, B, and C, is shown in Figure 12.9. As you can see, the first cell in the macro, at B5, is named \S. You therefore begin a run of the program by pressing Ctrl-S. This main part of the program consists of six lines of macro instructions. Here is a general description of what these lines do:

◆ B5: This first line chooses File New to create the worksheet, and then immediately enters the title *Daily Business Schedule* into cell A1. Then the program chooses the Style Font command and selects the Bold option to display this title in boldface type.

◆ B6: The program uses a macro command named {MenuCall} to display the time menu on the screen, and to respond to the option that you choose from the menu. You'll learn how to use the {MenuCall} command later in this chapter.

◆ B7: A second {MenuCall} instruction displays the date menu on the screen. The date you select or enter is copied to the schedule worksheet. The program then chooses the Range Format command to apply an appropriate date format to the entry.

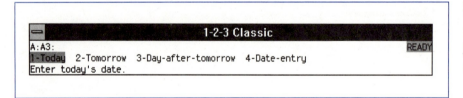

FIGURE 12.5:
The date selection menu from the first version of the schedule macro

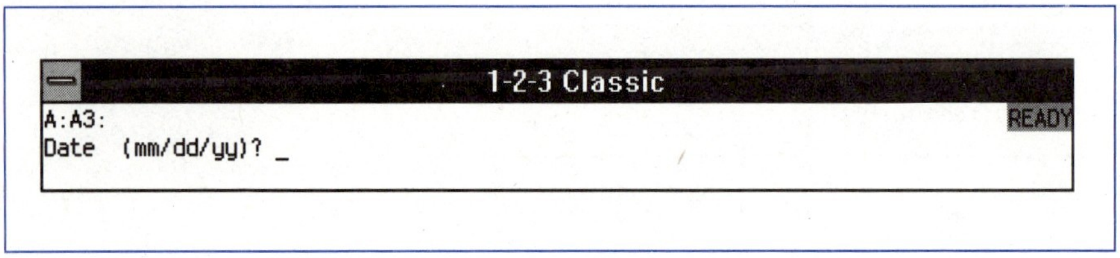

FIGURE 12.6:
The date input window

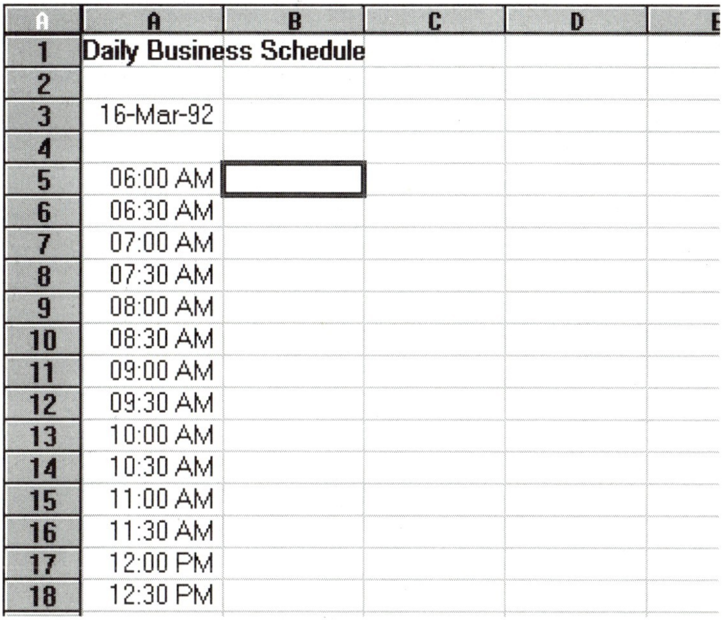

FIGURE 12.7:

A schedule worksheet with half-hour increments

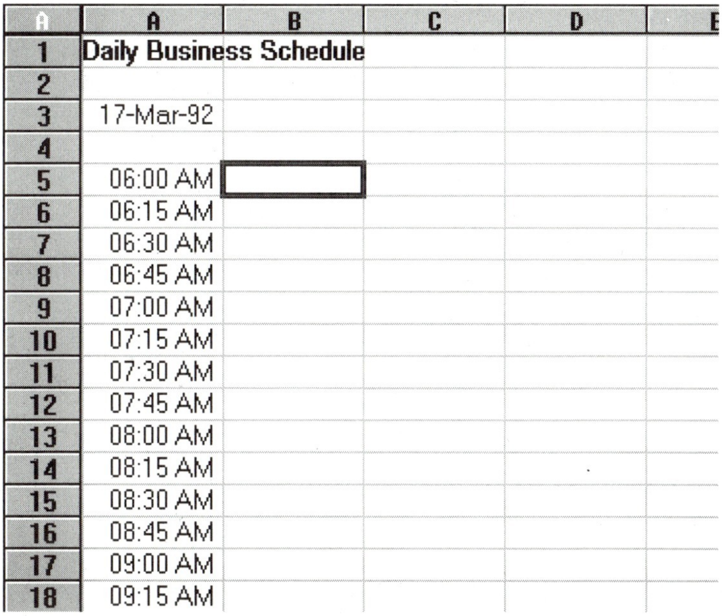

FIGURE 12.8:

A schedule worksheet with quarter-hour increments

- **B8:** The program next preselects the worksheet range in which the time entries will be displayed, and chooses Range Format to apply a time format to the entire range.

- **B9:** The {Alt}DF instruction chooses the Data Fill menu command. You'll recall that this command fills a selected range on the current worksheet with a sequence of values. To specify the contents of this sequence, the macro must enter values for the Start, Step, and Stop text boxes in the Data Fill dialog box. Accordingly, the program enters 6:00 AM as the Start value and 6:00 PM as the Stop value. Data Fill automatically converts these entries into the appropriate decimal numbers representing the time values: 0.25 and 0.75, respectively. The program's entry for the Step text box depends on the time increment you have selected from the time menu.

- **B10:** After entering the sequence of numbers, the program positions the cell pointer in column B, just to the right of the first time entry. The {Quit} command ends the program.

To display a menu in the 1-2-3 Classic window, a macro must include a specially organized menu definition. In the S1.WK3 worksheet, two such definitions appear in columns E through H, as shown in Figures 12.10. and 12.11. The definition for the time menu is in the range E1..G4, and the definition for the date menu is in E6..H9. The {MenuCall} commands in the main part of the program transfer control to these menu definitions.

Before you examine the precise structure of a menu definition, take the time to produce your own copy of the schedule macro. Open a new blank worksheet for the macro, and carefully enter the range names, macro instructions, and comments into columns A through H of the worksheet, as in Figures 12.9, 12.10, and 12.11. Once you have finished typing the contents of the

FIGURE 12.9:

The first version of the schedule macro

	A	B	C
1		Schedule Macro (C:\S1.WK3)	
2			
3	Incr		The increment amount.
4			
5	\S	{Alt}FNDaily Business Schedule~{Alt}SF{Alt "B"}~	Enter the title in bold.
6		{MenuCall TimeMenu}	Get the time choice.
7		{Down 2}{MenuCall DateMenu}{Alt}RF1~	Get user's date choice.
8		{Down 2}{Anchor}{Down 48}~{Alt}RF7~	Format the range.
9		{Alt}DF{Alt "S"}6:00 AM{Alt "T"}{Incr}{Alt "O"}6:00 PM~	Fill with time values.
10		{Right}{Quit}	Select the first time cell.

macro, here are the steps for completing your work:

Use the Range Name Label Create command to assign the labels displayed in cells A3 and A5 to the adjacent cells in column B; then use the command again to assign the labels in D1 and D6 to the adjacent cells in column E.

Choose the Worksheet Global Settings command and select the Protection option so that an X appears in the check box. Then click OK. This protects your macro worksheet from inadvertent revisions. Next, move the cell pointer to B3 and choose the Range Unprotect command. The program uses B3 as a storage place for the time increment you select from the time menu; the cell must therefore be unprotected.

Save the worksheet in the root directory of drive C as C:\S1.WK3. (Later, you'll be saving the two other versions of the program as

	D	E	F
1	TimeMenu	Sixty-minutes	Thirty-minutes
2		One-hour entries.	Half-hour entries.
3		{Let <<C:\S1.WK3>>INCR,"60min"}	{Let <<C:\S1.WK3>>INCR,"30min"}
4		{Return}	{Return}
5			
6	DateMenu	1-Today	2-Tomorrow
7		Enter today's date.	Enter tomorrow's date.
8		@TODAY{Calc}~	@TODAY+1{Calc}~
9		{Return}	{Return}
10			
11			

FIGURE 12.10:
The first two columns of menu definitions in S1.WK3

	G	H
1	Fifteen-minutes	
2	Quarter-hour entries	
3	{Let <<C:\S1.WK3>>INCR,"15min"}	
4	{Return}	
5		
6	3-Day-after-tomorrow	4-Date-entry
7	Two days from today.	You choose the date.
8	@TODAY+2{Calc}~	{GetNumber "Date (mm/dd/yy)? ",A3}
9	{Return}	{Return}
10		
11		

FIGURE 12.11:
The final two columns of menu definitions in S1.WK3

C:\S2.WK3 and C:\S3.WK3.) If you decide to save the macro worksheet in a different directory or under a different file name, you must revise the file references in cells E3, F3, and G3 accordingly.

When you finish your work, try running the macro a few times. Depending upon your selections in the time and date menus, the macro produces worksheets similar to those displayed in Figure 12.3, 12.7, and 12.8.

USING THE {MENUCALL} COMMAND

As this program illustrates, a custom menu is a clear and efficient way to elicit instructions from the user during a macro run. The {MenuCall} command displays a menu on the screen and waits for the user to choose one of the options in the menu. The command takes one argument, a reference to the location of the menu definition:

{MenuCall *reference*}

The *reference* argument can identify the entire range of the menu definition, or simply the upper-left corner cell of the range. For example, the {MenuCall} commands in the schedule macro contain references to the named cells located at the beginning of the time menu and date menu definitions, respectively:

{MenuCall TimeMenu}
{MenuCall DateMenu}

A menu definition is a range of columns in which you describe the commands in a custom menu. Each column in the range is devoted to one command in the menu, and provides three kinds of information for the command:

- The first cell in the column gives the command name as it is to appear in the 1-2-3 Classic window.

- The second cell in the column provides the command's description, which appears at the lower-left corner of the 1-2-3 Classic window when the command is highlighted. (See Figures 12.4 and 12.5 for examples of this description.)

♦ Subsequent cells down the column provide the macro instructions that 1-2-3 performs if the user chooses this command.

For example, here is the complete definition for the first command in the date menu:

1-Today

Enter today's date

@TODAY{Calc}~

{Return}

As you can see, the first cell contains the command's name as it appears in the menu: **1-Today**. (Here, the boldface display improves the clarity of the menu definition inside the macro worksheet itself; commands are not displayed in boldface inside the 1-2-3 Classic window.) The second cell is the description of the command. The two remaining cells are the macro instructions for this command. The first instruction enters the date number for today's date into the current cell. The second instruction, {Return}, returns control to the main part of the macro.

In effect, the {MenuCall} command treats each column in the menu definition as a subroutine. When the user chooses a command in the menu, {MenuCall} performs the instructions in the corresponding column of the menu definition. At the end of the subroutine, the control of the program returns to the instruction located immediately after the original {MenuCall} command. The optional {Return} command at the end of each subroutine represents this return of control. (The macro language also has a {MenuBranch} command that displays a menu on the screen; this command branches to the instructions for a selected command, but does not automatically return control to the main part of the macro.)

A menu that you define in a macro can contain up to eight commands. In other words, 1-2-3 recognizes as many as eight columns of individual command definitions in the range. In the schedule macro, the time menu has three commands, defined in columns E, F, and G; and the date menu has four commands, defined in columns E, F, G, and H.

Take a brief look at the second, third, and fourth columns in the date menu definition. The macro instruction corresponding to *2-Tomorrow* is

@TODAY+1{Calc}~ (in cell F8) and the instruction for *3-Day-after-tomorrow* is @TODAY+2{Calc}~ (in cell G8). In other words, these two commands enter the date numbers for tomorrow's date and the next day's date, respectively. The fourth column in the menu definition contains a different command:

4-Date-entry

You choose the date.

{GetNumber "Date (mm/dd/yy)? ",A3}

{Return}

Like the {GetLabel} command, {GetNumber} displays an input prompt in the 1-2-3 Classic window, and waits for the user's subsequent input. The only difference is that {GetNumber} expects a numeric entry, not a label. This particular {GetNumber} command is responsible for the input window shown back in Figure 12.6. Significantly, 1-2-3 accepts a date as the input in this window, and automatically converts the input into the corresponding date number.

In summary, each of the subroutines in the date menu definition enters a date in cell A3 of the schedule worksheet. When control of the program subsequently returns to the main part of the macro, the instruction *(Alt)RF1~* (in cell B7 of the macro worksheet) formats this entry as a date.

The subroutines in the time menu definition also perform data entries, but in the macro worksheet itself rather than in the schedule worksheet. Specifically, the selected subroutine records a time increment in the location named INCR, cell B3. Depending on the command you choose in the time menu, the program enters one of three labels into INCR: *60min*, *30min*, or *15min*. The Data Fill command accepts an entry in this format in the Step text box when the Start and Stop text boxes contain time values. For example, consider the Data Fill dialog box shown in Figure 12.12. Given Start, Step, and Stop entries of 6:00 AM, 15min, and 6:00 PM, respectively, Data Fill creates a column of time entries in quarter-hour increments.

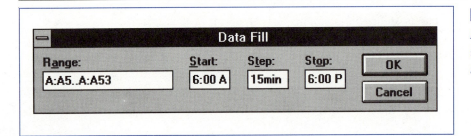

FIGURE 12.12:

Entering a time increment in the Step text box

Accordingly, the schedule program later copies the INCR label into the Data Fill dialog box as the Step value:

{Alt}DF{Alt "S"}6:00 AM{Alt "T"}{Incr}{Alt "O"}6:00 PM~

In the middle of this line of instructions, {Alt "T"} is the equivalent of pressing Alt-T to activate the Step text box in the Data Fill dialog box. Then the instruction {Incr} is a call to the subroutine at the cell named INCR. In this case, the subroutine consists simply of the sequence of characters; when this subroutine is performed, the macro copies characters into the active Step box.

To record the time increment in the INCR cell, the schedule program uses a macro command named {Let}.

USING THE {LET} COMMAND

The {Let} command simply enters a label or a value into a specified cell location:

{Let *reference,entry*}

The destination cell is identified by the first argument, *reference,* and the label or value to be entered into the cell is identified by the second argument, *entry.* For example, the following {Let} command enters the date number for today's date into a cell named DATEENTRY:

{Let DateEntry,@TODAY}

By default, {Let} enters a value into the worksheet file that is current at the time the macro is running. This creates an interesting problem for the schedule macro, because the macro worksheet is *not* the current worksheet during a run of the program. The solution to this problem is to choose a correct format for the reference argument in the {Let} command. In general, 1-2-3 follows two rules for evaluating references that appear as arguments in macro commands:

◆ In commands that send control of the program to a new location in the macro sheet—in other words, subroutine calls and branches of control—1-2-3 evaluates range arguments as references to the macro worksheet itself.

◆ In all other macro commands, 1-2-3 evaluates range arguments as references to the worksheet that is current at the time the macro is running.

For example, the instruction {MenuCall DateMenu} expects to find a cell named DATEMENU on the macro worksheet itself; but the instruction {Let DateEntry,@TODAY} makes an entry in the DATEENTRY cell on the worksheet that is current at the time the macro is running.

To override these default rules for references in macro commands, you must supply a file reference as part of the cell address or range argument. Here is how you write the {Let} command to enter a value or label in a cell location that is not in the current worksheet:

{Let <<*file*>>*reference,entry*}

For example, the subroutines of the time menu contain references to S1.WK3, the file name of the macro worksheet itself:

{Let <<C:\S1.WK3>>INCR,"60 min"}
{Let <<C:\S1.WK3>>INCR,"30 min"}
{Let <<C:\S1.WK3>>INCR,"15 min"}

Because of the distinct rules for evaluating references in macro commands, reference arguments are a common source of errors in programs. If 1-2-3 interrupts a macro and displays an *Invalid range* error message, check to see if a reference argument in the current instruction needs a file reference.

WORKING WITH LOOPS, DECISIONS, AND BRANCHES OF CONTROL

The second version of the schedule macro is similar to the first. When you run the second version, you'll see one main difference: The time menu now has four commands instead of three. As shown in Figure 12.13, the fourth command is named Other. This new command allows you to enter a time increment other than 60, 30, or 15 minutes for the time slots on the schedule worksheet. When you choose the Other command, an input window appears on the screen, as in Figure 12.14. In response to the *Minutes?* prompt, you

FIGURE 12.13:
The time menu from the second version of the schedule macro

enter the number of minutes you want to use as the increment. For example, you might enter a value of 10 to produce a range of time slots in ten-minute increments.

In addition to this change, the second version of the macro employs a new technique for entering the range of time values into the schedule worksheet. Specifically, this version illustrates the use of a macro command named {For} to create a loop in the program. In a repetitive process that is characterized by a start value, a stop value, and a step value, this {For} loop produces the time entries on the schedule worksheet one by one.

The main part of the new program appears in Figure 12.15, and the menu definitions are shown in Figures 12.16 and 12.17. To create this macro, you can start with your copy of the first version, S1.WK3. Here are the steps for making the appropriate revisions:

1. Close any schedule worksheets you created from the previous version of the program, and select S1.WK1. Choose the Worksheet Global Settings command and uncheck the Protection option. Click OK to confirm. This allows you to make changes on the macro worksheet.

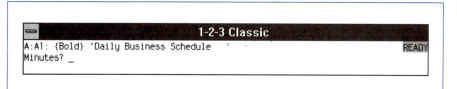

FIGURE 12.14:

The time input window

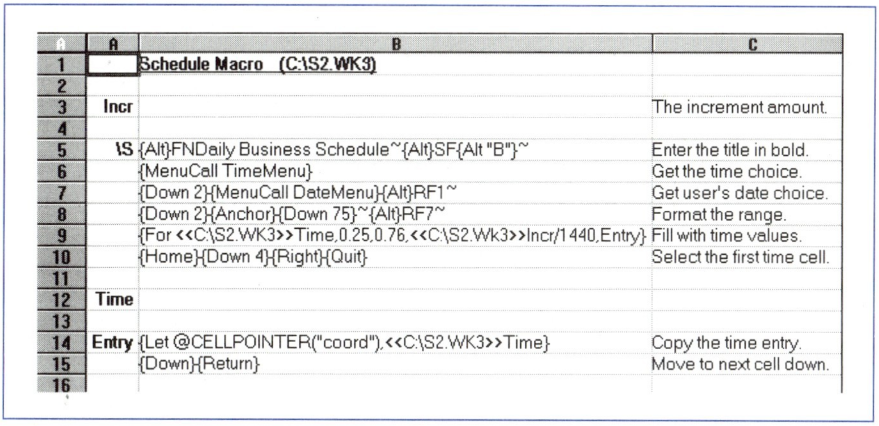

	A	B	C
1		Schedule Macro (C:\S2.WK3)	
2			
3	Incr		The increment amount.
4			
5	\S	{Alt}FNDaily Business Schedule~{Alt}SF{Alt "B"}~	Enter the title in bold.
6		{MenuCall TimeMenu}	Get the time choice.
7		{Down 2}{MenuCall DateMenu}{Alt}RF1~	Get user's date choice.
8		{Down 2}{Anchor}{Down 75}~{Alt}RF7~	Format the range.
9		{For <<C:\S2.WK3>>Time,0.25,0.76,<<C:\S2.Wk3>>Incr/1440,Entry}	Fill with time values.
10		{Home}{Down 4}{Right}{Quit}	Select the first time cell.
11			
12	Time		
13			
14	Entry	{Let @CELLPOINTER("coord"),<<C:\S2.WK3>>Time}	Copy the time entry.
15		{Down}{Return}	Move to next cell down.
16			

FIGURE 12.15:

The second version of the schedule macro

Pull down the Edit menu and choose the Find command. The Edit Find command performs search-and-replace operations, which can prove particularly useful for making global changes on a macro worksheet. In this case, you'll use it to change all the S1.WK3 refrences to S2.WK3.

Enter **S1.WK3** into the Search for text box. Select the Replace with option in the Action frame, and enter **S2.WK3** in the corresponding text box. Enter the range **A:A1..A:H20** in the Range text box. Keep the default Both option in the Search through frame. At this point, the Edit Find dialog box appears as in Figure 12.18. Click the Replace All button to perform the search-and-replace operation. In response, 1-2-3 changes all the file references in the macro worksheet. Press Home to move the cell pointer back to the beginning of the macro.

Delete the contents of cell B3. Then change the instructions in cells B8, B9, and B10, as shown in Figure 12.15. The comments for these lines, in C8, C9, and C10, are still correct. Enter the new labels, instructions, and

	D	E	F
1	TimeMenu	Sixty-minutes	Thirty-minutes
2		One-hour entries.	Half-hour entries.
3		{Let <<C:\S2.WK3>>INCR,60}	{Let <<C:\S2.WK3>>INCR,30}
4		{Return}	{Return}
5			
6	DateMenu	1-Today	2-Tomorrow
7		Enter today's date.	Enter tomorrow's date.
8		@TODAY{Calc}~	@TODAY+1{Calc}~
9		{Return}	{Return}
10			

FIGURE 12.16:
The first two columns of menu definitions in S2.WK3

	G	H
1	Fifteen-minutes	Other
2	Quarter-hour entries	You enter the time increment.
3	{Let <<C:\S2.WK3>>INCR,15}	{GetNumber "Minutes? ",<<C:\S2.WK3>>INCR}
4	{Return}	{Return}
5		
6	3-Day-after-tomorrow	4-Date-entry
7	Two days from today.	You choose the date.
8	@TODAY+2{Calc}~	{GetNumber "Date (mm/dd/yy)? ",A3}
9	{Return}	{Return}
10		

FIGURE 12.17:
The final two columns of menu definitions in S2.WK3

comments in the range A12..C15, also shown in Figure 12.15. Use the Range Name Label Create command to assign the labels in column A as the range names for the adjacent cells in column B. Adjust the widths of columns A, B, and C appropriately.

5. In the time menu definition, revise the {Let} instructions in cells E3, F3, and G3, as shown back in Figures 12.16 and 12.17. These instructions will now enter numeric values of 60, 30, or 15 into the INCR cell.

6. Enter the new subroutine for the Other option in the range H1..H4, as shown in Figure 12.17. Adjust the width of column H accordingly.

7. Choose the Worksheet Global Settings command and choose the Protection option; the X reappears in the check box. Click OK. Then select cell B12 and choose the Range Unprotect command. (Cell B3 retains its unprotected status from the previous version of the program.)

8. Choose the File Save As command and save the new version of the macro as C:\S2.WK3. (The former version remains unchanged on disk, saved as C:\S1.WK3.)

Now try running the macro two or three times. In particular, try choosing the Other command in the time menu and entering a value for the time increment. Just as in the first version, the program follows your instructions to produce a range of time entries in column A of the current schedule worksheet. But now the entries are produced by a {For} loop rather than 1-2-3's Data Fill menu command.

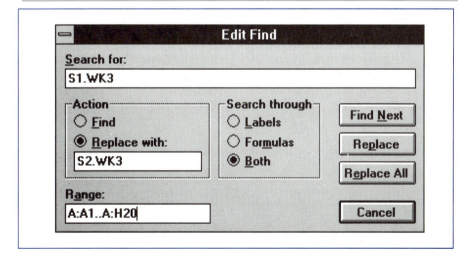

FIGURE 12.18:
Using the Edit Find command to make global changes in a macro

USING THE {FOR} COMMAND

The {For} command is 1-2-3's main tool for creating loops in a macro. {For} makes repeated calls to a subroutine while incrementing or decrementing the value stored in a designated *counter* cell. The command takes five arguments:

{For *reference,value1,value2,value3,subroutine*}

The first argument is a reference to the cell that {For} uses as a numeric counter to control the looping process. The next three arguments can appear as literal values, references to cells that contain values, or formulas that produce values. Specifically, *value1* is the start value for the loop, *value2* is the stop value, and *value3* is the step value. Finally, the fifth argument is a reference to the subroutine that the loop calls repeatedly.

The action of the {For} loop depends directly on the numbers you supply as the start, stop, and step values. If the step value is greater than zero, and the start value is less than or equal to the stop value, the subroutine is called once for each increment from start to stop. More specifically, here is how the loop proceeds:

- The start value is copied to the counter cell.

- If the value in the counter cell is less than or equal to the stop value, a call is made to the subroutine. When control returns from the subroutine, 1-2-3 increases the number in the counter cell by the step amount, and then repeats this entire step.

- At the point when the value in the counter cell is greater than the stop value, the action of the {For} command is terminated, and the macro continues with the next instruction.

In contrast, if the step value is negative, and the start value is greater than or equal to the stop value, the subroutine is called once for each step *decrement* from start down to stop:

- The start value, *value1*, is copied to the counter cell.

- If the value in the counter cell is greater than or equal to the stop value, a call is made to the subroutine. When control returns from the subroutine, 1-2-3 decreases the number in the counter cell by the negative step amount, and then repeats this entire step.

- At the point when the value in the counter cell is less than the stop value, the action of the {For} command is terminated, and the macro continues with the next instruction.

In the second version of the schedule macro, the {For} loop is responsible for producing time entries from 6:00 AM to 6:00 PM, in the time increment chosen from the time menu:

{For <<C:\S2.WK3>>Time,0.25,0.76,<<C:\S2.Wk3>>Incr/1440,Entry}

Here are descriptions of the arguments that appear in this instruction:

- The cell named TIME serves as the counter cell in this {For} command. Because TIME is on the macro worksheet, a file reference is required to identify the cell: <<C:\S2.WK3>>Time.

- The start value for the loop is 0.25, the decimal value that represents 6:00 AM.

- The stop value is 0.76, just slightly later than 6:00 PM. (There is a slight accumulation of error in the time calculations that the loop performs; for this reason, the looping sometimes stops before 6:00 PM if 0.75 is used as the stop value.)

- The step value is calculated from the value in the macro worksheet's INCR cell: <<C:\S2.WK3>>Incr/1440. The subroutine selected from the time menu uses a {Let} command to store a value such as 60, 30, or 15 in the INCR cell. Dividing this value by the number of minutes in a day, 1440, gives the corresponding time decimal.

- The subroutine call appears as *Entry*. Because the cell named ENTRY is on the macro worksheet itself, this call does not require a file reference.

The Entry subroutine, starting at cell B14 in the macro worksheet, uses a {Let} instruction to copy the time value from the TIME cell to the current cell in the schedule worksheet:

{Let @CELLPOINTER("coord"),<<C:\S2.WK3>>Time}

With a string argument of "coord," the @CELLPOINTER function returns the complete address of the current cell—that is, the current location of the cell pointer in the schedule worksheet. After copying a time value to this current cell, the Entry subroutine uses a {Down} instruction to move the cell pointer down to the next cell in column A of the schedule worksheet. Then a {Return} instruction sends control of the program back to the {For} command.

In the third and final version of the schedule macro, you'll explore the use of two additional macro commands, {If} and {Branch}.

USING THE {IF} AND {BRANCH} COMMANDS

The {If} command expresses a decision in a macro, and the {Branch} command sends control of the program to a new location in the macro worksheet. You can use these two commands together to create a repetition loop in a macro. For example, the third version of the schedule program illustrates these commands as a substitute for the {For} instruction. But in some programming contexts, {If} and {Branch} are the only appropriate tools for creating particular kinds of loops, as you'll see in the mailing list macro presented later in this chapter.

The third version of the schedule macro appears in Figure 12.19. Once again, you can start with the previous version, S2.WK3, to create this new file. Here are the steps:

1. Close any schedule worksheets you created with the previous version of the program. Select S2.WK3 and choose the Worksheet Global Settings command. Remove the X from the Protection option and click OK. Delete the contents of cells B3 and B12.

2. Use the Edit Find command to change all occurrences of S2.WK3 to S3.WK3. (Except for this change, the menu definitions in the third version of the program are identical to the second version.)

	A	B	C
1		Schedule Macro (C:\S3.WK3)	
2			
3	Incr		The increment amount.
4			
5	\S	{Alt}FNDaily Business Schedule~{Alt}SF{Alt "B"}~	Enter the title in bold.
6		{MenuCall TimeMenu}	Get the time choice.
7		{Down 2}{MenuCall DateMenu}{Alt}RF1~	Get user's date choice.
8		{Down 2}{Anchor}{Down 75}~{Alt}RF7~	Format the range.
9		{If <<C:\S3.WK3>>Incr<=0}{Let <<C:\S3.WK3>>Incr,60}	Correct a negative entry
10		{Let <<C:\S3.WK3>>Time,0.25}	Initialize the counter.
11	Loop	{Entry}	Call the Entry subroutine
12		{Let <<c:\s3.wk3>>Time,<<c:\s3.wk3>>Time+<<c:\s3.wk3>>Incr/1440}	Increment the counter.
13		{If <<C:\S3.WK3>>Time<0.76}{Branch Loop}	Test the counter.
14		{Home}{Down 4}{Right}{Quit}	Select the first time cell.
15			
16	Time		
17			
18	Entry	{Let @CELLPOINTER("coord"),<<C:\S3.WK3>>Time}	Copy the time entry.
19		{Down}{Return}	Move to next cell down.
20			

FIGURE 12.19:
The third version of the schedule macro

3. Delete the {For} command from cell B9, and the corresponding comment from cell C9. Preselect the range A10..C15 and click the range-move icon. Then click the mouse pointer (a pointing hand) in cell A14. The range A9..C13 is now blank.

4. Enter the five new macro instructions into B9..B13 and enter their corresponding comments into C9..C13, as shown in Figure 12.19. Enter the **Loop** label into cell A11, and use the Range Name Label Create command to assign this label as a range name to cell B11.

5. Choose the Worksheet Global Settings command and replace the X in the check box for the Protection option. Click OK. The cells B3 and B16 retain their unprotected status from the previous version of the worksheet.

6. Choose the File Save As command and save the file as **C:\S3.WK3**.

Try running the program. It works the same as the second version. The difference is in the logical structure of the new version: A sequence of {Let}, {If}, and {Branch} instructions have replaced the second version's {For} command.

The {If} command takes a single argument, a logical expression that results in a value of true or false. This expression represents a decision that the macro makes during a performance. In the same cell as the {If} command, you always include a second macro command:

{If *condition*} *command*

The result of {If} is as follows:

- If the *condition* is evaluated as true, 1-2-3 performs the *command* located in the same cell as the {If} instruction.

- If the *condition* is false, 1-2-3 skips the *command*, and instead continues to the next cell in the column of macro instructions.

Cell B9 in S3.WK3 contains a first example of an {If} instruction:

{If <<C:\S3.WK3>>Incr<=0}{Let <<C:\S3.WK3>>Incr,60}

This command examines the current contents of the INCR cell in the macro worksheet. If the cell contains a value that is less than or equal to zero, the user has made an invalid entry. For the program to work properly, the time increment must be greater than zero. Accordingly, if the expression <<C:\S3.WK3>>Incr<=0 is true, the subsequent {Let} command assigns a new valid value to the INCR cell. However, if the entry in INCR is already valid—that is, if the value in the cell is greater than zero—the performance skips the {Let} instruction and proceeds instead to the next command down the macro column.

Often the command located after {If} is a {Branch} command. {Branch} sends control of the program to a new location in the current macro. This instruction takes a single reference argument:

{Branch *reference*}

As usual, the *reference* argument can appear as a cell address or a range name. As long as the reference identifies a cell location in the current macro sheet, you do not need to include a file reference.

For example, consider the {If} and {Branch} statements in cell B13 of the new schedule macro:

{If <<C:\S3.WK3>>Time<0.76}{Branch Loop}

If the value in the cell named TIME is less than 0.76, the {Branch} instruction is performed, resulting in a jump back to the instruction stored at LOOP. Alternatively, if the value in TIME is 0.76 or greater, 1-2-3 skips the {Branch} instruction and instead moves on to the next line in the macro.

To put these two commands in context, here are brief descriptions of the instructions you've entered into this new macro in the range B9..B13:

- ◆ B9: The {If} instruction examines the value stored in the INCR cell. If the value is negative or zero (an invalid entry received from the {GetNumbers} operation), the subsequent {Let} command replaces it with a value of 60.

- ◆ B10: Another {Let} command stores an initial value of 0.25 (representing 6:00 AM) in the TIME cell.

- ◆ B11: The program makes a first call to the Entry subroutine. As a result, the current value of the TIME cell is copied to the current cell in the schedule worksheet.

- ◆ B12: A {Let} command replaces the current value of the TIME cell with an incremented value. The increment is calculated as *INCR/1400*.

- ◆ B13: An {If} command examines the current value of the TIME cell, and determines whether the value is less than 0.76. If this condition is true, the subsequent {Branch} statement sends control of the program back to the statement named LOOP in cell B11.

The loop represented by the statements in cells B11, B12, and B13 continues until the TIME cell contains a value that is greater than or equal to 0.76.

DEBUGGING A MACRO

The logical structure in a sequence of {If} and {Branch} statements presents many opportunities for error. Problems can result from a mistaken data entry, a faulty calculation, an incorrectly expressed condition, a misnamed cell, or any number of other common errors. In some cases, an error may actually cause an interruption in your program; 1-2-3 stops the macro at a particular instruction, and displays an error message that identifies the problem. At other times, however, a macro completes its performance from beginning to end without interruption, but fails to produce the results that you have planned. When this happens, you may need to examine the macro's actions step by step during a performance, in order to identify the instruction that is causing the trouble.

To help you in this effort, 1-2-3 has a special menu command named Tools Macro Debug. The dialog box for this command has two check boxes, labeled Single step and Trace. These two options represent features that you can turn on or off in advance of a given macro run. Both options are off by default. In most debugging procedures, you use these two options together; Figure 12.20 shows the two check boxes after they have both been selected. When you activate these options, 1-2-3 modifies the action of the subsequent macro performance:

◆ If the Single step option is active, 1-2-3 performs a macro in steps consisting of one instruction at a time. To proceed from one instruction to the next during the macro run, you press any key at the keyboard. (You can toggle in and out of the Step mode by pressing Alt-F2 at the keyboard.)

FIGURE 12.20:
The Tools Macro Debug dialog box

◆ If the Trace option is active, 1-2-3 displays a special Macro Trace window on the screen. This window displays the cell location and the contents of each macro instruction that 1-2-3 is about to perform. Figure 12.21 shows the Macro Trace window as it first appears on the screen, before you have started a macro's performance.

As an exercise with the Tools Macro Debug options, imagine that you have made the following error in the third version of the schedule macro: Rather than assigning the name LOOP to represent the instruction in cell B11, you have inadvertently assigned the range name to cell B12. If you want to experiment with the Debug options, you can actually create this error now in your copy of the program: Turn off the protection mode and reassign the LOOP range name to cell B12. When you next run the macro, the performance proceeds without interruption from beginning to end; 1-2-3 supplies no error message. But the output of the macro is incorrect. The program enters 6:00 AM in column A of the schedule worksheet, but makes no further entries.

As you think about this problem, your initial guess may be that you have made an error in the {If} command that controls the looping (in cell B13). But a close look at this instruction fails to reveal the problem; the {If} condition appears to be written correctly. This is an opportunity to take advantage of the Tools Macro Debug options. Here is how you proceed:

1. Pull down the Tools menu and choose the Macro command. Then choose the Debug command from the resulting cascade menu. Select both the Single step and Trace options, placing an X in each of the corresponding check boxes. Click OK to confirm.

2. Press Ctrl-S to run the schedule macro again. Press the Spacebar (or any other key) repeatedly to step through the initial instructions of the program. Select options from both of the program's menus when they appear on the screen.

3. Pause when the Macro Trace window first displays the instructions from cell B13, as shown in Figure 12.22. This is where you initially guessed the error was taking place. Press the Spacebar several more

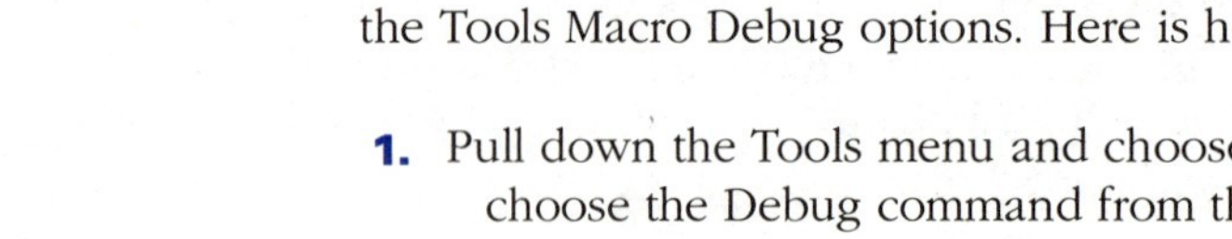

FIGURE 12.21:
The Macro Trace window as it first appears on the screen

times. As you do so, you discover that the loop is moving repeatedly between cells B12 and B13, without ever performing the subroutine call in cell B11. As you examine this action, you realize that the problem is not in the {If} instruction, but rather in the {Branch} command. {Branch Loop} is sending control of the program up to cell B12 rather than B11. This is a clear indication of the problem.

4. When the performance is complete, select the macro worksheet. Press the F5 function key to view a list of the range names defined on the worksheet. Double-click the name LOOP. When you do so, the cell pointer moves to cell B12, not B11.

5. Use the Range Name Create or Range Name Label Create command to reassign the name LOOP to the correct cell, B11.

6. Choose the Tools Macro Debug command and remove the Xs from both the Single step and Trace options. Click OK.

7. Press Ctrl-S to try running the program again. This time, the program runs as expected.

As you can see, the Single step and Trace options are simple features, but they can prove very helpful in the process of finding a logical error in a macro. This is your final exercise with the schedule macro. To prepare for the next program, you can now close the S3.WK3 worksheet and any schedule worksheets that you have created with the program.

CREATING A DATABASE MACRO

There are many useful ways to apply macro programming to a 1-2-3 database. For example, you might write macros for any of the following purposes:

◆ To simplify the process of entering records into a database

◆ To automate queries on the database

◆ To perform difficult database calculations

FIGURE 12.22:
The Macro Trace window during a macro run

Macro Trace	
A:B13	{If <<C:\S3.WK3>>Time<0.76}{Branc

◆ To produce special reports or lists from a database in formats that cannot otherwise be produced from 1-2-3

In the final programming exercise of this chapter, you'll work with a macro that creates a file of mailing labels from the instructor database. Figure 12.23 shows an example of this program's output. The program writes this list to disk as a text file, which can easily be printed out onto gummed mailing labels.

```
W. Ashford
Computing Conferences, Inc.
222 Allen Street
New York, NY 10103

S. Banks
Computing Conferences, Inc.
11 Maple Street
Dallas, TX 75210

L. Cody
Computing Conferences, Inc.
432 Market Avenue
Los Angeles, CA 90028

A. Daniels
Computing Conferences, Inc.
11 Maple Street
Dallas, TX 75210

G. Davis
Computing Conferences, Inc.
432 Market Avenue
Los Angeles, CA 90028

R. Eng
Computing Conferences, Inc.
11 Maple Street
Dallas, TX 75210

P. Gill
Computing Conferences, Inc.
432 Market Avenue
Los Angeles, CA 90028

P. Harris
Computing Conferences, Inc.
11 Maple Street
Dallas, TX 75210

J. Meyer
Computing Conferences, Inc.
222 Allen Street
New York, NY 10103
```

FIGURE 12.23:

A sample of the output from the mailing list macro

You'll create the mailing list macro in the same worksheet file as the database itself. In the completed project, the database file contains five worksheets, A through E, with the following contents:

◆ Worksheet A contains the office database.

◆ Worksheet B contains the instructor database.

◆ Worksheet C contains a criteria range that joins the office and instructor databases, as shown in Figure 12.24.

◆ Worksheet D contains the output range, with fields for each instructor's first and last name, office address, city, state, and zip code, as shown in Figure 12.25.

◆ Worksheet E contains the mailing list macro, shown in Figure 12.26.

Here are the instructions for preparing the database and creating this new macro:

1. Open your copy of the original INSTRUCT.WK3 file from disk. If necessary, use the Worksheet Unhide command to unhide worksheet D. Use the Worksheet Delete command to delete all the worksheets located after D. Then use Worksheet Insert to insert a new blank worksheet E.

2. Go to worksheet C. Delete the current contents of rows 3 and 4. As shown in Figure 12.24, enter **Instructdb.Region** as a boldface

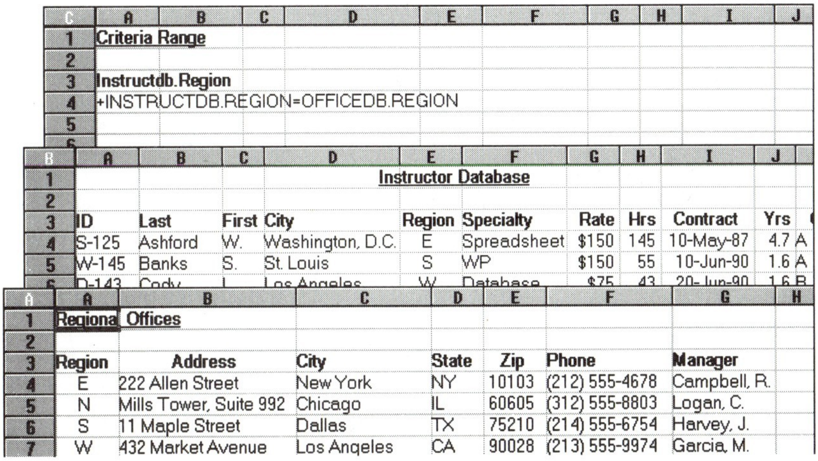

FIGURE 12.24:

Preparing the instructor database for the mailing list macro

label in cell C:A3, and enter the following formula in cell C:A4: **+IN-STRUCTDB.REGION=OFFICEDB.REGION**. While the cell pointer is still at C:A4, choose Range Format, select the Text option, and click OK. Then preselect the range C:A3..C:A4, choose the Range Name Create command, and enter **CRITERIA1** as the name for this range. (Note that this is a new definition for a range name that already exists. Type the name directly into the Range name box.) Click OK to confirm.

3. Go to worksheet D. Delete the current contents of rows 3 and below. Enter the six new field names into row 3, as shown in Figure 12.25, and adjust the column widths appropriately. Preselect the range D:A3..D:F3. Choose the Range Name Create command and enter **OUTPUT1** as the name for this range. (Again, this is a new definition for an existing range name.) Click OK to confirm.

4. Choose the Data Query command. Enter **INSTRUCTDB,OFFICEDB** in the Input range text box, **CRITERIA1** in the Criteria range text box, and **OUTPUT1** in the Output range text box. Click the Extract button, then click Cancel to close the dialog box. The instructors' names and addresses appear in the output range of worksheet D.

5. Preselect the range D:A4..D:F20, and choose the Data Sort command. Enter **D:B4** in the Primary key text box, and **D:A4** in the Secondary key text box. Select Ascending for both keys, and then click OK to complete the sort. Move the cell pointer to D:B1, and your worksheet appears as shown in Figure 12.25.

D	A	B	C	D	E	F
1	Output Range					
2						
3	Instructdb.First	Instructdb.Last	Officedb.Address	Officedb.City	Officedb.State	Officedb.Zip
4	W.	Ashford	222 Allen Street	New York	NY	10103
5	S.	Banks	11 Maple Street	Dallas	TX	75210
6	L.	Cody	432 Market Avenue	Los Angeles	CA	90028
7	A.	Daniels	11 Maple Street	Dallas	TX	75210
8	G.	Davis	432 Market Avenue	Los Angeles	CA	90028
9	R.	Eng	11 Maple Street	Dallas	TX	75210
10	P.	Gill	432 Market Avenue	Los Angeles	CA	90028
11	P.	Harris	11 Maple Street	Dallas	TX	75210
12	J.	Meyer	222 Allen Street	New York	NY	10103
13	D.	Perez	432 Market Avenue	Los Angeles	CA	90028
14	D.	Porter	Mills Tower, Suite 992	Chicago	IL	60605
15	M.	Porter	222 Allen Street	New York	NY	10103
16	F.	Ramirez	222 Allen Street	New York	NY	10103
17	P.	Roberts	Mills Tower, Suite 992	Chicago	IL	60605
18	W.	Sanchez	Mills Tower, Suite 992	Chicago	IL	60605
19	B.	Schwartz	222 Allen Street	New York	NY	10103
20	P.	Weinberg	11 Maple Street	Dallas	TX	75210

FIGURE 12.25:

An output range containing instructors' names and office addresses

6. Go to worksheet E. Enter the labels, instructions, and comments of the mailing list macro that are shown in Figure 12.26. Use the Range Name Label Create command to assign the labels in column A as range names to the adjacent cells in column B.

7. In column D of the macro worksheet, enter the following six labels in cells E:D1 through E:D6: **First**, **Last**, **Address**, **City**, **State**, and **Zip**. Preselect the range E:D1..E:D6, and click the bold and right-align icons. Then use the Range Name Label Create command to assign these six labels as range names to the adjacent cells in column E. Figure 12.27 shows what this range will look like after a run of the macro. As you can see, the macro uses this range to make a temporary copy of each record it reads from the output range of the database.

8. Choose the File Save As command and save the instructor database and the mailing list macro together under the name INSTMAIL.WK3.

Now you are ready to run the macro. Press Ctrl-M to begin. The macro begins by opening a new text file named MAILLIST.TXT in the root directory of drive C. Next, the macro moves record by record through the output range in worksheet D, copying the fields in each record to a temporary storage place in the range E:D1..E:D6. After reading each record, the program reorganizes the fields in the format of a mailing label, and writes lines of text to the MAILLIST.TXT file. When all the addresses have been written, the program closes the file and the performance is complete.

E	A	B	C
1		Mailing List Macro	
2	\M	{Goto}Output1~{Down}	Goto output range.
3		{Open "C:\MAILLIST.TXT",W}	Open a new text file.
4	Loop	{Contents First,@CELLPOINTER("coord")}{Right}	Copy the first initial.
5		{Contents Last,@CELLPOINTER("coord")}{Right}	Copy the last name.
6		{Contents Address,@CELLPOINTER("coord")}{Right}	Copy the address.
7		{Contents City,@CELLPOINTER("coord")}{Right}	Copy the city.
8		{Contents State,@CELLPOINTER("coord")}{Right}	Copy the state.
9		{Contents Zip,@CELLPOINTER("coord")}{Left 5}{Down}	Copy the zip code.
10		{Writeln @TRIM(First)&" "&Last}	Write full name to file.
11		{Writeln "Computing Conferences, Inc."}	Write company name to file.
12		{Writeln Address}	Write address to file.
13		{Writeln @TRIM(City)&", "&@TRIM(State)&" "&@TRIM(Zip)}	Write city and state to file.
14		{Writeln ""}	Write blank line to file.
15		{Writeln ""}	Write blank line to file.
16		{If @CELLPOINTER("type")<>"b"}{Branch Loop}	Test for end of database.
17		{Close}	Close the text file.
18		{Quit}	End of program.
19			
20			

FIGURE 12.26:
The mailing list macro

To view the program's output, minimize the 1-2-3 window and start up the Windows accessory application named Notepad. Pull down Notepad's File menu and choose the Open command. Select the MAILLIST.TXT file from the root directory of drive C. When the Notepad opens the file, you'll see the list of mailing labels shown back in Figure 12.23. If you wish, you can print this list by choosing the File Print command.

Return to 1-2-3 now, and look again at the macro instructions in worksheet E. The program illustrates several new macro commands. For one, the {Contents} command copies data from one cell to another in a worksheet. This command takes two references as its arguments:

{Contents *reference1,reference2*}

The command copies the contents of *reference2* to *reference1*. For example, here is how the mailing list program copies the first name field of each record to the cell named FIRST in worksheet E:

{Contents First,@CELLPOINTER("coord")}

Notice that the mailing list program does not need to use file references in the {Contents} commands, because the macro is stored in the same file as the database.

USING TEXT FILE COMMANDS IN A MACRO

The {Open}, {Writeln}, and {Close} commands are responsible for creating the text file on disk. The {Open} command takes two arguments: a string

E	D	E	F
1	First	P.	
2	Last	Weinberg	
3	Address	11 Maple Street	
4	City	Dallas	
5	State	TX	
6	Zip	75210	
7			

FIGURE 12.27:
The field cells on the mailing list macro

representing the file name, and a single letter code representing the operation for which the file will be opened:

{Open *file,code*}

The *code* argument can be R, W, M, or A, for reading, writing, modifying, or appending data. In the mailing list program, the MAILLIST.TXT file is opened for writing:

{Open "C:\MAILLIST.TXT",W}

Once a file is open in this mode, the {WRITELN} command sends a line of text to the open file. This command takes a single argument, a string or string expression:

{WRITELN *string*}

The mailing list program provides string arguments in a variety of formats for the {Writeln} command. For example, the argument in the program's first {Writeln} command is a concatenation of three strings, and includes a call to the @TRIM function to eliminate spaces from the end of the first string:

{Writeln @TRIM(First)&" "&Last}

After the last line of text is written to the file, a {Close} command is necessary to complete the write operation and to close the file. This command takes no arguments.

Here is a summary of the instructions in the mailing list program:

- ◆ E:B2: The macro selects the output range in worksheet D, and moves the cell pointer to the beginning of the first record in the range.

- ◆ E:B3: The {Open} command creates the file MAILLIST.TXT on disk. (If a previous version of the file already exists, it is deleted.)

- ◆ E:B4..E:B9: A sequence of {Contents} commands copies each field of the current record from the output range in worksheet D to the cells named FIRST, LAST, ADDRESS, CITY, STATE, and ZIP in worksheet E. At the end of this sequence, the cell pointer is positioned at the beginning of the next record in the output range.

- ◆ E:B10..E:B15: A sequence of {Writeln} commands format the record as a mailing label, and write each line of the label to the open text file.

- E:B16: An {If} instruction examines the contents of the current cell in the output range. If the cell is not empty, a {Branch} instruction sends control back up to the cell named LOOP, and the program once again begins reading a new record from the database. But if the cell is empty—that is, if the program has reached the end of the database—the {Branch} instruction is skipped.

- E:B17: A {Close} instruction closes the text file.

- E:B18: The {Quit} instruction represents the end of the program's performance.

This macro is easy to adapt for use in an address database that you use in your own work. After each {Contents} command, the program uses {Right}, {Left}, and {Down} instructions to move the cell pointer to a new field or record in the output range. Then a subsequent {Contents} command uses the @CELLPOINTER function to identify the address of the current cell. To revise this program, you simply need to make sure that the movement of the cell pointer matches the structure of your own database. In addition, you may want to change the name of the output file in the {Open} command in cell E:B3. And, of course, you should revise the {Writeln} command in E:B11, which currently writes the name Computing Conferences, Inc. as the second line of each mailing label.

SUMMARY

The 1-2-3 macro language provides commands for major categories of programming activity. In this chapter, you've seen a selection of these macro commands:

- *Data operations.* The {Let} command stores data values in cells and the {Contents} command copies values from one cell to another.

- *Input and output.* In an interactive program, the {GetLabel} and {GetNumber} commands display input prompts in windows on the screen, and accept the user's input from the keyboard. In addition, the {MenuCall} and {MenuBranch} commands display menus and respond to the user's menu choices. In a data file program, the {Open}, {Writeln}, and {Close} commands together create a file on disk and write lines of text as output to the file.

- *Decisions.* The {If} statement makes a decision that results in a choice between alternative courses of action during the macro performance.

- *Loops.* The {For} command is the main tool for creating loops in a macro. But when the loop cannot be based on specific start, stop, and step values, you can instead use the {If} and {Branch} commands to form a loop.

- *Subroutines and flow of control.* A subroutine call consists of a reference to the first cell in the subroutine, enclosed in braces. A {Branch} statement sends control of the program to a specified location without anticipating a return. Other commands that perform subroutines or branches include {For}, {MenuCall}, and {MenuBranch}.

This is just a small sampling of the many tools available in the 1-2-3 macro language. To explore the language further, study the wealth of information available on macro programming and on individual macro commands in the 1-2-3 Help window.

APPENDIX A

Installing Lotus 1-2-3 for Windows

otus 1-2-3 for Windows comes with an easy-to-use installation program named Install. It is stored on Disk 1 of the program disks that come with the 1-2-3 package. You run Install directly from Windows. While it is running, the program gives you complete instructions about the information you have to supply, and tells you when you need to swap disks. Install even has its own Help window that you can consult if you have questions during the installation process. When Install is finished, you are ready to run 1-2-3.

Here are the steps for installing 1-2-3 on your computer:

1. Start up Windows 3.0. Insert the Lotus 1-2-3 for Windows Install disk (Disk 1) into a floppy disk drive.

2. In the Windows Program Manager, pull down the File menu and choose the Run command. The Run dialog box appears on the screen. In the Command Line text box, type **A:INSTALL** if you have inserted Disk 1 in drive A, or **B:INSTALL** if Disk 1

is in drive B. Click the OK button, or press ↵. At the outset, a message box informs you that Install is copying its own working files to your hard disk.

3. A dialog box named Welcome to Install appears. This box contains the product's copyright notice. After you have read the information in the box, click the OK button to continue.

4. The Recording Name and Company Name box is displayed next on the screen. Enter your own name and your company name in the two text boxes provided. (After the first entry, you can press the Tab key to activate the second text box or you can click the second box with the mouse. Click Help if you want more information.) The Install program uses these names to initialize and identify your copy of the 1-2-3 program. When you have completed the two entries, click OK to continue. The subsequent dialog box asks you to confirm the two names you have entered. Click Yes if the entries are correct, or No if you want to reenter them. When you click Yes, a message tells you that Install is saving this information to disk.

5. Now the Install program's Main Menu is displayed. The menu box contains three icons, representing the three options of the menu. Click the first icon, labeled Install 1-2-3.

6. A dialog box named Type of Installation appears, as shown in Figure A.1. The icons in this box represent two approaches to the installation process. Click the second icon, Install with Options. As you'll see shortly, this option allows you to activate the Edit Undo command, which the Install program for Release 1.0 disables by default. (In Release 1.0a, Edit Undo is enabled by default.)

7. A dialog box named Specifying Files and Directories appears next. In the text box named Drives and space, the Install program shows the name of the first drive in which there is enough space to install 1-2-3.

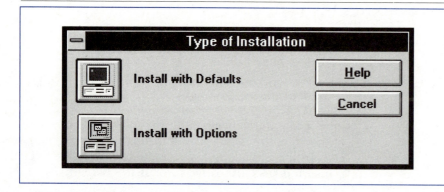

FIGURE A.1:
The Type of Installation dialog box

If you wish to save the program on a different drive, click the down-arrow icon displayed next to this text box. The resulting drop-down list shows you the hard drives available in your system. (Drives that do not have enough space for 1-2-3 appear in parentheses.) Click the name of the drive on which you want to install the program. For example, in Figure A.2, drive D has been selected. The Program Directory text box shows the name of the default directory in which Install saves the program, \123W. Do not change this name.

8. Use this same dialog box to select the parts of 1-2-3 that you want to install. By default, the installation includes the 1-2-3 program itself, a set of sample worksheets, and the dBASE DataLens Driver. (Click the Help command button if you want to know more about the various parts of the 1-2-3 package.) Click OK to confirm your selections.

9. A dialog box named Confirm Directory appears on the screen. Click the Yes button and the Install program creates the \123W directory on the drive that you have selected.

10. The Adding 1-2-3 Icons to a Program Manager Group dialog box appears next. This box displays the program icons that will appear inside the Lotus Applications group in the Windows Program Manager when you complete your installation. Click OK to accept these selections.

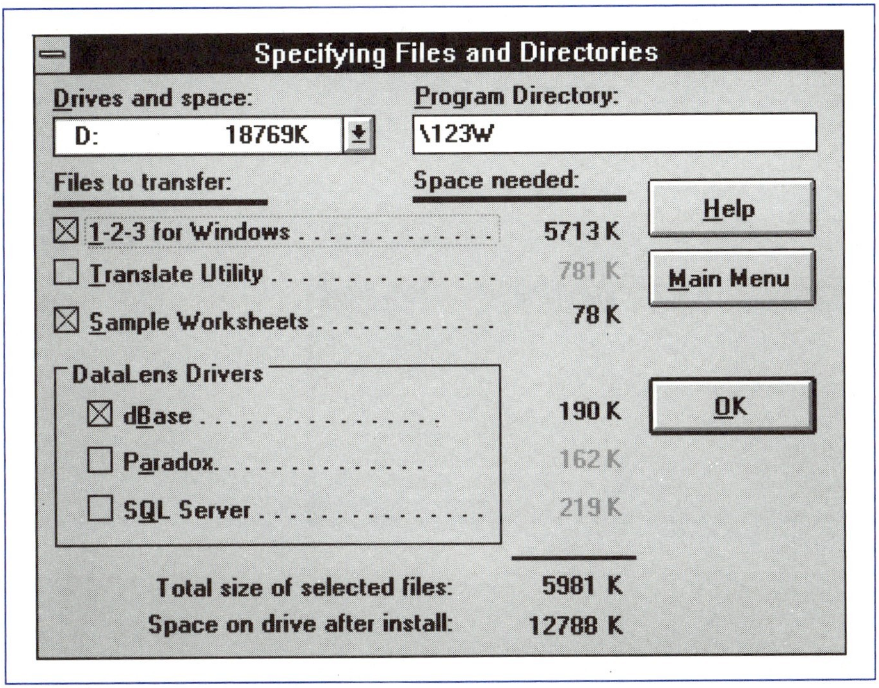

FIGURE A.2:
The Specifying Files and Directories Box

11. Next, the 1-2-3 Default Preferences dialog box displays options that you can turn on or off for your installation. If you are installing Release 1.0, click the Enable edit undo option, placing an X in the corresponding check box (as shown in Figure A.3). Then click OK. Another Confirm Directory box appears on the screen. Click Yes and the Install program creates the directory \123W\SAMPLE for the sample worksheets that will be copied to your disk.

12. Now the Install program begins copying the program files to your hard disk. This process takes several minutes. A dialog box named Transferring Files charts the progress of the installation. Whenever the Install program needs a new program disk, a box like the one in Figure A.4 appears on the screen, telling you which disk to insert in the floppy disk drive. After you swap disks, click the OK button to continue.

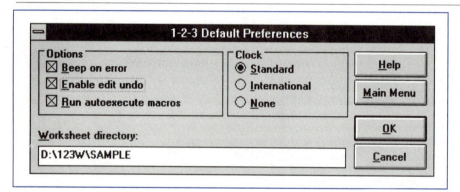

FIGURE A.3:
The 1-2-3 Default Preferences dialog box

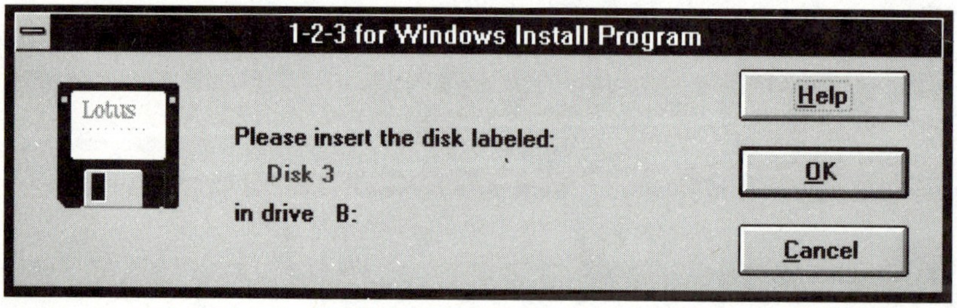

FIGURE A.4:
Instructions for swapping disks

13. After the Install program transfers files from all the 1-2-3 program disks, the 1-2-3 installation is complete. Read the Installation Finished box and then click OK.

14. You can now install the Adobe Type Manager, which comes with the 1-2-3 package. To do so, click the Yes button on the Option to Start ATM Installer dialog box.

15. Exit from the installation program by clicking the Exit Install button in the Main Menu dialog box. Back in the Windows Program Manager, you will now find a group named Lotus Applications. To start 1-2-3, double-click the 1-2-3 for Windows icon shown in Figure A.5.

At any time while you are working in 1-2-3, you can change the default preferences you have selected during installation. To do so, pull down the Tools menu and choose the User Setup command. In the resulting dialog box, shown in Figure A.6, you can activate or disable the Edit Undo command and you can enter a new name for the default directory.

FIGURE A.5:
The Lotus Applications group

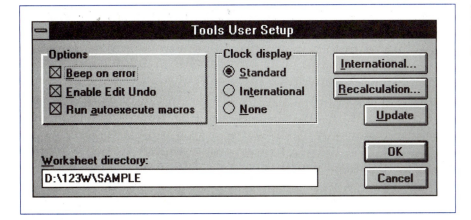

FIGURE A.6:
The Tools User Setup dialog box in 1-2-3

APPENDIX B

The @ Functions

elow is an annotated list of the @ functions available in 1-2-3 for Windows:

@@(*reference*) returns the contents of the cell identified in *reference*. For example, if cell A1 contains the label entry E19, and the cell E19 contains the value entry 123, then @@(A1) returns the value 123.

@ABS(*value*) gives the absolute value of its numeric argument. For example, @ABS(123) and @ABS(−123) both return the value 123.

@ACOS(*value*) returns the arccosine, or the angle in radians of a cosine argument. For example, @ACOS(−1) returns a value of π.

@ASIN(*value*) returns the arcsine, or the angle in radians of a sine argument. For example, @ASIN(1) returns a value of π/2.

@ATAN(*value*) returns the arctangent, or the angle in radians of a tangent argument. For example, the expression @ATAN(1)*4 gives a value of π.

@ATAN2(*x,y*) returns the arctangent, or the angle in radians of a line in an (*x,y*) coordinate system. For example, @ATAN2(1,1) gives a value of π/4.

@AVG(*list*) returns the average of the values in the list. The *list* argument can appear as any combination of values, addresses, ranges, or formulas.

@CELL(*info,reference*) supplies information about a cell at *reference*. The first argument, *info,* is a string that specifies the kind of information that @CELL will return. For example @CELL("format",A1) returns the current format of cell A1.

@CELLPOINTER(*info*) supplies information about the current location of the cell pointer. The argument is a string that specifies the kind of information the function will return. For example, @CELLPOINTER("contents") returns the contents of the current cell.

@CHAR(*integer*) returns a character from the LMBCS code. For example, @CHAR(76) returns "L".

@CHOOSE(*integer,list*) selects a value from a list or range of values. The first argument in a numeric offset, ranging from 0 to *n*–1, where *n* is the number of elements in the list. For example, @CHOOSE (1,"one","two","three") returns "two".

@CODE(*string*) returns the LMBCS code for the first character in the *string* argument. For example @CODE("L") is 76.

@COLS(*range*) returns the number of columns in a range. For example, if the range name DB represents a database range, @COLS(DB) returns the number of fields in the database.

@COORD(*worksheet,column,row,format*) supplies a cell reference. The arguments *worksheet, column,* and *row* are integers representing the elements of the reference. The *format* is an integer from 1 to 8 representing a reference format, where 1 is a completely absolute reference and 8 is a completely relative reference. For example, @COORD(2,2,2,1) gives the reference $B:$B$2.

@COS(*angle*) gives the cosine of an angle, where the argument is expressed in radians. For example, @COS(@PI) is –1.

@COUNT(*list*) counts the number of cells that contain entries in a range or list of ranges.

@CTERM(*rate,futurevalue,presentvalue*) calculates the number of compounding periods required to reach a *futurevalue* amount, given a one-time investment of *presentvalue* and a fixed periodic interest *rate.*

@DATE(*year,month,day*) returns the date number corresponding to the date specified in its three integer arguments. For example, @DATE(92,8,19) returns 33835, the date number corresponding to 19-Aug-92.

@DATEVALUE(*datestring*) returns the date number corresponding to a recognizable date string argument. For example @DATEVALUE ("19-Aug-92") returns 33835.

@DAVG(*database,field,criteria*) calculates the average of selected values in a *database* range. The target database column is identified by *field,* which may appear as a field name in quotes, or a column offset number. The calculation includes all *field* entries in records that match the expressions in the *criteria* range.

@DAY(*datenumber*) returns an integer from 1 to 31, representing the day of the month of *datenumber.* For example, @DAY(33835) returns 19, from the date 19-Aug-92.

@DAYS360(*date1,date2*) returns the number of days between two dates, *date1* and *date2*. The subtraction is based on a 360-day year.

@DCOUNT(*database,field,criteria*) returns a count of selected values in a *database* range. The target database column is identified by *field,* which may appear as a field name in quotes, or a column offset number. The count includes all *field* entries in records that match the expressions in the *criteria* range.

@DDB(*cost,salvage,life,period*) calculates the double-declining-balance depreciation of an asset, given the original *cost,* the *salvage* value at the end of useful life, the *life* of the asset in years, and the target *period* for which the depreciation is to be calculated.

@DGET(*database, field, criteria*) returns the *field* item from a single *database* record selected by the expressions in the *criteria* range. If two or more records match the criteria, @DGET returns an ERR value.

@DMAX(*database,field,criteria*) finds the largest value among selected entries in a *database* range. The target database column is identified by *field,* which may appear as a field name in quotes, or a column offset number. The largest value is selected from *field* entries in records that match the expressions in the *criteria* range.

@DMIN(*database,field,criteria*) finds the smallest value among selected entries in a *database* range. The target database column is identified by *field,* which may appear as a field name in quotes, or a column offset number. The smallest value is selected from *field* entries in records that match the expressions in the *criteria* range.

@DQUERY(*"function",arguments*) calls a function defined in an external database.

@DSTD(*database, field, criteria*) calculates the population standard deviation of selected values in a *database* range. The target database column is identified by *field,* which may appear as a field name in quotes, or a column offset number. The calculation includes all *field* entries in records that match the expressions in the *criteria* range.

@DSTDS(*database,field,criteria*) calculates the sample standard deviation of selected values in a *database* range. The target database column is identified by *field,* which may appear as a field name in quotes, or a column offset number. The calculation includes all *field* entries in records that match the expressions in the *criteria* range.

@DSUM(*database, field, criteria*) calculates the sum of selected values in a *database* range. The target database column is identified by *field*, which may appear as a field name in quotes, or a column offset number. The sum includes all *field* entries in records that match the expressions in the *criteria* range.

@DVAR(*database, field, criteria*) calculates the population variance of selected values in a *database* range. The target database column is identified by *field*, which may appear as a field name in quotes, or a column offset number. The calculation includes all *field* entries in records that match the expressions in the *criteria* range.

@DVARS(*database, field, criteria*) calculates the sample variance of selected values in a *database* range. The target database column is identified by *field*, which may appear as a field name in quotes, or a column offset number. The calculation includes all *field* entries in records that match the expressions in the *criteria* range.

@D360(*date1, date2*) returns the number of days between two dates, *date1* and *date2*. The subtraction is based on a 360-day year.

@ERR returns the value ERR.

@EXACT(*string1, string2*) returns a value of 1 (true) if *string1* is identical to *string2*, or a value of 0 (false) if the two strings are different.

@EXP(*value*) calculates e to the power of *value*. The natural constant e is given by @EXP(1) as 2.71828182845904524.

@FALSE returns the value 0, for false.

@FIND(*substring, string, pos*) searches for *substring*, starting from the offset position of *pos* inside *string*. If the search is successful, @FIND returns the offset location of the substring. For example, @FIND ("Co","Computing Conferences",5) returns a value of 10, the offset location of the second occurrence of "Co" in the string.

@FV(*payment,rate,term*) finds the future value of a series of equal periodic *payment* amounts over *term* periods at a fixed periodic interest *rate*.

@HLOOKUP(*value,table,row*) performs a lookup operation in a horizontally-arranged lookup *table*. Specifically, the function finds the largest number in the top row of the table that is less than or equal to *value*, then looks down the corresponding column to the cell located in *row*. @HLOOKUP returns the value in this target cell. (Alternatively, the function's first argument can appear as a string, in which case the first row of the lookup table contains labels.)

@HOUR(*timenumber*) returns an integer from 0 to 23, representing the hour of the decimal *timenumber* argument.

@IF(*expression,value1,value2*) returns *value1* if the logical *expression* is true, or *value2* if *expression* is false. For example, @IF(A1=0,"zero","not zero") returns *zero* if A1 contains a value of 0, or *not zero* if A1 contains a value other than 0.

@INDEX(*range,column,row,worksheet*) selects a label or a value from a worksheet table. The first argument, *range,* is the location of the table; and *column* and *row* are offset values identifying a cell location within the table. The optional *worksheet* argument refers to a table located on a different worksheet from the function itself.

@INFO(*info*) returns an item of information about the current 1-2-3 session. The *info* argument is a string that indicates the kind of information to be returned. For example, @INFO("directory") returns the current default directory path.

@INT(*value*) supplies the truncated integer portion of a numeric argument. For example, @INT(@RAND*10) gives random integers between 0 and 10.

@IRR(*guess,cashflows*) calculates the internal rate of return from a series of positive and negative cash flow amounts. The first argument is a reasonable *guess* for the internal rate of return, and the second is a reference to a worksheet range of positive and negative cash flow amounts.

@ISAAF(*name*) returns a value of 1 (true) if *name* is a defined add-in function, or a value of 0 (false) if *name* is not defined.

@ISAPP(*name*) returns a value of 1 (true) if *name* is a defined add-in application, or a value of 0 (false) if *name* is not defined.

@ISERR(*reference*) returns a value of 1 (true) if the cell at reference contains the value ERR or a value of 0 (false) if it does not. (The function's argument can also appear as a value or expression.)

@ISNA(*reference*) returns a value of 1 (true) if the cell at reference contains the value NA or a value of 0 (false) if it does not. (The function's argument can also appear as a value or expression.)

@ISNUMBER(*reference*) returns a value of 1 (true) if the cell at *reference* contains a numeric value or is blank. If the cell contains a label entry, @ISNUMBER returns a value of 0 (false). (The argument of @ISNUMBER can also appear as a value, label, or formula.)

@ISRANGE(*reference*) returns a value of 1 (true) if *reference* is a valid range name or a correctly expressed reference.

@ISSTRING(*reference*) returns a value of 1 (true) if the cell at *reference* contains a label entry or a formula that produces a label. If the cell is blank or contains a number, @ISSTRING returns a value of 0 (false). (The argument of @ISSTRING can also appear as a value, label, or formula.)

@LEFT(*string,n*) returns a substring consisting of the first *n* characters of *string*. For example, @LEFT("Computing Conferences, Inc.",9) returns the substring "Computing".

@LENGTH(*string*) returns the length, in characters, of its string argument. For example, @LENGTH("Computing Conferences, Inc.") returns 27.

@LN(*value*) supplies the natural logarithm of its argument, that is, the power of e that produces *value*.

@LOG(*value*) supplies the base-10 logarithm of its argument, that is, the power of 10 that produces *value*. For example, @LOG(1000) is 3.

@LOWER(*string*) returns a lower-case version of its string argument. For example, @LOWER("Computing Conferences, Inc.") returns "computing conferences, inc."

@MAX(*list*) returns the largest value in the list. The *list* argument can appear as any combination of values, addresses, ranges, or formulas.

@MID(*string,pos,n*) returns a substring consisting of *n* characters copied from *string*, starting at the position identified as *pos*. (The *pos* argument is the offset from the beginning of the string. The value of *pos* for the first character in the string is 0.) For example, @POS("Computing Conferences, Inc.",10,11) returns the substring "Conferences".

@MIN(*list*) returns the smallest value in the list. The *list* argument can appear as any combination of values, addresses, ranges, or formulas.

@MINUTE(*timenumber*) returns an integer from 0 to 59, representing the minutes in *timenumber*. The *timenumber* argument is a decimal time value. For example, @MINUTE(0.1875) returns 30, from the time 4:30 AM.

@MOD(*numerator,denominator*) supplies the remainder from the division of two integers. For example, @MOD(@TODAY,7) gives a value from 0 to 6 representing the day of the week from Saturday to Friday.

@MONTH(*datenumber*) returns an integer from 1 to 12, representing the month of *datenumber*. For example, @MONTH(33835) returns a value of 8, identifying the month in the date 19-Aug-92.

@N(*reference*) returns a copy of the value in the first cell of the range identified by *reference*. If this cell does not contain a value, @N returns 0.

@NA returns the value NA (for Not Available).

@NOW supplies a combined date-and-time number representing the current date and time. For example, @NOW returns 33835.25 for the date 19-Aug-92 at 6:00 AM.

@NPV(*rate,cashflows*) finds the net present value of a series of future periodic cash flow amounts, positive or negative. The *rate* is the periodic rate of return. The *cashflows* argument is a range of cash flow amounts.

@PI returns the value of π as 3.14159265358979324.

@PMT(*principal,rate,term*) calculates the periodic payment required to pay back a loan. The arguments are the original *principal* amount of the loan, the periodic *rate,* and the *term* of the loan. For a monthly payment result, the *rate* and *term* arguments must both be supplied as monthly amounts.

@PROPER(*string*) returns a new *string* version in which the first letter of each word is capitalized. For example, @PROPER("computing conferences, inc.") returns "Computing Conferences, Inc."

@PV(*payment,rate,term*) finds the present value of a series of equal future cash flow amounts. The *payment* argument is the cash flow at the end of each period in *term*. The *rate* is the periodic rate of return.

@RAND returns a random decimal value between 0 and 1. Multiplying this function by a maximum value produces random numbers in a specified range. For example, @INT(@RAND*100) supplies random integers between 0 and 100.

@RATE(*futurevalue,presentvalue,term*) calculates the interest rate corresponding to a fixed future return of *futurevalue,* given an initial investment of *presentvalue* and a specified investment *term*.

@REPEAT(*string,n*) generates a string consisting of *n* copies of *string*. For example, @REPEAT("*^",5) produces the string *^*^*^*^*^.

@REPLACE(*string,pos,n,substring*) returns a copy of *string* in which the *n* characters starting from *pos* have been replaced by *substring*. For example, @REPLACE("Computing Instructors, Inc.",10,11,"Conferences") returns the string "Computing Conferences, Inc."

@RIGHT(*string,n*) returns a substring consisting of the last *n* characters of *string*. For example, @RIGHT("Computing Conferences, Inc.",4) returns the substring "Inc."

@ROUND(*value,place*) returns a rounded value. The first argument is the *value* to be rounded, and the second argument is the decimal *place* at which rounding will occur. If *place* is positive, rounding occurs at the right side of the decimal point; if negative, rounding occurs at the left of the decimal. If *place* is zero, @ROUND returns the nearest integer.

@ROWS(*range*) returns the number of rows in the specified *range*. For example, if the range name DB represents a database range (not including the top row of field names), @ROWS(DB) returns the number of records in the database.

@S(*reference*) returns a copy of the label in the first cell of a range identified by *reference*. If this cell does not contain a label, @S returns an empty string.

@SECOND(*timenumber*) returns an integer from 0 to 59, representing the seconds in *timenumber*. The *timenumber* argument is a decimal time value.

@SHEETS(*range*) returns the number of worksheets in the specified *range*.

@SIN(*angle*) gives the sine of an angle, where the argument is expressed in radians. For example, @SIN(@PI) is 0.

@SLN(*cost,salvage,life*) calculates the straight-line depreciation of an asset, given the original *cost,* the *salvage* value at the end of useful life, and the *life* of the asset in years.

@SOLVER(*info*) returns information about the current Solver operation. For example, @SOLVER("done") returns a value of 1 if the Solver has completed its solution, 2 if the Solver is in the process of completing the solution, or 3 if the Solver is active but not in the process of finding a solution.

@SQRT(*value*) gives the square root of *value*. For example, @SQRT(81) is 9.

@STD(*list*) returns the standard deviation of the values in the list. The *list* argument can appear as any combination of values, addresses, ranges, or formulas. @STD is calculated as the square root of @VAR.

@STDS(*list*) returns the standard deviation of the values in the list. The *list* argument can appear as any combination of values, addresses, ranges, or formulas. @STDS is calculated as the square root of @VARS.

@STRING(*value,n*) produces a string from a numeric argument. The first argument, *value,* is the number to be converted to a string; and the second argument, *n,* is the number of decimal places that will appear in the result. For example, @STRING(123.456,1) produces the string "123.5" as its result.

@SUM(*list*) returns the sum of the values in the list. The *list* argument can appear as any combination of values, addresses, ranges, or formulas.

@SUMPRODUCT(*list*) returns the sum of the products of corresponding values in a list of ranges. For example, @SUMPRODUCT (RANGE1,RANGE2) mutliplies each value in RANGE1 by the corresponding value in RANGE2, and returns the sum of the products.

@SYD(*cost,salvage,life,period*) calculates the sum-of-the-years'-digits depreciation of an asset, given the original *cost,* the *salvage* value at the end of useful life, the *life* of the asset in years, and the target *period* for which the depreciation is to be calculated.

@TAN(*angle*) gives the tangent of an angle, where the argument is expressed in radians. For example, @TAN(@PI/4) is 1.

@TERM(*payment,rate,futurevalue*) calculates the number of equal *payment* amounts required to reach a specified *futurevalue,* given a fixed periodic interest *rate*.

@TIME(*hour,minutes,seconds*) returns the decimal time value corresponding to the time specified in its three integer arguments. For example, @TIME(4,30,0) returns 0.1875, the decimal corresponding to 4:30 AM.

@TIMEVALUE(*timestring*) returns a decimal time value corresponding to a recognizable time string. For example, @TIMEVALUE ("4:30 AM") returns 0.1875.

@TODAY supplies a date number representing the current date. For example, @TODAY returns 33835 for the date 19-Aug-92.

@TRIM(*string*) returns a copy of *string* without extraneous spaces. @TRIM removes all spaces from the beginning and end of the string, and multiple consecutive spaces from inside the string.

@TRUE returns a value of 1 for true.

@UPPER(*string*) returns an uppercase version of its string argument. For example, @UPPER("Computing Conferences, Inc.") returns "COMPUTING CONFERENCES, INC."

@VALUE(*string*) produces a number from a string of digits. For example, @VALUE("9876") returns the number 9876.

@VAR(*list*) returns the population variance of the values in the list. The *list* argument can appear as any combination of values, addresses, ranges, or formulas.

@VARS(*list*) returns the sample variance of the values in the list. The *list* argument can appear as any combination of values, addresses, ranges, or formulas.

@VDB(*cost,salvage,life,start,end,factor,switch*) calculates the variable-rate declining-balance depreciation of an asset, given the original *cost*, the *salvage* value at the end of useful life, the *life* of the asset in years, the *start* and *end* of the target period for which the depreciation is to be calculated, the optional accelerated depreciation *factor*, and a value of true or false for the optional *switch* argument. If *factor* is omitted, the default is 200%, the same as the double-declining-balance method. If *switch* is true (the default), the calculation changes to the straight-line method to maximize depreciation in the final years of useful life.

@VLOOKUP(*value,table,column*) performs a lookup operation in a vertically-arranged lookup *table*. Specifically, the function finds the largest number in the first column of the table that is less than or equal to *value*, then looks across the corresponding row to the cell located in *column*. @VLOOKUP returns the value in this target cell. (Alternatively, the function's first argument can appear as a string, in which case the first column of the lookup table contains labels.)

@YEAR(*datenumber*) returns an integer representing the year of *datenumber*. For example, @YEAR(33835) returns 92, the year in 19-Aug-92.

INDEX

Symbols

& (ampersand) to join text values, 249
* (asterisk)
  in data block, 478
  as wildcard, 382
@ (at sign)
  to begin function, 30, 237, 241, 254
  in header or footer text box, 224
\ (backslash)
  in header or footer text box, 224–225
  for label repeats, 176–177
  in macro names, 430–431, 438
{ } (braces) in macro names, 431–432, 438, 450, 453
^ (caret)
  for centering in cell, 173, 175
  for exponentiation, 243
) (close parenthesis) to complete summation formula, 120, 154, 256
, (comma) to separate arguments, 453–454, 540
$ (dollar sign) for absolute references, 147
>> (double angle brackets) as file reference, 436
" (double quotation mark) for right label alignment, 173
> (greater-than sign) in data block, 478
< (less-than sign) in label expression, 381
– (minus sign) to begin formula, 243
((open parenthesis)
  to begin formula, 243
  in function, 256
( ) (parenthesis) in order of operations, 153–154, 243
. (period) to anchor ranges, 68, 120
+ (plus sign) for starting formulas, 141–142, 240–241
# (pound sign) in header or footer text box, 224
? (question mark) as wildcard, 382
; (semicolon) to place note at end of formula, 242
' (single quotation mark) for left label alignment, 109, 114, 173
~ (tilde)
  to identify excluded value, 382
  in macros, 443
| (vertical bar)
  as excluded print range indicator, 177
  in header or footer text box, 225

A

About 1-2-3 commands in Help menu, 96
@ABS function, 270, 281–282, 579
absolute reference, 146–147
accelerated depreciation, 261

@ACOS function, 270, 272, 579
address, 8, 29
address box, 15, 79
adding
  graph to worksheet, 336–337
  objects to graph, 330–334
  objects to worksheet, 474–476
  titles and legend to worksheet, 326–330
adjustable cells, 502
aggregate columns, creating, 406–408
aligning labels, 22, 173–175
{Alt}, 433
  to activate menu bar, 11, 54, 59
  to activate tool in dialog box, 65
  to select options from dialog boxes, 443–445
  in writing macros, 440–443
Alt-Backspace, 112
Alt-Hyphen, 8, 86
Alt-Escape, 58
Alt-F4, 58
ampersand (&) to join text values, 249
anchoring, 68, 120
application, 532
area graphs, 339
arguments
  in database functions, 397
  in macro commands, 453
  reference, 453, 548, 560
  string, 453
arithmetic
  date, 192, 195–198
  matrix, 469–470
  time, 199, 201–205
arithmetic operators, 29
arrow keys, 9–11, 81
ascending sort order, 364
@ASIN function, 270, 272, 579
asterisk (*)
  in data block, 478
  for multiplication in formula, 141–142
  as wildcard, 382
at sign (@)
  to begin function, 30, 237, 241, 254

  in header or footer text box, 224
@ functions, 96, 579–592
@ATAN function, 270, 272, 579
@ATAN2 function, 272–273, 579
@@ as indirect cell reference function, 579
autoexecute macro, 459
automatic format, 189–190
@AVG function, 257, 580

B

Back button, 98
backslash (\)
  in header or footer text box, 224–225
  for label repeats, 176
  in macro names, 430–431, 438
Backspace key in edit line, 81
.BAK extension, 130
binary operators, 247
bin range, 482
bold icon, 220
bold option, 210
Bookmark menu, 98
borders, 214
braces ({ }) in macro names, 431–432, 438, 450, 453
{Branch} macro commands, 540, 558–561
Browse buttons, 98

C

calculated fields, 40, 359–361
calculations on database records, 396–408
call instruction, 438
cancel button, 22, 66, 79
caret (^)
  for centering in cell, 173, 175
  for exponentiation, 243
cascade menu, 62, 122
cell, 7–8
  adjustable, 502
  constraint, 502
  counter, 556

current, 8
  entering functions, 254–255
  optimal, 502
cell address, 16, 29
@CELL function, 580
Cell contents box, 218
cell pointer, 8
@CELLPOINTER function, 457, 557, 570, 580
changing
  data, 34–35
  data-entry mode, 189–191
  worksheets, 132–139
@CHAR function, 296, 580
Chart Headings dialog box, 326
Chart Legend dialog box, 326–327
Chart menu
  Axis command, 334
  Borders/Grids command, 335
  Ranges command, 317, 338
  Type command, 39, 317, 319–322
  Y command, 334
check boxes, 69–71
@CHOOSE function, 298, 580
clipboard, 6, 127
close parenthesis ( )) to complete summation formula, 120, 154, 256
@CODE function, 296, 580
coefficient matrix, 469
color range in creating graphs, 342
color in worksheets, 218–220
@COLS function, 580
column argument, 299
columns, 7
  changing widths, 166–170
  creating aggregate, 406–408
  creating computed, 402–406
  hiding, 170–173
  inserting, 136–139
column widths, changing, 166–170
columnwise method, 311, 322
comma (,) to separate arguments, 453–454, 540
comma format, 186
command buttons, 65–67
complete cell address, 16
computed columns, creating, 402–406

concatenation, 249
conditional branch, 537, 558–561
confirm button, 22, 79
constant matrix, 469
constraint cells, 502
contents box, 22, 79
context-sensitive help, 96–97
Control menu box, 8
control panel, 53
@COORD function, 580
copying
  formulas, 144–146
  ranges, 124–128
@COS function, 270–271, 581
cost, definition of, 261
@COUNT function, 257, 581
counter cell, 556
create-graph icon, 315–316
creating
  aggregate columns, 406–408
  computed columns, 402–406
  database macros, 563–570
  footers, 223–225
  graphs, 37–40
  headers, 223–225
  keystroke macros, 430–440
  links, 516–534
  one-way what-if tables, 491–494
  pie charts, 340–343
  three-way what-if tables, 495-499
  two-way what-if tables, 495–499
  worksheets, 26–35, 108–128
criteria, 373, 388–390
criteria range, 374–376
@CTERM function, 267, 581
Ctrl-PgDn, 15–16
Ctrl-PgUp, 15–16
currency format, 186
current cell, 8, 15
custom menu, 536, 548–551

D

data
  changing, 34–35
  creating graph from worksheet, 309–326
  entering, 27–28

moving ranges of, 133–136
transferring, 528–534
database, 5, 40. *See also* external database
　creating macro for, 563–570
　defining, 41–42, 353–357
　distinguishing from database table, 361
　entering, 358–361
　joining multiple, 408–413
　length of, 41
　multiple tables in, 361–364
　performing query operations in, 373–390
　performing sort and search operations in, 42–45
　sorting, 364–373
　working with external, 413–424
database functions
　@DAVG, 396–397, 581
　@DCOUNT, 396–397, 581
　@DMAX, 397, 582
　@DSTD, 397, 582
　@DSTDS, 397, 582
　@DSUM, 396–400, 417–418, 583
　@DVAR, 397, 583
　@DVARS, 397, 583
　using with an external database, 417–418
database operations, performing, 40–41
database records, performing calculations on, 396–408
database table, 355, 361
　distinguishing from database, 361
　multiple, 361–364
data block, 478
Data Connect to External dialog box, 415–416
data entry and mode indicator, 22–24
data-entry mode, changing, 189–191
DataLens driver, 413–414
Data Matrix Invert operation, 469
Data Matrix Multiply operation, 469–470
Data menu, 60
　Connect to External command, 415–416

Distribution command, 482–483
External Options command, 420
External Options Create Table command, 422–424
External Options Disconnect command, 424
External Options Send command, 422
External Options Paste Fields command, 420–422
Fill command, 239–240, 492
Matrix commands, 467–476
Parse command, 476–481
Query commands, 377–390
Query Delete command, 382–386, 420
Query Extract command, 379–382, 408
Query Find command, 377–379, 420
Query Modify command, 384, 386–388, 420
Query Modify Insert command, 424
Regression command, 484–487
Sort command, 364–367
Sort Extra Keys command, 367–371
What-if Table commands, 487–490
data ranges for graphs, 311–312, 339
date arithmetic, 192, 195–198
@DATE function, 284, 287–288, 360–361, 581
date functions, 282–291
date formulas, 244
@DATEVALUE function, 284, 288–289, 481, 581
date values, entering, 192–198
Data Matrix menu
　Invert command, 470
　Multiply command, 471
Data menu, 41
@DAVG function, 396–397, 581
@DAY function, 283, 581
@DAYS360 function, 284, 581
dBASE III Plus, 413
dBASE IV, 413
@DCOUNT function, 396–397, 581

@D360 function, 284, 583
@DDB function, 261, 582
DDE (Dynamic Data Exchange),
    514, 528–529, 532
debugging macro, 561–563
default directory, setting, 163–164
default font set, 212
default value, 14
delimited file, 480–481
Del key, 81, 110–111
deleting an entry, 110–112
dependent variable, 484
depreciation functions, 260–263
descending order, 364
destination file, 513, 522–525
@DGET function, 400–402, 582
dialog boxes, 13
  activating tools in, 65
  check boxes, 69–71
  command buttons, 65–67
  drop-down boxes, 73–74
  frames, 73
  list boxes, 69
  option buttons, 71–72
  selecting options from, 443–445
  text boxes, 67–69
directory list box, 75
@DMAX function, 397, 582
@DMIN function, 397, 582
documents, transferring data
    between, 528–534
dollar sign ($) for absolute
    reference, 147
double angle brackets (>>) as file
    reference, 436
double-declining-balance method,
    261, 263
double quotation mark (") for right
    label alignment, 173
@DQUERY function, 400, 424, 582
Draw menu
  Arrow command, 330, 332
  in creating graphs, 317
  Rearrange Clear command, 333
  Rearrange Flip command, 333
  Rearrange Turn command, 333
  Rectangle command, 330
drive list boxes, 75
drop-down boxes, 73–74

drop-shadow, 209
@DSTD function, 397, 582
@DSTDS function, 397, 582
@DSUM function, 396–400,
    417–418, 583
@DVAR function, 397, 583
@DVARS function, 397, 583
Dynamic Data Exchange (DDE),
    514, 528–529, 532

E

edit line, 79–81
Edit menu, 59–60
  Clear All command, 446
  Clear command, 110–111
  Clear Special command, 111
  Copy command, 124, 127–128,
      447, 532
  Cut command, 111
  Find command, 554
  Link Options command, 532
  Move Cells command, 132–136
  Paste command, 124, 127–128
  Paste Link command, 528, 532
  Quick Copy command, 124–126
  Undo command, 112–124
End key, 10, 81
entering
  data, 22–24, 27–28
  formulas, 141–144
  labels, 27–28, 108–110
entry, deleting, 110–112
equations, solving simultaneous,
    470–472
@ERR function, 583
errors, in formulas, 251–253
Escape key, 12, 54
@EXACT function, 294, 583
@EXP function, 273, 583
exponential functions, 273
exponentiation, 243
extensions
  .BAK, 130
  .FMB, 130
  .TXT, 477
  .WK3, 33, 477
external database

definition of, 395
performing queries on, 418–420
using database functions with, 417–418

F

factor argument, 262
@FALSE function, 583
field name, 40–41, 354, 356
fields, 40, 354, 359–361
file
  assigning password to, 131
  delimited, 480–481
File Exit dialog box, 24
file list box, 75
File menu, 59, 97–98
  Combine From command, 488–489, 525–526
  in creating graphs, 317
  Exit command, 24
  Import From Numbers command, 480
  Import From Text command, 476–477
  New command, 92, 190
  Open command, 92, 163–164
  Page Setup command, 221–223, 337
  Preview command, 68, 221
  Print command, 68, 222
  Printer Setup command, 220–221
  Save As command, 33, 129–131, 163–164
  Save command, 132
file name, 129
File Page Setup dialog box, 225
  Columns and Rows boxes, 226
  Compression frame, 226–227
file references, 513
File Save As dialog box, 130
financial functions, 260–269
@FIND function, 293, 583
fixed format, 186
.FMB extension, 130
fonts, 209–210
footers, creating, 223–225

{For} macro command, 537, 553, 556–557
format
  automatic, 189–190
  comma, 186
  currency, 186
  fixed, 186
  general, 186
  global, 188
  label, 189
  percent, 186
  +/−, 187
  range, 188
  text, 187
format line
  edit line, 79–81
  icon palette, 81–84
  mode indicator, 78
  status line, 84–85
formatting
  columns, 166–170
  values in worksheet, 184–187
formulas, 139–141
  arithmetic structure, 146
  categories of, 242–243
  copying, 144–146
  elements in, 139
  entering, 141–144
  finding errors in, 251–253
  logical, 246–248, 388–389
  numeric, 243–245
  order of precedence in, 153–154, 243
  reference types in, 146–153
  text, 249–251
  time and date, 244–245
  types of address references, 146
  writing, 29–31, 240–242, 388–390
frames, 73
function(s), 30, 253
  categories of, 257–302
  database, 396–402
  date, 282–291
  definition of, 237
  depreciation, 260–263
  elements of, 255–257
  entering in a cell, 254–255
  financial, 260–269
  logarithmic, 273

logical, 290–292
mathematical, 270–282
names of, 256
special, 298–302
statistical, 257–260
string, 292–298
time, 282–290
trigonometric, 270–273
function keys
　F1 (Help) key, 96, 432, 536
　F2 (Edit) key, 79–80, 175, 432
　F3 (Name) key, 254, 432, 517–518
　F4 (Anchor) key, 432
　F5 (Go to) key, 164–165, 179, 432
　F6 (Window), 433
　F7 (Query) key, 379, 419–420, 433
　F8 (Table), 433, 494–495
　F9 (Calc), 433, 458
　F10 (Menu bar), 11, 59, 433
function library, 253
@FV function, 264–265, 584

G

General format, 186
{GetLabel} command, 540
Global format, 188
graph(s), 307–308
　adding objects, 330–334
　adding titles and legend, 326–330
　adding to worksheet, 336–337
　area, 339
　columnwise format, 311, 322
　creating from worksheet, 36–40
　creating from worksheet data, 309–326
　creating in the rowwise format, 322–325
　designing, 37–40
　data ranges for, 311–312
　HLCO, 347–348
　line, 339
　making other changes in, 334–336
　mixed, 343–347
　performing what-if experiments with, 325–326
　pie charts, 340–343
　rowwise format, 322–325
　XY, 343–347
graphics, 5
Graph menu, 60
　choosing commands from, 312–316
　Add to Sheet command, 312, 336
　Go To command, 313
　Import command, 313
　Name command, 312
　New command, 312–315
　Refresh command, 313
　Size command, 313, 337
　View command, 312
graph window, 308
　icon palette in, 318–319
　menu bar for, 317–318
greater than sign (>) in data block, 478
grid lines, 28, 180–184

H

handles, 331
headers, 223–226
help
　finding context-sensitive, 96–97
　getting in Lotus 1-2-3 for Windows, 93–97
Help menu, 60
　About 1-2-3 command, 96
　in creating graphs, 318
　How Do I? command, 96
　For Upgraders command, 96
　Index command, 94
　Keyboard command, 96
　Macros command, 96, 541
　Using Help command, 96, 98
help window, 97–98
hiding columns, 170–173
HLCO graphs, creating, 347–348
@HLOOKUP function, 238, 300–302, 584
Home key, 11,
Horizontal scroll bar, 8, 178
@HOUR function, 283, 584

I

icon, attaching macro to, 449–453
icon palette, 17–20, 81–84
  customizing, 19, 81
  in graph window, 317–322
  style icons available in, 32
identity matrix, 470
@IF function, 247, 290–291, 360, 584
{If} macro command, 558–561
independent variable, 484
Index button, 98
@INDEX function, 299–300, 584
@INFO function, 584
information box, 67
input range, 374–376
installing Lotus 1-2-3 for Windows, 573–577
interactive macro, 453
Interior fill, 331
@INT function, 270, 274, 285–286, 584
invalid range error message, 552
@IRR function, 264, 268–269, 585
@ISAAF function, 585
@ISAPP function, 585
@ISERR function, 585
@ISNA function, 585
@ISNUMBER function, 290, 585
ISRANGE function, 585
@ISSTRING function, 585
italics icon, 220
item, 533

J

joining multiple databases, 408–413

L

LABEL mode, 78
label alignments, selecting, 173–175
Label format, 189
label prefixes, 173, 176–177
labels
  aligning, 22, 173–175
  entering, 27–28, 108–110
landscape orientation, 227
Layout menu in creating graphs, 317
@LEFT function, 292, 586
legend, adding to graph, 326–330
@LENGTH function, 294, 586
less-than sign (<) in label expression, 381
{Let} macro command, 551–552
life, definition of, 261
line graphs, creating, 339
lines, drawing, 215
links
  between documents, 527–534
  between worksheets, 516–526
list boxes, 69
literal strings, 250
@LN function, 586
logarithmic functions, 273
logical error, locating in macro, 537, 561–563
logical formulas, 246–248
logical functions, 290–292
logical operators, 247
@LOG function, 273, 586
Long International Date, 193
look-up table, 238
loops, 539
  {Branch} macro command, 558–561
  {for} macro command, 537, 553, 556–557
  {if} macro command, 558–561
Lotus Multibyte Character Set, 296
Lotus 1-2-3 interface, 6–7
@LOWER function, 294, 586

M

macro
  attaching to an icon, 449–453
  autoexecute, 459
  creating conditional branch in, 537, 558–561
  creating database, 563–570
  creating keystroke, 430–440

creating repetition loop in, 537, 556–557
debugging, 561–563
definition of, 61, 429
entering in a worksheet, 433–435
interactive, 453
locating logical error in, 537, 561–563
mailing list, 541
memo, 454–458
as menu shortcuts, 440–453
schedule, 541
as subroutines, 438–440
text file commands in, 568–570
transcript window to develop, 445–448
Macro Command Index, 96, 536
macro key names, 431–433
macro library, 430
macro programming, 539–542
macro programs, writing, 453–459, 542–552
mailing list macro, 541
margins, specifying, 225
mathematical functions, 270–282
matrix
  coefficient, 469
  constant, 469
  definition of, 467
  identity, 470
  solution, 470
  square, 469
matrix arithmetic, 469–470
maximize button, 8, 55
@MAX function, 257, 586
Memo macro, 454–458
Menu bar, 11–12
  Data menu, 60
  Edit menu, 59–60
  File menu, 59
  Graph menu, 60
  in graph window, 317–322
  Help menu, 60
  Range menu, 60
  Style menu, 60
  Tools menu, 60
  using menu commands, 61–77

  Windows menu, 60
  Worksheet menu, 60
{MenuCall} macro command, 536, 548–551
menu commands, 12–17, 61–77
MENU mode, 78
menus. *See also specific menus*
  cascade, 62
  writing macros as shortcuts, 440–453
Microsoft Word for Windows, 528, 530
@MID function, 293, 295, 298, 586
minimize button, 8, 55
@MIN function, 257, 586
minus sign (–) to begin formula, 243
@MINUTE function, 283, 586
mixed graphs, creating, 343–347
mode indicator, 12, 22–24, 78
@MOD function, 270, 280–281, 291–292, 295, 587
@MONTH function, 283, 587
mouse, 86
  in changing column width, 168
  in hiding column, 171
  in performing unhide operation, 173
  in sorting, 366
  in splitting worksheet into panes, 90
Multiple worksheet window, 11, 91

N

@NA function, 587
@N function, 295, 587
@NOW function, 283–284, 458, 587
@NPV function, 263–265, 587
numbers, entering, 114–115
numeric formats
  +/– format, 187
  Comma format, 186
  Currency format, 186
  Fixed format, 186
  General format, 186

Percent format, 186
Scientific format, 186
Text format, 187
numeric formulas, 243–245

O

objects
  adding to graph, 330–334
  adding to worksheet, 474–476
offset number, 293
OK button, 66
1-2-3 application window, 52–53, 77–78
1-2-3 classic window, 20–21, 543
1-2-3 window control menu
  Close command, 56–58, 570
  Maximize command, 56–57
  Minimize command, 56
  Move command, 56–57
  Restore command, 56–57
  Size command, 56–57
  Switch To command, 58
1-2-3 window title bar, 54
one-way what-if table, creating, 491–494
{Open} command, 568–569
open parenthesis (()
  to begin formula, 242
  in function, 256
operation(s)
  controlling the order of, 153–154
  definition of, 243
  Delete, 41
  Extract, 41
  Find, 41
  Modify, 41
  Sort and Search, 42–45
operators
  arithmetic, 29
  binary, 247
  logical, 247, 290, 389
  relational, 246, 290, 380–381, 389
  text, 249
  unary, 247
optimal cell, 502
option buttons, 71–72

order of precedence, 153–154, 243
orientation, selecting, 227
Other command, 552
output range, 374–376

P

panes, dividing worksheet window into, 88–91
Paradox, 413
parenthesis (( )) to control order of operations, 153–154, 243
password, assigning, 131
Percent format, 186
percent-labels range in creating graphs, 342
period, 261
period (.) to anchor range, 68, 120
Perspective option button, 13
pie charts, creating, 340–343
@PI function, 587
+/− format, 187
plus sign (+) for starting formula, 141–142, 240–241
@PMT function, 238, 264, 266, 587
POINT mode, 68, 78
population variance, 257
Portrait orientation, 227
pound sign (#) in header or footer text box, 224
precedence, order of, 153–154, 243
preview icon, 220
printed worksheet, compressing or expanding, 226–227
printer orientation, 227
print file, 476
printing
  headings, 226
  orientation for, 227
  worksheet, 220–231
print-range icon, 220
programming language, 539
prompt, 453
@PROPER function, 294, 587
protecting worksheet, 205–208
Protection option, 206
@PV function, 263–264, 588

Q

Quantity box, 14
queries
  definition of, 41
  performing, 373–390
  performing on external database, 418–420
  performing two-table operation, 411–413
  preparing ranges for two-table, 409–411
Query key, 379
question mark (?) as wildcard, 382

R

radians, 270
@RAND function, 270, 274–279, 588
range(s)
  anchoring with period, 120
  bin, 482
  copying, 124–128
  preparing for two-table query, 409–411
  selecting, 115–119
  values, 482
range box, 67
range-copy icon, 124–125, 198
Range format, 188
Range Format dialog box, 185
Range menu, 60
  Annotate command, 474–476
  Format command, 63, 185, 190, 492
  Goto command, 63, 164–165
  Justify command, 441
  Name command, 122
  Name Create command, 122, 448
  Name Label Create command, 433, 547
  Transpose command, 63, 473–474
  Unprotect command, 207
range name, creating, 121–124
Range Name Create dialog box, 122
@RATE function, 264, 268, 588
READY mode, 78
records, 354

reference argument, 453, 548, 560
reference types
  absolute and relative references, 146–149
  examining what-if scenarios, 154–156
  mixed references, 149–153
  understanding, 146
regression analysis, 484–487
relational operators, 246, 290, 380–381, 389
relative reference, 145
@REPEAT function, 294, 588
repetition loop, 537, 556–557
@REPLACE function, 293–294, 588
Reset command button, 65, 185
Restore button, 8, 55
revising source worksheet, 521–522
@RIGHT function, 292–293, 588
@ROUND function, 270, 279–280, 588
row argument, 299
rows, 7, 136–139
@ROWS function, 588
rowwise format, creating graph in, 322–325
R Squared value, 486–487
Run command, 447

S

salvage, 261
sample variance, 257
save-file icon, 198
saving worksheet, 128–131
schedule macro, 541–542
scientific format, 186
scroll box, 10
screen preview of printed page, 220
search button, 98
search operations, 42–45
@SECOND function, 283, 589
semicolon (;) to place note at end of formula, 242
@S function, 294–295, 589
shadings, 214
Sheet option, 14
@SHEETS function, 589

Shift-<, 20
Shift-Tab, 65
Short International Date, 193
single-quotation mark (') for left label alignment, 109, 114, 173
@SIN function, 270–271, 589
@SLN function, 261, 589
slash key (\) to display classic window, 20
solution matrix, 470
@SOLVER function, 589
sorting database, 364–373
sort operations, performing, 42–45
sort order, 372–373
source file, 513, 522–525
source worksheet
  building totals worksheet from, 518–521
  revising, 521–522
special functions, 298–302
specifying margins, 225
splitters, 90
spreadsheet, 5–7
SQL Server, 413
SQL Server DataLens, 424
@SQRT function, 273, 589
square matrix, 469
standard deviation, 257
Standard icons, 19
Standard icons box, 83
statistical functions, 257–260
status line, 53, 84–85
Std Err of Coef, 487
Std Err of Y Est, 487
@STDS function, 258, 589
@STD function, 258, 589
stock market graph, 347–348
straight-line depreciation, 263
string argument, 453
@STRING function, 296–297, 590
string functions, 292–298
strings, literal, 250
Style Color dialog box, 218
Style Font dialog box, 211–212
Style menu, 54, 60
  in adding objects to graph, 331
  Alignment command, 173, 175
  Border command, 214
  Color command, 218–220, 331
  in creating graphs, 317
  Font command, 209–210
  Name command, 215–217
  Shading command, 210, 214, 217
style names, defining, 215–217
subroutines, 438–440, 540
substring argument, 294
summation icon, 119–120
sum-of-the-years'-digits method, 261, 263
@SUMPRODUCT function, 590
@SUM function, 30, 120–121, 148, 257, 493–494, 590
@SUMPRODUCT function, 258–260
Switch argument, 262
@SYD function, 261, 590
Synchronize option, 375

T

Tab key, 65
@TAN function, 270–271, 590
Task List dialog box, 58
template, general-purpose, 107
@TERM function, 264, 267, 590
text boxes, 67–69
text file, 476
text file commands in macro, 568–570
Text format, 187
text formulas, 249–251
text operator, 249
three-dimensional worksheets, 11
three-way what-if table, creating, 495–499
tilde (~)
  to identify excluded value, 382
  in macros, 443
time arithmetic, 199, 201–205
time formulas, 244–245
@TIME function, 284, 590
time functions, 282–291
time values, entering, 199–205
@TIMEVALUE function, 284, 289, 590
Title bar, 7
titles, adding to graph, 326–330

@TODAY function, 283, 359–360, 458, 590
toggle, 20
Tools Icon Palette dialog box, 82
Tools menu, 54, 60
  Backsolver command, 499–501
  Icon Palette command, 19
  Macro Debug command, 557, 561–563
  Macro Run command, 436–437
  Macro Show Transcript command, 445–446
  SmartIcons command, 17, 80, 96, 317
  Solver command, 502–507
  User Setup command, 163–164, 188
  User Setup Recalculation command, 275
Tools SmartIcons dialog box, 72, 82–83
Tools SmartIcons Customize dialog box, 82–83
topic, 533
totals, finding, 119–122
totals worksheet, building, 518–521
transcript window, to develop macros, 445–448
transferring data, 528–534
trigonometric function, 270–273
@TRIM function, 294, 569, 591
@TRUE function, 591
two-way what-if table, creating, 495–499
.TXT extension, 477
type styles, 210

U

unary operations, 247
updating file, 132
@UPPER function, 294, 591

V

value, 22, 114, 184–187
VALUE mode, 78
values range, 482
@VALUE function, 296–298, 591
variable, 467
  dependent, 484
  independent, 484
variable-rate declining-balance method, 261, 263
variance, 257
@VAR function, 257–258, 591
@VARS function, 257–258, 591
@VDB function, 261–262, 591
vertical bar (|)
  as excluded print range indicator, 177
  in header or footer text box, 225
vertical scroll bar, 8
View command in Graph menu, 312
@VLOOKUP function, 300–302, 591–592

W

what-if experiments, performing with graphs, 325–326
what-if scenarios, 25, 154–156
what-if table
  creating one-way, 491–494
  creating two-way, 495–499
  creating three-way, 495–499
  recalculating with F8 function key, 494–495
wildcards in queries, 381–382
Window Display Options dialog box, 182, 184
Window menu, 60
  Cascade command, 93, 318
  Display Options command, 181
  in creating graphs, 317–318
  Insert command, 35
  Split command, 13, 15, 90, 375
  Tile command, 93, 318, 446
Windows Paintbrush program, 449–450
.WK3 extension, 33, 130
worksheet
  adding graph, 336–337
  adding objects, 474–476

applying colors, 218–220
changing, 132–139
changing column widths, 166–170
changing data, 34–35
changing data-entry mode, 189–191
copying range of values, 124–125
creating graph from, 36–40, 309–326
creating links between, 516–526
creating range names, 121–124
definition of, 6–7
deleting entries, 110–112
developing, 26–35
dimensions of, 7–11
entering date values into, 192–198
entering data, 27–28
entering labels, 27–28, 108–110
entering macros, 433–435
entering numbers, 114–115
entering time values, 199–205
finding totals, 119–122
formatting values, 184–187
hiding columns, 170–173
holding titles on screen, 178–180
inserting rows and columns, 136–139
label alignment, 173–175
label prefixes, 176–178
making adjustments, 166
multiple, 11–17
planning, 24–26
preparing for presentation, 32–34
printing, 220–231
protecting, 205–208
removing grid lines from, 180–184
resuming work on existing, 162–165
saving, 128–131
selecting global and range formats, 188
selecting ranges, 115–119
three-dimensional, 11
transferring data from another document, 532–534
transferring data to another document, 528–532
using Undo command, 112–124

working with formulas, 139–146
writing formulas, 29–31
Worksheet Global Settings dialog box, 188
Worksheet menu, 60
  Column Width command, 167, 358
  Delete command, 490
  Global Settings command, 166–167, 185, 188, 206, 363, 375, 547, 553
  Hide command, 170–171, 406, 482
  Insert command, 14–15, 358, 375, 406, 443, 446
  Page Break command, 221
  Titles command, 178–180
  Unhide command, 171–172
worksheet titles, holding on screen, 178–180
Worksheet window, 6–7, 86
  capacity of, 15
  characteristics of, 7
  control menu for, 56–58
  dividing into panes, 88
  getting help for, 93–94
  maximizing, 86
  menu bar for, 59–61
  minimizing, 86–87
  opening more than one, 91–93
  performing operations on, 86–87
  sizing and moving, 55–56
{WriteIn} command, 569–570
Writing formulas, 29–31, 240–242, 388–390
/WWC, 20–21

X

x data range, 311
X-range text box, 485
XY graph, 343–347, 484

Y

YEAR function, 283, 592
Y-intercept box, 485

Selections from The SYBEX Library

SPREADSHEETS AND INTEGRATED SOFTWARE

1-2-3 for Scientists and Engineers
William J. Orvis
371pp. Ref. 733-9

This up-to-date edition offers fast, elegant solutions to common problems in science and engineering. Complete, carefully explained techniques for plotting, curve fitting, statistics, derivatives, integrals and differentials, solving systems of equations, and more; plus useful Lotus add-ins.

The ABC's of 1-2-3 (Second Edition)
Chris Gilbert
Laurie Williams
245pp. Ref. 355-4

Online Today recommends it as "an easy and comfortable way to get started with the program." An essential tutorial for novices, it will remain on your desk as a valuable source of ongoing reference and support. For Release 2.

The ABC's of 1-2-3 Release 2.2
Chris Gilbert
Laurie Williams
340pp. Ref. 623-5

New Lotus 1-2-3 users delight in this book's step-by-step approach to building trouble-free spreadsheets, displaying graphs, and efficiently building databases. The authors cover the ins and outs of the latest version including easier calculations, file linking, and better graphic presentation.

The ABC's of 1-2-3 Release 2.3
Chris Gilbert
Laurie Williams
350pp. Ref. 837-8

Computer Currents called it "one of the best tutorials available." This new edition provides easy-to-follow, hands-on lessons tailored specifically for computer and spreadsheet newcomers—or for anyone seeking a quick and easy guide to the basics. Covers everything from switching on the computer to charts, functions, macros, and important new features.

The ABC's of 1-2-3 Release 3
Judd Robbins
290pp. Ref. 519-0

The ideal book for beginners who are new to Lotus or new to Release 3. This step-by-step approach to the 1-2-3 spreadsheet software gets the reader up and running with spreadsheet, database, graphics, and macro functions.

The ABC's of Excel on the IBM PC
Douglas Hergert
326pp. Ref. 567-0

This book is a brisk and friendly introduction to the most important features of Microsoft Excel for PC's. This beginner's book discusses worksheets, charts, database operations, and macros, all with hands-on examples. Written for all versions through Version 2.

The ABC's of Quattro Pro 3
Alan Simpson
Douglas Wolf
338pp. Ref. 836-6

This popular beginner's tutorial on Quattro Pro 2 shows first-time computer and spreadsheet users the essentials of electronic number-crunching. Topics range from business spreadsheet design to error-free formulas, presentation slide shows, the database, macros, more.

The Complete Lotus 1-2-3 Release 2.2 Handbook
Greg Harvey
750pp. Ref. 625-1

This comprehensive handbook discusses every 1-2-3 operation with clear instructions and practical tips. This volume especially emphasizes the new improved graphics, high-speed recalculation techniques, and spreadsheet linking available with Release 2.2.

The Complete Lotus 1-2-3 Release 3 Handbook
Greg Harvey
700pp. Ref. 600-6

Everything you ever wanted to know about 1-2-3 is in this definitive handbook. As a Release 3 guide, it features the design and use of 3D worksheets, and improved graphics, along with using Lotus under DOS or OS/2. Problems, exercises, and helpful insights are included.

Lotus 1-2-3 2.2 On-Line Advisor Version 1.1
SYBAR, Software Division of SYBEX, Inc.
Ref. 935-8

Need Help fast? With a touch of a key, the Advisor pops up right on top of your Lotus 1-2-3 program to answer your spreadsheet questions. With over 4000 index citations and 1600 pre-linked cross-references, help has never been so easy to find. Just start typing your topic and the Lotus 1-2-3 Advisor does all the look-up for you. Covers versions 2.01 and 2.2. Software package comes with 3½″ and 5¼″ disks. **System Requirements:** IBM compatible with DOS 2.0 or higher, runs with Windows 3.0, uses 90K of RAM.

Lotus 1-2-3 Desktop Companion SYBEX Ready Reference Series
Greg Harvey
976pp. Ref. 501-8

A full-time consultant, right on your desk. Hundreds of self-contained entries cover every 1-2-3 feature, organized by topic, indexed and cross-referenced, and supplemented by tips, macros and working examples. For Release 2.

Lotus 1-2-3 Instant Reference Release 2.2 SYBEX Prompter Series
Greg Harvey
Kay Yarborough Nelson
254pp. Ref. 635-9

The reader gets quick and easy access to any operation in 1-2-3 Version 2.2 in this handy pocket-sized encyclopedia. Organized by menu function, each command and function has a summary description, the exact key sequence, and a discussion of the options.

Lotus 1-2-3 Tips and Tricks (2nd edition)
Gene Weisskopf
425pp. Ref. 668-5

This outstanding collection of tips, shortcuts and cautions for longtime Lotus users is in an expanded new edition covering Release 2.2. Topics include macros, range names, spreadsheet design, hardware and operating system tips, data analysis, printing, data interchange, applications development, and more.

Mastering 1-2-3 (Second Edition)
Carolyn Jorgensen
702pp. Ref. 528-X

Get the most from 1-2-3 Release 2.01 with this step-by-step guide emphasizing advanced features and practical uses. Topics include data sharing, macros, spreadsheet security, expanded memory, and graphics enhancements.

Mastering 1-2-3 Release 3
Carolyn Jorgensen
682pp. Ref. 517-4

For new Release 3 and experienced Release 2 users, "Mastering" starts with a basic spreadsheet, then introduces spreadsheet and database commands, functions, and macros, and then tells how to analyze 3D spreadsheets and make high-impact reports and graphs. Lotus add-ons are discussed and Fast Tracks are included.

Mastering Enable/OA
Christopher Van Buren
Robert Bixby
540pp. Ref 637-5
This is a structured, hands-on guide to integrated business computing, for users who want to achieve productivity in the shortest possible time. Separate in-depth sections cover word processing, spreadsheets, databases, telecommunications, task integration and macros.

Mastering Excel on the IBM PC
Carl Townsend
628pp. Ref. 403-8
A complete Excel handbook with step-by-step tutorials, sample applications and an extensive reference section. Topics include worksheet fundamentals, formulas and windows, graphics, database techniques, special features, macros and more.

Mastering Excel 3 for Windows
Carl Townsend
625pp. Ref. 643-X
A new edition of SYBEX's highly praised guide to the Excel super spreadsheet, under Windows 3.0. Includes full coverage of new features; dozens of tips and examples; in-depth treatment of specialized topics, including presentation graphics and macros; and sample applications for inventory control, financial management, trend analysis, and more.

Mastering Framework III
Douglas Hergert
Jonathan Kamin
613pp. Ref. 513-1
Thorough, hands-on treatment of the latest Framework release. An outstanding introduction to integrated software applications, with examples for outlining, spreadsheets, word processing, databases, and more; plus an introduction to FRED programming.

Mastering Freelance Plus
Donald Richard Read
411pp. Ref. 701-0
A detailed guide to high-powered graphing and charting with Freelance Plus. Part I is a practical overview of the software. Part II offers concise tutorials on creating specific chart types. Part III covers drawing functions in depth. Part IV shows how to organize and generate output, including printing and on-screen shows.

Mastering Quattro Pro 2
Gene Weisskopf
575pp, Ref. 792-4
This hands-on guide and reference takes readers from basic spreadsheets to creating three-dimensional graphs, spreadsheet databases, macros and advanced data analysis. Also covers Paradox Access and translating Lotus 1-2-3 2.2 work sheets. A great tutorial for beginning and intermediate users, this book also serves as a reference for users at all levels.

Mastering Quattro Pro 3
Gene Weisskopf
618pp. Ref. 841-6
A complete hands-on guide and on-the-job reference, offering practical tutorials on the basics; up-to-date treatment of advanced capabilities; highlighted coverage of new software features, and expert advice from author Gene Weisskopf, a seasoned spreadsheet specialist.

Mastering Smartware II
Jonathan Paul Bacon
634pp. Ref. 651-0
An easy-to-read, self-paced introduction to a powerful program. This book offers separate treatment of word processing, data file management, spreadsheets, and communications, with special sections on data integration between modules. Concrete examples from business are used throughout.

Mastering SuperCalc5
Greg Harvey
Mary Beth Andrasak
500pp. Ref. 624-3

This book offers a complete and unintimidating guided tour through each feature. With step-by-step lessons, readers learn about the full capabilities of spreadsheet, graphics, and data management functions. Multiple spreadsheets, linked spreadsheets, 3D graphics, and macros are also discussed.

Mastering Symphony (Fourth Edition)
Douglas Cobb
857pp. Ref. 494-1

Thoroughly revised to cover all aspects of the major upgrade of Symphony Version 2, this Fourth Edition of Doug Cobb's classic is still "the Symphony bible" to this complex but even more powerful package. All the new features are discussed and placed in context with prior versions so that both new and previous users will benefit from Cobb's insights.

Teach Yourself Lotus 1-2-3 Release 2.2
Jeff Woodward
250pp. Ref. 641-3

Readers match what they see on the screen with the book's screen-by-screen action sequences. For new Lotus users, topics include computer fundamentals, opening and editing a worksheet, using graphs, macros, and printing typeset-quality reports. For Release 2.2.

Understanding 1-2-3 Release 2.3
Rebecca Bridge Altman
700pp. Ref. 856-4

This comprehensive guide to 1-2-3 spreadsheet power covers everything from basic concepts to sophisticated business applications. New users will build a solid foundation; intermediate and experienced users will learn how to refine their spreadsheets, manage large projects, create effective graphics, analyze databases, master graphics, more.

Understanding PFS: First Choice
Gerry Litton
489pp. Ref. 568-9

From basic commands to complex features, this complete guide to the popular integrated package is loaded with step-by-step instructions. Lessons cover creating attractive documents, setting up easy-to-use databases, working with spreadsheets and graphics, and smoothly integrating tasks from different First Choice modules. For Version 3.0.

Up & Running with Lotus 1-2-3 Release 2.2
Rainer Bartel
139pp. Ref 748-7

Start using 1-2-3 in the shortest time possible with this concise 20-step guide to the major features of the software. Each "step" is a self-contained, time-coded lesson (taking 15, 30, 45 or 60 minutes to complete) focused on a single aspect of 1-2-3 operations.

Up & Running with 1-2-3 Release 2.3
Robert M. Thomas
140pp. Ref. 872-6

Get a fast start with this 20-step guide to 1-2-3 release 2.3. Each step takes just 15 minutes to an hour, and is preceded by a clock icon, so you know how much time to budget for each lesson. This book is great for people who want to start using the program right away, as well as for potential 1-2-3 users who want to evaluate the program before purchase.

Up & Running with Lotus 1-2-3 Release 3.1
Kris Jamsa
141pp. Ref. 813-0

A 20-step overview of the new 3.1 version of 1-2-3. The first twelve steps take you through the fundamentals of creating, using and graphing worksheets. Steps 13 through 15 explain the database, and the balance of the book is dedicated to 3.1's powerful WYSIWYG capabilities.

Up & Running with Quattro Pro 3
Peter Aitken
140pp. Ref.857-2

Get a fast start with this 20-step guide to Quattro Pro 3. Each step takes just 15 minutes to an hour, and is preceded by a clock icon, so you know how much time to budget for each lesson. This book is great for people who want to start using the program right away, as well as for potential Quattro Pro 3 users who want to evaluate the program before purchase.

ACCOUNTING

Mastering DacEasy Accounting (Second Edition)
Darleen Hartley Yourzek
463pp. Ref. 679-0

This new edition focuses on version 4.0 (with notes on using 3.0), and includes an introduction to DacEasy Payroll. Packed with real-world accounting examples, it covers everything from installing DacEasy to converting data, setting up applications, processing work and printing custom reports.

Mastering Peachtree Complete III
Darleen Hartley Yourzek
601pp. Ref. 723-1

Presented from the business user's perspective, this practical, task-oriented guide can be used as a step-by-step tutorial or an easy reference guide. Detailed topics include: preparing your records for computer conversion; setting up and maintaining files; managing accounts payable and receivable; tracking inventory, and more. With a glossary of accounting and computer terms.

Up & Running with Quicken 4
Darleen Hartley Yourzek
139pp. Ref. 783-5

Enjoy a fast-paced introduction to this popular financial management program. In just 20 steps—each taking only 15 minutes to an hour—you can begin computerized management of all your financial transactions. Includes a special chapter for small business.

Understanding Quicken 4
Steve Cummings
506pp. Ref. 787-8

A practical guide to managing personal and business finances. Readers build a solid financial recordkeeping system, as they learn the ins and outs of using Quicken 4 to print checks; manage monthly bills; keep tax records; track credit cards, investments, and loans; produce financial statements, and much more.

HOME MONEY MANAGEMENT

Mastering Quicken 3
Steve Cummings
350pp. Ref. 662-6

With tips on personal financial planning by Pauline Tai of *Money Magazine*, this hands-on guide to both Quicken and Stock! portfolio manager centers on a variety of valuable examples. Covers simple check writing, budgeting, tax accounting, cash flow management, even payroll.

Understanding Managing Your Money
Gerry Litton
372pp. Ref. 751-7

A complete guide to the principal features of this practical software package. Replete with valuable examples and useful illustrations. Learn how various screens should be handled, and how to avoid trouble spots. Topics include: using the word processor and the calculator; managing a budget; maintaining a checkbook; estimating tax liabilities; calculating net worth; and more.

Will Builder™ The Complete Will-Writing Program
SYBAR, Software Division of SYBEX, Inc.
3½" and 5¼" disks Ref. 906-4

Designed by two experienced lawyers, Will Builder software provides you with all the information you need to create a solid, legally-binding will. Save on legal fees, write your will on your own computer in the privacy of your own home. On-Line

Expertise leads you through the process step-by-step. PLUS, you can create a Living Will and a Medical Power of Attorney to express your wishes in advance in case you ever need to be placed on a life-support system. You can also create a Financial Power of Attorney and Letter to Executor. Software program uses state-specific forms for powers of attorney and living wills. **System requirements:** IBM compatible with hard disk, minimum 512K RAM, DOS 2.0 or higher.

OPERATING SYSTEMS

The ABC's of DOS 4
Alan R. Miller
275pp. Ref. 583-2

This step-by-step introduction to using DOS 4 is written especially for beginners. Filled with simple examples, *The ABC's of DOS 4* covers the basics of hardware, software, disks, the system editor EDLIN, DOS commands, and more.

The ABC's of DOS 5
Alan Miller
267pp. Ref. 770-3

This straightforward guide will haven even first-time computer users working comfortably with DOS 5 in no time. Step-by-step lessons lead users from switching on the PC, through exploring the DOS Shell, working with directories and files, using essential commands, customizing the system, and trouble shooting. Includes a tear-out quick reference card and function key template.

ABC's of MS-DOS (Second Edition)
Alan R. Miller
233pp. Ref. 493-3

This handy guide to MS-DOS is all many PC users need to manage their computer files, organize floppy and hard disks, use EDLIN, and keep their computers organized. Additional information is given about utilities like Sidekick, and there is a DOS command and program summary. The second edition is fully updated for Version 3.3.

The ABC's of SCO UNIX
Tom Cuthbertson
263pp. Re. 715-0

A guide especially for beginners who want to get to work fast. Includes hands-on tutorials on logging in and out; creating and editing files; using electronic mail; organizing files into directories; printing; text formatting; and more.

The ABC's of Windows 3.0
Kris Jamsa
327pp. Ref. 760-6

A user-friendly introduction to the essentials of Windows 3.0. Presented in 64 short lessons. Beginners start with lesson one, while more advanced readers can skip ahead. Learn to use File Manager, the accessory programs, customization features, Program Manager, and more.

DESQview Instant Reference
Paul J. Perry
175pp. Ref. 809-2

This complete quick-reference command guide covers version 2.3 and DESQview 386, as well as QEMM (for managing expanded memory) and Manifest Memory Analyzer. Concise, alphabetized entries provide exact syntax, options, usage, and brief examples for every command. A handy source for on-the-job reminders and tips.

Essential OS/2 (Second Edition)
Judd Robbins
445pp. Ref. 609-X

Written by an OS/2 expert, this is the guide to the powerful new resources of the OS/2 operating system standard edition 1.1 with presentation manager. Robbins introduces the standard edition, and details multitasking under OS/2, and the range of commands for installing, starting up, configuring, and running applications. For Version 1.1 Standard Edition.

Essential PC-DOS (Second Edition)
Myril Clement Shaw
Susan Soltis Shaw
332pp. Ref. 413-5

An authoritative guide to PC-DOS, including version 3.2. Designed to make experts out of beginners, it explores everything from disk management to batch file programming. Includes an 85-page command summary. Through Version 3.2.

Graphics Programming Under Windows
Brian Myers
Chris Doner
646pp. Ref. 448-8

Straightforward discussion, abundant examples, and a concise reference guide to graphics commands make this book a must for Windows programmers. Topics range from how Windows works to programming for business, animation, CAD, and desktop publishing. For Version 2.

Hard Disk Instant Reference
SYBEX Prompter Series
Judd Robbins
256pp. Ref. 587-5

Compact yet comprehensive, this pocket-sized reference presents the essential information on DOS commands used in managing directories and files, and in optimizing disk configuration. Includes a survey of third-party utility capabilities. Through DOS 4.0.

Inside DOS: A Programmer's Guide
Michael J. Young
490pp. Ref. 710-X

A collection of practical techniques (with source code listings) designed to help you take advantage of the rich resources intrinsic to MS-DOS machines. Designed for the experienced programmer with a basic understanding of C and 8086 assembly language, and DOS fundamentals.

Mastering DOS (Second Edition)
Judd Robbins
722pp. Ref. 555-7

"The most useful DOS book." This seven-part, in-depth tutorial addresses the needs of users at all levels. Topics range from running applications, to managing files and directories, configuring the system, batch file programming, and techniques for system developers. Through Version 4.

DOS 3.3 On-Line Advisor Version 1.1
SYBAR, Software Division of SYBEX, Inc.
Ref. 933-1

The answer to all your DOS problems. The DOS On-Line Advisor is an on-screen reference that explains over 200 DOS error messages. 2300 other citations cover all you ever needed to know about DOS. The DOS On-Line Advisor pops up on top of your working program to give you quick, easy help when you need it, and disappears when you don't. Covers thru version 3.3. Software package comes with 3½" and 5¼" disks. **System Requirements:** IBM compatible with DOS 2.0 or higher, runs with Windows 3.0, uses 90K of RAM.

DOS Instant Reference
SYBEX Prompter Series
Greg Harvey
Kay Yarborough Nelson
220pp. Ref. 477-1

A complete fingertip reference for fast, easy on-line help:command summaries, syntax, usage and error messages. Organized by function—system commands, file commands, disk management, directories, batch files, I/O, networking, programming, and more. Through Version 3.3.

DOS 5 Instant Reference
Robert M. Thomas
200pp. Ref. 804-1

The comprehensive quick guide to DOS—all its features, commands, options, and versions—now including DOS 5, with the new graphical interface. Concise, alphabetized command entries provide exact syntax, options, usage, brief examples, and applicable version numbers. Fully cross-referenced; ideal for quick review or on-the-job reference.

FREE BROCHURE!

Complete this form today, and we'll send you a full-color brochure of Sybex bestsellers.

Please supply the name of the Sybex book purchased.

_____

How would you rate it?

____ Excellent   ____ Very Good   ____ Average   ____ Poor

Why did you select this particular book?

____ Recommended to me by a friend
____ Recommended to me by store personnel
____ Saw an advertisement in _____
____ Author's reputation
____ Saw in Sybex catalog
____ Required textbook
____ Sybex reputation
____ Read book review in _____
____ In-store display
____ Other _____

Where did you buy it?

____ Bookstore
____ Computer Store or Software Store
____ Catalog (name: _____)
____ Direct from Sybex
____ Other: _____

Did you buy this book with your personal funds?

____ Yes   ____ No

About how many computer books do you buy each year?

____ 1-3   ____ 3-5   ____ 5-7   ____ 7-9   ____ 10+

About how many Sybex books do you own?

____ 1-3   ____ 3-5   ____ 5-7   ____ 7-9   ____ 10+

Please indicate your level of experience with the software covered in this book:

____ Beginner   ____ Intermediate   ____ Advanced

Which types of software packages do you use regularly?

____ Accounting	____ Databases	____ Networks
____ Amiga	____ Desktop Publishing	____ Operating Systems
____ Apple/Mac	____ File Utilities	____ Spreadsheets
____ CAD	____ Money Management	____ Word Processing
____ Communications	____ Languages	____ Other _____
		(please specify)

Which of the following best describes your job title?

____ Administrative/Secretarial   ____ President/CEO

____ Director   ____ Manager/Supervisor

____ Engineer/Technician   ____ Other _____
(please specify)

Comments on the weaknesses/strengths of this book: _____

_____

_____

_____

_____

Name _____

Street _____

City/State/Zip _____

Phone _____

PLEASE FOLD, SEAL, AND MAIL TO SYBEX

SYBEX, INC.
Department M
2021 CHALLENGER DR.
ALAMEDA, CALIFORNIA USA
94501

SYBEX ®

MACRO KEY NAMES

MOVING THE CELL POINTER WITHIN A WORKSHEET

{Right} or {R}	→	{Home}	Home
{Left} or {L}	←	{Tab}	Tab
{Up} or {U}	↑	{BigRight}	Ctrl-→
{Down} or {D}	↓	{BigLeft} or {BackTab}	Ctrl-←
{PgUp}	PgUp		
{PgDn}	PgDn	{End}	End

MOVING THE CELL POINTER BETWEEN WORKSHEETS IN THE CURRENT FILE

{NextSheet} or {NS}	Ctrl-PgUp
{PrevSheet} or {PS}	Ctrl-PgDn
{FirstCell} or {FC}	Ctrl-Home
{LastCell} or {LC}	End Ctrl-Home

MOVING THE CELL POINTER BETWEEN ACTIVE FILES

{File}	Ctrl-End
{NextFile} or {NF} or {File}{NS}	Ctrl-End Ctrl-PgUp
{PrevFile} or {PF} or {File}{PS}	Ctrl-End Ctrl-PgDn
{FirstFile} or {FF} or {File}{Home}	Ctrl-End Home
{LastFile} or {LF} or {File}{End}	Ctrl-End End

PERFORMING FUNCTION KEY OPERATIONS

{Help}	F1	{Name}	F3
{Edit}	F2	{Anchor}	F4 (READY mode)